T0397527

Legislative Assemblies

Legislative Assemblies

Voters, Members, and Leaders

SHANE MARTIN
AND
KAARE W. STRØM

OXFORD
UNIVERSITY PRESS

OXFORD
UNIVERSITY PRESS

Great Clarendon Street, Oxford, OX2 6DP,
United Kingdom

Oxford University Press is a department of the University of Oxford.
It furthers the University's objective of excellence in research, scholarship,
and education by publishing worldwide. Oxford is a registered trade mark of
Oxford University Press in the UK and in certain other countries

Published in the United States of America by Oxford University Press
198 Madison Avenue, New York, NY 10016, United States of America

British Library Cataloguing in Publication Data

Data available

Library of Congress Control Number: 2023934323

ISBN 978–0–19–889082–9
ISBN 978–0–19–889084–3 (pbk.)

DOI: 10.1093/oso/9780198890829.001.0001

Printed and bound by
CPI Group (UK) Ltd, Croydon, CR0 4YY

Links to third party websites are provided by Oxford in good faith and
for information only. Oxford disclaims any responsibility for the materials
contained in any third party website referenced in this work.

MIX
Paper | Supporting
responsible forestry
FSC® C013604

Contents

Acknowledgments   viii
List of Figures   x
List of Tables   xi

1. Understanding Legislative Assemblies   1
    1.1 Why Legislative Assemblies?   4
    1.2 Institutional Functions   7
    1.3 Members, Leaders, and Voters   9
    1.4 Capacity   14
    1.5 Accountability   17
    1.6 Assembly Types   27
    1.7 Conclusion   34
    References   36

2. Comparing Legislative Assemblies   40
    2.1 Case Selection   41
    2.2 Assembly Organization and Functions   42
    2.3 Understanding Organizational Choices   48
    2.4 Data Collection   53
    2.5 Conclusion   56
    References   56

3. Electing the Legislative Assembly   58
    3.1 Restrictions on Membership   59
    3.2 Electoral Systems: Translating Votes into Seats   64
    3.3 Length of the Legislative Term   75
    3.4 Mechanisms of Recall, Censure, and Expulsion   78
    3.5 Conclusion   82
    References   84

4. Membership and Congruence   86
    4.1 The Ideal Agent   86
    4.2 Members' Partisan Affiliation   88
    4.3 Descriptive Representation and Congruence   93
    4.4 Conclusion   110
    References   110

5. Cameral Structures   113
    5.1 The Number of Chambers   115
    5.2 Membership Selection   121

5.3 Cameral Powers	126
5.4 The Future of Second Chambers	129
5.5 Conclusion	131
References	132
6. Organization and Leadership	**134**
6.1 The Size of the Chamber	135
6.2 Rules and Standing Orders	138
6.3 The Presiding Officer	144
6.4 Resources	149
6.5 Conclusion	155
References	157
7. Parties in the Assembly	**159**
7.1 Legislative Parties	160
7.2 The Number of Legislative Parties	161
7.3 Non-Party Legislators	166
7.4 Organizational Structure of Legislative Parties	167
7.5 Party Influence on Roll-Call Behavior	171
7.6 Conclusion	180
References	181
8. Committees	**184**
8.1 Why Committees?	186
8.2 Comparing Committee Systems	192
8.3 Conclusion	212
References	212
9. Lawmaking	**214**
9.1 Proposal Rights	218
9.2 Stages of Deliberation and Voting Mechanisms	224
9.3 Executive Agenda Control	226
9.4 External Veto Players	232
9.5 Legislative Productivity	233
9.6 Conclusion	235
References	237
10. The Budgetary Process	**239**
10.1 Measuring Budgetary Powers	241
10.2 Variation in Budgetary Powers	253
10.3 Conclusion	256
References	259
11. The Elective Function	**260**
11.1 Voters, Members, Leaders, and the Elective Function	260
11.2 Defining Regime Types	262
11.3 Government Formation under Parliamentarism	269

11.4 Patterns of Government Formation under Parliamentarism 272
11.5 Government Termination under Parliamentarism 277
11.6 Other Appointment Powers 278
11.7 Impeachment 285
11.8 Conclusion 288
References 288

12. Executive Oversight 291
12.1 Parliamentary Questions and Interpellations 293
12.2 Investigation and Inquiries 300
12.3 Financial Audits 301
12.4 War Powers 304
12.5 Treaties 306
12.6 Responsibility 309
12.7 Conclusion 309
References 310

13. Legislative Assembly Types 312
13.1 Operationalizing Ideal Types 313
13.2 A Members' Assembly Index 315
13.3 A Leaders' Assembly Index 326
13.4 A Voters' Assembly Index 335
13.5 Assembly Types in Comparison 346
13.6 Assembly Types and Regime Types 347
13.7 Conclusion 349
References 349

14. Incumbency and Re-election 352
14.1 Incumbency, Capacity, and Accountability 353
14.2 Comparing Incumbency Rates 354
14.3 Understanding Incumbency Rates 359
14.4 Modeling Re-election Decisions 362
14.5 Analysis 370
14.6 Addressing Endogeneity 377
14.7 Conclusion 379
References 380

15. Democratic Assemblies and Contemporary Challenges 383
15.1 The Forces that Shape Legislative Assemblies 385
15.2 Challenges to Legislative Assemblies 387
15.3 The Dictator's Assembly 388
15.4 Prospects 394
References 399

Index 401

Acknowledgments

We owe a particular debt of gratitude to Charles McClean, now at Yale University, for his invaluable research assistance. During his time at UC, San Diego, Charlie was central to the data collection efforts and his professionalism, attention to detail, and his intellectual curiosity and research skills were invaluable to us as we set about detailing how legislative assemblies are organized and how they function. Additionally, Chapter 14 is based on work to which Charlie contributed as a co-author—hopefully one of several publications which will emerge from the wider project.

We are extremely grateful to colleagues and other individuals who helped us with data collection, often answering very specific questions on individual legislative assemblies, sometimes requiring that they spend their valuable and limited time to investigate the questions and queries we raised. These include Claire Adida, Saeed Ahmad Maitla, Ronald Alfaro-Redondo, Rudy Andeweg, Audrey André, Nathan Batto, Jonathan Boston, Kathryn Baragwanath, Monica Buitrago, John Carey, Francesco Cavatorta, Adam Chabi Bouko, Gertrude Chebet, Mihail Chiru, Kendra Dupuy, Luis Estrada, Jorge Fernandes, Bonnie Field, Andrea Freitas, Omer Genckaya, Reuven Hazan, Alice Kang, Catherine Lena Kelly, Ihor Kohut, Phil Larkin, Don Lee, Fernando Limongi, Wolfgang C. Müller, Juan Munoz-Portillo, Lia Nijzink, Tamaki Ohmura, Anja Osei, Susan Ostermann, Nandini Patel, Duncan Pickard, Tapio Raunio, Irena Ristic, Olivier Rozenberg, Omar Rubiera, Federico Russo, Marek Rybar, Sebastian Saiegh, Jose Carlos Sanabria, Cameron Sells, Ulrich Sieberer, Frank Thames, Devesh Tiwari, Sarah Whitmore, Nikoleta Yordanova, and Radoslaw Zubek.

We are also extremely grateful to colleagues who read one or more of the chapters and provided thoughtful and constructive feedback: Eduardo Aleman, Lasse Aaskoven, Stefanie Bailer, Mihail Chiru, Jorge Fernandes, David Fortunato, William Heller, Bjørn Høyland, Christopher Kam, Heike Klüver, Tim Mickler, Valeria Palanza, Ulrich Sieberer, Joachim Wehner, Richard Whitaker, Thomas Winzen, and Thomas Zittle. We are especially indebted to Wolfgang C. Müller for his extremely insightful and valuable comments on our entire manuscript.

We gratefully acknowledge financial support from the Academic Senate of the University of California, San Diego, the Department of Government's Research Promotion Fund at the University of Essex, and the Norwegian Research Council (FriSam Project No. 222442, *The Evolution of Parliamentarism*).

Our sincere thanks to Dominic Byatt at Oxford University Press for his support, advice, and encouragement, and to Meghan Watson, Mark Ajin, and Martin Noble for their true professionalism during the production of the volume.

And last, but not least, a particular and heartfelt word of thanks to our respective spouses, Stephanie and Digna, for their continued support and encouragement throughout the time that this project has taken.

List of Figures

1.1. Delegation and accountability under parliamentary and presidential
government   19

4.1. Seniority in the US House of Representative, 114th Congress (2015–2017)   100

6.1. Population and chamber size   137

9.1. Legislative productivity by regime type   236

10.1. Index of legislative budget institutions   254

10.2. Average (mean) budget capacity by regime type   256

13.1. Members' assembly index   324

13.2. Leaders' assembly index   334

13.3. Voters' assembly index   345

14.1. Incumbency rates in 68 democracies (2000–2018)   359

14.2. Career paths for an incumbent legislator   363

14.3. Marginal effect of legislative resources on incumbency rate by
corruption level   376

List of Tables

1.1. Assembly types by capacity and accountability features   35

2.1. Major secondary sources employed in this study   54

3.1. Membership restrictions   60

3.2. Electoral systems and terms   65

3.3. Determinants of incentives to cultivate a personal vote   76

3.4. Determinants of term length   78

4.1. Vote-seat proportionality and mean district magnitude   90

4.2. Electoral disproportionality   93

4.3. Occupational background of British MPs, by party (2015)   96

4.4. Women legislators and gender quotas   104

4.5. Women legislators as a proportion of all members   109

5.1. Bicameralism   117

5.2. Membership selection in second chambers   122

5.3. The formal powers of second chambers   128

5.4. Second chamber budget authority   130

6.1. Size of assembly (number of members)   138

6.2. Final passage change and rules governing selection of presiding officer   142

6.3. The evolution of the American speakership   148

6.4. Salaries and resources   151

6.5. Staff per member   154

7.1. Legislative party systems   162

7.2. The effective number of legislative parties   165

7.3. The rate of non-party legislators   168

7.4. Party unity in 16 democracies   173

8.1. Committee system structures   194

8.2. Number of committees   205

9.1. Formal proposal rights   219

9.2. Executive authority and legislative productivity   228

9.3. Executive agenda control   231

9.4. External veto players   234

10.1. Budgetary powers   242

10.2. Reversionary budget that favors the assembly   248

10.3. Wehner Index of Budgetary Powers   257

11.1. Regime and investiture types   266

11.2. Presidential system   268

11.3. Parliamentary investiture   270

11.4. Government types in parliamentary and semi presidential regimes   280

11.5. Other appointment and dismissal powers   282

12.1. Oversight powers   296

12.2. Powers to question the executive   302

12.3. Assembly treaty power   307

14.1. Country elections included in our analysis   357

14.2. Legislative resources, corruption, and incumbency   372

14.3. Operationalization of independent variables   373

14.4. Summary statistics   374

14.5. Legislative resources, corruption, and incumbency (IV analysis)   378

1
Understanding Legislative Assemblies

> A good government implies two things: first, fidelity to the object of government, which is the happiness of the people; secondly, a knowledge of the means by which that object can be best attained. Some governments are deficient in both these qualities; most governments are deficient in the first.
>
> James Madison, *The Federalist Papers,* No. 62

James Madison wrote these words in his discussion of the design of what has become the world's most powerful and prestigious legislative chamber: The United States Senate. Madison was concerned about the ability of legislative assemblies, and in particular the proposed federal congress, to meet these challenges of "fidelity" and "knowledge of the means." In terms more familiar to twenty-first-century students of politics, Madison called his readers' attention to the twin challenges of popular accountability and institutional capacity. Madison saw accountability and capacity as critical tests that the newly designed institutions of his country, and especially its legislative assembly, needed to pass. Whereas to Madison popular accountability was always a central concern, institutional capacity became a pressing issue with the increasingly obvious weakness of the Congress of the Confederation.[1]

Even though the shortcomings of the Congress of the Confederation have long since been remedied, Madison's concerns are no less pressing for present-day assemblies than they were in 1788. Legislative assemblies are critical to liberal democracy. The emergence of democracy has rested on the evolution of popularly elected assemblies in which citizen concerns could be expressed with impunity and which could help shape government policy. Legislators and the assembly to which they belong thus somehow "represent" voters, sometimes uniquely. Especially in parliamentary monarchies and under unitary constitutions, the members of the legislative assembly are frequently the only national-level political representatives directly elected by the citizens. Under presidential or federal constitutions, this democratic responsibility is shared with other institutions, such as subnational

---

[1] The Congress of the Confederation (or Confederation Congress) was the unicameral legislative body set up in 1781 under the American Articles of Confederation. Its main weakness stemmed from its lack of taxation powers.

Legislative Assemblies. Shane Martin and Kaare W. Strøm, Oxford University Press.
© Shane Martin and Kaare W. Strøm (2023). DOI: 10.1093/oso/9780198890829.003.0001

assemblies or a directly elected chief executive. Yet, even under such constitutions, the national legislature remains a powerful vehicle of popular rule. As the branch of government that most directly represents the sovereign citizens, democratic assemblies face critical tasks. Such assemblies determine what becomes law and how public funds are raised and appropriated. They oversee the executive branch and hold various government agencies to account. And they are arenas of political socialization as well as recruitment for executive office. It is thus fitting that Roger D. Congleton (2011) titled his magisterial study of the emergence of liberal democracy *Perfecting Parliament*.

Like Madison, we believe that legislative assemblies cannot perform to the satisfaction of their citizens without capacity as well as accountability. For all their purposes, legislative assemblies need, as Madison noted, "knowledge of the means of government" and capacity to perform the various functions assigned to them. A well-functioning democracy also needs effective mechanisms by which citizens can hold their legislators to account. If fidelity to the people is found wanting in their legislative institutions, we see little hope of finding it anywhere else in politics. The ways in which members of these assemblies can be held to account by their citizens are therefore a critical issue for popular governance.

There can be no doubt that even the most venerable legislative assemblies can face problems of capacity as well as accountability. Ever since Bryce's (1921) classic work, there has been widely shared concern among scholars about the decline of representative assemblies in the United States as well as in Europe and other democracies. The dictates of party politics, the growing complexity of political issues, and the seemingly endless expansion of the executive branch have all circumscribed the autonomy of legislative assemblies and the quality and significance of their deliberations. In Polsby's (1975) terms, many assemblies have been reduced to "arenas" for partisan contestation and showboating, rather than decision-making bodies in which public policy can be designed and transformed.

Accountability concerns have also been prominent in much of the legislative studies literature. Social choice theorists have found flaws in all the various ways in which legislators can be elected and challenged the mandates that such elections can generate (Riker 1982). And studies of electoral systems have demonstrated their complexity and their susceptibility to failures of strategic coordination that can easily defeat the convergent tendencies of Downsian electoral competition (Cox 1997). In the United States in particular, there has also been serious concern about the ease with which legislative incumbents have won re-election, even in situations in which they have been embroiled in political scandals (Somit et al. 1994). In the early 1990s, such concerns gave rise to a movement to impose term limits on state legislators in many US states.

None of these concerns can be ignored, except at our peril. One reason is simply that the very presence of legislative assemblies in no way guarantees democratic governance. Indeed, most semi-democracies and even some decidedly autocratic states feature legislative assemblies (see Gandhi 2008; Schuler and Maleski 2014), though the powers and functions of these assemblies tend to be more limited than those of legislatures that operate under democratic rule. Sadly, the establishment of legislatures with powerful constitutional functions, such as the German Reichstag under the Weimar Constitution, has been no guarantee of democratic stability. Historically and even up to the present time, democracy has been rare and fragile. Throughout history, the great majority of ordinary citizens have been poor, politically ignorant, and lacking in many rights that readers of this book may take for granted. Even when such citizens have had broadly shared grievances against their government, they have often found it difficult to organize. And they have frequently met disinterest or fierce retaliation, even among representatives of the people, when they have pressed their concerns. We therefore cannot assume that once legislative assemblies have been established, they will be stable or effective, or that they will necessarily represent broadly shared public preferences. Parliaments may be historically important, virtually ubiquitous in the contemporary world, and even broadly appreciated and trusted, and yet inconsistent in their functions and vulnerable to institutional manipulation, as for example the recent history of the Russian Federation has shown. In a later chapter, we shall return to this threat and its significance.

This book has been written with these concerns in mind but in appreciation, though not unqualified admiration, of the role that legislative assemblies play in contemporary democracies globally. The challenges of legislative capacity and accountability are thus the topic of this book. In the rest of this chapter, we will begin by outlining the history and political functions of elected parliaments and legislatures. We will then discuss at greater length the challenges of capacity and accountability in legislative assemblies. Focusing on the three most critical classes of actors that shape or inhabit legislative assemblies, we develop three ideal-typical models of legislative assemblies: the members' assembly, the leaders' assembly, and the voters' assembly. We then discuss the institutions and operations that characterize these models and how they relate to the challenges of capacity and accountability, respectively. Briefly put, one model prioritizes capacity, a second accountability, whereas the third represents more of a compromise between these concerns.

In the chapters that follow, we analyze real-world national legislative assemblies with the help of this framework. Going beyond Madison, our concern is with legislative institutions not only in a new and rapidly expanding democracy, but also in a largely new and, we hope, expanding democratic world. We therefore examine legislative assemblies in the 68 most populous democracies in the world, from Finland to Papua New Guinea. These assemblies may in their respective societies be known as parliaments, congresses, diets, councils, courts, senates, or the like. Whatever their names, these bodies are the cornerstone of modern representative democracy. There is no contemporary democratic state that does without a national assembly. Indeed, a national assembly in which at least one chamber is popularly elected is the only necessary institutional condition in Przeworski et al.'s (2000) influential definition of democracy. In 11 empirical chapters, we compare institutional features and procedures in these 68 democracies and discuss their relevance for legislative capacity and accountability. On the basis of data presented in these various chapters, in Chapter 13 we build an index for each of our assembly types and score each national legislature on each of these indices. In the following chapter, we analyze the importance of legislative institutions for one important issue that has already been raised in the discussion above: turnover in legislative assemblies and the ease with which incumbents can gain re-election. In the concluding chapter, we then discuss trends and prospects in contemporary legislative assemblies, as well as the threat that democratic backsliding can pose to these democratic institutions.

1.1 Why Legislative Assemblies?

Before we begin exploring the inner world of legislative assemblies, however, let us consider why such organizations exist in the first place. There are at least two ways to answer this question, one historical and the other functional. We begin with the historical answer, which points to the circumstances and places in which the assemblies that gave rise to contemporary legislatures emerged.

Although legislative assemblies today exist across the world and have evolved in various ways and under different political and cultural influences, most have been inspired by the ancient assemblies of Athens and Republican Rome. Yet, the design of many contemporary assemblies evolved more organically out of the European parliaments that existed from the Middle Ages onward. The emergence of a variety of such precursors of modern parliaments during the Middle Ages had much to do with the division of Europe into numerous empires, kingdoms, principalities, and occasionally republics. This multitude of political units allowed for mutual competition and frequently outright conflict but also for institutional experimentation and dissemination.

To protect themselves, build their communities, and acquire riches for themselves and their followers and compatriots, kings and other rulers typically needed more money than was in their personal possession or coffers. And to confiscate, tax, or borrow the necessary funds, they needed not just coercive capacity, but commonly also the assent of at least some wealthier members of their communities, their potential creditors. For ambitious but financially strapped rulers, accommodation was of course less nasty and risky than coercion and confiscation, and this is essentially the story of how England under a weak and needy monarch got its Magna Carta in 1215, which in turn set the stage for the gradual evolution of the Model Parliament and its subsequent division into the House of Lords and the House of Commons (Turner 2003). And although these privileges would be sorely tested under the Stuart monarchs (1603–88), Parliament would eventually sustain and build on the fiscal and legislative prerogatives it had obtained under Magna Carta.

Several factors paved the way for the Mother Parliament, which in turn has influenced the emergence of legislative assemblies in so many parts of the world. One was that England already had a tradition of strong assemblies empowered not only to make and adjudicate law but also to elect the kings themselves (Maddicott 2010). With the age of global exploration, the Protestant Reformation, and the rise of capitalism, Parliament increasingly came to be influenced by commercial interests set apart from the monarchy and by thinkers and religious leaders who were apt to question the king's authority, especially when the latter embraced the notion of an absolute monarchy and a divine right of kings. The Glorious Revolution of 1688–89 resulted in the triumph of the anti-absolutist forces and a decisive strengthening of Parliament as a forum in which their interests would generally be protected.

Although the English parliamentary tradition has become particularly well-known, influential, and celebrated, the country was not alone in its historical reliance on legislative assemblies. Such assemblies did in fact exist across much of northern Europe and were part of the Germanic political tradition. In the Nordic countries such institutions (known as "tings" or "things") similarly existed from the Viking age on, with the best-known and historically most powerful one being the Swedish Riksdag (see Metcalf 1987). Yet, the Icelandic Althingi justly celebrates its status as the oldest existing national assembly in the world. First established in 930 AD, the Althingi could be attended by all free men. The birth of the Althingi also more or less coincided with the establishment of the first Icelandic law code (Ferguson 2010: 165). From the beginning, the assembly had broad legislative powers and at the same time functioned as a court of law, as well as a debating chamber and a general social fair for Icelanders from all over the country.

The broad powers that the Althingi came to enjoy were at least in part due to the peculiar characteristics of Icelandic society at the time of its foundation. Iceland around the tenth century was a thinly settled country largely populated by settlers (as well as outcasts and political refugees) from various parts of Northern Europe, mainly Scandinavia and Ireland. Unlike most of the rest of Europe, Iceland had no king and no strong central government. Icelandic society also was not dominated by any network of clans such as existed in Ireland and Scotland. Instead, coercive and political power was decentralized and privatized, and its politics dominated by the coexistence and rivalry of a number of local chieftains (Byock 2001). This dispersion of power facilitated the rise of a powerful assembly.

The strong parliamentary traditions of England and the Nordic countries may be due to some of the same historical conditions, such as decentralized political authority and the relative absence of serfdom and other forms of social stratification and inequality that characterized Continental European feudalism. England and the Nordic region also had in common a long and strong legal tradition, in the former area reflected in its distinctive common law heritage. The rule of law was also highly valued in the Nordic area. In the words of the Norwegian Frostathing Law, as recorded about 1260 AD, "land shall be built by laws, but desolated without them." A similar statement is found in the preamble to the Danish Jutland Law of 1241. Norwegian king Magnus Lagabøter's (Magnus Lawmender) claim to fame was his compilation in 1274–76 of a codified national law, one of the first in Europe. Large parts of this legal code remained in force for more than 400 years.[2] The legislative assemblies of these nations were the arenas in which these laws were made, amended, interpreted, and applied.

Legislative assemblies waxed and waned in power over the ensuing centuries and were generally at their most vulnerable during the heyday of royal absolutism. Yet, even the most powerful monarchs, such as the French Bourbons or the British Stuarts, could not entirely extinguish their legislative assemblies, in large part because revenue concerns became a near-permanent, rather than occasional, royal preoccupation. Another perennial threat, even to powerful kings, was military defeat or death, such as happened to Charles I of England (1625–49) and Karl XII of Sweden (1697–1718). Such royal tragedies often paved the way for legislative resurgence. The historical record of these legislative assemblies thus suggests that they were most likely to gain power when they were useful to financially needy rulers. It also suggests that critical events, such as wars or the fall or death of rulers, often created opportunities for parliamentary empowerment. And finally, strong parliaments may have been most likely to emerge in relatively egalitarian and decentralized societies with a strong legal tradition.

With decolonization and the emergence of new democracies, national assemblies have become more numerous and diverse. Yet, the British and later US legislative models have inspired the design of many such assemblies in the Commonwealth and the Western hemisphere, respectively. In some cases, other legislative blueprints have been influential as well, such as the French one, especially in North Africa, and the Soviet one, the latter admittedly largely in regimes that could hardly be called democratic. But even when such models have been imported, they have often been adapted for local purposes in various ways. Thus, with the 1889 Meiji Constitution, Japan adopted a largely British blueprint, including a bicameral design with a hereditary upper house, but reserved a more exalted and significant role for the Emperor. In Latin America, largely US-style legislatures have been designed with a variety of electoral systems. And in such African countries as Ghana and Tanzania, national assemblies evolved organically out of the British model but were subsequently reformed for the purposes of single-party politics.

---

[2] Property law in Shetland and Orkney is still based in part on Udal Law, which is derived from the Norse legal tradition.

1.2 Institutional Functions

An alternative, or complementary, way to understand the evolution of democratic legislative assemblies is to consider the functions they perform. The functional perspective points to the distinctive organizational forms that legislative assemblies have taken and the political roles that these forms have allowed them to perform. Despite common references to political leaders as dictators or strongmen, making public policy is always a collective endeavor. As Bueno de Mesquita and Smith (2011: 1) put it, "To understand politics properly, we must modify one assumption in particular: we must stop thinking that leaders can lead unilaterally." The loosely organized bodies of individuals who historically advised and assisted rulers in making policy decisions, and who sometimes gained the right to take part in these decisions, were the precursors of modern national assemblies.

Roger D. Congleton (2011) argues that the evolution of such bodies of policy advisors and assistants to princely rulers into national legislatures was a path historically favored due to the distinctive advantages of the "king-and-council template." Congleton contends that this form of political organization, in which a singular strong executive is supported by and shares power with a collegial body of lieutenants, helps reduce information problems, contain intra-organizational conflict, and provide institutionalized and credible procedures for leadership transition and successions. These advantages, Congleton maintains, are the reason that king-and-council institutions became so prevalent in medieval Europe. Yet, the political history of these states from the Middle Ages to the age of democracy was one of constant tension between the two components of this template: the monarch and the assembly. In this "tug-of-war" each side had its weakness. The council often suffered from collective action problems and internal conflicts, which the monarch could exploit to his advantage. On the other hand, kings would vary more in their political ability and commitments, and less capable or committed monarchs, such as James II (1685–88) of England or Christian VII (1766–1808) of Denmark, would leave themselves vulnerable to usurpation of power by members of the council.

Since legislative assemblies have been empowered and institutionalized, scholars and pundits have sought to understand their functions in modern polities. Such concerns have been addressed in numerous classical works, including Walter Bagehot's (1867) analysis of the British Constitution. Assembly functions have also been a topic in the more contemporary literature on comparative legislatures, beginning around the 1960s. The most obvious purpose of such assemblies is lawmaking, a function so essential that it is inherent in the very noun ("legislature") we commonly use to describe these assemblies (at least for presidential democracies). Indeed, most democratic constitutions stipulate lawmaking as a core assembly function. Such constitutions typically also detail the process by which laws are to be made and prescribe the assembly's role within this process. If the rule of law is indeed the supreme governing principle of any democratic state, then the role of the people and their representatives in the lawmaking process must be carefully designed and protected.

Yet as we shall see in Chapter 9, the lawmaking procedures found in most democracies (and especially in parliamentary ones) grant extensive agenda powers to the executive branch and effectively to civil servants working at least nominally under the direction of their respective cabinet members. Commonly, the assembly also delegates much of the implementation of new laws to the same civil servants. Contemporary legislatures thus delegate extensive policy making powers to the cabinet and indirectly to the civil service, specialized agencies, and local adminis- trators. Such delegation frequently includes the authority to set specific standards for broad swaths of goods and services, as well as responsibilities for enforcement and adjudication of legislative decisions. For these reasons, oversight and control of the executive branch, including the civil service, is another critical legislative function. Various oversight and audit procedures help the assembly to keep a tab on the management and implementation decisions of the executive agencies to which it delegates, as well as to police malfeasance and financial irregularities in these agencies.

Fiscal policy, or public taxing and spending, is another key assembly function. The rise of the English Parliament from Magna Carta through the Glorious Rev- olution had much to do with its increasing power of the purse (see Cox 2016). Gradually, Parliament wrested control over taxation and public spending away from the monarch. And, more than anything else, this critical evolution subjected the king and his advisors to the will of the parliamentary majority. The importance of this development was duly noted by contemporary observers. Montesquieu (1989 [1748]: 164) thus saw the parliamentary power of the purse as critical to the protection of liberty: "If the executive power enacts on the raising of public funds without the consent of the legislature, there will no longer be liberty, because the executive power will become the legislator on the most important point of legisla- tion." And in Federalist No. 58, James Madison (2009 [1788]: 298) concurred that "power over the purse may, in fact, be regarded as the most complete and effec- tual weapon with which any constitution can arm the immediate representatives of the people, for obtaining a redress of every grievance, and for carrying into effect every just and salutary measure."

Lawmaking and budgeting are jointly associated with a legitimization function, which has been stressed by analysts as far back as Bagehot and more recently including Packenham (1970) and Norton (2018). Legitimization, in a narrow sense, means approving bills and spending requests from the executive branch. In a broader sense, it refers to the assembly's power to attach a voice of support for these demands and thus to reconcile the requests of the governors (the executive) with the approval of the citizens (through their representatives).

Important purposes of legislative assemblies also include socialization and recruitment of political leaders. Particularly in Westminster democracies but indeed throughout the democratic world, the legislative assembly is the primary arena in which aspiring politicians receive their on-the-job political training and prove their skills and worthiness as candidates for higher office. Even under presidential constitutions, the legislative assembly is often the springboard for the pursuit of executive office. Thus, since 2000 six out of nine major-party candidates for the US presidency, including every single presidential candidate fielded by the Democratic Party, have had prior experience in the federal legislature.

Parliament may even play a direct role in selecting the chief executive. Under positive parliamentarism, the assembly (or one of its chambers) actively votes in the occupants of the cabinet and especially the prime minister (see Bergman 1993; Rasch et al. 2015). Even Bagehot insightfully singled out the electoral function of Parliament as its most critical purpose: "The elective function is now the most important function of the House of Commons. It is most desirable to insist, and be tedious on this, because our tradition ignores it" (Bagehot 1867: 117). Besides the chief executive, as we shall explore in Chapter 11, legislative assemblies are typically empowered to appoint cabinet members, executive agency heads, judges, ambassadors, and CEOs of major state enterprises.

Legislative assemblies have emerged under a range of historical circumstances and perform a broad set of political functions. Yet, it is likely no coincidence that legislative assemblies have historically been particularly powerful and prominent in areas with a strong commitment to property rights and the rule of law, such as England and the Nordic region. If rulers could make their own law, as was more feasible under a feudal system of seigneurial justice, there would be less need for legislative assemblies. Similarly, if a king could simply confiscate the property he wanted, he would have less need of a parliament. At the same time, powerful assemblies surely also reinforced legal protections of persons and property.

1.3 Members, Leaders, and Voters

Legislative assemblies are complex organizations populated by elected representatives, their political assistants and advisors, professional civil service staffers, staff hired by political parties, media personnel, non-political service personnel such as janitors, security officers, and chauffeurs, and so on. The set of individuals whose lives are affected by what happens in legislatures is even much larger, as in democratic societies these assemblies make significant and binding decisions on behalf of their entire society, affecting virtually every citizen and resident.

But who are critical individuals in these complex environments? And whom do such assemblies serve? The answers to these two questions are interrelated. Despite their complexity, we can understand much of what legislative assemblies are and do by focusing on three key sets of actors: (1) the ordinary members of the assembly, (2) the leaders of the organizations designed to compete for control of the assembly and the legislative process (and in some political systems, the executive branch), and (3) ordinary citizens with the right to select and deselect legislators through the voting process. We will refer to these actors as members, leaders, and voters, respectively.

Members

Out of these three classes of legislative actors, members come first, chronologically as well as analytically. Assemblies needed members before leaders could emerge. And voting by ordinary citizens is only one way, and a relatively recent one, in which members could be selected. Although the members of the various democratic assemblies of the contemporary world have much in common, the social origins of legislators have over time varied substantially. Some historical assemblies have been remarkably inclusive in their membership. In Viking-age assemblies such as the Icelandic Althingi, for example, all free men could in principle participate in debates and decisions. Similar principles governed the assemblies of some local communities in the North Atlantic colonies, most notably the town hall assemblies of Massachusetts, which themselves were modeled on local governments in East Anglia (Fischer 1989). Yet, even the Icelandic inclusiveness was not quite as remarkable as it may sound. Not all men were free; some were slaves or serfs who did not have the same participation rights. Women were generally also not permitted to participate. And some free men were surely freer than others, at least in the sense of being able to gain an audience at the assembly.

The members of the English Parliament of the thirteenth century were knights sent by the county sheriffs to advise the King on financial matters and to assent to his requests for new taxes. The Model Parliament of 1295 included representatives selected from the various counties, boroughs, and cities, as well as noblemen and lower clergy. Early in the following century, these various types of members sorted themselves into a House of Lords (spiritual and temporal) and a House of Commons. Such separate chambers of estates representation were common in Europe until the 1789 French Revolution and beyond. In Sweden, for example, the four-chamber estates Riksdag, with a separate chamber for free farmers, survived until 1866. And, of course, the British House of Lords, though variously reformed since 1911, still exists today.

Contemporary legislative assemblies typically consist of hundreds, though rarely thousands, of members. As we shall see in Chapter 3, the membership size of most democratic parliaments correlates loosely with overall population. Thus, all else equal, more populous countries tend to have larger legislative assemblies. Yet even though the country is only middling in overall population, the world's largest democratic assembly is the UK Parliament, with well over 1,400 members between the House of Commons and the House of Lords. Our main concern in this book will be with the lower (or first) legislative chambers (such as the House of Commons), since they tend to be the more powerful and accountable ones, and since about half of our democracies do not have an upper (or second) chamber. These lower chambers are, at least in democratic societies, designed to be representative bodies. Each member is the designated representative of some set of citizens and residents, and typically elected by some subset of them.

Leaders

The smallest, most exclusive, and most powerful set of players in democratic assemblies are their leaders. Elected legislative chambers are typically collegial, in the sense that all members are elected with the same constitutional general rights and responsibilities. Yet, legislative bodies depend for their success on cooperation and coordination among their members. And legislative leaderships are the main vehicle of such cooperation. From the very inception of assembly politics, some members have had greater authority and power than others. In medieval Europe, such leadership functions often came with membership in the nobility or the clergy, which in turn might be bestowed by the monarch. Yet assembly leaders could emerge from the bottom up as well as from the top down. Thus, some assembly leaders held their positions and power by appointment from the monarch, whereas others derived them from their support among the assembly membership.

Leadership offices were surely created in part to satisfy personal desires for power, but also for specific functional reasons. Then as now, legislative assemblies needed expertise and coordination. Their early leadership officers were often designated as speakers. Thus, the Althingi's presiding officer was the Lawspeaker, "a man with an approved reputation for wisdom and a lawyer well versed in the technicalities of the law" (Ferguson 2010: 166). He was elected for a three-year period and could be re-elected. In England, the continuous history of the speakership of the House of Commons dates back to 1376 and Sir Peter de la Mare.

While in many democracies, the Speaker (or assembly president) continues to outrank all others in formal protocol, the actual power of this office has in many places been eclipsed since the emergence of parliamentary parties. Thus, in 1721 Robert Walpole became the first modern British prime minister by virtue of his leadership of the Whigs and his support in the House of Commons. Similarly, Arvid Horn rose to the position as President of the Swedish Privy Council Chancellery in 1720 based on his Riksdag support among members of the Caps Party (Mössorna), a party largely supported by commoners and the lower classes. Horn held his position of preeminence for 18 years, almost as long as his contemporary Walpole.

The emergence of legislative leaders and hierarchy stems at least in part from the fact that without them assembly decision making can degenerate into parody through bickering and gridlock. And in a democratic society leaders and members alike serve at the pleasure of the voters, largely as channeled through political parties. In contemporary assemblies, the keys to legislative leadership thus lie with the political parties with which most members are affiliated. Contemporary legislative leaders are therefore almost invariably also party leaders.

Note that by leaders, we mean not only the members who hold the official leadership position in the legislative caucus of their respective parties, but also other individuals with privileged positions in the party hierarchy, the set that Cox and McCubbins (2005) characterize as the "senior partners" of their respective parties. These could include committee chairs, speakers, or members of the assembly presidency, members of the party's legislative steering body, the chief whip and his or her main assistants, and possibly others. In Westminster democracies, the front benches on both sides of the floor well encompass this set of leaders. In other democracies, the boundaries of the leadership set may be more fluid and may also include individuals whose main source of influence lies outside the parliamentary party, for example in their ties to powerful business leaders, labor unions, or the chief political executive.

Voters

In the first historical assemblies, voters were hardly a separate category of assembly actors. In small-scale communities such as medieval Iceland or seventeenth-century Massachusetts townships, all enfranchised citizens had the opportunity to participate personally and directly in political decisions. In larger-scale societies, individuals might be selected as assembly members based on their noble titles, the offices (spiritual or temporal) they held, their financial resources, or the monarch's appointment or invitation.

When elections became more common, the electoral process was often manipulable or outright corrupt, and the franchise restricted by property, gender, ethnicity, age, or religious denomination. Even the most democratic national constitutions of the early 1800s generally restricted voting rights to men with a minimum of property. And even at a time when life expectancies were radically lower than today, the right to vote was typically limited to individuals well into their 20s or beyond. In the democratizing United Kingdom, Catholics had no voting rights until 1829. In many countries, including parts of the United States, racial or ethnic minorities might have no voting rights at all. In Norway, the 1814 Constitution explicitly denied citizenship rights to all Jews and members of Catholic orders.[3]

---

[3] The ban on Jews was rescinded in 1851, whereas the denial of citizenship rights to Catholic orders (specifically Jesuits) survived until 1956.

Only in the late 1800s did (at first mostly propertied) women begin to gain voting rights in the democracies of that time. Thus, in 1893 New Zealand became the first country to extend the franchise to all adult women and men. This most Caledonian outpost of the British Empire was followed by Australia in 1902, Finland in 1906,[4] and Norway in 1913 (Przeworski 2018: 37). In many parts of Europe and in various emerging democracies, women's voting rights did not arrive until after World War II. Note, however, that several American states were remarkable pioneers in extending voting rights to women. Thus, New Jersey allowed women with independent property to vote in every election from 1776 until 1807. And women gained the right to vote in Wyoming in 1869 and in Utah in 1870, a generation before this happened in any European country.[5]

The assemblies we analyze in this book represent the world's 68 most populous democracies. The populations of these countries range from just over four million to approximately 1,390 million in the case of India. Of course, not all these residents are necessarily citizens or voters. Some may be foreign nationals, living temporarily in one of the states in our sample. Others may be immigrants who have not gained citizenship. And large numbers will be children, who have not yet reached voting age. Finally, some may have lost their citizenship or voting rights due to criminal convictions, emigration, or other circumstances (Blais, Massicotte, and Yoshinaka 2001). And although those with voting rights will in most cases still make up a majority of the population, in many countries large numbers of eligible voters do not in fact turn out for any given election. Yet, with all these caveats, voters are a very large social category who numerically dwarf the number of assembly members and leaders. At the same time, however, the great majority of voters are political amateurs and part-timers, who rarely pay much attention to day-to-day legislative politics.

We can and will think about the purposes of legislative assemblies from the perspectives of these three sets of actors and their respective objectives. A legislature can thus be explored meaningfully by clarifying the relationships between the members who serve in it, the leaders who seek to control and coordinate the assembly, and the voters who select its members. And assemblies vary in the extent to which they reflect the interests of one of these types of actors over the others. Thus, the three types of assemblies that we will introduce and discuss in this chapter are the members' assembly, the leaders' assembly, and the voters' assembly. What most clearly differentiates these assembly types are the distinctive interests they embody. Thus, a members' assembly is organized in such a way as to privilege the members' interests, a leaders' assembly the aspirations of its leaders, and a voters' assembly those of its voters. All three types are, or can be, democratic assemblies, but they serve the public interest in different ways

---

[4] The Finnish case is remarkable in that when females gained voting rights and parliamentary eligibility in 1906, a large number of women actually ran for office, and 19 were elected (out of a parliament of 200) in the very first election in which women had voting rights.

[5] Colorado followed suit in 1893 and Idaho in 1896.

and perhaps to different degrees. Note also, however, that an elective legislature can be part of an autocratic state and that assemblies designed to serve democratic purposes can indeed become institutions over which voters have little or no influence.

In the chapters to come we will examine a broad range of legislative rules, powers, and processes and ask to what extent they serve the purposes of members, leaders, or voters. By purposes we mean the interests and preferences that such individuals tend to have by virtue of their political offices and endowments. This is not to say that institutions that serve the purposes of say, party leaders, were necessarily designed with this intent. These institutions may have originated for totally different reasons, but once established may survive because they nicely serve the interests of those who can most easily sustain or change them.

1.4 Capacity

The broad and critical functions that legislatures perform are the main reason that students of democratic politics have given them so much attention. Yet, legislative assemblies face substantial challenges in exercising their constitutional responsibilities. What, then, enables legislative assemblies to perform their functions? As Madison noted, the object or purpose of government is the happiness of the people. Representative bodies ideally have the task of making authoritative public decisions consistent with the interests of the citizens. For any such task, legislative assemblies obviously need powers and capacity. Hence, in democratic constitutions the founders often devote a great deal of attention to the powers, structures, and processes of their national assemblies. Many national constitutions explicitly refer to their respective legislatures as the representatives of the people, authorized to legislate, tax, and appropriate on the citizens' behalf. According to the Swedish Constitution (the Instrument of Government), for example, "The Riksdag is the principal representative of the people" (Chapter 1, Art. 4). No more, no less. The idea that the purpose of a national assembly is to represent the interests of ordinary citizens is therefore fundamental and well-entrenched.

A legislative assembly hence needs organizational means and capacity; or it may be no more than a "parchment" institution whose real influence falls far short of its formal authority (Carey 2000). In other words, the actual assembly powers may, by accident or design, not reflect its lofty ambitions and responsibilities. Each and every legislator may have been fairly and properly elected by their constituents, and yet the legislative output may not be to anyone's satisfaction. Such assemblies may still lack critical properties for effective decision making. But under what conditions are legislatures capable of responding effectively to citizen demands, and when are they simply parchment, or sham, institutions? These are questions concerning legislative capacity.

Legislative capacity in turn depends on three critical conditions: Authority, resources, and efficacy. For a legislative assembly to have lawmaking or budgetary capacity, it first needs to have the formal right, or authority, to make decisions in these policy domains. Such authority may rest on constitutional and statutory provisions that allow assemblies to examine possible policy initiatives, collect information, propose policies, deliberate on such proposals, make binding policies and decisions, and oversee their implementation. This authority, which includes proposal power, agenda control, and veto power, can be granted or circumscribed in any number of ways. In subsequent chapters, we shall examine these aspects of legislative authority.

Secondly, legislative capacity depends on resources. Formal authority means little if the assembly does not have the resources necessary to exercise this power. Resources refer to the human and material assistance, including labor, time, and financial support, available to assembly members and subunits as they make policy. Critical resources also include staffing and funding, as well-staffed and well-funded assemblies are likely to have greater capacity, all else equal, than those that lack these endowments. Another critical resource is time. Assemblies with long electoral terms and lengthy sessions clearly have substantial advantages over those that meet only occasionally and perhaps have short terms to boot, such as has been the case with many US state legislatures. Finally, the assembly's access to information is critical. And information points to the need for assembly members to have access to knowledge about existing social conditions, policy options, the potential consequences of these options, and the preferences and behaviors of the social actors that would be affected. Informationally, the assembly is virtually always at a disadvantage compared to the executive branch. Hence, assemblies jealously protect their right to solicit and receive truthful and complete information from executive agencies.

Finally, legislative capacity depends on the efficacy of the assembly, on the ease with which the assembly can make and sustain collective decisions. Efficacy can be lacking if many assembly decisions require qualified majorities or complicated procedures involving many stages of deliberation and corresponding veto points. Assemblies can also face efficacy challenges if they lack control of their own timetable, for example if it is easy for subgroups of members to filibuster or if the head of state can unilaterally adjourn or dissolve the assembly at short notice. Finally, efficacy can be compromised if the assembly is not resolute—if it is easy for any group of members to overturn, delay, or compromise decisions the assembly has already made. This latter concern with resoluteness is hardly novel. In Federalist No. 62, James Madison indeed lamented the "mutability" of the new republic's existing legislative bodies.

Legislative capacity is a function of all these factors: authority, resources, and efficacy. In large part, deficiencies in one aspect can be compensated for by strengths in another. Thus, exceptional resource endowments can, for example, make up for some weakness in formal authority. Yet, at extreme levels of deficiency, things are not quite so simple. Thus, an assembly totally lacking in authority cannot simply make up for this through generous staffing or highly efficacious decision-making procedures. It therefore makes sense to think about the relationship between authority, resources, and efficacy as multiplicative rather than additive. Thus:

$$\text{Capacity} = \text{Authority} \times \text{Resources} \times \text{Efficacy}$$

This formulation implies that a minimum of each of these three factors is necessary for legislative capacity. Above this minimum level, surpluses in one factor can compensate for deficiencies in others, yet assemblies that score particularly low on any one of these dimensions will be severely limited in their overall capacity.

Whereas the formal authority of legislative assemblies is typically in large part given by the existing constitution and legal framework, resources and efficacy can more easily vary and be manipulated. Different forms of legislative organization reflect attempts to secure resources, including information. Hierarchy is an important element of internal legislative organization and a mechanism by which an assembly can secure capacity and especially efficacy. Assembly members may benefit from centralized decision-making hierarchies that control their careers and information flows. And for these purposes, centralized, programmatic, and cohesive legislative parties have in many assemblies become their main instruments (see Aldrich 2011). Parties function as control and coordination devices inside parliaments, with powers to coordinate across policy jurisdictions, enforce policy commitments, and control the legislative agenda (Cox and McCubbins 2005). Parties are therefore by far the most important and effective hierarchies within legislatures. In contemporary legislatures, the most powerful actors are therefore the leaders of the major political parties.

Yet, different forms of democracy yield different kinds of parties, with systematic ramifications for the ability of these parties to aggregate popular preferences and manage the legislative agenda. The ideal setting for strong and cohesive political parties is a unitary parliamentary regime in which the national assembly is unicameral or asymmetrically bicameral (meaning that the lower house is dominant) with a pure or modified majoritarian electoral system, such as the United Kingdom or New Zealand. Various constitutional provisions can, however, pose challenges to such party cohesion. Samuels and Shugart (2010) show that compared to pure parliamentarism, regimes with directly elected presidents (whether presidential or semi-presidential) tend to feature less cohesive parties, because these regime forms generate divergent electoral incentives between the legislative and the presidential party branches. These points can be generalized to other constitutional divisions of authority, such as federalism and symmetric bicameralism, which similarly permit differentiated electoral incentives. And where mayorships of large cities constitute valuable political prizes (as in Brazil), even the power and lure of such offices can further threaten party cohesiveness. One of the ways in which these various constitutional features can weaken party cohesion is by facilitating progressive ambition among politicians, as we will discuss below and particularly in Chapter 14.

Assemblies can also build capacity by facilitating differentiation and specialization among their members. If thus empowered, even ordinary members can respond to voter demands, especially when these demands have to do with case work or issues of local or specialized interest, and where members are elected in low-magnitude (e.g., single-member) districts. Such specialization typically takes place most notably through permanent legislative committees and can generate a hierarchy defined less by party structures than by policy specialization and differentiation (Krehbiel 1991). Seniority rules and well-policed deference to legislative committees provide incentives for members to build expertise in well-defined policy areas.[6] Seniority may have consequences for committee assignments and the prospects of gaining a legislative committee chair, with further ramifications for members' ability to "bring home the bacon." Voters who value fiscal transfers to their district or experienced (and favorable) handling of their special policy concerns may respond by re-electing incumbents who have invested in expertise and agenda power in specialized policy areas.

High incumbent re-election rates, especially for members holding key offices (such as committee chairs), may allow legislatures to develop capacity through stable and efficient procedures, policy expertise, and strong institutional memories (Krehbiel 1991: 141–143). If in contrast turnover is high, the result may be inexperienced leadership, a lack of expertise, and low professionalism. High legislative turnover may also blunt effective oversight functions and in general adversely impact assembly capacity. Thus, as the re-election rate rises, the assembly may gain capacity, though possibly at the cost of accountability.

1.5 Accountability

Even if legislative assemblies can develop sufficient capacity to perform their constitutional functions, it is far from obvious that they will faithfully and effectively represent the interests of their voters. Madison's second concern was about legislators' fidelity to the citizens' happiness, in other words legislative accountability. As Madison suggested, this may be an even more daunting challenge than capacity. Although ostensibly designed to represent the people, legislative assemblies are

---

[6] As witnessed in the US Congress, seniority norms may be particularly likely to operate within assembly subunits such as committees and legislative presidencies (speakerships), and to some extent within legislative parties.

mostly inhabited by professional politicians and thus operate through delegation of power, with the various pitfalls that such an organizational design implies.

Delegation, which means voluntarily and conditionally transferring authority to others, occurs in many social contexts for a variety of reasons (see Dahl 1990). One is capacity: I may delegate gardening tasks because I do not have the time to mow the lawn and weed the flowerbed regularly. Another motivation is competence: Even if I had the time to fix my car's transmission, I would not know what to do. A third may be coordination: A family might be able to take care of its gardening, yard, and maintenance work if all chipped in and divided the tasks, but that requires agreement on who does what when, as well as monitoring of their agreed responsibilities. It might be more efficient to entrust all these tasks (or at least the coordination of them) to a single person. Finally, groups may delegate to avoid collective action problems in which each member behaves in a narrowly self-interested way to the detriment of all, as in the tragedy of the commons examples of overgrazing or overfishing (or emptying the fridge without restocking it).

All these rationales for delegation apply in politics. Most citizens certainly do not have the time or resources to acquaint themselves with all issues facing their community. Most of us (the present authors included) do not feel that we have the information and skills necessary to determine the optimal central bank lending rate or the safety standards for the nuclear power industry. And there are myriad circumstances in which we delegate to our representatives to improve coordination or avoid collective action problems.

The Principal-Agent (PA) framework is a conceptual apparatus that can help us understand political relationships of delegation and accountability. Principals are individuals, groups, or organizations in which sovereignty, the ultimate right to decide, is vested. In democratic societies, this generally includes every adult citizen with voting rights. Agents are those whom the principals have conditionally designated to take or suggest decisions within their respective fields of responsibility. Principals and agents are by mutual consent engaged in a delegation relationship by which the former conditionally empower the latter. In politics, elected representatives are among the most important such agents.

Contemporary democracies require political delegation, and democratic constitutions define the terms on which legislative candidates become the agents of the citizens.[7] Through further political delegation those who initially receive delegated authority can further transfer it onto others. Thus, democratic decision making takes the form of a chain of delegation, in which ultimate authority (sovereignty) rests with ordinary citizens, who can through elections delegate this authority to their representatives. These representatives may in turn delegate further to cabinet members and agency heads. The agency head delegates to her subordinates, with

---

[7] Not all theories of representation characterize the responsibilities of legislators to their constituents as an agency relationship, but we find this conception useful for our purposes here.

increasingly specific competencies and responsibilities, who in turn delegate to their assistants. There is a corresponding, reverse chain of accountability, in which agents answer to their respective principals. As occasions when voters can make and unmake political grants of delegation, popular elections provide the initial and critical democratic bridge from ordinary citizens to their political representatives.

Democratic delegation regimes vary, as Figure 1.1 illustrates. Here we contrast in simplified form a Nordic-style unicameral parliamentary democracy with a US-style bicameral presidential democracy.[8] In parliamentary democracies, citizens typically elect only legislators (parliamentarians), who in turn help select the executive with its further stages of internal delegation. Thus, under parliamentarism, legislators are at the same time the agents of the citizens and the principals of the prime minister and the cabinet. In presidential democracies, citizens elect both legislators and executives, who in turn jointly (or in competition) delegate to

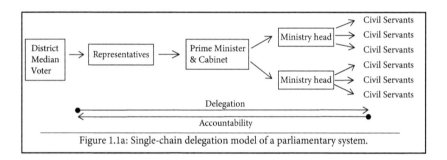

Figure 1.1a: Single-chain delegation model of a parliamentary system.

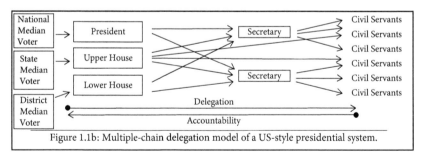

Figure 1.1b: Multiple-chain delegation model of a US-style presidential system.

Figure 1.1 Delegation and accountability under parliamentary and presidential government

Source: Strøm et al., 2003: 65.

---

[8] Bicameral parliamentary regimes generally have delegation regimes that in complexity fall between these two polar types. Yet, the majority of parliamentary regimes are unicameral, and most bicameral parliamentary assemblies are asymmetrical, meaning that the upper (second) chamber has significantly weaker powers than the lower chamber, as in the UK House of Lords versus the House of Commons. Parliamentary regimes are also less likely to have popularly elected and powerful heads of state. For these reasons, parliamentary delegation regimes are generally significantly less complex than presidential ones.

unelected agents. In ideal-typical form, the parliamentary chain of delegation is simple, unitary, and hierarchical. Agents answer to only one principal and know who their boss is. The presidential chain of delegation is more complex. To begin with, voters elect more agents with differentiated responsibilities. Down the chain of delegation, several principals may have common agents, and agents may have to answer to more than one principal.

Under either design, the delegation of authority from voters to their elected representatives is the first and critical link in the chain of relationships that make democracies democratic. Yet, the assembly's role differs. In presidential systems, the president and the legislature are complementary or competing agents of the voters and at the same time principals of the civil servants. Under bicameralism, whether presidential or parliamentary, both chambers are typically also designed to represent the people (except for non-elected or only partially elected second chambers), though sometimes according to diverging electoral designs. Thus, it is in unicameral parliamentary regimes that the responsibility of representing the citizens falls most squarely on a single elected body and where effective delegation from voters to parliament matters most. Assemblies in bicameral and/or presidential regimes face this challenge less acutely, though they may instead confront issues of cooperation and coordination that could result in inefficiencies and gridlock.

All the motivations for delegation exist within legislative assemblies as well as between the members and voters. Given the multitude of political proposals and demands at any time, time is always scarce and capacity a perennial problem. Legislative assemblies typically do not meet for considerable periods every year, and even when the assembly is in session, members must find time for party activities, constituency service, receptions, excursions, outside occupations, and perhaps even family time. Competence is equally a challenge. Competence problems in this context need not mean that legislators generally lack skills (although that may sometimes be true), but rather that for the assembly to be effective, members must develop expertise across a broad range of specialized domains. Even though many members are impressively gifted and credentialed, most are generalists who lack expert knowledge of many issues they are called upon to decide. Even professional skills that may seem basic to the task of legislative assemblies may be missing. Thus, for eight consecutive years the Norwegian *Storting* had no licensed lawyer among its members. Coordination issues mean that assembly members must find ways of efficiently husbanding their scarce resources, such as meeting time and debate opportunities. And if all members insist on flogging their own respective hobbyhorses, they are bound to encounter collective action problems.

Any delegation of authority entails a risk that our agents may not faithfully use the power we grant them in our best interest. They may skimp on the time or resources they devote to their task. Or they may pursue their own interests even as we ask them to look after ours. Or they may simply not be very good at the responsibilities we give them. To avoid such problems, we need mechanisms of accountability, such that the person or organization to whom authority is transferred stands responsible to the grantor and that the grantor can renegotiate or terminate the delegation relationship.

We can discuss the risks of political delegation in terms of the potential for agency loss, which refers to any discrepancy in the principal's payoff between what results from the agent's actions compared to what the principal would have chosen if she had had the agent's information and choice set. Such agency loss can derive from omission (or "shirking"), when the agent fails to act in the best interest of the principal, or from commission, when the agent takes positive action contrary to the principal's interest.[9]

Agency loss may happen when the agent's preferences differ from those of the principal, and when the latter also lacks the means (i.e., information and mechanisms of enforcement) to monitor and police every action the agent takes on her behalf.[10] The risk of agency loss thus exists whenever, compared to the principal, the agent has different preferences and superior information. Such asymmetric information may take two forms: (1) hidden information (when principals do not fully know the competences or preferences of their agents or the exact demands of the task at hand), and (2) hidden action (when principals cannot fully observe the actions of their agents). Whereas the former condition may lead the principal to choose an unsuitable agent, the latter may cause the principal to be unable to police unsuitable agent behavior. Adverse selection (hidden information) and moral hazard (hidden action) are problems that may arise, respectively, out of such information asymmetries. In the context of democratic legislatures, adverse selection refers to the risk of selecting members that do not have the skills, preferences, and inclinations most beneficial to the citizens. Moral hazard has to do with the risk of shirking or malfeasance by members in contexts where the citizens cannot observe their representatives' behavior or its consequences.

Principals can try to prevent or contain agency loss through various devices, many of which apply in assembly politics. Before delegating, principals can seek to gain information through practices such as signaling (by the agent) or screening (by the principal). In electoral politics, signaling may mean that the prospective agent (the candidate) tries to provide evidence of his competence (I have a degree from Yale Law School) or dedication (I served my country honorably in the Marines or the Peace Corps). In screening the burden of investigating such competence falls on the voters (the principals). Contract design is a way in which the principal can structure the delegation "contract" to align the incentives of the agent with her own preferences (if the results please the voters, the representative gets a "bonus"). After authority has been delegated, principals can hold their

---

[9] By interests, we here simply mean the preferences held by this actor.
[10] For simplicity, we use female pronouns for principals and male pronouns for agents.

agents to account through monitoring (by the principal), reporting requirements (falling on the agent), or by the checks or "fire alarms" conducted by interested third parties, such as interest groups with interests similar to those of the principal (see Kiewiet and McCubbins 1991; Lupia 2003).

Democratic delegation thus needs to be complemented by effective mechanisms of accountability. Citizens can control their representatives at several points. Their right to choose these members through free and fair elections is indeed a core tenet of democracy. And the design of the electoral system—how votes are translated into legislative seats—has real and substantive consequences for electoral accountability. Citizens also need to be able to monitor incumbent legislators contemporaneously, so as to respond to their decisions and possibly reverse undesirable ones. Finally, citizens must be empowered to decide whether to return their incumbent deputies to office (if indeed these members seek re-election). Such ex post control rests on formal voting rights and ballot access rules. It also effectively depends on the citizens' ability to assess their assembly members' (or their respective parties') performance in office. When these conditions obtain, retrospective voting is indeed a key mechanism of democratic accountability.

Are these conditions realistic? To what extent is the relationship between voters and their representatives beset with such problems? And are the accountability mechanisms likely to be effective? These questions have no general and precise answers, but in Mitchell's (2000: 336) view, "Of all the links in the delegation chain from individual voter to Prime Minister, the link from voter to MP may be fraught with the greatest dangers." This is primarily because of the great asymmetry of information between ordinary voters and professional politicians and recognizing that the latter can be counted upon to have self-serving preferences (such as re-election and generous compensation) that are not shared by the voters.

To address these issues more adequately, however, we need to consider several features of effective delegation that should thus be reflected in the relationship between citizens and their democratic assembly (see, e.g., Miller 2005):

Consent. Delegation from citizens to members is by mutual consent. Thus, citizens cannot be forced to engage a particular assembly member, and no one can be forced to serve as an elected representative.

Citizen Sovereignty. Citizens define the purpose of delegation (the tasks of their elected representatives).

Delegation of Authority. Members have conditional authority to act or propose action on the citizens' behalf.

Citizen Veto. Citizens can approve or reject the proposals or actions of their elected representatives.

Citizen Termination Rights. Citizens are free to extend or withdraw the authority they have delegated to their elected representatives and to re-elect or replace them in office.

A perfectly accountable assembly should reflect these features of effective delegation. Citizens should through competitive elections be free to select their representatives (Condition 1). Members should be free, if elected, to accept or reject the privileges and responsibilities of office (Condition 1). Citizens should be entitled to define the assembly's political agenda, in practical terms most likely by choosing among alternative policy bundles at election time (Condition 2). Elected assembly members should then have the power to make or propose legislation and other decisions on the citizens' behalf (Condition 3). Ideally, citizens should also have the right ex post to approve or reject policy initiatives proposed by the members, for example through a confirmatory or abrogative referendum (Condition 4). Finally, citizens should be entitled subsequently to extend or terminate the tenure of their representatives, at the next scheduled election or through a recall procedure (Condition 5).

While no real-world assembly perfectly exhibits the full set, constitutional and other provisions in democratic states typically provide at least some semblance of these features. Competitive elections contested by programmatic political parties thus help underpin Conditions 1 and 5 above. Other constitutional and statutory provisions typically empower legislative assemblies and thus support Condition 3. And while in any real-world society Condition 2 (citizens' right to determine the political agenda) may in strict terms be a fiction, election laws at a minimum systematically order citizen choices over the options that parties and candidates present. Finally, Condition 4 (citizens' right to veto or reverse assembly decisions) is constitutionally entrenched for only a small set of assembly decisions, typically constitutional amendments, in a limited number of democracies (such as Denmark and Ireland, plus a few US states). To a limited extent, this shortage can be remedied by the citizens' power to deselect incumbents and replace them with members empowered to reverse decisions of which these citizens disapprove.

Since in most representative democracies conditions 2 and 4 (citizens' agenda control and veto power) are at best conditionally satisfied, and since (as we shall see in a later chapter) recall mechanisms are few and far between, effective democratic delegation hinges in large part on electoral accountability through political parties (conditions 1 and 5). Of course, all functional democracies (and many semi-democracies and outright autocracies) hold regular elections. But to carry the load that effective delegation requires, such elections must be inclusive, transparent, fair, free, and competitive. These can be higher hurdles, and the most consequential of them is competitiveness.

Electoral Accountability and Competition

A critical requirement for legislative accountability thus concerns the process by which members are selected and deselected. There are multiple well-established ways of selecting representatives of the people, many of which effectively pre-empt democratic accountability. In ancient Athens, assembly members were randomly chosen by lot (among free men exclusively). Similar lottery-based procedures (including "sortition") are still used in jury selection and have their normative advocates (see Tridimas 2012). Such procedures may result in an assembly that roughly represents the demographics and preferences of the citizenry, or at least that part of the population from which the sample is drawn, but it leaves ordinary citizens with no direct influence over the selection of their legislators. It is also unlikely to generate a body of members with the skills, experience, and interest necessary to perform the legislature's functions well, as James Madison argued in Federalist No. 10. But most fundamentally, it precludes any mechanism by which the citizens can hold their representatives to account.

More commonly in non-democratic societies, assembly members gain their offices through heredity, auction, or appointment, or some combination of these mechanisms. Heredity, of course, means that offices are passed on from generation to generation within the same families, typically drawn from the more affluent and influential segments of society. While this principle may seem archaic, some legislatures still have a hereditary component. As of August 2022, the UK House of Lords included 92 hereditary peers out of a total membership of approximately 800. Moreover, several African legislative assemblies have a chamber reserved for regional, hereditary chiefs. Thus, the Senate of the Kingdom of Lesotho comprises 22 traditional regional chiefs, as well as 11 senators appointed by the King. And even in democratically elected assemblies, heredity matters indirectly, as membership in a political dynasty may provide competitive advantages in the contest for elective office (Smith 2018) and/or progression to leadership positions (Smith and Martin 2017).[11]

Appointment implies that legislator selection is at the discretion of other political officials, though assembly candidates may have to meet specific criteria, such as ethnic, faith, or gender requirements. While such requirements may be compatible with democracy, they do restrict voters' choice. Auction means that offices are filled through a (formal or informal) bidding process, in which those prevail who are willing to pay the most. Where clientelism is rampant, appointment procedures may in practice turn into informal auctions. Compared with heredity, auction may produce representatives more committed to their political functions, yet those who buy their offices are also more likely to abuse them to "recoup their investments." Moreover, none of these procedures generates much hope for less affluent or well-connected members of society. Nor do they provide any mechanism by which citizens can hold their representatives to account.

---

[11] Smith (2018: 3) defines a democratic dynasty, as "any family that has supplied two or more members to national-level political office" and notes that in recent years approximately ¼ of the members of the Japanese Diet have belonged to a democratic dynasty.

Thus, the only mechanism that can satisfy even the most basic requirements of democratic delegation is popular voting, which is why regimes with no popularly elected legislative chamber simply cannot qualify as democracies. Moreover, elections must happen regularly and elected members must be permitted to perform their functions. King Charles I's third English Parliament was first assembled in March 1628, but dissolved just over a year later, and then for 11 years no election was held and no parliament convened. Not surprisingly, civil war followed. The formal right to vote and periodic elections are not in themselves sufficient, however. North Korea regularly holds elections, as did Iraq under Saddam Hussein, and yet neither regime qualifies (or would have qualified) for inclusion in this book. Democratic elections must be free and fair, and they must be reasonably frequent. Citizens who so aspire must have the right and opportunity to run for office, and citizens as well as candidates must be free to exercise their rights without discrimination, harassment, or fear of subsequent retaliation (see Dahl 1971).

Besides providing for some mechanism of accountability, electoral laws must facilitate political competition. Competition in the relationship between voters and representatives refers to the discretion that voters enjoy in their selection of political contenders for office. Competition is commonly held to be a key prerequisite of democracy (see especially Dahl 1971 and Przeworski 1991). Any degree of competition presumes that there is (or can be) more than one candidate or electoral list.[12] We can think of electoral competitiveness (from the voter's perspective) as the degree of choice, or (from the incumbent member's perspective) as the degree of risk, that the election presents.

Przeworski (1991) conceives of electoral competitiveness as the ex-ante uncertainty of the contest for office. While ex ante uncertainty is an important precondition for political competitiveness, however, it is not sufficient. Consider an (hypothetical, we hope) assembly in which each political party's representation is determined by a random number generator (or a roulette wheel). Such a device would satisfy the condition of ex ante uncertainty but do nothing to empower citizens at election time. We therefore prefer to think of electoral competitiveness as performance sensitivity, as the extent to which the representation of the various parties (or candidates) reflects the voters' retrospective judgments of their past record and/or prospective assessments of their campaign commitments. Performance sensitivity is low when elections are decided by factors beyond politicians' control, such as the voters' demographics, pandemic diseases, shark attacks, or the weather on election day. Performance sensitivity thus requires ex ante uncertainty (the election result cannot be given in advance), but also that the payoff for each party or candidate positively reflects the voters' judgment of their performance (see Strøm 1992). Unsurprisingly, assessing competitiveness in actual

---

[12] More precisely, we can think of an election as contestable if it is legal and feasible for more than one candidate to contest it and competitive if more than one candidate actually does.

elections is challenging. Measuring ex ante electoral uncertainty is clearly difficult in a world where we mainly observe ex post results. And even aggregate results give us few clues about performance sensitivity, though reasonable proxies may exist in incumbent re-election rates, or in the actual margin of victory in individual races (see Cox, Smith, and Fiva 2020).

Sadly, high interparty competitiveness is not to be expected in the real world, as politicians generally do not want it. Left to their own devices, politicians, just like businesspeople, strive to become monopolists (see Thiel 2014). If that is not feasible, they will, as noted by Adam Smith, incline to form cozy cartels. Political leaders of different colorations thus seek mutual accommodations at the expense of the voters, such as in the common (though declining) practice in bipartisan legislative redistricting in the United States of carving out mutually safe seats.

Yet electoral accountability depends on individual candidates as well as on political parties, especially where the latter are not highly programmatic and disciplined. Hence, one factor affecting accountability is political ambition among the candidates for office and specifically their interest in re-election. Joseph Schlesinger (1966) seminally differentiated between discrete, static, and progressive political ambition. Discrete ambition refers to office-seeking for a single term only, whereas static ambition underlies the quest for re-election to a given office and progressive ambition pertains to the pursuit of one elective office as a steppingstone to a higher or more desirable one.

An assembly dominated by static ambition, where most members aspire to be re-elected to their existing offices, would constitute an optimal setting for individual electoral accountability. The most famous portrait of such static ambition may be David Mayhew's (1974) depiction of members of the United States House of Representatives as single-minded seekers of re-election. In contrast, assemblies characterized by discrete ambition, where few or no incumbents seek re-election, will not be conducive to individual electoral accountability. The starkest cases of such lack of static ambition may be assemblies with term limits, such as in Costa Rica, Bolivia, the Philippines, and formerly Mexico, in which members are restricted to a limited number of terms or may not even be permitted to run for re-election once.

The effect of progressive ambition on individual accountability depends on constitutional features. Under parliamentary and unicameral constitutions, higher ambition would only reinforce the re-election motive, since there is hardly any alternative political office for which an ambitious MP would want to give up his or her seat. Instead, progressive ambition focuses on cabinet positions, the route to which goes through parliament and the ruling party or coalition. Similarly, members who aspire to "mega-seats" such as committee chairs or party caucus leadership positions will tend to seek re-election and their party's good graces (see Strøm 2012; Martin 2014). In contrast, under federalism ambitious members may want to pursue governorships and in bicameral systems "elevation" to the upper or more prestigious chamber may beckon. The lure of alternative offices thus depends on regime properties, such as federalism, presidentialism, and bicameralism, which compared to the alternatives (unitarism, parliamentarism, and unicameralism, respectively) all tend to expand the set of attractive alternative offices. Thus, progressive ambition will generally only depress the re-election motive in bicameral, presidential, and/or federal regimes.[13]

1.6 Assembly Types

For democratic assemblies, capacity and accountability are separate and mutually independent challenges. Successfully meeting these challenges is by no means a given. Thus, real-world legislative assemblies can satisfy one challenge, neither, or both. Thus, an assembly whose members are motivated to be responsive to their constituents but lack capacity will be one in which "the spirit is willing but the flesh is weak" (Matthew 26: 41). Conversely, an assembly can have great legislative capacity but little accountability. The latter possibility, of course, reflects Madison's concern about fidelity. Sadly, legislatures can also be ineffective and unaccountable at the same time.

One pitfall of legislative design is that the very institutional features that promote assembly capacity may at the same time impede accountability. Thus, the powers of political parties, for example, may at the same time facilitate capacity and permit serious abuses of power. Even ordinary members may abuse their power discreetly and within confined constituencies and areas of responsibility, but they can rarely put serious coercive force behind their transgressions. Assembly leaders are in a much more obvious position to do so, especially if the machinery of the executive branch stands at their disposal, as may be particularly likely in parliamentary regimes, and if judicial authorities and oversight procedures are weak. Yet, there is no necessary trade-off between capacity and accountability. Enhancing legislative capacity does not necessarily mean sacrificing the interests of the voters. Yet, legislative assemblies may cluster in ways that effectively prioritize one of these challenges (capacity and accountability) at the expense of the other.

Assemblies may differ in such ways because they are shaped (through deliberate design or organic evolution) in ways that favor the interests of one or other of the three sets of their critical actors: members, leaders, or voters. In the rest of this chapter, we shall therefore discuss three ideal-typical assemblies: the members' assembly, the leaders' assembly, and the voters' assembly. Later chapters will

---

[13] Occasionally, incumbent legislators may pursue alternative office even in countries that have none of these institutional characteristics. For example, some members may run for mayor of a major city or hanker after a central bank governorship or some other executive appointment. Or, in member countries, some legislators may seek European Union offices.

ask whether these ideal-typical conceptions help us make sense of the legislative assemblies of the world's 68 largest democracies.

The Members' Assembly

Let us therefore now consider, in the context of capacity and accountability, three ideal-typical legislatures based on the interests of members, leaders, and voters, respectively. The first such ideal type, the members' assembly, is configured to suit the interests of assembly members. More specifically, a members' assembly is one in which members benefit from opportunities to promote their interests (including career ambitions), through secure tenure, decentralized decision making, and autonomy from assembly leaders as well as from voters.

The preferences and ambitions of members of legislative assemblies naturally focus strongly on their own careers and benefits. Prominent among these preferences are the desires for secure tenure and re-election. Politicians, it has been said, have two objectives: to be elected and then to be re-elected (McChesney 1997: 47). Hence, a members' assembly will have long and fixed terms, no term limits, no recall procedures, and no constitutional provisions for early parliamentary dissolution. Members' assemblies should also tend to have decentralized, rather than centralized, candidate selection procedures and electoral systems that allow members to cultivate a personal vote (Carey and Shugart 1995). Moreover, a members' assembly will ideally be lodged within a constitution that permits multiple avenues for progressive ambition that are not strictly under the control of assembly leaders. Thus, presidential, semi-presidential, and federal regimes will be more conducive to members' assemblies than parliamentary and unitary ones.

Yet, overall opportunities for static, rather than progressive, ambition surely matter more for the majority of ordinary members. The traditional organization of the US Congress, with its strong and decentralized committee system and opportunities for members to pursue personal votes, was arguably singularly well suited for the electoral needs of its members. As Mayhew (1974) suggests, many of the institutional features of the US House of Representation serve the purposes of incumbent members remarkably well by enhancing incumbency re-election rates and reducing turnover.

Some members' assemblies may be so organized as to allow members use their perquisites of office to protect their tenure but do little else. Members' assemblies, especially if they fail to promote specialization, may have little capacity to serve the more general interests of the population through broad legislation. The British House of Commons prior to the major reform acts of the nineteenth century had many of these characteristics (Cox 1987), with extensive privileges and opportunities for individual members but collective bottlenecks and inefficiencies. Yet, a members' assembly can build capacity through a wide range of legislative features, such as committee systems, opportunities for legislative initiatives and questions, mechanisms of executive oversight, access to discretionary "pork-barrel" grants, and generous staffing and remuneration schemes. By empowering individual members, this legislative model can promote responsiveness to voter demands, especially to the extent that these demands have to do with case work or issues of local or sectoral interest, and where members are elected in low-magnitude (often single-member) districts.

A members' assembly will most likely build capacity through permanent and specialized committees, especially if those have substantial agenda powers and if committee leadership positions are not strictly controlled by the assembly majority. Such committees may have a hierarchy at least partly defined not by party structures but by the accumulation of seniority in office—the total time served as an assembly member relative to that of other members.[14] Seniority may matter for committee assignments and the prospects of gaining a legislative committee chair, with further ramifications for members' ability to "bring home the bacon." Voters who value fiscal transfers to their district may under such a hierarchical, seniority-based system be inclined to re-elect well-placed incumbents. Indeed, it was long assumed that the seniority system in the US Congress thus motivated voters to re-elect incumbents. Today, in a more partisan Congress, the impact of seniority has diminished, so that "a senior member of Congress, on average, brings no more pork to her district than the counterfactual freshman representing the same district at the same time" (Fowler and Hall 2015: 42).

The members' assembly is a form to which collegial assemblies may be easily drawn and much in line with what Madison and the Federalists had in mind for the US Senate. Incumbent politicians will naturally favor institutions that reduce their electoral risk, and members' assemblies can do so by generating policies informed by expertise and political experience as well as by distributive and particularistic ("pork-barrel") outputs and favors. Powerful committees may build considerable expertise and prestige in their respective jurisdictions and thus aid their members at election time. But members' assemblies may be less successful at aggregating interests across policy areas in cost-effective ways. Their main strategy for such aggregation will generally be mutual deference according to jurisdictional boundaries and expertise, which may be relatively safe but costly, especially if the dominant members also tend to be "high demanders" in their areas of specialization.

The Leaders' Assembly

A second type of legislature is the leaders' assembly. A leaders' assembly is as if designed for the purposes of legislative leaders—those individuals capable of

---

[14] As witnessed in the US Congress, seniority norms can operate within an assembly as a whole, within subunits such as committees, within individual legislative parties, or some mix of the above.

dominating the assembly agenda and competing for control of the executive branch and the national policy process. The leaders that dominate the chain of delegation in contemporary legislatures are those of the major political parties. As Saalfeld and Strøm (2014: 377) note, political parties underpin and mediate this democratic chain of delegation. Parties provide candidates with labels that voters can use in their voting decisions. Parties also shape their members' legislative behavior and can disrupt their role as agents of the voters who elected them. In fact, legislators in leaders' assemblies have two principals: their respective voters and their party leaders.

In a leaders' assembly, accountability operates via the competing political parties. As Gregory M. Luebbert (1986: 46) noted, party leaders "are motivated above all by a desire to remain party leaders." In addition, those party leaders that matter most, those capable of winning control of the legislative assembly for their own party or a coalition in which they participate, will wish to control assembly decision making and the fruits thereof. Leaders prefer the electoral term to be long, but early dissolution may well be feasible, as long as it is under the control of the assembly leadership (the majority party or coalition). There should, however, be no opportunity for voters to recall their members before the end of the regular electoral term. Candidate selection should be centralized and controlled by the respective party leaders. Ballots in Proportional Representation systems will be closed list or with very limited opportunities for voters to affect candidate choice. Party unity is easier to achieve in a parliamentary regime than in a presidential or semi-presidential one (Samuels and Shugart 2010). Similarly, we expect stronger party cohesion in a unicameral assembly than under bicameralism, particularly if the latter is symmetric and incongruent, such that the two chambers have relatively equal powers but are elected under diverging electoral systems (see Lijphart 2012).

Within a leaders' assembly, party leaders dominate their members through centralized decision making, hierarchy, agenda powers, and control of legislators' careers, campaign funds, and information flows. In a leaders' assembly hierarchy is defined by party leadership position rather than seniority. "Backbench" members in a leaders' assembly find their incentives for legislative careers dominated by their respective party leaders. This helps facilitate party cohesion (Kam 2009) and simplifies voters' decision making. Party leaders are likely to have their own forms of static and progressive ambition focusing on majority control and personal promotion. Party leaders first and foremost want to control the assembly majority, but each individual leader also wants to rise in the ranks. The higher a particular politician is in the party hierarchy, however, the more static her ambition is likely to be.

Party leaders are in the business of winning elections. And the best way to win elections is generally to build (minimal winning) coalitions by offering tangible benefits to sufficiently broad coalitions of voters, tacitly at the expense of others.

Thus, assembly leaders will need to make trade-offs between policy, office, and vote pursuits (Strøm 1990; Müller and Strøm 1999). The broader the constituencies they seek to win, the more their policy promises will focus on public goods and broadly redistributive issues. Hence, party leaders will be office-seekers and in multiparty parliamentary regimes coalition-builders, but at the same time they first and foremost need to remain party leaders. Being able to rein in their legislative co-partisans is thus critically important and controlling the reward structure and the flow of information inside the assembly party imperative.

The elections game can be rough and brutal. Party leaders expected to win elections typically do not survive long unless they do. And the more party power is concentrated in the hands of one leader, as in a parliamentary system with a single or dominant chamber, the higher the price of electoral losses. As one-time Conservative grandee Enoch Powell famously observed, all such political lives tend to end in failure.

As Martin (2016) notes, certain leadership positions in a governing party may produce specific electoral rewards. Parties are not strictly unitary actors, and legislators within the same party may have divergent interests, which complicates party decisions. Holding a ministerial portfolio may confer an electoral advantage, and so, in contrast to their co-partisans, cabinet ministers may not face as a stark a conflict between their electoral prospects and their pursuits of office. Thus, differentiating between the electoral incentives of party leaders versus their co-partisans may help explain why political parties often choose to enter government despite the evident electoral costs they will encounter (Rose and Mackie 1983, Strøm 1985; Narud and Valen 2008).

Party leaders use their powers to aggregate policies from various jurisdiction so as to serve the party interest (and their own). In their analysis of the US Congress, Gary Cox and Mathew McCubbins (2005) point to agenda control as the critical power that allows party leaders to create "procedural cartels." Agenda control comes in a positive form—the ability to force bills onto the legislative agenda, and a negative form—the ability to prevent bills from receiving consideration on the floor. Cox and McCubbins especially stress the role of party leaders in exercising negative agenda control and thus preventing the assembly from even considering bills that might otherwise gain majority support and impose a policy the same leaders disfavor. Such agenda control is rarely exercised overtly, since it may imply suppressing bills with considerable popular support outside (or even inside) the governing party. Where leaders exercise strong agenda control, transparency is thus a weak spot.

Leaders' assemblies will tend to produce redistributive policies. And more so than members' assemblies, leaders' assemblies are perfectly capable of imposing substantial losses on particular groups of citizens, especially those that tend to support competing parties. Party leaders seek to attract winning coalitions of voters but also to generate rents for themselves. The competitive context limits the rents they can generate and the magnitude of the costs they can inflict, but majoritarian decision rules mean that they can nevertheless impose costs (though preferably hidden ones) on citizens outside their winning coalition.

A leaders' assembly may emerge from a members' assembly when the inefficacy of the latter becomes particularly pressing. In many countries, assembly leaderships have thus been strengthened during times of war, systemic threats, or economic crises (Koss 2018). In the United Kingdom, the transition from a members' assembly to a leaders' assembly happened during the great economic transformations of the nineteenth century amid the growing demands for a broader political franchise that accompanied that process.

Our description of a leaders' assembly assumes that these leaders freely compete for control of the assembly with a realistic expectation of turnover. This obviously contrasts with an assembly dominated by a singular leader in which there is no prospect of leadership alternation and perhaps no plausible scenario in which such a change could happen. We call this type of legislature a *dictator's assembly*. Since it is associated with autocracy, rather than democracy, this assembly type will occupy the least of our attention in this book, but we shall return to it in the final chapter.

The Voters' Assembly

Finally, the voters' assembly is a body in which citizens can exercise a direct and immediate influence over policies.[15] Voters differ from members and leaders in several ways. First and foremost, compared with professional politicians, voters labor under severe informational asymmetries. They are far less able to understand and follow political events from day to day or week to week. Voters are also likely to have shorter time horizons and to be more concerned about the immediate responsiveness of politicians. Finally, voters are likely to have more particularistic and local concerns than party leaders or even members. The voters' assembly is therefore an assembly type designed to lessen voters' informational disadvantages and characterized by high electoral accountability, transparency, and immediacy. This assembly type thus has much in common with the blueprint for the US House of Representatives presented by Madison and the Federalists.

A voters' assembly in our conception has short electoral terms and fixed election dates that cannot be manipulated by party leaders. Indeed, in Federalist No. 52, Madison argued that democratic assemblies "should have an immediate dependence on, and an intimate sympathy with, the people. Frequent elections are unquestionably the only policy by which this dependence and sympathy can be

---

[15] Our argument applies to voters as well as to the broader category of citizens. For simplicity, however, we shall generally refer to voters. We shall correspondingly refer to the type of legislative assembly that privileges voter/citizen interests as a voters' assembly, which helps us avoid any confusion that might arise from use of the term "citizens' assembly."

effectually secured." Electoral systems under this form of assembly would feature candidate preference voting and opportunities for cross-partisan voting, such as the Single Transferable Vote (STV). Candidate selection is decentralized, involving primary elections or other avenues by which ordinary voters can defy the dictates of central party leaders. And a pure voters' assembly should feature opportunities for member recall initiated by the voters.

Since voters' information problems are often severe, actual voter influence depends on transparency. While legislative assemblies vary in this respect, they are typically the most open and transparent branch of government. Executives, in contrast, more often operate behind closed doors. Judiciaries rarely disclose the details of their deliberations and may not even need to provide a rationale for their decisions. But even though assemblies are the most transparent branch, such transparency may be ineffective unless the actions and behavior of legislators are communicated to voters.

Many reform efforts designed to promote voters' assemblies have to do with the pursuit of institutional virtues such as information transparency and access. Transparency means openness and the free dissemination of information relevant to the deliberations and operations of the assembly. In the electoral arena, voters' assemblies will thus typically feature sustained efforts toward voter-friendly electoral reform and member responsiveness, including for example recall provisions and primary elections. Such efforts are designed to keep legislative members on a "short leash," so that they remain mindful of their electoral accountability and their needs to satisfy the demands of their voters, often at short notice.

The pursuit of transparency has in many assemblies also meant introducing open committee hearings and televised coverage of legislative debates and deliberations. The UK House of Commons, for example, has introduced a petition process, whereby citizens through a sign-up process can force the assembly to debate issues of the citizens' choosing. By promoting such reforms as youth parliaments and various forms of citizen engagement, parliamentary leaders have also attempted to make Parliament more familiar and accessible to ordinary citizens. Finally, voters' assemblies will often prioritize the development of permanent committee systems and professional staff services. None of these reforms should be understood purely as attempts to make legislative assemblies more responsive to voter interests, but surely such rationales surely have helped justify many of them.

Yet, all legislative assemblies face a challenge in selling their role and communicating their activities to the public, since much of the work of a legislative assembly is technical and unexciting—regardless of how important and consequential its decisions are. On the other hand, political theater within legislatures—such as the weekly Prime Minister's Questions in the British House of Commons—may attract an audience, entertain, and put leading politicians to a test of their knowledge and debating skills, but do little to give the voters reliable policy information.

While our concept of a voters' assembly is an abstraction for which there is no pure example in the real world, it is an important analytical benchmark. In brief, it is an assembly form focused on transparency, openness to civil society, and immediate responsiveness and accountability. Our conceptual discussion also helps us understand different ways in which legislative assemblies can depart from this characterization. And there are good reasons that most real-world assemblies do not resemble the voters' assembly model. Simply put, legislative assemblies are most likely to be governed in ways that benefit the most powerful actors within them, which generally means leaders and sometimes members but rarely voters.

1.7 Conclusion

As James Madison perceptively noted, the likelihood that legislative assemblies will faithfully serve their citizens depends on two conditions: (1) the capacity of the assembly to act effectively in pursuit of the voters' interests and (2) the strength and credibility of the electoral mechanisms by which the citizens can hold their representatives to account. These are the conditions of capacity and popular accountability, respectively, and meeting them both is no easy task. Thus, real-world legislative assemblies can successfully meet one of these challenges of capacity and accountability, neither, or both. There is not necessarily a trade-off between capacity and accountability. Enhancing legislative capacity does not necessarily mean sacrificing the interests of the voters. Sadly, it is also possible for legislatures to be ineffective and unaccountable at the same time. Yet, legislative assemblies may, as we have suggested, cluster in ways that effectively prioritize one of these challenges at the expense of the other.

Legislative assemblies in the democratic world differ in many ways that affect their capacity as well as their accountability, and this chapter has suggested that much of this variation can be understood in view of the ways in which these assemblies reflect the interests of the members and leaders that populate these institutions and the voters that elect them. We have thus identified three democratic assembly ideal types, based on the extent to which the assembly's rules and procedures favor one or another of these actors: A members' assembly, a leaders' assembly, and a voters' assembly.

Assembly capacity depends on authority, resources, and efficacy. Accountability depends largely on the efficiency of electoral competition. In turn, there are myriad institutional features that impact on these preconditions for capacity and accountability, and which are systematically related to the distinctive features of a members', leaders', or voters' assembly. We include some of the most important ones in Table 1.1. In this table, we characterize our three assembly types according to some of their most important capacity and accountability mechanisms. The models in Table 1.1 thus represent the interests of one of the categories of actors around whom this book is organized: Members, leaders, and voters.

What determines the relative power of members, leaders, and voters in legislative politics? The assembly rules and routines certainly matter. Some rules, typically those concerning cameral structure, eligibility, and voting rights, are constitutional and thus often well entrenched and of long standing. Others are statutory and contained in ordinary legislation. Much of the fine print of legislative organization and procedure, however, is typically found in the standing orders which are easily amendable by the assembly itself (Sieberer et al. 2016). Yet other rules exist simply by convention. Thus, Norway has the second oldest written constitution in the democratic world, dating back to 1814. But many contemporary rules that govern the legislative process in Norway bear little resemblance to the formal provisions of its Constitution. And even the basic principle of ministerial responsibility to parliament was not incorporated into the Norwegian Constitution until 2007, although it had been universally accepted as binding more than a century earlier. Thus, the effective rules governing legislative assemblies may diverge from the formal ones and evolve over time.

This evolution will be shaped by the actors that populate and control the legislative arena: members, leaders, and voters. Among these sets of actors, voters

Table 1.1 Assembly types by capacity and accountability features

	Members' Assembly	Leaders' Assembly	Voters' Assembly
Electoral Term and Recall	Long and fixed, with no recall procedure	Long and subject only to dissolution power, with no recall procedure	Short and fixed, with recall procedure
Electoral System	Candidate-centered	Party-centered	Cross-partisan and candidate-centered
Candidate Selection	Decentralized	Centralized	Decentralized and cross-partisan
Agenda Powers	Decentralized	Centralized	Decentralized, including citizen groups
External Institutional Constraints	Weak	Weak, except for executive branch	Strong, especially concerning citizen rights
External Transparency	At the discretion of members and legislative subunits	Low	High
Member Resources and Compensation	Large and non-discretionary	Variable and at the discretion of assembly leaders	Moderate, task-related, and subject to public scrutiny

are undoubtedly in the weakest position to influence the "living constitution" of their legislative assembly. Hence, we expect real-world assemblies to drift away from the voters' assembly model over time, except at the rare times when institutional reform is a particularly salient issue for politicians as well as voters, such as the Progressive Era in the United States or constitutional moments in emerging democracies.

Chapter 2 will set out our empirical strategy for assessing how the ideal types presented in this chapter match the structures, processes, and powers of the national assemblies of our 68 major contemporary democracies. It also reviews existing approaches to comparing and classifying legislatures, provides a rationale for our selection of the institutional features on which we focus, and discusses the background conditions which may affect these features. Moreover, we will discuss case selection and data collection strategies. The subsequent ten chapters discuss different features of contemporary legislative assemblies. Chapter 13 applies the ideal types developed in this chapter to generate indices of legislative assembly types and map our 68 national legislatures accordingly. Chapter 14 develops and tests a model of how various institutional features affect what we believe is a critical internal dynamic in all democratic assemblies: the success of incumbent members in winning re-election to their respective offices. We conclude in Chapter 15 by discussing the consequences different forms of legislative organization may have for democratic quality and their prospects in the contemporary world.

References

Aldrich, John H. 2011. *Why Parties? A Second Look.* Chicago: The University of Chicago Press.

Bagehot, Walter. 1867. *The English Constitution.* London: Chapman & Hall.

Bergman, Torbjörn. 1993. "Formation Rules and Minority Government." *European Journal of Political Research* 23(1): 55–66.

Blais, André, Louis Massicotte, and Antoine Yoshinaka. 2001. "Deciding Who Has the Right to Vote: A Comparative Analysis of Election Laws." *Electoral Studies* 20(1): 41–62.

Bryce, James. 1921. *Modern Democracies.* London: Macmillan.

Bueno de Mesquita, Bruce, and Alastair Smith. 2011. *The Dictator's Handbook.* New York: Public Affairs.

Byock, Jesse. 2001. *Viking Age Iceland.* London: Penguin.

Carey, John M. 2000. "Parchment, Equilibria, and Institutions." *Comparative Political Studies* 33(6-7): 735–761.

Carey, John M., and Matthew S. Shugart. 1995. "Incentives to Cultivate a Personal Vote: A Rank Ordering of Electoral Formulas." *Electoral Studies* 14(4): 417–439.

Congleton, Roger D. 2011. *Perfecting Parliament.* Cambridge: Cambridge University Press.

Cox, Gary W. 1987. *The Efficient Secret.* Cambridge: Cambridge University Press.

Cox, Gary W. 1997. *Making Votes Count.* Cambridge: Cambridge University Press.

Cox, Gary W. 2016. *Marketing Sovereign Promises*. Cambridge: Cambridge University Press.

Cox, Gary W., Jon H. Fiva, and Daniel M. Smith. 2020. "Measuring the Competitiveness of Elections." *Political Analysis* 28(2): 168–185.

Cox, Gary W., and Mathew D. McCubbins. 2005. *Setting the Agenda: Responsible Party Government in the US House of Representatives*. Cambridge: Cambridge University Press.

Dahl, Robert A. 1971. *Polyarchy*. New Haven: Yale University Press.

Dahl, Robert A. 1990. *After the Revolution? Authority in a Good Society*. Revised edition. New Haven: Yale University Press.

Ferguson, Robert. 2010. *The Hammer and the Cross: A New History of the Vikings*. London: Penguin.

Fischer, David Hackett. 1989. *Albion's Seed: Four British Folkways in America*. New York: Oxford University Press.

Fowler, Anthony, and Andrew B. Hall. 2015. "Congressional Seniority and Pork: A Pig Fat Myth?" *European Journal of Political Economy* 40: 42–56.

Gandhi, Jennifer. 2008. *Political Institutions under Dictatorship*. New York: Cambridge University Press.

Kam, Christopher J. 2009. *Party Discipline and Parliamentary Politics*. New York: Cambridge University Press.

Kiewiet, D. Roderick, and Mathew D. McCubbins. 1991. *The Logic of Delegation*. Chicago: University of Chicago Press.

Koss, Michael. 2018. *Parliaments in Time*. Oxford: Oxford University Press.

Krehbiel, Keith. 1991. *Information and Legislative Organization*. Ann Arbor: University of Michigan Press.

Lijphart, Arend. 2012. *Patterns of Democracy*. 2nd edition. New Haven: Yale University Press.

Luebbert, Gregory M. 1986. *Comparative Democracies*. Berkeley: University of California Press.

Lupia, Arthur. 2003. "Delegation and Its Perils." In Kaare Strøm, Wolfgang C. Müller, and Torbjörn Bergman (eds.), *Delegation and Accountability in Parliamentary Democracies*. Oxford: Oxford University Press, 33–54.

Maddicott, John R. 2010. *The Origins of the English Parliament*. Oxford: Oxford University Press.

Madison, James. 2009 [1788]. *The Federalist Papers*, No. 58. New Haven: Yale University Press.

Martin, Shane. 2014. "Why Electoral Systems Don't Always Matter: The Impact of 'Mega-seats' on Legislative Behaviour in Ireland." *Party Politics* 20(3): 467–479.

Martin, Shane. 2016. "Policy, Office and Votes: The Electoral Value of Ministerial Office." *British Journal of Political Science* 46(2): 281–296.

Mayhew, David. 1974. *Congress: The Electoral Connection*. New Haven: Yale University Press.

McChesney, Fred S. 1997. *Money for Nothing: Politicians, Rent Extraction, and Political Extortion*. Cambridge, MA: Harvard University Press.

Metcalf, Michael. 1987. *The Riksdag: A History of the Swedish Parliament*. New York: St. Martin's Press.

Miller, Gary J. 2005. "The Political Evolution of Principal-Agent Models." *Annual Review of Political Science* 8: 203–225.

Mitchell, Paul. 2000. "Voters and Their Representatives: Electoral Institutions and Delegation in Parliamentary Democracies." *European Journal of Political Research* 37(3): 335–351.

Montesquieu, Charles de S. 1989 [1748] *The Spirit of the Laws*. New York: Cambridge University Press.

Müller, Wolfgang C., and Kaare Strøm (eds.). 1999. *Policy, Office, or Votes?: How Political Parties in Western Europe Make Hard Decisions*. Cambridge: Cambridge University Press.

Narud, Hanne Marthe, and Henry Valen. 2008. "Coalition Membership and Electoral Performance." In Kaare Strøm, Wolfgang C. Müller, and Torbjörn Bergman (eds.), *Cabinets and Coalition Bargaining: The Democratic Life Cycle in Western Europe*. Oxford: Oxford University Press, 369–402.

Norton, Philip. 2018. "The House of Commons at Work." In Bill Jones, Philip Norton, and Oliver Daddow (eds.), *Politics UK*. Oxford: Routledge, 371–73.

Packenham, Robert A. 1970. "Legislatures and Political Development." In Allan Kornberg and Lloyd D. Musolf (eds.), *Legislatures in Developmental Perspective*. Durham: Duke University Press, 521–537.

Polsby, Nelson W. 1975. "Legislatures." In Fred I. Greenstein and Nelson W. Polsby (eds.), *Handbook of Political Science*. Reading, MA: Addison Wesley, 257–319.

Przeworski, Adam. 1991. *Democracy and the Market: Political and Economic Reforms in Eastern Europe and Latin America*. New York: Cambridge University Press.

Przeworski, Adam. 2018. *Why Bother with Elections?* Medford, MA: Polity Press.

Przeworski, Adam, R. Michael Alvarez, Michael E. Alvarez, Jose Antonio Cheibub, and Fernando Limongi. 2000. *Democracy and Development: Political Institutions and Well-being in the World, 1950–1990*. New York: Cambridge University Press.

Rasch, Bjørn Erik, Shane Martin, and Jose Antonio Cheibub (eds.). 2015. *Parliaments and Government Formation*. Oxford: Oxford University Press.

Riker, William H. 1982. *Liberalism against Populism*. San Francisco: W.H. Freeman.

Rose, Richard, and Thomas Mackie. 1983. "Incumbency in Government: Asset or Liability." In Hans Daalder and Peter Mair (eds.), *Western European Party Systems: Continuity and Change*. London: Sage, 115–137.

Saalfeld, Thomas and Kaare W. Strøm. 2014. "Political Parties." In Shane Martin, Thomas Saalfeld, and Kaare W. Strøm (eds.), *The Oxford Handbook of Legislative Studies*. Oxford: Oxford University Press, 371–398.

Samuels, David J., and Matthew S. Shugart. 2010. *Presidents, Parties, and Prime Ministers*. New York: Cambridge University Press.

Schlesinger, Joseph. 1966. *Ambition and Politics: Political Careers in the United States*. Chicago: Rand McNally.

Schuler, Paul, and Edward J. Maleski. 2014. "Authoritarian Legislatures." In Shane Martin, Thomas Saalfeld, and Kaare W. Strøm (eds.), *The Oxford Handbook of Legislative Studies*. Oxford: Oxford University Press, 676–695.

Sieberer, Ulrich, Peter Meißner, Julia F. Keh, and Wolfgang C. Müller. 2016. "Mapping and Explaining Parliamentary Rule Changes in Europe: A Research Program." *Legislative Studies Quarterly* 41(1): 61–88.

Smith, Daniel M. 2018. *Dynasties and Democracy*. Stanford: Stanford University Press.

Smith, Daniel M., and Shane Martin. 2017. "Political Dynasties and the Selection of Cabinet Ministers." *Legislative Studies Quarterly* 42(1): 131–165.

Somit, Albert, Rudolf Wildenmann, Bernhard Boll, and Andrea Römmele (eds.). 1994. *The Victorious Incumbent: A Threat to Democracy?* Aldershot: Dartmouth.

Strøm, Kaare. 1985. "Party Goals and Government Performance in Parliamentary Democracies." *American Political Science Review* 79(3): 738–754.

Strøm, Kaare. 1990. "A Behavioral Theory of Competitive Political Parties." *American Journal of Political Science* 34(2): 565–598.

Strøm, Kaare. 1992. "Democracy as Political Competition." *American Behavioral Scientist* 35(4-5): 375–396.

Strøm, Kaare. 2003. "Parliamentary Democracy and Delegation." In Kaare Strøm, Wolfgang C. Muller, and Torbjorn Bergman (eds.), *Delegation and Accountability in Parliamentary Democracies*. Oxford: Oxford University Press, 55–106.

Strøm, Kaare. 2012. "Roles as Strategies: Towards a Logic of Legislative Behavior." In Magnus Blomgren and Olivier Rozenberg (eds.), *Parliamentary Roles in Modern Legislatures*. Abington: Routledge, 85–100.

Thiel, Peter. 2014. *Zero to One: Notes on Startups, or How to Build the Future*. New York: Crown Business.

Tridimas, George. 2012. "Constitutional Choice in Ancient Athens: The Rationality of Selection to Office by Lot." *Constitutional Political Economy* 23: 1–21.

Turner, Ralph V. 2003. *Magna Carta through the Ages*. London: Pearson Longman.

2

Comparing Legislative Assemblies

In Chapter 1 we argued that we can meaningfully classify legislative assemblies based on the interests of key institutional actors, specifically ordinary members of the assembly, its leaders, and voters. We thus proposed three assembly types, based on the extent to which the assembly's rules and procedures favor one or another of these actors: A members' assembly, a leaders' assembly, and a voters' assembly. These three types are all compatible with democracy and are therefore the ones on which this book will focus. Moreover, these concepts are ideal types in the sense that each is defined by a set of characteristics that are commonly clustered for reasons of design or historical evolution. They are also pure or polar types that we are unlikely to encounter in the real world of legislative politics, but that help us identify common empirical correlates and patterns. Ideal types such as these are thus designed to help us understand and compare the institutions they describe by highlighting their most critical features and the relationships among them.

In the rest of this book, we will examine the legislative assemblies of the world's major democracies and employ the ideal types presented in Chapter 1 to help us understand them. How closely do real-world legislative assemblies in the world's major democracies correspond to these ideal types? And to what extent do such differences help us understand important ways in which these assemblies function and make policy? This chapter sets out our strategy to explore the design and functioning of legislative assemblies in the democratic world. Our ambition is to identify the memberships, powers, and processes of real-world legislative assemblies and the extent to which the ideal types set out in Chapter 1 help us understand them.

In developing a typology of legislative assemblies, and using this typology to understand and simplify real-world variety, we are following in the footsteps of many distinguished legislative scholars. Students at least as far back as Bagehot (1867) have focused on the functions that democratic legislatures serve and sought to identify important assembly types accordingly. In more contemporary scholarship, Polsby (1975) identified "arena" and "transformative" legislatures and the critical differences between them: "for arenas the impact of external forces is decisive in accounting for legislative outcomes. For transformative legislatures, what is decisive are variables depicting internal structure and sub-cultural norms" (Polsby 1975, 141). Based on each assembly's policy-making powers and its level of external support, Mezey (1979) differentiates between active, reactive, minimal, vulnerable, and marginal Legislatures. More recently, Kreppel (2014) explores

Legislative Assemblies. Shane Martin and Kaare W. Strøm, Oxford University Press.
© Shane Martin and Kaare W. Strøm (2023). DOI: 10.1093/oso/9780198890829.003.0002

differences in institutional and partisan autonomy, distinguishing between weak congresses, strong congresses, weak parliaments, and strong parliaments. Institutional autonomy is thus defined in large part by regime type and especially by the constitutional relationship between the assembly and the executive power, whereas partisan autonomy refers to the ability of legislative parties to withstand pressure from the executive or from their own extra-parliamentary organizations and their members.

Recognizing the contributions of this literature in defining critical variables that constrain assembly powers and functions, our project is based on the belief that any effort to understand legislatures must also appreciate the goals and strategies of the critical actors that select and populate them: members, leaders, and voters. Thus, in approaching the world's democratic assemblies we are guided by the objectives of the major players within these institutions, the ways in which these actors shape their arenas, and the consequences of such design features. We do not assume that the objectives of members, leaders, and voters necessarily conflict with one another. In other words, there may be assembly features that two different types of actors, or perhaps all three, find desirable. For example, both members and leaders (though not necessarily voters) may appreciate long terms between elections. Moreover, both voters and ordinary members (though not necessarily leaders) may value strong executive oversight capabilities. And all three sets of actors may prefer not to waste precious time and resources on fruitless pursuits. Preferences over assembly features and processes must in our view be considered case by case. In this and the following chapters, we shall pursue this agenda by identifying the features of legislative assemblies to which we will apply our perspective. We will then use our classification scheme to derive expectations about the value of different forms of legislative organization to different types of actors.

A second task in this chapter is thus to provide the rationale for and survey the most important such assembly structures and processes. Our dataset includes over 300 variables on 10 general themes concerning the membership, structures, processes, and powers of legislative assemblies in our 68 democratic countries. We hope that these data, in addition to helping us determine the empirical usefulness of our ideal types, will serve as a basic infrastructure for many scholars interested in comparative legislative organization and design.

Finally, this chapter will present the methods used to collect and create the data we examine empirically and outline the ways in which these data will be discussed and analyzed in subsequent chapters. For this purpose, we need to address a number of research design challenges, beginning with our selection of cases.

2.1 Case Selection

This is a study of national legislative assemblies in democratic countries. Our empirical focus in this book is thus on the structures, processes, and powers of the national legislatures in 68 major contemporary democratic states. By major states we in this context mean sovereign countries with a population of four million inhabitants or more. By democracies we mean states that as of the end of 2015 had at least one legislative chamber elected in regular and reasonably free and fair elections in which virtually all adult citizens were qualified to vote.[1]

Our focus on countries with a population of four million or more is driven by real-world relevance as well as data availability concerns, since information on the institutions of small democracies is generally more difficult to ascertain, and since these assemblies obviously affect fewer lives than those of larger countries such as India or the United States. Some smaller democracies may also be able to function with less institutionalized and professional assemblies than larger democracies. All the world's democracies with a population of four million or more do in fact have national legislatures, and the great majority of these assemblies operate on a full-time basis. These societies are generally large enough to need and be able to support a professional and institutionalized legislature. We should emphasize that the decision to focus on relatively larger democracies was not an easy one, and that it remains our ambition to expand this study to a larger number of contemporary democracies.

Finally, in terms of case selection, note that our focus is on national legislatures. We do not, therefore, include supranational legislatures, such as the European Parliament. Nor do we include subnational legislatures, for example the state legislatures of California or Texas, as important and powerful as these may be. That is not to suggest that our typology cannot fruitfully be applied to these and other supranational or subnational cases. But we believe that sovereignty matters, especially for institutions that are often constitutionally designated as the main representation of national popular interests. And our focus here will be on legislative assemblies in sovereign states. Our 68 democracies nevertheless represent a broad set of continents and environments, though predictably more affluent and stable parts of the world are better represented than regions that are less prosperous and stable. In geographical terms, 12 of our assemblies represent Sub-Saharan Africa, eight are Asian, three are Oceanic, three are Middle Eastern/North African, 17 are American, and 25 are European.

2.2 Assembly Organization and Functions

Legislative assemblies are as heterogeneous in organization and design as they are ubiquitous. Legislatures are too complex for us to be able to map every institutional feature, requiring us to make hard choices with regards to what aspects of

---

[1] As Chapter 3 will demonstrate, there is some modest cross-national variation in age requirements for the right to vote in legislative elections. Some democratic countries also restrict voting rights on the basis of insanity or criminal convictions, and most reserve voting rights for those who have citizenship.

legislative design we study and which we do not. A key task, therefore, is to identify the core set of design features that help us identify the interests that different forms of legislative organization serve. In other words, what features of legislatures allow us to score them as a members', leaders', or voters' assembly? In so doing, we aim to discover patterns in these properties, and their sources, in historical and societal contexts. We aim systematically to select those features of legislative life that are particularly important to members, leaders, and voters, respectively. For this purpose, we explore 10 important aspects of legislative assemblies, with a subsequent chapter dedicated to each of these themes. Each aspect can, to a greater or lesser extent, tell us something about the degree to which any given assembly aligns with each of our ideal types.

Membership Selection Rules

Our first focus is on membership selection, on the rules and procedures governing who gains membership in the legislative assembly. This issue is clearly fundamental to the problem of agency discussed in Chapter 1. Citizens' ability to choose who represents them and hold these representatives to account at the next election is central to our concept of a voters' assembly. Likewise, the rules governing membership have important consequences for the degree to which leaders can manage and control the assembly or the degree to which members can behave independently of party leaders.

Specifically, we will focus on (1) rules that govern who can become a legislator, (2) the electoral system used to elect the members, (3) the maximum inter-electoral period, and (4) the rules shaping the degree to which individual legislators are secure in office between elections. The specific design of these rules, we suggest, can privilege or constrain citizens in their capacity to select and control who represents them. In a perfect voters' assembly, citizens have direct and immediate influence over the selection of members as well as the ability to remove and replace these representatives through future elections or other processes. These rules, we suggest, also privilege or constrain members and leaders and in particular the degree to which a legislator is accountable to, or relatively independent from, leaders and voters.

Membership

The purpose of selection rules, of course, is to influence who gets to occupy legislative office. Next, we therefore explore the actual membership composition of the legislative assemblies in our study. Whereas in some political bodies (such as assemblies in ancient Athens, or juries in many democracies) the members are drawn more or less randomly from the (adult) population, contemporary legislative assemblies rarely come close to mirroring the demographics of their respective electorates. Indeed, compared to their electorates, most legislatures include more middle-aged and senior individuals, more men, more well-educated people, and more affluent individuals, whereas women and ethnic and religious minorities are often under-represented. All these biases may be noteworthy and consequential, but not all of them are equally undesirable from the perspectives of voters, members, and leaders.

We will discuss various facets of assembly membership but focus on two in particular: (1) the degree to which the partisan composition of the chamber reflects the partisanship of the voters and (2) the proportion of the assembly's members that are women. We do so because we believe both aspects provide important insights into whether legislative assemblies serve the interest of voters, members, or leaders. In general, we suggest that a voters' assembly will have a membership that broadly reflects the partisanship of the voters and in which both genders are significantly represented. At the same time, we believe that leaders, in the interest of facilitating majority construction in the assembly, may wish for less partisan proportionality.

Cameral Structure

Cameral structure is our next topic for investigation. A legislative assembly's cameral structure describes the number of chambers it contains. Though in the nineteenth century, both Sweden and Finland had four-chamber assemblies, contemporary democracies tend to have one or two. In the cases of bicameral (two-chamber) assemblies, the similarities and differences between the chambers also matter. One of them is the division of authority between the chambers. Thus, in his influential analysis Arend Lijphart (2012) distinguishes between symmetrical (where power is fairly equally divided between the two chambers) and asymmetrical bicameralism (where the lower chamber dominates). Lijphart's second distinction is, according to the method of selection, between congruent and incongruent bicameralism. Under congruent bicameralism, both chambers are elected under similar rules, whereas incongruent bicameralism means that the rules differ markedly.

Such differences in bicameralism may matter significantly to voters, members, and leaders. Leaders (who are typically found in the lower chamber) may have mixed views on cameral structure. Party leaders are most likely to favor a second chamber that is appointed (because it offers opportunities for patronage or a political "retreat") or congruent (elected under similar rules) and asymmetric (less powerful than the lower chamber). Congruent and asymmetric upper chambers are likely to have a partisan composition similar to the lower chamber and limited powers of opposition. While a relatively powerless second chamber may thus be convenient, an independently elected and powerful second chamber is much more likely to stand in the way of the ambitions of the leaders of the lower house. Bicameralism is more likely to serve the interest of members. The presence of a second chamber may offer an avenue for promotion and thus satisfy what Schlesinger (1966) terms "progressive ambition." Even when "elevation" to the second chamber is more of a euphemism than a promotion, an upper chamber may offer a comfortable and prestigious avenue for senior politicians to scale back their activities (or be gracefully "kicked upstairs"). In contrast, voters' interests will only be served under bicameralism if both chambers are democratically selected. For all its potential utilities, an unelected second chamber is the polar opposite to our notion of a voters' assembly—an open legislative assembly where members are highly responsive and accountable to citizens.

Legislative Organization

Next we will look at internal legislative organization, which Alemán (2015: 145) defines as "the set of procedures that regulate the legislative process and the related set of offices with internal authority." These procedures may have a variety of rationales, but they rarely provide a "level playing field" for all members. Real-world legislative organization thus typically contrasts with what Cox (2006: 141) calls the legislative state of nature—"an assembly in which members wield equal parliamentary rights and in which access to plenary time is unregulated."

How a legislature is organized by way of rules, procedures, and its allocation of powers and resources between members is of vital importance to voters, members, and leaders alike. A members' assembly associates with a structure in which authority and resources are decentralized to individual members and the procedural rights of ordinary members protected. In contrast, a more centralized legislative organization will characterize a leaders' assembly—with party leaders holding significant formal authority over procedural rights and resources. Voters may be more conflicted over this issue, but we assume that in general they prefer to vest power in their direct, rather than indirect, agents. This preference seems particularly likely for assemblies with candidate-centered electoral systems.

Our survey of legislative organization, which encompasses a series of chapters in this book, will focus on two particularly important "nerve centers" of legislative assemblies, namely political parties and standing (or permanent) legislative committees. In most assemblies, these are the venues in which the most consequential decisions are made.

Political Parties

Though constitution makers from James Madison and the Federalists onward have been wary of political parties, they are the most important decision-making units in most contemporary legislatures. We therefore next turn our attention to legislative parties. Parties do many things, but one critical function in legislative assemblies is to provide a hierarchical decision-making structure. The most powerful leaders in modern legislatures are almost without exception the leading members of the most powerful political parties within these assemblies. A core empirical concern in our study is the degree to which parties, and in particular party leaders, through their control of ballot access, committee assignments, or funding, have the capacity to control members and thus define the relationship between voters and their representatives. A leaders' assembly is one in which this capacity is high, whereas in a members' assembly the power of party leaders is more conditional and circumscribed.

Legislative Committees

Next we turn to committees and especially permanent (standing) committees with substantive responsibilities for the preparation of bills in designated policy areas. Alongside parties, committees are frequently cited as amongst the most important internal organizational features of a legislative assembly. Whereas legislative parties represent the development of hierarchy within legislative assemblies, committees are typically vehicles of differentiation and specialization. We believe that, all else equal, a system of permanent and specialized committees enhances the capacity and expertise of that legislative assembly to the benefit of members and citizens and sometimes to the detriment of party leaders.

Lawmaking Authority

After analyzing these critical legislative fora, we shall examine rules and procedures with respect to four critical assembly functions: (1) lawmaking, (2) budgeting, (3) appointments, and (4) oversight of the executive. While we may think of legislative assemblies as all having a similar set of functions, there is in fact significant variation in what different legislative assemblies do. Our first task in this regard will be to explore variation in the authority and capacity of legislative assemblies to make laws. This legislative capacity may vary along several dimensions. One has to do with the laws and regulations that empower particular office-holders or institutions to introduce legislative bills (proposed pieces of legislation).

Another aspect of lawmaking authority has to do with the control that the executive branch has over the assembly's agenda.

Budgetary Authority

The budgetary powers of legislative assemblies are a critical aspect of their capacity. Making budgetary decisions is one of the key functions of democratic legislatures and, as with lawmaking more generally, the assembly's ability to perform this function speaks to the capacity challenge that we discussed in Chapter 1. Cox (2014: 710) thus argues that "any measure of legislative power should be mostly about the legislature's power over the purse. If that power fails, the others will likely be illusory." Yet, legislative assemblies may be more or less involved in determining exactly how much the government taxes, borrows, and spends across different policy areas. We expect an assembly's budgetary capacity to be related to its purposes. A members' assembly may use the budgetary process to seek rents or win personal votes for its members (or at least the more influential ones), to the detriment of fiscal discipline. In contrast, a voters' assembly and a leaders' assembly will in different ways seek to overcome the collective action problems of budgeting for many discrete local constituencies. But while a voters' assembly will seek to minimize the slack and waste in such a budget, a leaders' assembly will instead focus on how to capture the rents from this process for the party leadership. While we may expect different levels of legislative power over the budgetary process to have different consequences, the first task in studying budgetary processes is to capture empirically the wide variation in budgetary powers. In this process, we shall rely in large measure on pioneering previous work by Joachim Wehner (2010).

Elective and Appointment Authority

Next, we turn to the elective function that legislative assemblies perform. Selecting, appointing, and/or sanctioning the head of government and other high public officials is a critical function of most democratic legislatures. And legislative assemblies in many presidential as well as parliamentary regimes routinely appoint a number of other office holders that may not subsequently be accountable to the assembly majority, such as judges, directors of public enterprises, ambassadors, and commissioners. Such elective powers have consequences for the degree to which particular legislatures fit the mold of members', leaders', or voters' assemblies. In a pure leaders' assembly, it is permissible and easy for legislative leaders to take control of executive office for themselves or their co-partisans, and difficult to displace their appointees. A members' assembly, in contrast, will feature a broad range of permissive appointment and dismissal powers vested in the assembly itself. Finally, a voters' assembly will have appointment powers largely in technical areas (such as the selection of a central bank governor), but not with respect to the most important political offices, such as the cabinet. In other words, we assume that voters prefer to have the power to elect the chief political executive directly, even if they prefer to leave personnel choices concerning offices requiring greater technical expertise in the hands of their elected representatives.

Oversight Authority

Finally, legislative assemblies have important oversight functions. The capacity to oversee the executive echoes the fundamental nature of the voters' assembly. A voters' assembly should have a high capacity to monitor, and high transparency, as voters need information on the performance of the incumbent powers to decide whom to support at election time. A leaders' assembly, in contrast, may be less inclined to develop and employ tools of executive oversight. A members' assembly should ensure that executive oversight is sufficiently strong such that individual legislators can monitor the executive in pursuit of their own goals, be those re-election, progressive ambition, or some other objective. To explore oversight capacity we will examine a numbers of tools at the disposal of legislators, including parliamentary questions, investigations, audit functions and offices, and, ultimately, the right to remove the executive.

2.3 Understanding Organizational Choices

The chapters that follow will thus provide a wealth of information on the legislative assemblies of contemporary democracies. They will also be designed to help us understand the cross-national variation in these properties. For example, whereas the US House of Representatives has a fixed two-year term, the Liberian House of Representatives is elected for an electoral period of six years. Benin's Assemblée Nationale has just five standing committees while the House of Representatives in neighboring Nigeria has 84. In Ireland, voters can use their vote to benefit individual candidates from not just one, but several parties, whereas Norwegian voters can support only one party and effectively have no opportunity to affect the selection of candidates from within that party's list. These examples only begin to illustrate the variation we observe in how legislatures are designed and organize. But what factors may account for the choice of institutional design and functions in the first place? Alongside describing how legislatures vary (and ultimately mapping such variation onto our typology of legislative assemblies), we are interested in understanding the sources of institutional variation.

Legislative assemblies and their functions must be understood in context. In particular we are interested in the degree to which legislative structures and roles correlate with history, geography, economy, society, and political regimes. Note that we will be looking for correlations, or associations, between assembly features and characteristics of the societies in which they have emerged. Such correlations may or may not represent causal relationships. It may indeed be that some assembly properties, such as for example rules concerning the conditions under which elections can be called, tend to result from features or events in the societies they represent. On the other hand, as we shall discuss later in this volume, the causal directions may be reversed, so that assembly features and procedures influence the societies in which they exist. Moreover, there may be cases, as could well be suggested for the UK House of Commons or the US Congress, in which particularities of one country's legislature have effects well beyond its own borders (see e.g., Power and Rae 2006).

Yet, we need to be cautious in interpreting any empirical association we find as causal. In a strict sense, causation implies that one variable, the putative cause, is a necessary and sufficient condition for a particular outcome, the putative effect. In other words, the cause will always produce this particular effect, and the effect will never appear in the absence of the cause. This is a very strong claim, which we will rarely make. In a less demanding sense, scholars often invoke causal language to refer to conditions under which one variable systematically influences the incidence of another. We believe such causal influences exist among some assembly characteristics, though we cannot always identify the mechanisms by which these relationships work, or exclude alternative explanations. We shall therefore endeavor to uncover associations between legislative features and their geographical, historical, social, and political environments, but it is often beyond our capacity here to determine whether these associations are truly causal.

For example, as we shall see, the number of staff members per legislator tends to increase with a country's population size, as well as with its affluence. We find it plausible to think that this association may have causal foundations, as increasing population size and affluence may influence political decisions to expand legislative staffing levels. We also believe that this direction of influence is more plausible than the reverse (that expansive legislative staffing increases wealth or population growth). But we will not in this book attempt to trace such political processes. Nor will we exhaustively try to eliminate alternative explanations, such as for example that both staffing levels and prosperity stem from common cultural features or historical influences.

In seeking to map and understand the range of assembly features that we will consider, we shall apply standard quantitative methods such as ordinary-least-squares and logistic regressions with a set of predictors (independent variables) that represent societal, geographical, historical, economic, and political factors that we expect might correlate with assembly features. We shall employ these background variables in standard clusters in each of our various chapters. Because of the complexity of the task, we will not, for each of these background variables and each assembly feature, develop explicit hypotheses concerning their effects. In some cases, plausible expectations could be derived from existing scholarship. In other cases, our predictors should simply be considered as standard control variables. In some models, however, we will specifically identify and include institutional and other variables that existing scholarship has identified as potentially important determinants of the legislative feature in question.

Our regression models will report coefficients that estimate the effect of a change in the independent variable on the dependent variable. We will also report a coefficient of determination that estimates the amount of variance in the dependent variable that is explained by the set of independent variables in that model. Finally, we report standard significance levels for each of the coefficients in each model. These should be interpreted cautiously for a number of reasons. For one thing, our set of 68 observations (in some cases even fewer) is small enough that statistical significance is generally hard to obtain. More fundamentally, it is not obvious what statistical significance tells us about our set of legislative assemblies. Our data set is one that includes all national legislatures of democracies above a certain population size. It is not a random sample of anything, and it is unclear what larger population it might be argued to represent. For example, since we have deliberately included only societies with a population of four million or more, our data is clearly not a representative sample of all democratic societies. Similarly, since all our assemblies are described as of the end of 2015, we cannot strictly make generalizations about legislatures across time, or about patterns of historical development within them. Our findings, then, should be understood as an exercise in mapping and description in the interest of understanding, but not as a set of strict causal claims. We do hope that more specific and causal claims can and will be made in the relevant literatures (and some obviously have been in existing works) and that our exercise can contribute to such research agendas.

Let us then turn to the background factors against which we will seek to understand our legislative assemblies. First, we are interested in whether legislative instruments associate with how long a state has existed as an independent and sovereign entity. Some countries are old, others relatively new. Forty-one of the countries in our study were already independent in 1900 and have been so continually since then. Three countries gained independence in the 1910s (South Africa, Finland, and Poland). Ireland gained independence in the 1920s. Six countries gained independence in the 1940s, followed by two counties (Tunisia and Ghana) in the 1950s. Nine countries gained independence in the 1960s, followed by one state (Papua New Guinea) in the 1970s, and four in the 1990s. The newest country in our study is Serbia, which became a sovereign state on June 5, 2006, following Montenegro's secession.

Legislative structures, rules and functions may date from the time of sovereignty, as such moments are usually critical moments constitutionally and more generally in the design of political organizations. And as Cheibub et al. (2014) note, "in order to predict the powers of a country's executive and legislature, it is more useful to know where and when the constitution was written than whether the country has a presidential or parliamentary system." In particular, the first two decades of the twentieth century were a time when many new states emerged and democratized, especially in the industrializing world. Similarly, many regimes in developing countries date from the first two decades after World War II. Such waves of decolonization and democratization may have left similar imprints on the societies involved. We therefore want to place our democracies within these temporal parameters in particular. In the regressions reported in the subsequent chapters, the variable sovereignty is the date of most recent tradition to independence post-1900. Cases of pre-1900 sovereignty are coded as if these transitions occurred in the year 1900, since precise dating in these cases can be more problematic and since we are less convinced that exact dates matter as much for the oldest democracies (full details of all variables including the source are available in Appendix 1).

Our second variable which may help explain variations among legislative assemblies is a measure of a country's economic wealth. GDP per capita provides such a measure, controlling for the population size of the country. Wealth is often used in studies of politics as an explanatory variable or as a theoretically informed control variable. For example, Przeworski et al. (2000) find a strong relationship between a moderate to high level of economic development and democracy. It also stands to reason that a country's wealth may impact its capacity to invest in political institutions, including its legislative assembly. In overall income terms, Burundi is the poorest country in our study with a GDP per capita of USD 275.98, while Switzerland has the greatest wealth with a GDP per capita of USD 80,214.73. The per capita income ratio between these two countries is thus close to 300 to 1, powerfully underscoring the variance in affluence among the world's contemporary democracies.

We also consider whether income inequality—the degree to which a nation's income is spread across its citizenry or is generated (and enjoyed) by a small minority of citizens—relates to legislative instruments. Boix (2003), for example, argues that income inequality hinders the prospects for democracy, since under high income inequality the wealthy would resist enfranchisement of the poor, out of fear that the latter would confiscate the property of the former through the ballot box. In this scenario, we might expect highly unequal societies to be inimical to voters' assemblies. In contrast, Ansell and Samuels (2014) find democratization to be most likely under land equality but income inequality (see also Deaton

2013). The implications for assembly types would thus be contested. In empirical studies, the Gini coefficient of income inequality is a commonly adopted measure, with higher scores indicating higher levels of income inequality. A Gini coefficient of zero would thus mean that income is perfectly equally distributed, so that no person receives any more than anyone else, whereas a coefficient of one represents perfect inequality, with one person claiming the entire national income. On this variable, the Ukraine exhibits the highest equality in our sample, while South Africa is our most economically unequal democracy in terms of income distribution.

Overall population size also may impact how a legislature works. And even though our sample of legislative assemblies has been selected in part on population size, it still exhibits a great deal of variation on this count. By population, the smallest country in our study is Croatia (with just under 4.4 million inhabitants) while the largest is India, with a population of roughly 1.3 billion. In our analysis, we log population size to avoid giving disproportionate weight to outliers such as India. The variable log(Population) is thus our measure of a country's population size. All else equal, we expect that such variables as membership size, staffing levels, and committee numbers will scale with population size.

We will also explore whether ethnic fractionalization—the degree to which a country is ethnically diverse—correlates with assembly features. Some countries are relatively ethnically homogenous while others are heterogeneous, and research has demonstrated consequences for how political institutions are designed (Fearon 2003). South Korea has the lowest ethnic diversity in our sample, while Papua New Guinea is the most fractionalized society. From our perspective, ethnic fractionalization is likely to impact the allocation of legislative power and resources, especially where such diversity is constitutionally recognized. Thus, powersharing arrangements in ethnically diverse societies may favor certain forms of legislative organization, most likely such in which minorities are guaranteed some access and power (see Strøm et al. 2017).

When exploring the correlates of legislative assembly types, we also want to control for geographic location and specifically for world regions. While our globalized world may ultimately break down the consequences of geography, a country's physical position in the world has long been associated with certain trends and institutional norms. Most democracies in the Western hemisphere, for example, are presidential (Canada being an obvious but rare exception). Political institutions and other political features often cluster spatially, possibly because of political diffusion whereby countries that are located nearby one another learn from their neighbors' experiences and/or copy institutional designs and reforms from their neighboring regimes (O'Loughlin et al. 1998).

Finally, in exploring variation in legislative assemblies, we control for colonial history. A large majority of the countries included in our study have experienced colonial rule, with many gaining independence after extended periods of colonialism. Yet, colonial histories vary greatly. Fifteen of our countries were British colonies, two (Belgium and Indonesia) were Dutch colonies, one (Burundi) was a Belgian possession, three (Benin, Niger, and Senegal) were French colonies, 15 Spanish, one (Brazil) was a Portuguese colony, one (Poland) was at times ruled by Germany, three (Croatia, the Czech Republic, and the Slovak Republic) were parts of the Austro-Hungarian Empire, one (Ukraine) was Russian, six were Turkish, one (South Korea) was Japanese, while the remaining 19 countries in our study were never colonized.

A colonial legacy is often present in political institutions (Abramson and Barber 2019). In part, colonial powers often transposed their political institutions and framework (although typically in a less than democratic context) to their colonies. For example, many (but not all) features of the Irish Parliament can be traced back to Westminster and the legacy of British rule in Ireland (and Irish MPs in the House of Commons). And when Nigeria emerged from British rule in 1960, many of its institutions looked remarkably similar to Westminster. Similarly, many former French colonies have inherited features typical of the French republican tradition. Such institutional dissemination was presumably more likely in cases (such as Nigeria) in which decolonization happened peacefully and by mutual consent than where it happened through national uprisings or anti-colonial wars (such as in Vietnam or Poland). Wehner (2006), for example, finds that colonial legacy—and even more so the specific colonial power—influences the formal role of legislatures in the budgetary process, particularly in African countries. To account for the potential impact of colonial powers, we therefore include control for whether the legislative assembly operates in a country that was part of the British Empire, was controlled by another colonial power, or did not experience colonialism.

2.4 Data Collection

In this study, we want to understand how legislatures are organized, why, and with what consequences. To gain such understanding and be able to compare real-world legislative assemblies with our ideal types, we embarked on a major multi-year data collection exercise. As noted above, our study covers 68 countries. Some legislatures are sufficiently communicative and information-rich as to make data collection relatively easy; other cases required extensive research, including engagement with the legislative assemblies themselves or calling on national experts for help. In assembling our data, we have not discriminated on regional grounds or by levels of development, even though data for some parts of the world are clearly more easily available, and perhaps more reliable, than those for other regions.

Our empirical approach to data collection involved a number of sequential steps discussed below.[2] Basic information on all variables used in our analysis and their sources are included alongside further supplementary information and, to aid replication, coding decisions online (available at www.legislatures.pub). Here, we want to review briefly the various sources on which we relied and the methods we used to locate data for all 68 cases. As a first step, in our data collection effort we have relied on a number of existing datasets, including the major datasets listed in Table 2.1.

Table 2.1 Major secondary sources employed in this study

Inter-Parliamentary Union	1. Parline database: http://www.ipu.org/parline-e/parlinesearch.asp 2. Global Parliamentary Report: http://www.ipu.org/gpr/gpr/downloads/index.htm#data
Parliamentary Powers Index	http://polisci.berkeley.edu/people/person/m-steven-fish
Database of Political Institutions	http://go.worldbank.org/2EAGGLRZ40
African Legislatures Project	http://www.cssr.uct.ac.za/alp
Europa World Online	http://www.europaworld.com/welcome
World Values Survey	http://www.worldvaluessurvey.org/wvs.jsp
Index of Economic Freedom	http://www.heritage.org/index/download
Human Development Index	http://hdr.undp.org/en/content/human-development-index-hdi
Polity	http://www.systemicpeace.org/polity/polity4.htm
Freedom House	https://freedomhouse.org/
OECD Budget	http://www.oecd.org/gov/budgeting/internationalbudgetpracticesandproceduresdatabase.htm
Democratic Electoral Systems Around the World	http://mattgolder.com/elections
World Bank	http://data.worldbank.org/
COW Project	http://cow.dss.ucdavis.edu/
The ICOW Colonial History Data Set	http://www.paulhensel.org/icowcol.html
Boix-Miller-Rosato (BMR) coding of democracy	https://sites.google.com/site/mkmtwo/data
Gallagher Index	http://christophergandrud.github.io/Disproportionality_Data/
Electoral Systems and the Personal Vote	Joel W. Johnson; Jessica S. Wallack. "Electoral Systems and the Personal Vote," http://hdl.handle.net/1902.1/17901

---

[2] Despite our multiple strategies of data collection, we still miss data on a limited set of legislative features for a small number of countries. Wherever such data are missing, we make it clear in the relevant analysis.

As helpful as these existing sources are, they go only some way toward providing us with the information we needed to complete this study. Actually, the majority of data presented and analyzed in this book are based on primary research. In order to collect (and in some cases confirm) data on legislative assemblies we followed a sequential data collection effort based on a number of potential sources. Our first step was to consult national constitutions, which are frequently available on government websites. As a second step we consulted the official website of national legislatures for which we needed information. In the absence of an English-language version of this website (or where the English-language version was clearly truncated relative to the local language version), we relied on Google Translate to help us locate information within the parliamentary website. Some national legislatures have dedicated data websites (for example http://www.data. parliament.uk/), although in our experience most do not. Still, assembly websites can be a valuable source of information which can be quantified or otherwise analyzed. Within this broad category, an invaluable source of information was the assembly's standing orders.

For information that we could not obtain via secondary sources, or by consulting a country constitution, the legislative assembly's standing orders, or its website, our next port of call was direct communication with the legislature itself. Typically, we did this via email or other online communication addressed to the legislature's presiding officer. In cases of non-response, we followed up with communication to the senior assembly official.

A final avenue was national experts. For the legislative assemblies of countries for which we were missing data, we developed a list of up to five country experts. By country experts we mean social scientists (and mostly political scientists) with a field knowledge of, and interest in, a particular country, and preferably in legislative politics in that country. In the first instance we relied on our own professional networks to populate this database. In other cases we first conducted a bibliographical search using country and institution keywords on Google Scholar (and follow-up literature searches) to try to identify country (and institution) experts. We then contacted these experts, one at a time, to see if they could help. In virtually all cases, we received prompt and very helpful answers, or recommendations as to where else to look (including alternative contacts). Note that we did not survey experts on institutional features for which we were able to get the information elsewhere. Rather, country experts were contacted to help obtain missing data or to help clarify questions that made coding difficult.

The end result, we believe, is a fairly complete picture of how legislative assemblies in the world's 68 largest democracies are organized and function, in terms of membership rules, member characteristics, cameral structures, internal organization and procedures, the structure and role of parties and committees, and the legislative assembly's capacity to engage in lawmaking, budgeting, appointments, and oversight.

2.5 Conclusion

How closely do real-world legislative designs correspond to our ideal-type legislative assemblies set out in Chapter 1, and with what consequences? This chapter has set out our strategy in answering these questions by presenting the criteria by which we have selected the assemblies in our study, mapping their legislative organization, providing a rationale for our selection of the institutional features we focus on in the next set of chapters, and discussing the background variables with which we believe these organizational features may correlate. We have discussed our interpretation of any associations we might observe, as well as our strategies in collecting our data. The next 10 chapters will discuss these features of contemporary legislative assemblies before we return in Chapter 13 to seeing whether the empirical variation we observe can fruitfully be understood through the application of the concepts developed in Chapter 1. In the following chapter, we examine the effects of a range of assembly features on an outcome in which members, leaders, and voters all have an interest: the rate at which legislative incumbents get re-elected. We will conclude our analysis by discussing what broader economic, social, and political consequences different forms of legislative organization may have.

References

Abramson, Scott F., and Michael J. Barber 2019. "The Evolution of National Constitutions." *Quarterly Journal of Political Science* 24(1): 89–114.

Alemán, Eduardo. 2015. "Legislative Organization and Outcomes," in Jennifer Gandhi and Rubén Ruiz-Rufino (eds.), *The Routledge Handbook of Comparative Political Institutions*. Abingdon: Routledge, 145–161.

Ansell, Ben W., and David J. Samuels. 2014. *Inequality and Democratization: An Elite-Competition Approach*. Cambridge: Cambridge University Press.

Bagehot, Walter. 1867. *The English Constitution*. London: Chapman & Hall.

Boix, Carles. 2003. *Democracy and Redistribution*. New York: Cambridge University Press.

Cheibub, José Antonio, Zachary Elkins, and Tom Ginsburg. 2014. "Beyond Presidentialism and Parliamentarism." *British Journal of Political Science* 44(3): 515–544.

Cox, Gary W. 2006. "The Organization of Democratic Legislatures." In Barry R. Weingast, and Donald Wittman, (eds.), *The Oxford Handbook of Political Economy*. Oxford: Oxford University Press, 141–161.

Cox, Gary W. 2014. "Reluctant Democrats and Their Legislatures." In Shane Martin, Thomas Saalfeld, and Kaare W. Strøm (eds.), *The Oxford Handbook of Legislative Studies*. Oxford: Oxford University Press, 696–716.

Deaton, Angus. 2013. *The Great Escape*. Princeton: Princeton University Press.

Fearon, John D. 2003. "Ethnic and Cultural Diversity by Country." *Journal of Economic Growth* 8(2): 195–222.

Kreppel, Amie. 2014. "Typologies and Classifications." In Shane Martin, Thomas Saalfeld, and Kaare W. Strøm (eds.), *The Oxford Handbook of Legislative Studies*. Oxford: Oxford University Press, 82–102.

Lijphart, Arend. 2012. *Patterns of Democracy*. 2nd edition. New Haven: Yale University Press.

Mezey, Michael, 1979. *Comparative Legislatures*. Durham: Duke University Press.

O'Loughlin, John, Michael D. Ward, Corey L. Lofdahl, Jordin S. Cohen, David S. Brown, David Reilly, Kristian S. Gleditsch, and Michael Shin. 1998. "The Diffusion of Democracy, 1946–1994." *Annals of the Association of American Geographers* 88(4): 545–574.

Polsby, Nelson. 1975. "Legislatures." In Fred I. Greenstein and Nelson Polsby (eds.), *Handbook of Political Science (Vol. V)*. Reading: Addison-Wesley Press, 557–622.

Power, Timothy Joseph, and Nicol C. Rae (eds.). 2006. *Exporting Congress: The Influence of the U.S. Congress on World Legislatures*. Pittsburgh: University of Pittsburgh Press.

Przeworski, Adam, R. Michael Alvarez, Michael E. Alvarez, José Antonio Cheibub, and Fernando Limongi. 2000. *Democracy and Development: Political Institutions and Well-being in the World, 1950–1990*. New York: Cambridge University Press.

Schlesinger, Joseph A. 1966. *Ambition and Politics: Political Careers in the United States*. Chicago: Rand McNally.

Strøm, Kaare W., Scott Gates, Benjamin A.T. Graham, and Håvard Strand. 2017. "Inclusion, Dispersion, and Constraint: Powersharing in the World's States, 1975–2010." *British Journal of Political Science* 47 (1): 165–185.

Wehner, Joachim. 2006. "Assessing the Power of the Purse: An Index of Legislative Budget Institutions." *Political Studies* 54(4): 767–785.

Wehner, Joachim. 2010. *Legislatures and the Budget Process: The Myth of Fiscal Control*. Basingstoke: Palgrave Macmillan.

3
Electing the Legislative Assembly

Many constitutions explicitly designate the national legislators as the representatives of the people. In most parliamentary systems, they are the only branch of government that stands in this direct agency relationship to the citizens. Under presidentialism, there is at least one other popularly elected institution, yet legislators typically remain the representatives that are closest in proximity to the ordinary voter. In order to serve their representative function, democratic legislatures are directly elected by, and thus accountable to, the citizens. Indeed, in all democratic states, at least one legislative chamber (which we generally refer to as the lower house) is directly elected by popular vote.[1]

In many ways, the direct election of a legislative assembly, and the electoral accountability that this entails, is the very cornerstone of our concept of a voters' assembly. Citizens' ability to choose who represents them, and to hold these representatives to account at the next election (by either re-electing or replacing the incumbents), places voters (those citizens who exercise these voting rights) at the heart of all legislative politics—and reflects Madison's concern regarding popular accountability. Thus, one may be forgiven for thinking that any democratically elected legislative assembly is, by definition, a voters' assembly. Yet, as we will see, ordinary citizens can be privileged or constrained by the rules governing who gets to serve in a legislative assembly. Likewise, the rules governing membership have important consequences for the degree to which leaders can manage and control members or the degree to which members can behave independent of their party leadership.

This chapter focuses on four such rules: (1) rules that govern who can become a legislator, (2) rules which determine how legislators are elected, (3) the rule specifying the maximum inter-electoral period, and (4) rules shaping the degree to which individual legislators are secure in office between elections. The specific design of these rules, we will suggest, can privilege or constrain citizens in their capacity to select and control who represents them. These rules also privilege or constrain leaders in terms of their capacity to control an incumbent's ability to remain in office, and ultimately the degree to which a legislator is accountable to, or relatively independent from, leaders and voters.

---

[1] For cases in which the legislature has two chambers, we will focus on the lower of these, such as the House of Commons in the United Kingdom or the Diet in Japan.

Legislative Assemblies. Shane Martin and Kaare W. Strøm, Oxford University Press.
© Shane Martin and Kaare W. Strøm (2023). DOI: 10.1093/oso/9780198890829.003.0003

Particularly relevant here is the challenge of agency which we discussed in Chapter 1—the challenge to select members able and willing to be responsive to the interests and demands of the citizenry. The rules governing who can seek election, the mechanism by which votes are translated into seats (the electoral system), term length, and removal rules, we will suggest, significantly impact the agency relationship between voters, members and leaders.[2] Selection, duration, and removal rules also privilege or constrain members and leaders, as we will discuss. As a result, membership rules play an important role in shaping the degree to which a country has a voters', members' or leaders' assembly.

Membership selection and removal rules are a complex topic, often raising issues of significance for how a democracy functions. We begin with a discussion of membership restrictions (who can, or cannot, stand for election), spend the bulk of the chapter discussing electoral systems (how votes are translated into legislative seats and in particular the autonomy available to citizens to select who represents them in the assembly), before we discuss term lengths and whatever mechanisms exist to remove a legislator between elections. Our core task is to explore how, if at all, members, leaders, or voters are privileged or constrained by the rules governing who gets to serve in the legislative assembly and for how long.

3.1 Restrictions on Membership

Dahl (1989: 233) identifies the right of "most adults" to run for elected office as an essential element of democracy. In a voters' assembly, we would expect minimal restrictions, other than a citizenship requirement, on who has the right to serve. Minimal membership restrictions maximize the voters' choice set of potential assembly representatives. Yet, even consolidated democracies often impose additional restrictions, typically to ensure that legislators are likely to be competent and have the interests of their constituents at heart. In addition to citizenship, we thus consider three such restrictions on eligibility for legislative office: (1) a minimum-age requirement, (2) a residency requirement, and (3) term limits. Table 3.1 summarizes these membership restrictions by country.

All countries included in this study have citizenship requirements for members of their respective national assemblies.[3] Generally, this means that candidates for membership of a country's national legislature are required to be citizens. There

---

[2] Some legislatures may divide their time into terms or sessions, but for our purpose a legislative term means the maximum time permitted between legislative elections, or in other words the inter-electoral period. Terms may be fixed (as in Norway, Switzerland, or the United States) or have a maximum-specified length (as in most parliamentary democracies).

[3] The Oxford English Dictionary defines citizenship as "The position or status of being a citizen of a particular country," further defining a citizen as "A legally recognized subject or national of a state or commonwealth, either native or naturalized."

Table 3.1 Membership restrictions

Country	Residency Requirement	Minimum Age Restriction	Term Limits
Argentina	in district	25	No
Australia	no requirement	18	No
Austria	no requirement	18	No
Belgium	in country	18	No
Benin	in country	25	No
Bolivia	no requirement	25	2 consecutive terms
Brazil	in district	21	No
Bulgaria	no requirement	21	No
Burundi	in district	25	No
Canada	in country	18	No
Chile	in district	21	No
Colombia	no requirement	25	No
Costa Rica	no requirement	21	2 consecutive terms
Croatia	no requirement	18	No
Czech Republic	no requirement	21	No
Denmark	no requirement	18	No
Dominican Republic	in district	25	No
Ecuador	no requirement	30	No
El Salvador	no requirement	25	No
Finland	no requirement	18	No
France	no requirement	18	No
Germany	in country	18	No
Ghana	in district	21	No
Greece	no requirement	25	No
Guatemala	no requirement	18	No
Honduras	in district	21	No
Hungary	no requirement	18	No
India	no requirement	25	No
Indonesia	no requirement	21	No
Ireland	no requirement	21	No
Israel	no requirement	21	No
Italy	no requirement	18	No
Japan	no requirement	25	No
Kenya	no requirement	18	No
Liberia	no requirement	25	No
Malawi	no requirement	21	No
Mexico	in district	21	4 consecutive terms
Nepal	no requirement	25	No
Netherlands	no requirement	18	No
New Zealand	no requirement	18	No
Nicaragua	no requirement	21	No
Niger	no requirement	21	No

Country	Residency Requirement	Minimum Age Restriction	Term Limits
Nigeria	no requirement	30	No
Norway	no requirement	18	No
Pakistan	no requirement	25	No
Papua New Guinea	in district	25	No
Paraguay	no requirement	25	No
Peru	no requirement	25	No
Philippines	in district	25	3 consecutive terms
Poland	in country	21	No
Portugal	no requirement	18	No
Romania	in country	23	No
Senegal	no requirement	25	No
Serbia	in country	18	No
Sierra Leone	no requirement	21	No
Slovak Republik	in country	21	No
South Africa	in district	18	No
South Korea	no requirement	25	No
Spain	no requirement	18	No
Sweden	no requirement	18	No
Switzerland	no requirement	18	No
Taiwan	no requirement	20	No
Tunisia	no requirement	23	No
Turkey	no requirement	25	No
Ukraine	in country	21	No
United Kingdom	no requirement	18	No
United States	in region	25	No
Zambia	in country	21	No

are some exceptions, which extend the rights to stand for election to related territories. For example, although the Republic of Ireland and the United Kingdom are now separate countries, citizens of either country can stand for election in either country.[4] In other cases our data suggests that the citizenship rule is simpler: To be a national legislator, citizenship of that country is an essential requirement.[5]

Residency—where one lives—may be another barrier to standing for election to the national legislature. Such residency restrictions limit the choice of would-be representatives available to citizens while also possibly imposing limitations on the ability of incumbent members to reside wherever they want or change the location

[4] This uncommon rule reflects the fact that Ireland was until the 1920s part of the United Kingdom.
[5] Australian citizens who are also citizens of another country (dual citizens) are barred from membership of the federal Parliament of Australia. This has caused several Australian federal legislators to resign or be removed from office when it emerged that they held citizenship of another country (Morgan 2018).

in which they seek re-election. A strict residency requirement is that a candidate be registered as living in the legislative district prior to or at the time of election; 11 countries have such a district residency requirement. The exact nature of residency requirements can vary: For example, a prospective legislator may need to spend a minimum period of time in the district to establish residency—perhaps weeks, months, or years. In Argentina for example, a candidate must have been born in the district or have two years of immediate residence therein. In the United States, a candidate for the House of Representatives need not live in the district, but must be a resident of the state in which the district is based. For a further 10 countries in our study, residency in the district or region is not mandatory but residency in the country is. At the other end of the scale, just over two-thirds of our countries have no residency requirement, thus allowing even citizens living abroad to run for elective office (see Table 3.1).

Dahl's reference to "most adults" having the right to seek elected office reminds us that adulthood means different things in different cultures. The legal age of adulthood or majority is 16 in the United Kingdom but up to 21 in the United States, depending on state. Regardless of how we classify adulthood, however, the minimum voting age in contemporary democracies tends to converge. Blais et al. (2001) find that over 90% of the countries in their study have set the voting age at 18. Age restrictions are on the whole more common with respect to eligibility for office than for the right to vote (see Table 3.1). Such minimum age restrictions could be motivated by the belief that legislators should be sufficiently old to be financially independent. Moreover, with age comes experience (allegedly), and some minimum life experience may be considered a desirable personal trait for effective citizenship—or perhaps even to contribute to institutional capacity.

In our sample of 68 countries, none permits individuals under the age of 18 to be a national legislator.[6] Just over one-third of the countries in our study have set 18 as the minimum age to stand for election to the lower chamber. A number of countries specify a minimum age greater than 18. Taiwan sets the minimum age for national legislative office at 20, whereas 19 countries set this limit at 21. Two countries set the age minimum at 23 and several others (including the United States) at 25. The most extreme lower-chamber age restrictions are found in Ecuador and Nigeria, both of which require legislators to be 30 years old. Across all countries in

---

[6] We are unaware of any democratic lower chamber that specifies a maximum age requirement for membership. As we will see in Chapter 5, however, bicameral systems often have different age requirements for lower and upper chambers. Members of the Canadian House of Lords for example can serve only until age 75, at which point they must retire. We discuss the financial benefits of legislative office in Chapter 6, but it is worth noting that pension regulations may impact the incentive for legislators to retire rather than seek re-election. In some countries, pensions may be available only after an extended period of service. And welfare arrangements for legislators exiting at the end of term (due to failure to get re-elected or reselected or of their own choosing) likely shapes post-career financial returns and the incentive to seek re-election.

our study, the mean minimum age is 21.5 years. Thus, on average, the age bar to serve in the national assembly is slightly higher than the bar to vote in legislative elections. Such membership age restrictions mean that the voice of young people may be somewhat under-represented in the legislative arena, a theme we will return to in Chapter 4.

One controversial restriction on membership is the imposition of a term limit. A term limit is a restriction of the right of an office-holder to seek re-election to the same office. As we will see in later chapters, some legislators acquire impressive records of seniority in office. In particular, legislators who win their seat at an early age can often accumulate remarkable seniority. In the United States House of Representatives, individual legislators have had up to 60-year careers, despite the fact that all members are up for re-election every two years.[7] Such seniority is not always beneficial, especially when name recognition, the accumulation of wealth or political connections, or lack of partisan competitiveness allows member to serve into their 80s or even 90s. One way to limit long political careers is through term limits. While term limits may open opportunities for younger candidates or under-represented groups (Carey 1998), such restrictions tend to run counter to the notion of a voters' assembly because they limit the ability of citizens to choose their representatives freely.

Term limits for membership of national legislative assemblies are not very common—only four of our 68 countries have such limitations.[8] In Bolivia and Costa Rica, legislators are limited to serving two consecutive terms. In other words, any legislator who has served two successive terms cannot immediately seek re-election and must wait for a later election to seek legislative office again. In the Philippines, legislators are limited to three consecutive terms. And in Mexico, legislators can serve at most four consecutive terms. Prior to 2014, members of Mexico's Cámara de Diputados were limited to a single consecutive term—in other words, re-election was not a possibility. As one newspaper noted, the softening of this "no re-election" rule was designed to allow for greater accountability and more incentive for Mexican legislators to do national-level legislative work:

> Many observers say re-election would benefit the legislative process by giving lawmakers time to garner experience and expertise on specific issues, while allowing voters to make their representatives more accountable since they could be punished or rewarded at the ballot box for their performance.[9]

---

[7] Representative John D. Dingell, Jr. (D—MI) served Michigan's 12th congressional district for 30 successive terms—a tenure of 59 years and 21 days. John D. Dingell, Jr. thus served under 11 different presidents and became the longest-serving member of the U.S. Congress in history. See also Chapter 14.

[8] Again, our focus is on the lower chamber of each country's national legislative assembly. Subnational legislatures may have term limits even if the national legislature does not, as is the case in a number of US state legislatures.

[9] https://www.wsj.com/articles/mexico-edges-toward-ending-some-term-limits-1380322809.

Term limits reduce or eliminate the ability of voters to hold individual legislators to account at the next election. Such accountability is an important form of ex-post control between principals (voters) and their agents (legislators). Hence, term limits reduce the incentives for incumbents to be responsive to the needs and policy preferences of those who elected them, which creates a form of moral hazard. Term limits may also reduce the ability of leaders to control members, as term-limited members may be less inclined to build or maintain a relationship with the party leadership within the chamber. On the other hand, term limits may induce incumbent politicians to look to the wider party leadership for post-legislative career opportunities. Ultimately, term limits bear little congruence with our notion of a members' assembly, since such restrictions prevent members from building a long-term career within the legislature.

Of course, other factors affect the degree to which incumbent legislators need to be responsive and accountable to voters and/or leaders. And in this regard the most important institution, to which we now turn, is the electoral system.

3.2 Electoral Systems: Translating Votes into Seats

As already noted, electoral systems can be thought of as the mechanism by which votes in an election are transformed into legislative seats. The choice of mechanism has, as we will see, many consequences for which parties and individuals win seats in the legislature (and thus its composition).[10] The choice of electoral system even affects public policy making and economic outcomes (Persson and Tabellini 2005; Rickard 2018). Little wonder then that the choice of electoral system constitutes a crucial decision for constitutional engineers.

The choice of electoral system fundamentally impacts the relationships between voters, members, and leaders. Comparing and classifying electoral systems and their effects is a difficult task because as Farrell (2011: 3) has noted, no two countries have the same electoral system. We therefore have to focus on the most critical "moving parts" of these systems, and identifying these parts in turn depends on the research question that we are asking. Our main goal here is to understand how the electoral system affects the voter-, member- or leader-centeredness of the legislative assembly. Thus, our core interest is in the degree to which an electoral system gives either voters or leaders control over which individuals get to serve in the legislative assembly. Relatedly, we want to understand the degree to which party leaders or voters control an incumbent legislator's re-election prospects. This control differs greatly depending on the design of the electoral system and specifically the degree to which it permits voters to make a choice between political parties (a

---

[10] In the next chapter, we will focus on the degree to which the electoral system produces a proportional partisan outcome—a situation where a parties' share of seats in the legislature tends to correlate highly with the party's share of the national vote.

party-centered system) or between individual candidates (a candidate-centered system). Whereas party-centered electoral systems are conducive to leaders' assemblies, candidate-centered electoral systems will tend to generate a members' assembly. A members' assembly will be elected by a candidate-centered rather than party-centered electoral system because the former rules maximize the autonomy and independence of members from leaders. Citizens' influence over who represents them in the legislative assembly is enhanced in candidate-centered electoral systems where voters can choose between several candidates from their favored political party, thus inducing intra-party differentiation and competition among candidates. In the most candidate-centered systems, voters can even give their support to several candidates from different political parties. Such electoral systems are particularly conducive to voters' assemblies. Table 3.2 provides an overview of electoral rules for all countries in our study.

Table 3.2 Electoral systems and terms

Country	Electoral Rule	Mean District Magnitude	ICPV	Term	Fixed Term
Argentina	Closed List	10.7	1	4	Yes
Australia	Alternative Vote	1	8	3	No
Austria	Closed List	20.3	3	5	No
Belgium	Closed List	13.63	3	5	No
Benin	Closed List	3.46	1	4	Yes
Bolivia	Mixed Member	1.69	10	5	Yes
Brazil	Open List	19	7	4	Yes
Bulgaria	Mixed Member	7.74	1	4	No
Burundi	Closed List	5.88	1	5	No
Canada	SMDP	1	10	4	No
Chile	Closed List	2	5	4	Yes
Colombia	Closed List	5	12	4	Yes
Costa Rica	Closed List	8.1	1	4	Yes
Croatia	Closed List	13.39	3	4	No
Czech Republic	Open List	14.29	2	4	No
Denmark	Open List	10.5	3	4	No
Dominican Republic	Closed List	6.1	3	4	Yes
Ecuador	Closed List	2.74	3	4	Yes
El Salvador	Closed List	8.24	1	3	Yes
Finland	Open List	13.33	3	4	No
France	Two-Round System	1	10	5	No
Germany	Mixed Member	1.9	10	4	No

Continued

Table 3.2 *Continued*

Country	Electoral Rule	Mean District Magnitude	ICPV	Term	Fixed Term
Ghana	SMDP	1	10	4	Yes
Greece	Mixed Member	5.4	3	4	No
Guatemala	Closed List	10.72	1	4	Yes
Honduras	Closed List	7.1	1	4	Yes
Hungary	Mixed Member	13.82	10	4	No
India	SMDP	1	10	5	No
Indonesia	Closed List	16.47	3	5	Yes
Ireland	Single Transferrable Vote	4	4	5	No
Israel	Closed List	120	1	4	No
Italy	Closed List	22.5	10	5	No
Japan	Mixed Member	1.54	11	4	No
Kenya	SMDP	1	10	5	Yes
Liberia	SMDP	1	6	6	Yes
Malawi	SMDP	1	10	5	Yes
Mexico	Mixed Member	80.6	6	3	Yes
Nepal	Mixed Member	195.59	10	4	No
Netherlands	Closed List	8.3	3	4	No
New Zealand	Mixed Member	21.42	10	3	No
Nicaragua	Closed List	7.6	1	5	Yes
Niger	Mixed Member	7	10	5	No
Nigeria	SMDP	1	10	4	Yes
Norway	Closed List	8.9	2	4	Yes
Pakistan	SMDP	1	10	5	No
Papua New Guinea	Alternative Vote	1	10	5	No
Paraguay	Closed List	4.4	1	5	Yes
Peru	Closed List	4.8	5	5	No
Philippines	Mixed Member	1.1	10	3	Yes
Poland	Closed List	11.2	3	4	No
Portugal	Closed List	10.5	1	4	No
Romania	Mixed Member	1	1	4	No
Senegal	Mixed Member	4.3	1	5	No
Serbia	Closed List	250	1	4	No
Sierra Leone	SMDP	1	10	5	Yes
Slovak Republic	Closed List	150	3	4	No
South Africa	Closed List	44.4	1	5	No
South Korea	Mixed Member	6.38	10	4	Yes
Spain	Closed List	6.7	1	4	No
Sweden	Closed List	11.6	3	4	No
Switzerland	Open List	7.7	3	4	Yes
Taiwan	Mixed Member	11.5	11	4	No
Tunisia	Closed List	7.56	1	5	No

Country	Electoral Rule	Mean District Magnitude	ICPV	Term	Fixed Term
Turkey	Closed List	7	1	4	Yes
Ukraine	Closed List	450	10	5	No
United Kingdom	SMDP	1	10	5	No
United States	SMDP	1	10	2	Yes
Zambia	SMDP	1	10	5	No

Note: SMDP = Single Member District Plurality.

We refer to electoral systems which require voters to choose only between political parties as a party-centered electoral system. A closed-list Proportional Representation (PR) electoral system with centralized candidate selection is arguably the best example of such a party-centered electoral system, in which voters opt for a political party rather than for individual candidates. Parties compete in multi-member districts and present an ordered (ranked) list of candidates. Under centralized candidate selection, party leaders control the ranking of candidates. Seats in the legislative assembly are allocated to parties in (approximate) proportion to the share of the vote that the party receives. Which candidates within the party win assembly seats depends on the number of votes the party receives and the candidates' placement on the party list.

In a closed-list system, voters have minimal say in which individuals represent them in the legislative assembly. While the overall distribution of votes decide how many seats each party obtains in the legislative assembly, the party's ballot control and the ordering of the candidates on its list determine which individuals ultimately get elected. Closed-list systems are thus "party-centered" because voters only choose between parties and because the party organization (often through its leaders) determines the order in which individual candidates will fill these seats.

The party-centered nature of the closed-list system obviously matters for candidate responsiveness and accountability, since such responsiveness depends on who holds the keys to the candidate's electoral prospects. Recall that legislators and candidates for such office serve two masters: their voters and their respective party leaders. Closed-list electoral systems typically empower leaders over voters because leaders play a significant role in determining a candidate's probability of election. A candidate at the top of the list will have a good chance of being elected even with minimal effort and even in a "bad year." In contrast, a candidate in a lowly list position often has no chance, regardless of her personal appeal and how hard she campaigns.

The ability to determine the ordering of the party list gives leaders significant influence over members and induces loyalty to the party leadership. Thus, in a closed-list system with centralized ballot control, a member is as much, if not more, an agent of the party leadership as an agent of the citizens in his or her district. A legislative assembly selected by means of a closed-list electoral system is likely to be party-centered, all else equal, with party leaders able to use their control of list placement at the next election as a means to inspire political loyalty. An incumbent member's autonomy is, we believe, most constrained when she needs to respond to the party leadership more than to constituency voters in order to be re-elected. Thus, all else equal, we do not associate a members' assembly with closed-list (or more generally, party-centered) electoral systems. Closed-list electoral systems are relatively popular around the world: 32 countries (47% of the cases) in our study use a closed-list electoral system to elect their national legislature.

The opposite of a party-centered electoral system is a candidate-centered one with the potential for cross-partisan voting. In a candidate-centered electoral system, citizens vote for individual candidates rather than for political parties. In the most candidate-centered systems, voters can even support candidates from several different parties. Candidate-centered systems create incentives for politicians to cultivate/seek/try to win what scholars refer to as a "personal vote." A personal vote can be defined as the part of a candidate's vote that is based on his or her individual characteristics or record (Cain et al. 1987). This personal element of a vote can be contrasted with a party vote—the part of a candidate's vote that is based on his or her party affiliation and label. We can ask then: To what degree is a voter voting for a party or candidate, and if for a candidate is the vote based on the candidate's personal characteristics or party affiliation? To the extent that personal votes matter, we classify the electoral system as having candidate-centered features.

The degree to which the personal vote matters depends on the electoral system. In a seminal contribution, Carey and Shugart (1995) suggest that different electoral systems provide different incentives to cultivate personal votes. The authors show how electoral systems can be characterized meaningfully based on the extent to which they require individual legislators seeking re-election to build a personal reputation. Legislators elected via party-centered systems have the least incentive to respond actively to individual constituents, and are thus least likely to focus on building and maintaining a direct link with the electorate. In contrast, where ballot structures are candidate-centered, the candidates' need to cultivate personal votes is greatest.

Unfortunately, psephologists and legislative scholars disagree somewhat as to what makes electoral systems most candidate-centered (André et al. 2016). Yet, the incentives to cultivate a personal vote are arguably strongest among candidates in a Single Transferrable Vote (STV) electoral system. Linking surveys of legislators across mostly European countries to the electoral system used to elect them, André et al. (2016) indeed conclude that STV is the most candidate-centered electoral system used to elect national legislatures. Only one country in our study—Ireland—employs STV to elect the lower chamber of its national assembly—the Dáil Eireann (see Box 3.1). The district magnitude (number of legislators per electoral district) in Irish elections ranges from three to five, depending on the population of the district.[11] Voters can on their ballots express an ordered preference for as many candidates as they like by putting "1" opposite the name of their first choice candidate and, if they wish, "2" opposite the name of their second choice and so on until they are indifferent as to the remaining candidates. Candidates from the largest parties in particular are likely to be competing for votes against co-partisans. As a consequence, such candidates can't rely upon their party label alone to win votes and may therefore actively compete and campaign against other co-partisan candidates. STV maximizes the options available to citizens by allowing them choice between candidates—and often between candidates with the same party label. STV therefore incentivizes Irish legislators to spend significant time in their constituency and dedicate significant effort to constituency service (Martin 2014).

Box 3.1 The Single Transferrable Vote

The Single Transferrable Vote (STV) electoral system is used to elect members of Dáil Eireann, the lower chamber of the Irish Parliament. STV (or PR-STV) was first introduced to Ireland under British rule and was seen as a way to provide representation in parliament for the minority Protestant population. Voters express an ordered preference for as many of the listed candidates as they like. Voters mark the ballot paper by putting "1" opposite the name of their first choice candidate and, if they wish, "2" opposite the name of your second choice and so on until they are indifferent as to the remaining candidates.

Continued

---

[11] In fact, district magnitude often differs significantly not only across different electoral systems but within the same polity. In Germany, for example, some legislators are elected in districts with just one member, whereas Germany also features multi-member districts ranging between 6 and 142 members.

While casting a vote is relatively simple (as noted above, a voter rank orders candidates until they are indifferent as to the remaining candidates), the counting of votes and filling of seats is anything but simple. Indeed, counting of votes at Irish elections can last several days (in 1992 it took one constituency 10 days to declare a full result). Central to understanding how votes are translated into seats in the STV system is the concept of a quota. The quota is the minimum number of votes necessary to guarantee a candidate's election. The quota is calculated by dividing the total number of valid ballot papers by one more than the number of seats to be filled and adding one to the result. Any candidate reaching or exceeding the quota is elected. Their "surplus" votes—the votes they receive beyond the quota—are then distributed. This distribution is based on the lower preferences given by voters who voted for the elected candidate. Candidates who receive the fewest votes may also be eliminated with their ballots redistributed based on those voters' lower preferences.

Particularly for the largest parties, a candidate is likely to be competing for votes against other candidates from the same party. As a consequence, party label alone can't be relied upon to win votes. STV maximizes the choice available to citizens by allowing them choice between candidates—and often candidates from the same party label. In terms of voting behavior, evidence suggests that the Irish electorate vote for individual candidates rather than strictly along party lines. Asked in a survey to explain their voting choices, 45 percent of respondents indicated that a candidates' personal attributes were the reason for voting for that candidate, whereas only 10 percent indicated that party label influenced their choices (Marsh 2007).

Competition from candidates of the same party greatly enhances the need for Irish legislators to cultivate personal votes. STV thus incentivizes Irish legislators to spend a great deal of time in their constituency and dedicate significant effort to constituency service. Even the presence of the informal bailiwick system in Ireland, whereby co-partisan candidates are expected to focus on different geographical parts of the constituency at election time, seems to do little to eliminate intra-party rivalry.

Personal vote cultivation in Ireland follows many of the usual patterns, including case work, attending meetings in the constituency, asking parliamentary questions on behalf of individual constituents or groups of constituents, as well as interacting with the government bureaucracy on behalf of constituents. And as Whitaker (1996; np) notes: "in Ireland constituents tend to make representations to more than one member—indeed in a five-member constituency they may approach all five. The burden of constituency work entailed both for deputies and for the Departments and agencies to which they convey the representations is thereby multiplied."

But vote cultivation can take unusual forms as well: For example, attendance at a constituent's funeral is almost a prerequisite for most Irish parliamentarians, even for government ministers. Interaction with the (grieving) family, friends, and neighbors is used to win support while showing the member's willingness to be present in the constituency.

STV remains very popular, both among voters and political elites (although some voices do raise concerns regarding the inability of legislators to focus on national political issues). Two referendums to replace STV with a SMP system have failed (in 1959 and again in 1968). A 2013 Constitutional Convention (comprising 66 citizens, 33 parliamentarians, and an independent Chairman) voted decisively in favor of keeping the current STV electoral system. Asked whether to replace the existing STV electoral system with a Mixed-Member Proportional (MMP) system, such as the one used in Germany, 20 voted yes, 79 voted no, and 1 offered no opinion. Despite the personal-vote nature of the electoral system, party voting unity in the Irish parliament is very high (Martin 2014) because personal vote seeking focuses on non-political/non-national issues that need not contradict party unity.

Five countries in our study—Brazil, the Czech Republic, Denmark, Finland, and Switzerland—have multi-member districts with open-list electoral systems. An open-list electoral system differs from a closed-list system in that under open lists voters get to indicate their preferences among the candidates on their preferred party's list. An open-list system differs from the above-discussed STV in that in an open-list system seats are first allocated to parties and only subsequently to specific individuals. In an open-list system, each party still produces a list of candidates, but voters can affect the order in which these candidates are elected in one of several ways. In the least "open" list format, parties still list candidates in declining order of priority, but voters can change this order by giving their support to candidates lower on the list. Alternatively, the list may be unordered by the party. In Brazil, for example, the list is unordered and the allocation of seats to individual candidates within each list is based on the number of preference votes each candidate receives.

As with STV, in an open-list system legislators from the same party must compete with each other to win office. And again, compared to the closed-list variety, open-list electoral systems enhances the intra-party choice available to citizens by allowing them to choose among candidates within their party—thus creating a direct link between representative and voter. All else equal, open-list electoral systems thus reduce the influence of party leaders over incumbent members who seek re-election. Open-list systems diverge from STV in not allowing voters to express preferences for candidates from more than one party. In open-list as well as in STV systems, members (or prospective members) can build personal reputations with voters and thus insulate themselves from the control of party leaders. In Ireland, for example, electorally popular incumbents have been expelled from their party by the party leadership only to be re-elected to their parliamentary seat at the next election. This highlights the comparative autonomy and independence from the party leadership that members may enjoy under open lists.

Twelve countries in our study use a Single Member District Plurality (SMDP), or First-past-the-Post (FTP), electoral system. Under this system, each district elects one (a single) assembly member. In a plurality version, in each electoral district the candidate that receives the greatest number of votes wins the election. It can be difficult to classify the candidate-centeredness or party-centeredness of the plurality SMDP electoral system. In the United Kingdom, most voters seem to make their electoral choices on the basis of party label, even if they are technically selecting an individual MP to represent them in the House of Commons (Cain et al. 1987). In contrast, American voters often value their politicians' personal characteristics and may or may not select their representatives based on party label alone. Thus, the same electoral system (SMDP is used for both the UK House of Commons and the US House of Representatives) procedures different personal vote incentives. US politicians have strong incentives to cultivate a personal vote, in part because of the primary election system (see below); British MPs significantly less so. Hence, some scholars consider voting in single-member plurality systems to be for parties, whereas others label plurality systems as candidate-centered (André et al. 2016). Still others consider it impossible to categorize all SMDP systems alike—as some are more party-centered and others more candidate-centered (André et al. 2016). Certainly, SMDP is less party-centered than a closed-list system (voters can choose to vote based on the candidates' personal characteristics) but also less candidate-centered than STV or open-list systems (due to the lack of competition for votes between candidates from the same party, except in primary elections). In Britain, for example, most incumbent MPs engage in some form of personal-vote cultivation despite the high level of partisanship among the voters.

France operates a two-round system to elect members of the National Assembly, and is the only country in our study to do so. All members are elected in single-member districts. To win election in the first round, a candidate must win a majority of the votes cast. If no candidate wins a majority of votes, a second or "run-off" round is held. In such run-offs, the number of candidates allowed to compete may be reduced. In France, only candidates who received at least 12.5 percent of the eligible vote in the first round are allowed to stand in the second round, in which the candidate who receives more votes than anyone else (a plurality) is elected. As with the SMDP system, it can be difficult to classify the two-round format as more candidate—or more party-centered than open-list systems.

Two countries in our study—Australia and Papua New Guinea—use a system known as the Alternative Vote. Again, the country is divided into electoral districts and each district elects one legislator. Each Australian district thus returns one member to their House of Representatives. However, voters in Australian House elections are permitted to rank-order candidates. Any candidate that receives a majority of first preference votes is elected. If no candidate receives a majority of first preference votes, however, the lowest-polling candidate (the candidate with fewest first preference votes) is eliminated and this candidate's ballot papers are transferred to candidates based on the second preferences of the eliminated candidate's supporters. This successive elimination procedure continues until one candidate receives enough transfer votes to obtain a majority of votes. The alternative vote is sometimes known as the Instant Run-off system because voters who supported losing candidates are instantly able to have their votes transferred to other candidates. In its operation, this system is also akin to a single-member-district version of the STV.

Fifteen of our countries have a mixed electoral system that combines party-centered and candidate-centered features (ballots). The German Bundestag provides an example of a mixed electoral system. Approximately half of the Bundestag is elected under a single-member plurality (SMDP) electoral system and the other half under a proportional electoral system. We refer to such systems as "mixed" because they combine two separate ways to elect the chamber. In effect, there are two alternative routes to the legislature. Such systems often offer illuminating opportunities to study the behaviors of legislators in the same chamber elected under different electoral systems. Thus, we may be able to draw inferences about the effects of how members are elected on their behavior in the chamber. There is, for example, some evidence that German legislators seeking re-election via the party list part of the electoral system are more sensitive to their party leadership, whereas legislators seeking re-election via the plurality route are more likely to build relations with and be responsive to constituents (for an overview, see Zittel 2018). Mixed-member systems may represent the "best of both worlds," or at least a mix of their attractions and liabilities, allowing for a citizens' element (via the plurality electoral system) but also allowing for a party-based one (via the closed list element). The precise mix of these effects will depend in part on the number of members elected under each. Members too have a choice: they can work to be re-elected under the district element of the system or under the list element of the system (or under both, where this is allowed).

The party- or candidate-centeredness of electoral systems also depends on candidate selection procedures, on the process by which individuals can get their names placed on the ballot as candidates for office. Ballot access of course affects the degree to which voters can determine the selection of candidates. Ballot access procedures vary in the characteristics of the selectorate (those empowered to grant ballot access), in the centralization of the process, and in its nature (openness, competitiveness). The most consequential of these dimensions is the nature and size of the selectorate, which most importantly varies in its inclusiveness, from one in which candidate selection is at the discretion of a single party leader to the most inclusive procedures, in which all party members or even ordinary voters can participate (Hazan 2014). The greatest inclusiveness is found in a primary elections system, as in the United States, which allows ordinary voters to make candidate as well as party choices, though not necessarily at the same time.

Candidate selection processes are largely determined by the political parties themselves. Only rarely are they legally prescribed, as in the United States, though even here there are variations from state to state. Thus, the "top two" primary system used in California is extreme in its candidate-centeredness in the sense that the distribution of the candidate vote in the primary may prevent a major party from running any candidate in the general election. Other democracies, such as Finland, Germany, and New Zealand, regulate candidate selection less extensively. But overall candidate selection processes mainly take place within different political parties and are largely unregulated by law (Hazan and Rahat 2010). A more inclusive candidate selection process will in general be associated with a members' or voters' assembly, whereas a more centralized and exclusive process correlates with a leader's assembly and party unity (Sieberer 2006). At the same time, however, high inclusiveness also tends to correlate with higher incumbent re-election rates and lower social representativeness among the elected members (Hazan 2014). And finally, it is important to recognize that candidate selection procedures can vary from party to party within the same political system—reinforcing or weakening the impact of the electoral system (Martin 2014; Shomer 2014, 2017; Fernandes et al. 2019), which means that a full account of their effects is beyond the scope of our analysis.

While we have seen that the party- vs. candidate-centeredness of electoral systems depends on a number of specific features, political scientists have sought to come up with aggregate indices of such effects. One empirical measure of how different electoral systems shape incentives to cultivate a personal (as distinct from a party) vote is provided by Johnson and Wallack (2012). These authors seek to empirically quantify the dimensions of the personal vote identified by Carey and Shugart by looking at party control over access to the ballot, the extent to which votes are shared with co-partisans, whether votes are primarily cast for parties or candidates, and district magnitude.[12] Johnson and Wallack combine these elements to create a measure of the incentives to cultivate a personal vote. Their measure is reported in Table 3.2. Their ordering of electoral systems is not uncontroversial: for example, whereas most scholars view STV as being highly candidate-centered, Johnson and Wallack (2012) score many SDMP systems as

---

[12] Johnson and Wallack (2012) is missing information on the personal vote for nine of our countries: Benin, Burundi, Liberia, Nepal, Senegal, Serbia, Sierra Leone, Tunisia, and Turkey. Our coding decisions for these cases are set out in the online appendix www.legislatures.pub to this book.

more candidate-centered than STV (compare the scores for Ireland and the UK in Table 3.2).

What characterizes countries in which assembly elections present incentives to cultivate a personal vote? Table 3.3 presents a regression analysis in which the dependent variable is each assembly's score on the Johnson and Wallack index of Incentives to Cultivate a Personal Vote (ICPV). ICPV ranges from 1 to 12, following Johnson and Wallack's coding. A higher value suggests that the electoral system creates greater incentives for the personal vote. In this regression model, we include measures of economic, social, culture, and historical factors that might influence this choice of electoral institutions, details for which are presented in Chapter 2. Due to our limited number of observations and the risk of collinearity, we present five different specifications of our model.

The results in Table 3.3 suggest that more populous countries, Asian/ Oceanic countries, and former British colonies tend to have electoral systems with greater incentives for the personal vote. Conversely, non-British colonies and countries with greater income inequality (higher GINI coefficients) tend to adopt electoral systems with fewer incentives for the personal vote.

As we will see in subsequent chapters, the degree to which an electoral system is candidate-centered or party-centered has significant consequences for the behavior of legislators and in particular for what they prioritize in order to be re-elected. For now, we want to emphasize that a voters' assembly is one which gives electors maximum control of candidate selection through the electoral system. This matters not just in terms of selection, but also in terms of control—the ability of voters to hold individual legislators accountable at the next election. This, we believe, is maximized in a candidate-centered/personal-vote electoral system. In contrast, a closed-list electoral system significantly privileges party leaders in determining which individuals get to serve in the legislative assembly. Again, this privilege extends not just to choosing who sits in the assembly, but also to the "link" between leaders and members. Where leaders effectively control a member's chances of re-election through their control over the party list, members must be more sensitive to the needs and preferences of their leaders, as we will discuss in subsequent chapters.

3.3 Length of the Legislative Term

One other feature of the electoral system that has a clear implication for the degree to which legislators must think about re-election is the length of the legislative term. How long voters must wait to hold their legislators to account (and hence how long the latter are "safe"), and the immediate security in office that members enjoy, varies dramatically from polity to polity. National assemblies also differ as to whether their terms are fixed or open-ended, which relates to the power of leaders to dissolve the assembly. We code a fixed-term assembly as one in which election

Table 3.3 Determinants of incentives to cultivate a personal vote

	Incentive to Cultivate a Personal Vote				
	(1)	**(2)**	**(3)**	**(4)**	**(5)**
Sovereignty	0.0001			0.01	
	(0.02)			(0.02)	
log(GDP per Capita)	−0.20				
	(0.42)				
GINI	−0.12*				−0.05
	(0.07)				(0.06)
log(Population)	1.50***			1.02***	1.01***
	(0.36)			(0.37)	(0.34)
Ethnic Fractionalization	2.79			3.23	
	(2.25)			(2.11)	
Africa and Middle East		1.03		−1.14	
		(1.32)		(1.70)	
Asia and Oceania		4.86***		2.71*	2.27*
		(1.44)		(1.53)	(1.15)
Americas		0.09		−1.12	
		(1.28)		(1.32)	
Eastern Europe		−0.72		−1.47	
		(1.54)		(1.74)	
British Colony			3.02**		2.43**
			(1.21)		(1.20)
Other Colony			−2.14**		−1.49
			(1.00)		(0.98)
Constant	−14.75	4.50***	5.84***	−33.40	−10.10*
	(35.48)	(0.92)	(0.80)	(36.44)	(5.57)
N	68	68	68	68	68
R^2	0.28	0.21	0.26	0.34	0.44
Adjusted R^2	0.22	0.15	0.24	0.26	0.39

*$p < 0.1$; **$p < 0.05$; ***$p < 0.01$.
Notes: The dependent variable, Incentives to Cultivate a Personal Vote (ICPV), ranges from 1 to 12, following Johnson and Wallack's coding. A higher value suggests that the electoral system creates greater incentives for the personal vote.

dates are constitutionally or statutorily mandated and immovable in normal circumstances. In a Members' Assembly, the legislative term will be long and fixed, providing members with relatively greater job security. In a Leaders' Assembly terms will be long but with the ability for the leadership to dissolve the assembly. And in a in a Voters' Assembly the legislative term will be short and fixed, giving voters maximum ability to hold their legislators to account at predictable times.

In all, 28 assemblies have fixed terms, whereas 40 legislatures do not. Almost all parliamentary systems have open-ended terms, though the conditions under which assemblies are subject to "premature" dissolution (and early elections) vary a great deal. So do the decision rules under which such early elections can be called. Presidential systems typically have fixed terms. Among the 28 fixed-term assemblies, 26 are presidential. Norway is the only parliamentary system with fixed terms. Switzerland also has a fixed-term legislature. No semi-presidential systems in our sample have fixed terms. Two Presidential systems (Burundi and Zambia) have legislatures without fixed terms. We do not include either Canada or the UK as having fixed-term parliaments. Both countries have passed legislation implementing fixed terms, but early dissolutions are still possible. In the United Kingdom, the Fixed-term Parliaments Act 2011 removed the power of the Prime Minister to unilaterally dissolve Parliament and call an election. Yet, even then the House of Commons could be dissolved early via a vote of no confidence in the government, or by a two-thirds majority vote in the House of Commons. The latter occurred in 2017. In March 2022, the Dissolution and Calling of Parliament Act became law, repealing the Fixed-term Parliament Act and returning to the Prime Minister the power to request a parliamentary dissolution.

Legislators in democratic countries are typically elected for a maximum term of between three and five years. Table 3.2 shows the breakdown by country. The most common term is four years, and the average for our countries is 4.28 years. The shortest length of the legislative term in our study is the two-year term of the US House of Representatives. Five countries in our study—Australia, El Salvador, Mexico, New Zealand, Philippines—have a three-year term. 37 countries have a four-year term, while 24 countries have a five-year term. The Liberian House of Representatives alone has a six-year term. All else equal, a voters' assembly would have relatively short terms. Short terms arguably make incumbents seeking re-election most responsive to the needs and policy preferences of voters, exactly because incumbents know that the next election is never far away. The shadow of future elections is greater, all else equal, the shorter the (maximum or average) inter-electoral period. Members, on the other hand, value longer inter-electoral periods as this increases career (and employability) certainty and arguably their opportunities to devote themselves to policy specialization. Even the most seasoned electoral campaigner presumably fears the judgment of the voters when elections are due. Yet, as we will see below, voters may need not wait to the next election to hold an incumbent legislator to account.

Table 3.4 presents a regression analysis in which the dependent variable is the maximum length of the assembly's term (its constitutional inter-electoral period) in years. The results in Table 3.4 suggests that wealthier countries tend to have shorter constitutional terms between elections. There is suggestive evidence in model 4 that countries with greater ethnic fractionalization tend to have longer terms. Countries in the Americas and Eastern Europe tend to have shorter terms.

Table 3.4 Determinants of term length

	Term Length				
	(1)	**(2)**	**(3)**	**(4)**	**(5)**
Sovereignty	0.0000			0.005	
	(0.003)			(0.003)	
log(GDP per Capita)	−0.21***				−0.19***
	(0.07)				(0.06)
GINI	−0.02				
	(0.01)				
log(Population)	−0.05			−0.05	
	(0.06)			(0.07)	
Ethnic Fractionalization	0.20			0.71*	0.10
	(0.40)			(0.39)	(0.37)
Africa and Middle East		0.36		−0.16	
		(0.23)		(0.31)	
Asia and Oceania		−0.28		−0.46	
		(0.25)		(0.28)	
Americas		−0.38		−0.53**	−0.45**
		(0.23)		(0.24)	(0.18)
Eastern Europe		−0.26		−0.62*	−0.29
		(0.27)		(0.32)	(0.22)
British Colony			0.02		
			(0.24)		
Other Colony			−0.08		
			(0.20)		
Constant	7.43	4.37***	4.32***	−3.66	6.06***
	(6.30)	(0.16)	(0.16)	(6.70)	(0.67)
N	68	68	68	68	68
R^2	0.22	0.16	0.004	0.24	0.27
Adjusted R^2	0.16	0.11	−0.03	0.15	0.22

*p < 0.1; **p < 0.05; ***p < 0.01.
Note: The dependent variable, Term Length, is a continuous variable measuring the constitutional maximum inter-electoral period in years.

3.4 Mechanisms of Recall, Censure, and Expulsion

In all democratic countries, the responsibility of the members of at least one assembly chamber to the citizens hinges on the electoral connection. Representatives are elected for a limited term and are in most countries eligible for re-election. Voters get to choose the representatives they want, under such constraints as we have discussed above. The same voters can in most cases pass judgment on their representatives in later elections, provided that the constitution allows member to stand for re-election and that they choose to do so. In more technical terms, we can say that in this delegation relationship, voters can hold legislators to account at the end of the electoral term.

But in many relationships of delegation, representatives (agents) are also subject to ongoing scrutiny, and their "contracts" can be terminated at short notice before the end of the term they have been given. Professional football managers, for example, typically sign multi-year contracts with their respective clubs, but nonetheless many of them find themselves without a job much sooner than they had hoped or expected. Thus, Sir Alex Ferguson notes that during his long tenure (1986–2013) at Manchester United, the 48 clubs that made up the remaining members of the English Premier League (and previously the First Division) went through no fewer than 267 permanent managers, not including caretakers. High-flying teams such as Chelsea and Manchester City accounted for 13 and 14 of these, respectively, and some less successful teams for many more (Ferguson 2015: 227).

Legislators lead much more secure work lives than football managers. The great majority of legislators serve out the terms for which they have been elected or at least stay in office until the next general election. Most of those who don't resign on their own, for example because they have been elected or appointed to an office that is incompatible with continued service in their legislative chamber (for example, service in a different assembly, a governorship, or an ambassadorship). Other terms are cut short for less happy reasons, such as death, illness, scandal, or disability.

Then there are several ways in which legislators can be forced to leave office before their term expires. One is impeachment—removal from office through a judicial or quasi-judicial decision. Another is a recall election, which is a process whereby citizens can petition to trigger a vote, between regular elections, on whether an incumbent representative is permitted to continue in office. Though both are mechanisms of expulsion, recall differs from impeachment in that it is a political rather than a legal process—the judgment is not one of legal guilt but of political preference. Such recall provisions are very rare cross-nationally; in fact they exist in only three of our 68 democracies: Ecuador, Nigeria, and the United Kingdom.

The Recall of MPs Bill was passed by the British House of Commons in 2015 (see Box 3.2). There are three circumstances under which recall can be triggered: first, when an MP is convicted of an offence and receives a prison sentence, second, when the House of Commons suspends the member for a minimum period of time, or third, if the MP has been found guilty of false or misleading parliamentary expenses claims. For the recall election to be held, 10 percent of the registered electorate in the relevant constituency will need to sign a petition, after which the seat is vacated and a by-election held. The former MP may stand again in the by-election as long as this candidate meets the normal conditions for eligibility. At the time of writing (summer 2023), three petitions to recall a sitting UK MP have been initiated: the first petition did not achieve the necessary 10 percent support, the second did and the incumbent MP was removed and did not seek re-election, in the third case the MP was also removed but contested the subsequent by-election, albeit unsuccessfully.

Box 3.2 Recall of UK Parliamentarians

As a result of a parsimoniously titled piece of legislation—the Recall of MPs Act 2015—MPs in the UK House of Commons can now be recalled by their constituents, albeit in a process triggered only by a relatively specific set of circumstances.

Ahead of the 2010 general election, each of the three main parties—the Conservatives, Labour, and the Liberal Democrats—promised in their electoral manifesto to introduce legislation to allow voters to recall their MP for certain wrongdoings. For the Liberal Democrats, for example, this was a way to "empower people" and part of their broader constitutional reform agenda. Arguably, all three political parties were motivated by public dissatisfaction with the behavior of some MPs. In particular, British politics had been impacted by an expenses scandal in 2009 which saw revelations concerning the amount and nature of expenses and allowances paid to some MPs. Many thoughts such payments—including expenses to cover such things as an MP's home birdhouses and cleaning a moat at the MP's country estate—excessive and beyond what the allowance and expense system was meant to cover. Following the 2010 general election, the incoming coalition government committed itself to introducing a recall process. There was some resistance from MPs. A Political and Constitutional Reform Select Committee concluded that "a system of full recall may deter MPs from taking decisions that are unpopular locally or unpopular in the short-term, but which are in the long-term national interest."[13]

Among the public however, recall was more popular. A YouGov opinion poll conducted in March 2012 found that 79 percent of respondents suggested they felt recall was a good idea, 10 percent felt it was a bad idea, and 11 percent didn't know.[14] That same opinion poll questioned respondents on the causes for which an MP should face recall. In order of popularity, they were (with percentage indicating they would support a recall process for these scenarios):

1. Committing a crime serious enough to receive a prison sentence (91%)
2. Taking bribes (91%)
3. Being caught claiming expenses to which they are not entitled (87%)
4. Being caught lying in Parliament (80%)
5. Making racist or offensive comments (70%)

6. Not holding surgeries or responding to constituents' letters (60%)
7. Committing a less serious crime, which does not receive a prison sentence (56%)
8. Switching to a different political party (53%)
9. Breaking a promise made in their election leaflets (50%)
10. Having an affair/cheating on their spouse (22%)
11. Supporting a policy with which you disagree (10%).

The Government aimed for a recall process which would "give the public their say on whether an MP who has been found guilty of serious wrongdoing should retain their seat in this House."[15]

Ultimately, under the new law constituents themselves cannot initiate a recall petition. Rather, the recall process could be triggered if a Member is sentenced to a prison term, is suspended from the House for at least 10 sitting days, or is found guilty of misuse of parliamentary expenses. Petitions would then be open for signing for six weeks. If at the end of that period at least 10 percent of the eligible electors in the constituency had signed the petition, the seat would be declared vacant and a by-election would follow. Thus the hurdle is relatively low once a petition has been initiated. No provision is made to disagree with the petition. As with all seats vacated between general elections in the UK Parliament, any vacancy arising from a successful petition is filled by a parliamentary by-election. The loss by an MP of his or her seat as a result of a recall petition under this Act does not prevent him or her standing in the resulting by-election.[16] In 2018, the Northern Irish MP Ian Paisley Jr. became the first MP to face a recall. Constituency members had the opportunity to sign the petition at one of three petition locations. Ultimately, 7,099 constituents signed the recall petition, less than the 7,543 (10% of registered voters) required to force a by-election.

---

[13] p. 28; https://publications.parliament.uk/pa/cm201213/cmselect/cmpolcon/373/373.pdf.
[14] The question was as follows: The government has said that voters should have a means to "sack" MPs who are guilty of "serious wrongdoing." It proposes to allow voters in individual constituencies to vote on whether to recall their MP—that is, to hold a by-election—if more than 10 percent of voters sign a petition calling for one to take place. In principle, do you think this is a good idea or a bad idea?
[15] Hansard, House of Commons.
[16] Source: https://services.parliament.uk/bills/2014-15/recallofmps.html.

The United States has no recall provisions for federal legislators, though 19 states, plus the District of Columbia, permit the recall of state officials such as legislators, executives, and even judges. An even larger number of states have such provisions for locally elected officials. Such provisions were typically introduced during the Progressive Era, when major reforms were introduced in state politics to combat corruption and strengthen the accountability of elected politicians to their "masters" in the electorate. California was the first state to introduced the recall election in 1903, and exactly a century later it was successfully used to unseat Governor Gray Davis (Democrat).

The second way in which legislators can be removed from office prior to the end of their term is through some mechanism of expulsion by the legislature itself or through a legal provision or procedure. These are not very common procedures, and unfortunately, we only have full data for 48 of our countries. This data shows that the most common reason legislators have to leave their elected offices between election is because they have been elected or appointed to some office that is incompatible with a seat in the legislature, such as a judgeship or an office at a different level of government (see the discussion above); 38 of our countries have such rules of incompatibility.

Expulsion may alternatively happen if a legislator is found guilty of a serious criminal offense, such as bribery or embezzlement. Thus, 25 countries have rules that force legislators to resign if they are convicted of certain crimes. In some countries, legislators may be shielded from criminal investigations and trials. For example, members of the German Bundestag are legally shielded from legal investigations under immunity rules.[17] Other circumstances in which legislators are forced to leave their seats include situations in which they become ineligible for legislative office, for example by taking citizenship in a different country (24 countries), unexcused absence (12 countries), or personal bankruptcy (eight countries). It is particularly in countries with a British heritage (including Australia, Ghana, India, Kenya, Pakistan, and Zambia) that a member is forced to resign if he or she declares bankruptcy.

3.5 Conclusion

Rules governing who can be a legislator, how members are elected and for how long are fundamental: they determine who gets to be a member to begin with, and they are the principal means by which voters can exercise the sovereignty that democracy gives them. But electoral laws are, perhaps for these very reasons, complex and often far from transparent in their operations and effects.

Since electoral rules are so fundamental, it is no surprise that they matter to the purposes of voters, legislative members, and political leaders alike. Since voters, we assume, want to maintain control of their representatives, the same voters should

---

[17] Members of the Bundestag cannot be prosecuted under Germany's basic law. However, immunity can be lifted as a result of a decision made by one of the standing Bundestag committees, with jurisdiction on this matter.

prefer systems that keep legislators on a short leash, subject them to frequent re-election, and give voters the opportunity to pass differentiated judgments on their representatives (where they have more than one). This involves selecting not only the party label of their representative but also the individual candidate. Members, on the other hand, will be best served by systems that enhance their likelihood of re-election, for example by limiting competition, stipulating long legislative terms, and curtailing the opportunities for voters or leaders to penalize them or remove them from office outside of regularly scheduled elections. Finally, leaders will presumably prefer systems that give them control of access to the ballot, and also rules that allow them to sanction and reward ordinary members in electorally relevant ways.

The electoral rules of existing democracies clearly make different trade-offs between these various purposes, but in general they seem better suited to the purposes of members and leaders than to those of ordinary citizens. Mayhew's (1974) classical claim is that in the US House of Representatives these rules (like most other properties of the legislative arena) almost perfectly fit the purposes of ordinary members and their interest in re-election. While the short two-year electoral term of the House does not seem to fit this picture (US Senators, with their six-year term, would in this perspective seem much better placed), the low competitiveness of most US House races and the limited ability of party leaders to control candidate selection or to sanction members electorally or financially are indeed consistent with Mayhew's claim. Closed-list systems, particularly in parliamentary systems in which party leaders control both ballot access, election timing, and ability to control promotion to executive offices, would seem much better suited to the purposes of party leaders.

It is more difficult to point to existing selection and control mechanisms that seem perfectly designed for the purposes of ordinary citizens. Very few constitutions (currently only three) allow citizens to recall their representatives other than at election time. Legislative terms are in most countries fairly long (four or five years), and in many countries they are also fixed, or early dissolution is constrained by restrictive constitutional rules. Moreover, even when early dissolution is permitted, the discretion is typically placed in the hands of leaders such as the prime minister or the president. Candidate choice is in most cases restricted by the fact that single-member districts typically offer only two viable candidates (Cox 1997), or by the fact that many PR systems are closed-list, in which party leaders typically maintain control of each party's representatives. Interestingly, the electoral systems that offer voters the greatest control of candidate choice, such as the Single Transferable Vote or the Alternative Vote, are quite rare in the contemporary world and have found little acceptance outside of advanced industrial democracies.

While these limitations do not mean that popular elections are a sham, they do point to several ways in which electoral reform in many countries might benefit ordinary voters. Whether such reform is always a good thing is of course a different matter. A set of electoral rules that institutionalizes deference to responsible and well-informed politicians capable of coordinating a variety of social interests might of course have advantages over a more populist form of democracy (see for example Almond and Verba 1963). But this is not a debate that we can settle in this chapter.

References

Almond, Gabriel Abraham, and Sidney Verba. 1963. *The Civic Culture: Political Attitudes and Democracy in Five Nations*. Princeton: Princeton University Press.

André, Audrey, Sam Depauw, and Shane Martin. 2016. "The Classification of Electoral Systems: Bringing Legislators Back In." *Electoral Studies* 42: 42–53.

Blais, André, Louis Massicotte, and Antoine Yoshinaka. 2001. "Deciding Who Has the Right to Vote: A Comparative Analysis of Election Laws." *Electoral Studies* 20(1): 41–62.

Cain, Bruce, John Ferejohn, and Morris Fiorina. 1987. *The Personal Vote: Constituency Service and Electoral Independence*. Boston: Harvard University Press.

Carey, John M., 1998. *Term Limits and Legislative Representation*. Cambridge: Cambridge University Press.

Carey, John M., and Matthew Soberg Shugart. 1995. "Incentives to Cultivate a Personal Vote: A Rank Ordering of Electoral Formulas." *Electoral Studies* 14(4): 417–439.

Cox, Gary W. 1997. *Making Votes Count*. Cambridge: Cambridge University Press.

Dahl, Robert A. 1989. *Democracy and Its Critics*. New Haven: Yale University Press.

Farrell, David M., 2011. *Electoral Systems: A Comparative Introduction*. London: Macmillan.

Ferguson, Alex. 2015. *Leading*. New York: Hachette.

Fernandes, Jorge M., Lucas Geese, and Carsten Schwemmer. 2019. "The Impact of Candidate Selection Rules and Electoral Vulnerability on Legislative Behaviour in Comparative Perspective." *European Journal of Political Research* 58(1): 270–291.

Hazan, Reuvan Y. 2014. "Candidate Selection: Implications and Challenges for Legislative Behaviour." In Shane Martin, Thomas Saalfeld, and Kaare W. Strøm (eds.), *The Oxford Handbook of Legislative Studies*. Oxford: Oxford University Press, 213–231.

Hazan, Reuven Y., and Gideon Rahat. 2010. *Democracy within Parties: Candidate Selection Methods and Their Political Consequences*. Oxford: Oxford University Press.

Johnson, Joel W., and Jessica S. Wallack. 2012. Electoral Systems and the Personal Vote. Dataverse Network Project.

Marsh, Michael. 2007. "Candidates or Parties? Objects of Electoral Choice in Ireland." *Party Politics* 13(4): 500–527.

Martin, Shane. 2014. "Why Electoral Systems Don't Always Matter: The Impact of 'Mega-seats' on Legislative Behavior in Ireland." *Party Politics* 20(3): 467–479.

Mayhew, David R. 1974. *Congress: The Electoral Connection*. New Haven: Yale University Press.

Morgan, James. 2018. "Dual Citizenship and Australian Parliamentary Eligibility: A Time for Reflection or Referendum?" *Adelaide Law Review* 39(2): 439–451.

Persson, Torsten, and Guido Tabellini. 2005. *The Economic Effects of Constitutions*. Boston: MIT Press.

Rickard, Stephanie J. 2018. *Spending to Win: Political Institutions, Economic Geography, and Government Subsidies.* New York: Cambridge University Press.

Shomer, Yael. 2014. "What Affects Candidate Selection Processes? A Cross-national Examination." *Party Politics* 20(4): 533–546.

Shomer, Yael. 2017. "The Conditional Effect of Electoral Systems and Intraparty Candidate Selection Processes on Parties' Behavior." *Legislative Studies Quarterly* 42(1): 63–96.

Sieberer, Ulrich. 2006. "Party Unity in Parliamentary Democracies: A Comparative Analysis." *Journal of Legislative Studies* 12: 150–178.

Whitaker, T. Kenneth (ed.). 1996. *Report of the Constitution Review Group.* Dublin: The Stationery Office.

Zittel, Thomas 2018. "Electoral Systems in Context: Germany." In Erik S. Herron, Robert J. Pekkanen, and Matthew S. Shugart (eds.), *The Oxford Handbook of Electoral Systems.* Oxford: Oxford University Press, 781–801.

4

Membership and Congruence

Legislative assemblies are bodies of individual politicians, referred to in their national context as members, representatives, deputies, or by other designations. Chapter 3 explored the formal routes to becoming a legislator including rules governing who could become a legislator, and for how long. This chapter explores the actual composition of legislative assemblies (with a continuing focus on lower chambers under bicameralism). As with any multi-person body, the composition of a chamber can be analyzed according to an almost-infinite set of characteristics. We could ask, for example, what assemblies have in their ranks the greatest number of redheads, the most philatelists, parents of the largest families, the most accomplished badminton players, or the best sopranos. Interesting as these questions may be to some, however, they rarely cause much political fervor in their respective countries or scholarly concern among political scientists.

Yet, many scholars and voters do seem convinced that the partisan, demographic, economic, and professional characteristics of legislators may matter a great deal. As we shall see, this is presumably because these characteristics affect how well and faithfully legislators can be expected to serve their masters, the voters. In this chapter, we explore in particular two of the most important and commonly studied dimensions by which the membership of legislative chambers has been assessed: (1) the degree to which the membership of the chamber reflects the partisanship of the citizenry and (2) the proportion of assembly members that are female. We do so because we believe both aspects are important to popular representation in any assembly. Specifically, a voters' assembly will have a membership that broadly reflects the partisanship of the voters and in which both genders are significantly represented. We discuss the importance of such member–voter congruence in the next section.

4.1 The Ideal Agent

Why is it important to explore a chamber's membership? As we suggest throughout this study, a legislature can be explored meaningfully by thinking about the relationship between voters who select it, members who serve in it, and leaders who somehow control and shape what members do. The relationship among these sets of players is defined by the democratic chain of delegation, in which voters (as principals) delegate authority to their elected representatives (their agents), who

Legislative Assemblies. Shane Martin and Kaare W. Strøm, Oxford University Press.
© Shane Martin and Kaare W. Strøm (2023). DOI: 10.1093/oso/9780198890829.003.0004

in turn delegate to (party) leaders they select among themselves. In this chain, agents are supposed to act faithfully and efficiently in the interests of their respective principals—in line with our concept of a voters' assembly. Yet, as we discussed in Chapter 1, delegation is rarely perfect in these terms, and agency losses may arise when agents have preferences and information that differ from those of their principals. And in real-life assemblies, members typically differ from their respective voters in their preferences as well as in their information and skill levels. The challenge for voters is to minimize the adverse consequences of these differences and sometimes to make trade-offs among them. For example, when do we prefer to be represented by a brilliantly capable legislator, even when we know this person's preferences to differ from our own? And when would we rather have a less skilled or experienced member whose beliefs we trust to be more similar to our own?

So voters have to find their own devices by which to assess the suitability of political candidates and make the necessary judgments. Voters can thus rely on the signals that political candidates send through position taking, parties or organizations they represent, causes they have espoused, skills or experiences they have acquired, and costly action they have taken to prepare themselves for office (Chapter 3). Or citizens may be able to screen candidates based on their background characteristics or past record in office. None of these methods is foolproof. Members do not always wear their true preferences on their sleeves, and rarely do politicians admit to being anything but perfectly capable and dedicated to their responsibilities. Voters therefore often have to rely on simpler "proxies," such as whether the candidates share important objective characteristics with them or belong to organizations, such as political parties, that will enforce certain policy principles.

A commonly espoused normative principle in democratic theory is thus that a legislature's composition should somehow reflect the characteristics of the voters who select it. In other words, because a legislative assembly is a "representative body," the chamber should be a microcosm of the general population.[1] In general, districts should be relatively well apportioned (see Box 4.1 below) such that each legislator represents approximately the same number of people (or eligible voters). By congruence we mean the degree to which a legislative chamber reflects, and is descriptively compatible with, the population that elected it. A legislative assembly that matches the characteristics of its electorate is said to be congruent. In contrast, a legislative assembly that demographically differs from the population

---

[1] Note the difference between the characteristics of "voters" and those of the "population." A population contains individuals who are not enfranchised, for example young citizens below the minimum voting age and those who are not citizens. The difference can be important for the apportionment of electoral districts based on "population" criteria. In *Evenwel v. Abbott*, [136 S. Ct. 1120, 578 U.S., 194 L. Ed. 2d 291 (2016)], the US Supreme Court ruled that total population rather than total voting-eligible population should form the basis of Congressional boundaries. In contrast, the United Kingdom uses the size of the electorate (those entitled and registered to vote) in determining constituency boundaries.

is incongruent. And the criteria by which we assess congruence between voters and members can be anything that people consider a politically salient individual characteristic.

Box 4.1 Malapportionment

Legislative malapportionment can be defined as "the discrepancy between the shares of legislative seats and the shares of population held by geographical units" (Samuels and Snyder 2001: 652). A perfectly apportioned polity is one in which each representative represents the same number of people (or eligible voters). In contrast, malapportionment occurs when representatives represent a different number of people. As an example of malapportionment consider the Canadian case. At the 2015 Canadian Federal elections, the Member elected to represent the district of Labrador represented 26,728 people (20,084 voting-eligible persons). In contrast, the MP for Brant represented 132,443 individuals (95,616 voting-eligible persons). Such differences raise the issue of equality between voters within a country—the principle of "one person, one vote." Malapportionment deviates from that principle. Samuels and Snyder (2001) find that malapportionment is highest in poor, recently established democracies. Malapportionment is also most common in African and in Latin American countries, although political systems in the British Westminster tradition often have high levels of malapportionment as well. Looking at the consequences of malapportionment, Barkan et al. (2006) note that the "rural bias" (rural areas tend to have more representatives per head of population) means that agricultural sectors are often overrepresented in the legislature, possibly leading to public policies that favor agricultural producers over consumers.

Scholars pay particular attention to policy congruence. Policy congruence refers to the extent to which legislators' policy preferences correspond to those of the voters in the members' district. Although such matching might not be desirable from a broader philosophical perspective if voters are ignorant, bigoted, envious, or spiteful, policy congruence is generally considered to be a good quality in a democracy and, from our perspective, in a voters' assembly in particular.

4.2 Members' Partisan Affiliation

Partisanship is the most important way in which politicians signal their policy preferences, and a legislature's partisan distribution is therefore the most obvious way to analyze that chamber's policy congruence. In a voters' assembly, the partisan distribution of the members should correspond, at least approximately, to the partisan preferences of the voters. Not all assemblies permit partisanship, however. A notable feature of autocratic assemblies is that we often find only one political party represented, or none at all. Thus, Svolik (2012: 35) reports that all parties were banned in 17 percent of all country-years under autocratic rule between 1946 and 2008, whereas only a single party was allowed in 36 percent of these observations, and multiple parties in 47 percent (see also Schuler and Malesky 2014). Yet, the number of autocracies that ban political parties outright has fallen sharply since the fall of European communism around 1990. Even when opposition parties are permitted, their power is typically sharply curtailed (Wegmann 2022) and electoral laws often deliberately stacked against them. This lack of partisan diversity and free competition is of course an important reason why we characterize these regimes as autocratic in the first place. Because legislative assemblies in autocratic regimes are not, in any meaningful way, selected by voters, can't be held to account by voters, and have little incentive to represent the needs and policy preferences of voters, such assemblies are the antithesis of our concept of a voters' assembly.

In this volume, we focus on democratic assemblies, in which multiple parties are at least permitted to contest for representation. A multiparty legislature is one in which multiple different parties in fact hold legislative seats. Elections determine how many parties are represented and the relative size of each party group. Thus, for any legislature a very basic question concerns how many parties are represented, and the relative size of each party. Scholars have taken an interest in two-party legislatures—a special case of multiparty legislatures in which only two political parties are represented. A very important question concerning any assembly, as we will see in subsequent chapters, is whether a single party controls a majority of the seats. This is typically the case in two-party legislatures (except where independent deputies make up a sizeable and sometimes pivotal bloc) but is much less common in multiparty assemblies.

Partisan congruence can be measured by comparing the partisan preferences of citizens who turned out to vote and the party composition of the chamber—since it may be worthwhile but impossible to measure the partisan preferences of the entire population, including those that did not vote. Such data allows us to determine the degree to which the assembly's partisan composition corresponds to the partisan distribution of the electorate, as measured at the legislative election. Table 4.1 reports data on the proportionality of legislative seats to votes, as measured by the Gallagher Index of Disproportionality. This index has been designed to measure how well the shares of seats parties receive in the legislative assembly correspond to their vote shares. A low score on the Index of Disproportionality means a high degree of proportionality—indicating that the partisan composition of the chamber well reflects, or is congruent with, the voters' partisan

Table 4.1 Vote-seat proportionality and mean district magnitude

Country	Proportionality	Mean District Magnitude
Argentina	4.82	10.7
Australia	9.54	1
Austria	3.31	20.3
Belgium	4.6	13.63
Benin	3.39	3.46
Bolivia	5.53	1.69
Brazil	2.14	19
Bulgaria	2.52	7.74
Burundi	5.49	5.88
Canada	12.42	1
Chile	8.04	2
Colombia	6.68	5
Costa Rica	6.34	8.1
Croatia	12.31	13.39
Czech Republic	6.12	14.29
Denmark	0.73	10.5
Dominican Republic	2.17	6.1
Ecuador	15.93	2.74
El Salvador	3.9	8.24
Finland	2.95	13.33
France	17.66	1
Germany	7.83	1.9
Ghana	5.76	1
Greece	9.98	5.4
Guatemala	9.33	10.72
Honduras	5.6	7.1
Hungary	17.8	13.82
India	17.53	1
Indonesia	2.79	16.47
Ireland	8.69	4
Israel	2.77	120
Italy	17.34	22.5
Japan	16.32	1.54
Kenya	8.26	1
Liberia	11.14	1
Malawi	7.43	1
Mexico	6.87	80.6
Nepal	6.09	195.59
Netherlands	0.99	8.3
New Zealand	3.72	21.42
Nicaragua	6.41	7.6
Niger	2.83	7

Country	Proportionality	Mean District Magnitude
Nigeria	7.87	1
Norway	2.56	8.9
Pakistan	12.56	1
Papua New Guinea	23.66	1
Paraguay	11.51	4.4
Peru	10.23	4.8
Philippines	6.17	1.1
Poland	5.95	11.2
Portugal	5.68	10.5
Romania	6.2	1
Senegal	19.8	4.3
Serbia	12.3	250
Sierra Leone	6.09	1
Slovak Republic	9.77	150
South Africa	0.37	44.4
South Korea	7.15	6.38
Spain	6.93	6.7
Sweden	2.64	11.6
Switzerland	3.76	7.7
Taiwan	9.07	11.5
Tunisia	7.43	7.56
Turkey	7.4	7
Ukraine	3.59	450
United Kingdom	15.1	1
United States	4.35	1
Zambia	3.39	1

Notes: Data refers to lower chamber only in where multiple chambers exist. Vote-Seat proportionality is calculated using the Gallagher Index of Electoral Proportionality.

preferences.[2] In a voters' assembly, the partisan composition of the membership should be largely proportional with that of the voters. Such congruence means that the legislative assembly represents the partisan preferences (and thus the policy preferences) of the electorate (or those who voted).

Using this metric, South Africa has the highest correspondence between voter preferences and chamber membership in our study. In contrast, Senegal has the highest disproportionality—meaning that it has the lowest level of partisan congruence between voters and members. As subsequent chapters will show, the partisan composition of the legislative assembly matters for a whole number of reasons, such as which preferences get represented in legislative deliberations,

[2] A score of zero on the index indicates a perfectly proportional election outcome.

which party or parties control an assembly majority and, in some cases, who gets to form the executive branch and thus dominate policy development and implementation. And to the extent that political parties structure the chain of political delegation from voters to policy makers, a high level of disproportionality is a potential problem, especially if the same parties are consistently overrepresented or underrepresented over time.

What explains variation in votes-to-seats proportionality? The electoral system plays a crucial role. Some electoral systems are designed to produce proportional outcomes; other systems may or may not. Unsurprisingly, a large family of multi-member-district electoral systems generally referred to as Proportional Representation (PR) systems are designed to result in high proportionality. Of the electoral systems described in Chapter 3, Open-List, Closed-List, and STV are generally considered to be proportional. Mixed-member systems, such as in Germany, are also often designed to promote proportionality. The SMDP system is typically seen as the least proportional, followed by the Two Round system and the Alternative Vote. Amongst our cases, the most proportional system is the Open List (an average Gallagher Index score of 3.1), followed by Closed List (6.5). Mixed systems and STV each average 8.7 on the Gallagher Index. Our SMDP cases have an average score of 9.3, followed by the Two Round at 11.9. The Alternative Vote systems are the most disproportional with a Gallagher Index score of 16.6.

An electoral system's district magnitude (the number of legislators elected in each district) can also significantly affect its partisan congruence. Indeed, high district magnitude correlates with proportionality. Yet, the correlation between district magnitude and proportionality is far from perfect. Italy, for example, has a relatively high mean district magnitude (the average number of legislators per district across the country) but also relatively high disproportionality. The overall size of the assembly also matters. Taagepera (2007: 17) demonstrates that assembly size affects the chances of smaller parties winning legislative seats, with the number of parties positively correlated with the number of legislators. Farrell (2011: 159) similarly suggests that the number of seats affects the levels of proportionality. Table 4.1 reports the mean district magnitude for each country in our study.

Since partisan congruence thus is an important characteristic of legislative assemblies (especially to the extent that they strive to be voters' assemblies), we examine in Table 4.2 the factors that correlate with Gallagher's index of disproportionality. We include in this regression model both socio-economic and historical variables and features of the electoral system such as its electoral formula and district magnitude.

As expected, the results in Table 4.2 suggest that countries with majoritarian electoral systems tend to have higher levels of electoral disproportionality. There is suggestive evidence that this may be most true for more populous countries (Model 2) and Asian/Oceanic democracies (Model 3).

Table 4.2 Electoral disproportionality

	Electoral Disproportionality					
	(1)	(2)	(3)	(4)	(5)	(6)
Majoritarian	4.68***				5.57***	3.68**
	(1.48)				(1.78)	(1.46)
Mixed	2.38				2.64	
	(1.45)				(1.71)	
Mean District Magnitude	−0.001				−0.01	
	(0.01)				(0.01)	
Sovereignty		0.02			0.04	
		(0.02)			(0.03)	
log(GDP per Capita)		−0.64				
		(0.59)				
GINI		−0.07				
		(0.10)				
log(Population)		0.88*			0.18	0.02
		(0.50)			(0.53)	(0.52)
Ethnic Fractionalization		−4.04			−3.85	
		(3.18)			(3.00)	
Africa and Middle East			−0.29		−2.54	
			(1.80)		(2.40)	
Asia and Oceania			3.50*		0.44	2.59
			(1.96)		(2.32)	(1.68)
Americas			0.27		1.41	
			(1.75)		(1.82)	
Eastern Europe			1.58		0.84	
			(2.09)		(2.55)	
British Colony				0.60		
				(1.75)		
Other Colony				−1.21		
				(1.45)		
Constant	6.17***	−28.59	6.92***	8.17***	−81.31	6.18
	(0.83)	(50.11)	(1.25)	(1.16)	(55.44)	(8.57)
N	68	68	68	68	68	68
R^2	0.15	0.09	0.07	0.02	0.27	0.15
Adjusted R^2	0.11	0.01	0.01	−0.01	0.14	0.11

*$p < 0.1$; **$p < 0.05$; ***$p < 0.01$
Notes: DV: Gallagher Index of Electoral Proportionality. Higher values suggest greater disproportionality. Ranges from 0.37 to 23.66 in our dataset.

4.3 Descriptive Representation and Congruence

The term descriptive representation refers to how well the frequency of some salient demographic characteristic in the population is matched in the legislative assembly's membership. Thus, if gender is a salient demographic characteristic, and if 50 percent of the population are women, a descriptively representative chamber would have approximately 50 percent women legislators. If race is our concern, and 30 percent of the population belong to a racial minority, then 30 percent of the members of a congruent legislature should belong to that racial minority. And if a religious minority makes up 20 percent of the population, then the assembly should have a similar proportion of members from this community. Thus, for any given legislature, we can examine its congruence with respect to particular demographic characteristics.

Descriptive representation may be important because it recognizes particular sub-groups in society and represents them politically. Dahl (1971) thus identified inclusiveness as an important aspect of representative democracy. Moreover, descriptive representation is important to the extent that it promotes what scholars term substantive representation. Substantive representation refers to the degree to which a particular group's preferences are being represented and considered in the policy process. For example, continuing our example of gender, descriptive gender representation refers to the percentage of women legislators. Substantive gender representation refers to the degree to which women's interests are actively represented by the legislature. In an influential contribution, Phillips (1995) suggests that women are best able to represent the interests of women; thus, having women legislators is a necessary (but not necessarily sufficient) condition for substantive women's representation. In the parlance of principal-agency theory, women legislators are according to this argument the best agents of women voters. They understand and are more likely to respond to the interests and preference of fellow women. A voters' assembly then should have a sufficient proportion of women so that the interests and preferences of women are fairly represented in the assembly decision making.

The argument that a demographic sub-group is best represented by someone from within that group may apply to many demographic categories, but not necessarily to all. Most people would probably agree that the interests of children or the very elderly can often best be represented by individuals who do not share those characteristics. This is because effective representation (the quality of democratic agents) depends not only on preference congruence, but also on information and skills. Many people would presumably also agree that the interests of middle-aged citizens could reasonably be represented by members who are not themselves middle-aged. This is because older people will remember what it was like to be middle-aged and many younger people will anticipate becoming middle-aged, and because most people have at some point lived with middle-aged people in their households and understand their concerns.

In the case of gender, things are more complicated. While most people have lived in households that included both genders, males and females tend to have different life experiences from early on. In the case of racial or religious differences, the contrasts may be even greater. In many societies, most ordinary voters from majority groups have few interactions with individuals from certain racial, ethnic, or religious minorities, and most majority voters surely do not expect to become members of those minority communities.

Beyond the possible policy advantages of having a chamber be representative of the wider population, descriptive representation may be important for reasons of recruitment. In many political systems, membership of a legislative chamber is a stepping-stone to more senior political office. For example, in many parliamentary systems, members of the cabinet must or tend to be drawn from the legislature. In such cases, a country's legislature is a recruitment ground for high political office. If diversity in high political office is considered desirable, then diversity in the legislative chamber is likely to help break the glass ceiling in executive politics. We explore the politics of gender and legislative assemblies in more detail in the next section.

There are a multitude of interesting characteristics of legislators, including socio-economic background (such as wealth, education, and previous careers), age profiles, legislative experience, race, ethnicity, disability, religion, and sexual orientation, to name but a few. For some demographic characteristics, such data is readily available on members of national assemblies across the world. We can, for example, with relative ease register the gender composition of legislative assemblies, as most contemporary legislatures keep tabs on such characteristics of their membership.

Yet, for many other background variables, comparable data are surprisingly hard to come by, either because such information is in some countries considered private or uninteresting, or because the politically relevant variables differ so much from country to country. For example, even on a seemingly salient characteristic such as religious affiliation, information is very incomplete for the Norwegian Storting—a well-resourced legislature in a rich and stable democracy. The lack of comparable data on demographic characteristics means that an in-depth cross-national analysis of most membership characteristics is beyond the scope of this study. In such cases, we shall discuss available data from some existing cross-national or single-country studies of better-researched assemblies. Note, however, that in many cases it should be possible to collect such membership data, and that we see such systematic data collection as an obvious agenda for the comparative study of legislatures.

Socio-Economic Background

Representation is not only about partisanship, but also about other salient characteristics of voters and representatives. One of them is social class. A person's class is shaped by their social and economic status in society. Sociologists have identified different ways in which societies are stratified into different classes. Karl

Marx thus wrote of the bourgeoisie and proletariat as the most important classes in industrial societies and drew the distinction between them based on whether they controlled any economic assets other than their own labor (Marx 1867). Contemporary measures of social class tend to focus on a broader set of criteria, such as a person's income, wealth, education, or occupation, and to rely on more fine-tuned stratification measures.

The occupations that legislators had before entering politics are a key indicator of their class membership. Table 4.3 thus describes the occupation background of British MPs elected at the 2015 general election. MPs are here characterized as coming from one of the following occupations: (1) the professions, (2) business, (3) miscellaneous, or (4) manual careers. As Table 4.3 amply illustrates, there are significant party-based difference in the career backgrounds of British MPs, but also thoroughgoing ways in which all MPs differ from the general population. The professions are well represented in all parties, from 28 percent in Labour to a staggering 75 percent in the (admittedly small) caucus of the Liberal Democrats. These proportions are, of course, far higher than in the population at large. Among the professions, lawyers clearly dominate across all three British parties.

Professional, and especially legal, backgrounds are common also among US legislators. The US House of Representatives elected in 2020 included 75 Members who worked in education, 13 doctors, seven ordained religious ministers, 15 former judges, 32 prosecutors, 203 former state legislators, 70 congressional staffers,

Table 4.3 Occupational background of British MPs, by party (2015)

	Percentage			
	Conservative	Labour	Liberal Democrat	Scottish National Party
Professions	32%	28%	75%	30%
Solicitor	8%	7%	25%	7%
Barrister	8%	4%	0%	2%
Teachers: University/college	0%	5%	0%	5%
Teacher: school	2%	3%	25%	4%
Civil service/local govt	1%	4%	25%	4%
Accountant	4%	0%	0%	2%
Armed services	4%	0%	0%	0%
Doctor/dentist/optician	2%	0%	0%	4%
Business	44%	11%	25%	34%
Miscellaneous	23%	54%	0%	36%
Politician/Political organizer	12%	25%	0%	14%
Publisher/Journalist	5%	6%	0%	7%
Public relations	2%	1%	0%	2%
Manual Workers	1%	7%	0%	0%

as well as 22 farmers, ranchers, or cattle farm owners, one flight attendant and one pilot.[3] Though lawyers may be well represented in many national assemblies, this is not universally true. In the Norwegian Storting, for example, lawyers have for decades made up only a handful or less of the currently 169 representatives. Thus, the Judiciary Committee has at times operated without any member from the legal profession, and for two consecutive terms there was not a single MP with a law degree in Parliament.

Business owners are also represented in the House of Commons well above their share of the general population, especially among Conservative and Scottish National Party (SNP) MPs. On the other hand, more than half of the Labour Party members fall into the "miscellaneous" category, many of them presumably in middle-class public sector occupations. The other especially well represented category in the Labour Party is politicians and political organizers, in other words the class of professional politicians. Finally, in another reflection of the prominence of the "talking professions" in the British House of Commons, publishers and journalists are well represented across all political parties.

The occupational class that is spectacularly missing in most legislative assemblies is the working class—manual or blue-collar workers (Barnes and Saxton 2019). Even in the British Labour Party, originally founded to serve the interests of precisely such workers, only 7 percent of MPs are actually drawn from the working class. Among Conservatives, the number is 1 percent, and in the SNP and the Liberal Democrats none at all. The mix between academics and trade unionists has a long and at times tense history in the British Labour Party, but since the Blairite period the middle-class professionals have clearly been in the ascendancy. This underrepresentation of manual workers is hardly unique to the British House of Commons (Elsässer and Schäfer 2022). In the US Congress, members drawn from working-class occupations are effectively extinct. In Canada, the picture is only marginally different (Erickson 1997). Even in the Nordic parliaments, where social democratic parties have traditionally been even stronger than in the United Kingdom, a study conducted in the 1990s found that the share of blue-collar members varied only between 0 (Iceland) and 16 percent (Sweden) (Narud and Valen 2000: 88).

Our focus in this section has been on member's careers before entering political office. But the temporal focus on past occupations may be inaccurate for two reasons. First, some legislators may choose to continue their professional careers (although it may be challenging to do so this given the heavy demands placed on most full-time legislators). Second, members of some assemblies may not actually serve full time. Switzerland's national parliament is a militia parliament—meaning that it meets only part time and members are expected to have other careers. The 200-member Swiss National parliament thus holds four ordinary sessions per year,

---

[3] https://sgp.fas.org/crs/misc/R45583.pdf.

each lasting three weeks. Because members have other jobs, they remain more closely linked to "ordinary" citizens, at least in theory. Yet, having part-time legislators brings challenges. As Kriesi (2001: 61) notes, "as a consequence of its 'militia' status, the Federal Assembly as a whole lacks time, information and professional competence and is consistently disadvantaged compared with the government and the federal administration."

Education

An alternative measure, or correlate, of class is education. The US case illustrates how legislative assemblies tend to have members who have much higher levels of education than the general population. Thus, while 58 percent of the US population have no college or university degree, only 5 percent of the members of the House of Representatives fall into the same category. And 31 percent of House members have an advanced (graduate or professional) degree, compared to just 12 percent of the general population. In other words, US House legislators are considerably better (formally) educated than their voters.

In the United Kingdom—often considered a class-conscious society—education is also a major aspect, or correlate, of class. Following the 2020 election, an estimated 29 percent of those MPs educated in the UK had attended private, fee-paying, secondary/high schools. This compared to 7 percent of the general population.[4] Of the 87 percent of the MPs who had attended a UK university, 22 percent had gone to Oxford or Cambridge. As the authors of a report on the topic note, the educational background of MPs is important because: "[t]he social backgrounds of MPs are still vastly different to those of the general population, which may mean that the concerns and priorities of all parts of society are not adequately reflected in parliament."[5]

At the same time, education is one domain in which congruence is not necessarily desirable, because congruence in this respect may conflict with skills—and thus the notion of capacity as discussed in Chapter 1. Few of us would consult a physician whose formal training in the medical profession was no better than our own. To the extent that we value information and expertise in our political agents similarly, we might therefore prefer a representative who has a higher level of formal education than we do ourselves. And even to the extent that a voter's assembly might perhaps reflect the educational profile of the electorate, a leader's assembly presumably would not. Party leaders need "senior partners" (Cox and

---

[4] There are also substantial partisan differences. 44 percent of Conservative MPs attended fee-paying schools, compared to 38 percent for the Liberal Democrats and 19 percent for Labour. *Source:* https://researchbriefings.files.parliament.uk/documents/CBP-7483/CBP-7483.pdf.

[5] https://www.suttontrust.com/wp-content/uploads/2017/06/Parliamentary-privilege-2017_FINAL_V2.pdf.

McCubbins 2005) to whom they can delegate important gate-keeping functions such as committee chairs, presidencies, and membership on important rules or steering committees. It stands to reason that they would want these legislators to be among the "best and brightest," rather than a cross-section of the electorate at large. To the extent that legislative committees serve important specialized functions (e.g., drafting detailed financial regulations or health care provisions), party leaders may also ideally wish to have members at their disposal with a range of advanced specialized skills.

Legislative Experience

A related aspect of membership composition is how long its members have served. As noted in the previous chapter, few legislatures disallow re-election or impose other term limits, which means that the great majority of legislative incumbents across the world can seek re-election. Figure 4.1 shows that the average number of consecutive terms served by the members of the US House of Representatives (in which there are no term limits) elected in November 2016, was 4.7. Representative John Conyers (D–Michigan) was in 2018 the member of the US House of Representatives with the greatest seniority, serving his 27th term since he was first elected in 1964.[6]

The rate of seniority is influenced primarily by two factors: the number of incumbent legislators seeking re-election and the proportion of those seeking re-election that are successful. In the case of the US House of Representatives in 2016, 393 out of 435 members (90.3%) sought re-election, and 380 of these (96.7%) were in fact re-elected. Such high re-election rates were not always the case. As Glassman and Hope Wilhelm (2017: Summary) note: "during the early history of Congress, turnover in membership was frequent and resignations were commonplace, and that during the 20th century, congressional careers lengthened as turnover decreased and Congress became more professionalized." In other countries, such as India, the career of an elected politician may be more precarious, with re-election a real battle for many incumbents.

Some legislatures have a "seniority system" which grants certain privileges to individual members based on time served in the legislature. In the US case, for example, seniority is important in the allocation of committee assignments and in particular committee chairs. Custom and practice dictates that the ranking member from the majority party (the member longest serving on that committee from the party with a majority of seats in the chamber) takes the prized position of committee chair.

---

[6] http://clerk.house.gov/member_info/Terms_of_Service.pdf.

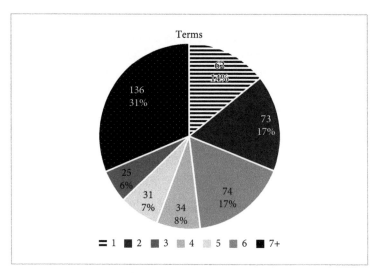

Figure 4.1 Seniority in the US House of Representative, 114th Congress (2015–2017)

Source: "Seniority." US House of Representatives. September 6, 2016. https://pressgallery.house.gov/member-data/seniority.

Legislatures tend to be large organizations, with internal working procedures and operations that are often complex and technical. Recognizing the informational disadvantage faced by inexperienced members, legislative officials may provide training programs for new legislators. Induction and training programs help new legislators (sometimes referred to as freshmen or first-termers) adjust smoothly to legislative rules and norms. Such information and support help reduce any disadvantage members new to the legislature may face—compared to long-serving members or new members from political dynasties (Smith and Martin 2017). Still, the description of someone as a "career politician" does not normally have positive connotations. We will return in the concluding chapters to the issue of incumbency.

Age Profiles

Legislators also tend to differ systematically from their voters in age. In the simplest of terms, legislators are almost always on average older than their voters. According to the 2010 US Census, the median age in the United States is 35.3 years.[7] In contrast, the mean age of members of the House of Representatives at the outset of the 115th Congress was 57.8 years. The average age of a newly elected member

[7] https://www.census.gov/prod/cen2010/briefs/c2010br-03.pdf.

was not much lower at 50.8 years.[8] Part of the explanation is institutional. As noted in Chapter 3, constitutions often impose minimum age requirements on members. Such requirements result in an obvious divide between the age profile of the general population and that of the legislature. The ineligibility of young adults for political office has led some countries to create "Youth Parliaments" to represent the voices and preferences of the young (see Shephard and Patrikios 2012), although such efforts seem to us mostly symbolic.

But it is not just the young who may be descriptively underrepresented in many legislatures. Young adults (18–40) and even the middle-aged (40–60) are likewise descriptively underrepresented in many assemblies. Since in most countries the minimum age of eligibility is not much higher than the minimum voting age, this cannot be the main reason that people in their 20s or 30s tend to be underrepresented in national assemblies. A more important cause of this underrepresentation is probably that in most democracies election to the national assembly is close to the pinnacle of political careers and that successful candidates need to have proven their qualities in lower offices, often at the local or regional level. And the larger and more stratified the political system is, the stronger this age bias may be.

Witness the contrast between the large, federal, and multi-tiered United States and the much smaller and more centralized Scandinavian countries. In the Nordic countries, the 36–44 age group was in the 1990s only marginally underrepresented, whereas the 45–54 age group was much better represented than older citizens or the population at large (Narud and Valen 2000). Overall, the Norwegian Parliament has in recent years been slightly younger than the population at large (Allern, Karlsen, and Narud 2014). In general, however, younger people seem to be underprepresented in legislative assemblies, and with consequences for which age groups are favored in public policy making (McClean 2021).

Race, Ethnicity, and Faith

According to the American Sociological Association, the term race refers to physical differences that groups and cultures consider socially significant, whereas the term ethnicity refers to individuals' "shared culture, such as language, ancestry, practices, and beliefs." Thus skin color is a racial feature while country of origin is an ethnic characteristic. What constitutes an ethnic, racial, or religious minority will vary from country to country, although most countries have at least one such minority group. Iceland is one of the few countries that at least until recently have had very little ethnic or religious diversity, whereas India and Nigeria rank among the most ethnically diverse countries in the world.

The descriptive representation of religious, ethnic and/or racial groups can be particularly salient in societies where such tensions are present, often stemming

---

[8] Source: https://fas.org/sgp/crs/misc/R44762.pdf.

from experiences of discrimination or unequal endowments. As Crisp et al. (2016:1) have argued: "the election of members from traditionally underrepresented groups is important because those members share a heritage and set of experiences that make them more likely to attend to the issues and concerns of their groups." In the United States, for example, racial divisions have roots especially in African American slavery in the eighteenth and much of the nineteenth century. Until well after the Civil Rights movement of the 1950s and 1960s, American blacks were substantially underrepresented in virtually all political offices. Part of this discrepancy still exists today, but it has been greatly reduced.

Ethnic and religious minorities are often, but far from always, similarly underrepresented. In most Western European countries ethnic minorities, and especially those made up largely of recent immigrants and their offspring, tend to be underrepresented. Even in Norway, where closed-list PR makes it possible for party leaders closely to control the composition of their respective party groups, only one member with a non-Western immigrant background had ever been elected prior to 2013. In quantitative terms, this minority made up 0.6 percent of the MPs of the 2009–13 Storting, compared with its 4.4 percent share of the electorate and its 6.4 percent share of the population at large (Allern, Karlsen, and Narud 2014). In the United States, Jews, Mormons, and Muslims make up religious minorities of roughly similar size. Yet, their political representation differs significantly. In the Congress elected in 2016, there were 30 Jews, 13 Mormons, and two Muslims. In fact, no Muslim had been elected to Congress prior to Keith Ellison (D–MN) in 2006. Yet, even minorities that are small nationally can gain a substantial presence regionally. Thus, as of 2018 all six members of Utah's congressional delegation (two senators and four representatives) were Mormon, whereas between 1993 and 2017 both of California's senators were Jewish (both females from the San Francisco Bay Area).

Proportional Representation electoral systems are often said to benefit the representation of social (for example, racial, ethnic, or religious) minorities. One other (and not necessarily incompatible) way to guarantee seats for minorities is to reserve some assembly seats for them. Lundgren and Strøm (2014) define reserved seats as "elective offices with full voting rights in the national legislature for which only members of specific demographic minority groups are eligible." For reserved seats, demographic criteria thus determine who is eligible to hold the seat, but similar restrictions may be placed on the electorate that is allowed to vote to select that seat holder. Twelve countries in our study have reserved seats in their national legislature (the lower chamber in bicameral systems): Belgium, Burundi, Colombia, Croatia, Finland, India, Nepal, New Zealand, Niger, Pakistan, Romania, and Taiwan. Reserved seats for demographic minorities are more common in newer democracies with ethnic diversity and in countries that have experienced UN peacekeeping interventions (for a review, see Lundgren and Strøm 2014). These correlates suggest that reserved seats are commonly adopted in response to significant ethnic tension or instability. Thus, reserved seats can be used to guarantee descriptive representation in the interest of containing social tension, but this device is in most cases used only for relatively small ethnic or other minorities.

Yet reserved seats exist even in very stable and well-established democracies. Thus, the 120-member New Zealand Parliament reserves seven seats for indigenous Māori people. The system of reserved seats dates back to 1867, when four "Māori seats" were created. Since the 1970s, every Māori voter can choose whether to enroll to vote with the general electorate or in the special Māori electorate, with the number of reserved seats depending on how many Māori choose to register in the Māori electorate. The New Zealand system of reserved seats is a source of ongoing controversy because it might tend to perpetuate and cement social differences. During the 2017 New Zealand general election campaign, one party hence called for the abolition of the reserved seats, referring to them as "race-based seats."[9] Crisp et al. (2016) find that substantive representation of Māori interests is stronger from Māori legislators elected via the Māori reserved seats. In contrast, Māori MPs elected via the general list are not as focused on Māori interests.

Gender

Despite the near-balanced rate of women to men in the general population, most democratic legislatures have significantly fewer women than men. For our 68 national assemblies, the mean rate of women legislators is 25.1 percent. In other words, on average approximately three out of every four legislators are men. The two legislatures closest to this rate is the Honduran Congreso Nacional with 25.8 percent women members and the Canadian House of Commons with 26.0 percent.

Yet, there is significant cross-national variation in the rate of women legislators. Papua New Guinea has the lowest share of women legislators of any assembly in our study, with just 2.7 percent females in the lower chamber as of late 2015. The 2017 General Election in Papua New Guinea went even further—returning no women legislators to the 111-member chamber—despite a record number of women (167) standing in the election. Since independence, the Papua New Guinea National Parliament has never at any given moment had more than three women members. In contrast, Bolivia has the highest percentage of women legislators in our study. Of the 130 members in Bolivia's Cámara de Diputados, 53.1 percent are women. In fact, Bolivia is the only chamber in our study with a majority female membership. Table 4.4 reports the rate of women members for all 68 countries.

---

[9] https://theconversation.com/new-zealand-elections-maori-seats-once-again-focus-of-debate-83,293.

Table 4.4 Women legislators and gender quotas

Country	Percent Women Legislators	Gender Quotas
Argentina	35.8	Yes (Party Quotas)
Australia	28.67	No
Austria	30.6	No
Belgium	39.33	Yes (Party Quotas)
Benin	7.23	No
Bolivia	53.08	Yes (Party Quotas)
Brazil	9.94	Yes (Party Quotas)
Bulgaria	20	No
Burundi	36.36	Yes (Reserved Seats For Women)
Canada	26.04	No
Chile	15.83	No
Colombia	19.88	Yes (Party Quotas)
Costa Rica	33.33	Yes (Party Quotas)
Croatia	15.23	Yes (Party Quotas)
Czech Republic	20	No
Denmark	37.43	No
Dominican Republic	26.84	Yes (Party Quotas)
Ecuador	41.61	Yes (Party Quotas)
El Salvador	32.14	Yes (Party Quotas)
Finland	41.5	No
France	26.17	Yes (Party Quotas)
Germany	36.45	No
Ghana	10.91	No
Greece	19.67	Yes (Party Quotas)
Guatemala	13.92	No
Honduras	25.78	Yes (Party Quotas)
Hungary	10.1	No
India	11.97	No
Indonesia	17.12	Yes (Party Quotas)
Ireland	15.06	Yes (Party Quotas)
Israel	26.67	No
Italy	31.43	No
Japan	9.47	No
Kenya	19.14	Yes (Reserved Seats For Women)
Liberia	10.96	No
Malawi	16.67	No
Mexico	42.4	Yes (Party Quotas)
Nepal	29.58	Yes (Party Quotas)
Netherlands	37.33	No
New Zealand	31.4	No
Nicaragua	42.39	Yes (Party Quotas)

Country	Percent Women Legislators	Gender Quotas
Niger	14.62	Yes (Reserved Seats For Women)
Nigeria	5.56	No
Norway	39.64	No
Pakistan	20.59	Yes (Reserved Seats For Women)
Papua N.Guinea	2.7	No
Paraguay	15	Yes (Party Quotas)
Peru	21.54	Yes (Party Quotas)
Philippines	27.34	No
Poland	27.39	Yes (Party Quotas)
Portugal	34.78	Yes (Party Quotas)
Romania	13.72	No
Senegal	42.67	Yes (Party Quotas)
Serbia	34	Yes (Party Quotas)
Sierra Leone	12.4	No
Slovak Republic	16	No
South Africa	41.67	No
South Korea	15.67	Yes (Party Quotas)
Spain	40	Yes (Party Quotas)
Sweden	43.55	No
Switzerland	32	No
Taiwan	33.63	Yes (Party Quotas)
Tunisia	31.34	Yes (Party Quotas)
Turkey	14.91	No
Ukraine	12.02	No
United Kingdom	29.58	No
United States	19.4	No
Zambia	10.76	No

Note: Lower chambers only in the case of bicameral legislatures.

Does descriptive representation translate into substantive representation for women? As noted above, Phillips (1995: 67–68) suggests that having more women legislators should translate into better representation for and of women's interests:

Women have distinct interests in relation to child-bearing (for any foreseeable future, an exclusively female affair); and as society is currently constituted they also have particular interests arising from their exposure to sexual harassment and violence, their unequal position in the division of paid and unpaid labor and their exclusion from many arenas of economic or political power.

The empirical evidence seems to suggest that within the legislative arena women legislators generally engage themselves more in women's rights and family-related issues than their male colleagues (for a wider discussion see O'Brien and Piscopo 2019). Evidence that women are more likely to advance interests traditionally associated with women (such as welfare and education) is more mixed (Taylor-Robinson 2014). And recent research suggests that women legislators have a different working style from many of their male colleagues. Looking at the Argentinian case, Barnes (2016) finds that women legislators are more likely to engage in cross-party collaboration. They collaborate with other women to overcome structural barriers and to attain political power.

What explains the significant cross-national variation in the rate of women legislators? The extensive academic literature on this topic discusses a number of possible causes. Thus, Pippa Norris (1997) distinguishes between (1) institutional factors, such as electoral and constitutional provisions (Barnes and Holman 2020), (2) recruitment procedures (Bjarnegård and Kenny 2015), (3) the pipeline and supply of candidates (Thomsen and King 2020), and (4) the demands of voters and gatekeepers, including perhaps societal attitudes (Teele et al. 2018). In this volume, we shall focus on the first and second of these factors. Building on the relevant scholarly literature, we discuss a number of explanations of why women are generally under-represented in national legislature, as well as why some legislatures have a higher rate of women legislators than others.

1. Compared with majoritarian ones, proportional electoral systems are said to favor the election of women candidates. In particular, a higher district magnitude appears to facilitate women's access to legislative office. In other words, the more legislators returned per district, the higher the rate of women elected. The specifics of the electoral system also matter. Research suggests that due to the influence of party leaders, closed-list PR facilitates the election of women better than open-list PR (see, for example, Wängnerud 2009; Roberts, Seawright and Cyr 2013; Taylor-Robinson 2014). Yet, closed-list PR only favors the election of women legislators when party leaders care about gender balance. Party leaders who want to promote women's representation may choose to place more women on the party list and closer to the top. Thus, if a political party (or whoever determines the party's candidate list) is inclined to equality, closed-list PR produces more women legislators; if parties are disinclined toward equality, open-list PR is more favorable to the election of women.

2. A gender quota is a statutory or party-based rule whereby a certain number or proportion of legislative seats or candidates on the electoral ballot must belong to a specific gender (typically women). The emergence and spread of gender quotas is frequently cited as the major cause of increased rates of women legislator over the last few decades (Krook 2009; O'Brien and Rickne 2016). Thirty-six countries in our study have no gender quota, four have reserved seats for a specific gender and a further 28 have party-based gender quotas (see Table 4.4). Reserved seats for women are seats in the legislature that only women can hold. Four countries in our study have such reserved seats for women: Niger, Kenya, Pakistan, and Burundi. In Niger, any party winning more than three seats must ensure that the proportion of elected candidates of either sex should not be less than 10 percent.

In Kenya, 47 of 350 seats in the lower chamber are reserved for women. In Pakistan 60 of the total 342 seats in the National Assembly are reserved for women. In Burundi, it is a requirement that 30 percent of the members of the National Assembly must be women. Burundi reserves seats for both women and ethnic minorities (see box 4.2).

Box 4.2 Reserved Seats in Burundi's National Assembly

Burundi is unusual in that assembly seats are reserved both for ethnic groups and for women. A former Belgian colony, Burundi is an ethnically divided country. The major ethnic groups are Hutus (85%), Tutsis (14%), and Twa (1%). Civil war followed the 1993 assassination by Tutsi extremists of Burundi's first democratically elected Hutu president. A peace process foreshadowed the eventual end of the civil war in 2005. A new constitution formed part of the settlement. Vandeginste (2009: 64) describes the constitution as creating a "multi-layered and multi-faceted power-sharing arrangement."

As part of this power-sharing arrangement, Article 164 of the 2005 Burundian constitution stipulates that:

The National Assembly is composed of at least 100 deputies at the rate of 60% Hutu and 40% Tutsi, with a minimum of 30 percent of women, elected by direct universal suffrage for a mandate of five years, and three deputies from the Twa co-opted ethnicity conforming to the electoral code. Where the results of the vote do not reflect the above percentages, a co-optation mechanism provided under the electoral code will proceed to address the imbalance.*

Members of the Assemblée Nationale du Burundi are elected by closed-list PR. Article 168 of the constitution facilitates ethnic and gender diversity in the list composition by requiring that: "These lists must have a multiethnic character and maintain the equilibrium between women and men. For three candidates listed in a row, only two may belong to the same ethnic group, and at least a quarter of the candidates must be women."

At the June 2015 elections, 75 men and 25 women were elected, of whom 70 were Hutus and 30 were Tutsis. In accordance with the Constitution, the country's electoral commission then co-opted 18 women (three Hutus and 15 Tutsis) and three Twa representatives (one woman and two men). Co-optation consisted of selecting from the party lists candidates from the relevant demographic groups who did not otherwise win a seat. The result was to being the total number of women to 44 and the total membership of the lower chamber to 118.**

---

* Available at https://www.constituteproject.org/constitution/Burundi_2005.pdf.
** Source: http://www.ipu.org/parline-e/reports/2049_E.htm.

Candidate gender quotas require political parties to nominate a minimum percentage of women candidates. Such quotas are an alternative mechanism to facilitate the election of more women, although they tend not to be as effective as reserved seats. Gender quotas place the responsibility on political parties to ensure that women are placed on the ballot in sufficient numbers to allow voters to elect more females. Argentina, for example, which operates a closed-list system, adopted a 30 percent gender electoral quota in 1991. Moreover, parties are not allowed simply to position women candidates at the bottom of the list: women candidates must be in "electable positions" on the party list. Although quotas are seen as an effective way to bring greater balance to a legislative chamber, one disadvantage is the fear that members elected via a quota may be considered less legitimate than legislators elected independently of a quota system. Also, by their very nature, quotas reduce the choice available to voters.

To explore the relative impact of electoral rules and gender quotas on the share of women legislators, Table 4.5 reports a linear regression model where the dependent variable is the percentage of a country's lower chamber members who are women. Party Quota and Reserved Seats are both binary variables that take the value of 1 if a country has either formal party quotas or reserved seats for women, respectively.

The results in Table 4.5 show that countries that are majoritarian, gained sovereignty later, are more populous, former British colonies, and countries from the African/Middle Eastern, Asian/Oceanic, and Eastern European regions tend to have fewer women serving in the lower or unicameral chamber of the legislature. In the final model (6), however, only majoritarianism and the regional dummies remain significant. Scandinavian countries are often considered to be pioneers in promoting women to political office. Indeed, countries such as Sweden (43.6 %), Finland (41.5%), Norway (39.6 %), and Denmark (37.4 %) have achieved some of the highest rates of female representation without any statutory requirement, though many parties in these countries have their own rules of gender balance. These cases likely also point to an important factor in explaining the rate of women legislators: social attitudes toward women and their place in society and the workforce. There are aspects of a political career which may make it unattractive for women to seek elected office and to build a career in politics once elected. For example, important deliberations in the British House of Commons and many other legislatures typically take place in the late afternoon and evening and often into the wee hours, a schedule that is unattractive to women (and men) with family responsibilities and that also fosters a culture of late-night pub-going that may not always be healthy or female-friendly. Also, one factor that may limit the female presence in many legislatures is that women legislators may tend to serve fewer terms than men and retire earlier. The fact that Scandinavian legislators on average tend to be comparatively young (rarely older than 60) may, for example, limit the effect of this possible "differential retirement effect." Finally, colonial history

Table 4.5 Women legislators as a proportion of all members

	Women as a Proportion of All Members					
	(1)	(2)	(3)	(4)	(5)	(6)
Gender Quota	2.85				3.63	
	(2.36)				(2.40)	
Reserved Seats	−1.15				0.39	
	(3.77)				(3.74)	
Majoritarian	−10.83***				−6.27	−9.10*
	(3.49)				(3.97)	(4.61)
Mixed	−1.14				1.72	
	(3.45)				(3.69)	
Mean District Magnitude	−0.01				0.02	
	(0.02)				(0.02)	
Sovereignty		−0.12**			−0.06	−0.02
		(0.05)			(0.06)	(0.05)
log(GDP per Capita)		1.58				
		(1.27)				
GINI		−0.10				
		(0.21)				
log(Population)		−1.99*			−1.26	−0.88
		(1.08)			(1.13)	(1.12)
Ethnic Frac-tionalization		4.46			3.26	
		(6.84)			(6.65)	
Africa and Middle East			−13.28***		−10.09*	−9.11**
			(3.78)		(5.22)	(4.50)
Asia and Oceania			−12.67***		−10.22**	−8.93*
			(4.12)		(5.10)	(4.57)
Americas			−5.47		−7.48*	−5.29
			(3.67)		(4.06)	(3.55)
Eastern Europe			−14.69***		−15.34***	−14.86***
			(4.39)		(5.61)	(5.12)
British Colony				−11.76***		0.43
				(3.83)		(4.63)
Other Colony				−4.49		
				(3.18)		
Constant	26.81***	275.77**	33.41***	29.95***	173.96	92.45
	(2.36)	(107.91)	(2.63)	(2.55)	(125.97)	(107.43)
N	68	68	68	68	68	68
R^2	0.18	0.21	0.24	0.13	0.40	0.35
Adjusted R^2	0.11	0.15	0.19	0.10	0.27	0.26

*$p < 0.1$; **$p < 0.05$; ***$p < 0.01$
Note: DV: Percentage of members in the lower/unicameral chamber that are women. Ranges from 2.70 to 53.08 in our dataset.

on the whole seems to have a negative effect on women's representation, although only Other Colony is significant (and only in Model 5). This may once again reflect the greater presence of women in Western European countries, which presumably make up a great part of the omitted category (countries without a colonial history). Regardless of the reason for why some legislative assemblies have so few female legislators, our key take-home point is that a voters' assembly should have a significant proportion of women members.

4.4 Conclusion

In this chapter, we have examined the membership composition of the national assemblies in our 68 democracies with specific focus on the similarity or congruence of the assembly relative to the voters it represents. Congruence is the extent to which assembly members resemble their constituents in preferences (policy congruence) and socio-economic characteristics (demographic or descriptive congruence). In a voters' assembly we expect this congruence to be high, since it makes it more likely that the actions of the members will reflect the concerns of the voters. We have focused on assembly composition and specifically its breakdown by political party and demographic properties such as class, religion, ethnic, faith, education, and prior occupation or service. Our most intensive focus, though, has been on gender, and we have sought to identify various institutional features that may account for the large differences in the representation of women that we observe across the world. Thus, we have examined the effects of electoral systems written large. We have also examined the presence of statutorily reserved seats for women as well as party-specific rules concerning gender representation, and we have found evidence that all these institutions matter in their own ways.

References

Allern, Elin Haugsgjerd, Rune Karlsen, and Hanne Marthe Narud. 2014. "En representativ forsamling?" in H. M. Narud, K. Heidar, and T. Grønlie (eds.), *Stortingets historie 1964–2014*. Oslo: Fagbokforlaget, 316–336.

Barkan, Joel D., Paul J. Densham, and Gerard Rushton. 2006. "Space Matters: Designing Better Electoral Systems for Emerging Democracies." *American Journal of Political Science* 50(4): 926–939.

Barnes, Tiffany D. 2016. *Gendering Legislative Behavior*. New York: Cambridge University Press.

Barnes, Tiffany D., and Mirya R. Holman. 2020. "Gender Quotas, Women's Representation, and Legislative Diversity." *The Journal of Politics* 82(4): 1271–1286.

Barnes, Tiffany D., and Gregory W. Saxton. 2019. "Working-class Legislators and Perceptions of Representation in Latin America." *Political Research Quarterly* 72(4): 910–928.

Bjarnegård, Elin, and Meryl Kenny. 2015. "Revealing the 'Secret Garden': The Informal Dimensions of Political Recruitment." *Politics & Gender* 11(4): 748–753.

Cox, Gary W., and Mathew D. McCubbins. 2005. *Setting the Agenda: Responsible Party Government in the US House of Representatives.* Cambridge: Cambridge University Press.

Crisp, Brian F., Betul Demirkaya, Leslie A. Schwindt-Bayer, and Courtney Millian. 2016. "The Role of Rules in Representation: Group Membership and Electoral Incentives." *British Journal of Political Science* 48(1): 47–67.

Dahl, Robert A. 1971. *Polyarchy.* New Haven: Yale University Press.

Elsässer, Lea, and Armin Schäfer. 2022. "(N) One of Us? The Case for Descriptive Representation of the Contemporary Working Class." *West European Politics* 45(6): 1334–1360.

Erickson, Lynda. 1997. "Canada." In Pippa Norris (ed.), *Passages to Power: Legislative Recruitment in Advanced Democracies.* New York: Cambridge University Press, 33–55.

Evenwel v. Abbott. 2016. 136 S. Ct. 1120, 578 U.S. 54, 194 L. Ed. 2d 291.

Farrell, David M., 2011. *Electoral Systems: A Comparative Introduction.* London: Macmillan.

Glassman, Matthew E., and Amber Hope Wilhelm. 2017. *Congressional Careers: Service Tenure and Patterns of Member Service, 1789–2015.* Washington, DC: Congressional Research Service.

Kriesi, Hanspeter. 2001. "The Federal Parliament: The Limits of Institutional Reform." *West European Politics* 24(2): 59–76.

Krook, Mona Lena. 2009. *Quotas for Women in Politics: Gender and Candidate Selection Reform Worldwide.* New York: Oxford University Press.

Lundgren, Lydia L., and Kaare W. Strøm. 2014. "Explaining Reserved Seats for Minorities in National Legislatures: A Global Analysis." Paper presented at the Joint Sessions of the European Consortium for Political Research, Salamanca.

Marx, Karl. 1867. *Das Kapital: Kritik der politischen Ökonomie.* Hamburg: Verlag von Otto Meisner.

McClean, Charles T. 2021. *Does the Underrepresentation of Young People in Political Institutions Matter for Social Spending?* Working Paper. Ann Arbor: University of Michigan.

Narud, Hanne Marthe, and Henry Valen. 2000. "Does Social Background Matter?" In Peter Esaiasson and Knut Heidar (eds.), *Beyond Westminster and Congress: The Nordic Experience.* Columbus: Ohio State University Press, 83–106.

Norris, Pippa. (ed.) 1997. *Passages to Power: Legislative Recruitment in Advanced Democracies.* New York: Cambridge University Press.

O'Brien, Diana Z., and Jennifer M. Piscopo. 2019. "The Impact of Women in Parliament." In Susan Franceschet, Mona Lena Krook, and Netina Tan (eds.), *The Palgrave Handbook of Women's Political Rights.* London: Palgrave Macmillan, 53–72.

O'Brien, Diana Z., and Johanna Rickne. 2016. "Gender Quotas and Women's Political Leadership." *American Political Science Review* 110(1): 112–126.

Phillips, Anne. 1995. *The Politics of Presence.* Oxford: Oxford University Press.

Roberts, Andrew, Jason Seawright, and Jennifer Cyr. 2013. "Do Electoral Laws Affect Women's Representation?" *Comparative Political Studies* 46(12): 1555–1581.

Samuels, David, and Richard Snyder. 2001. "The Value of a Vote: Malapportionment in Comparative Perspective." *British Journal of Political Science* 31(4): 651–671.

Schuler, Paul, and Edward J. Malesky. 2014. "Authoritarian Legislatures." In Shane Martin, Thomas Saalfeld, and Kaare W. Strøm (eds.), *The Oxford Handbook of Legislative Studies*. Oxford: Oxford University Press, 676–695.

Shephard, Mark, and Stratos Patrikios. 2012. "Making Democracy Work by Early Formal Engagement? A Comparative Exploration of Youth Parliaments in the EU." *Parliamentary Affairs* 66(4): 752–771.

Smith, Daniel M. and Shane Martin. 2017. "Political Dynasties and the Selection of Cabinet Ministers." *Legislative Studies Quarterly* 42(1): 131–165.

Svolik, Milan W. 2012. *The Politics of Authoritarian Rule*. New York: Cambridge University Press.

Taagepera, Rein. 2007. *Predicting Party Sizes: The Logic of Simple Electoral Systems*. Oxford: Oxford University Press.

Taylor-Robinson, Michelle M., 2014. "Gender and Legislatures." In Shane Martin, Thomas Saalfeld, and Kaare W. Strøm (eds.), *The Oxford Handbook of Legislative Studies*. Oxford: Oxford University Press, 250–266.

Teele, Dawn Langan, Joshua Kalla, and Frances Rosenbluth. 2018. "The Ties that Double Bind: Social Roles and Women's Underrepresentation in Politics." *American Political Science Review* 112(3): 525–541.

Thomsen, Danielle M., and Aaron S. King. 2020. "Women's Representation and the Gendered Pipeline to Power." *American Political Science Review* 114(4): 989–1000.

Vandeginste, Stef. 2009. "Power-sharing, Conflict and Transition in Burundi: Twenty Years of Trial and Error." *Africa Spectrum* 44(3): 63–86.

Wängnerud, Lena. 2009. "Women in Parliaments: Descriptive and Substantive Representation." *Annual Review of Political Science* 12: 51–69.

Wegmann, Simone. 2022. "Policy-making Power of Opposition Players: A Comparative Institutional Perspective." *The Journal of Legislative Studies* 28(1): 1–25.

5

Cameral Structures

A legislative assembly's cameral structure describes its number of chambers and, in the case of a legislature with two or more chambers, the similarity and differences between these chambers. This chapter explores the design of cameral structures from the perspectives of voters, members, and leaders. Many legislatures have only one chamber (unicameralism); whereas bicameralism means that the assembly has two chambers. More specifically, Tsebelis and Money (1997: 1) suggest that the "defining characteristic of bicameral legislatures is the requirement that legislation be deliberated in two distinct assemblies." Of the legislative assemblies included in our study, 33 have two chambers while 35 have just one.[1] Although all the current national legislatures we examine are unicameral or bicameral, some states have in the past had legislatures with more than two chambers. South Africa, for example, between 1984 and 1994 had a three-chamber (tricameral) legislature. And prior to an 1866 reform, the Swedish Riksdagen had no fewer than four chambers.

Cameral structures impact the type of legislative assembly a country has. Citizens, we presume, value bicameralism. A second chamber—sometimes referred to as an upper chamber and often called a senate—may provide an extra check on the executive (thus adding to transparency in government) and on the lower chamber (thus allowing for more reflective lawmaking).[2] As Russell (2001) notes, requiring a second chamber to scrutinize proposed legislation makes it more likely that any flaws in a bill can be ironed out before it becomes law—a role which fits well with the concept of capacity as outlined in Chapter 1. The British House of Lords is often considered a revising chamber, in that it typically takes draft legislation from the House of Commons and seeks to improve it. Second chambers may thus serve as a constraining or slowing influence on the ability of the majority in the first chamber to make new policy.

But voters' interests may not be well served by a second chamber that is unelected or only partially elected. In a voters' assembly, citizens benefit from their direct and immediate influence over member selection and their ability to remove and replace these representatives in future elections. This will not be possible in a second chamber that is unelected (and only partially possible in a partially elected

---

[1] Because we focus on larger democracies, this number likely overestimates the rate of bicameralism around the world. Tsebelis and Money (1997) suggest that approximately one-third of countries have a bicameral legislature.

[2] The word senate is derived from the Latin word *senex* (the Senate was an important political institution in ancient Rome) which translates "council of old men" (Russell 2013: 42).

Legislative Assemblies. Shane Martin and Kaare W. Strøm, Oxford University Press.
© Shane Martin and Kaare W. Strøm (2023). DOI: 10.1093/oso/9780198890829.003.0005

chamber). For all its potential utilities, an unelected second chamber is the polar opposite to our notion of a voters' assembly—an open legislative assembly where members are highly responsive and accountable to citizens.

Equally, if for different reasons, bicameralism may also serve the interest of members. While a second chamber may reduce the influence of a lower-chamber legislator (Diermeier and Myerson 1999) exactly because legislative power is somehow shared between the two chambers, members may nevertheless prefer the presence of a second chamber in their nation's legislative assembly. The presence of a second chamber may offer an avenue for promotion, thus enabling what Schlesinger (1966) terms "progressive ambition."[3] In the United States, for example, members of the House of Representatives may wish to become Senators. In the United Kingdom, some MPs—including former prime ministers—move from the House of Commons to the House of Lords. Examples of former prime ministers moving to the House of Lords include Margaret Thatcher and John Major. And in other countries, a second chamber may be an opportunity for politicians who failed to get re-elected to the lower chamber to remain in politics at the national level, possibly again seeking office in the lower chamber in a subsequent election.[4]

Leaders (in the lower chamber) will have mixed preferences over cameral structure. On the one hand, leaders may benefit from the ability to influence the composition of the second chamber, particularly where the second chamber is unelected or only partially elected. The UK Prime Minister, for example, decides who, if anyone, is appointed to the House of Lords, often rewarding loyal colleagues or financial contributors.[5] On the other hand, leaders will prefer to centralize decision making in one chamber, thereby enhancing their legislative influence. Bicameralism requires inter-cameral bargaining, as the leaders of the US House of Representatives and US Senate know only too well. All else equal, under unicameralism leaders have the greatest control over the lawmaking process in the assembly. In a bicameral legislature, this leadership power is to a lesser or greater degree shared. Exactly how power is shared between chambers is, as we will see, an important question. But, while leaders may be happy to have a second chamber, and in particular a relatively weak second chamber whose composition they can influence, they have little strategic interest in a strong and directly elected one.

Constitutional engineers—a term to describe individuals and organizations who advise on and draft new, or amend existing, constitutions—often have a

---

[3] For an application of the progressive ambition framework see Sieberer and Müller (2017).

[4] For example, Michael W. D'Arcy lost his seat in the lower house (the Dáil Éireann) at the 2011 Irish general election. Shortly after, he was elected to the Irish senate (which is not popularly elected). At the subsequent general election in 2016 he won back his seat in the lower chamber.

[5] https://www.gov.uk/government/news/dissolution-peerages-2015.

particular fascination with cameral structures. When Norway adopted its constitution in 1814, the choice between a unicameral and a bicameral parliament was one of the most hotly debated issues, which was only resolved through an inelegant and ultimately ineffectual compromise (Holmøyvik 2012).[6] In many countries today, the status of second chambers is the subject of significant attention from political elites and voters, with calls for fundamental reform (for example in the United Kingdom and Italy). Some second chambers have faced the threat of elimination (for example, in Ireland—see MacCarthaigh and Martin 2015). Some second chambers have indeed been eliminated (for example, in Croatia in 2001 and in Peru in 1993). At the same time, other countries have amended their constitutions to (re)establish a second chamber (for example, Kenya in 2010, effective 2013, and Nepal, effective in 2018).

Bicameral constitutions are not all the same, and rather than treating unicameralism and bicameralism as binary categories, it often makes more sense to think of different degrees of cameral differentiation. We begin, however, by exploring the choice between having one or two chambers. The core of this chapter then discusses variation in cameral structures with a focus on how members of second chambers are selected and what legislative powers they have. It thus becomes possible to speak of strong versus weak bicameralism according to the division of power between the chambers and their respective modes of selection (Tsebelis and Money 1997; Lijphart 2012; Russell 2013).

5.1 The Number of Chambers

Second chambers have long fascinated scholars. For many, the number of chambers is an obvious starting point in efforts to compare and contrast legislatures cross-nationally. The number of chambers is relatively easily identified (although see Norton 2004). As noted in the introduction, of the 68 legislative assemblies in our study, 33 are bicameral while 35 have just one chamber. Why do some countries have bicameral legislatures while others choose unicameralism? A number of possible explanations can be put forward, as we discuss below. It is worth noting that cameral structure is today typically defined in a nation's constitution (Heller and Branduse 2014). Thus, the design of cameral structure tends to be a topic of constitutional design and redesign and is not easily manipulated by political parties and their leaders in the short run.

---

[6] The Norwegian Constitution of 1814 divided the Storting (Parliament) into two divisions or quasi-chambers, the Lagting (1/4 of the total number of members) and the Odelsting (3/4). These were to be jointly elected and the assignment of members to one division or the other to be determined by the elected representatives themselves. The two divisions would deliberate separately only on non-financial bills and in impeachment cases. After partisan politics took hold in the 1880s, the partisan composition of the two divisions became effectively identical and deliberations in the Lagting largely superfluous. The Lagting was abolished by constitutional amendment in 2007, effective with the 2009 election.

Population

Legislatures are the cornerstone of representative democracy, providing a link between citizens and those who govern. It is plausible to think that in this process there is an optimal ratio of legislators to voters, or at least a desirable range. A very large ratio (e.g., 1 to 2) would be unwieldy and inefficient, as legislative assemblies may grow so large as to make them ineffective and inefficient. Cox (2006) for example, has written of the "plenary bottleneck" problem: as legislative chambers are busy places, demand for plenary time to debate and vote may far exceed the total time available to members. Countries with larger populations may, all else equal, require more governance and a larger number of members (see Chapter 3), meaning that the plenary bottleneck will be particularly acute in such countries. On the other hand, a very low ratio of legislators to voters (e.g., 1 to 10 million) would unduly diminish the influence of the individual voter.

Such extreme ratios are indeed rare, and the number of national legislators tends to vary with the country's population. According to Taagepera (1973), the membership of a national legislature tends to be about the cube root of its population. The largest lower chamber amongst countries included in our study is the House of Commons of the United Kingdom with 650 MPs. Britain also has the largest total number of national legislators when both chambers are counted.

Of course, the United Kingdom does not have the largest population in the democratic world, so exactly what is the relationship between population size and the incidence of bicameralism? Table 5.1 presents the results of a regression analysis where the presence or absence of a second chamber is the dependent variable. The results in Table 5.1 suggest that more populous and federal countries are more likely to have bicameral legislatures, whereas countries that gained sovereignty later are less likely to be bicameral. There is also some evidence, depending on the model specifications, that Asian/Oceanic countries are less likely to have bicameral legislatures.

Federal versus Unitary Countries

Scholars have suggested that bicameralism is associated with federal systems of government (Tsebelis and Money 1997; Russell 2001)—with some evidence provided in Table 5.1 above. A federal system is one in which different levels of government have constitutionally differentiated powers and functions. The United States is a classic example, with the federal government operating alongside state governments, each with constitutionally defined competencies. In contrast, in a unitary state, government power is centralized. The central government in such states may devolve authority to lower levels, but can take such power back at any stage.

Specifically, second chambers may exist to represent territorial interests at the federal level. Filippov et al. (2004: 280) identify a second chamber as part of the essential criteria for sustainable federalism. The German political system

Table 5.1 Bicameralism

	Bicameral Legislature					
	(1)	(2)	(3)	(4)	(5)	(6)
Presidential	0.05				0.10	
	(0.11)				(0.16)	
Federal	0.56***				0.36**	0.34**
	(0.14)				(0.16)	(0.14)
Sovereignty		−0.004*			−0.004	−0.003**
		(0.002)			(0.002)	(0.002)
log(GDP per Capita)		0.06				
		(0.05)				
GINI		−0.004				
		(0.01)				
log(Population)		0.17***			0.15***	0.15***
		(0.04)			(0.05)	(0.05)
Ethnic Fractionalization		0.24			−0.06	
		(0.28)			(0.27)	
Africa and Middle East			−0.29		−0.13	
			(0.18)		(0.24)	
Asia and Oceania			−0.17		−0.33*	−0.25*
			(0.20)		(0.19)	(0.15)
Americas			−0.04		−0.19	
			(0.18)		(0.22)	
Eastern Europe			−0.29		0.04	
			(0.21)		(0.22)	
British Colony				0.07		
				(0.17)		
Other Colony				−0.11		
				(0.14)		
Constant	0.35***	4.87	0.62***	0.53***	4.96	4.67
	(0.08)	(4.40)	(0.13)	(0.12)	(4.55)	(3.21)
N	68	68	68	68	68	68
R^2	0.21	0.30	0.06	0.02	0.37	0.36
Adjusted R^2	0.18	0.24	0.003	−0.01	0.28	0.32

*p < 0.1; **p < 0.05; ***p < 0.01.
Note: DV: 1 = Bicameral Legislature, 0 = Unicameral Legislature.

exemplifies the relationship between federalism and bicameralism. Germany's second chamber, the Bundesrat, is designed to represent the governments of Germany's regional states (Länder). The Bundesrat is composed of ministers of the regional governments rather than elected members—with the size of each Land's delegation based in part on the population of the Länder. The Bundesrat can veto proposals related to the Länder. Voting is by Länder rather than by delegate. The Bundesrat is thus clearly designed to provide Länder representation at the federal level in Germany – see Box 5.2.

Box 5.2 Bicameralism in Germany

Germany has a particularly interesting system of bicameralism at the federal level. As we have noted elsewhere, the lower chamber of the Germany parliament is the Bundestag, directly elected and currently comprising 736 members (Summer 2022). By some accounts, including its own self-description, the Bundestag is Germany's federal parliament.[7]

But most scholars of bicameralism would classify Germany as having a bicameral system—with the second or upper chamber being the federal council (Bundesrat). The Bundesrat represents Germany's 16 states (Länder) at the federal level. Some of the atypical characteristics of the Bundesrat add to the confusion over whether it is the second chamber of the federal parliament, or whether it should be characterized differently. Relevant properties include the fact that the Bundesrat meets in one of two different places (Bonn or Berlin) and that rather than popularly elected representatives, its membership comprises delegations from each of the 16 Länder—typically the state's premier minister and senior state cabinet members (the size of each delegation depends in part on the state's population size, although all states have a minimum of three members in the Bundesrat and a maximum of six). Unlike most legislative assemblies, the Bundesrat is never dissolved, but at any time comprises the delegates from each Land's government. The Bundesrat's status as a second chamber revolves around its constitutional role in German lawmaking. Like most upper chambers, the Bundesrat has no role in government formation or termination. Proposed legislation passes through the Bundesrat, which can veto any legislation within the policy domain of state governments. The Bundesrat can also oppose proposed legislation not in the policy domain of the states but the Bundestag can vote to override any such objection. Still, inter-cameral conflict is not unusual, particularly when the partisan legislative coalitions differ between the two chambers—a phenomenon known as Blockadepolitik.

Germany's form of bicameralism recognizes the distinct roles of Länder in German politics. Although only indirectly elected at the state level, the Bundesrat arguably serves to protect the interests of state-level government and, given its malapportionment (with small states over-represented), the interests and preferences of smaller German states (such as Bremen, with three votes and population 680,000), over larger states (such as North Rhine—Westsphalia, with six votes and population 18 million).

[7] https://www.bundestag.de/en/teasertext-startteaserbildtext-692028.

The United States Senate represents another example of how sub-federal units may be represented in the federal political system. Each state in the United States elects two members of the US Senate. As states vary in population size, relatively small states are by design significantly overrepresented in the Senate compared to big states—a phenomenon referred to as malapportionment. Voters in Wyoming (population circa 586,000) have equal representation with voters in California (population circa 39 million) in the Senate. This malapportionment ensures small states a significant voice in federal decision making. Thus, a second chamber may in a federal system provide a forum for the individual states to counterbalance population-based representation in the lower chamber.[8]

Of the 68 countries included in this study, only one federal system had a uni-cameral parliament as of 2015—Nepal. And Nepal transitioned to a bicameral legislature in 2018 as part of a new Constitution adopted in 2015. The remaining 13 federal states in our study all have bicameral parliaments. However, 20 uni-tary states also have a bicameral parliament, meaning that the correlation between federalism and bicameralism is far from perfect. While federal systems tend to be bicameral, not all bicameral systems are federal.

Broader Representation

Second chambers may be created to facilitate the representation of groups that for some reason lack representation, or are under-represented, in the first chamber. Thus bicameralism may allow for representation of different interests within the country. As we saw in Chapter 4, the composition of a legislative assembly can depend on a number of factors including the rules used to elect members. Varying the electoral system used to elect each chamber may produce two chambers that are demographically very different.

One way to see whether second chambers allow for the representation of dif-ferent interests is to compare the rate of women members in the chambers of bicameral parliaments. Women tend to be under-represented in lower chambers relative to the general population (Chapter 4). The evidence that second cham-bers provide for a greater proportion of women legislators is mixed: In 19 of the second chambers in our study, women form a lower proportion of members than in that legislature's lower chamber. In the remaining 14 bicameral assemblies, the differences are reversed. For example, in the Dominican Republic, women hold 27 percent of seats in the first chamber but just 9 percent of seats in the second chamber. At the other extreme is the Irish Parliament where women comprise 30 percent of the second chamber compared to just 15 percent in the first chamber.

---

[8] In contrast, Wyoming has one seat and California 52 in the US House of Representatives.

Higher Quality Representation

When the American Founders debated the organization of their new national assembly, they quickly converged on a preference for a bicameral one. This preference was in substantial part based on the expectation (or hope) that the upper chamber would deliberate with a greater level of wisdom, restraint, or reflection than a larger chamber more directly or frequently accountable to ordinary citizens. As James Madison [1961] noted, "The necessity of a senate is not less indicated by the propensity of all single and numerous assemblies to yield to the impulse of sudden and violent passions, and to be seduced by factious leaders into intemperate and pernicious resolutions."

Similar considerations of capacity may have underpinned the design of other bicameral assemblies. How a higher quality of deliberation can be attained is of course a tricky question, but one common way to promote such qualities has been a higher age requirement for upper chamber members. Wisdom, thus defined by the proxy of age, provides some insight into the design of second chambers. The average minimum age of eligibility for all lower chambers in our study is 21.5 years. In contrast, the average for upper chambers is 27.7 years. In 10 of our 33 cases of bicameralism, there is no difference in age requirement between chambers. The most significant gap is in Italy, with 40 being the minimum age to serve in the Senate, compared to 18 for the Chamber of Deputies. Differences in minimum age requirements may reflect the fact that upper chambers are designed to be more reflective, mature, and possibly less partisan than their lower-chamber counterparts.

The quality of deliberation can presumably also be enhanced by having smaller chambers in which members have more opportunity and incentive to interact in an ongoing manner. Bicameralism may also be one way to broaden participation, enhance deliberation, and overcome such legislative bottlenecks as concern Cox. Two chambers can function simultaneously, allowing more legislators to be involved in deliberation and debate.

Most second chambers are smaller than their counterpart first chamber. Of the 33 bicameral systems in our study, only the United Kingdom has a second chamber that is larger than the first chamber. The British House of Lords currently has 23 percent more members than the House of Commons (a percentage which would have been greater in 1999 when the House of Lords comprised 1,330 members). At the other extreme is the Philippines with 297 members of the House and just 24 Senators. On average, second chambers have just 40 percent of the membership number of first chambers. The smaller size of most second chambers is politically important. The US Senate, with 100 members, is often described as being more collegial than the House of Representatives, with 435 members.

Regional and Historical Effects

The 68 legislative assemblies that we analyze in this book did not all evolve through mutually independent trajectories. On the contrary, there has been a great deal of diffusion, learning, and emulation involved in their respective histories. The dominant legislative models that have been diffused throughout the world are those that originated in the United Kingdom and the United States of America, respectively. Two forces are particularly likely to have influenced the adoption and design of upper chambers: colonial history and regional diffusion. Colonial history is in large part responsible for the diffusion of many aspects of Westminster parliamentary design and procedure throughout the Commonwealth. Thus, when Nigeria gained independence in 1960, the country adopted a bicameral format including an upper house known as the House of Chiefs and modeled after the British House of Lords, even as the latter had largely become considered obsolete in its home country and had undergone important reforms. There is some evidence from Table 5.1, depending on the model, that Asian/Oceanic assemblies are less likely to be bicameral whereas former British colonies are more likely to have bicameralism. The results in Table 5.1 also suggest that countries that gained sovereignty later are less likely to have bicameralism.

Regional diffusion and homogenization is another source of the adaption of different legislative designs. Whereas the British model of bicameralism was dispersed in large part through colonial imposition or borrowing, the American model has spread more through regional diffusion, particularly in Latin America, but also in parts of Asia and Africa. But even the British model has of course spread not only within the former British Empire but also in other countries in which the British cultural influence has been strong, such as Denmark. In more recent times, diffusion has also occurred within such regions as Scandinavia, in which all five independent states have over time converged on a unicameral legislative format.

By spreading workload and allowing for greater levels of representation, second chambers can help serve the needs and interests of a country's citizens. But the degree to which bicameralism serves the interests of citizens depends on the degree to which citizens can hold the members of any second chamber to account. It is therefore important to discuss exactly how second chambers are selected.

5.2 Membership Selection

Second chambers differ in how their membership is selected. As we saw in earlier chapters, the rules used to elect an assembly are important for several reasons. Table 5.2 presents basic information on upper chamber selection rules (we use the term "selection rules" as in some second chambers elections do not form part of the path to membership). The first level of differentiation is between chambers that are somehow "directly elected" and chambers who are unelected or only partially elected.

Twelve upper chambers in our study are appointed or somehow indirectly elected, rather than popularly elected—a relatively high proportion and somewhat surprising given that our cases include only democracies. But even within this broad characterization, the process by which upper chamber members are selected can vary dramatically. In Germany, as we have already noted, members of the Bundesrat comprise representatives selected by the 16 German states (Länder). State delegations within the Bundesrat typically comprise senior members of the cabinet from each state government. In the United Kingdom, the House of Lords is comprised of hereditary peers and life peers. Also, 26 of the most senior Church of England archbishops and bishops serve in the Lords ex officio. Until 1999 all hereditary peers were entitled to sit in the House of Lords but the House of Lords Act 1999 reduced the number of hereditary peers serving in the House of Lords to 92.[9] Today, most Lords are appointed. Other than these groups, the Prime Minister

Table 5.2 Membership selection in second chambers

Elected*	Not Directly Elected
Argentina (Limited Vote)	Austria
Australia (Single Transferable Vote)	Belgium
Bolivia (List Proportional Representation)	Burundi
Brazil (Block Vote)	Canada
Chile (List Proportional Representation)	France
Colombia (List Proportional Representation)	Germany
Czech Republic (Two-Round System)	India
Dominican Republic (Single Member District Plurality)	Ireland
Italy (List Proportional Representation)	Netherlands
Japan (Mixed Independent)	Pakistan
Kenya (Single Member District Plurality)	South Africa
Liberia (Block Vote)	United Kingdom
Mexico (Mixed Independent)	
Nigeria (Single Member District Plurality)	
Paraguay (List Proportional Representation)	
Philippines (Block Vote)	
Poland (Single Member District Plurality)	
Romania (List Proportional Representation)	
Spain (Limited Vote) (NB: part appointed)	
Switzerland (Two-Round System)	
United States (Single Member District Plurality)**	

Notes: *With electoral system in parenthesis; **DM = 2, but typically 1 Senator per district (State) is elected at any one election.

[9] The reduction was designed as an interim measure pending further reforms to how members of the House of Lords are selected—reforms which have not progressed further at the time of writing.

has the power to appoint members (though formally appointments of members of the House of Lords are made by the King on the advice of the Prime Minister). In addition, the House of Lords Appointments Commission nominates a small number of non-political individuals for membership. Appointed members serve for life, or until they decide to retire. Most appointees are political supporters—having served the ruling party in some capacity. A Prime Minister may also reach out to other parties for nominations of potential members of the House of Lords.

The Irish senate (Seanad Éireann) has one of the most distinctive selection processes, involving a mix of indirect elections and appointment. 43 Irish Senators are elected by six vocational panels. Select panels are comprised of elected members of local government, members of the lower chamber, and members of the outgoing Seanad. Each panel in theory represents a particular vocational interest—Culture and Education, Agriculture, Labour, Industry and Commerce, and Public Administration. A further six Senators are elected in an election involving graduates of two universities. Finally, 11 senators are appointed by the prime minister (Taoiseach).

By their very nature, unelected assemblies present a fundamental problem for political systems that otherwise operate on a democratic principle: How can it be acceptable for a group not selected by the general electorate, and thus not responsible to the population at large, to have a central role in policy making? One rationale is that an unelected chamber frees members from the shackles of short-term responsiveness: Members of the Canadian Senate, for example, can serve continually until they reach the mandatory retirement age of 75. As such, once appointed, Canadian Senators face no career pressures from party leaders or voters. Thus they are free to act, in the words of the political philosopher Edmund Burke, as trustees rather than delegates. But few would contend that unelected second chambers, particularly appointed chambers, have democratic legitimacy. Lijphart (2012) suggests that a lack of legitimacy may undermine a second chamber's formal powers: "[s]econd chambers that are not directly elected lack the democratic legitimacy, and hence the real political influence, that popular election confers." Yet Russell suggests that popular support, which she refers to as "perceived legitimacy," may be more important in shaping the power of a second chamber: "legitimacy of a second chamber may depend on more than its composition alone; potentially being affected by how it acts, and by broader factors such as political culture." Thus, the evolution of the British House of Lords from a hereditary chamber to one where the vast majority of Lord's are appointed by the Prime Minister potentially shifts the chamber's perceived legitimacy. Although still unelected, the Lords may be perceived as more legitimate, having mostly shed its hereditary basis. This legitimacy may be helped by the Lord's reluctance, owing to its self-acknowledged lack of legitimacy, to use its delaying powers to disrupt the will of the House of Commons (see below and Box 5.1).

Box 5.1 The Salisbury Convention

The British Parliament consists of a directly elected House of Commons and a part-hereditary, part-appointed House of Lords. Over time, the formal legislative power of the House of Lords has been curtailed. Under the 1911 Parliament Act, the Lords lost the right to veto legislation, instead being able to delay for two years any non-financial bills passed by the House of Commons (the 1949 Parliament Act reduced the power to delay to one year). Historically, the center-right Conservative Party enjoyed a majority in the House of Lords. This created difficulty for Labour Governments that struggled to get their legislative program approved in a timely fashion. In the 1940s the Conservative and Labour leaderships in the House of Lords made an agreement to the effect that the Lords would not seek to block any policy proposals which formed part of a Government's manifesto commitments. Today, manifesto commitments can be considered anything written in a political party's electoral platform (manifesto). In a speech on the floor of the House of Lords, the Conservative Leader in the chamber, Viscount Cranborne (later Lord Salisbury), explained the basis of what would later become known as the Salisbury convention:

Whatever our personal views, we should frankly recognize that these proposals were put before the country at the recent General Election and that the people of this country, with full knowledge of these proposals, returned the Labour Party to power. The Government may, therefore, I think, fairly claim that they have a mandate to introduce these proposals. I believe that it would be constitutionally wrong, when the country has so recently expressed its view, for this House to oppose proposals which have been definitely put before the electorate (House of Lords, Hansard, August 16, 1945, vol. 137, col. 47).

As Russell (2010) summarizes: "the 'Salisbury convention' required [the House of Lords] not to reject completely any bill implementing a government manifesto commitment." In other words, the Salisbury convention can be seen as an attempt to deal with the lack of legitimacy of the House of Lords.

The convention is not just a piece of British political history. It continues to influence the behavior of the House of Lords. Following a Supreme Court decision, the British Government was in 2016 forced to get Parliament's approval before triggering the process to exit the European Union. The House of Commons voted to trigger Article 50, but the House of Lords wanted to see certain amendments, notably a protection for EU citizens currently living in the UK. The House of Lords passed the amendment which was then rejected by the House of Commons. The Lords could have delayed the process by one year, but members choose not further to confront the House of Commons and Government. As a Financial Times contributor noted "the 2015 Conservative

> manifesto also promised that there would be a referendum on the membership
> issue and the referendum result is without doubt a mandate for the UK to leave
> the EU. This means there is no scope under the Salisbury convention for the
> Lords to block it."*
>
> * http://blogs.ft.com/david-allen-green/2017/01/16/brexit-leaving-the-single-market-and-
> the-constitution/.

The appointment of members of the House of Lords presents a good example
of how an unelected form of bicameralism may suit the interests of lower-chamber
legislators but not those of ordinary citizens. As noted, members of the House of
Lords are appointed or elected by a small group of hereditary Lords. Former MPs
often end up in the House of Lords (though Lords may not stand for election to
the House of Commons). But to whom is a member of the UK House of Lords
accountable? The simple answer is to themselves, and themselves only (on this
earth at least!). They can't ordinarily be removed, voters never got to select them,
and the same voters have no opportunity to replace them.

Certainly, some see this "freedom" as a strength of the House of Lords exactly
because Lords need not be accountable to either party leaders or voters—as in
the Canadian case mentioned above. Philip Norton—a distinguished legislative
scholar and member of the House of Lords—suggest that an appointed House
of Lords is not undemocratic but rather perfectly consistent with representative democracy. As he (2004: 199) writes: "The present arrangements ensured
accountability. There is one body—the party-in-government—responsible for
public policy. It is elected on a particular platform and if it fails to meet its promises
then electors know who to hold to account. They can sweep it out at the next
election. The second chamber does not challenge this core accountability." Nevertheless, a second chamber is useful only if it has some legislative power and it
is willing to use such powers. As the French political theorist Abbé Sieyès's rather
dismissively wrote of bicameralism, "if a Second Chamber dissents from the First,
it is mischievous; if it agrees, it is superfluous" (quoted in Campion 1953: 17).

Still, the majority of second chambers in our study are directly elected. As we can
see from Table 5.2, the electoral systems used to elect senators vary from legislature
to legislature, just as in the case of lower chambers. A majority of second chambers use some form of proportional representation electoral system. The United
States Senate is a notable exception. Each of the 50 states selects two senators. However, generally only one Senator is elected by each state at each election, meaning
that the electoral system is effectively single member district plurality—as used in
elections to the House of Representatives.[10]

---

[10] The United States Senate has staggered elections. The various states choose their own electoral system, which in some cases is single-member district majority, or the alternative vote ("ranked-choice"),

Lijphart (2012: 194) defines incongruent bicameralism as a situation where the two chambers differ in their composition, typically caused by differences between their electoral systems. By cameral congruence, we thus mean the degree to which similar electoral systems are used in both chambers. Incongruence occurs if, for example, Proportional Representation is used in the lower chamber but not in the upper chamber, or if electoral districts are very differently drawn, or if voting rights are very differently designed. For Lijphart (2012) incongruence is one of two defining features of strong bicameralism (alongside symmetry of formal powers, as we will discuss below). Congruent chambers imply that the majority preferences are likely to be similar across both chambers, meaning that the second chamber is unlikely to want to contest or veto any proposals accepted by the first chamber. Crucially then, the election rules for each chamber shapes the level of cameral congruence. Incongruence may, however, result from factors other than divergences between their electoral formulas. For example, district size may be different. In the US, for example, each state is a district for the purpose of Senate elections; yet for most states districts for House of Representative elections are (geographically) much smaller, and the social heterogeneity of House districts is much greater than that of states. Only two countries in our study have the same district structure for lower and upper chamber elections: Switzerland and the Dominican Republic.

5.3 Cameral Powers

Thus far, the focus of this chapter has been on whether the legislature is bicameral or unicameral and how any second chamber is selected. Another question concerns how the chambers in a bicameral assembly relate to each other in roles, functions, and relative powers. The relationship between the chambers determines what political scientists call the strength of bicameralism. The strength of bicameralism is defined by the degree to which each chamber's formal powers are balanced. In a strong bicameral system, both chambers have equal or similar formal powers. Each chamber, for example, would be able to veto bills from becoming law (what is termed an absolute legislative veto). Law making is a central function of a legislative assembly, and in the presence of mutual veto powers one chamber cannot ignore the preferences of the other chamber in this legislative process. When a legislative chamber is unable to veto proposed legislation, this significantly reduces its influence over the lawmaking process and lowers the strength of bicameralism.

In some cases, the second chamber cannot absolutely veto proposed legislation but can instead delay a bill from becoming law for a certain period of time, what

rather than plurality. In most legislative assemblies, the entire chamber is elected at the same time. In chambers with staggered elections, not all members are elected at the same time. Willumsen and Goetz (2015) note that 20 democracies have a bicameral legislature in which the members of the upper house are elected based on a staggered schedule.

scholars call a suspensory veto. A suspensory veto keeps a bill from becoming law in the knowledge that it will become law after a fixed period of time. One of the earliest provisions for a suspensory veto was provided for in the 1911 Parliament Act in the United Kingdom. The 1911 Act replaced the veto power of the British House of Lords with the right to delay legislation for two years (the time frame was changed in 1949 to a one-year delay). In passing the 1911 Parliament Act the House of Lords voted to dramatically reduced its legislative powers.[11]

Other rules may reduce the ability of a second chamber to veto legislation. Its authority to legislate may be limited to certain policy areas and topics. In Belgium for example, both chambers have equal authority concerning bills concerning the constitution, laws governing the relationship between linguistic communities, and laws governing the organization of the judiciary and the political system. On other matters, the Senate merely has the right to delay. A more frequently observed limitation on the powers of second chambers relates to the right to amend money bills. A money bill is a bill which concerns a country's taxation, other sources of revenue (such as borrowing), or the spending of public money. In many parliamentary systems, the cabinet has sole authority to introduce money bills. The second chamber's role in the legislative process may also be different for money bills, compared to non-financial legislation. The 1911 Parliament Act mentioned above excluded the British House of Lords from vetoing money bills. Thus, in the United Kingdom a bill designated (by the Speaker of the House of Commons) as a money bill becomes law one month after it has been passed by the Commons, regardless of whether it is approved by the House of Lords.

Australia provides another example of how financial bills are treated differently from non-financial ones. Under the Commonwealth of Australia Constitution Act "the Senate shall have equal power with the House of Representatives in respect of all proposed laws" except that: "The Senate may not amend proposed laws imposing taxation, or proposed laws appropriating revenue or moneys for the ordinary annual services of the Government. The Senate may not amend any proposed law so as to increase any proposed charge or burden on the people." Instead, the Senate "may at any stage return to the House of Representatives any proposed law which the Senate may not amend, requesting, by message, the omission or amendment of any items or provisions therein. And the House of Representatives may, if it thinks fit, make any of such omissions or amendments, with or without modifications." In other words, while the Australian Senate is co-equal with the lower chamber on non-financial matters, it can only make recommendations to the lower chamber on financial legislation, which the lower chamber can accept or reject as it wishes.

The middle columns of Table 5.3 set out the powers of second chambers over financial and non-financial legislation. Notably, most second chambers in our study have the right to veto legislation that is not money bills. The Kenyan case

---

[11] The House of Lords voted to pass the Parliament Bill 1911 by a 131–114 vote.

appears an outlier, which we code as having no veto power with respect to legislation. This reflects, in part, the role of the Kenyan Senate that was re-established as part of the 2010 Constitution. Under that constitution, significant power was devolved to sub-national units (counties), and the Senate became the national-level focus of representation for the counties. The Kenyan Senate does play a role in any proposed legislation related to the counties but is otherwise relatively powerless in the legislative process.

Table 5.3 The formal powers of second chambers

Country	Power over Financial bills	Power over non-Financial Bills	Role in Government Formation
Argentina	Power to Veto	Power to Veto	No Role
Australia	No legislative powers	Power to Veto	No Role
Austria	No legislative powers	Power to Delay	No Role
Belgium	No legislative powers	Power to Delay	No Role
Bolivia	Power to Veto	Power to Veto	No Role
Brazil	Power to Veto	Power to Veto	No Role
Burundi	No legislative powers	Power to Veto	No Role
Canada	No legislative powers	Power to Veto	No Role
Chile	Power to Veto	Power to Veto	No Role
Colombia	Power to Veto	Power to Veto	No Role
Czech Republic	No legislative powers	Power to Veto	No Role
Dominican Republic	Power to Veto	Power to Veto	No Role
France	Power to Veto	Power to Veto	No Role
Germany	Power to Delay	Power to Veto	No Role
India	No legislative powers	Power to Veto	No Role
Ireland	No legislative powers	Power to Delay	No Role
Italy	Power to Veto	Power to Veto	Formal Role
Japan	Power to Delay	Power to Veto	No Role
Kenya	No legislative powers	No legislative power	No Role
Liberia	Power to Veto	Power to Veto	No Role
Mexico	No legislative powers	Power to Veto	No Role
Netherlands	Power to Veto	Power to Veto	No Role
Nigeria	Power to Veto	Power to Veto	No Role
Pakistan	No legislative powers	Power to Veto	No Role
Paraguay	Power to Veto	Power to Veto	No Role
Philippines	Power to Veto	Power to Veto	No Role
Poland	Power to Veto	Power to Veto	No Role
Romania	Power to Veto	Power to Veto	Formal Role
South Africa	Power to Delay	Power to Veto	No Role
Spain	Power to Veto	Power to Veto	No Role
Switzerland	Power to Veto	Power to Veto	Formal Role
United Kingdom	No legislative powers	Power to Delay	No Role
United States	Power to Veto	Power to Veto	No Role

Table 5.4 presents the results of a regression analysis which explores factors which correlate with a second chamber's budgetary powers. The dependent variable captures the financial legislative power of the second chamber, with the value zero indicating no financial legislative power, a score of one indicating the power to delay, and a value of two indicating the power to veto. The results in Table 5.2 show that presidential countries are more likely to have a second chamber with budget authority, whereas countries that gained sovereignty later and former British colonies are less likely to have a second chamber with strong fiscal powers.

In his influential work on different forms of democracy, Lijphart (2012: 193) combines measures of the relevant chambers' formal powers and democratic legitimacy to determine what he terms the level of bicameral symmetry. Symmetrical chambers are those with equal or only moderately unequal constitutional powers and democratic legitimacy. Asymmetrical chambers are highly unequal in these respects. Symmetrical and incongruent chambers, in Lijphart's view, make for strong bicameralism. In contrast, having one chamber dominate in term of formal power and democratic legitimacy makes for weak bicameralism.

5.4 The Future of Second Chambers

As noted at the beginning of this chapter, the status of second chambers is in many countries a salient political issue, with calls for second chambers to be reformed or even abolished. Having a second chamber can be considered a costly luxury, particularly in times of fiscal stress. Where second chambers are not elected, and however competent and well-intentioned the members, their democratic legitimacy may be questioned. Some second chambers lack the power to contribute very much to oversight or policy making. Where second chambers are powerful, they may make decision making too difficult, leading to bicameral gridlock—a situation in which one chamber is in conflict with the other, resulting in each chamber's policy proposals being vetoed by the other.

Indeed, several countries have simply abolished their second chamber. For example, Peru did away with its second chamber in 1994. As Llanos and Nolte (2003: 56) note, the decision of Peruvian political elites to move to unicameralism can be considered part of a strategy to concentrate power in the hands of the President: "a unicameral legislature would pave the way for an unconstrained executive because favorable political majorities are easier to build." While this may have been the true rationale for unicameralism in Peru, the authors note that in public the government emphasized other goals "such as the simplification of the lawmaking processes, the reduction of parliamentary costs, and the eradication of duplicated administrative and control organisms" (Llanos and Nolte 2003: 56).

Table 5.4 Second chamber budget authority

	Second Chamber Budget Authority					
	(1)	(2)	(3)	(4)	(5)	(6)
Presidential	0.64**				1.24**	0.64**
	(0.31)				(0.50)	(0.28)
Federal	−0.51				−0.51	
	(0.31)				(0.33)	
Sovereignty		−0.02**			−0.02***	−0.01**
		(0.01)			(0.01)	(0.01)
log(GDP per Capita)		−0.12				
		(0.14)				
GINI		0.02				
		(0.02)				
log(Population)		−0.02			0.19	
		(0.12)			(0.12)	
Ethnic Fractionalization		−0.22			0.49	
		(0.71)			(0.72)	
Africa and Middle East			−0.10		−0.63	
			(0.52)		(0.73)	
Asia and Oceania			−0.50		−0.64	
			(0.52)		(0.48)	
Americas			0.50		−0.82	
			(0.42)		(0.61)	
Eastern Europe			0.23		0.86	
			(0.62)		(0.58)	
British Colony				−0.84**		−0.51
				(0.41)		(0.34)
Other Colony				0.03		
				(0.37)		
Constant	1.11***	36.40**	1.10***	1.40***	41.78***	26.70**
	(0.24)	(15.91)	(0.30)	(0.28)	(13.54)	(11.49)
N	33	33	33	33	33	33
R^2	0.20	0.27	0.13	0.17	0.54	0.37
Adjusted R^2	0.15	0.14	0.01	0.11	0.37	0.31

*$p < 0.1$; **$p < 0.05$; ***$p < 0.01$.
Notes: DV: Captures the financial legislative power of the second chamber; 0 = No financial legislative power; 1 = Power to delay; 2 = Power to veto.

Less radical are attempts to reform rather than abolish second chambers. In December 2016, Italian voters went to the polls to consider a number of political reforms. The bulk of the measures sought to reform the composition and powers of the Italian Senato della Repubblica. Under the reform proposals, the number of senators was to be dramatically reduced and their mechanism of selection differentiated. Under the existing rules, 315 Senators were directly elected via a form of list PR, the President appointed up to five Senators for life, and former Presidents of the Republic were also life members. Under the reform proposal, 95 Senators would be elected by the regional governments. The President would appoint five senators for seven-year terms and past presidents of Italy would continue to be members for life. The proposals would substantially differentiate the methods by which the first and second chamber are selected.

In addition to its membership and form of selection, the powers of the second chamber were to be dramatically cut. As things stood, both chambers had full legislative authority; a bill only became law if both chambers passed it in identical form. As Tsebelis (2017: np) describes it, Italy was a case of "full and symmetric bicameralism, with the effect that the "legislature tends to be unsuccessful in passing consequential legislation." Indeed this legislative gridlock was a significant argument for reform of the second chamber. The proposed reforms would have stripped the second chamber of veto power over proposed legislation in areas other than matters of constitutional law. In addition, the Italian cabinet would no longer need to have the confidence of the upper chamber (whereas under existing rules government formation and termination in Italy were matters for both the first and the second chamber). Ultimately, in the referendum 59.1 percent of the voters rejected the government's package of proposed reforms, with a turnout just below 66 percent. Having seen his core political reform proposal fail, Matteo Renzi soon after resigned the prime ministership. Because Senate reform was not the only aspect of the reform proposal, however, we cannot attribute the vote outcome to Italian citizens' preferences concerning their Senate.

5.5 Conclusion

Cameral structures represent one of the most commonly studied aspects of legislative organization. We have noted the often-heated debate on the role of, and need for, second chambers. We have also discussed the rationale for bicameralism over unicameralism and observed the great variation in the selection provisions and powers of upper chambers where they exist.

Our data show that a significant number of second chambers lack powers and in many cases the popular accountability that tends to sustain legitimacy. Are such weak forms of bicameralism redundant and an unnecessary waste of political resources? Not necessarily. In their seminal comparative study of bicameralism, Tsebelis and Money (1997: 211) observe that "all second chambers exercise influence even if they are considered weak or insignificant" noting that "second chambers may be bad (depending on one's point of view), but they are certainly not useless." The reason for their importance, is that "[b]icameralism increases stability through promotion of the status quo; in other words, it makes the status quo more difficult to defeat" (Tsebelis and Money 1997: 216). The authors point to France, the United Kingdom, and Italy as cases where the second chamber has shaped legislation.

From our perspective, different forms of bicameralism may suit the interests of voters, members, or leaders. Voters may value having a second avenue of policy input and an additional source of institutional capacity, a chamber which they select and whose membership they can hold accountable. Members of the lower chamber may for reasons of progressive ambition or employment security value an unelected or partially appointed second chamber, particularly one which does not distract from their power in the lower chamber. Leaders in the lower chamber may prefer not having to engage in inter-cameral bargaining with a second chamber, but may on the other hand relish the prospects of having a second chamber for which they could exercise cartel-like appointment powers.

References

Campion, Lord. 1953. "Second Chambers in Theory and Practice." *Parliamentary Affairs* 7(1): 17–32.

Cox, Gary W. 2006. "The Organization of Democratic Legislatures." In Barry R. Weingast and Donald Wittman, (eds.), *The Oxford Handbook of Political Economy*. Oxford: Oxford University Press, 141–161.

Diermeier, Daniel, and Roger B. Myerson. 1999. "Bicameralism and Its Consequences for the Internal Organization of Legislatures." *American Economic Review* 89(5): 1182–1196.

Filippov, Mikhail, Peter C. Ordeshook, and Olga Shvetsova. 2004. *Designing Federalism: A Theory of Self-sustainable Federal Institutions*. New York: Cambridge University Press.

Heller, William B., and Diana M. Branduse. 2014. "The Politics of Bicameralism." In Shane Martin, Thomas Saalfeld, and Kaare W. Strøm (eds.), *The Oxford Handbook of Legislative Studies*. Oxford: Oxford University Press, 332–351.

Holmøyvik, Eirik. 2012. *Maktfordeling og 1814*. Oslo: Fagbokforlaget.

Lijphart, Arend. 2012. *Patterns of Democracy: Government Forms and Performance in Thirty-six Countries*. New Haven: Yale University Press.

Llanos, Mariana, and Detlef Nolte. 2003. "Bicameralism in the Americas: Around the Extremes of Symmetry and Incongruence." *The Journal of Legislative Studies* 9(3): 54–86.

MacCarthaigh, Muiris, and Shane Martin 2015. "Bicameralism in the Republic of Ireland: The Seanad Abolition Referendum." *Irish Political Studies* 30(1): 121–131.

Madison, James. 1961. "No 62: The Senate." In *The Federalist Papers*, edited by Clinton Rossiter. New York: Signet Classic, 374–380.

Norton, Philip. 2004. "How Many Bicameral Legislatures Are There?" *The Journal of Legislative Studies* 10(4): 1–9.

Norton, Philip. 2004. "Reforming the House of Lords: a View from the Parapets." *Representation* 40(3): 185–199.

Russell, Meg. 2001. "What Are Second Chambers For?" *Parliamentary Affairs* 54(3): 442–458.

Russell, Meg. 2013. *The Contemporary House of Lords: Westminster Bicameralism Revived.* Oxford: Oxford University Press.

Schlesinger, Joseph A. 1966. *Ambition and Politics: Political Careers in the United States.* Chicago: Rand McNally.

Sieberer, Ulrich, and Wolfgang C. Müller. 2017. "Aiming Higher: The Consequences of Progressive Ambition among MPs in European Parliaments." *European Political Science Review* 9(1): 27–50.

Taagepera, Rein. 1973. "Seats and Votes: A Generalization of the Cube Law of Elections." *Social Science Research* 2(3): 257–275.

Tsebelis, George. 2017. "Compromesso Astorico: The Role of the Senate after the Italian Constitutional Reform." *Italian Political Science Review* 47(1): 87–104.

Tsebelis, George, and Jeannette Money. 1997. *Bicameralism.* Cambridge: Cambridge University Press.

Willumsen, David M., and Klaus H. Goetz. 2015. "Staggered Political Institutions: Design and Effects." *Journal of European Public Policy* 22(7): 1040–1051.

6

Organization and Leadership

This chapter begins our look at how chambers within a legislative assembly are organized, what scholars tend to refer to as legislative organization (or sometimes internal legislative organization). Alemán (2015: 145) defines legislative organization as "the set of procedures that regulate the legislative process and the related set of offices with internal authority." Legislative organization may depart significantly from what Cox (2006: 141) calls the legislative state of nature—"an assembly in which members wield equal parliamentary rights and in which access to plenary time is unregulated." In Cox's legislative state of nature, all legislators are equal in formal authority and capacity. While some legislative assemblies may at one time have existed in this primeval state of nature, today all legislative assemblies that we know of are governed by rules, leadership structures, and resource allocations that often set them apart considerably from such equalities.

Contemporary legislatures vary significantly in how they are organized, including how big they are, and how authority and resources are allocated internally. Chamber size and legislative rules, procedures, and resource allocations among members help determine legislative accountability and capacity. A members' assembly associates with authority and resources decentralized to individual members, with any chamber leadership functions focused on protecting the rights of members. These features affect legislative capacity as well as accountability. Members' assemblies may be designed so as to contain collective action problems by ensuring that all members have substantial powers and interact with some level of collegiality. Decentralized authority and member specialization may also help the assembly deal effectively with matters of strong localized impact or with highly specialized issues. On the other hand, such a decentralized legislature, with power and resources in the hands of individual members, may create capacity problems, resulting in socially inefficient policy making. For example, powerful members may use their legislative resources to help win re-election by passing collectively inefficient policies designed to make them popular in their respective districts. In contrast, a more centralized organizational legislative structure may associate with our concept of a leaders' assembly—with party leaders holding significant formal authority over procedural rights and resources. While such centralization may help avoid wasteful effects of decentralized authority, it may also allow assembly leaders to reap large rents and to impose large costs on assembly minorities and their constituents.

Legislative Assemblies. Shane Martin and Kaare W. Strøm, Oxford University Press.
© Shane Martin and Kaare W. Strøm (2023). DOI: 10.1093/oso/9780198890829.003.0006

In this chapter we explore variation in organizational and leadership structures across legislative assemblies. In particular, we focus on four questions. First, we explore assembly size as reflected in the number of members. Legislatures have evolved from the legislative state of nature often because too many members were chasing too little plenary time, which raises the question of whether chambers have an optimal size. Second, we explore the sources of rules and organizational structures. Who decides what the rules are? Third, we look in closer detail at authoritative legislative offices and in particular the office of presiding officer. Whose interests do such leaders represent? At one end of the spectrum, the office of presiding officer can be a tool for party leaders—at the other end of the spectrum it can be designed to serve the interest of ordinary members. Finally, we look at the resources available to members (both collectively and individually) to perform their duties and ensure legislative capacity. We dedicate the subsequent two chapters to two specific organizational features of particular importance: how political parties structure the ways in which legislative assemblies work and what role, if any, legislative committees play in the organization of the legislative assembly. We begin, however, by exploring an issue which shapes the core nature of any chamber: the number of its members.

6.1 The Size of the Chamber

Alongside cameral structure (see the previous chapter), one of the first questions any constitution-framer must consider is the size of the legislature. By size of legislature we mean the number of ordinary members it contains. There is significant variation in the size of the national legislature among the countries in our study. The smallest national legislature is Costa Rica's *Asamblea Legislativa* with 57 members.[1] The largest (lower) chamber in our study is the British House of Commons with 650 members. The average (mean) chamber size is 266.

Assembly size is important for a number of reasons. First, in a voters' assembly, legislators serve as an important link between citizens and government. If legislators are to interact with citizens, the ratio of voters to legislators needs to be sufficient low to make interaction possible and meaningful. To this end, many national constitutions specify a minimum and maximum number of voters per representative. Changes in a country's total population may require the legislature to be resized. For example, in 2015 the Canadian House of Commons increased in size from 308 to 338.

What determines the size of a legislative chamber? Some of the factors that affect assembly size are intrinsic to the assembly itself. Members need a sufficient

---

[1] In the case of bicameral legislatures (a legislature with two chambers), our numbers pertain to the lower chamber, unless otherwise noted.

number of colleagues to ensure legislative capacity and allow legislative work to be conducted responsibly without over-working the members. It is rare to meet a legislator who complains of having too little work to do! Combining work within the legislature with any outside demand (such as attending district meetings or meeting constituents, for example) makes the workload of most assemblies even more challenging. In some parliaments, senior members of the executive must simultaneously serve in the assembly, reducing the number of "backbenchers" available to conduct ordinary legislative business. A report on the New Zealand Parliament thus concluded that "an increase in the number of MPs is necessary for parliamentary committees to function effectively" (Royal Commission on the Electoral System 1986: 125).[2] Observers of the Israeli Knesset sometimes worry that the small number of Knesset Members (MKs) constrains the influence of its committees. This is because the governing coalition needs to maintain a majority in each committee, despite having its ministers and deputy ministers withdrawn from its ranks of eligible representatives. Consequently, available government MKs are spread out over multiple committees and have little time to acquaint themselves with their work (see, for example, Hazan 2001: 61).

Having too many members may make it equally difficult for the assembly to work effectively, since it may generate a plenary bottleneck—which means that there is too little time to deal with the legislative demands of all the members (Cox 2006). Having a larger legislature may also affect members' access to promotion—which party leaders often use to incentivize loyalty among backbenchers (Kam 2009). And, of course, legislators cost money, in terms of direct salary costs and indirect support costs. Under Prime Minister David Cameron (2010–16) the British House of Commons was due to decrease in size from 650 to 600 members. One of that government's stated rationales for this reduction the number of MPs was to save money. Looking at comparative evidence, Jacobs and Otjes (2015: 287) note that "economic recessions sometimes lead to a reduction in the size of legislative chambers." In Ireland, for example, political reform following an economic crisis resulted in a reduction of seats from 166 to 158. Thus, in the most practical of ways, the size of the legislature impacts the degree to which the interests of citizens and members are safeguarded.

Other factors that may affect assembly size are extrinsic, having to do with the political system and national community in which the assembly operates. In a 1972 article aptly titled "The size of national assemblies" Rein Taagepera suggests a relationship between the number of legislators and a country's population: the larger the population, the larger the legislature. Such a relationship is intuitively appealing: for representative, communications, and governance purposes, countries with

---

[2] http://www.elections.org.nz/voting-system/mmp-voting-system/report-royal-commission-electoral-system-1986.

larger populations require more legislators. Specifically, Taagepera suggests that the size of a legislature correlates with the cube root of the country's population.[3]

We use our data on legislative size and national population to examine Taagepera's Cubed Root theory in Figure 6.1. Population size appears to be a good if imperfect predictor of chamber size. To explore the issue further, Table 6.1 reports the results of a regression analysis in which chamber size is the dependent variable and various societal features are predictors. The results in Table 6.1 suggest that population size is an important correlate of the size of national legislatures. Unsurprisingly, countries with bicameral legislatures, which are often federal and diverse, also tend to have larger assemblies. On the other hand, countries in the African/Middle East, Asian/Oceanic, and Americas regions, as well as former non-British colonies, have smaller legislatures. Countries with greater income inequality (higher GINI coefficients) also tend to have smaller legislatures.

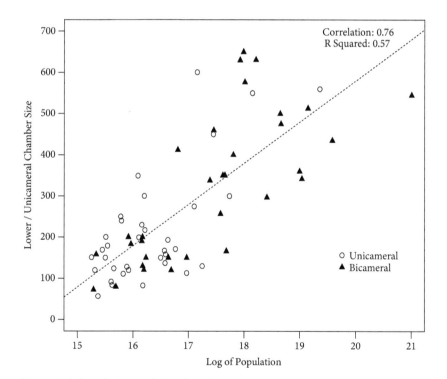

Figure 6.1 Population and chamber size

[3] According to https://www.mathsisfun.com/definitions/ "The cube root of a number is a special value that, when used in a multiplication three times, gives that number. Example: 3 × 3×3 = 27, so the cube root of 27 is 3."

Table 6.1 Size of assembly (number of members)

	Number of Members					
	(1)	(2)	(3)	(4)	(5)	(6)
Bicameral	218.16***				56.47	47.20
	(62.11)				(44.72)	(42.95)
Federal	44.09				−81.60	
	(76.77)				(55.28)	
Sovereignty		−1.01			−1.15	
		(0.79)			(0.81)	
log(GDP per Capita)		9.11				
		(19.78)				
GINI		−6.57**				1.62
		(3.20)				(3.60)
log(Population)		151.99***			166.80***	153.09***
		(16.91)			(18.65)	(18.42)
Ethnic Fractionalization		−93.43			−39.09	
		(106.65)			(93.02)	
Africa and Middle East			−204.55**		−169.67**	−216.67***
			(88.81)		(75.31)	(64.08)
Asia and Oceania			−58.99		−221.78***	−239.42***
			(96.78)		(66.67)	(61.76)
Americas			−201.87**		−249.99***	−224.84***
			(86.07)		(56.85)	(72.80)
Eastern Europe			−132.03		−21.06	
			(102.96)		(75.04)	
British Colony				−128.20		
				(83.51)		
Other Colony				−210.50***		−60.02
				(69.25)		(41.72)
Constant	213.25***	−94.48	450.81***	461.74***	−138.31	−2,165.43***
	(38.67)	(1,682.75)	(61.78)	(55.47)	(1,566.72)	(300.81)
N	68	68	68	68	68	68
R^2	0.22	0.60	0.11	0.12	0.71	0.69
Adjusted R^2	0.19	0.56	0.06	0.10	0.67	0.66

Notes: DV is the size of the national-level assembly (all chambers).
*$p < 0.1$; **$p < 0.05$; ***$p < 0.01$.

6.2 Rules and Standing Orders

Political scientists have a long-standing fascination with rules and institutional structures, not least as they set out the parameters within which politics and politicians must operate. Much of this book is concerned with formal rules: how members are selected, the formal roles of assemblies, and the procedures they employ in undertaking these roles. Formal or less formal rules govern almost every facet of the legislative assembly. As in any aspect of life, some rules are more important than others. Rules can vary from the apparently superficial (for example, a dress code for members) through to the more consequential (for example, seating arrangements for members in the plenary assembly) all the way to the critically important (for example, procedures for final passage of legislation).

Rules can be more or less formal. The latter include norms of behavior that guide practice which may be based on precedent. Thus, the rules that shaping the operation of the legislative assembly may have multiple sources. Formal rules are written. Existing written sources of rules, and thus legislative organization, include:

1. **The National Constitution**. A country's constitution will typically specify many rules relevant to the assembly, including how it is elected, for how long (the maximum inter-electoral period), and the assembly's formal role in governance. But constitutions can be more or less silent on how the legislature is to be organized. Some constitutions define the broad outlies of the legislative process. Other constitutions may delegate the task of making rules to the legislative assembly itself. For example, Article 57 of the South African Constitution (*Internal arrangements, proceedings and procedures of National Assembly*)—provides that:

(1) *The National Assembly may—*
   (a) *determine and control its internal arrangements, proceedings and procedures; and*
   (b) *make rules and orders concerning its business, with due regard to representative* and participatory democracy, accountability, transparency and public involvement.
(2) *The rules and orders of the National Assembly must provide for—*
   (a) *the establishment, composition, powers, functions, procedures and duration of its committees;*
   (b) *the participation in the proceedings of the Assembly and its committees of minority parties represented in the Assembly, in a manner consistent with democracy;*
   (c) *financial and administrative assistance to each party represented in the Assembly in proportion to its representation, to enable the party and its leader to perform their functions in the Assembly effectively; and*
   (d) *the recognition of the leader of the largest opposition party in the Assembly as the Leader of the Opposition.*

It is often assumed that rules governing how a legislative assembly operates are determined by the assembly itself. In other words, in the parlance of social science, legislative organization is endogenous to the assembly itself. The implication is that legislators design how the assembly operates and can change (redesign) the organization of the legislature. But all legislative assemblies must organize and operate within the boundaries imposed by the constitution. These boundaries can be broader (as in the South African case) or narrower. Thus, the Constitution of France's Fifth Republic goes so far as to specify the maximum number of legislative committees which each chamber is permitted to have.

While the South African Constitution states that the South African Parliament may "determine and control its internal arrangements, proceedings and procedures" and "make rules and orders concerning its business," these must be constructed "with due regard to representative and participatory democracy, accountability, transparency and public involvement." Moreover, other constitutional provisions—such as free speech and the right to natural justice, must be protected by the rules of the assembly.

On occasions, the judiciary may be called upon to adjudicate when members believe their constitutional rights are being impinged by legislative rules, or by the actions of the legislative leadership based on legislative rules. For example, in the case of *De Lille and Another v. Speaker of the National Assembly* [1998 (3) SA 430], the South African Supreme Court was asked to quash the suspension of a member. The National Assembly voted to suspend Patricia De Lille from the Assembly for 15 days in response to her making serious accusations against named members during a debate in the National Assembly.[4] While the court acknowledged that the South African Constitution permitted the National Assembly to make and enforce its own internal arrangements, proceedings and procedures, including dealing with behavior which is obstructing or disruptive or unreasonably impeding orderly business in the Assembly, it ruled that the suspended member had a right to free speech and that the suspension was not lawful. In short, all legislative organization exists in the shadow of the country's constitution. Members nor leaders never have a completely free hand to determine their chamber's rules and procedures. Of course, as we will see, in some democracies there are no other hurdles for (some) constitutional changes than a vote or votes in the legislative assembly.

2. **The Assembly's Standing Orders.** Every legislative assembly that we are aware of has a set of written rules. These rule-books may be referred to by different titles in different assemblies, including Rules of Procedure or Standing Orders (hereafter we will refer to all such compilations of rules as standing orders). Regardless of name, these sets of written rules are designed to regulate the proceedings and working operations of the legislative assembly. Standing orders can and do change, as Sieberer et al. (2016) have noted, with potentially important implications for how the legislature works and where power resides—especially the balance of power between members and party leaders. And assembly rules can interact with a nation's constitution to shape the relationship between the

---

[4] http://www.casac.org.za/wp-content/uploads/2015/02/The-South-African-Parliament-in-2015. pdf.

executive and legislature and, under bicameralism, the relationship between each chamber of the legislative assembly (Sin 2015).

3. **Assembly Manuals and Guide Books.** In addition to constitutional provisions and standing orders, operating manuals and legislative guides may provide legislative assemblies with supplementary details on assembly rules and procedures. After all, not all details governing how an assembly works are likely to be incorporated into the country's constitution or the assembly's standing orders. Perhaps the most famous guide to parliamentary practice is *Erskine May*. Originally drafted in 1844 by Thomas Erskine May (a senior parliamentary official), and formally titled *A Treatise on the Law, Privileges, Proceedings and Usage of Parliament*, this volume is considered "the most authoritative reference book on parliamentary procedure" in the UK Parliament.[5] Such guides can include important precedents and rulings which never found their way into formal standing orders. In other cases, these guides live alongside the rule book. For example, the Rules of the US House of Representatives include relevant constitutional provisions, rules, and Jefferson's Manual on Parliamentary Procedures, originally written by Thomas Jefferson in 1801.[6]

To explore the sources of legislative rules, we have collected data on how rules governing the final passage of a bill can be changed. Virtually all legislative assemblies have one thing in common: they have an authoritative role in making laws. Exploring the source of the rule governing the final passage of a bill helps us understand which sources of rules most critically impact legislative organization. The data are reported in Table 6.2.

In 60 of our 68 cases, changes to the rules governing final passage of a bill may require a change to the country's constitution. Thus, in the vast majority of cases, we must look to the national constitution for rules governing final bill passage. Enshrining some rules on bill passage in a constitution means that a change to some aspects of legislative organization require a constitutional amendment. Amending a constitution may be more or less challenging, depending on whether such rules changes require a favorable referendum, the involvement of multiple veto players, or the sequential involvement of the assembly in making and later confirming and enacting the change to the constitution. Thus, all else equal, constitutionalizing legislative organization is a way to prevent the legislature itself from changing important aspects of how it does business. Such constraints may serve to protect members and citizens over party leaders.

In a minority of eight of our democracies, rules concerning final passage can be changed without a constitutional amendment. In one case (Austria), statutory law governs bill passage, and the regulation of bill passage can thus be changed by amending the law. In other cases, the legislature itself can amend rules governing

---

[5] https://www.parliament.uk/site-information/glossary/erskine-may/.
[6] https://rules.house.gov/HouseRulesManual115/front.xml.

Table 6.2 Final passage change and rules governing selection of presiding officer

Country	Source of regulation for final bill passage	Decision rule for selection of presiding officer	Vote to select of presiding officer
Argentina	Constitutional	Plenary majority	Open
Australia	Constitutional	Plenary majority	Secret
Austria	Statutory	Plenary supermajority	Secret
Belgium	Constitutional	Plenary majority	Secret
Benin	Constitutional	Plenary majority	Secret
Bolivia	Constitutional	Plenary supermajority	Secret
Brazil	Constitutional	Plenary majority	Secret
Bulgaria	Constitutional	Plenary majority	Secret
Burundi	Constitutional	Plenary majority	Open
Canada	Constitutional	Plenary majority	Secret
Chile	Constitutional	Plenary majority	Secret
Colombia	Constitutional	Plenary majority	Open
Costa Rica	Constitutional	Plenary majority	Secret
Croatia	Constitutional	Plenary majority	Open
Czech Republic	Constitutional	Plenary majority	Secret
Denmark	Constitutional	Plenary majority	Open
Dominican Republic	Constitutional	Plenary majority	Secret
Ecuador	Constitutional	Plenary majority	Open
El Salvador	Constitutional	Plenary majority	Open
Finland	Constitutional	Plenary majority	Secret
France	Constitutional	Plenary majority	Secret
Germany	Constitutional	Plenary majority	Secret
Ghana	Constitutional	Plenary majority	Secret
Greece	Constitutional	Plenary majority	Secret
Guatemala	Constitutional	Plenary majority	Open
Honduras	Constitutional	Plenary majority	Open
Hungary	Constitutional	Plenary majority	Secret
India	Constitutional	Plenary majority	Open
Indonesia	Constitutional	Plenary majority	Open
Ireland	Constitutional	Plenary majority	Open
Israel	Constitutional	Plenary majority	Open
Italy	Plenary (Absolute majority)	Plenary supermajority	Secret
Japan	Constitutional	Plenary majority	Secret
Kenya	Constitutional	Plenary supermajority	Secret
Liberia	Constitutional	Plenary majority	Open
Malawi	Constitutional	Plenary majority	Open
Mexico	Constitutional	Plenary majority	Secret
Nepal	Constitutional	Plenary majority	Open
Netherlands	Constitutional	Plenary majority	Secret
New Zealand	Plenary (majority)	Plenary majority	Open
Nicaragua	Constitutional	Plenary majority	Open

Country	Source of regulation for final bill passage	Decision rule for selection of presiding officer	Vote to select of presiding officer
Niger	Constitutional	Plenary majority	Secret
Nigeria	Constitutional	Plenary majority	Secret
Norway	Plenary (plurality)	Plenary majority	Secret
Pakistan	Constitutional	Plenary majority	Secret
Papua New Guinea	Constitutional	Plenary majority	Secret
Paraguay	Constitutional	Plenary majority	Open
Peru	Plenary (Absolute majority)	Plenary majority	Secret
Philippines	Plenary (supermajority)	Plenary majority	Open
Poland	Constitutional	Plenary majority	Open
Portugal	Constitutional	Plenary majority	Secret
Romania	Constitutional	Plenary majority	Secret
Senegal	Constitutional	Plenary majority	Secret
Serbia	Constitutional	Plenary majority	Secret
Sierra Leone	Constitutional	Plenary supermajority	Secret
Slovak Republic	Constitutional	Plenary majority	Secret
South Africa	Constitutional	Plenary majority	Secret
Spain	Constitutional	Plenary majority	Secret
South Korea	Constitutional	Plenary majority	Secret
Sweden	Constitutional	Plenary majority	Secret
Switzerland	Constitutional	Plenary majority	Secret
Taiwan	Constitutional	Plenary majority	Secret
Tunisia	Constitutional	Plenary majority	Secret
Turkey	Constitutional	Plenary supermajority	Secret
Ukraine	Constitutional	Plenary supermajority	Secret
United Kingdom	Plenary (plurality)	Plenary majority	Open
United States	Plenary (majority)	Plenary majority	Open
Zambia	Constitutional	Plenary majority	Open

final passage. In the case of the House of Representatives of the Philippines, the Italian House of Representatives and the Peruvian Congress, a two-thirds majority is required to amend the final passage rule. In two other cases (the New Zealand Parliament and the US House of Representatives) the final passage rule can be changed by a simple majority. Finally, in Norway and the United Kingdom the decision rule for a change to procedural rules governing final passage is plurality.

In summary, legislative rules may be exogenous or endogenous and, within each of these two categories, more or less difficult to change. Many political scientists consider legislative organization to be relatively "sticky"—meaning that rules and procedures are hard to change, although Sieberer et al. (2016) have challenged this wisdom.

6.3 The Presiding Officer

Virtually all legislative assemblies endow certain members with pre-eminent authority and responsibilities. As noted above, the nation's Constitution or other documents may provide for leadership positions within the legislature. Carroll, Cox, and Pachón (2006) refer to such positions as "mega-seats." Candidates compete in legislative elections to become legislators. Legislators may be formally equal at the point of election. However, legislative elections are typically followed by a second selection process within the assembly itself—the selection of mega-seat holders. Examples of mega-seats include committee positions, executive posts such as cabinet portfolios (in parliamentary systems) and positions overseeing the operation of the legislative assembly. The selection of mega-seat holders represents a second chapter of electoral democracy, with legislators delegating power and authority among themselves, just as voters delegated power and authority to legislators in the previous chapter (the election). How these mega-seats are allocated, and the power their office-holders acquire, shape the extent to which voters, members or leaders are privileged in legislative organization.

From the perspective of internal legislative organization, one of the most significant mega-seats is the office of presiding officer. Presiding officers are known by different titles in different legislatures, including the Speaker, Chairman or President (of the assembly). Each lower chamber in our study has a clearly identifiable presiding officer. Indeed, we know of no legislative chamber that lacks a presiding officer.[7] Perhaps the most obvious and certainly most visible function of the presiding officer is to chair and preside over debates when the chamber is in plenary session. This is understandable given the need for some form of chairship for bodies that in some cases are vast and whose members are often keen to be heard. The primary role of the Speaker in the Chair is to call members to speak. In this regard both precedent and the rules of the chamber determine the actual powers of the chair. In some cases, the Speaker is free to call whoever he or she wishes and to set time limits. In other cases, representatives of the political parties decide in advance who shall speak and for how long. Speaking time during plenary meetings—what political scientists call "access to the plenary" is in many legislatures highly coveted (Proksch and Slapin 2015; Bäck, Debus, and Fernandes 2021).

The power of the presiding office to end a debate is one of the more controversial functions of this office. Closure, defined as the ability of the presiding officer to cut short debate and call for a vote or move onto other business, originated in the British House of Commons in the 1880s. It came about following attempts by Irish separatist members to obstruct the business of the parliament by protracting

---

[7] Prior to reforms that came into effect in 2006, the UK House of Lords lacked a full-time presiding officer. Instead, the Lord Chancellor presided over meetings of the House of Lords. The reforms of 2005 saw the creation of a presiding officer with the title The Lord Speaker. The US Vice President serves as President of the US Senate.

debate. The Standing Orders were revised to allow the Speaker to conclude debate after a reasonable time. The motivation behind closure is that it prevents what we might now consider to be a filibuster, the talking out of a bill or amendment by protracting debate until time runs out. The ability of an individual legislator, or a small group of members, to filibuster is a powerful tool and the ability to filibuster is today heavily constrained in most legislative assemblies around the world.

In some legislatures, the presiding officer may have other very specific roles. For example, the Speaker of the Swedish *Riksdag* plays an important role in government formation (see Chapter 11). Following a general election, the Speaker consults with party leaders to identify a possible government. The Speaker then presents a candidate prime minister to parliament which votes to accept or reject the Speaker's choice.[8]

The presiding officer may have responsibility for the overall management of the legislative assembly. This includes such functions as the allocation of offices and the running of ancillary services such as research services for members and committees or the production of transcripts of parliamentary debates. Of course, the presiding officer is assisted in this task by a bureaucracy, as we will see below. Writing on the allocative powers of Speakers in general and on the US Speaker in particular, Bach (1999: 211) explores the potential benefits which this power can bring:

> The Speaker can exercise significant influence over the assembly's facilities—buildings, staff, information resources and so on. In part as a consequence, the Speaker may be intimately involved in setting and allocating the assembly's budget. These powers enable the Speaker to affect the wellbeing of the assembly and its individual members who, in anticipation or as a result, can become beholden to him. In ways sometimes obvious and sometimes subtle, a clever Speaker who is so inclined can translate administrative responsibility into political influence.

The British model of a neutral presiding officer (see Box 6.1) contrasts sharply with the situation in many other legislative assemblies, including the United States House of Representatives. The Speaker of the US House of Representatives is not, and is not perceived as being, neutral. In the US House of Representatives, the Speaker's job, in addition to being the presiding officer, is to be leader of the majority party. The US Speaker is not just an active member of her political party but a leader of the party in Congress. No other member of Congress arguably possesses the visibility and authority of the Speaker of the House. Although, and unlike Euro-

---

[8] As Wockelberg (2015: 235) notes, "[i]f the Speaker fails all four attempts to suggest a candidate that is tolerated by the *Riksdag*, a new general election is called."

pean political parties, it is notoriously difficult to attach the label "leader" to US political parties, it is generally recognized that the Speaker serves as a leader of the Congressional majority party.

Box 6.1 Speakers and Neutrality

The original function of the Speaker of the English House of Commons was to represent the Commons before the King. In 1376 it was recorded that one of the Commoners, Sir Peter de la Mere, was given a presiding role over the debates and a role in communicating with outside bodies: "Because the said Sir Peter de la Mere had spoken so well and had so wisely repeated the arguments and opinions of his colleagues, and because he had told them much that they did not know, they begged him to take responsibility for expressing their wishes." Over time, the role of the Speaker was institutionalized. On January 4, 1642, King Charles I entered the House of Commons to arrest five Members of Parliament for high treason. Addressing the Speaker, Charles shouted: "By your leave, Mr. Speaker, I must borrow your chair a little." The King then turned to the Speaker, whom he regarded as his servant, and asked: "Is Mr Pym here?" The apparently brave Speaker replied:

> May it please your Majesty, I have neither eyes to see, nor tongue to speak in this place, but as the House is pleased to direct me, whose servant I am here, and I humbly beg your Majesty's pardon that I cannot give any other answer than this to what your majesty is pleased to demand of me.

These words are often quoted to this day as signaling the emergence of a Speaker dedicated to the whole chamber rather than to political interests—and the newly elected Speaker in the British House of Commons is still "dragged" to the chair to reflect the (historical) dangers of the role. Today, the principle of neutrality continues to define the Speakership of the British House of Commons. Neutrality implies impartiality between members and between parties. Non-partisanship requires that once elected as Speaker, a politician breaks his or her ties with the party, or at the very least refrains from active participation. As Laundy (1964: 125) writes:

> Once in the chair the Speaker becomes in the true sense a House of Commons man. He sheds all his party affiliations and dedicates himself exclusively to the impartial discharge of his functions. It is inconceivable today that any Speaker would be consciously partisan.

We are left with a picture of a presiding officer devoted not to a political party, ideology, or administration but solely to the wellbeing of the House which he or she now serves. This perspective fits well with our conception of a members' assembly—the presiding officer serves the interests of members. The presiding officer in the British tradition is thus not a servant of one faction or party but an agent of the chamber as a whole. This model places members, rather than parties and their leaders, at the center of legislative leadership.

The historical events which shaped the nature of the presiding officers in US state legislative assemblies include the War of Independence fought between the North American colonies and the United Kingdom. Faced with the need for strong political opposition to the British government, the colonies' assemblies became the focus of such leadership and within each the Speaker was the leader of the opposition to British rule—a very political role—"the history of the American colonial period, in which the colonial assemblies often acted in direct opposition to the mandates of the royal governors, produced the unique concept of a Speaker as not only the arbiter of debate but as a leader of the opposition against the crown" (National Democratic Institute 1996: 7).

By the time the US Constitution was drafted there was no tradition of a neutral Speaker (Peters 1997). The Speakership—as one of only four offices mentioned in the Constitution—quickly became the subject of political bargaining. Having failed to get either the Presidency, Vice-Presidency or Supreme Court Chief Justiceship, the state of Pennsylvania was rewarded with the office of the Speaker. Although the unique circumstances prevailing at the time of preparation for and transition to independence are commonly seen as the reason for the US Speakership being as it is, Peters (1997) argues that the nature of the Speakership evolved either because of what he terms environmental factors or alternatively as a result of a forceful personality taking office. While Peters identifies four main periods in the evolution of the Speakership (see Table 6.3), the office's fundamental partisan character has remained remarkably resilient to long-term change. A legislative assembly with a partisan presiding officer corresponds closely to our concept of a leaders' assembly. In contrast, a non-partisan presiding officer corresponds to our concept of a members' assembly—with the Speaker being an agent of the membership rather than the party leadership (see Table 6.3).

How political or partisan are presiding officers across the legislative assemblies in our study? To help answer this question, we explore the rules governing how the presiding officer is selected. Generally, the presiding officer is somehow selected by the membership of the relevant chamber. We explore variation in rules governing the selection of presiding officer along two dimensions: the decision rule

Table 6.3 The evolution of the American speakership

Description	Period	Characteristics
Parliamentary Speakership	Independence to Civil War	Weak Congress; internally disorganized; weak Speaker
Partisan Speakership	Civil War to departure of Speaker Cannon in 1910	Strong Speaker, individual strengths allied with highly partisan Congress
Feudal Speakership	Post Cannon to departure of Rayburn	Weaker Speaker, sharing power with new center of power, namely committee chairs
Democratic Speakership	Post Rayburn to date	Speaker has procedural authority but is agent of party as much as leader.

Source: adapted from Peters (1997: 6: Figure 1).

(which could range from plurality to some form of super-majority) and the level of transparency in the vote (secrecy versus open).

As a general rule, the greater the hurdle presented by the decision rule for election of the presiding officer, the more likely it is that the individual elected will be non-partisan (Jenny and Müller 1995). The decision rules governing the selection of the presiding officer are reported in Table 6.2. In 62 of our 68 cases the relevant decision rule is a majority of the members voting. In other words, to be elected Speaker a majority of the members voting must support the candidate in question. In the British House of Commons, a vacancy in the Speakership is filled by MPs voting sequentially in rounds until one candidate is victorious. Since 2017, the presiding officer of the Irish *Dáil* is selected by the alternative vote electoral system, with the winner being the candidate who ultimately secures an absolute majority of votes cast (the selected candidate must then be formally approved by the whole chamber in a yes/no vote).

In six cases (Bolivia, Italy, Kenya, Sierra Leone, Turkey, and the Ukraine), the support of a supermajority of legislators is required to become the presiding officer, setting the bar even higher and likely requiring cross-party support. For example, to be elected *Presidente della Camera dei deputati* (President of the Italian Chamber of Deputies) on the first ballot, a candidate needs a two-thirds majority of all members. If this is not achieved, a candidate can be elected in a second round by a two-thirds majority of those legislators voting. If again this fails to produce a presiding officer, the decision rule is lowered to an absolute majority requirement in the third round.

A second dimension with consequences for the partisanship or neutrality of the office of presiding officer revolves around the transparency of the vote. For example, in the Italian case just cited, voting to elect the president of the chamber is secret. And indeed in 44 of our cases, voting to elect the presiding officer is conducted in secret. In 24 cases, voting is conducted in the open. Secret voting should typically enhance the neutrality of the presiding officer by removing or reducing partisan and leadership influences in the selection and election process. For example, the UK Speaker is now elected by secret ballot (when the incumbent Speaker is not seeking re-appointment). In Ireland, a 2016 reform similarly introduced a secret ballot to select the *Ceann Comhairle*. Under the changes, the *Ceann Comhairle* is selected by secret ballot and the person selected is then formally elected (or not) by an open vote in the Dáil. The second part of this process is necessitated by the fact that the Constitution required an open and recorded vote on final decisions within the Irish parliament. Clearly, we are seeing a move towards more secret voting in the selection of the presiding officer in at least some countries. In the Irish case at least, this reflects a desire to strengthen the position of presiding officer by reducing the role of party leaders relative to ordinary members in the selection process. Such a trend associates with a strengthening of some of the features of a members' assembly.

Interestingly, all seven legislative assemblies with a supermajority requirements for selecting the presiding officer also conduct the vote via a secret ballot. These seven cases arguably represent a rules-based attempt to help select only a presiding officer who has broad support within the chamber, free from discipline-based legislative voting. For the remaining cases, the majority requirement also means that the presiding officer must win the support of a majority of members voting. That approximately two-thirds of presiding officers are selected by secret vote implies to us that the UK-type Speakership focused on neutrality and serving all members is in practice preferred to the US-type Speakership where the presiding officer represents factional and partisan interests—and in particular the leadership of one party—in the chamber.

6.4 Resources

An often overlooked aspect of legislative organization is the resources available to members. The reason for the lack of focus on resources is that it is a difficult task to compare and contrast the resources and in-kind entitlements available to legislators around the world. Resources include everything from the physical estate from where the legislative assembly operates, through to the salary paid to legislators.[9]

---

[9] Managing the legislative estate can be a challenge. At the time of writing the UK Parliament is considering options to renovate its estate, including one controversial option to move Parliament to temporary locations away from the Palace of Westminster for a number of years. Some countries look to foreign governments for support in building and maintaining their national legislature. The Chinese Government funded the construction of a new building for the legislature for Lesotho, formally handed over in 2012. The Chinese Government continue to play a role in maintaining the building (http://www.lestimes.com/lesotho-renews-agreement-with-china/).

In this section, we explore three types of relatively comparable resources: members' salary, the staffing of the legislature and the overall budget of the legislative assembly.

Who gets to allocate resources has consequences for the distribution of power in a legislative assembly between members and party leaders. Ultimately, resources shape how well legislators are able to perform their duties and the degree to which they are interested in building a career as a legislator—both crucial aspects of legislative capacity.

The average annual salary for a lower-chamber legislator across our study is USD $63,732 (USD equivalents). The lowest salary is in Senegal (USD$2,330 per annum), followed by India (2,893). Members of the US House of Representatives have the highest salaries, at $174,000.[10] The salaries for each legislative assembly are reported in Table 6.4. Salaries are self-evidently important in that they help define the attractiveness of any office. Moreover, setting the "right" salary for legislatures is a challenging task: A very high salary adds to the attractiveness of the office but may create a distance between voters and members. A low salary means that politicians won't be drawn into public office for personal gain (leaving aside the financial benefits that flow from being a current or former legislator) but a low salary may also dissuade the "best and brightest" from a career in politics. Why be subjected to a low salary and all the challenges of public office when one could have an easier life as a banker or academic?

We acknowledge that it is difficult to compare salaries across countries and this challenge may apply particularly to legislative salaries for at least two reasons. In some countries, legislative salaries are tax-free, whereas in others, legislators pay taxes like all other citizens. Members may also receive other financial benefits not accounted for in the salary data, such as pension schemes, housing or travel benefits, and various expense accounts. In some countries, these expenses may be a significant component of a legislator's overall income.

Of course, legislators' levels of salaries and expenses can be a politically contentious issue. Some citizens may fear that legislators and other politicians are "just in it for the money" or otherwise abusing their office for personal financial gain. For example, in 2009, a major scandal erupted in British politics when a national newspaper began reporting details of the expenses of members of the UK House of Commons. As Pattie and Johnston (2012: 733) note, a low base salary for MPs meant that some MPs "seem to have used the expenses system as a means of recompensing themselves for foregone salary increases." The foregone salary increases resulted from the Chamber setting MPs salaries and MPs not wanting to be seen to give themselves a pay increase. In the wake of this controversy, the expenses system was overhauled and the determination of MPs salaries delegated to an independent body.

[10] Note that we do not have salary data for four countries (Liberia, Malawi, Nicaragua, and Niger).

Table 6.4 Salaries and resources

Country	Salary ($USD)	Staff	Staff Per Member	Budget ($USD)	Budget (PPP)	% State Budget
Argentina	60,000	6619	20.1			
Australia	142,201	309.7	1.4	162,903,687	117,405,820	0.05
Austria	131,286	415.2	1.7	205,298,013	181,665,583	0.2
Belgium	94,032	974	4.6	283,174,033	246,787,131	0.352
Benin	16,252	300	3.6	20,390,415	42,863,373	0.9
Bolivia	34,800	780	4.7			
Brazil	102,674	5583	9.4			
Bulgaria	19,244	510	2.1	35,883,548	78,172,178	0.63
Burundi	20,244	380	2.3	10,690,265	22,561,754	1.2
Canada	120,729	2636	6.3	478,468,071	403,475,825	0.2
Chile	154,322	775	4.9	162,309,704	205,406,365	0.361
Colombia	98,604	571	2.1	205,804,877	310,495,543	0.29
Costa Rica	77,988	683	12	40,945,102	62,647,279	0.53
Croatia	35,027	250	1.7	26,662,059	37,830,583	0.12
Czech Republic	31,890	531	1.9	83,251,345	115,367,361	0.137
Denmark	101,812	726	4.1	173,379,622	122,500,088	0.14
Dominican Republic	5,372	979	4.4	137,484,396	245,579,911	1.3
Ecuador	72,000	1213	8.9			
El Salvador	27,737	387	4.6			
Finland	83,999	472	2.4	176,494,040	145,325,375	0.3
France	93,086	2381	2.6	1,165,430,464	998,863,436	0.23
Germany	119,069	2992	4.3	884,924,503	821,185,642	0.28
Ghana	23,419	485	1.8	25,776,023	32,641,021	0.47
Greece	70,710	1318	4.4	262,235,762	274,114,221	0.38
Guatemala	36,000	1701	10.8			
Honduras	28,986	378	3			
Hungary	31,441	603	3	79,825,274	124,403,569	0.1
India	2,893	3691	4.7	121,933,572	296,095,092	0.039
Indonesia	12,163	3734	6.7	332,833,210	485,094,980	0.28
Ireland	95,333	818	4.9			
Israel	112,800	428	3.6	167,909,067	168,156,680	0.17
Italy	153,441	1916	2			
Japan	128,857	2989	4.1	1,706,925,944	1,345,138,700	0.15
Kenya	42,948	913	2.2	89,381,313	188,459,564	0.71
Liberia		71	0.7			
Malawi		151	0.8	19,331,039	49,393,534	1
Mexico	48,000	7257	11.6	702,608,916	1,116,543,848	0.25
Nepal	5,097		1.8			
Netherlands	111,439	603.45	2.7			
New Zealand	102,790	1329	11.1	112,082,556	112,454,683	0.2

Continued

Table 6.4 *Continued*

Country	Salary ($USD)	Staff	Staff Per Member	Budget ($USD)	Budget (PPP)	% State Budget
Nicaragua		540	5.9	19,230,000	47,022,719	1.3
Niger			8.5			
Nigeria	42,000		14.8	1,057,340,534	2,043,739,537	
Norway	103,856	445	2.6	158,516,476	106,302,307	0.1
Pakistan	9,491	1028	2.3	29,809,202	79,162,457	0.084
Papua New Guinea	32,116		2.8			
Paraguay	61,440	2098	16.8			
Peru	57,084	2177	16.7			
Philippines	42,604	3922	12.2	168,710,508	310,580,223	0.752
Poland	30,509	1548	2.8	201,324,046	323,991,995	0.19
Portugal	40,058	380	1.7	151,625,010	180,570,010	0.14
Romania	15,600	1406	2.4	93,137,823	176,536,923	0.27
Senegal	2,330		9.5			
Serbia	7,223	410	1.6			
Sierra Leone	25,080	51	0.4	2,748,396	6,947,330	0.77
Slovak Republic	25,710	385	2.6	38,489,142	56,130,280	0.17
South Africa	67,025		17.5			
Spain	67,075	844	1.4	194,508,225	204,242,486	0.069
South Korea	117,337	1454	4.8			
Sweden	85,340	654	1.9	210,163,152	167,618,215	0.2
Switzerland	77,692	217	0.9	106,433,406	73,487,877	0.17
Taiwan	86,253	1039	9.2			
Tunisia	18,900	486	2.2			
Turkey	98,765	2696	4.9	341,274,118	517,991,036	0.16
Ukraine	8,005	1127	2.5	116,476,789	257,907,430	0.274
United Kingdom	109,695	2367	1.6	536,172,859	532,608,948	0.05
United States	174,000	15,907	29.7	5,120,000,000	5,120,000,000	0.2
Zambia	25,006	540	3.2	56,195,353	69,550,324	1.31

Next, we explore the level of staffing in legislative assemblies—another critical ingredient of legislative capacity (Otjes 2023). We measure staffing levels by the number of full-time equivalent (or FTE) positions.[11] Note also that we only count staff whose payroll is processed by the legislative assembly. The data in this paragraph refers to paid staff across the legislative assembly (not just the lower chamber

---

[11] This means we are measuring the number of full-time staff, or their equivalent. For example, a staff member working only 50 percent of the normal working week has a FTE score of 0.5. Ten staff working at 50 percent would equal five FTEs. As such, FTE does not measure the total number of individuals employed in an organization but the number or number equivalent to full-time employees.

in bicameral systems), excluding legislators.[12] The average staff FTEs across the legislative assemblies in our study is 1,622. While this may appear high, the staffing levels in a legislature still tend to be small relative to staffing levels in the executive. Indeed, the resource inequality in terms of staffing variation between the legislature and the executive is often held to be a weakness of the legislature and one of the reasons it may find it difficult to perform its lawmaking and executive oversight functions. We find significant variation in staffing levels across different legislative assemblies. The US Congress has the highest level of staffing with 15,907 FTE staff. All four of the highest-staffed legislatures are in the Americas, but even within the region, the US Congress stands out with more than double the number of staff compared to the next highest-staffed legislature (Mexico = 7,257 FTE). You would have to add together the staff of the 34 least staffed legislatures to get the staff levels of the US Congress. The Parliament of Sierra Leone has the fewest staff of any legislative assembly in our study (with 51 FTEs), followed by Liberia (71 staffers) and Malawi (151 staff).

The number of assembly chambers may well impact overall staff size and to account for this we next look at staffing levels in the lower chamber only (for bicameral assemblies). Note that for Austria and Ireland it was not possible to separate staff by chamber and these countries are therefore excluded from the analysis here. The average number of lower-chamber (or unicameral chamber) staff is 1,221 across our study. The highest number of staff are employed in the US House of Representatives (9,808 FTEs). The lowest level of lower-chamber staffing is in Liberia, where the House of Representatives has a staff of 41 individuals.

Next, we examine the number of staff members per legislator. After all, the membership size of the legislative assembly determines the demand for staff support for many purposes, such as secretarial assistance, transportation, meals, security, etc. Small chambers should require fewer staff, all else equal. On average, our legislative assemblies have five staff members per legislator. In other words, for every legislator, there are the equivalent of five full-time staff employees on average. But again, we observe significant variation in the ratio of staff to legislators. In the US House, there are just under 30 FTE staff per legislator. In Sierra Leone there is one staff member for just under every two members.

Table 6.5 reports the results of a regression analysis where staff per legislator is the dependent variable. The results in Table 6.5 indicate that we find larger staffs per legislator in presidential, wealthier, more unequal (higher GINI coefficients), and more populous countries, as well as in countries from the Asian/Oceanic and Americas regions, and in countries that were non-British colonies. Conversely, there is uneven evidence regarding whether the number of staff per legislator correlates with the overall size of the legislature.

---

[12] We have no data on staff for the following countries: Nepal, Niger, Nigeria, Papua New Guinea, Senegal, and South Africa.

Table 6.5 Staff per member

	Staff per Member					
	(1)	(2)	(3)	(4)	(5)	(6)
Presidential	3.63***				0.004	2.27
	(1.33)				(1.80)	(1.83)
Size of Legislature	0.001				−0.01*	−0.01**
	(0.003)				(0.004)	(0.003)
Sovereignty		−0.01			−0.01	
		(0.02)			(0.02)	
log(GDP per Capita)		1.15*				1.21**
		(0.62)				(0.50)
GINI		0.29***				−0.07
		(0.11)				(0.12)
log(Population)		0.92*			2.05**	2.08***
		(0.48)			(0.86)	(0.78)
Ethnic Fractionalization		1.46			−2.67	
		(3.10)			(2.71)	
Africa and Middle East			−0.40		−0.15	
			(1.65)		(2.59)	
Asia and Oceania			3.54**		0.58	0.50
			(1.75)		(2.35)	(1.87)
Americas			7.37***		5.92**	5.54***
			(1.47)		(2.38)	(1.87)
Eastern Europe			−0.45		0.37	
			(1.75)		(2.15)	
British Colony				2.86		
				(1.92)		
Other Colony				3.31**		0.24
				(1.52)		(1.19)
Constant	3.28**	−7.42	2.74**	2.88**	−2.03	−38.94***
	(1.30)	(52.45)	(1.05)	(1.21)	(47.57)	(14.05)
N	62	62	62	62	62	62
R^2	0.11	0.27	0.40	0.08	0.47	0.51
Adjusted R^2	0.08	0.21	0.36	0.05	0.38	0.44

Notes: We are missing data on staff for 6 countries. The DV is the average number of staff members per legislator.
*$p < 0.1$; **$p < 0.05$; ***$p < 0.01$.

Finally in this section on resources, we explore the overall budget of the legislative assembly. Budgets cover everything from lights to staff to external consultancy. We take three budget measures: Total budget in US dollars, total budget in Purchasing Power Parity, and the legislative assembly's total budget as a percentage of the overall state budget. Note that we are missing budgetary data for 22 countries in our study. For the remaining countries, we again see significant variation. Using the US dollar measure, for example, the legislature with the largest budget is the

US Congress (see Table 6.4), followed as a distant second by Japan and then France and Nigeria. Sierra Leone, Burundi, and Nicaragua spend the least money (in terms of USD equivalents). Using purchasing-power-parity does not significantly alter the above results. Finally, we should consider the budget of the legislature as a percentage of the overall government budget. This does impact the rank ordering of countries. In terms of the legislative assembly's share of the national budget, the least well-resourced legislatures are to be found in India (0.039% of the government budget spent on the legislature), Australia (0.05%) and the United Kingdom (0.05%). At 0.2% of the government budget, the United States is in the mid-range of spending. The largest share of the government budget dedicated to the legislature occurs in Zambia (1.31) followed closely by the Dominican Republic and Nicaragua (both at 1.3).

Significant evidence exists to suggest that legislative capacity—including factors such as salaries, staffing, and total budgets, impacts the ability of legislative assemblies to perform their lawmaking, representative, and oversight functions. For example, the capacity of US state legislatures to review and hold accountable the police is impacted by the legislatures' capacity (Cook and Fortunato 2023), and the ability of state legislatures to be responsive to changing public preferences is also impacted by the assembly's capacity (Fortunato and Turner 2018), a phenomenon observed in other jurisdictions as well (Appeldorn and Fortunato 2022).

6.5 Conclusion

Today, very few—if any—legislatures operate in what Cox (2006) calls the legislative state of nature, in which all members have equal and undifferentiated resources and responsibilities. All members may be equal at the point of election to the chamber, but as soon as the assembly has convened, chosen its officers, and begun its deliberations, not all members of the same chamber enjoy equal parliamentary rights and equal access to plenary time. Rather, the internal legislative organization privileges some individuals and groups over others in shaping what the legislature does, and how resources are allocated. As we have seen in this chapter, legislatures vary significantly in how they are organized, including how big they are, how well they are resourced, and how leadership positions are selected.

First, we explored the number of members. Legislatures have evolved from the legislative state of nature often because too many members were chasing too little plenary time, raising the question of whether chambers have an optimal size. In a voters' assembly, legislators serve as an important link between citizens and government. If legislators are to interact with citizens, the ratio of legislators to voters needs to be sufficient low to make interaction and accountability both possible and meaningful. To have legislative capacity, members need enough colleagues to allow specialized and painstaking legislative work to be conducted without getting over-worked or having work go undone. Having too many members may make it equally difficult for the assembly to work effectively, since it may add to a plenary bottleneck as large numbers of members clamor for speaking time and opportunities to get recognized.

Second, we explored the sources of rules and organizational structures. Who decides what the rules are? It is often assumed that rules governing how a legislative assembly operates is determined by the legislative assembly itself (Bucur et al. 2018)—allowing the emergences of a members' legislature or a leaders' legislature. The implication is that legislators design and can change (redesign) the organization of the legislature. But all legislative assemblies must organize and operate within the boundaries specified by a statutory framework, often entrenched in the constitution. In the vast majority of cases, we have to look to a national constitution for rules governing, for example, the final passage of bills. Constitutionalizing legislative organization may serve to protect members and citizens from the dictates of party leaders.

Third, we explored the office of presiding officer. At one end of the spectrum, the office of presiding officer can be a tool for party leaders—at the other end of the spectrum it can be designed to serve the interest of ordinary members. Secret voting generally enhances the neutrality of the presiding officer by removing or reducing partisan influences in the selection and election process. In 44 of our cases, voting to elect the presiding officer is indeed conducted in secret, whereas in 24 cases, voting is conducted in the open. Thus, in about two-thirds of our democracies the speakership seems designed to protect the interests of ordinary members, rather than party leaders.

Finally, we explored the financial rewards and resources available to members to perform their duties. How much should a policy spend on their legislative assembly, and how well resourced and remunerated should members be? Members' salaries, the staffing of the legislature, and the overall budget of the legislative assembly shape how well legislators can perform their duties and their incentives to build a career as a legislator. Setting the "right" legislator salary is a challenging task: A very high salary adds to the attractiveness of the office but may privilege the members such as to distance them from the concerns of the voters. A low salary may force the members to "feel the pain" of the voters but at same time reduce the quality of legislative candidates. A low salary thus means that politicians won't be motivated to seek public office for personal gain (leaving aside "irregular" gains and the financial benefits that may flow from being a former legislator) but the low salary may also dissuade the "best and brightest" from a career in politics. Staff resources also matter. Indeed, the resource inequality in staffing between the legislature and the executive is often held as a critical weakness of the former branch and one reason the legislature may find it difficult to perform its lawmaking and executive oversight functions. We move in the next chapters to discuss two more specific aspects of legislative organization: political parties and legislative committees.

References

Alemán, Eduardo 2015. "Legislative Organization and Outcomes." In Jennifer Gandhi and Rubén Ruiz-Rufino (eds.), *The Routledge Handbook of Comparative Political Institutions*. Abingdon: Routledge, 145–161.

Appeldorn, Niels H., and David Fortunato. 2022. "Legislative Capacity in Germany's Parliaments." *Legislative Studies Quarterly* 47(2): 309–328.

Bach, Stanley. 1999. "The Office of Speaker in Comparative Perspective." *The Journal of Legislative Studies* 5(3–4): 209–254.

Bäck, Hanna, Marc Debus, and Jorge Fernandes (eds.). 2021. *The Politics of Legislative Debate*. Oxford: Oxford University Press.

Bucur, Cristina, José Antonio Cheibub, Shane Martin, and Bjørn Erik Rasch. 2018. "Constitution Making and Legislative Involvement in Government Formation." In Jon Elster, Roberto Gargarella, Vatsal Naresh, and Bjørn Erik Rasch (eds.), *Constituent Assemblies*. Cambridge, MA: Cambridge University Press, 186–206.

Carroll, Royce, Gary W. Cox, and Mónica Pachón. 2006. "How Parties Create Electoral Democracy, Chapter 2." *Legislative Studies Quarterly* 31(2): 153–174.

Cook, Scott J., and David Fortunato. 2023. "The Politics of Police Data: State Legislative Capacity and the Transparency of State and Substate Agencies." *American Political Science Review* 117(1): 280–295.

Cox, Gary W. 2006. "The Organization of Democratic Legislatures." In Barry R. Weingast and Donald Wittman (eds.), *The Oxford Handbook of Political Economy*. Oxford: Oxford University Press, 141–161.

Fortunato, David, and Ian R. Turner. 2018. "Legislative Capacity and Credit Risk." *American Journal of Political Science* 62(3): 623–636.

Hazan, Reuven Y., 2001. *Reforming Parliamentary Committees: Israel in Comparative Perspective*. Columbus: Ohio State University Press.

Jacobs, Kristof, and Simon Otjes. 2015. "Explaining the Size of Assemblies. A Longitudinal Analysis of the Design and Reform of Assembly Sizes in Democracies around the World." *Electoral Studies* 40: 280–292.

Jenny, Marcelo, and Wolfgang C. Müller. 1995. "Presidents of Parliament: Neutral Chairmen or Assets of the Majority." In Herbert Döring, (ed.), *Parliaments and Majority Rule in Western Europe*. Frankfurt: Campus Verlag & New York: St. Martin's Press, 326–364

Kam, Christopher. 2009. *Party Discipline and Parliamentary Politics*. New York: Cambridge University Press.

Laundy, Philip. 1964. *The Office of Speaker*. London: Cassell.

National Democratic Institute for International Affairs. 1996. *Presiding officers: Speakers and Presidents of Legislatures*. Legislative Research Series Paper No. 1, Washington, D.C.: National Democratic Institute.

Otjes, Simon. 2023. "What Explains the Size of Parliamentary Staff?" *West European Politics* 46(2): 374–400.

Pattie, Charles, and Ron Johnston. 2012. "The Electoral Impact of the UK 2009 MPs' expenses scandal." *Political Studies* 60(4): 730–750.

Peters, Ronald M. 1997. *The American Speakership: The Office in Historical Perspective.* Baltimore: The Johns Hopkins University Press.

Proksch, Sven-Oliver, and Jonathan B Slapin. 2015. *The Politics of Parliamentary Debate.* Cambridge: Cambridge University Press.

Royal Commission on the Electoral System. 1986. *Report of the Royal Commission on the Electoral System.* Wellington: Government Printer.

Sieberer, Ulrich, Peter Meißner, Julia F. Keh, and Wolfgang C. Müller. 2016. "Mapping and Explaining Parliamentary Rule Changes in Europe: A Research Program." *Legislative Studies Quarterly* 41(1): 61–88.

Sin, Gisela. 2015. *Separation of Powers and Legislative Organization.* New York: Cambridge University Press.

Taagepera, Rein. 1972. "The Size of National Assemblies." *Social Science Research* 1(4): 385–401.

Wockelberg, Helena. 2015. "Weak Investiture Rules and the Emergence of Minority Governments in Sweden" In Rasch, Bjørn Erik, Shane Martin, and José Antonio Cheibub (eds.), *Parliaments and Government Formation: Unpacking Investiture Rules.* Oxford: Oxford University Press, 233–249.

7

Parties in the Assembly

Political parties are teams of individuals united for the purpose of winning elections and controlling government (Downs 1957). Parties exist in many social arenas, but first emerged in modern form inside legislative assemblies. Although parties have in most democracies enrolled the majority of national legislators for well over a century, or in some cases two, many constitutions are still silent on the legislative roles parties play and effectively treat them as private and voluntary organizations. Indeed, classical democratic theorists and constitutional framers such as James Madison were, at least initially, critical of parties and their consequences for democratic governance. Yet, as Schattschneider (1942: 1) notes, "political parties created democracy and modern democracy is unthinkable save in terms of the parties." Legislative parties are typically the most important organizational feature of a legislative assembly. This chapter explores the nature of legislative parties, how legislative parties organize and how party leaders shape and perhaps even control what members do. Indeed, the role and functioning of political parties, and the hierarchies they create, are central to our notion of a leaders' assembly.

Parties do many things, but most importantly they provide a critical hierarchical governance structure in legislative assemblies. The most powerful leaders in modern assemblies are almost without exception the leading members of the most powerful political parties within these legislatures. These individuals possess their power largely because of the benefits that parties provide for their elected representatives and arguably for their voters (see Robertson 1976; Ware 1987; Schlesinger 1991; Cox and McCubbins 1993, 2005; Aldrich 1995; Müller 2000). While other officeholders, such as committee chairs or independently elected speakers, may sometimes perform important leadership functions, the heads of political parties are without question the most powerful class of leaders in modern legislative assemblies—often also holding important executive positions such as prime minister. And parliamentary party organizations are most important vehicle by which leaders and members interact. A core theme in this chapter is the degree to which parties, and in particular party leaders, control members and thus encroach on the relationship between voters and members. The level of control plays a central role in determining the type into which the legislature falls: a voters', members' or leaders' assembly.

Legislative Assemblies. Shane Martin and Kaare W. Strøm, Oxford University Press.
© Shane Martin and Kaare W. Strøm (2023). DOI: 10.1093/oso/9780198890829.003.0007

From the perspectives of capacity and accountability discussed in Chapter 1, political parties undeniably impact the chain of delegation from voters to their elected representatives in modern democracies. As Saalfeld and Strøm (2014: 377) note, "political parties underpin and mediate this chain of delegation." Parties variously select their candidates and provide them with labels that voters can employ in their decision-making at election time. Parties also shape or control legislators' behavior, and they may constrain the ways in which these legislators act on behalf of the voters that elected them. In fact, we can usefully think of most democratically elected legislators as having two principals: their respective voters and their party leaders (Carey 2007). Legislators may need to balance their responsiveness to voters with following the call of their respective parties. In many situations, serving their party may come at a cost to their constituents, and vice versa. Having multiple principals thus complicates an assembly member's opportunity structure, particularly where the preferences of these principals differ.

7.1 Legislative Parties

Our primary focus in this chapter is on legislative parties—that part of the party which organizes in the legislative assembly and typically comprises the assembly members affiliated with that party. The legislative party is arguably the core of most political parties, consisting as it is of those individuals elected to national legislative office. Historically, this is where parties first emerged, such as in the seventeenth and eighteenth centuries the Whigs and Tories in England or the Hats and Caps in Sweden. The legislative party is thus one component of Key's (1964) "party in government" and one part of May's (1973) "party leaders." Note however, that in this book we use the term "party leaders" for the designated and typically elected leaders of the party's legislative organization, though we recognize that parties' sets of influentials also include individuals such as Cox and McCubbins' (2005) "senior partners"—established politicians with important specialized responsibilities within the party, for example committee chairs or senior whips. Yet, from our perspective an ordinary (backbench) legislator is not a party leader.

Exactly which legislators constitute the legislative party and what this organization is titled varies across political systems. In bicameral assemblies, the legislative party may be composed of members from just the lower chamber (as in the case of the British Parliamentary Labour Party) or from both chambers (as in the Irish case). In some countries, transnational legislators (for example Members of the European Parliament) may have a seat in their domestic party's legislative party. Legislative parties may also be known by different terms in different countries. Parliamentary Party Group (PPG) and party caucus are two such labels (Heidar and Koole 2003).

Individuals occupying different positions within a party may have very different policy preferences and interests. Private goods that derive from control of the legislative arena or the executive branch flow disproportionately to party leaders, who therefore greatly value such control. That in turn may incline such leaders to pursue electoral victory rather than policy purity, or to value successful bargains with other party leaders, even if they compromise party policy. Backbench members in competitive districts or unsafe list positions will likely want to maximize their votes locally, whereas their counterparts in safer seats may be more concerned with policy principles or with satisfying the party faithful. And where elections are staggered, members who face upcoming elections will value votes more than members whose next elections is far away in time, or those that are term-limited or planning to retire (Schlesinger 1966, 1991; May 1973; Cox and McCubbins 1993; Strøm 1997). At the same time, the behavior of co-partisans is constrained by the interdependence of the various components of the party. Thus, legislators are not free to pursue exclusively their own interests and preferences or those of their peers, they must also consider the interests and preferences of their party leaders as well as of ordinary party members and the broader electorate.

7.2 The Number of Legislative Parties

When thinking about legislative parties, one of the most critical questions concerns the number of different parties with which assembly members are affiliated. One-party assemblies work very differently from competitive two-party legislatures, which in turn diverge sharply from institutions in which the members are divided among a plethora of parties, none of which has any prospect of gaining a majority. Assemblies in which membership is restricted by law or fiat to a single party, such as the former Soviet Union for most of its lifespan, violate the basic requirements of democracy and are therefore excluded from this study. Of course, single-party legislatures do exist in some contemporary non-democratic political regimes, such as China. Yet no legislative assembly in this study is composed entirely of members belonging to just one party. This is not surprising given that democracy requires multi-party elections and at least the possibility that more than one party will be represented. Yet, there is substantial variation in the number of parties in the assemblies featured in this study. The number of legislative parties for each country in our study is presented in the second column of Table 7.1. Across all our cases, the average (mean) number of parties is 11.6.

Our 68-country dataset contains two examples of pure two-party legislatures. The 124-member Parliament of Sierra Leone comprises legislators from just two parties—the All People's Congress and the Sierra Leone People's Party (by 2022, however, Sierra Leone had a multiparty parliament). The US House of Representatives elected in November 2016 similarly comprised just two parties: 188

Table 7.1 Legislative party systems

Country	Number of Legislative Parties	Effective Number of Legislative Parties	Number of Party Groups	Non-Party Members	Percent Non-Party Members
Argentina	37	4.28	20	0	0.00
Australia	7	2.14	7	2	1.33
Austria	6	4.24	6	3	1.64
Belgium	12	8.42	12	0	0.00
Benin	11	2.64	11	0	0.00
Bolivia	3	1.85	3	0	0.00
Brazil	27	10.44	27	0	0.00
Bulgaria	25	3.34	8	13	5.42
Burundi	4	2.39	4	0	0.00
Canada	5	2.4	5	1	0.30
Chile	9	5.64	8	7	5.83
Colombia	14	4.95	14	0	0.00
Costa Rica	9	3.9	9	0	0.00
Croatia	20	2.61	14	7	4.64
Czech Republic	7	4.51	7	8	4.00
Denmark	12	5.61	12	0	0.00
Dominican Republic	10	2.01	10	0	0.00
Ecuador	11	3.46	9	3	2.19
El Salvador	5	2.94	5	1	1.19
Finland	8	5.83	8	0	0.00
France	14	2.49	5	28	4.85
Germany	5	4.83	4	0	0.00
Ghana	3	2.12	2	3	1.09
Greece	8	2.59	8	4	1.33
Guatemala	13	4.15	13	0	0.00
Honduras	7	2.3	7	4	3.13
Hungary	9	2	4	1	0.50
India	36	5.01	36	3	0.55
Indonesia	10	6.13	10	0	0.00
Ireland	7	3.46	5	14	8.86
Israel	10	6.77	10	0	0.00
Italy	13	3.07	7	0	0.00
Japan	7	2.1	7	13	2.74
Kenya	20	3.52	3	1	0.29
Liberia	12	6.41	12	9	12.33
Malawi	6	2.49	6	52	26.94
Mexico	8	2.75	7	1	0.20
Nepal	30	2.4	30	2	0.33

Country	Number of Legislative Parties	Effective Number of Legislative Parties	Number of Party Groups	Non-Party Members	Percent Non-Party Members
Netherlands	11	6.74	11	7	4.67
New Zealand	7	2.98	7	0	0.00
Nicaragua	3	1.79	3	0	0.00
Niger	16	3.72	8	0	0.00
Nigeria	6	1.75	5	0	0.00
Norway	8	4.07		0	0.00
Pakistan	18	4.61	20	9	2.63
Papua New Guinea	21		20	16	14.41
Paraguay	5	3.43	5	1	1.25
Peru	6	3.97		0	0.00
Philippines	61	3.84	9	6	2.02
Poland	7	3	7	4	0.87
Portugal	7	2.96	7	0	0.00
Romania	9	3.6	6	42	10.19
Senegal	13	1.31	6	0	0.00
Serbia	16	3.48	12	0	0.00
Sierra Leone	2	2.54	2	0	0.00
Slovak Republik	6	4.01	6	0	0.00
South Africa	13		13	3	0.75
South Korea	4	2.87	3	3	1.00
Spain	13	2.36	8	0	0.00
Sweden	8	4.51	8	1	0.29
Switzerland	11	5.58	7	1	0.50
Taiwan	5	1.75	5	1	0.88
Tunisia	18		18	0	0.00
Turkey	4	2.35	4	0	0.00
Ukraine	11	3.3	8	46	10.22
United Kingdom	11	2.57	12	4	0.62
United States	2	1.97	2	1	0.23
Zambia	5		5	3	1.80

Democrats and 247 Republicans. In contrast, some other legislatures are highly fragmented in partisan terms. The 2013 elections to the Philippines' House of Representatives resulted in 61 different parties having at least one seat in the lower chamber. The Argentinian Chamber of Deputies elected in October 2015 had members from 37 parties.

Such figures can be slightly misleading if not all parties are of relatively equal size. A legislature could, for example, have just one or two large parties—comprising the vast majority of members—but also many parties with only a handful of representatives. A measure called the *Effective Number of Legislative Parties* helps overcome this problem by weighting the number of parties by their relative size (Laakso and Taagepera 1979). The Effective Number of Legislative Parties (EnLP) is reported in Table 7.1. In our study, Brazil has the largest EnLP, at 10.44 parties. Senegal has the lowest EnLP at 1.31 parties and provides a good example of the difference between the absolute and the effective number of legislative parties; 13 parties are represented in Senegal's *Assemblée Nationale*. However, one party (United in Hope) controls 119 of the 150 seats. The remaining seats are spread across 12 parties, seven of which have only one legislator. Thus, the EnLP score for Senegal highlights the degree to which the chamber is dominated—in quantitative membership terms—by a single legislative party, despite the presence of 12 other parties.

What factors correlate with a country's EnLP? To explore this, Table 7.2 reports the results of a regression analysis where EnLP is the dependent variable. Following Duverger (1959), we would expect a country's electoral system to shape its legislative party system (although, see also Blais 2016). A majoritarian electoral system is said to associate with a two-party system, while a proportional representation (PR) electoral system correlates with a multiparty system. The results in Table 7.2 provide at least some support for Duverger, as they suggest that countries with majoritarian or mixed electoral systems, as well as countries from the African/Middle Eastern (MENA) and Americas regions, tend to have a smaller number of effective political parties.

Parties with only a small number of legislators may find it difficult to be formally recognized as a legislative group. The rules of the assembly may grant certain rights, prerogatives, and perquisites to legislative party groups. Such recognition rules may include access to plenary speaking time, membership of the governing board, rights to a certain portion of committee seats and access for the group and group members to resources such as salaried administrative and research assistance. In some cases, the legislature's rule book specifies that a party must have a minimum number of legislators to enjoy such group rights. Thus, the seven parties in the Senegal legislature with just one member each are unlikely to have the same group access rights and resources as the party with 119 seats. In fact, only six party groups are recognized in the Senegalese legislature. The number of recognized party groups in each country is reported in Table 7.1. Legislative party groups refer to a legislative party or technical grouping which is recognized by the rules of the assembly as having certain legislative privileges, as described above. A technical group is a group of members from different legislative parties, or no legislative

Table 7.2 The effective number of legislative parties

	Effective Number of Parties					
	(1)	(2)	(3)	(4)	(5)	(6)
Majoritarian	−0.78				−1.14*	−0.68
	(0.52)				(0.64)	(0.53)
Mixed	−1.37***				−1.69***	−1.53***
	(0.51)				(0.61)	(0.51)
Mean District Magnitude	0.001				0.001	
	(0.003)				(0.004)	
Sovereignty		0.00001			0.001	
		(0.01)			(0.01)	
log(GDP per Capita)		0.22				
		(0.21)				
GINI		−0.03				
		(0.03)				
log(Population)		0.02			0.06	
		(0.18)			(0.19)	
Ethnic Fractionalization		0.91			1.51	
		(1.12)			(1.07)	
Africa and Middle East			−1.21*		−1.53*	−0.88
			(0.62)		(0.86)	(0.53)
Asia and Oceania			−0.59		0.04	
			(0.68)		(0.83)	
Americas			−0.67		−1.12*	−0.61
			(0.60)		(0.65)	(0.49)
Eastern Europe			−0.84		−0.92	
			(0.72)		(0.91)	
British Colony				−0.61		
				(0.60)		
Other Colony				0.09		
				(0.50)		
Constant	4.14***	1.92	4.33***	3.78***	2.22	4.53***
	(0.29)	(17.67)	(0.43)	(0.40)	(19.82)	(0.34)
N	68	68	68	68	68	68
R^2	0.12	0.04	0.06	0.03	0.21	0.16
Adjusted R^2	0.07	−0.04	−0.001	−0.004	0.07	0.10

Notes: The DV is the Effective number of legislative parties;
*p < 0.1; **p < 0.05; ***p < 0.01.

parties, who form a (typically loose) internal legislative association to share such benefits within the legislature that derive from meeting any such minimum size threshold.

7.3 Non-Party Legislators

A non-party legislator is a member who does not affiliate with any political party. Non-party legislators are sometimes referred to as independent legislators or independents.[1] Note, however, that candidates can run as non-partisans for electoral purposes and then join one of the legislative parties once they have been elected. In contrast, there may also be cases in which a member is elected on a partisan slate but later resigns or is ousted from his or her party. As Weeks notes (2014: 605), independents may thus be a relatively heterogeneous group: "Some are party mavericks, others represent interest groups, while some are quite anti-party and run for office to provide a genuine independent choice for voters." The presence of one or more non-party legislator can reflect the strength of voters and members relative to party leaders, to the extent that it signifies that voters have been able to elect non-party representatives. Yet, if non-partisans are mainly members elected on a party slate who have subsequently left (or been expelled by) their party, this inference may be less warranted. The critical issue in such cases may be what prospects such members have of being re-elected. The ability to be elected or re-elected without a party label is thus a more reliable measure of the power of members relative to party leaders, as party leaders may be less capable of sanctioning members when the member knows she could gain re-election without the party label. A study of the election and re-election rates of non-partisan legislators could therefore make a valuable contribution to our understanding of the limits of party politics in legislative settings.

Thirty-eight of the 68 legislatures in our study have at least one non-party legislator. This finding runs counter to prevailing assumptions that non-party legislators are uncommon, being a feature of a very small number of cases only. In our study, the highest incidence of non-party legislators is in Malawi.[2] Fifty-two independent members (almost 27% of the membership) took their seats following the 2014 National Assembly election—admittedly almost double the number elected at the previous election. In Malawi, independents are a larger political grouping than any single political party (the largest party—the Democratic Progressive Party—had 50 MPs). Patel and Wahman (2015: 86) suggest that the high number of independents in Malawi reflects the weakness of voters' attachment to

---

[1] A non-party election candidate is typically defined as "someone who is running for office not on behalf of a party" (Weeks 2014: 605).

[2] A legislature with (some) non-party members is very different from a legislature without (any) parties. Weeks (2015) identifies a number of sub-national legislatures that operate without recognized political parties, including the Tasmanian Legislative Council, the Nebraskan State Assembly, and the Legislative Assemblies of the Northwest Territories and Nunavut in Canada, as well as the assemblies in the Isle of Man, the Channel Islands, and the Falkland Islands.

political parties but also the fact that in some cases "popular parliamentary candidates lost nominations and contested the election on an independent ticket." Four hundred and twenty-one of the 1290 candidates who stood for election in Malawi in 2014 were independents.

Note that Malawi uses a single-member district plurality (SMDP) electoral system to elect its national assembly. Other countries with high rates of Independents include Papua New Guinea (14.4%), Liberia (12.3%), Ukraine (10.2%), Romania (10.2%), and Ireland (8.9%). Larger district magnitudes and candidate-centered electoral systems are often held to favor the emergence of independent legislators (Weeks 2014). Table 7.3 reports results of a regression analysis where the dependent variable is the percentage of the legislative assembly that is comprised of non-party legislators. The results in Table 7.3 suggest that majoritarian countries with SMD elections tend to have a higher percentage of non-party legislators, as we would expect. In addition, there is some evidence that wealthier and more populous countries have fewer non-party legislators.

Independent legislators can play a pivotal role in some legislatures. Following the 2016 general election in Ireland, a number of independent members (TDs) provided important legislative support to the minority government that formed. In return, three independent legislators were appointed to the cabinet. Thus, although political parties are core to modern-day politics, and legislative politics in particular, not all legislators belong to a political party, and some such independents may gain legislative bargaining power and even access to executive office.

7.4 Organizational Structure of Legislative Parties

Legislative parties tend to be strongly hierarchical organizations. For example, legislative parties commonly have a clearly identifiable leader, often elected by and responsible to his or her co-partisans in the assembly. In the case of bicameral legislatures, party leaderships may be common to both chambers, or each legislative party in each chamber may have its own leader. In the United States Congress, for example, the Speaker of the House of Representatives is leader of the majority party in that chamber. The House Minority Leader leads the minority party in that same House. The Senate Minority Leader heads the minority party in the Senate, while the Majority Leader leads the Senate majority party. But neither party has one Congressional party leader that commands its caucus in both chambers.

In many political systems, the leader of the legislative party (or the legislative party in the lower chamber) may be recognized as the national leader of that party. How legislative parties choose their leader varies from party to party. Some party

Table 7.3 The rate of non-party legislators

	Proportion of Non-Party Members					
	(1)	(2)	(3)	(4)	(5)	(6)
ICPV	−0.001				0.001	
	(0.002)				(0.002)	
Majoritarian	0.04**				0.04*	0.03***
	(0.02)				(0.02)	(0.01)
Mixed	0.01				0.001	
	(0.02)				(0.02)	
Mean District Magnitude	0.0001				0.0001	
	(0.0001)				(0.0001)	
Sovereignty		0.0001			−0.0001	
		(0.0002)			(0.0003)	
log(GDP per Capita)		−0.01*				−0.01
		(0.01)				(0.003)
GINI		−0.0003				
		(0.001)				
log(Population)		−0.004			−0.01*	−0.01**
		(0.004)			(0.005)	(0.004)
Ethnic Fractionalization		−0.02			−0.01	
		(0.03)			(0.03)	
Africa and Middle East			0.01		0.01	
			(0.02)		(0.02)	
Asia and Oceania			0.01		0.01	
			(0.02)		(0.02)	
Americas			−0.01		0.001	
			(0.02)		(0.02)	
Eastern Europe			0.03		0.03	
			(0.02)		(0.02)	
British Colony				0.02		
				(0.01)		
Other Colony				0.0003		
				(0.01)		
Constant	0.01	−0.04	0.01	0.02	0.27	0.20***
	(0.01)	(0.43)	(0.01)	(0.01)	(0.51)	(0.08)
N	68	68	68	68	68	68
R^2	0.11	0.11	0.06	0.05	0.21	0.17
Adjusted R^2	0.06	0.03	−0.0001	0.02	0.05	0.14

Notes: The DV is Percentage of non-party MPs in the lower chamber;
*$p < 0.1$; **$p < 0.05$; ***$p < 0.01$.

rules place the decision on/about leadership selection entirely in the hands of the members of the legislative party. In other cases, all party members in the electorate may participate in the selection of the party leader. The degree to which the selection of party leader is centralized (in the hands of the legislative party, for example) or decentralized (through a one member, one vote selection process, for example) has important implications for who becomes the party leader. And changes in the rules governing leadership selection can affect the type of candidate who can win such contests, as recent events in the British Parliamentary Labour Party demonstrate (Quinn 2016). And the 2022 UK Conservative Party competition is another case in point. The candidate most favored by Conservative MPs (at the shortlisting stage) was not the candidate ultimately selected by the party membership to become party leader (and Prime Minister). Box 7.1 explores another case: how Japan's Liberal Democratic Party (LDP) selects its party leader.

Box 7.1 Electing the LDP Leader

The Leader of the Liberal Democratic Party (LDP), Japan's largest political party, serves for a three-year term, although the office holder is permitted to serve three consecutive terms. The election of LDP leader in September 2021 illustrates how the LDP chooses its leader and the person who typically soon after becomes Prime Minister.

To be a candidate for party leader, the individual must be a member of the Diet and must be nominated by at least 20 LDP legislators. After nominations have closed and candidates are confirmed, a period of campaigning is allowed.

The selectorate—the group of people voting to select the party leader—consists of two groups: (1) LDP members of the Diet (LDP legislators) and (2) with certain restrictions, LDP party members and senior office holders. LDP members of the Diet vote on leadership election day by casting a vote for their preferred candidate. Party members can cast their vote in one of a number of ways, including most commonly postal balloting.

An electoral college determines the outcome. Each LDP legislator receives a vote and the party membership receives a vote equal to the number of LDP legislators. In 2021, 383 LDP legislators meant that there were also 383 "Party Member Votes."

To be elected party leader, a candidate needs to receive a majority of votes in this electoral college. If no candidate receives a majority of votes in the first round, a runoff between the top two candidates from the first round is held, with a modified allocation of votes between legislators and members—reducing greatly the influence of party members, with voting weights allocated by party prefecture. In any second round, LDP legislators vote again but the

Continued

party element of the vote changes: instead of constituting half of the selectorate, the 47 prefectural chapter representatives receive one vote each, with the first-round results of party members in each prefecture determining which candidate will receive these prefecture votes.

In 2021, four candidates were nominated but no candidate won a majority of votes in the first round. Taro Kono topped the poll with 44 percent of the vote (supported by 22 percent of Diet LDP legislators and 44 percent of party members), with Fumio Kishida winning 39 percent of LDP legislators and 29 percent of party members—placing him on 29 percent overall. In the second round, however, while Kone still polled very well with party members (supported by 83 percent of party members, and 17 percent of LDP legislator), the greater weighting afforded Diet LDP legislators in the second round meant that Fumio Kishida was elected party leader. Kishida was invested as Prime Minister following a formal vote in the Diet on October 4, 2021.

Party leaders play important roles in managing their legislative party and negotiating with other parties. In some parliamentary systems, the prime ministership is typically filled by the leader of one of the largest parties in the most recent election (as we will discuss in Chapter 11). In the classic models of political delegation and accountability in such systems, voters select legislators and legislators select the head of government. In parliamentary systems that feature coalition governments, the leader of one of the parties that form the executive is likely to become the head of government. Thus, who gets to choose the party leader has significant implications for who can become the chief political executive.

The party's assembly leader is generally assisted in his or her leadership tasks by a leadership group of fellow party legislators. Many parties thus have a collective leadership body selected by the party leader or elected by the party caucus. In the US House of Representatives, for example, each party has a leadership body of a dozen or so members, in addition to the chairs and ranking members of the various standing committees. In some legislatures, this creates a division between legislators with a party leadership position (often referred to as "the frontbench") and legislators with no party leadership position (often referred to as "backbenchers"). In Westminster systems members of the frontbench are typically at the same time cabinet members, or shadow cabinet members, with responsibility for specific policy areas (portfolios)—either acting as ministers if their party is in government or if in opposition shadowing a government minister. As we will discuss later, the interests and influence of frontbench and backbench legislators may differ greatly.

One member of the party leader's inner circle may be the Party Chief Whip. Party Whips are responsible for managing members of the legislative party and to assure that backbench legislators follow leadership requests. In larger assemblies, such as the British House of Commons, the Chief Whip may be helped by a number of assistant whips. The term "whip," which conjures up unpleasant images of legislators been whipped into line, derives from fox hunting, where whippers-in or whips are used to look after the hounds and prevent them from straying (Richards, 1972: 55, n. 1). Porritt (1903) claims that the first attempt to organize and inform British MPs can be traced back to the early 1620s when followers of King James I received regular reports detailing what was happening in Parliament and what they were required to do. As we will see in the next section, the Party Whip is responsible for ensuring that colleagues turn up to participate in legislative votes (divisions), and to vote in accordance with the party line, if there is one. As we have seen, legislative organization and rules may privilege party leaders over other members, giving rise to our notion of a leaders' assembly. An assembly in which ordinary members are subject to, and regularly succumb to, whipping, is one form that a leaders' assembly may take, as we will now discuss.

7.5 Party Influence on Roll-Call Behavior

Legislators are called upon to perform many different roles and duties. They make speeches, they serve on committees, some appear in the media, and many engage directly with constituents and interest groups. Ultimately, one of the most critical duties of a legislator involves casting a vote in what in Westminster parliaments is known as legislative divisions, or the final vote on bills before the assembly.

Voting unity is the extent to which legislators from the same political party vote the same way in legislative divisions. In a party with 100 legislators, if 50 co-partisans were to vote "No" and the remaining 50 vote "Yes," we could say that the legislative party is perfectly divided, and therefore is totally lacking in voting unity. The index of voting unity on any division is computed as the absolute difference between the proportion of party members voting in favor and the proportion of party members voting in opposition, multiplied by 100 to obtain a number ranging from 0 to 100 (Rice 1925). Voting unity scores in roll-call votes are typically presented at the party level and compared across parties. In the above example, the voting unity score would equal zero. Knowing only the party affiliation of a member in this party would provide no indication of their voting behavior. In contrast, if all 100 members of a legislative party were to vote together, their party's voting unity score would equal 100, representing perfect voting unity.

A particular challenge in roll-call analysis relates to interpreting abstentions. An abstention can take one of two different forms, depending on the legislative assembly. In the Italian Senate, for example, Senators can vote to abstain. This vote generally counts as a "No" vote in arriving at a formal decision. Italian Senators can also decide not to vote—an abstention rather than a vote to abstain. Such abstentions do not count in the overall decision—assuming that the quorum (the minimum number of votes cast required for an authoritative decision) has been met. Scholars of roll-call analysis have long struggled to interpret abstentions in legislative divisions. An abstention may simply reflect that a member is not in the chamber at the time of the vote and may have her party's permission (if the member belongs to a party) to miss that vote. A famous example of an (allegedly) accidental abstention happened when Danish Social Democrat Erhard Jakobsen missed a critical vote of confidence in the *Folketinget* in the 1970s, leading to the fall of his party's government, because his car ran out of fuel on the way to Parliament.

We do not have comparable data on the level of unified party voting for all the countries in this study. However, we can report some historical data on the voting behavior of legislators in over 90 parties in 16 legislatures. As Table 7.4 demonstrates, party voting unity scores for the 16 legislatures reported are lowest in Finland and highest in Ireland and Denmark. In Ireland, party unity is at a remarkable 100 percent, whereas in Denmark it differs from that lofty number only by rounding error. Yet, even in Finland party unity is above 88 percent, and nowhere else does it fall below 93 percent. In other words, Danish and Irish legislators hardly ever vote against their party in legislative divisions (Depauw and Martin 2008), and in most other countries in this study disunity is quite rare. In fact, in many legislatures, voting along party lines is so common that scholars have not bothered to collect systematic data on legislative voting behavior. This is particularly true for parliamentary regimes, and it is worth noting that all the countries in the survey discussed above are in fact parliamentary.

But why is voting unity so high? Relatedly, what explains variation in party voting unity, both across different parties in the same legislature, across different legislatures, and over time? One way to approach voting unity is to ask why a legislator may choose to vote with or against (a majority of) their party colleagues. The answer may lie in party cohesion or in party discipline. Understanding the difference between these concepts of cohesion and discipline is a useful first step in answering this question.

Legislative party cohesion refers to the degree to which legislators in the same party share policy preferences. A cohesive legislative party is one in which members intrinsically share the same outlook on policy matters. A shared ideology—a broad approach or understanding of politics and society—may help shape policy preferences on specific issues and foster coherent preferences among co-partisans. An ideologically cohesive party should associate with high party unity in voting; legislators from that party vote similarly because they all share the same preferences over the relevant issues. In contrast, ideological heterogeneity within a legislative party may lead to low levels of voting unity (we say "may," because

Table 7.4 Party unity in 16 democracies

Country	Period covered	No. of Parties	Mean	St.dev
Australia	1996-98	3	99.07	0.15
Austria	1995-97	5	98.68	1.45
Belgium	1991-95	9	99.06	0.75
Canada	1994-95	4	97.60	2.24
Denmark	1994-95	7	99.93	0.11
Finland	1995-96	7	88.63	2.59
France	1993-97	4	99.33	0.63
Germany	1987-90	3	96.33	1.79
Iceland	1995-96	6	96.93	2.84
Ireland	1992-96	3	100.0	0.00
Israel	1999-00	10	96.88	1.15
Italy (1st Republic)	1987-92	9	97.52	1.60
Italy (2nd Republic)	1996-01	11	96.46	1.44
New Zealand	1993-94	2	93.17	0.65
Norway	1992-93	6	95.90	0.52
Sweden	1994-95	7	96.57	1.51
United Kingdom	1992-97	2	99.25	0.49

Source: Depauw and Martin (2008).

factors other than ideological preference could drive members' roll-call behavior, as we discuss below).

Why would legislative parties be ideologically cohesive? The obvious answer is that individuals join political parties that reflect their policy preferences. A would-be politician who believes in the virtues of the free market is unlikely to join a communist party, to use an obviously extreme example. To the extent that they have an interest in policy, politicians therefore self-select into parties with like-minded individuals. Moreover, politicians who wish to rise in the ranks may want to join a party in which most other legislators share their policy preferences and are likely to entrust them with policy-making responsibilities. Yet, their ability to join a party with like-minded individuals depends on a number of factors, most especially the set of available parties. In general, the greater the number of competitive parties in a democracy, the more likely it is that would-be politicians can find a party that suits their policy preferences. In a multiparty system, it may be possible to have an economically and socially liberal party, an economically liberal but socially conservative one, an economically redistributive and socially liberal option, and an economically redistributive and socially conservative party. Along these two policy dimensions (an economic and a social one) at least, it would then be possible for most would-be politicians to find a home that *fits* their policy preferences. In a pure two-party system, by contrast, it may be more difficult to find the right fit. The consequence is that one or both legislative parties in a two-party system are often described as "broad churches"—the spectrum of policy opinions within each legislative party is wide, so that internal party policy disagreements are frequent. Sometimes a legislator will switch parties (see Box 7.2), often because of disenchantment with the party's policy positions.

Box 7.2 Party Switching

The term party switching refers to "any recorded change in party affiliation on the part of a politician holding or competing for elective office" (Heller and Mershon 2009, 8). Most legislators remain a member of the same party for their entire political career. Yet, some make the decision to divorce their party and possibly join a new party. In some countries, party switching is, or has been, common. Between 1996 and 2001, 22 percent of Italian legislators changed their parliamentary party affiliation.

Why would a legislator change parties? One possibility is that the legislator has grown unhappy with her party. This may be because of unhappiness with the party's policy, for example because the party changed its policy or reacted to new issues or events in ways that were not in keeping with preferences of those members. To the extent that such policy change drives defections, party switching may be more common in newly democratized systems, as new parties define and refine their policy platforms. Thus a member may find that another party better reflects her preferences. In 2011, Ehud Barak thus resigned as leader of the Israeli Labour Party to establish a new political party (O'Brien and Shomer 2013).

Legislators may also change parties because of unhappiness with how they are treated by their party leadership. If legislators are eager to be promoted but fail to get such rewards, they may consider switching parties. The assumption here is that such legislators are motivated above all else by "office" and the quest for what some scholars term "mega-seats."

A legislator may also switch parties for electoral purposes. In 2009, US Senator Arlen Spector, after 44 years as a Republican, left his party to become a Democrat. Accused of political opportunism to hold onto his seat, however, Spector failed to win the Democratic party nomination for his seat the following year. As Mershon (2014: 420) notes, "legislators exit parties that are likely to reduce their chances for re-election and favor parties likely to boost those chances." If true, a party that is losing support between elections (as measured, for example, in opinion polls), should be most susceptible to losing legislators to other parties or to independent status.

Of course, political institutions shape the degree to which party switching is feasible. Some constitutions require that a legislator resign their seat if they choose to switch parties, a rule that would presumably restrict the number of party switchers, all else equal. Other constitutions or standing orders might withhold legislative resources or prerogatives from members who leave (or get expelled from) their parties.

Regardless of its source, party cohesion—the degree to which members of a party share similar preferences—is one obvious source of voting unity (Ozbudun 1970). But a lack of party cohesion does not necessarily lead to low voting unity. The reason is party discipline. In the legislative context, the term discipline refers to the ability of party leaders to enforce party unity in voting, even to the extent that members will vote against their own preferences. In other words, discipline occurs when a legislator agrees to vote with her party against her personal preferences.

The level of observed party unity in any roll-call vote may be the combined result of party cohesion and party discipline. If cohesion is high, party discipline is less necessary to produce unified party voting. If cohesion is low, strong discipline may still yield the same result. On occasion, scholars and commentators will characterize legislative parties as highly disciplined or cohesive without carefully considering whether party unity is mainly due to one or the other of these factors. The truth is that we really only observe (where votes are public and recorded) the level of party voting unity. We can't normally directly observe levels of cohesion or levels of discipline.

One way to try to observe cohesion more directly is to focus on votes that are unwhipped. An unwhipped legislative division is a vote where party leaders do not instruct their members whether or how to vote. In some legislatures, for example, divisions related to matters of personal conscience are unwhipped. Observing members behavior on unwhipped votes provides us opportunity to observe the level of voting cohesion absent party discipline. The problem with such votes, however, is that they typically concern issues that are atypical and often matters of very personal beliefs, and that they are unwhipped precisely because there is no intra-party agreement. So a focus on unwhipped or unobserved votes could easily lead us to underestimate party cohesion (Hug 2010).

Typically though, scholars infer cohesion through such means as surveys of legislators to measure their ideological preferences. We can then map each legislative party's ideological spectrum. Scholars can also study the words of legislators, either in legislative debates or through other communication channels. In some legislatures, the German *Bundestag* for example, members can provide short speeches to explain their vote (Sieberer 2015). To assess the direct effect of discipline on voting we would ideally want to know the preferences of each member prior to or absent any application of partisan carrots or sticks. But such a measure is very difficult to get at, partly because so much of the pressure party leaders bring to bear on their members takes place behind closed doors and partly because so much of it is anticipated and therefore not actually observed.

Party leaders and Whips have a number of tools at their disposal to induce party unity. Indeed, these tools are central to our concept of a leaders' assembly. In his analysis of Westminster democracies, Christopher Kam (2009) distinguishes between three such mechanisms: (1) advancement, (2) discipline, and (3) socialization. Whereas we often think of the mechanisms by which party leaders induce unity in terms of "sticks" (negative sanctions), it is important to note that "carrots" such as advancement are often more common and effective. And whereas we might naively think of cohesion as a "natural" result of the self-selection of political candidates, it may in fact be brought about by successful socialization efforts by which the party leadership seeks to train and inform its activists and candidates.

Among the mechanisms of discipline and advancement are the power of party leaders to affect an incumbent's re-selection as a party candidate for the next legislative election, to otherwise assist or hinder with electioneering and campaigning, and the ability to act as gatekeepers over members' promotion from the legislative backbenches to positions of power within the legislature and in the executive (Strøm 1997; Kam 2009). If incumbent legislators wish to be re-elected, they must first get re-selected by their respective parties—in effect secure a position on the ballot, or under closed-list electoral systems as high a position as possible. Only once re-selection has been secured can the candidate focus on maximizing electoral support. The degree of control party leaders exert over the candidate re-selection process can vary. In some systems, local or national party leaders may need to endorse an incumbent who is seeking re-election. In other systems, incumbents have a right to be on the ballot as a party candidate. In yet other polities, such as Iceland or the United States, reselection may be decided by the voters in primary elections (Lundell 2004; Hazan and Rahat 2010).

Whether a legislator needs the permission of party leaders to run for re-election may have behavioral consequences for this member's willingness to vote against the party position. A rebel (someone voting against the party position) may be refused re-selection, or in the case of closed-list PR, be placed low on the party list so that re-election is unlikely. In essence, the more control the party leader exercises, the less likely individual legislators will be to diverge from their party in their legislative votes, resulting, all else equal, in a leaders' assembly. In contrast, where candidate selection is controlled by local party members or their local constituency organization, an incumbent is less beholden to the party leadership but may need to be more attuned to local issues and preferences. A leaders' assembly provides party leaders with the resources and capacity to enforce party discipline; a members' assembly in contrast, serves to "protect" individual members from the power and control of party leaders.

As noted in Chapter 3, one way to compare electoral systems is to examine the incentives they provide legislators to cultivate a personal vote (Carey and Shugart 1995). Incentives for a personal vote are typically assumed to reduce the incentive members have to vote the party line. In the US context, Cox and McCubbins (1993) argue that the ties that bind candidates' electoral fates together are responsible for party unity. These ties reflect their party's reputation based on the state of the economy, major pieces of legislation, and the reputation of the president. Legislators will more readily comply with party directives when an unfavorable party reputation might seriously damage their own electoral prospects. Furthermore, party unity will typically decrease as district magnitude increases (Depauw and Martin 2008). With higher district magnitude, the information demands on voters increase rapidly. Voters can hardly keep up with the voting records of multiple incumbents. In a similar vein, Shugart et al. (2005) argue that increased district magnitude reduces the number of candidates who have local roots or have served in local elected positions within the district—but only in closed-list systems. In "pure" open-list systems, larger district magnitude increases this number: as candidates hope to attract a personal vote, social distinctiveness becomes more important. This presents a problem as party unity might suffer when candidates try to gain credibility as spokespersons for distinctive constituencies. Ultimately, if a legislator needs to cultivate a personal vote to win re-election, she may occasionally need to be seen to vote against her party in the assembly.

Upward political ambition is often at the discretion of the party leader. In effect, party leaders can use the potential for promotion to cabinet (or other high rank) as a source of control over individual legislators.[3] The tight grip governments typically hold over the legislative agenda in parliamentary systems makes ministers the prime initiators of policies—to the virtual exclusion of all other legislators. While the practice of including only (or mainly) elected legislators in the cabinet varies from country to country, promotion to cabinet rank is mostly in the hands of party leaders, which provides a powerful incentive to ordinary assembly members not to dissent too often. The more opportunities exist for promotion and the more such promotions are controlled by the party leadership, the more legislators will be inclined to obey their party leaders. In a leaders' assembly the allocation of these mega seats (see Box 7.2) is cartelized in the party leadership—members wishing to be promoted need to be responsive to their party leadership.

In sum, in parliamentary systems legislators' progressive ambition, the perquisites of ministerial office, and the ability of party leaders to cartelize the allocation of these prized offices provide strong incentives for legislators to be loyal to their party leaders (Martin 2014). But what happens when legislators have competing goals, for example, when electoral incentives clash with enticements

---

[3] As Benedetto and Hix (2005) put it, rebels consist of the rejected, the ejected, and the dejected, a phrase evoking Prime Minister John Major's quip about the dispossessed and the never-possessed.

to win prized post-election positions? When party leaders cartelize the allocation of mega-seats (such as, committee chairs, the presiding officership and cabinet seats), the effects may be strong (united) legislative parties even under a candidate-centered electoral system.[4] Ireland represents a good example: highly disciplined parties within the legislative arena co-exist with a highly candidate-centered electoral system.

For some, the high levels of unified party voting in many legislatures lead to the conclusion that these assemblies have become little more than rubber-stamps. As Huber (1996: 280) notes, "scholars have devoted thousands of pages to parliamentary forms of government, and a good share of these pages have stressed the subordination of members of parliaments to leaders in governments." Modern parliaments are said to perform a mere "rubber-stamp" function, readily agreeing to the executive's legislative proposals. Under parliamentarism, the perception is that the executive does what it wants and gets the legislation it wants, particularly if it controls a majority of parliamentary seats. Of course, one of the aims of this book is to explore the degree to which legislative assemblies vary, including in the degree to which leaders control members and outcomes.

There are multiple explanations, sometimes complementary, sometimes competing, for why party hierarchy has emerged in parliamentary regimes especially. Amongst the most prominent is the concept of the *efficient secret*—the combination of executive and legislative leadership in the cabinet. For Bagehot (1867), the cabinet's control of both executive power and (*de facto*) legislative power in parliamentary regimes contrasts with the situation under presidentialism where the constitution priorities a separation of executive and legislative powers. As he (Bagehot 1867: 48) writes:

> The efficient secret of the English Constitution may be described as the close union, the nearly complete fusion, of the executive and legislative powers. No doubt by the traditional theory, as it exists in all the books, the goodness of our constitution consists in the entire separation of the legislative and executive authorities, but in truth its merit consists in their singular approximation.

But how did the cabinet come to obtain such significant influence in lawmaking? In a seminal contribution on the nineteenth-century British House of Commons, Gary Cox (1987) suggests that an increase in parliamentary business and in particular the volume of legislation arising from industrialization and modernization drove a change in the legislature's procedural rights. The "plenary bottleneck"

---

[4] There are many other "carrots" and "sticks" that party leaders can use to enforce party discipline. Folklore suggests that Party Whips at Westminster keep records—"little black books"—on each of their backbenchers' personal lives. Any indiscreet behavior—such as an affair, financial impropriety, or other possible scandal—can be used to encourage wayward members to toe the party line.

arising from greater volumes of legislation necessitated the erosion of the legislative powers of individual MPs—including the right to introduce bills, control the debate agenda, and make speeches. Such procedural prerogatives passed from individual MPs to the cabinet. Whereas Ostrogorski (1902) viewed the rise of party organizations following franchise extension as contributing to the rise of partisan voting among the electorate, Cox suggests that party-centered elections in Britain followed rather than caused the rise of party voting within the legislature.

Indeed, when contrasted with presidential systems, assemblies in parliamentary systems (see Chapter 11) tend to have higher levels of party voting unity (Sieberer 2006; Carey 2009; Depauw and Martin 2008; Kam 2009). For John Huber, one important source of legislative discipline in parliamentary systems is the vote of confidence procedure—"an institutional prerogative that permits the government to attach the vote on a specific policy or program to an up or down vote on the government" (Huber 1996: 269). The consequences of this procedure are significant but simple: A head of government can threaten to dissolve parliament (and call a new election) unless the assembly votes for the government's policies. What makes this threat credible is the vote of confidence procedure. Under parliamentarism, the government must resign if it loses a vote of confidence. As a consequence, the fate of the cabinet and the legislature can be tied directly to the fate of any of the cabinet's bills, if the cabinet so wishes. When a confidence vote has been introduced, dissenting members of the government's legislative coalition face a dire choice: support the government or cause the government's fall and possibly a general election, with all the personal and collective costs and risks associated with the latter. Ultimately, confidence vote procedures serve to strength assembly leaders at the expense of members, even if the former would be advised to use such procedures sparingly in order to produce short-term loyalty.

Samuels and Shugart (2010) argue that all systems with a directly elected and powerful head of state, including various forms of semi-presidentialism as well as presidentialism, tend to diminish party unity, as they weaken the electoral unity of purpose of governing parties. One factor that may contribute to this weakening of unity is that opportunities for progressive ambition in such systems will be less tightly controlled by the leaders of the assembly party. The president thus may have substantial influence over cabinet and other executive appointments.

But similar effects should be expected for other constitutional separations of power as well. Bicameralism, for example, will tend to reduce the control of the lower chamber party leaders over progressive ambition, especially when this bicameralism is symmetrical, meaning that the powers of the two chambers are roughly balanced. Some members of the lower chamber may then position themselves for election to the upper chamber, even when this means taking positions at odds with their party leaders in the chamber in which they currently serve. Presidential constitutions may similarly weaken party unity also because they feature other directly elected offices, for which assembly members may wish to compete. And federalism and other forms of decentralization (such as devolution in the United Kingdom) may mean the presence of attractive governorships, cabinet offices, or mayoral positions at the subnational level. Access to these offices can rarely be effectively controlled by the leaders of the party in the national assembly, and candidates for these offices may well need to appeal to a very different constituency from the one they faced as assembly members.

Thus, it is mainly in parliamentary and unitary states with a unicameral or asymmetrically bicameral national assembly, such as New Zealand, Ireland, or the Scandinavian democracies, that we would expect assembly party leaders to be able to use their control over opportunities for progressive ambition to cement party unity. But of course assembly party leaders may have other powers at their disposal as well, such as control of over committee assignments, legislative resources, or candidate selection procedures.

7.6 Conclusion

In this chapter, we have examined the most important organizations that operate within legislative assemblies: political parties. Parties are relatively modern organizations, and they are virtually ubiquitous in the contemporary world of legislatures. They are so common partly because they enable legislative assemblies to function more effectively. Many scholars also see them as critical to the democratic chain of delegation in that they allow for an orderly process of decision making that ordinary citizens can understand, influence, and sanction. Parties are also the vehicles by which the most powerful assembly leaders emerge and operate. The powers and functions of these leaders are therefore of critical importance for the democratic chain of delegation through elected legislators—allowing both capacity and accountability.

Legislative assemblies operate quite differently depending on the number of parties they contain. For democratic quality, it is thus not only the presence of parties that matters, but also their numbers. Assemblies that permit only one party to operate cannot be truly competitive and therefore also not truly democratic. Thus, none of the assemblies covered in this volume restricts representation to one party and in fact none of our assemblies features only one party. Assemblies dominated by two parties and the competition between them also tend to be different, and specifically more majoritarian in their operation, than assemblies that routinely harbor a large number of parties, none of which has a majority or is perpetually in control of the executive branch. These are differences that we shall explore in many other chapters in this book.

Most assemblies, and especially those operating under parliamentary democracy, exhibit high levels of party unity in voting. The members of most parties vote as a bloc in most legislative divisions. There are two main reasons for this partisan convergence: cohesion and discipline. Cohesion means that most members of the same parties have similar policy preferences and vote the same way for those reasons. Discipline means that within parties leaders have powers of reward and punishment that permit them to control the voting behavior of their respective members, regardless of the sincere policy preferences of these members. While political scientists have found ways of measuring the level of party unity in legislative voting, it is much more difficult to determine whether such unity results from cohesion or from discipline. It is highly plausible that observed unity results from both of these sources even though we often cannot separate them empirically.

Yet, as important and dominant as parties are, many legislatures operate with a goodly number of non-partisan members. Thus, while the world of party politics is in general well recognized and studied among students of legislative assemblies, there are still questions about party politics about which we need to know more. And the presence and influence of such independent members can be an important source of knowledge about the distribution of power within legislatures. If no assembly member can operate outside of political parties, it suggests that the power of party leaders is likely to be substantial. Where, in contrast, independent members can be numerous and successful, the discretion and power of ordinary members are likely to be greater.

References

Aldrich, John H. 1995. *Why Parties? The Origins and Transformation of Political Parties in America*. Chicago: The University of Chicago Press.

Bagehot, Walter. 1867. *The English Constitution*. London: Chapman & Hall.

Benedetto, Giacomo, and Simon Hix. 2005. "The Rejected, the Ejected, and the Dejected: Explaining Government Rebels in the 2001–2005 British House of Commons." *Comparative Political Studies* 40: 755–781.

Blais, André, 2016. "Is Duverger's Law Valid?" *French Politics* 14(1): 126–130.

Carey, John M. 2007. "Competing Principals, Political Institutions, and Party Unity in Legislative Voting." *American Journal of Political Science* 51(1): 92–107.

Carey, John M. 2009. *Legislative Voting and Accountability*. Cambridge: Cambridge University Press.

Carey, John M., and Matthew Soberg Shugart. 1995. "Incentives to Cultivate a Personal Vote: A Rank Ordering of Electoral Formulas." *Electoral Studies* 14: 417–439.

Cox, Gary W. 1987. *The Efficient Secret*. Cambridge: Cambridge University Press.

Cox, Gary W. and Mathew D. McCubbins. 1993. *Legislative Leviathan*. Cambridge: Cambridge University Press.

Cox, Gary W., and Mathew D. McCubbins. 2005. *Setting the Agenda: Responsible Party Government in the US House of Representatives*. Cambridge: Cambridge University Press.

Depauw, Sam, and Shane Martin 2008. "Legislative Party Discipline and Cohesion in Comparative Perspective." In Daniela Giannetti and Kenneth Benoit (eds.), *Intraparty Politics and Coalition Government*. London: Routledge, 119–136.

Downs, Anthony. 1957. *An Economic Theory of Democracy*. New York: Harper.

Duverger, Maurice. 1959. *Political Parties: Their Organization and Activity in the Modern State*. Second English Revised edn. London: Methuen & Co.

Hazan, Reuven Y., and Gideon Rahat. 2010. *Democracy within Parties: Candidate Selection Methods and Their Political Consequences*. Oxford: Oxford University Press.

Heidar, Knut, and Ruud A. Koole (eds.). 2003. *Parliamentary Party Groups in European Democracies*. London: Routledge.

Heller, William, and Carol Mershon (eds.). 2009. *Political Parties and Legislative Party Switching*. New York: Palgrave Macmillan.

Huber, John D. 1996. *Rationalizing Parliament*. Cambridge: Cambridge University Press.

Hug, Simon. 2010. "Selection Effects in Roll Call Votes." *British Journal of Political Science* 40(1): 225–235.

Kam, Christopher J. 2009. *Party Discipline and Parliamentary Politics*. New York: Cambridge University Press.

Key, V.O., Jr. 1964. *Politics, Parties, and Pressure Groups*. New York: Thomas Crowell.

Laakso, Markku, and Rein Taagepera. 1979. "'Effective' Number of Parties: A Measure with Application to West Europe." *Comparative Political Studies* 12: 3–27.

Lundell, Krister. 2004. "Determinants of Candidate Selection: The Degree of Centralization in Comparative Perspective." *Party Politics* 10(1): 25–47.

Martin, Shane. 2014. "Committees." In Shane Martin, Thomas Saalfeld, and Kaare W. Strøm (eds.), *The Oxford Handbook of Legislative Studies*. Oxford: Oxford University Press, 352–370.

May, John D., 1973. "Opinion Structure of Political Parties: The Special Law of Curvilinear Disparity." *Political Studies* 21(2): 135–151.

Mershon, Carol. 2014. "Legislative Party Switching." In Shane Martin, Thomas Saalfeld, and Kaare W. Strøm (eds.), *The Oxford Handbook of Legislative Studies*. Oxford, Oxford University Press, 418–435.

Müller, Wolfgang C. 2000. "Political Parties in Parliamentary Democracies: Making Delegation and Accountability Work." *European Journal of Political Research* 37(3): 309–333.

O'Brien, Diana Z., and Yael Shomer. 2013. "A Cross-National Analysis of Party Switching." *Legislative Studies Quarterly* 38(1): 111–141.

Ostrogorski, Moisei. 1902. *Democracy and the Organization of Political Parties*, 2 vols. New York: Macmillan.

Özbudun, Ergun, 1970. *Party Cohesion in Western Democracies: A Causal Analysis*. Beverly Hills: Sage.

Patel, Nandini, and Michael Wahman. 2015. "The Presidential, Parliamentary and Local Elections in Malawi, May 2014." *Africa Spectrum* 50(1): 79–92.

Porritt, Edward, and Annie G. Porritt. 1903. *The Unreformed House of Commons: Parliamentary Representation before 1832*. Cambridge: Cambridge University Press.

Quinn, Tom. 2016. "The British Labour Party's Leadership Election of 2015." *The British Journal of Politics and International Relations* 18(4): 759–778.

Rasch, Bjørn Erik 1995. "Parliamentary Voting Procedures." In Herbert Döring (ed.), *Parliaments and Majority Rule in Western Europe*. New York: St. Martin's, 488–527.

Rice, Stuart A. 1925. "The Behavior of Legislative Groups: A Method of Measurement." *Political Science Quarterly* 40(1): 60–72.

Richards, Peter G. 1972. *The Backbenchers*. London: Faber.

Robertson, David Bruce. 1976. *A Theory of Party Competition*. London: John Wiley.

Saalfeld, Thomas, and Kaare W. Strøm. 2014. "Political Parties and Legislators." In Shane Martin, Thomas Saalfeld, and Kaare W. Strøm (eds.), *The Oxford Handbook of Legislative Studies*. Oxford: Oxford University Press, 371–398.

Samuels, David, and Matthew S. Shugart. 2010. *Presidents, Parties, and Prime Ministers*. New York: Cambridge University Press.

Schattschneider, Elmer Eric. 1942. *Party Government*. New York: Rinehart.

Schlesinger, Joseph. 1966. *Ambition and Politics: Political Careers in the United States*. Chicago: Rand McNally.

Schlesinger, Joseph. 1991. *Political Parties and the Winning of Office*. Ann Arbor: University of Michigan Press.

Shugart, Matthew Søberg, Melody Ellis Valdini, and Kati Suominen. 2005. "Looking for Locals: Voter Information Demands and Personal Vote-Earning Attributes of Legislators under Proportional Representation." *American Journal of Political Science* 49: 437–449.

Sieberer, Ulrich. 2006. "Party Unity in Parliamentary Democracies." *Journal of Legislative Studies* 12: 150–178.

Sieberer, Ulrich. 2015. "Using MP Statements to Explain Voting Behaviour in the German Bundestag: An Individual Level Test of the Competing Principals Theory." *Party Politics* 21 (2): 284–294.

Strøm, Kaare. 1997. "Roles, Reasons, and Routines: Legislative Roles in Parliamentary Democracies." *Journal of Legislative Studies* 3: 155–174.

Ware, Alan. 1987. *Citizens, Parties, and the State*. Princeton: Princeton University Press.

Weeks, Liam, 2014. "Crashing the Party. Does STV Help Independents?" *Party Politics* 20(4): 604–616.

Weeks, Liam. 2015. "Parliaments without Parties." *Australasian Parliamentary Review* 30(1): 61–71.

8

Committees

Throughout this book we have been examining the various forms of legislative organization in contemporary democratic assemblies and asking whether—through the lenses of capacity and accountability—legislative assemblies serve the purposes of citizens, members, or leaders. Alongside legislative parties, committees are frequently cited as amongst the most important internal organizational features of a legislative assembly. The Oxford English Dictionary defines a committee as "a group of people appointed for a specific function by a larger group and typically consisting of members of that group."[1] Mattson and Strøm (1995: 249) define a legislative committee as "a subgroup of legislators, normally entrusted with specific organizational tasks." Committees are not a necessary feature of legislative organization, yet they are a ubiquitous part of today's democratic assemblies. Legislative assemblies could in principle conduct their work exclusively in the plenary body—where all members of the chamber have a seat. However, none of the ones covered in this volume do. Alternatively, a legislative assembly could in theory perform all its functions through a system of committees, in which such subgroups were authorized to make final policy decisions, although we know of no such case, either. In the real world of contemporary democratic legislatures, committees play a partial, but important, role.

Committees exist in substantial part to enhance legislative capacity. As noted in Chapter 1, the challenge of capacity has to do with the assembly's ability to enact effective policies and to select policy instruments that serve these goals efficiently. And as we have also noted, hierarchy and differentiation are two organizational features that are often employed for this purpose. Whereas legislative parties manifest the development of hierarchy within legislative assemblies, committees are typically viewed as vehicles of differentiation and specialization. This is especially the case when these committees are made permanent and given specific policy jurisdictions and memberships that are effectively fixed for the entire legislative term.[2] We believe that, all else equal, a system of permanent and specialized committees enhances the capacity of that legislative assembly to the benefit of members and citizens and sometimes to the detriment of leaders. Committees can enhance the legislative assembly's capacity vis-à-vis the executive through specialization

---

[1] https://en.oxforddictionaries.com/definition/committee.
[2] But as we shall see, it is also possible to see committees as another aspect of hierarchy, one that might even work hand in hand with the way that political parties structure the legislative process of deliberation and lawmaking.

Legislative Assemblies. Shane Martin and Kaare W. Strøm, Oxford University Press.
© Shane Martin and Kaare W. Strøm (2023). DOI: 10.1093/oso/9780198890829.003.0008

and gains from trade. In this sense, committees allow for a division-of-labor that enhances the productivity of the chamber as a whole. A system of committees may also benefit *individual* incumbent members by meeting their electoral, representational, or policy-making needs. To the extent that they permit members to serve the needs of their particular constituents, committees may benefit ordinary citizens as well. From this perspective we expect a voters' assembly and a members' assembly both to have a well-developed system of committees. In contrast, we would expect a leader-centered assembly to feature a more centralized policy process with less deference to committees, since backbenchers might otherwise use their committee assignments to develop policy agendas that could conflict with those of their leaders. Yet, as we shall see, at least one existing theory recognizes that committees may alternatively (or additionally) serve the needs of party leaders. From our perspective, however, a critical function of committees is that they provide alternative and specialized loci of power suited to the interests of ordinary members. Thus, how a legislature organizes its committee system provides important insights into whether an assembly is designed primarily to serve the interests of voters, its members, or the party leaders.

Our main task in this chapter is to describe the primary contours and variation in how real-world legislative committees are designed and relate such organizational design to our concepts of voters', members', and leaders' assemblies. Formal structures and powers define a legislative assembly's committee system. Our focus will be on the number of committees, their membership, and their powers. This will help identify the degree to which committees play a significant role in the life of a legislative assembly. It will also aid our understanding of whom, if anyone, this legislative organization privileges, and how.

Having described the components of a legislative committee system, our second objective is to understand variation in their structure across different assemblies. Why do some countries have a small number of committees with broad jurisdictions, whereas others feature many committees with much more specialized remits? Why do individual members in some assemblies serve on several different committees, whereas in other legislatures some members get no committee assignment at all? Why do committees dominate decision making in some legislative assemblies, whereas in others they rarely alter the bills they consider?

We begin, however, by discussing why a legislative assembly would create and empower a system of committees. This may seem like an obvious question with a self-evident answer. Yet, we should at least consider the possibility that legislatures might function without such subunits. And at the very least the historical record includes cases in which constitutional "engineers" have deliberately sought to reduce the importance and powers of legislative committees. The scholarly literature on committees has offered competing explanations of why committees have been such a popular form of legislative organization. This chapter therefore begins with a review of the four most prominent explanations.

8.1 Why Committees?

Students of legislatures have long sought to understand why a legislative assembly would delegate certain powers or functions to a system of committees. Here we discuss four of the leading explanations: the informational theory of committees, the distributive theory, the cartel-party theory, and the bicameral-conflict theory. In addition to providing insights into the roles and functions of committees, these theories also serve to illuminate more general issues of legislative organization which interest us in this book: how legislatures are designed to meet the, sometimes competing, interests of citizens, members and/or party leaders.

The Informational Perspective and Efficiency

The political roles and functions of a legislative assembly—from the appointment or confirmation of executive office holders, through citizen representation, constituency service, lawmaking, and budgeting, to executive oversight—are a complex and time-consuming business. Legislators have only so many hours in the day and balancing their legislative and extra-legislative roles is demanding. Performing well in these various roles is perhaps even more challenging when the legislature confronts a larger and better-resourced executive with much greater staff and research capacity.

Creating subunits within the legislature and delegating authority away from the plenary allows for the effective and efficient use of members' time. This organizational advantage of committees applies not only to legislatures; any organization can benefit from creating subunits that allow members to specialize and that permit multiple tasks to be done simultaneously. Consequently, a system of committees can dramatically increase an assembly's workload capacity. As Cox (2006) notes, plenary bottlenecks arise when the demand for legislation exceeds the assembly's capacity to find sufficient plenary time to consider all the proposals before it. Assemblies may face a bottleneck exactly because plenary time is limited (by practical time constraints or by members' ability to attend). Plenary bottlenecks can be overcome by delegating plenary authority, for example to a part of the executive (allowing ministers to issue decrees or giving them broad powers of implementation) or to committees within the legislative assembly. The latter option allows the assembly to retain stronger control of the policy process and is therefore less susceptible to agency loss. A system of committees allows the members to work simultaneously on different responsibilities—from proposed legislation in specific policy areas to executive oversight. Individual committees can probe more deeply into issues than can the plenary, while in most cases ultimately reporting back to the "floor." This way, a system of committees can exponentially increase the feasible overall legislative workload and output and through specialization and division of labor allow members to differentiate themselves and play identifiable roles. Thus, legislative organization that places committees at the heart of the chamber's work and allows ordinary members opportunities for influence and exposure would correspond closely with our notion of a members' assembly.

Yet, it is important to remember that committees (as any academic will tell you) come at a cost! A system of committees requires legislators to join committees and engage in committee work. And even if committees allow the assembly to get more work done, it is not necessarily the case that individual legislators will want to have committee responsibilities. Committee work can be time-consuming for members who may wish to focus their attention elsewhere—for example within their legislative party or in their electoral constituency. Getting members to perform such tasks can also become a collective action problem; all members know that their assembly is better off if the committee work gets done, but every member may hope that someone else will do the job.

Gilligan and Krehbiel (1987) suggest an informational rationale for committees in the US Congress and explain how this legislature overcomes its collective action problem with respect to committee work. These authors argue that committees provide a mechanism by which legislators can focus and specialize in particular policy areas. Therefore, committees do not just allow more work to be done, through specialization they also allow committee members to accumulate informational advantages and tacit knowledge resulting in better legislation, which benefits the entire chamber. Thus, committee service provides policy expertise that functions as a collective good for all members of the chamber. In return for developing such specialist knowledge, members—through committee service—are granted certain decision-making prerogatives in their respective policy jurisdictions, which they can use to claim credit for policies in these areas. Members are thus incentivized to specialize and undertake committee work because it gives them certain privileges in their chosen policy domain.

From the informational perspective, committees will be given the greatest discretion when they are a microcosm of the policy preferences of the parent chamber. Such policy congruence between the committee and the chamber, coupled with the opportunity to develop specialized knowledge, ensures that the committee will act in the best interest of the chamber. Thus, appointments of members to committees should serve not to facilitate constituents' particular interests but rather to maximize members' personal expertise and knowledge.

The informational efficiency perspective also associates clearly with our concept of a voters' assembly. By allowing members to specialize, and by ensuring that the composition of the standing committee reflects the composition of the chamber, committees can make better informed decisions that serve the interests of the citizens as well as members. Specialized committees can make well-informed decisions and help legislators choose policy instruments that serve their purposes effectively and cost-efficiently. Creating specialized committees thus allows the legislative chamber to perform its roles and functions more effectively and efficiently. And whatever specific policy goals citizens have, we assume that in their government institutions they prefer efficiency over waste.

The Distributive Perspective

The distributive theory gains its designation from the suggestion that committees exist to allow committee members to distribute benefits to their constituents. Benefits could include specific policies favored by voters in the member's district or so-called pork-barrel projects—initiatives that are geographically targeted and locally beneficial though in a broader context often wasteful. To understand the distributive theory of legislative organizations, we need to begin with the assumption that legislators are self-interested and that their primary motivation is to be re-elected (Mayhew 1974). In order to win re-election, members seek to build personal reputations (a personal vote) among their respective constituents by providing benefits to the constituency and by aligning their policy concerns with those of their voters (Fenno 1978). Legislators will also seek to pass locally favored legislation for which they can claim credit, and what gets them such credit will obviously vary from district to district. For example, voters in a Michigan district that is home to various automobile industry suppliers may have different policy concerns from voters in rural Kansas or in New York City. While New York City constituents may emphasize issues concerning public transport or the environment, the concerns of Michigan voters may center on protecting domestic manufacturing, whereas Kansas voters may prefer policies that promote agriculture or build rural infrastructure. To be re-elected, incumbents must adopt policies most salient to their constituents, control public policy, and allocate scarce resources to sectors (for examples through subsidies—see Rickard 2018) that enhance their credentials with voters.

Yet, in a plenary-centered legislature in which policy is enacted by simple majority vote, all legislators are equal in their ability to influence all proposals. Thus, unless representatives from rural areas control a majority of the plenary, they cannot control and claim credit for agricultural policy. Moreover, given the existence of multiple salient policy issues, it is unlikely that any one interest can maintain control of the plenary agenda very long.

Shepsle and Weingast (1981) view committees as an institutional solution to these problems by compartmentalizing policy making such that members with particular policy interests are able to control their respective policy areas. The price each of the members of these policy communities pays is to relinquish control in policy domains about which they care less. Thus, representatives from agricultural districts will seek to control agricultural committees with influence over farm policies—effectively shifting power from the plenary to those members who have the most to gain or lose in that policy area. Likewise, representatives from districts that value urban housing or support for local military communities will seek to dominate committees that control those policy areas. Put slightly differently, committees prevent the breakdown of cooperation among groups with different policy priorities by dividing up policy responsibility by the intensity of policy concern (Weingast and Marshall 1988). On the motivations that drive members to look for such solutions, Katz and Sala (1996) note that the emergence of the candidate-centered ballot in US elections created the need for legislators to claim credit among their constituents.

This distributive perspective relies on a number of assumptions. First, committees must have the ability to control the policy agenda and thereby the policy outcomes within their respective policy jurisdictions—commonly known as "gate-keeping powers." The plenary, thus, must delegate significant authority to committees, making them veto players in policy making and oversight. Second, members must be able to self-select into their preferred committees (Shepsle 1978). Third, and relatedly, committees should predominantly be composed of "policy outliers" (Shepsle and Weingast 1987). In other words, in their respective policy areas, committees will not represent the median policy position in the assembly but instead overrepresent members with extreme policy preferences (typically "high demanders"). Thus, an agricultural committee will consist mostly of members committed to supporting farming and ranching, with few members from urban districts preferring to keep food cheap or its contents rigidly regulated. As such, the committee will be unrepresentative of the chamber. Crucially, the policies emanating from the legislative assembly will then poorly represent the views of the assembly majority—precisely because each committee consists of policy outliers and controls the agenda in its policy area.

The distributive perspective arguably associates with a members' assembly. The legislature is organized around a system of committees which permit incumbents to tailor policies and fiscal transfers to the preferences of their constituents. And by benefitting constituents, committees ultimately help incumbent legislators build their reputation among their own voters, thus enhancing their popularity and likelihood of re-election.

The Cartel Party Perspective

Cox and McCubbins (1993, 2005) suggest that that the aforementioned perspectives on Congressional committees both miss an important element: that political parties play a crucial role in shaping the committee system and its effects. In their view, the committee system, far from being the focal point of power in the US Congress, is a structure created to allow parties to influence members' behavior. In Cox and McCubbins' model of a partisan cartel, committees are not the dominant source of policy influence that traditional accounts of congressional organization suggest.

One way in which these authors question the distributive perspective concerns the process by which members get assigned to committees. Party leaders, Cox and McCubbins suggest, play a far more significant role in the assignment process than previously acknowledged, especially when parties are cohesive. Members of the US Congress are not always assigned to their most preferred committees. Instead, party leaders control the allocation of assignments and use them strategically to reward loyal partisans and punish members who have defied the leadership on roll-call votes. Cox and McCubbins find a similar pattern of control in cases where legislators request to be reassigned to a different committee. In short, their argument is that focusing on the power of congressional committees obscures the fact that parties control who serves on which committee.

This partisan control shapes not only the composition of the committees, but also by extension their policy profiles. The correct view of internal assembly decision making may not be one of committees versus parties, but of party leaders carefully managing committees. Cox and McCubbins (1993) uncover significant evidence of partisanship, which, they suggest, confirms the role and impact of party leaders. For example, bill sponsorship aligns along partisan divisions. Thus, legislative committees are not alternatives to assembly parties but instead reflect the predominance of party. And the most important means by which party leaders dominate the policy process is their power to set the agenda through such bodies as the Rules Committee in the US House of Representatives (Cox and McCubbins 2005). Compared to the model of a "committee-centered Congress," the cartel party theory interprets decision making in the US Congress as more similar to parliamentarism, in which scholars have long understood parties, and not committees, as the central organizational structure. And in the broader sense that Chapter 1 discusses legislative assemblies, the party cartel theory is most compatible with our concept of a leaders' assembly. Yet, as noted in the introduction to this chapter, we see a system of specialized and permanent committees as the internal assembly structure most capable of competing with the powers and resources of the party leadership. This is not to reject Cox and McCubbins' (1993) thesis that parties may significantly control committees even under US presidentialism, but to argue that within a legislative assembly committees are the most likely locus for any opposition to party control of policy influence and resource-allocation rights. Ultimately therefore, the cartel party theory notwithstanding, we expect leader-centered legislatures to be the least likely to have strong and independent committee systems.

The Bicameral Rivalry Perspective

The foundation for the fourth model of committees again arises from the US Congressional context and assumes that committees are institutional vehicles by which members seek to attain their goals. In the bicameral-rivalry theory, however, the proximate goal of legislators is neither re-election nor policy influence, but the maximization of political rents in the form of payments by lobbyists. Committees are thus understood as mechanisms by which members extract payments from lobbyists. And the designation bicameral-rivalry theory derives from the argument that success in this endeavor depends on whether the legislature consists of one or two chambers (Groseclose and King 2001).

Diermeier and Myerson (1999) suggest that cameral structure (whether the assembly has a single or multiple chambers) shapes the incentives to establish committees as a core organizational feature. Diermeier and Myerson's model relies on a vote-buying perspective in which lobbyists use bribes to influence legislative outcomes. In this game, legislators desire to maximize their monetary payoffs, and under bicameralism they do so by creating within each chamber institutional hurdles, such as within-chamber veto points and supermajority requirements. Their purpose is effectively to extract payments from interested parties seeking favors and their lobbyists. And payments increase in the number of veto points in the chamber. Thus, if one chamber has such hurdles and the second not, members of the first chamber will extract disproportionately more "bribes" (or campaign contributions) from lobbyists. In equilibrium, both chambers should maximize their hurdles in order to the largest possible share of bribes. A strong committee system with delegated authority is arguably an obvious way for a chamber to create a significant internal hurdle. Committees can thus serve as an internal veto gate to maximize the monetary returns that incumbents can derive from lobbyists seeking preferential legislation.

Many—ourselves included—would question the assumption that legislators in democratic countries generally design the internal organization of their chamber to maximize monetary payments from lobbyists. However, as Groseclose and King (2001) astutely observe, it is possible to retain the Diermeier and Myerson (1999) model and its predictions while replacing bribes as the core motivation of legislators with "power" or "policy influence." From this perspective, chambers in a bicameral system compete for policy-making influence by manipulating their internal structure and process. In such circumstances, the approach suggested by Diermeier and Myerson (1999) would yield exactly the same expectations: a chamber in competition with another chamber for policy influence would create internal hurdles to maximize influence. Committees, apparently, are ideal internal hurdles.

The bicameral-rivalry theory marries elements from our notion of a members' assembly with those of a leaders' assembly. With the distributive model, it shares the assumption that the policy-making process is driven by the incentives of individual legislators. At the same time, it relies, like the party cartel model, on the assumption that political leaders (here: cameral rather than partisan) are able to design and police forms of legislative organization that serve their own purposes as well as those of ordinary members.

Ultimately, each of the four perspectives represents a stylized abstraction from reality which is not likely to fully explain the emergence and operation of legislative committees. Three theories (the efficiency/informational, the distributive and the bicameral rivalry) stress the legislator as the central unit of analysis, discounting, if not entirely ignoring the role of political parties in shaping legislative organization. In contrast, the cartel party model reminds us that legislative parties often play a dominant role in shaping the ways in which legislative assemblies work. And in a different way, the informational perspective stands out by being the only one that focuses on information uncertainty and incentives to produce *better* public policy and hold the executive to account more effectively.

8.2 Comparing Committee Systems

Having surveyed the major theoretical accounts of legislative committees and how these relates to our typology of legislative assemblies, we now turn our attention to the characteristics of committee systems in our 68 democratic assemblies. Our focus in this chapter is on what we call substantive permanent committees. By substantive we mean that the committee is encharged with policy deliberation, rather than for example primarily administrative or housekeeping functions. By permanent we mean that the committee exists for at least the length of the legislative term (for example until the chamber is dissolved ahead of a legislative election). Substantive legislative committees fall into three general categories: (1) ad hoc committees, appointed for a limited time to deliberate on a specific policy issue, typically a bill; (2) functional committees, whose jurisdictions are defined by specific constitutional functions of the legislature, such as budgeting, lawmaking, executive oversight, constitutional deliberation, etc.; and (3) committees defined by policy area, such as education, defense, or transport, often corresponding to the jurisdictions of the various ministerial departments in that country. Cross-nationally ad hoc committees are much less common than categories 2 and 3. Over time, there also has been a trend for national assemblies to replace functional committees (category 2) with policy-based ones (category 3).

Our focus in this chapter is not on ad hoc committees—created for a limited time with a highly specific remit—or on housekeeping committees—which serve an administrative role in the running of the legislative assembly but not in policy deliberation. We will also ignore more informal committees that are sometimes formed by members with similar social backgrounds or interests, such as members of ethnic or religious minorities, members interested in opera or amateur theatre, or members interested in policy issues such as disarmament or child poverty. This is not to say that such committees are unimportant. For example, housekeeping committees can be procedurally important—determining the rules for the passage of a bill—as in the US Congress.

Each of the 68 legislatures in our study has a system of substantive permanent committees. In other words, no legislature in our study is without at least one substantive permanent committee. Yet, this ubiquity of committees could hide significant variation in how committees are organized and what formal roles they play. Table 8.1 reports data on committee structures for each country in our study. Our description of legislative committees focuses on three core features: (1) the number of committees, (2) committee appointments, and (3) the powers and capacity of committees. Together, these features indicate how central committees are to the functioning of a legislative assembly, and, as noted above, they help determine where power and influence resides—whether it is decentralized to individual members or more centralized, with the party leadership wielding significant influence and whether committee structures serve the interest of voters, members, or leaders.

The Number of Committees

Once it has been decided to create a system of assembly committees, a series of questions need to be considered. One of the most basic ones relates to the number of such committees. The number of assembly committees matters for several reasons: too few committees mean that the possible advantages of committees—including allowing members specialize and allowing a range of topics and proposed legislation be considered simultaneously by the legislative assembly—are diluted. On the other hand, while a large number of committees helps the assembly deal with many specialized tasks simultaneously and may give each member multiple avenues of influence, too many committees may also result in legislators being overburdened with committee work. Thus, there is likely some tradeoff between maximizing the assembly's effectiveness and productivity and burdening members with unreasonable workloads. Yet, for the assembly's overall effectiveness, more committees is generally better. Thus, Martin and Vanberg (2011: 49) find that the overall number of permanent committees is the single indicator most closely related to their measure of legislative policing strength—the ability of legislators to scrutinize and amend legislative proposals introduced by the executive. We therefore expect that a member-centered or citizen-centered assembly will have relatively more committees than a leader's assembly.

How does the number of permanent (or standing) committees vary across the legislatures of the democratic world? We count a total of 1418 such substantive

Table 8.1 Committee system structures

Country	No of Committees	Member/ Committee Ratio	Multiple Member-ship?	At Least One Mem-bership?	Committee Membership Tenure	Committee Chair Control	Committee-Ministry Congruence	Legislative Process?	Budgetary Process?
Argentina	45	5.7	Yes	Yes	Entire Term	All Majority Chairs	Mostly Congruent	Yes	Budgetary Committee (Only)
Australia	15	10.0	Yes	Yes	Entire Term	All Majority Chairs	Mostly Congruent	No	Portfolio Committee
Austria	38	4.8	Yes	Yes	Entire Term	Some "Opposition" Chairs	Mostly Congruent	Yes	Budgetary Committee (Only)
Belgium	11	13.6	No	Yes	Entire Term	All Majority Chairs	Mostly Congruent	Yes	Budgetary Committee (Only)
Benin	5	16.6	No	Yes	Entire Term	Some "Opposition" Chairs	Mostly Congruent	Yes	Budgetary Committee (Only)
Bolivia	12	10.8	No	Yes	Not Entire Term	Some "Opposition" Chairs	Mostly Congruent	Yes	Portfolio Committee
Brazil	20	25.7	No	Yes	Entire Term	All Majority Chairs	Mostly Congruent	Yes	Budgetary Committee (Only)

Bulgaria	20	12.0	Yes	Yes	Entire Term	All Majority Chairs	Mostly Congruent	Yes	Budgetary Committee (Only)
Burundi	8	15.1	No	Yes	Entire Term	Some "Opposition" Chairs	Mostly Congruent	Yes	Budgetary Committee (Only)
Canada	24	14.1	Yes	Yes	Entire Term	Some "Opposition" Chairs	Mostly Congruent	Yes	Budgetary Committee (Only)
Chile	18	6.7	Yes	No	Entire Term	Some "Opposition" Chairs	Mostly Congruent	Yes	Budgetary Committee (Only)
Colombia	7	23.7	No	Yes	Entire Term	Some "Opposition" Chairs	Strongly Congruent	Yes	Budgetary Committee (Only)
Costa Rica	6	9.5	No	Yes	Entire Term	All Majority Chairs	Mostly Congruent	No	Budgetary Committee (Only)
Croatia	29	5.2	Yes	Yes	Entire Term	All Majority Chairs	Mostly Congruent	Yes	Budgetary Committee (Only)

Continued

Table 8.1 *Continued*

Country	No of Committees	Member/ Committee Ratio	Multiple Member- ship?	At Least One Mem- bership?	Committee Membership Tenure	Committee Chair Control	Committee- Ministry Congruence	Legislative Process?	Budgetary Process?
Czech Republic	7	28.6	Yes	Yes	Entire Term	Some "Opposition" Chairs	Mostly Congruent	Yes	Budgetary Committee (Only)
Denmark	26	6.9	Yes	Yes	Entire Term	All Majority Chairs	Mostly Congruent	Yes	Budgetary Committee (Only)
Dominican Republic	39	4.9	Yes	Yes	Not Entire Term	Some "Opposition" Chairs	Mostly Congruent	Yes	Budgetary + Portfolio
Ecuador	13	10.5	No	Yes	Entire Term	Some "Opposition" Chairs	Mostly Congruent	Yes	Budgetary Committee (Only)
El Salvador	20	4.2	No	Yes	Entire Term	All Majority Chairs	Mostly Congruent	Yes	Budgetary Committee (Only)
Finland	16	12.5	Yes	Yes	Entire Term	All Majority Chairs	Strongly Congruent	Yes	Budgetary + Portfolio
France	8	72.1	No	Yes	Entire Term	Some "Opposition" Chairs	Strongly Congruent	Yes	Budgetary Committee (Only)
Germany	23	27.4	No	Yes	Entire Term	Some "Opposition" Chairs	Strongly Congruent	Yes	Budgetary Committee (Only)

Ghana	15	18.3	Yes	Yes	Entire Term	All Majority Chairs	Mostly Congruent	Yes	Budgetary Committee (Only)
Greece	6	50.0	No	Yes	Entire Term	Some "Opposition" Chairs	Strongly Congruent	Yes	Budgetary Committee (Only)
Guatemala	33	4.8	Yes	Yes	Entire Term	All Majority Chairs	Mostly Congruent	Yes	Budgetary Committee (Only)
Honduras	29	4.4	Yes	Yes	Entire Term	Some "Opposition" Chairs	Mostly Congruent	Yes	Budgetary Committee (Only)
Hungary	14	14.2	No	No	Entire Term	Some "Opposition" Chairs	Mostly Congruent	Yes	Budgetary Committee (Only)
India	40	13.6	Yes	Yes	Not Entire Term	Some "Opposition" Chairs	Mostly Congruent	Yes	Budgetary Committee (Only)
Indonesia	17	32.9	Yes	Yes	Entire Term	Some "Opposition" Chairs	Mostly Congruent	Yes	Budgetary Committee (Only)
Ireland	19	8.3	Yes	Yes	Entire Term	Some "Opposition" Chairs	Mostly Congruent	Yes	No Involvement

Continued

Table 8.1 Continued

Country	No of Committees	Member/ Committee Ratio	Multiple Member- ship?	At Least One Mem- bership?	Committee Membership Tenure	Committee Chair Control	Committee- Ministry Congruence	Legislative Process?	Budgetary Process?
Israel	12	10.0	Yes	Yes	Entire Term	Some "Opposition" Chairs	Mostly Congruent	Yes	Budgetary Committee (Only)
Italy	14	45.0	No	Yes	Entire Term	All Majority Chairs	Strongly Congruent	Yes	Budgetary Committee (Only)
Japan	17	27.9	Yes	Yes	Entire Term	All Majority Chairs	Mostly Congruent	Yes	Budgetary Committee (Only)
Kenya	12	29.2	Yes	Yes	Entire Term	Some "Opposition" Chairs	Mostly Congruent	Yes	Budgetary Committee (Only)
Liberia	33	2.2	Yes	Yes	Entire Term	Some "Opposition" Chairs	Mostly Congruent	Yes	Budgetary Committee (Only)
Malawi	16	12.1	No	Yes	Entire Term	Some "Opposition" Chairs	Mostly Congruent	Yes	Budgetary Committee (Only)
Mexico	52	9.6	Yes	Yes	Entire Term	All Majority Chairs	Mostly Congruent	Yes	Budgetary Committee (Only)
Nepal	14	42.9	No	No	Entire Term	Some "Opposition" Chairs	Mostly Congruent	Yes	Budgetary + Portfolio

Country									
Netherlands	14	10.7	Yes	Yes	Entire Term	Some "Opposition" Chairs	Mostly Congruent	Yes	Budgetary Committee (Only)
New Zealand	18	6.7	No	Yes	Entire Term	Some "Opposition" Chairs	Mostly Congruent	Yes	Portfolio Committee
Nicaragua	18	5.1	Yes	Yes	Entire Term	Some "Opposition" Chairs	Mostly Congruent	Yes	Budgetary Committee (Only)
Niger	8	21.4	Missing	Yes	Entire Term	Missing	Missing	Yes	Budgetary + Portfolio
Nigeria	84	4.3	Yes	Yes	Entire Term	All Majority Chairs	Mostly Congruent	Yes	Budgetary Committee (Only)
Norway	12	14.1	No	Yes	Entire Term	Some "Opposition" Chairs	Mostly Congruent	Yes	Budgetary Committee (Only)
Pakistan	32	10.7	Yes	Yes	Entire Term	Some "Opposition" Chairs	Strongly Congruent	Yes	Budgetary Committee (Only)
Papua N.Guinea	11	10.1	No	Yes	Entire Term	All Majority Chairs	Mostly Congruent	Yes	Budgetary Committee (Only)

Continued

Table 8.1 *Continued*

Country	No of Committees	Member/ Committee Ratio	Multiple Member- ship?	At Least One Mem- bership?	Committee Membership Tenure	Committee Chair Control	Committee- Ministry Congruence	Legislative Process?	Budgetary Process?
Paraguay	30	2.7	Yes	Yes	Entire Term	Some "Opposition" Chairs	Mostly Congruent	Yes	Budgetary Committee (Only)
Peru	24	5.4	Yes	Yes	Entire Term	Some "Opposition" Chairs	Mostly Congruent	Yes	Budgetary Committee (Only)
Philippines	58	5.1	Yes	Yes	Entire Term	Some "Opposition" Chairs	Mostly Congruent	Yes	Budgetary + Portfolio
Poland	25	18.4	Yes	Yes	Entire Term	Some "Opposition" Chairs	Mostly Congruent	Yes	Budgetary Committee (Only)
Portugal	12	19.2	Yes	Yes	Entire Term	Some "Opposition" Chairs	Mostly Congruent	Yes	Budgetary Committee (Only)
Romania	14	29.4	No	Yes	Not Entire Term	Some "Opposition" Chairs	Mostly Congruent	Yes	Budgetary Committee (Only)
Senegal	11	13.6	Yes	Yes	Entire Term	All Majority Chairs	Mostly Congruent	Yes	Budgetary Committee (Only)
Serbia	20	12.5	Yes	Yes	Entire Term	Some "Opposition" Chairs	Mostly Congruent	Yes	Budgetary Committee (Only)

Country									
Sierra Leone	26	4.8	Yes	Yes	Entire Term	Some "Opposition" Chairs	Mostly Congruent	Yes	Budgetary Committee (Only)
Slovak Republik	16	9.4	Yes	Yes	Entire Term	Some "Opposition" Chairs	Mostly Congruent	Yes	Budgetary Committee (Only)
South Africa	37	10.8	No	Yes	Entire Term	All Majority Chairs	Mostly Congruent	Yes	Budgetary Committee (Only)
South Korea	16	18.8	Yes	Yes	Entire Term	All Majority Chairs	Mostly Congruent	Yes	Budgetary Committee (Only)
Spain	17	20.6	Yes	Yes	Entire Term	Some "Opposition" Chairs	Mostly Congruent	Yes	Budgetary Committee (Only)
Sweden	15	23.3	No	No	Entire Term	Some "Opposition" Chairs	Mostly Congruent	Yes	Budgetary Committee (Only)
Switzerland	9	22.2	No	Yes	Entire Term	All Majority Chairs	Mostly Congruent	Yes	Budgetary Committee (Only)
Taiwan	8	14.1	No	Yes	Not Entire Term	Some "Opposition" Chairs	Mostly Congruent	Yes	Budgetary Committee (Only)

Continued

Table 8.1 *Continued*

Country	No of Committees	Member/ Committee Ratio	Multiple Member- ship?	At Least One Mem- bership?	Committee Membership Tenure	Committee Chair Control	Committee- Ministry Congruence	Legislative Process?	Budgetary Process?
Tunisia	9	24.1	Yes	No	Entire Term	Some "Opposition" Chairs	Mostly Congruent	Yes	Budgetary Committee (Only)
Turkey	18	30.6	No	No	Not Entire Term	All Majority Chairs	Mostly Congruent	Yes	Budgetary Committee (Only)
Ukraine	27	16.7	No	No	Entire Term	All Majority Chairs	Mostly Congruent	Yes	Budgetary Committee (Only)
United Kingdom	38	17.1	Yes	Yes	Entire Term	Some "Opposition" Chairs	Mostly Congruent	No	Budgetary Committee (Only)
United States	20	21.8	Yes	Yes	Entire Term	All Majority Chairs	Mostly Congruent	Yes	Budgetary Committee (Only)
Zambia	18	9.3	No	No	Entire Term	Some "Opposition" Chairs	Mostly Congruent	Yes	Budgetary Committee (Only)

committees across our 68 democratic assemblies. This means that the mean (average) number of legislative committees is 20.8. However significant variation in the number of committee exists between legislative assemblies, as the variable *No. of Committees* in table 8.1 demonstrates. Benin's *Assemblée Nationale* has just five committees, followed by the Costa Rican and Greek cases, each with six committees. At the other end of the scale, the Nigerian House of Representatives has 84 committees (see Box 8.1).

Box 8.1 Legislative Committees in Nigeria

The legislative assembly in our dataset with the largest number of parliamentary committees is the Nigerian House of Representatives. With 84 permanent committees it has significantly more such subunits than any other national legislatures. Indeed, the number has increased further since 2015, with Siefken and Rommetvedt (2021: 14) reporting a rise to 109 at the most recent count. This latest increase reflects a pattern since 1999 of increasing the number of committees for each parliamentary term. Thus, during the 1999–2003 session (the first under the Fourth Republic Constitution) the House of Representatives had only 45 committees.

What explains the number and the expansion in the number of committees in Nigeria? Regarding the formal rules concerning committees, it is worth noting that Section 62(1) of the 1999 Nigerian Constitution explicitly allows each chamber to set up as many committees as it wishes. In a mixed review of the role and performance of Nigeria's parliamentary committees, Ekeyi (2021: 210) cites the increased complexity of governance, the heavy workload of existing committees, and a need to avoid jurisdictional conflict and overlap between committees as explanations for the increased number of committees.

Other motivations may also be at play. Agunyai and Ojakorotu (2021: 97) suggest that "political corruption among parliamentary committee members aggravates constituency woes and impedes socio-economic development in Nigeria" and suggest that committees are an avenue by which many legislators engage in corruption and graft—often to help "recoup the money spent to win their seats" (Agunyai and Ojakorotu 2021: 114). Nwozor and Olanrewaju 2019: 176) argue that "[m]ost of the scandals involving the National Assembly originated from the operations of its committees," further noting that "[t]he number of committees has made it possible for every senator to be either a committee chairman or vice-chairman and for every other House member to be the same" (Nwozor and Olanrewaju 2019: 178). The personal gains and financial rewards to being a committee member (most Nigerian legislators serve on between three and five committees) as well as the possibility of being a committee chair—with extra benefits—make an increase in the number of committees one avenue by which party leaders can distribute rewards to members. Unfortunately, far from adding to legislative capacity, enhancing accountability, or reducing corruption, the burgeoning of Nigeria's committee system has had the opposite motives and impact: to facilitate graft at the expense of good public policy making and oversight.

What explains this variation in the number of legislative committees? One possible answer is the size of the legislature. Committees probably need to have some minimum number of members to be effective, and if the assembly is small, it limits the number of effective committees it can contain. Larger legislative assemblies have more members available to serve on committees, thus allowing more committees to be created, all else equal. This supply-side argument (driven by the availability of members to serve on committees) complements a demand-side argument which suggests having more committees is one way to allow members to serve on several committees (increasing committee size being another solution). With 83 members, Benin has a relatively small assembly (the fourth smallest in our sample), perhaps explaining that legislature's small number of committees. Moreover, not every legislator is available to serve on committees—particularly in those parliamentary systems where cabinet members often serve simultaneously as legislators. We would therefore expect small assemblies in parliamentary regimes to have particularly low numbers of committees.

We can get a rough measure of how many members serve on each committee if we assume that all members are available to do so (a significant abstraction from reality) and that no member serves on more than one committee (which in some cases is an even greater stylization). As reported in Table 8.1, the lowest ratio of members to committees is in Liberia—its lower chamber comprises 73 members and 33 committees, giving a hypothetical 2.2 members per committee, if the committees were populated only by members of the lower chamber and every member was available to take one and only one committee assignment. At the other end of the scale is France, with a lower chamber of 577 members and just eight committees, which translates into 72.1 members per committee. The French case is telling as the Constitution explicitly limits the number of legislative committees; one of a number of constitutional measures adopted at the birth of the Fifth Republic to weaken the legislature and prevent the hyper-instability that had characterized the cabinets of the Fourth Republic between 1946 and 1958 (Huber 1996).

Table 8.2 presents a fuller analysis of the correlates of the number of standing committees. The results suggest that more populous, presidential, and federal countries tend to have a larger number of standing committees. Contrary to

Table 8.2 Number of committees

	(1)	(2)	(3)	(4)	(5)	(6)
log(Size of Lower Chamber)	4.58*				−0.02	2.50
	(2.63)				(5.33)	(4.15)
Presidential	7.98**				8.19*	6.95*
	(3.10)				(4.82)	(3.50)
Federal	10.24**				10.63**	9.27**
	(3.90)				(4.69)	(4.20)
Sovereignty		−0.03			−0.03	
		(0.06)			(0.07)	
log(GDP per Capita)		−0.59				
		(1.53)				
GINI		0.04				
		(0.25)				
log(Population)		3.79***			2.61	1.40
		(1.31)			(2.76)	(2.16)
Ethnic Fractionalization		3.52			−1.43	
		(8.26)			(8.08)	
Africa and Middle East			3.80		1.68	
			(4.95)		(7.21)	
Asia and Oceania			5.36		−0.50	
			(5.39)		(6.28)	
Americas			7.12		−1.23	
			(4.80)		(7.16)	
Eastern Europe			3.33		8.48	
			(5.74)		(6.61)	
British Colony				7.19		
				(4.68)		
Other Colony				2.26		
				(3.88)		
Constant	−9.18	18.04	17.00***	18.21***	26.32	−20.92
	(14.35)	(130.28)	(3.44)	(3.11)	(136.31)	(23.15)
N	68	68	68	68	68	68
R^2	0.23	0.15	0.04	0.04	0.26	0.23
Adjusted R^2	0.19	0.08	−0.03	0.01	0.13	0.18

Notes: Dependent variable is the number of permanent/standing committees.
*$p < .1$; **$p < .05$; ***$p < .01$.

expectations, Size of Lower Chamber is significant at the 10 percent level in Model 1 (controlling for Presidential and Federal constitutions), but not significant in the fuller models.

Committee Membership

Next, we explore committee membership in more detail. Mattson and Strøm (1995: 271) suggest that "[s]pecialisation and expertise will be reinforced if the committee members concentrate their work on one, and only one, committee." Where legislators commonly serve on more than one committee, they can pay less attention to each committee assignment, all else equal. This is especially true in assemblies such as the Israeli Knesset, where committees typically meet simultaneously, and members literally cannot be in two places at the same time. Membership of multiple committees, in other words, makes it more difficult for legislators to specialize, thus reducing the efficiency and effectiveness of the committee system as a whole. Limiting membership to one committee per member is thus good for the membership of the chamber. It is also good for citizens in that the same benefits of capacity, efficiency and effectiveness benefit citizens through the delivery of well-considered legislation and effective oversight of the executive. At the same time, where members serve on only one committee, the breadth of their influence is likely to be narrower.

Table 8.1 demonstrates that in 40 of our cases, legislators commonly serve on more than one committee. In 27 cases, members do not commonly serve on more than one committee.[3] Despite considerable cross-national variation, this pattern indicates that most legislatures are designed to promote committee effectiveness over each member's breadth of influence. Note also that the US Congress, in which members can serve on four or five committees simultaneously, is highly atypical.

Mattson and Strøm (1995: 271) also suggest that a committee system's specialization and expertise will be reinforced if all (available) legislators belong to one committee apiece. Expecting all legislators—with the exceptions of senior office-holder such as the presiding officer, party leaders, or government ministers—to do committee duty maximizes the capacity of the committee system to meet the needs of members and citizens. Spreading the workload amongst all eligible legislators ensures that the maximum workload can be achieved. In the vast majority (60 out of 68) of legislative assemblies in our study, all legislators (presiding officers and cabinet ministers excluded) serve on at least one committee. The eight assemblies where not all legislators commonly serve on at least one committee are those of Chile, Hungary, Nepal, Sweden, Tunisia, Turkey, Ukraine, and Zambia. Thus, being assigned to a committee has become a regular feature of the legislative workload for most legislators around the democratic world (although see Box 8.2).

---

[3] We are missing data on the number of committee assignments per legislator for Niger.

> **Box 8.2 Members without Committee Assignments in Sweden**
>
> The Swedish Riksdag consists of 349 representatives, whereas the standing committees only accommodate 255 regular members. There are 15 standing committees, each of which has 17 members. Each party has a proportional share of these 17 seats, and this "quota" is the same for all committees. What happens to the 94 Swedish parliamentarians who do not get a regular committee assignment? Most of these individuals become deputy members of one of the committees, which means that they may take the place of one of their co-partisans if that person is not able to participate or is for example "elevated" to a cabinet position. Sometimes deputy members are also permitted to participate in committee deliberations alongside the regular members, but without voting rights. But the actual participation of deputy committee members varies a great deal and some such members see hardly any committee "action." A few members of the Riksdag get no committee assignment at all. But these individuals are not typically the "rejected" or marginal members, but rather parliamentary party leaders or other members with heavy existing political commitments (Hagevi 1998). Thus, these features of the Swedish Riksdag reflect a leaders' assembly, in which committee assignments are largely controlled by, and serve the purposes of, the political parties and their leaderships.

Committee membership tenure—how long a legislator can expect to serve on the same committee—also matters. Security of tenure until the next legislative election constrains the ability of leaders to shift members across committees as they may wish. Relatedly, security of committee tenure helps members adopt a time horizon necessary to develop expertise, with concomitant benefits for citizens. In 62 of our 68 cases, legislators serve on the same committee (or committees) for the entire legislative term (by which we mean the period during which the legislature is in session between general elections). In some cases, it may be possible to remove a legislator from a particular committee (for example, if this legislator switches parties during the legislative term). Typically, however, a legislator can expect to serve on his or her assigned committee until the next election. And in many assemblies, re-elected members who wish to retain their committee assignments are given preferential consideration. The tenure that such practices foster provides an incentive for legislators to specialize and become more expert on the topics covered by their respective committees.

In six cases, legislators do not serve on the same committee for an entire legislative term: Bolivia, the Dominican Republic, India, Romania, Taiwan, and

Turkey. Similarly, in the European Parliament, MEPs switch committee assignments at the mid-point of their five-year term. Whitaker (2011: 36) notes that these assignment changes "provide a chance for members unhappy with their current position to move to another committee provided that space is available and party group and national party leaders are in agreement." Note the caveat about leadership agreement, which again points to the preference of party leaders for flexible assignments.

The rules and norms concerning committee assignments are useful indicators of assembly type. In a members' assembly, as modeled by for example Shepsle and Weingast, members self-select for committees (presumably based on the preferences of their constituents) and can expect to retain their assignments over time, unless they gain access to more prestigious or valuable committees. In a voters' assembly, committee assignments should principally enhance capacity and accountability. Hence, initial committee assignments should be based on skills and experience and constituency preferences rather than party needs or members' special interests, but members who have been successfully re-elected should expect to retain their committee assignments so that they can deepen their expertise. In a leaders' assembly, committee assignments are made by party leaders according to party needs, and members must expect that they can be reassigned over time.

To the extent that committee structures resemble a leaders' assembly, we would expect majority parties or coalitions to secure control of one special position within each committee: the committee chair. The committee chair typically plays an important role in setting the agenda and controlling committee resources. Committee chairs can be allocated under any number of rules including by a vote of the committee itself (as in most cases), by a vote of the plenary (as in the United Kingdom), or through bargaining between party leaders (as in Ireland). In countries where coalition governments are common, committee chairs may be allocated through the coalition agreement between the coalition parties.

One way to explore committee chair assignments is to examine whether the majority party or, absent a majority, the party of the president (in a presidential system) or the governing party or coalition (in a parliamentary system) controls all committee chairs. As table 8.1 reports, the majority group control all committee chairs in approximately one-third of legislative assemblies in our study (24 out of 67—we are missing such data for Niger). In 43 assemblies, the chair of at least some committees is held by a legislator from a party other than the majority party or governing party/coalition.

Committee Powers

Our task here is to explore the capacity of legislative committees to influence the production of public policy and engage in executive oversight. The latter includes the post-legislative implementation of public policy by the executive. As with any other part of the legislature, it is difficult to measure the power and influence of legislative committees directly. For example, it is sometimes proposed that the rate of amendments made to government bills at committee stage provides a direct measure of committee influence. Proponents of this approach see amendments to the bill adopted in committee as the direct effect of legislative committees—the bill changed because the committee was part of the legislative process. But we don't know whether the changes would have happened absent committees, as amendments could have been tabled at later stages of the legislative process. If the assembly majority agreed to the changes at committee stage, might they not alternatively have agreed to the same changes at some other stage? If so, committees had no independent effect on the legislative outcome, they were just suitable avenues for amendments that otherwise would have happened elsewhere.

Moreover, a lack of amendments to government bills at committee stage cannot be taken as evidence of a lack of committee influence. After all, a rational ministry would do its best to ensure that the bill was in accordance with the preferences of a powerful legislative committee. Ministers are typically astute politicians who recognize the foolishness of bringing a proposal to the legislature which lacks support among the minister's legislative coalition. Because the bill's sponsors anticipate the committee's response, we may not be able to observe the true influence of the committee, as the data would show no (successful) amendments.

Because it is so challenging to make such inferences from legislative records, our discussion of committee strength will focus on capacity. Thus, rather than trying to measure the number of amendments (and their quality and significance), we will examine three measures of the capacity of legislative committees to influence policy: (1) the degree of committee-ministry jurisdictional congruence, (2) the formal role of committees in lawmaking, and (3) the formal role of committees in the budgetary process.

If a manual existed on how to create a strong legislative committee system, it would most likely suggest above all else jurisdictional congruence between official ministries and committee portfolios. In other words, the policy responsibilities of legislative committees should mirror those of the executive departments (Strøm 1990). For example, if the executive has an education ministry, then the legislature should have an education committee; if the executive lacks an education ministry, the legislature should not have such a committee. This paralleling or congruence provides several advantages for the legislature: it generates efficiencies by maximizing oversight capacity, with the committee able to accumulate expertise concerning the entire policy remit of the relevant ministry or department. Similarly, the ministry becomes accustomed to dealing with and being scrutinized by a single legislative committee. The committee's expertise affects not just oversight of the executive, but may allow the legislative committee a greater formal and informal role in the legislative process.

For example, the committee may be able to influence the content of proposed government legislation because the ministry knows the committee's preferred policies. In contrast, if the policy jurisdictions of committees and government ministries don't correspond, with one committee overseeing multiple ministries—or just part of one ministry—the level of shared knowledge will tend to be lower, as will likely the level of mutual trust. A lack of congruence thus makes it difficult for a legislative committee to track the actions and non-actions of a specific ministry. For these reasons, we expect leaders to disfavor jurisdictional correspondence— the more a committee shadows the leaders, the more accountable the leaders are to committees. In contrast, both members and citizens should favor jurisdictional correspondence, since it allows them greater capacity to influence public policy and hold the executive to account.

In the real world, congruence is rarely perfect. Only seven of our countries, Colombia, Finland, France, Germany, Greece, Italy, and Pakistan, display a perfect or almost perfect jurisdictional congruence between legislative committees and government ministries. It is far more common, however, to find a pattern of general congruence with some significant exceptions. In 60 cases, the majority of committees thus have jurisdictions which mostly coincide with government departments (we are missing data for Niger). We find no case of substantive permanent committees whose respective areas of policy responsibility diverge radically from the jurisdictions of their ministerial departments. And over time the trend seems to favor congruence, as legislatures in Denmark, India, Portugal, Sweden, and Switzerland have shifted from functionally defined to policy-based committees, which has generally also led to higher levels of congruence (Davidsson 2003: 127). The take-home point here is that in all the world's major democracies, committee-ministry jurisdictional congruence is now a very common feature of legislative committee systems. And the trend toward congruence seems to have been particularly strong in Europe.

Most likely, in designing its committee system the legislative assembly responds to the structure of the government, rather than vice versa. In other words, where congruence exists, committee jurisdictions tend to be designed to fit government structures. We don't think executive ministries tend to structure themselves to "fit" legislative committee jurisdictions and know of no example of that kind of adaptation. Executive ministries are simply much larger and "heavier" organizations, so that structural reform comes at a much steeper cost. Of course, the design of government ministries changes—in some countries not infrequently—with various policy areas being shifted between government departments. In such circumstances, the onus is then on the legislature to update its committee system if it wishes its committees to maintain jurisdictional congruence with the restructured government ministries.

Next, we explore the formal role of legislative committees in the legislative process. After all, law making is a crucial function of a legislative assembly, as we will explore in the next chapter. To what degree are legislative committees, then, involved in the legislative process? A key measure of committee capacity to influence law production is whether or not proposed legislation (in other words, a bill) must be considered and voted on by a committee (as defined in this chapter, a permanent substantive committee), with the bill unable to be adopted if it fails to pass a vote within the committee. In other words, we want to know whether a committee can veto proposed legislation. If it can, the committee holds significant "gatekeeping powers" over policy within its jurisdiction. And if a committee can veto proposed legislation, it also means that the assembly has in effect delegated to the committee the right to prevent policy change. A committee system with such gatekeeping powers empowers members and may also benefit voters, but reduces the influence of leaders, unless a cartel party or coalition can keep the committees on a short string.

Do committees in fact have such gatekeeping powers? In all but three cases in our dataset, proposed legislation must pass through a permanent committee. The three exceptions are Australia, Costa Rica, and the United Kingdom. In the United Kingdom bills go through a "committee stage" but this typically does not involve a permanent committee. Rather, the bill is considered either by a specially created ad hoc committee (which reviews the bill, and that bill alone, before then disbanding) or by the plenary meeting as a committee—known as a "committee of the whole house." In the remaining 65 democracies, permanent committees must formally consider and vote on proposed legislation. Clearly, there are likely to be major differences among these countries in the actual influence that legislative committees can have on proposed legislation. In some legislatures, committees may simply "rubber-stamp" proposed government legislation (as the plenary may also do); in other assemblies, committees may be far more independent and guard closely their right to accept, reject or amend proposed legislation.

Finally, we explore the role of legislative committees in the budgetary process. As we will see in Chapter 10, the government's budgetary process is a significant event in every political system and legislative assemblies can be more or less influential. Involving legislative committees in the budgetary process enhances the budgetary role of the legislature but also reflects how significant legislative committees are in the legislature's organization. The overall picture of assembly involvement in the budgetary process is striking. In all but one case (Ireland), legislative committees are engaged in the budgetary process in one way or another. Fifty-nine legislative assemblies feature a specific budgetary committee. In contrast, in the Irish parliament (the Houses of the *Oireachtas*), legislative committees play no formal role in passing the nation's budget, although Oireachtas committees now do receive and review pre-budget submissions from various interest and lobby groups. Overall, however, legislative committee have a formal and often significant role in the budgetary process in virtually all major democracies.

8.3 Conclusion

Woodrow Wilson's once observed that, "Congress in session is Congress on public exhibition, whilst Congress in its committee-rooms is Congress at work" (Wilson 1981 [1885], 69). Today, the conventional notion is that a strong system of committees, however defined, is a necessary if not sufficient condition for the legislature to operate effectively, not least in terms of influencing the content of legislation and holding the executive accountable. The evidence in this chapter suggests that while all assemblies feature committees, legislatures differ in how they organize them. This variation extends to, among other things, the number of committees, rules governing membership of committees, who controls committee chairs, the congruence between committee portfolios and executive portfolios and the formal role of committees in the legislative and budgetary process. In combination, these variables shape the degree to which a legislature has a strong versus weak committee system. In a strong committee system, committees are a focal point in the legislature and legislative process, giving committee members significant influence and authority. In contrast, committees may be only weakly organized or lack the powers to impact what a legislature does. As we have discussed in various sections of the chapter above, we expect to find strong and independent committees in a members' assembly and in most respects also in a voters' assembly. On the other hand, we expect a leader's assembly to have less strong and independent committees.

References

Agunyai, Samuel Chukwudi, and Victor Ojakorotu. 2021. "The Nigerian Legislative Committee System, Corruption, and Constituency Woes: Lessons Nigerians Can Learn from the Singaporean Legislative Committee System." *Taiwan Journal of Democracy* 17(2): 97–123.

Cox, Gary W. 2006. "The Organization of Democratic Legislatures." In Barry R. Weingast and Donald Wittman (eds.), *The Oxford Handbook of Political Economy*. Oxford: Oxford University Press, 141–161.

Cox, Gary W., and Mathew D. McCubbins. 1993. *Legislative Leviathan*. Berkeley: University of California Press.

Cox, Gary W., and Mathew D. McCubbins. 2005. *Setting the Agenda*. New York: Cambridge University Press.

Davidsson, Lars 2003. "Riksdagen." In Ingvar Mattsoon and Olof Petersson (eds.), *Svensk författningspolitik*. Stockholm: SNS Förlag, 112–129.

Diermeier, Daniel, and Roger B. Myerson. 1999. "Bicameralism and Its Consequences for the Internal Organization of Legislatures." *American Economic Review* 89: 1182–1196.

Ekeyi, Benjamin. 2021. "Exploring the Gap between Theory and Practice in Lawmaking and Oversight by Committees of the Nigerian National Assembly." In Sven T. Siefken, and Hilmar Rommetvedt (eds.), *Parliamentary Committees in the Policy Process*. London: Routledge, 206–223.

Fenno Jr, Richard F. 1978. *Homestyle: Members of Congress in Their Constituencies.* New York: Little, Brown.

Gilligan, Thomas W., and Keith Krehbiel. 1987. "Collective Decision-Making and Standing Committees: An Informationale Rationale for Restrictive Amendment Procedures." *Journal of Law, Economics, and Organization* 3: 287–335.

Groseclose, Tim, and David C. King. 2001. "Committee Theories Reconsidered." In Lawrence C. Dodd, and Bruce I. Oppenheimer (eds.), *Congress Reconsidered*, 7th edition, Washington: CQ Press, 191–216.

Hagevi, Magnus. 1998. *Bakom riksdagens fasad.* Gothenburg: Akademiförlaget Corona.

Huber, John D. 1996. *Rationalizing Parliament: legislative institutions and party politics in France.* New York: Cambridge University Press.

Katz, Jonathan N., and Brian R. Sala. 1996. "Careerism, Committee Assignments, and the Electoral Connection." *American Political Science Review* 90(1): 21–33.

Martin, Lanny W., and Georg Vanberg. 2011. *Parliaments and Coalitions: The Role of Legislative Institutions in Multiparty Governance.* Oxford: Oxford University Press.

Mattson, Ingvar, and Kaare Strøm. 1995. "Parliamentary Committees." In Herbert Döring (ed.), *Parliaments and Majority Rule in Western Europe.* Frankfurt: Campus Verlag, 249–307.

Mayhew, David R. 1974. *Congress: The Electoral Connection.* New Haven: Yale University Press.

Nwozor, Agaptus, and John Shola Olanrewaju. 2019. "Oiling the Legislature: An Appraisal of the Committee System in Nigeria's National Assembly." In Joseph Yinka Fashagba, Ola-Rotimi Matthew Ajayi, and Chiedo Nwankwor (eds.), *The Nigerian National Assembly.* New York: Springer, 165–187.

Rickard, Stephanie J. 2018. *Spending to Win: Political Institutions, Economic Geography, and Government Subsidies.* New York: Cambridge University Press.

Shepsle, Kenneth A. 1978. *The Giant Jigsaw Puzzle: Democratic Committee Assignments in the Modern House.* Chicago: University of Chicago Press.

Shepsle, Kenneth A., and Barry R. Weingast. 1981. "Structure-induced Equilibrium and Legislative Choice." *Public Choice* 37: 503–519.

Shepsle, Kenneth A., and Barry R. Weingast. 1987. "The institutional foundations of committee power." *American Political Science Review* 81(1): 85–104.

Siefken, Sven T., and Hilmar Rommetvedt. 2021. "A Black Box that Deserves More Light: Comparative Findings on Parliamentary Committees in the Policy Process." In Sven T. Siefken and Hilmar Rommetvedt (eds.), *Parliamentary Committees in the Policy Process.* London: Routledge, 206–223, 9–37.

Strøm, Kaare. 1990. *Minority Government and Majority Rule.* Cambridge: Cambridge University Press.

Weingast, Barry R., and William J. Marshall. 1988. "The Industrial Organization of Congress; or, Why Legislatures, Like Firms, Are Not Organized as Markets." *The Journal of Political Economy* 96: 132–163.

Whitaker, Richard. 2011. *The European Parliament's Committees: National Party Influence and Legislative Empowerment.* Abingdon: Routledge.

Wilson, Woodrow. 1885 [1981]. *Congressional Government.* Baltimore: The Johns Hopkins University Press.

9

Lawmaking

This chapter explores the role of legislative assemblies in lawmaking, and in particular where power resides when it comes to making laws. By definition, a legislative assembly is one that makes laws, and by almost universal accord, lawmaking is a central function of any legislative assembly. Norton (2013: 1) even defines a legislature as "a body created to approve measures that will form the law of the land." Yet, lawmaking is in most democracies neither an exclusive property of the national legislature nor its only significant function. A country's legislative assembly may have other functions, and this assembly may not be the only source of a nation's set of laws. Judicial precedents (particularly in common law systems) and judicial decisions may be an alternative source of law. Moreover, in many systems, executives enjoy significant authority to issue decrees, a form of delegated authority to make and implement public policy (Carey and Shugart 1998; Palanza 2019). In some democracies, including various US states, law may be made by ordinary citizens through initiatives and referendums. Also, the governments of all nations are expected to respect international law and most contemporary democracies have signed international agreements which may reduce the authority of their legislative assembly to make new laws or change existing ones.[1] Finally, we should note that the lawmaking authority of national legislative assemblies may be limited by their respective constitutions. Such caveats notwithstanding, our focus in this chapter is on the lawmaking function of democratic legislative assemblies, and the resulting laws, sometimes referred to as statutes, acts, or statutory law.

Particularly in parliamentary monarchies, legislative assemblies are the principal, and in many cases the only, decision-making body directly elected by the people. If the legislature under these conditions does not adequately represent citizens, then it is difficult to identify an institution that plausibly could perform the function of passing laws that serve the interests and preferences of the citizens at large. Thus, de Montesquieu (1989 [1748]) proffered a system of government with a strong lawmaking function for the legislature. And the founders of the US Constitution clearly looked to Congress (and the state legislatures) to provide the impetus and the initiative for much of country's lawmaking activity. Yet, the contemporary literature does not portray the lawmaking capacity of democratic legislatures

---

[1] For some supporters of the United Kingdom's exit from the European Union, leaving provides an opportunity to give back to the UK Parliament its role as the country's ultimate (sovereign) lawmaking body.

Legislative Assemblies. Shane Martin and Kaare W. Strøm, Oxford University Press.
© Shane Martin and Kaare W. Strøm (2023). DOI: 10.1093/oso/9780198890829.003.0009

in very hopeful terms. Scholars have lamented the passing of many legislative assemblies' de facto significance in lawmaking. Instead many modern legislative assemblies, are said to perform a mere "rubber-stamp" function, readily agreeing to the executive's legislative proposals. Particularly under parliamentary constitutions (see Chapter 11), the perception is that the executive proposes and gets the legislation it wants, especially if it controls a majority of seats in the legislature. As Mezey (1979: 3) noted in a now-classical work on the topic: "research on western European parliaments demonstrated quite conclusively that the lawmaking function of these 'established' legislatures had long since passed to executives that controlled disciplined parliamentary majorities."

Lawmaking typically takes place in several stages. The initiative for new legislation may come from different sources, such as parties, citizens' groups, experts, heads of state or others, though in most contemporary democracies the executive is responsible for the preparation, and often the introduction, of a large share of all legislative bills. Such government bills may in turn be the result of the work of commissions representing not only governing parties and bureaucrats, but also experts, representatives of affected interests, major interest groups, and the like. Once a bill has been introduced, or a legislative proposal made, it is most often subject to several rounds of hearings in the assembly. Such hearings provide an occasion to notify members that the bill has been introduced, will be debated, or has been deliberated in committee. After the initial hearing, the bill may be assigned to one or several committees for more intensive scrutiny and deliberation. Its fate may be decided in committee, or the bill may be reported back to the assembly for a plenary decision. Once an assembly decision has been made, the bill may face further scrutiny in a second chamber or by the executive. In cases of disagreement, there may additional stages of deliberation through such vehicles as conference committees, or attempts to override any executive veto (Palanza and Sin 2014). See Box 9.1 for more details on the lawmaking process in the Italian case.

Our specific aim in this chapter is to explore variation in the authority and capacity of legislative assemblies to make laws. This legislative capacity of legislative assemblies may vary along several dimensions. One has to do with the laws and regulations that empower particular office-holders or institutions to introduce legislative bills (proposed pieces of legislation). In that context, we shall also consider rules that allow leaders to preclude potential bills from consideration, also known as gate-keeping power. Such rules are of course particularly relevant to the power of legislative leaders, or individual members, to control their respective assemblies. Given our interest in legislative assemblies as vehicles of citizen representation, we shall also examine different ways in which ordinary citizens can put their own proposals on the assembly's agenda. It may even be the case that laws (e.g., decrees) can be made without the prior consent and deliberation of the legislative assembly.

The initial stages of deliberation on proposed laws can have a huge impact on the eventual result. As a result, one recent innovation has been the introduction in some systems of pre-legislative scrutiny (see Box 9.2) The process of agenda setting helps determine which of the multitude of possible proposals will be considered and what form and sequence this deliberation will take. One way to explore the capacity to make new laws or amend existing laws is therefore through the lenses of legislative agenda-setting institutions. Rasch (2014: 455) defines agenda-setting institutions as the rules that "regulate which issues and proposals are to be considered, and how the issues are finally decided." We begin by exploring the first aspect of agenda setting—formal proposal rights, or in other words who can make formal proposals to change laws. We then explore various tools which the leadership may have at its disposal to control the agenda. Next, we explore how decision making, and in particularly voting, takes place within legislatures. We then discuss the degree to which an external actor, such as a head of state, can veto legislation proposed by a legislative assembly. We conclude with an exploration of whether lawmaking productivity—the volume of legislation passed by a legislative assembly—varies across the countries included in our study. Throughout the chapter, we want to understand the degree to which the rules governing how laws are made privilege the interests of citizens, member, or leaders.

Box 9.1 Parliamentary Stages of the Legislative Process in Italy

The Italian lawmaking process is particularly interesting because it includes different procedures: an ordinary legislative procedures and two forms of abbreviated legislative procedure.

The ordinary legislative procedure involves the introduction of a bill by the government or a member of one of the chambers, referral to a parliamentary committee and then a debate and vote in the plenary. The committee stage represents the first review of the bill, and includes a report by a rapporteur which is made available for the debate in the plenary. At the plenary stage, the rapporteur introduces the bill and a debate is held on the content of the bill. Any amendments recommended by the committee is voted on and finally the bill with any agreed amendments is voted on. If both chambers approve identical versions of the bill, the law is promulgated by the Italian President.

The first form of abbreviated legislative procedure places greater responsibility on the parliamentary committee. Under this procedure, the committee acts as the legislative assembly, reviewing and approving the bill—a procedure known as in sede legislative. To ensure that the actions of the committee represent the will of key actors, if the Government, or 10 percent of the deputies, or one-fifth of the Committees, request it, the procedure is usurped and the bill is sent to the plenary.

Under a second form of abbreviated legislative procedure, the plenary can delegate to the committee the preparation of a bill, which will subsequently be reviewed by the plenary in an up-or-down vote, with no amendments permitted.

Box 9.2 Pre -Legislative Scrutiny: A New Way to Engage?

Pre-legislative scrutiny (PLS) is a process whereby a legislative assembly analyses draft bills and reports its observations and/or recommendations to the executive. As Smookler (2006: 522) notes, pre-legislative scrutiny "typically involves scrutiny by a parliamentary committee before the final drafting of a Bill has been decided and before the formal legislative process begins." The aim of this process is to enhance the effectiveness of a legislative assembly's role in lawmaking. Pre-legislative scrutiny can be contrasted with examination of a bill as it progresses through the formal lawmaking process within a legislative assembly. Again, in contrast, post-legislative scrutiny involves the scrutiny of enacted legislation to determine the degree to which the objectives of the legislation were and are being achieved.

Pre-legislative scrutiny is a relatively recent innovation and appears to be still limited to a minority of national assemblies. The United Kingdom Parliament was one of the first national legislative assemblies to experiment with PLS. Most commentary on PLS in the UK indicates that the experimentation has been positive for the role of Parliament in lawmaking. A 2006 Modernization Committee report on the UK's Legislative Process concluded that:

[T]here is little doubt that pre-legislative scrutiny produces better laws. As the Law Society told us, "it would probably be difficult to prove scientifically that more pre-legislative scrutiny has improved legislation, but it would seem unarguable in practice that it has. . . ." Effective consultation procedures and processes, such as publication and consideration of Bills in draft, would appear to have greatly improved the text presented to Parliament, or to have identified drawbacks in the draft text which require rethinking.

Norton (2013: 84) suggests that "[b]y being able to have some input at the formulation stage, parliamentary influence is maximised." Smookler (2006: 534) concluded that PLS has a "proven record of influencing a Bill's content before it is entrenched, and providing a locus of guidance for parliamentarians,

Continued

demonstrating its value as a significant contributor towards the development of better legislation." However, as Russell and Gover (2017: 229) note, most Bills are not subject to PLS in the UK Parliament. The Government decides which Bills are subject to PLS and for how long it is possible to scrutinize the Bill (Norton 2013: 84).

Looking at the Irish case, Lynch and Martin (2020) assesses the impact of PLS on legislative outcomes by focusing on (a) the degree to which legislative committees makes recommendations as part of PLS and (b) whether these recommendations are accepted by the executive in the Bill as presented to the Irish Parliament. Their content analysis of 50 PLS cases finds a high level of engagement, thus an average of 9.34 recommendations per completed PLS. Their analysis of 31 PLS reports and the content of the subsequently published Bills indicates that the executive accepted 146 of 350 recommendations. Given this overall rate of acceptance (41.7%), and notwithstanding some individual cases in which no recommendations were accepted, it appears that in the Irish case PLS is having a direct impact on the content of Government legislation.

9.1 Proposal Rights

Proposal rights determine who can initiate the formal process to change a country's statutory laws. Simply proposing changes to a body of law may not result in any actual change, but proposal rights represent an important gatekeeping power: the ability to decide what proposed new laws a legislative assembly will consider. In this section we look at who can formally propose changes to laws, and specifically nonfinancial legislation. We focus on non-financial legislation here as we consider financial legislation in the next chapter. In many systems, the executive may have a near-monopoly on the introduction of financial legislation, so that it is useful to consider these two processes separately.

It is important to note that our focus is on *formal* proposal rights. Many groups or even individuals, ranging from lobbyists to individual firms or wealthy politically minded individuals may seek to influence the content of legislation and may lobby for changes to the law. A significant body of research explores which policy issues get on the political agenda, helping us understand why politicians focus on certain policy topics at any given time (Baumgartner and Jones 2010). In contrast, our focus in this chapter is on *who* can formally initiate an attempt to change the lawmaking process. The assignment of proposal rights can give us useful information on the powers of members, parties, committees, and executives in different national assemblies. Table 9.1 presents a survey of exactly who has formal proposal rights with respect to non-financial legislation in our various assemblies.

Table 9.1 Formal proposal rights

Country	Executive	Individual Legislator	Group of Legislators	Party	Committee	Court	Citizens Agenda Initiative	Citizen Initiative	Citizen Amendment	Citizen Referendum
Argentina	Yes	Yes	No	No	No	No	Yes	No	No	No
Australia	Yes	Yes	No	No	No	No	No	No	No	No
Austria	Yes	No	Yes	No	No	No	Yes	No	No	No
Belgium	Yes	Yes	Yes	No	No	No	No	No	No	No
Benin	Yes	Yes	No	No	No	No	Yes	No	No	No
Bolivia	Yes	Yes	No	No	No	Yes	Yes	No	No	Yes
Brazil	Yes	Yes	No	No	No	Yes	Yes	No	No	No
Bulgaria	Yes	Yes	No	Yes	No	No	No	No	No	No
Burundi	Yes	Yes	No	No	No	No	No	No	No	No
Canada	Yes	Yes	Yes	Yes	No	No	No	No	No	No
Chile	Yes	Yes	Yes	No	No	No	No	No	No	No
Colombia	Yes	Yes	No	No	No	Yes	Yes	Yes	Yes	Yes
Costa Rica	Yes	Yes	No	No	No	No	Yes	Yes	Yes	No
Croatia	Yes	Yes	No	Yes	Yes	No	No	Yes	No	Yes
Czech Republic	Yes	Yes	Yes	No	No	No	No	No	No	No
Denmark	Yes	Yes	No	No	No	No	No	No	No	No
Dominican Republic	Yes	Yes	No	No	No	Yes	No	No	No	No
Ecuador	Yes	No	Yes	Yes	No	Yes	Yes	Yes	No	Yes
El Salvador	Yes	Yes	No	No	No	Yes	No	No	No	No
Finland	Yes	Yes	No	No	No	No	No	No	No	No
France	Yes	Yes	Yes	Yes	No	No	No	No	No	No
Germany	Yes	No	Yes	Yes	No	No	No	No	No	No

Continued

Table 9.1 *Continued*

Country	Executive	Individual Legislator	Group of Legislators	Party	Committee	Court	Citizens Agenda Initiative	Citizen Initiative	Citizen Amendment	Citizen Referendum
Ghana	Yes	Yes	No	No	No	No	No	No	No	No
Greece	Yes	Yes	No	No	No	No	No	No	No	No
Guatemala	Yes	Yes	No	No	No	Yes	Yes	No	No	No
Honduras	Yes	Yes	No	No	No	Yes	Yes	No	No	No
Hungary	Yes	Yes	No	No	Yes	No	Yes	Yes	Yes	Yes
India	Yes	Yes	No	No	No	No	Yes	No	No	No
Indonesia	Yes	Yes	No	No	No	No	No	No	No	No
Ireland	Yes	Yes	Yes	No	No	No	No	No	No	No
Israel	Yes	Yes	Yes	No	Yes	No	No	No	No	No
Italy	Yes	Yes	No	No	No	No	Yes	No	No	Yes
Japan	Yes	No	Yes	Yes	Yes	No	No	No	No	No
Kenya	No	Yes	No	No	Yes	No	No	No	No	No
Liberia	No	Yes	No	No	No	No	No	No	No	No
Malawi	Yes	Yes	No	No	No	No	No	No	No	No
Mexico	Yes	Yes	Yes	No	No	No	No	No	No	No
Nepal	Yes	Yes	No	No	No	No	No	No	No	No
Netherlands	Yes	Yes	Yes	No	No	No	Yes	No	No	No
New Zealand	Yes	Yes	No	No	No	No	No	Yes	No	No
Nicaragua	Yes	Yes	No	No	No	Yes	Yes	Yes	No	No
Niger	Yes	Yes	No	No	No	No	Yes	No	No	No
Nigeria	Yes	Yes	No	No	No	No	No	No	No	No
Norway	Yes	Yes	No	No	No	No	No	No	No	No
Pakistan	Yes	Yes	No	No	No	No	No	No	No	No
Papua New Guinea	Yes	Yes	No	No	No	No	No	No	No	No

Paraguay	Yes	Yes	No	No	No	Yes	Yes	No	No
Peru	Yes	Yes	No	No	No	No	No	No	Yes
Philippines	No	Yes	No	No	No	No	Yes	Yes	Yes
Poland	Yes	Yes	No	No	No	No	No	No	No
Portugal	Yes	Yes	Yes	No	No	No	No	No	No
Romania	Yes	Yes	No	No	No	No	No	No	No
Senegal	Yes	Yes	No	No	No	No	No	No	No
Serbia	Yes	Yes	No	No	No	No	No	No	No
Sierra Leone	Yes	Yes	No	No	No	No	No	No	No
Slovak Republic	Yes	Yes	No	Yes	No	Yes	No	Yes	No
South Africa	Yes	Yes	No	Yes	No	Yes	No	No	No
South Korea	No	No	Yes	No	No	No	No	No	No
Spain	Yes	Yes	No	No	No	Yes	No	No	No
Sweden	Yes	Yes	Yes	No	No	No	No	No	No
Switzerland	Yes	No	Yes	Yes	Yes	No	No	Yes	Yes
Taiwan	Yes	No	Yes	No	Yes	No	Yes	No	No
Tunisia	No	Yes	No	No	No	No	No	No	No
Turkey	Yes	No	No	No	No	No	No	No	No
Ukraine	Yes	No	No	No	No	No	Yes	No	No
United Kingdom	Yes	Yes	Yes	No	No	No	No	No	No
United States	No	No	Yes	Yes	No	No	No	No	No
Zambia	Yes	No	No	No	No	No	No	No	No

The government (by which we mean the executive or cabinet) can introduce proposed legislation (bills) into the formal legislative process in 64 of the 68 countries in our study. Overall then, it is highly common for a country's government to be recognized as a formal player in the lawmaking process. All else equal, this indicates that the executive is recognized as playing an active and legitimate role in the process of proposing laws (in the form either of new laws, or amendments to existing laws). This runs contrary to de Montesquieu's (1989 [1748]) above-mentioned vision of a separation of lawmaking and law-implementing bodies. In these cases, leaders are privileged in the lawmaking process, especially when the parties that control the executive branch also tend to control the assembly, in keeping with our notion of a leaders' assembly. In four countries in our study—Kenya, Liberia, Philippines, and the United States of America—the government cannot formally place proposed legislation before the legislative assembly. In the United States, for example, the President has no authority to formally introduce a bill to the United States Congress. Such cases privilege members at the expense of the executive. Rather, the bill must be initiated within the Congress itself (as we will discuss in further detail below). Liberia and the Philippines are countries in which the American political influence has been strong, which may help account for their similarity in this respect.

In 62 of our 68 cases, an individual legislator can introduce a (non-financial) bill. This prerogative is rarely exclusive, as most of these countries also permit the government to introduce such bills. In Liberia, however, only individual legislators can introduce legislative proposals. In this context at least, Liberia appears to fit our concept of a members' assembly. In contrast, six legislative assemblies prohibit individual members from introducing bills: Austria, Ecuador, Germany, Japan, South Korea, and Tunisia. In 18 countries, a group of legislators can combine to introduce legislative bills. Examples of these cases include Canada, Japan, Germany, and the United States. Technically, in the US House of Representatives, only one member can sponsor any proposed legislation, but other members can "co-sponsor" a bill. Which members come together to signal their approval of a bill in this way has created an important research agenda, with scholars searching for partisan, social and ideological connections, or "networks" between legislators who co-sponsor bills (Fowler 2006). Yet, such co-sponsorship arrangements are rare cross-nationally. In 50 countries, no provision is available for a group of legislators to come together to introduce proposed legislation.

In 12 of our democracies, including Bulgaria, Ecuador, and Japan, a party group can formally propose legislation. Such arrangements benefit party leaders. Surprisingly given the central role of party groups in many legislative arenas, the vast majority of assemblies in our study—56 cases—have no provision for a party group to introduce legislation. As we saw in Chapter 8, committees are often another important institution within a legislative assembly, partly determining its effectiveness. In 9 countries, including Croatia, Israel, Kenya, and the

United States, committees can introduce proposed legislation. By providing an alternative avenue to party leaders, committees with agenda-setting authority in lawmaking may privilege members over leaders, in keeping with our notion of a members' assembly. Yet, such committee rights are the exception rather than the rule. In the remaining 59 cases, committees have no lawmaking proposal rights. The inability to table (here meaning to introduce) proposed legislation reduces a committee's legislative influence, as under such circumstances the committee's power will derive mainly from its ability to review legislation proposed by others.

Occasionally, the power to propose legislation may also be vested in institutions outside the democratic chain of delegation from voters to their representatives. Thus, in 11 countries in our study a court can formally introduce legislation. This is interesting for two reasons: In some countries, the judiciary may enjoy the right to reject laws passed by a legislative assembly, particularly when such laws conflict with the national constitution or international legal obligations. Second, when considering cases before it, a court may wish that the statutory position was clearer, and may make such a formal proposal. Proposal rights for courts go beyond such powers of ex post judicial review but may be driven by similar considerations.

Finally, some constitutions empower citizens outside the legislative assembly to propose changes to the law directly. One way to allow ordinary citizens to exercise such powers is to allow citizens to place a proposal on the legislative agenda, which is sometimes referred to as an agenda initiative process. The agenda initiative process can be defined as: "[a] direct democracy procedure which enables citizens to submit a proposal which must be considered by the legislature but is not necessarily put to a vote of the electorate" (IDEA 2008: 84). In 24 countries, citizens have such formal proposal rights. Examples include Argentina, Italy, Niger, and Spain. Typically, this involves a minimum group of citizens petitioning the legislative assembly to formally consider changes to the law. In Austria, for example, an initiative (*Volksbegehren*) requires the signatures of 100,000 voters, and the initiative "may take the form of a bill, i.e. contain the concrete wording of a text to be adopted, but it is also sufficient if the movers' concern is described in detail."[2] The ability of citizens to formally set the legislative agenda potentially tallies with our concept of a voters' assembly, in which citizens benefit from direct and immediate influence over members and policies. Of course, it could be that the general interests of citizens may not be well met by the ability of a faction of citizens to set the legislative agenda.

Sixteen countries have a citizens' initiative (as distinct from the above-described citizen agenda initiative). As defined by IDEA (2008: 10) the citizen initiative process allows "the electorate to vote on a political, constitutional or legislative measure proposed by a number of citizens and not by a government, legislature, or other political authority." Examples of countries with citizen initiatives include

---

[2] https://www.parlament.gv.at/ENGL/PERK/GES/WEG/INITIATIVE/index.shtml.

Spain, Taiwan, and the Ukraine. In federal political systems, citizen initiatives may also be important at the state level—in California, for example, initiatives are a common feature of the electoral cycle. Initiatives allow the legislature to be bypassed in the lawmaking process, effectively allowing citizens to become legislators (Bowler, Donovan, and Tolbert 1998). Relatedly, nine countries permit a citizen-called referendum. Examples include Switzerland, Colombia, Hungary, and the Philippines. A referendum is a procedure "which give the electorate a direct vote on a specific political, constitutional or legislative issue" (IDEA 2008: 10). A citizen referendum is a referendum which can be initiated by citizens and in this sense is similar to an initiative process. Referendums need not focus on ordinary laws but may also consider issues ranging from the constitution to decisions on who is entitled to citizenship, as in some parts of Switzerland. Citizens' initiatives certainly empower citizens and provide one example whereby laws can be made without the involvement of the legislature, as we discussed in the introduction. For this reason, such procedures reduce the relative powers of members and leaders, thus correlating negatively with our concepts of a members' and leaders' assembly, respectively.

9.2 Stages of Deliberation and Voting Mechanisms

Once a bill has been introduced, the legislative process can vary in many ways. One aspect, as discussed above, is the ability of the executive to control the legislative process. This raises the more general question of how a bill becomes law. In the case of legislative assemblies with more than one chamber, this may involve a bill moving between chambers or the need to reconcile the content of bills between each chamber's version. Box 9.1 sets out the legislative process in Italy. In the United States the following is the prescribed legislative process, as described by the House of Representatives:[3]

> Laws begin as ideas. First, a representative sponsors a bill. The bill is then assigned to a committee for study. If released by the committee, the bill is put on a calendar to be voted on, debated or amended. If the bill passes by simple majority (218 of 435), the bill moves to the Senate. In the Senate, the bill is assigned to another committee and, if released, debated and voted on. Again, a simple majority (51 of 100) passes the bill. Finally, a conference committee made of House and Senate members works out any differences between the House and Senate versions of the bill. The resulting bill returns to the House and Senate for final approval. The Government Printing Office prints the revised bill in a process called enrolling. The President has 10 days to sign or veto the enrolled bill.

---

[3] https://www.house.gov/the-house-explained/the-legislative-process.

Votes within a chamber are key to the lawmaking process. A legislative division is a vote within the legislature to decide an issue. In most cases, such votes are undifferentiated, so that each member has one vote and all votes count the same. Thus, the outcome of the vote can be decided by a simple count of votes, though the decision rule need not be simple majority. Divisions commonly take place in the plenary but can also occur in committees. Legislators may need to cast votes at multiple stages of the legislative process. And of course, members vote on many matters in addition to legislative bills. Legislators may thus have to vote to select or confirm various officeholders, including, in many cases, the chamber's presiding officer or members of the executive or judiciary. Legislative divisions may also be employed in some countries to remove officeholders. Members may also vote on procedural matters, such as whether to permit amendments or end debate. Legislators may spend hours, days or even weeks debating an issue in committees, party caucuses, in leadership meetings, and in the "corridors," but actual decisions are typically made by a formal vote in a plenary session.

Legislative voting mechanisms vary by legislature, chamber, and possibly even by the topic of the vote. One source of variation has to do with the options available to the members. Some chambers give members the options to vote yes, vote no, or to abstain, whereas others require all members present to vote "up or down." A second important variable is quorum requirements, which refer to the number or proportion of members that must participate in a vote to make its decision valid. Higher quorums or the ability to abstain privilege members because these empower ordinary members over leaders.

Other variations have to do with voting procedure.[4] Some legislative divisions are decided by acclamation, with the presiding officer deducing the outcome by means such as a show of hands or the volume of verbal responses (ayes or nays). In such cases, the outcome of the vote is likely recorded but there may be no way of knowing which individual legislator voted which way. An alternative mechanism is for the official parliamentary record to show how each member voted. In some legislatures, the name of each member is read out and their reply recorded—a system known as roll-call voting. In fact, the term *roll-call* is now synonymous with legislative voting—thus scholars refer to "roll-call" analysis and "roll-call" behavior when discussing legislative divisions in which each member's vote can be identified, even when this is not the precise legislative voting mechanism used. In a number of assemblies, members have the opportunity to vote electronically. In some cases, voting is secret, so that the ultimate outcome of the vote—the decision— is recorded, but we have no way of knowing which legislator voted which way (assuming the vote was not unanimous). Secret voting has its pros and cons. It reduces the ability of voters (and party leaders) to hold individual legislators to

---

[4] See Rasch (1995) for an excellent survey of voting procedures in European parliaments and their implications.

account for their roll-call behavior. At the same time, this procedure allows legislators to vote their true preferences, without fear of retribution from party or constituents.

Voting procedures can be important for the outcome of legislative deliberations. Unrecorded votes, such as voice votes or votes by acclamation, make it easy for legislators to pass bills which they personally favor, but which their constituents might feel differently about (such as pay raises for the members themselves). Secret voting similarly makes it challenging for voters or party leaders to shape legislators' voting behavior. Both of these procedures should therefore correlate with a members' assembly. Ordinary recorded roll-call votes are the least forgiving for legislators, since their votes are on record and their attendance can also be ascertained.

When we can identify how members voted on any particular bill, their voting behavior provides us with important insights into political motivations. In particular, scholars have been long fascinated with the degree to which legislators from the same party vote together. As discussed in Chapter 7 and noted in the introduction to this chapter, legislators may face competing demands from competing principals—their voters versus their party—when deciding how to cast their roll-call vote. For any given vote, each legislator may have their own preferences but may also have to take into account (when voting is open and recorded) the preferences of voters as well as those of the party leadership. Often, the preferences of one or more of these actors may differ, requiring the legislator to choose between competing demands. Thus, legislators may have to weigh up the competing demands of voters, their party and their own personal policy preference and/or intuition. For this reason, the voting mechanism within a legislative assembly may have important consequences for, and privilege, voters, members or leaders.

9.3 Executive Agenda Control

The executive may have certain privileges with regard to the lawmaking process once the process has begun, possibly allowing these leaders to control the legislative assembly's timetable. Modern assemblies face what Cox (2006) describes as a plenary bottleneck. Plenary bottlenecks arise when the demand for legislation exceeds a legislature's capacity to find sufficient plenary time to consider all the proposed laws and amendments. One way to manage such plenary bottlenecks is to give some individual or group control of the chamber's agenda, or what is often referred to as the business of the chamber. In some legislatures (for example, Ireland since 2016), the legislative agenda is set by a business committee in which there is an attempt to get a consensual agreement of all party groups. In some legislative assemblies the government alone may determine the plenary agenda. In 17 of our countries (see table 9.2), the executive possesses some mechanism or combination of mechanisms to control the chamber timetable to effectively decide what bills get placed on the legislative agenda and debated. In one-quarter of the countries in our study, the executive thus has the authority to control the plenary timetable and holds significant de facto control over what issues and bills are debated. Executive gatekeeping refers to the ability of the executive to keep something off the legislature's agenda. Countries where the executive holds significant agenda powers include Chile, the United Kingdom, and the Philippines. In a majority of countries in our study, however, the executive has no capacity to keep issues off the legislative agenda.

Rasch (2014: 456) notes that agenda control can involve "agenda-setting (or generating), blocking (or delaying), and sequencing (or ordering) of alternatives before or until an outcome is reached." In many parliamentary systems, the executive controls the legislature's timetable (Cox 1987; Döring 2001), enjoys a near-monopoly on drafting power (Rasch 2014), and often has at its disposal rights to close debate, reject amendments, or exclusively offer the cabinet's own amendments.

Huber (1996) sheds light on agenda-setting and agenda-controlling instruments which on the face of it would seem to aid the executive's legislative hegemony. In particular, he focuses on the package vote (*vote bloqué*) arising from Article 44.3 of the Constitution of the French Fifth Republic. The package vote procedure allows the government to demand a vote in either chamber of the French legislature on all or part of a bill, retaining only the amendments that the government has proposed or accepted. It is generally acknowledged that the framers of France's Fifth Republic thus aimed to strengthen the executive by means of restrictive legislative procedures favoring the cabinet. Yet, Huber (1996 28) cautions that, "The prime minister . . . has institutional prerogatives that permit the government to influence policy proposals and voting. As in any parliamentary system, the prime minister can only exercise these prerogatives by maintaining the support of a majority in parliament."

Another significant agenda control tool available to the executive is the ability to curtail the legislative process of deliberation. In 20 of our countries, the executive has some such capacity to curtail the legislative process to its advantage. In the remaining 48 countries, however, the executive enjoys no such power to curtail the legislative process. Strong executive agenda control mechanisms of this kind are thus relatively rare, found in less than one-third of our assemblies. Table 9.3 reports results of a regression analysis where executive curtailment is the dependent variable. By curtailment, we mean the ability of the executive to, for example, set time limits on debate of a bill and/or bring a bill to a vote. The results in Table 9.3 provide suggestive evidence that majoritarian and economically more unequal (GINI) countries are more likely to grant agenda control to the executive. Conversely, countries with greater ethnic fractionalization are less likely to grant this power to the executive.

Table 9.2 Executive authority and legislative productivity

Country	Exec Control	Exec Gatekeeping	External Veto	Veto Override	Productivity
Argentina	No	No	Head of State, only	Yes, supermajority	110.7
Australia	Yes	Yes	No	NA	180
Austria	No	No	No	NA	125.6
Belgium	No	No	No	NA	165.8
Benin	No	No	Head of State, only	Yes, simple majority/plurality	20
Bolivia	No	No	Head of State, only	Yes, supermajority	125
Brazil	Yes	Yes	Head of State, only	Yes, simple majority/plurality	3111
Bulgaria	No	No	Head of State, only	Yes, simple majority/plurality	144.4
Burundi	Yes	Yes	Head of State, only	Yes, simple majority/plurality	
Canada	Yes	Yes	No	NA	32.7
Chile	Yes	Yes	Head of State, only	Yes, supermajority	
Colombia	Yes	Yes	Head of State, only	Yes, simple majority/plurality	
Costa Rica	No	Yes	Head of State, only	Yes, supermajority	85.7
Croatia	No	No	Courts, only	0	224
Czech Republic	No	No	Head of State, only	Yes, simple majority/plurality	98.6
Denmark	No	No	No	NA	218
Dominican Republic	No	No	Head of State, only	Yes, supermajority	
Ecuador	No	Yes	Head of State, only	Yes, supermajority	10.5
El Salvador	No	No	Head of State, only	Yes, supermajority	17
Finland	No	No	Head of State, only	Yes, simple majority/plurality	221.8
France	Yes	Yes	No	NA	50.6
Germany	No	No	No	NA	140

Ghana	Yes	Yes	Head of State, only	Yes, supermajority	23.25
Greece	Yes	Yes	Head of State, only	Yes, simple majority/plurality	99.2
Guatemala	No	No	Head of State, only	Yes, supermajority	47.2
Honduras	No	No	Head of State, only	Yes, supermajority	236.3
Hungary	No	No	Head of State or Courts	Yes, simple majority/plurality	203.2
India	No	No	Head of State, only	0	24.3
Indonesia	No	Yes	No	NA	34.8
Ireland	Yes	Yes	Courts, only	0	46.2
Israel	No	Yes	No	NA	157
Italy	No	No	Head of State, only	Yes, simple majority/plurality	90.2
Japan	No	No	No	NA	103.1
Kenya	No	No	Head of State, only	Yes, supermajority	26
Liberia	No	No	Head of State, only	Yes, supermajority	31.5
Malawi	Yes	Yes	Head of State, only	Yes, simple majority/plurality	
Mexico	No	No	Head of State, only	Yes, supermajority	97.5
Nepal	No	No	No	NA	
Netherlands	No	No	No	NA	?
New Zealand	No	No	No	NA	114.2
Nicaragua	No	No	Head of State, only	Yes, simple majority/plurality	
Niger	No	Yes	Head of State, only	Yes, simple majority/plurality	
Nigeria	No	No	Head of State, only	Yes, supermajority	26.5
Norway	No	No	Head of State, only	Yes, simple majority/plurality	112.9
Pakistan	No	No	Head of State, only	Yes, simple majority/plurality	14.7
Papua N.Guinea	No	No	No	NA	47.3

Continued

Table 9.2 *Continued*

Country	Exec Control	Exec Gatekeeping	External Veto	Veto Override	Productivity
Paraguay	Yes	No	Head of State, only	Yes, simple majority/plurality	256
Peru	No	No	Head of State, only	Yes, simple majority/plurality	104
Philippines	Yes	No	Head of State, only	Yes, supermajority	43.3
Poland	Yes	No	Head of State, only	Yes, supermajority	189.8
Portugal	No	Yes	Head of State, only	Yes, simple majority/plurality	84
Romania	No	No	Head of State, only	Yes, simple majority/plurality	318.2
Senegal	No	No	Head of State, only	Yes, supermajority	
Serbia	No	No	Head of State, only	Yes, simple majority/plurality	149.2
Sierra Leone	No	No	Head of State, only	Yes, supermajority	11.8
Slovak Republik	No	No	Head of State, only	Yes, simple majority/plurality	127
South Africa	No	No	Head of State or Courts	Yes, simple majority/plurality	
South Korea	No	Yes	Head of State, only	Yes, supermajority	1444.3
Spain	No	No	No	NA	39.4
Sweden	No	No	No	NA	204
Switzerland	No	No	Other Institutions	0	121
Taiwan	No	No	No	NA	210
Tunisia	No	No	Head of State or Courts	Yes, simple majority/plurality	
Turkey	Yes	Yes	Head of State, only	Yes, simple majority/plurality	159.4
Ukraine	No	No	Head of State, only	Yes, supermajority	253.4
United Kingdom	Yes	Yes	No	NA	32.2
United States	No	No	Head of State, only	Yes, supermajority	190.8
Zambia	Yes	No	Head of State, only	Yes, supermajority	24

Table 9.3 Executive agenda control

	Executive Agenda Control					
	(1)	(2)	(3)	(4)	(5)	(6)
Presidential	0.12				0.20	
	(0.11)				(0.16)	
Federal	−0.10				−0.12	
	(0.13)				(0.16)	
Majoritarian	0.25*				0.37**	0.40***
	(0.14)				(0.16)	(0.12)
Mixed	−0.06				−0.03	
	(0.13)				(0.15)	
Mean District Magnitude	−0.001				0.0001	
	(0.001)				(0.001)	
Sovereignty		0.0000			−0.003	
		(0.002)			(0.003)	
log(GDP per Capita)		−0.02				
		(0.05)				
GINI		0.02**				0.02***
		(0.01)				(0.01)
log(Population)		0.05			0.05	
		(0.04)			(0.05)	
Ethnic Fractionalization		−0.51*			−0.59**	−0.66***
		(0.27)			(0.28)	(0.22)
Africa and Middle East			0.08		0.18	
			(0.16)		(0.24)	
Asia and Oceania			−0.07		−0.09	
			(0.17)		(0.21)	
Americas			0.04		0.01	
			(0.15)		(0.21)	
Eastern Europe			−0.14		0.11	
			(0.18)		(0.23)	
British Colony				0.24		
				(0.15)		
Other Colony				0.08		
				(0.12)		
Constant	0.20**	−0.81	0.25**	0.16	4.44	−0.35
	(0.09)	(4.25)	(0.11)	(0.10)	(5.00)	(0.23)
N	68	68	68	68	68	68
R^2	0.12	0.12	0.03	0.04	0.24	0.23
Adjusted R^2	0.05	0.05	−0.03	0.01	0.07	0.19

Notes: The dependent variable is Can the executive curtail the legislative process? (1 = Yes; 0 = No); *$p < .1$; **$p < .05$; ***$p < .01$.

9.4 External Veto Players

As we have already noted, a legislative assembly may not have a complete monopoly on the generation of new laws. Beyond alternative sources of laws, one other factor may critically impinge on the lawmaking capacity of the legislative assembly: the presence of a player external to the legislative assembly itself who can veto assembly decisions. Tsebelis (1995: 293) defines a veto player as "an individual or collective actor whose agreement is required for a policy decision." An external veto player with regard to lawmaking is an individual or collective actor outside of the legislative assembly who can veto bills approved by the legislative assembly and thus prevent them from becoming law.

In 18 of the 68 countries in our study, no external agent can veto a bill passed by the legislative assembly and thus prevent it from becoming law (see Table 9.2). This is the case, for example, in Belgium, Germany, Israel, and Taiwan. In a number of such countries, the head of state may play a formal role by signing the bill into law (in some political systems this is referred to as giving royal-assent to the bill), but the head of state has no discretion—the bill as presented by the legislative assembly must be signed. This is the case, for example, in a number of the constitutional monarchies around Europe, including the United Kingdom, where the monarch formally signs a bill into law. In the United Kingdom, this royal assent has not been refused by a monarch since 1707.[5] In 1990, the then King of Belgium, Baudouin I, was temporarily suspended as head of state by the Belgian government after he expressed unease at signing a bill related to abortion. Using a constitutional procedure, the government deemed the King temporarily "unable to govern," assumed the King's powers, promulgated the abortion law, and thereafter worked with the Belgian parliament to immediately reinstate the King.[6]

In five countries—Croatia, Hungary, South Africa, Tunisia, and Ireland—a court can veto proposed legislation.[7] In three of these cases (Hungary, South Africa, and Tunisia), either the court or head of state can veto proposed legislation. In Ireland, a bill passed by Parliament is sent to the President for signing. The President has two options: He can sign the bill into law or he can refer the bill to the Supreme Court for the court to decide on the bill's compatibility with the Constitution. If the Supreme Court rules that the bill is compatible with the Constitution, the President must then sign it into law.[8] If the Supreme Court rules

---

[5] Absent a written constitution, we therefore code the United Kingdom as being a country without an external veto-player.

[6] https://www.nytimes.com/1990/04/05/world/belgian-king-unable-to-sign-abortion-law-takes-day-off.html.

[7] To clarify, veto power in this context relates to the formal capacity of the court to review and permit or veto proposed legislation. In most political systems, enacted law may be subject to constitutional review.

[8] The "cost" or difficulty of this process is that the constitutionality of any part of the law cannot subsequently be challenged by individuals in the court system.

otherwise, the bill fails. Thus in the Irish case, the President is not a veto player but can set the agenda with regard to whether or not the Supreme Court becomes a veto player in that particular case.

In 47 of our 68 cases the head of state can veto proposed legislation. For example, the United States President can veto a bill passed by the United States Congress. He must, however, accept or veto the bill in its entirety. The alternative approach is known as a line-item or partial veto; which means that the veto player can choose to approve some parts of the bill and reject others. In *Clinton v. City of New York*, 524 US 417 (1998), the US Supreme Court ruled that a US President does not have the right to partial veto.

The veto power of a head of state may not be water-tight. In fact, for those countries with an external veto, some form of veto-override is very common. Only three countries—India, Croatia, and Ireland—permit no veto override. In 22 countries in our study, a special majority of the legislative assembly can override the external veto. As discussed above, the United States permits the legislative assembly to override a veto by a two–thirds vote of each house. For example during the Presidency of Barack Obama, the President vetoed 12 pieces of legislation, with Congress over-riding the presidential veto on one occasion. In another 24 countries, a veto can be overcome by a simple majority/plurality vote in the legislative assembly. This is the case for example in Paraguay and Italy.

Table 9.4 presents the results of a regression analysis where the dependent variable is the presence of an external veto player with respect to bills passed by the legislature. The dependent variable takes the value equal to one if an external agent can veto legislation passed by the legislature, and zero otherwise. The results in Table 9.2 suggest that presidential countries, former colonies, and more unequal societies (GINI) are more likely to have external veto players. By comparison, richer countries are less likely to have an external veto player.

9.5 Legislative Productivity

If lawmaking is a core function of a legislative assembly, one way to assess its performance is to look at legislative productivity—the number of bills passed into law.[9] In this section, we explore legislative productivity by looking at the average no of bills passed into law per annum between 2005 and 2015.[10]

---

[9] Thus we should differentiate between legislative productivity—the measure of laws passed—and the productivity of the legislature—a more general measure encompassing the various roles and functions of a legislative assembly.

[10] We were unable to collect, and therefore are missing data on legislative productivity for the following cases: Burundi, Chile, Colombia, Dominican Republic, Malawi, Nepal, Nicaragua, Niger, Senegal, South Africa, and Tunisia. Where data were available for only some of the years 2005–15, our measure is the mean of the years for which data were available.

Table 9.4 External veto players

	External Veto Players					
	(1)	(2)	(3)	(4)	(5)	(6)
Presidential	0.40***				0.31**	0.23
	(0.10)				(0.14)	(0.14)
Federal	−0.15				−0.03	
	(0.13)				(0.14)	
Majoritarian	−0.11				−0.14	
	(0.13)				(0.14)	
Mixed	−0.04				0.04	
	(0.13)				(0.13)	
Mean District Magnitude	0.001				−0.001	
	(0.001)				(0.001)	
Sovereignty		0.002			0.003	
		(0.002)			(0.002)	
log(GDP per Capita)		−0.10**				−0.04
		(0.05)				(0.04)
GINI		0.02**				0.003
		(0.01)				(0.01)
log(Population)		−0.03			0.04	
		(0.04)			(0.04)	
Ethnic Fractionalization		−0.19			0.02	
		(0.25)			(0.24)	
Africa and Middle East			0.50***		0.20	0.23
			(0.13)		(0.21)	(0.16)
Asia and Oceania			−0.07		−0.24	
			(0.14)		(0.18)	
Americas			0.50***		0.22	0.22
			(0.13)		(0.18)	(0.18)
Eastern Europe			0.56***		0.48**	0.54***
			(0.15)		(0.20)	(0.16)
British Colony				0.31**		0.06
				(0.14)		(0.14)
Other Colony				0.49***		0.09
				(0.11)		(0.14)
Constant	0.62***	−1.87	0.44***	0.42***	−5.14	0.70
	(0.09)	(4.00)	(0.09)	(0.09)	(4.27)	(0.53)
N	68	68	68	68	68	68
R^2	0.23	0.25	0.37	0.22	0.46	0.44
Adjusted R^2	0.17	0.19	0.33	0.20	0.35	0.37

Notes: The dependent variable measures whether an external agent veto legislation? (1 = Yes; 0 = No);
*p < 0.1; **p < 0.05; ***p < 0.01.

Across all our cases, the average legislature produced 189 laws per annum. There is significant variation in the volume of legislation passed between different legislative assemblies (see Table 9.2). We find the lowest levels of lawmaking productivity in Ecuador (an average of 10.5 laws per annum), followed by Sierra Leone (11.8 bills per annum) and Pakistan (14.7 bills per annum). At the other end of the scale, Romania has the third-highest rate of legislative productivity, with an average of 318.2 bills past per year. Two outliers round off the upper-end of the productivity score: In South Korea, 1444.3 pieces of legislation were enacted on average. In Brazil, this number was even higher at 3111 per annum. Thus, for every law passed by the Ecuadorian legislature, the assembly in neighboring Brazil adopts roughly 300.

What explains this large variation in legislative productivity? We begin by looking at whether or not the regime type (parliamentary, semi-presidential, or presidential) affects legislative productivity. It may be that elected presidents constitute the most consequential veto players. The presence of a veto player in the form of an elected president may reduce the rate of legislative productivity. At a very first look, this seems to be what Figure 9.1 demonstrates. Looking first at the mean number of bills passed across regime types, presidential regimes seem the most productive. Indeed, presidential regimes are on average more than twice as productive as parliamentary regimes, with semi-presidential regimes falling in-between. This is a counter-intuitive finding, and may be driven by particularly high or low levels of productivity in a small number of assemblies, such as for example Brazil or Ecuador. Looking at the median scores, the picture is very different. Using median scores, legislative assemblies in presidential systems pass far less legislation than either semi-presidential or parliamentary systems. Interestingly, the median scores suggest that assemblies in semi-presidential systems pass the highest numbers of bills.

9.6 Conclusion

Law making is a key function of democratic assemblies. In fact, in many countries laws can only formally be made or unmade by the national assembly. Even in democracies where other institutions, such as executives and/or courts, play a major role in this process, they often cannot do so without the participation or at least toleration of the assembly. The lawmaking process is often complex and arcane, and its formalities may baffle all but the most knowledgeable aficionados. At the same time, however, it is useful and typically fairly easy to identify the formal role that the assembly plays in the introduction, scrutiny, amendment, and final passage (or rejection) of proposed legislation. In this chapter, we have examined various stages of the lawmaking process, from the proposal stage to the end of the legislative process, terminating either in legislative passage, rejection by the

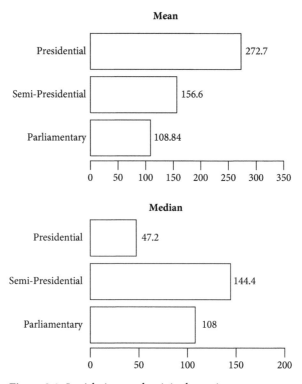

Figure 9.1 Legislative productivity by regime type

assembly, or the intervention and possible veto by other institutional agents such as executives or courts.

In democratic societies, law making is rarely the province of any single institutional actor. In the great majority of the countries in our study, the right to propose new laws, or amendments to existing ones, is given to political executives as well as to ordinary members of the assembly. In smaller numbers of countries, other actors share this prerogative as well. Thus, in some countries (about one-fourth of our sample), political parties are recognized as having this right. A similar and apparently growing number of countries allow ordinary citizens the same opportunity. Thus, on the whole executives rarely enjoy complete legislative gatekeeping powers, and their control of the making of non-financial laws is generally weaker than that of financial legislation.

The legislative assembly is often thought of as the end point of the process of law making, but in fact many democracies allow executive vetoes or judicial review of legislation. In the case of executive vetoes, there is typically an opportunity for a legislative override, whereas in the case of judicial review, there is rarely any arguing with the court's decision, though the legislature may well decide to reconsider a version of the bill that is more to the court's liking.

It is difficult to compare the outcomes of the lawmaking process from one country to another, but in this chapter we have examined the average (mean) number of bills passed in each of our democracies between 2005 and 2015. As we have seen, the variation is huge, with Brazil passing roughly 300 times as many bills per year as neighboring Ecuador. Since both of these regimes are presidential, it is hard to see regime type as having a strong determining effect on legislative productivity, and in fact our results do not suggest any strong such regularity. Yet, we do find indications that better-resourced assemblies in more affluent countries tend to be more productive than those in poorer countries and those with fewer resources. Whether a high output of laws per annum is good or bad for society at large, however, is a matter that we cannot settle in this chapter.

References

Baumgartner, Frank R., and Bryan D. Jones. 2010. *Agendas and Instability in American Politics*. University of Chicago Press.

Bowler, Shaun, Todd Donovan, and Caroline J. Tolbert. 1998. *Citizens as Legislators: Direct Democracy in the United States*. Columbus: Ohio State University Press.

Carey, John M. and Matthew S. Shugart (eds.). 1998. *Executive Decree Authority*. New York: Cambridge University Press.

Cox, Gary W. 1987. *The Efficient Secret: The Cabinet and the Development of Political Parties in Victorian England*. Cambridge: Cambridge University Press.

Cox, Gary W. 2006. "The Organization of Democratic Legislatures." In Barry R. Weingast and Donald Wittman (eds.), *The Oxford Handbook of Political Economy*. Oxford: Oxford University Press, 141–161.

Döring, Herbert. 2001. "Parliamentary Agenda Control and Legislative Outcomes in Western Europe." *Legislative Studies Quarterly* 26(1): 145–165.

Fowler, James H. 2006. "Connecting the Congress: A Study of Cosponsorship Networks." *Political Analysis* 14(4): 456–487.

Huber, John D. 1996. *Rationalizing Parliament: Legislative Institutions and Party Politics in France*. New York: Cambridge University Press.

IDEA. 2008. *Direct Democracy The International IDEA Handbook*. Available online: http://www.eods.eu/library/IDEA.Direct-DemocracyEN.pdf.

Lynch, Catherine, and Shane Martin. 2020. "Can Parliaments Be Strengthened? A Case Study of Pre-legislative Scrutiny." *Irish Political Studies* 35(1): 138–157.

Modernisation Committee, *The Legislative Process*. September 7, 2006, HC 1097 2005–06.

Montesquieu, Charles de S. 1989 [1748] *The Spirit of the Laws*. New York: Cambridge University Press.

Mezey, Michael L. 1979. *Comparative Legislatures*. Durham, NC: Duke University Press.

Norton, Philip (2013). *Parliament in British Politics*. Basingstoke: Palgrave Macmillan.

Palanza, Valeria. 2019. *Checking Presidential Power: Executive Decrees and the Legislative Process in New Democracies*. New York: Cambridge University Press.

Palanza, Valeria, and Gisela Sin. 2014. "Veto Bargaining and the Legislative Process in Multiparty Presidential Systems." *Comparative Political Studies* 47(5): 766–792.

Rasch, Bjørn Erik. 1995. "Parliamentary Voting Procedures." In Herbert Döring (ed.), *Parliaments and Majority Rule in Western Europe*. Frankfurt: Campus, 566–589.

Rasch, Bjørn Erik. 2014. "Institutional Foundations of Legislative Agenda Setting." In Shane Martin, Thomas Saalfeld, and Kaare W Strøm (eds.), *The Oxford Handbook of Legislative Studies*. Oxford: Oxford University Press, 455–480.

Russell, Meg, and Daniel Gover. 2017. *Legislation at Westminster: Parliamentary Actors and Influence in the Making of British Law*. Oxford: Oxford University Press.

Smookler, Jennifer. 2006. "Making a Difference? The Effectiveness of Pre-legislative Scrutiny." *Parliamentary Affairs* 59(3): 522–535.

Tsebelis, George. 1995. "Decision Making in Political Systems: Veto Players in Presidentialism, Parliamentarism, Multicameralism and Multipartyism." *British Journal of Political Science* 25: 289–325.

10

The Budgetary Process

Politics is often conceived as fundamentally being about "who gets what, when, and how" (Lasswell 1936). The budgetary process determines many of these distributive questions. Few public policies are costless to implement. Government (in the broad sense), no matter how limited and small, involves some expenditure. And it must secure enough revenue to fund such expenditure. Some public policies have greater distributive consequences than others. Public policies such as welfare, national defense, education, and healthcare may require governments to spend significant resources. Such expenditure must be paid for—either from taxing individuals or corporations, from any surplus the government can generate through public enterprises, from selling natural resources such as oil, or through government borrowing, which is in effect a form of deferred taxation. Today, government expenditure accounts for a significant proportion of economic activity in democratic countries—61.4 percent in France, 51.5 percent in the United Kingdom, 47.8 percent in the United States, and 33.9 percent in Korea, to list but a few.[1] What such data reveals is that notwithstanding noteworthy cross-national variation in the extent of government involvement, public expenditure today constitutes a significant part of national economic activity.

Making budgetary decisions is clearly one of the key functions of democratic legislatures. Yet, because budgetary powers are so critical, there is no shortage of claimants, and legislative assemblies may be more or less involved in determining exactly how much the government taxes and borrows and spends across different policy areas. The extent of involvement of a legislative assembly in the budgetary process is often referred to as the legislature's "power of the purse." Cox (2014: 696) defines the power of the purse as "the power to deny, amend, or approve new taxes; new sovereign debt; and the state's annual expenditures." In many countries these powers are deeply rooted in history. Thus, Cox (2014) notes that while the power of the purse was established in the UK Parliament by the mid-1690s, executives across the world have often been very reluctant to yield such powers to the national assembly and creative in the ways in which they have loaded the dice in their own favor in the struggle for control over public spending. Fast-forward a few centuries, and in one of the few book-length treatments of the subject Wehner (2010) writes

---

[1] Source: https://data.oecd.org/gga/general-government-spending.htm. These figures represent total general government spending, as a percentage of Gross Domestic Product, 2020 or latest available. Accessed August 17, 2022.

Legislative Assemblies. Shane Martin and Kaare W. Strøm, Oxford University Press.
© Shane Martin and Kaare W. Strøm (2023). DOI: 10.1093/oso/9780198890829.003.0010

of the decay of budgetary control by national legislatures and the "myth of fiscal control."

The capacity of legislative assemblies to regulate government income and expenditure is an important, if understudied, aspect of executive-legislative relations. Cox (2014: 710) argues that "any measure of legislative power should be mostly about the legislature's power over the purse. If that power fails, the others will likely be illusory." He goes on (Cox 2014: 712) to suggest that:

> Legislatures can effectively hold executives accountable for their actions if and only if they are armed with a secure power over the purse. Indeed, I would argue that the distinction between regimes with and without fiscally strong legislatures may be more fundamental than the canonical distinction between presidential, semi-presidential, and parliamentary regimes.

This focus on the significance of budgetary rules for legislative assemblies, and the operation of government more generally, has a long lineage. For Montesquieu (1989[1748]: 164) the power of the purse defined the very notions of liberty versus tyranny: "If the executive power enacts on the raising of public funds without the consent of the legislature, there will no longer be liberty, because the executive power will become the legislator on the most important point of legislation." In *Federalist* No. 58, James Madison (2009 [1788]: 298) noted that "power over the purse may, in fact, be regarded as the most complete and effectual weapon with which any constitution can arm the immediate representatives of the people, for obtaining a redress of every grievance, and for carrying into effect every just and salutary measure."

This chapter explores the role of legislative assemblies in the budgetary process. Our primary objective is to explore current-day cross-national variation in legislative assemblies' power of the purse. We expect an assembly's budgetary capacity to be related to its purposes. A members' assembly may use the budgetary process to seek rents or win personal votes for incumbent members (or at least the more influential ones), to the detriment of fiscal discipline. In contrast, a voters' assembly and a leaders' assembly will in different ways seek to overcome the collective action problems of budgeting for a large number of discrete local constituencies. Leaders' assemblies will tend to pursue budgetary policies with broader sets of beneficiaries and preferably diffuse costs, falling mainly on the supporters of the political "outs." Voters' assemblies will under favorable circumstances tend to seek policies that are either close to Pareto efficiency (no net losers) or that generate sufficiently large net benefits that any broad set of losers can be compensated. On the other hand, voters' assemblies (and other types as well) may be driven in their budgetary decisions by wishful thinking and fiscal illusions or time inconsistency problems, such that their budgetary decisions for example favor current generations over future ones, or those with voting rights over others affected by budgetary decisions. If having a weak role for legislative assemblies in the budgetary process therefore deflates the budget and reduces over-spending, then citizens, as a whole and over the long run, will benefit.

10.1 Measuring Budgetary Powers

While we may expect different levels of legislative power over the budgetary process to have different consequences, the first task in studying budgetary processes is to capture empirically the wide variation in budgetary powers. Given the institutional complexity of such decisions, this is no easy task. Thankfully, we can be guided in this process by Wehner's (2006) seminal analysis. To understand better and measure legislative assemblies' power of the purse, we discuss below six aspects of the budgetary process identified by Wehner: (1) the degree to which the legislative assembly can amend the proposed budget, (2) what happens if no budget is agreed (the budgetary reversion), (3) the degree to which the executive has flexibility during budget implementation, (4) the amount of time available to the legislative assembly to consider the budget, (5) the role and significance of legislative committees in the budgetary process, and (6) the level of budgetary information available to the legislative assembly. Following Wehner (2006), we will use these data to create an index of the cross-national variation in the legislature's power of the purse. This index, we will see, can be related to our three ideal-type legislative assemblies. We begin by discussing each component in detail.

Amendment Powers

The national assembly is rarely the institution that makes the first move in the budgetary process. As Cox (2014: 701) notes, the executive "under almost all constitutions, has the right to make the first proposal on the budget." Thus, the budgetary process can be considered a sequential game, in which the executive makes the first (visible and formal) move. Exactly how a legislative assembly can respond, and in particular its power to amend the executive's proposed budget, may vary greatly. The first component of Wehner's (2006) index seeks to capture this variation in the ability of the legislative assembly to amend the proposed budget. At one end of the scale, the legislative assembly may only be able to vote to accept or reject the proposed budget, with no right to offer or make amendments. As Table 10.1 (column titled *Amendment Powers*) reports, this is the case in no more than three countries in our study (Ecuador's *Asamblea Nacional*, Greece's Parliament of the Hellenes and Ireland's Houses of the *Oireachtas*). In these three cases, the legislative assembly has no opportunity to make amendments to the government's proposed budget. South Africa had a similar budgetary rule but this

Table 10.1 Budgetary powers

Country	Amendment Powers	Reversion	Withhold	Reallocate	Reserve Funds	Flexibility	Time	Budget Cttee.	Portfolio Cttee.	Audit Cttee.	Cttee. Index	Research Office	Index
Argentina	6.7	6.7	3.3	0	3.3	6.7	3.3	3.3	0	3.3	6.7	0	50.2
Australia	3.3	3.3	3.3	0	0	3.3	0	3.3	0	3.3	6.7	10	44.3
Austria	10	6.7	3.3	0	0	3.3	3.3	3.3	0	3.3	6.7	10	66.7
Belgium	10	6.7	3.3	0	0	3.3	3.3	3.3	3.3	1.7	8.3	0	52.7
Benin	6.7	0	3.3	3.3	0	6.7	3.3	3.3	0	0	3.3	10	50.0
Bolivia	10	0	3.3	0	3.3	6.7	3.3	3.3	0	0	3.3	0	38.8
Brazil	6.7	6.7	0	0	0	0	3.3	3.3	0	0	3.3	10	50.0
Bulgaria	10	6.7	0	0	0	0	0	3.3	0	0	3.3	0	33.3
Burundi	6.7	6.7	0	0	0	0	3.3	3.3	0	0	3.3	0	33.3
Canada	3.3	3.3	3.3	3.3	0	6.7	0	0	3.3	3.3	6.7	10	50.0
Chile	3.3	0	3.3	0	0	3.3	3.3	3.3	3.3	0	6.7	0	27.7
Colombia	6.7	0	0	3.3	0	3.3	3.3	3.3	0	3.3	6.7	0	33.3
Costa Rica	6.7	3.3	3.3	3.3	3.3	10	3.3	3.3	0	3.3	6.7	0	50.0
Croatia	6.7	10	0	0	0	0	0	3.3	0	0	3.3	0	33.3
Czech Republic	6.7	6.7	3.3	0	0	3.3	6.7	3.3	0	1.7	5	0	47.3
Denmark	10	6.7	3.3	3.3	0	6.7	3.3	3.3	0	3.3	6.7	0	55.7
Dominican Republic	10	6.7	3.3	3.3	0	6.7	3.3	3.3	0	3.3	6.7	10	72.3
Ecuador	0	0	0	0	3.3	3.3	0	3.3	0	0	3.3	10	27.7
El Salvador	3.3	6.7	0	3.3	3.3	6.7	3.3	3.3	0	3.3	6.7	10	61.2
Finland	10	0	3.3	3.3	0	6.7	3.3	3.3	0	0	3.3	0	38.8
France	3.3	6.7	0	0	0	0	3.3	3.3	0	1.7	5	10	47.2
Germany	10	6.7	3.3	0	3.3	6.7	6.7	3.3	0	1.7	5	0	58.5
Ghana	3.3	10	0	3.3	3.3	6.7	0	3.3	0	0	3.3	0	38.8
Greece	0	6.7	3.3	0	0	3.3	0	3.3	0	1.7	5	10	41.7
Guatemala	10	6.7	0	0	3.3	3.3	3.3	3.3	0	0	3.3	0	44.3
Honduras	10	6.7	3.3	0	3.3	6.7	3.3	3.3	0	0	3.3	10	66.7
Hungary	10	10	3.3	3.3	0	6.7	3.3	3.3	0	3.3	6.7	10	77.8

India	10	3.3	0	3.3	0	3.3	0	0	3.3	3.3	6.7	0	38.8
Indonesia	6.7	6.7	3.3	3.3	3.3	10	3.3	3.3	0	3.3	6.7	0	55.7
Ireland	0	10	3.3	3.3	3.3	10	0	0	3.3	3.3	6.7	0	44.5
Israel	6.7	6.7	3.3	3.3	0	6.7	3.3	3.3	0	3.3	6.7	10	61.3
Italy	6.7	0	3.3	3.3	0	6.7	3.3	3.3	0	0	3.3	10	50.0
Japan	10	10	3.3	3.3	0	6.7	0	3.3	0	3.3	6.7	10	77.8
Kenya	6.7	10	0	0	0	0	0	3.3	0	3.3	6.7	10	55.7
Liberia	10	10	3.3	0	3.3	6.7	0	3.3	0	3.3	6.7	10	72.3
Malawi	10	6.7	3.3	3.3	3.3	10	3.3	3.3	0	3.3	6.7	10	72.3
Mexico	10	10	0	0	0	0	0	3.3	3.3	3.3	10	10	72.2
Nepal	10	6.7	0	3.3	0	3.3	0	3.3	0	3.3	6.7	0	44.5
Netherlands	6.7	6.7	3.3	0	0	3.3	0	0	3.3	0	3.3	10	55.5
New Zealand	10	3.3	3.3	3.3	0	6.7	0	3.3	3.3	0	6.7	0	44.5
Nicaragua	6.7	0	3.3	3.3	0	6.7	3.3	3.3	0	3.3	6.7	10	55.7
Niger	6.7	0	0	0	3.3	3.3	3.3	3.3	0	3.3	6.7	10	50.0
Nigeria	10	6.7	0	3.3	0	3.3	0	3.3	0	3.3	6.7	10	61.2
Norway	10	10	3.3	3.3	0	6.7	0	3.3	3.3	0	6.7	0	61.2
Pakistan	3.3	3.3	0	0	0	0	0	3.3	0	3.3	6.7	0	22.2
Papua New Guinea	3.3	6.7	3.3	0	0	3.3	0	3.3	0	0	3.3	0	33.2
Paraguay	6.7	0	0	0	3.3	3.3	3.3	3.3	0	3.3	6.7	0	33.3
Peru	3.3	0	3.3	3.3	3.3	10	3.3	3.3	0	3.3	6.7	0	38.8
Philippines	3.3	6.7	0	0	0	0	0	3.3	0	3.3	6.7	10	50.0
Poland	6.7	0	3.3	0	0	3.3	0	3.3	0	3.3	6.7	10	50.0
Portugal	10	6.7	3.3	0	0	3.3	0	3.3	0	0	3.3	10	61.0
Romania	6.7	6.7	3.3	3.3	3.3	10	3.3	3.3	0	3.3	6.7	10	66.8
Senegal	6.7	0	0	0	0	0	0	3.3	0	0	3.3	0	16.7
Serbia	6.7	10	3.3	3.3	0	6.7	0	3.3	0	3.3	6.7	0	50.2
Sierra Leone	6.7	0	0	0	3.3	6.7	0	3.3	0	3.3	6.7	0	33.5

Continued

Table 10.1 *Continued*

Country	Amendment Powers	Reversion	Withhold	Reallocate	Reserve Funds	Flexibility	Time	Budget Cttee.	Portfolio Cttee.	Audit Cttee.	Cttee. Index	Research Office	Index
Slovak Republik	10	6.7	0	0	3.3	3.3	3.3	3.3	0	0	3.3	0	44.3
South Africa	10	0	3.3	3.3	3.3	10	0	3.3	3.3	3.3	10	10	66.7
South Korea	3.3	6.7	3.3	0	0	3.3	3.3	3.3	0	0	3.3	10	49.8
Spain	6.7	6.7	0	0	0	0	3.3	3.3	0	1.7	5	0	36.2
Sweden	10	10	3.3	3.3	0	6.7	3.3	3.3	3.3	0	6.7	10	77.8
Switzerland	10	10	3.3	3.3	0	6.7	3.3	3.3	0	3.3	6.7	0	61.2
Taiwan	3.3	10	3.3	3.3	3.3	10	3.3	3.3	3.3	3.3	10	10	77.7
Tunisia	6.7	0	0	0	0	0	0	3.3	0	3.3	6.7	10	39.0
Turkey	6.7	3	3.3	0	0	3.3	3.3	3.3	0	0	3.3	0	32.7
Ukraine	10	6.7	0	3.3	0	3.3	3.3	3.3	0	3.3	6.7	10	66.7
United Kingdom	3.3	3.3	3.3	0	0	3.3	0	0	3.3	3.3	6.7	0	27.7
United States	10	10	3.3	3.3	0	6.7	10	3.3	3.3	0	6.7	10	89.0
Zambia	3.3	0	0	0	0	0	3.3	3.3	0	3.3	6.7	0	22.2

Notes: For Amendment Powers, 0 = accept or reject only; 3.3 = cuts only or other severe restrictions; 6.7 = aggregate constraint; 10 = unfettered power to amend. For Reversion, the reversionary budget, 0 = executive budget proposal, 3.3 = vote on account (see text); 6.7 = last year's budget, and 10 = legislature approves interim measure. For Withhold, 0 = may withhold funds without legislature approval, 3.3 = may not withhold funds or only with legislative approval. For Reallocate, 0 = may reallocate funds without legislature approval, 3.3 = may not reallocate funds or only with legislative approval. Reserve Funds equals 0 if reserve fund; 3.3 = no reserve fund. Flexibility is calculated as the sum of the last three variables (Withhold + Reallocate + Reserve Funds), ranging from 0 = full executive flexibility to 10 = no executive flexibility. Time is coded as 0 = up to 2 months; 3.3 = up to 4 months; 6.7 = up to 6 months, and 10 = more than 6 months. Budget Cttee = Scores 0 = if no budget committee or 3.3 = budget committee. Portfolio Cttee. scores 0 =if portfolio committees play no substantive role; 3.3 = decide departmental budgets. Audit Cttee. Scores 0 = no specialized audit committee; 1.7 = audit sub-committees; 3.3 = specialized audit committee. Cttee. Index is calculated as the sum of the last three variables (Budget Cttee. + Portfolio Cttee. + Audit Cttee.), and ranges from zero (no committee capacity) to 10 = (full committee capacity). Research Office equals one if national legislature have a specialized research office/unit to conduct analyses of the budget; zero otherwise. Index is the sum of the six main variables divided by 0.6.

rule was changed in 2009 so that the South African Parliament can now propose budgetary amendments. The "take it or leave it" nature of the no-amendment decision rule disadvantages members of the legislative assembly. We know that such "accept or reject" scenarios give bargaining advantages to the proposer (Romer and Rosenthal 1978; Baron and Ferejohn 1989). Since the executive gets to set the agenda which the legislature can then only accept or reject, the assembly should accept any proposal that is better than the reversion for its decisive members, even if there are many feasible alternatives that a majority of the members would prefer.

At the other end of the scale, a legislative assembly may have unfettered authority to amend the executive's proposed budget. This is the case in 27 countries in our study, ranging from Austria to the United States. All else equal, such unfettered rights to amend the budget, including total spending and the allocation of resources across policy domains, empower the legislature to the maximal extent. Between these two extremes, we can identify two intermediate levels of amendment rights. In 14 countries in our study, the legislative assembly can make limited amendments. Wehner (2006: 779) describes these as "amendments which reduce existing items but not those which shift funds around, increase items or introduce new ones." Examples of countries in this category include Australia, Canada and the United Kingdom but also countries as diverse as Chile, France, Taiwan, and Zambia. In Chile for example "[a]fter the executive submits the budget proposal to congress, the legislature may only reduce the size of budget items, and cannot reallocate the budget (even if it were to compensate any potential increases in an item with decreases in another one" (Ardanaz and Scartascini 2014: no pagination). Finally, in 24 countries in our study, the legislative assembly may amend the details of the budget but the aggregate totals in the draft budget must be maintained. This aggregate constraint allows the assembly to reassign spending but not to increase or decrease the executive's proposed overall expenditure. Argentina and Turkey represent two cases where the executive's proposed level of expenditure cannot be changed by their respective legislative assemblies, though spending can be shifted among policy areas within this constraint.

The scope of budgetary amendment powers has clear relevance for the assembly's purposes and issues of capacity and accountability. We expect a members' assembly to have stronger amendment powers. The implications for a voters' assembly are less straightforward. A concentration of fiscal power in the executive may serve to empower citizens to the extent that it avoids the inefficiencies and collective action problems that may result from a more inclusive budgetary process. On the other hand, a more decentralized budget process may generate greater transparency (and accountability) and permit more options favored by citizens to be considered. As will become clear, such trade-offs characterize many of the features of the budgetary process. Leaders' assemblies should tend to have weaker budget powers, members' assemblies stronger ones, whereas for voters' assemblies there will often be a trade-off that cannot easily be resolved in one direction or the other.

Reversionary Budget

Wehner's second variable relates to what happens if the legislative assembly fails to pass a budget, sometimes referred to as the reversionary budget or reversionary point in the budgetary process. As with amendment powers, the reversion point impacts the relative bargaining strengths of the executive and the legislative assembly. Some budgetary reversion points empower the legislative assembly in budget negotiations, whereas other reversionary points advantage the executive. Of course, the reversion point has real-world implications, particularly where the government or parts of the government may have to stop functioning in case of a lack of an agreed budget. For example, in 2013 (parts of) the US Federal Government "shut down" for 13 days, with further "shutdowns" in 2018 and 2019.

What are the possible reversion points when a legislative assembly fails to pass a budget? One possible reversion point in the absence of an agreed budget is that the executive's proposed budget is implemented. In other words, if the legislative assembly has failed to accept the proposed budget but passed no alternative budget, the executive can nevertheless implement its proposal. This occurs in 17 of our 68 cases, including Peru and Italy (see column headed *Reversion* in Table 10.1). Such implementation of the proposed budget could take the form of either a definitive implementation of the executive's proposal, or the proposed budget could be implemented on an interim basis or as an emergency budget until agreement is reached between the executive and legislative assembly.

In a further eight countries in our study, the reversionary point is what Wehner (2006) describes as a "vote on account." Here the legislative assembly approves interim spending, typically policy-area by policy-area. We find this occurring in the United Kingdom and a number of English-speaking Commonwealth countries such as Australia and Canada, but also in Costa Rica. For example, in Australia: "75–80 per cent of the Budget has ongoing legislative approval and will continue. The remainder that does not have approval will cease" (OECD 2013). In Canada "[t]he legislature must approve a portion of the Expenditure estimates before the start of the fiscal year with the remainder approved within three months of the start of the fiscal year" (OECD 2013).

In 29 countries, failure to agree on a budget means that last year's budget is implemented on an interim basis until the new budget is approved by the legislative assembly. This occurs in countries such as Argentina, South Korea, and Spain. In Hungary, for example, "[i]f the Parliament has not adopted the act on the central budget by the beginning of the calendar year, the Government shall be authorized to collect the revenues determined in the relevant legislation and, within the framework of the appropriations set out in the act on the central budget for the previous year, make the expenditures as commensurate" (OECD 2013).

Finally, 10 countries feature special interim measures. These may include the legislative assembly voting in cases where government expenditures are not allowed without legislative approval. Countries in this category include the United States, Switzerland, and Sweden. In Sweden, for example, "The legislature decides about each appropriation to the extent needed until the budget is approved" (OECD 2013).

For Cox (2014: 701), a reversion budget is "executive-favoring" when "the reversion is either the executive's proposal or last year's budget." Cox further notes that (2014: 697) reluctant democrats (politicians who seek to preserve "the appearance of legislative accountability while avoiding its reality") around the globe [have] succeeded, over the course of the twentieth century, in rewriting the budgetary reversion … to advantage the executive." Following Cox, we expect that leaders' assemblies will have reversionary provisions more favorable to the executive than will members' assemblies.

Table 10.2 presents the results of a regression analysis where the reversionary budget is the dependent variable. More specifically, the variable measures whether the reversionary budget favors the legislature or the executive, with values ranging from zero (executive budget proposal is the reversionary budget) through to ten (the legislature approves an interim budget). The intermediate value 3.3 indicates a vote on account and a value of 6.7 indicates that last year's budget is employed. We expect that presidential and federal regimes will be more likely to have reversionary provisions favorable to the legislature, since leaders' assemblies are less likely under such constitutions. The results in Table 10.2 suggest that more unequal societies (higher GINI) and countries from the African/Middle East and Americas regions are less likely to have a reversionary budget that favors the legislature. This may also be true for non-British former colonies. By comparison, there is some suggestion that presidential and federal countries are more likely to have a legislature-favoring reversionary budget, but these results are not clear.

Executive Flexibility during Implementation

Another aspect of fiscal powers has to do with the executive's ability to modify the budget after it has been formally adopted. The government budget, once agreed, may be more or less flexible during the financial year, or in other words susceptible to change by the executive without the need for legislative approval. Wehner (2006: 770) suggests that "If the executive can withhold funds, transfer between items and initiate fresh funding without the consent of the legislature, it has significant leeway unilaterally to alter the approved budget, which diminishes

Table 10.2 Reversionary budget that favors the assembly

	Reversionary Budget that Favors the Assembly					
	(1)	(2)	(3)	(4)	(5)	(6)
Presidential	−0.33				3.42**	3.16**
	(0.93)				(1.30)	(1.20)
Federal	1.25				2.38*	1.05
	(1.13)				(1.28)	(1.05)
Majoritarian	0.63				1.41	
	(1.18)				(1.31)	
Mixed	1.05				1.45	
	(1.12)				(1.24)	
Mean District Magnitude	0.01				0.01	
	(0.01)				(0.01)	
Sovereignty		0.01			0.01	
		(0.02)			(0.02)	
log(GDP per Capita)		0.45				
		(0.40)				
GINI		−0.15**				−0.17**
		(0.07)				(0.08)
log(Population)		0.17			−0.38	
		(0.35)			(0.41)	
Ethnic Fractionalization		0.80			−2.01	
		(2.18)			(2.23)	
Africa and Middle East			−2.49*		−4.22**	−2.47*
			(1.25)		(1.94)	(1.34)
Asia and Oceania			−0.41		−2.04	
			(1.36)		(1.72)	
Americas			−2.55**		−4.97***	−2.45
			(1.21)		(1.71)	(1.64)
Eastern Europe			0.58		0.12	
			(1.45)		(1.87)	
British Colony				−1.73		
				(1.22)		
Other Colony				−2.31**		−0.95
				(1.01)		(0.93)
Constant	4.59***	−11.05	6.47***	6.84***	−2.15	11.83***
	(0.79)	(34.39)	(0.87)	(0.81)	(40.26)	(2.62)
N	68	68	68	68	68	68
R^2	0.07	0.17	0.13	0.08	0.28	0.27
Adjusted R^2	−0.01	0.10	0.07	0.05	0.12	0.20

Notes: The dependent variable measures whether the reversionary budget favors the legislature or the executive, and ranges from 0 to 10, with 0 = executive budget proposal; 3.3 = vote on account; 6.7 = last year's budget; 10 = legislature approves interim measure.
*p < .1; **p < .05; ***p < .01.

legislative control over implementation." To measure the level of budget flexibility enjoyed by the executive, we consider three factors in turn: (1) whether the executive has the authority to cut/cancel/rescind mandatory spending once the budget has been approved by the legislative assembly (what is referred to as withholding power), (2) whether ministers in charge of specific portfolios can re-allocate funds within their own budget envelope (reallocation power), and (3) whether the annual budget includes any central reserve funds to meet unforeseen expenditures (central fund).[2] To the extent that any of these sorts of executive discretion exist, the budgetary powers of the assembly are weakened.

Looking first at the executive's withholding power, the executive may withhold budgeted expenditure without legislative approval in 26 of our 68 countries. This is the case, for example, in Brazil, France, and India. In the remaining 42 countries, in contrast, the executive may not withhold budgeted expenditure or may do so only with prior legislative approval. This is the case, for example, in Denmark, Israel, and the United States. Next, we look at the power of the executive to reallocate budgeted expenditure. Specifically, we explore whether line ministers (ministers in charge of specific executive portfolios) can re-allocate funds within their own budget envelope. In 36 countries, just over half our sample, ministers may thus reallocate funds within their spending authority without the need for legislative approval. This is the case, for example, in Argentina, Germany, and Niger. In the remaining 32 countries, including Malawi, Sweden, and Ukraine, ministers may not reallocate funds or may do so only with legislative approval.

Third, we explore whether in different countries the government possesses a central reserve fund to meet unexpected expenditure during the financial year. Such short-term "rainy day" funds could serve various purposes, including the capacity to fund responses to unexpected events such as natural disasters, pandemics, or to help correct any budgetary forecasting errors concerning income or expenditure. The presence of a central fund provides executive independence from the legislative assembly in that the former has at its disposal a pot of money to spend, or not, as it sees fit. In 47 countries, the budget includes a reserve fund. This is the case, for example, in Nicaragua, Tunisia, and Spain. In 21 cases, including Bolivia, Romania, and Taiwan, no such reserve fund is included in the budget.

These three elements—the ability to withhold, reallocate or call upon a central fund—can be aggregated to arrive at an overall measure of executive flexibility during budget implementation. This variable and component parts are reported in Table 10.1. Following Wehner (2006), the value of the variable *Flexibility* can range from full executive flexibility to no executive flexibility. In 13 countries in our study, the executive has full flexibility during budget implementation, as defined above. This is the case, for example, in France, Kenya, and Mexico. In eight

---

[2] Our wording here follows closely the relevant survey questions reported in OECD (2013).

countries, including Taiwan, Ireland, and South Africa, no executive flexibility exists during budget implementation.

The majority of countries in our study fall into some intermediate level of flexibility: In 23 countries, there are what we can classify as high but not perfect levels of budget flexibility. This is the case, for example, in Colombia, United Kingdom, and Papua New Guinea. In 24 cases, there is a low but greater than zero level of executive flexibility. Examples in this category include Argentina, Japan, and Germany. We expect leaders' assemblies to have high flexibility and members' assemblies low levels of the same. In this case, however, we believe voters' assemblies will have high flexibility, as rigidity and the threat of budgetary gridlock will tend to be important disadvantages from citizens' point of view.

Time for Scrutiny

Another feature of the budgetary process that relates to assembly power is the amount of time available to the assembly to scrutinize and review the budget. One way to think about the time available for scrutiny is to explore the length of time between when the budget is presented to the legislative assembly and the beginning of the government's new financial year, by which time the budget would begin to be implemented. More time for the assembly to deliberate on the budget associates with more legislative influence on the budgetary process. Members' assemblies should thus have extensive time for scrutiny, leaders' assemblies less so. In this case, we expect that informational transparency associated with longer time for scrutiny to weigh heavily in the design of voters' assemblies, which we thus expect to resemble members' assemblies in this respect.

The timeframe for budget review is presented in Table 10.1 (column titled *Time*). We observe significant variation in the time available to legislative assemblies to consider the draft budget. The only polity where the legislative assembly is given more than six months to review the executive's draft budget is the United States. Two countries (The Czech Republic and Germany) allow their respective legislative assemblies up to six months for budgetary deliberation. In 41 cases, or well over half our sample, the time limit for legislative review is four months. Examples in this category include Hungary, Japan, and Nicaragua. Finally, in 24 cases, including Canada, Ecuador, and Liberia, the legislative assembly is given two months or less to perform its budgetary functions.

Legislative Committees

As we noted in Chapter 8, committees are one of the most important organizational features of modern legislative assemblies. Amongst other things, a system of committees permits legislators to obtain gains from specialization.

Wehner (2006: 771) thus suggests that "a well-designed committee structure enables budget scrutiny and oversight of implementation." Wehner's (2006) measure of committee capacity with regard to budgeting has three component parts: (1) whether or not the draft budget is considered by a specialized budget or finance committee (2) whether or not the draft budget is considered by sectoral or department committees (what we term portfolio committees), and (3) whether there is committee capacity for the consideration of audit reports of public finances (audit committee).

Looking first at the presence or absence of a specialized budget committee, we find that such committees are very common amongst the countries included in our study: As reported in Table 10.1, 61 of the 68 legislative assemblies have a specialist committee to review the executive's draft budget. Specialist committees enhance the ability of legislative assemblies and legislators to engage with the draft budget by allocating specific resources and effort to the task and by building up expertise within the assembly. The exceptions—where no specialized budget committee exists—are Switzerland, Canada, India, Ireland, the Netherlands, the United Kingdom, and Nepal. We note that five out of these seven have a history of British rule. And note that since 2015, Ireland has created a specialized budget committee, part of a reform following the 2008 fiscal crisis to enhance the capacity of the Irish Parliament to oversee the public finances.

Next, we explore the role of portfolio committees in the budgetary process. Portfolio committees shadow specific government departments or "portfolios." The typical pattern is that such sectoral committees play no or only an advisory role in the formulation of their respective sectors' budget. In 54 of our 68 cases, sectoral committees thus play no substantive role in the budgetary process. In 14 cases, portfolio committees have actual authority over department budgets. Examples where portfolio committees have a substantive role include Belgium, South Africa, and the United States. Note that in arriving at these calculations we follow Wehner (2006: 774), who argues that to play a substantive role, portfolio committees must "have actual authority over departmental budgets" and that merely being "consulted or submit non-binding recommendations while a finance or budget committee retains full authority" is not a substantive role.

Finally, we consider the capacity of the committee system to review audits of government expenditure. A members' or voters' assembly should be able to review how governments spend the money allocated to them in the budgetary process, including spending effectiveness, corruption avoidance and value-for-money. Giving an executive a budget without any oversight of how the budget is implemented signifies a weak role for the legislative assembly in the budgetary process and limited opportunities for accountability. And in the majority of our democracies, the assembly does have an institutionalized vehicle for budgetary review. 36 countries thus have a specialized audit committee. In five countries (Belgium, The Czech Republic, France, Germany, Greece, and Spain) there is an audit function at the sub-committee level. Yet, in 24 cases, there is no specialized audit committee. Examples of systems without a specific audit committee or sub-committee include Benin, Italy, and the United States. The absence of such a committee is thus not a sure-fire sign of assembly weakness in the budgetary process. Audit committees—sometimes referred to as public accounts committees, can be particularly influential even in legislative assemblies that otherwise have relatively weak budgetary powers. In many Commonwealth countries, these public accounts committees attempt to focus on policy implementation, efficiency, and value-for-money in government expenditure rather than on more partisan policy-making issues (Wehner 2003). Noting the practice in the UK Parliament's Public Accounts Committee, *Erskine May* (1844 [1983]: 728) noted that

> The Committee does not seek to concern itself with Policy; its interest is in whether policy is carried out efficiently, effectively and economically. Its main functions are to see that public moneys are applied for the purposes prescribed by Parliament, that extravagance and waste are minimised and that sound financial practices are encouraged in estimating and contracting, and in administration, generally.

Following Wehner (2014) we arrive at an overall measure of committee influence in the budgetary process by combining scores on these three factors—a specialized budget committee, the authority of portfolio committees over sector budgets, and the capacity to review audits of public expenditure. This variable is reported as *Cttee. Index* in Table 10.1.

Interestingly, all legislative assemblies have some committee capacity, although their capacity levels vary significantly. The score of three legislative assemblies—Mexico's *Congreso de la Unión*, the Parliament of South Africa, and Taiwan's *Legislative Yuan*—indicates maximum committee capacity in their budgetary process. These are followed closely by Belgium's federal Parliament. A plurality of assemblies—38 countries—score a medium-high (our label for a score of 6.7). Finally, 19 countries have weak committee capacity with regard to the budget. Examples of polities in this range include Benin, South Korea, and Turkey.

Access to Budgetary Information

Wehner's sixth and final variable pertains to the ability of the legislature to access information on the budget. As we have discussed in various chapters, the executive often enjoys an informational advantage over the legislative assembly. The executive is more generously staffed, better resourced, and may not always be willing to fully and openly reveal information to the legislative assembly. We therefore expect both members' and voters' assemblies to be committed to public access to budgetary information. As Wehner (2006) notes, it is difficult to compare and classify levels of access to budgetary information. One way to do so it to look at the presence or absence of a specialized research office/unit tasked to conduct analyses of the budget. In exactly half our cases, such a specialized budget research unit exists. In the other half, no such research unit exists (see the variable *Research Office*, Table 10.1).

10.2 Variation in Budgetary Powers

In his study, Wehner (2006) derives an index of parliamentary capacity for budgetary scrutiny in 36 countries from data on the above-discussed budgetary procedures. We replicate this approach using new data for the 68 countries in our study. The index is constructed by adding together the values of each component variable and dividing by 0.6 (this approach generates a scale with hypothetical bounds of zero and 100). Low values mean that the legislative assembly has little capacity to engage in budgetary scrutiny, while a higher score reflects greater capacity for budgetary scrutiny. The results are displayed graphically in Figure 10.1.

As with many variables in our study, the index of budgetary strength displays significant cross-institutional variation. Scoring just under 17 out of 100, Senegal's *Assemblée Nationale* has the weakest budgetary capacity of any of our legislatures, followed by the legislative assemblies of Pakistan and Zambia. At the other end of the scale is the United States Congress, with the strongest capacity of any legislative assembly in our study to engage in budgetary oversight. The US Congress scores 89 out of 100 on budgetary capacity. Although the patterns are broadly similar for the cases which we have in common with Wehner (2006), our data shows evidence of some shifts over time (see Box 10.1).

What explains the variation in the budgetary capacity of our 68 legislative assemblies? As a starting point, we consider whether budgetary capacity may correlate with the fundamental constitutional choice between parliamentarism, presidentialism or semi-presidentialism. As noted above, Cox (2014; 712) suggested that the distinction between systems with "fiscally strong" versus "fiscally weak" legislatures (analogous to our notion of legislative budget capacity) may tell us more about how politics works than the distinction between presidential, semi-presidential, and parliamentary regimes. But regime type and legislative budgetary capacity may be related. For example, the separation-of-powers inherent in presidential systems may give the legislature more budgetary influence vis-à-vis the executive (as appears to be the case in the United States). A cursory look at Figure 10.1 indicate that this may not be the case given that many parliamentary systems have legislative assemblies with strong budgetary capacity (for example, Sweden—a parliamentary regime). Meanwhile, some presidential systems have legislative assemblies with relatively weak budgetary capacities. Thus, Zambia and Chile, with the third- and fourth-weakest budgetary capacity scores,

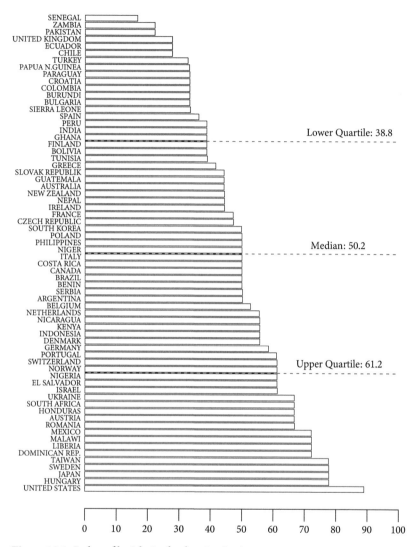

Figure 10.1 Index of legislative budget institutions

are both presidential. And Senegal, the country with the weakest legislative budget institutions, is semi-presidential.

Figure 10.2 displays the average (mean) budget capacity scores broken down by regime type. There does not seem to be a great difference between regime types—legislative assemblies in presidential systems score an average of 51.5 (out of 100) in terms of budgetary capacity, semi-presidential-regimes an average of 48.5 and parliamentary regimes an average of 50.3. In other words, regime type does not seem to be a predictor of the budgetary capacity of a country's national assembly.

Box 10.1 Reforming Legislative Budgetary Processes

Although the patterns are broadly similar for the cases which we have in common with Wehner (2006), our data shows evidence of some shifts over time. In both studies, the strongest budgetary powers are those of the assemblies of the United States, followed by Hungary and Sweden. Norway slips in budgetary capacity when our new data is considered. Perhaps the most striking shift, however, concerns South Africa. Wehner (2006) found the South African Parliament to have the weakest budgetary capacity of all his 36 cases, scoring 16.7 on his 100-point scale. South Africa now has a much higher placement in terms of budgetary capacity, with a score of 66.7. In fact, South Africa has gone from having one of the weakest budgetary capacities to the 12th strongest (out of 68 cases), in large part due to a new budgetary framework introduced in 2009 which significantly enhanced the budgetary powers of Parliament (Verwey 2009). Reform of budgetary capacity is not limited to South Africa. Today, Sweden shares the second highest score on budget capacity. But the Swedish *Riksdag* did not always have a strong role in the budgetary process. As Wehner (2007: 313) notes, historically, the *Riksdag* "was widely blamed for contributing to [Sweden's] poor fiscal performance" and this led to calls for reforms and ultimately the introduction of a new budget process effective from 1996 (see also Molander 1999). Thus, budgetary institutions can change, often dramatically. Another example of this is Ireland: In Wehner's (2006) study, Ireland's legislative assembly had the second-weakest budgetary oversight capacity; in our study Ireland climbed to stand 27th from the bottom. Ongoing reforms include the creation of a Committee on Budgetary Oversight and the establishment in 2017 of a Parliamentary Budget Office (PBO) to provide information, analysis, and advice to parliamentarians on budgetary matters.

And reform of legislative assemblies' budgetary procedures is not limited to advanced industrial democracies. Many international organizations such as the World Bank and International Monetary Fund have traditionally been reluctant to encourage a strengthening of the role of national legislatures in the budgetary process (Wehner 2010) – presumably fearing that legislative engagement would lead to budgetary indiscipline. Increasingly however, international donors and aid agencies have stressed the need for better public finances and transparency to ensure value for money for donors while also reducing misspending, corruption, and graft. One way to minimize these problems is to empower legislative assemblies to be more engaged in the budgetary process – from budget planning to auditing of public expenditure.

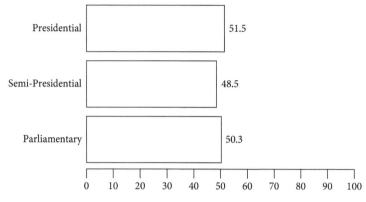

Figure 10.2 Average (mean) budget capacity by regime type

To further explore the correlates of budgetary capacity, Table 10.3 presents results of a regression analysis with the index of budgetary capacity as the dependent variable and various social, political, and economic indicators as independent variables. The results in Table 10.3 suggest that former colonies tend to have budget institutions that favor the executive over the legislature. Conversely, there is some evidence in Model 5 that countries with a higher district magnitude (and typically Proportional Representation) have more legislature-favoring budget institutions.

10.3 Conclusion

Raising government revenue and deciding how to expend it for public purposes are among the most critical functions of contemporary democratic polities. Yet, the budgetary process is one in which legislative assemblies are at a decided disadvantage relative to the executive branch. This disadvantage is driven by asymmetries of information and institutional capacity, as well as in many cases shortages of time available for deliberation. Nonetheless, there are substantial differences in budgetary capacity from one national assembly to another. Building on Wehner's (2006) seminal work, we have examined a variety of institutional features that contribute to variation in the capacity of legislative assemblies to affect budgetary decisions.

We have found substantial differences in budgetary capacity, with the United States and several European countries coming in at the high end of budgetary capacity and less economically developed nations generally scoring much lower. In our analysis, we find that economic development seems to account for a substantial share of such differences, whereas somewhat surprisingly regime type

Table 10.3 Wehner Index of Budgetary Powers

	Wehner Index of Budgetary Powers					
	(1)	(2)	(3)	(4)	(5)	(6)
Presidential	1.75				6.16	
	(4.07)				(6.14)	
Federal	6.44				6.51	
	(4.95)				(6.05)	
Majoritarian	−3.75				0.58	
	(5.14)				(6.21)	
Mixed	3.42				3.17	
	(4.90)				(5.88)	
Mean District	0.03				0.06*	0.04
Magnitude	(0.03)				(0.04)	(0.03)
Sovereignty		−0.08			−0.16	
		(0.07)			(0.10)	
log(GDP per		1.49				
Capita)		(1.84)				
GINI		−0.28				
		(0.30)				
log(Population)		0.93			0.31	
		(1.57)			(1.94)	
Ethnic		3.53			−10.98	
Fractionalization		(9.93)			(10.55)	
Africa and			−5.23		3.58	
Middle East			(5.78)		(9.16)	
Asia and Oceania			−3.32		−2.48	
			(6.30)		(8.12)	
Americas			−1.62		−4.96	
			(5.60)		(8.10)	
Eastern Europe			−0.09		5.53	
			(6.70)		(8.85)	
British Colony				−9.06*		−8.57
				(5.32)		(5.30)
Other Colony				−9.38**		−10.07**
				(4.41)		(4.41)
Constant	47.44***	190.48	52.28***	56.86***	350.85*	56.16***
	(3.44)	(156.69)	(4.02)	(3.53)	(190.44)	(3.55)
N	68	68	68	68	68	68
R^2	0.06	0.08	0.02	0.07	0.15	0.10
Adjusted R^2	−0.02	0.01	−0.05	0.04	−0.04	0.05

Notes: The dependent variable is the Wehner Index of Legislative Budget Institutions, which ranges from 0 (executive favoring) to 10 (legislature favoring).
*$p < 0.1$; **$p < 0.05$; ***$p < 0.01$.

has no statistically significant effect. Yet, regardless of economic circumstances, it seems possible to build the institutional capacity necessary for assembly effectiveness. Thus, we have noted that institutional reforms in such countries as Ireland, South Africa, and Sweden have in various ways enhanced the budgetary capacity of these assemblies.

Budgetary capacity might sound like an assembly characteristic upon which all democratically inclined persons would agree. But in real-world politics, not all actors will tend to look favorably on such an assembly. This is because assemblies compete with other political institutions for control of the budgetary process. In most polities, budgetary proposals originate in the executive branch, and under many constitutions there are strict limitations on the amendments that the legislature can introduce and pass. Thus, legislative assemblies often compete with the executive branch over these decisions, and the competition is one in which the executive often has substantial advantages. Other political institutions, such as independent central banks, regional governments, or even courts, may also have their own related powers.

Budgeting and legislative politics can be viewed as a classic collective action problem: voters and members want to maximize the government expenditure allocated to them while ensuring that the tax burden to fund this expenditure is shared by taxpayers more broadly and diffusely (Ardanaz and Scartascini, 2014). Pork-barrel politics, in legislative jargon, "fiscal legislative particularism," refers to the practice of spending national tax revenues on economically inefficient, often geographically targeted projects. The avoidance of such expenditure helps to achieve fiscal discipline (balance the government budget) and may be associated with a weaker role for the legislative assembly in the budgetary process (see, for example, Poterba and Von Hagen 1999). Indeed, international economic organizations such as the World Bank or the International Monetary Fund appear reticent to encourage the strengthening of parliamentary capacity in the budgetary process, lest such strengthening leads to higher budget deficits (Wehner 2010). On the other hand, some scholars argue the need for effective engagement by representative bodies in the budgetary process to ensure accountability and good public policy (Santiso 2009; for a review of both perspectives in the debate, see Wehner 2014).

Within the world of legislative assemblies, we expect budgetary capacity to be lower under conditions approaching the model of leaders' assemblies, compared with either members' or voters' assemblies. But members' and voters' assemblies may favor budgetary capacity for different reasons. In a members' assembly, budgetary capacity may be high because of the desire of legislators to affect particularistic policies through their appropriations. In contrast, a voters' assembly may feature a high level of budgetary capacity to maximize the economic efficiency of policy outputs and reduce the rents that the politicians controlling the executive wish to enact to benefit themselves and their constituents and supporters at the expense of other groups of citizens.

References

Ardanaz, Martin, and Carlos Scartascini. 2014. "The Economic Effects of Constitutions: Do Budget Institutions Make Forms of Government More Alike?" *Constitutional Political Economy* 25(3): 301–329.

Baron, David P. and John A. Ferejohn. 1989. "Bargaining in Legislatures." *American
Political Science Review* 83(4): 1181–1206.

Cox, Gary W. 2014. "Reluctant Democrats and Their Legislatures." In Shane Martin,
Thomas Saalfeld, and Kaare W Strøm (eds.), *The Oxford Handbook of Legislative
Studies*. Oxford: Oxford University Press, 696–716.

Lasswell, Harold D. 1936. *Who Gets What, When, and How?* New York: McGraw-Hill.

Madison, James. 2009[1788]. *Federalist No. 58*. New Haven: Yale University Press.

May, Thomas Erskine 1983 [1844]. *A Treatise upon the Law, Privileges, Proceedings and
Usage of Parliament*. London: Butterworths.

Molander, Per. 1999. "Reforming Budgetary Institutions: Swedish Experiences." In Rolf
R. Strauch and Jürgen von Hagenvon Hagen (eds.), *Institutions, Politics and Fiscal
Policy*. Boston: Kluwer Academic Publishers, 191–214.

Montesquieu, Charles de S. 1989[1748]. *Spirit of the Laws*. Cambridge: Cambridge
University Press.

OECD. 2013. *International Budget Practices and Procedures Database* Available
online: http://www.oecd.org/governance/budgeting/internationalbudgetpractices
andproceduresdatabase.htm

Poterba, James M., and Jurgen Von Hagen. 1999. *Fiscal Institutions and Fiscal Performance*. Chicago: NBER and University of Chicago Press.

Romer, Thomas, and Howard Rosenthal. 1978. "Political Resource Allocation, Controlled Agendas, and the Status Quo." *Public Choice 33*(4): 27–43.

Santiso, Carlos. 2009. *The Political Economy of Government Auditing: Financial Governance and the Rule of Law in Latin America and Beyond*. New York: Routledge.

Verwey, Len (ed.). 2009. *Parliament, the Budget and Poverty in South Africa. A Shift in
Power*. Cape Town: Idasa.

Wehner, Joachim. 2003. "Principles and Patterns of Financial Scrutiny: Public
Accounts Committees in the Commonwealth." *Commonwealth & Comparative
Politics* 41(3): 21–36.

Wehner, Joachim. 2006. "Assessing the Power of the Purse: An Index of Legislative
Budget Institutions." *Political Studies* 54(4): 767–785.

Wehner, Joachim. 2007. "Budget reform and legislative control in Sweden." *Journal of
European Public Policy* 14(2): 313-332.

Wehner, Joachim. 2010. *Legislatures and the Budget Process: The Myth of Fiscal Control*.
Basingstoke: Palgrave Macmillan.

Wehner, Joachim. 2014. "Legislatures and Public Finance." In Shane Martin, Thomas
Saalfeld, and Kaare W Strøm (eds.), *The Oxford Handbook of Legislative Studies*.
Oxford: Oxford University Press, 514–525.

11

The Elective Function

In his famous book *The English Constitution*, Walter Bagehot a century and a half ago identified "the elective function" as the main function of the British House of Commons. In his words, "The House of Commons is an electoral chamber; it is the assembly which chooses our president." In emphasizing this function, Bagehot (1867) thus compared the House of Commons not to the United States Congress, but to the Electoral College. Obviously, the role of the legislative assembly as an electoral institution varies greatly, particularly between parliamentary and presidential regimes, but Bagehot's observation was both prescient and acute. Selecting, appointing, and sanctioning the head of government and other high public officials is a critical function of most democratic legislatures.

This chapter explores the role, if any, of legislative assemblies in selecting the government and other important office holders. By government we mean the political executive and specifically the members of the cabinet and the person identifiable as the head of government. In some political systems, the national legislature plays a key role in determining which individuals and parties comprise the government and for how long. Elsewhere, legislatures are less involved in selecting or removing the chief political executive, but may nevertheless play some role in executive appointments. Legislative assemblies commonly also have other elective functions, typically concerning high government offices not directly accountable to the cabinet, in the judicial branch, or in government enterprises. Here we will focus on two such offices, namely those of the head of the highest court in the judiciary (or the constitutional court, where such courts exist) and the governor of the central bank.

The elective functions of a national assembly depend in the first instance on whether the political regime is parliamentary, presidential, or some mix of these. Indeed, it is in large part for this reason that one of the most fundamental constitutional decisions facing any country is whether to adopt a parliamentary form of government, a presidential one, or some mix of the two.

11.1 Voters, Members, Leaders, and the Elective Function

The elective functions of a legislative assembly differ substantially, greatly depending on the regime type within which the assembly operates. Laver (2006) suggests that legislative assemblies are fundamentally different animals depending on

Legislative Assemblies. Shane Martin and Kaare W. Strøm, Oxford University Press.
© Shane Martin and Kaare W. Strøm (2023). DOI: 10.1093/oso/9780198890829.003.0011

whether they exist in a parliamentary or presidential system, proposing that par-liaments exist in parliamentary systems and legislatures in presidential systems.[1] Certainly, the elective function of legislative assemblies can vary substantially between parliamentary and presidential systems. Thus, the chain of delegation and the nature of accountability, discussed in Chapter 1, look very different in presidential as distinct from parliamentary systems. Parliamentary regimes tend to have simple, hierarchical, and indirect chains of delegation. Parliament is typi-cally the only national body that voters directly elect, and the executive branch is directly responsible to parliament (or most commonly its lower house in bicam-eral systems) and to parliament only. Presidential systems tend to have more agents directly elected by the people, and more complex lines of delegation and accountability between them and the voters (Strøm 2000).

Delegation implies selection through processes such as election or appointment. We will look at differences between and within these regime types in the legis-lature's role in appointing and removing cabinet members and other executive office-holders. Moreover, as we shall discuss below, national assemblies in many presidential as well as parliamentary regimes routinely appoint a number of other office-holders, such as judges, directors of public enterprises, ambassadors, and commissioners, who are not subsequently accountable to the assembly majority. Hence, the elective function in itself cannot usefully distinguish parliamentarism from other forms of democracy. As we will see, the role of the national assembly in appointing and dismissing the executive varies, often dramatically, among parlia-mentary systems. But one thing remains constant: in a *pure* parliamentary system, the legislative assembly (or at least one of its chambers) can remove the executive at will.

Roughly, and with important qualifications, parliamentary systems grant their assemblies decisive powers to seat and unseat cabinets, but leave other appoint-ment powers largely in the hands of the cabinet. In presidential systems, this pattern is reversed: the legislature may select and appoint such officials as judges and bank governors, but has little or no say in the appointment or dismissal of members of the national cabinet. The rest of this chapter will expand on these patterns. For now, note simply that the decision to enshrine into the constitution a parliamentary versus presidential form of government (or a mix of each) has significant consequences for the electoral role of the national legislatures.

Elective powers have consequences for the degree to which particular legisla-tures fit the mold of voters', members', or leaders' assemblies. In a pure leaders' assembly, it is permissible and easy for legislative leaders to take control of exec-utive office, and difficult to displace those who do so. Other appointment powers will be vested primarily in the chief executive. A members' assembly, in contrast,

---

[1] As we discuss in Chapter 1, we do not follow Laver's nomenclature. Rather we use the terms parliament, legislative, assembly, congress and legislative assembly interchangeably.

will feature a broad range of permissive appointment and dismissal powers vested in the assembly itself. Finally, a voters' assembly will have appointment powers largely in technical areas (such as the selection of a central bank governor), but not with respect to the most important political offices such as the cabinet. In other words, we assume that voters prefer to have the power to elect the chief political executive directly and that they will only prefer to have such appointment powers vested in the assembly for offices for which voters expect massive information asymmetries between themselves and the office-holders.

11.2 Defining Regime Types

But what exactly defines parliamentarism versus presidentialism? As we will see, the role of the legislature in choosing and maintaining the executive is a core criterion of differentiation. In a parliamentary system of government, the executive somehow emerges from, and remains responsible to, a legislative assembly. In other words, the cabinet stems from the legislature and is formally accountable to it. Some confusion surrounds the exact defining feature of parliamentarism.[2] For example, Lijphart (1984: 68) defines parliamentary government as "a form of constitutional democracy in which executive authority emerges from, and is responsible to, legislative authority." Müller, Bergman, and Strøm (2003: 13) define parliamentary government as "a system of government in which the Prime Minister and his or her cabinet are accountable to any majority of the members of parliament and can be voted out of office by the latter, through an ordinary or constructive vote of no confidence." The latter definition places more emphasis on the power of the legislative assembly in parliamentary regimes to hold governments responsible, and if a majority of the legislators wishes to, ultimately remove them.

We will discuss various types of such procedures later; for now, note that confidence procedures are mechanisms which permit the legislature to remove the executive. As Laver (2003: 122) notes, in a parliamentary system a "government that loses a legislative vote of no confidence is constitutionally deemed dismissed ... if such a provision is not in the constitution, then the country concerned does not have a parliamentary government system." Note that members of the legislative opposition, even if they draw no direct benefits from the government and disagree with its policies, may prefer not to vote a government out of office. The reason may be that there is no feasible alternative that these members view more favorably. Thus, under parliamentarism, governments may come into and remain in office as long as they are *tolerated* by a legislative majority. As we will see later,

---

[2] A note on terminology: Scholars tend to use the terms "parliamentary government," "parliamentary systems," "parliamentary regimes," and "parliamentarism" interchangeably. The same applies for similar terms used to describe presidential government and semi-presidential government.

different legislatures have different mechanisms to test tolerance for the formed or about-to-be-formed government.

The United Kingdom represents a classic case of parliamentary government. At the general election, voters elect MPs to the House of Commons, thus shaping the partisan composition of the chamber. If one party wins a majority of seats in the House of Commons, that party forms the government. The head of state (currently the King) formally appoints a Prime Minister (invariably the leader of the majority party if such a party exists). The Prime Minister then selects her cabinet. The government continues to govern as long as it has the support or toleration of a majority of the members of the House of Commons. If the government loses a confidence vote, it must resign. Otherwise, the government can stay in office until a new government is formed after the next general election.[3]

Similarly, the Swiss government is elected by the Swiss legislative assembly. Once formed, however, the Swiss executive is not dependent on the assembly's confidence to stay in office. In other words, the Swiss legislature cannot remove the executive from office. Some political scientists classify Switzerland as having a parliamentary constitution (because the government "comes from" the legislatures), whereas other scholars classify the country as non-parliamentary (because the Swiss government is not "responsible [or accountable] to" the legislature). We agree with the latter, preferring to classify the Swiss political system as non-parliamentary. The Swiss case nicely illustrates that although "emerging from the legislature" is a common feature of parliamentary government, the defining feature should be "political responsibility"—the need for the government to have the continued confidence of a majority in the legislative assembly.

Parliamentary government is most commonly contrasted with presidential government. In presidential government, sometimes referred to as presidentialism or a presidential system, legislative assemblies exist, but they play little or no role in determining who occupies the chief executive positions. In presidential systems, the legislature and the head of the government are independently elected, typically for a fixed term. The legislature plays no role in selecting the head of government. Moreover, the head of government is not politically responsible to the legislative assembly. As Linz (1990: 52) notes, "in presidential systems an executive with considerable constitutional powers-generally including full control of the composition of the cabinet and administration-is directly elected by the people for a fixed term and is independent of parliamentary votes of confidence."

The United States is the original presidential system of government. Voters elect a federal legislature—the US Congress. Separately, voters indirectly select

---

[3] Cox (2014, 2017) argues that it was the anticipation that they might be denied supply (tax revenue) and ultimately impeached that after the Glorious Revolution induced English cabinet members to recognize their responsibility to Parliament. Thus, the confidence relationship that characterizes parliamentary regimes may rest on an expectation of credible sanctions even in the absence of a formal constitutional requirement of parliamentary control.

a President through the Electoral College. The President serves as Head of Government and Head of State for a four-year term and can be re-elected once. The President selects his cabinet (although in a deviation from *pure* presidentialism, as we will see below, the cabinet appointees are subject to confirmation by the Senate). Congress cannot remove the President at will. Again, as we will see below, Congress can remove the President via an impeachment process, but this is a procedure to be used in cases of "high crimes and misdemeanors" and which requires a two-thirds majority in the Senate for conviction. Congress thus cannot remove the President just because it has no confidence in him, and in fact no president has ever been successfully impeached. Thus, while a British Prime Minister can be removed by the House of Commons at any time, for any reason the Commons deems worthy, the same is not true of the US President and the US Congress. The executive in a presidential system is not politically responsible or accountable to the legislature but, once elected, remains head of government whether or not he or she has the support of a legislative majority.

A lively debate exists regarding the relative advantages of presidential versus parliamentary constitutions. Linz (1990) provokingly suggested that parliamentarism is superior, observing that "the vast majority of the stable democracies in the world today are parliamentary regimes," whereas "the only presidential democracy with a long history of constitutional continuity is the United States" (Linz 1990: 52). With an additional generation or so of hindsight, one could surely add a number of other stable presidential democracies, such as Chile, Costa Rica, Taiwan, and others. At any rate, the merits of presidentialism versus parliamentarism remain a matter of debate.

Not all political systems fit well into the presidential versus parliamentary framework. A semi-presidential system involves a combination of a popularly elected President (head of state) and a Prime Minister (head of government) responsible to the legislature. As with parliamentarism, definitions of what constitutes semi-presidentialism vary. Duverger (1980: 166) defines semi-presidentialism as a regime type which combines a directly elected president who "possesses quite considerable powers," and "has opposite him, however, a prime minister and ministers who possess executive and governmental power and can stay in office only if the parliament does not show its opposition to them." A core problem with this approach is identifying exactly what is meant by "quite considerable powers" (Elgie 1998). For example, Ireland has a directly elected President, who co-exists with a prime minister and cabinet responsible to the legislature. Ireland's President has certain political powers (for example, the right to refuse a dissolution of parliament under certain circumstances) but on the whole these powers could not be considered "considerable." In response to these classification challenges, Elgie (1999: 13) proposed a simpler definition of semi-presidentialism: "the situation where a popularly elected fixed-term president exists alongside a prime minister and cabinet who are responsible to parliament."

The semi-presidential regime type is sometimes referred to as Dual System, Hybrid System or Presidential-parliamentary democracy (see also Shugart and Carey 1992 and Cheibub 2007).

France is the classical example of a semi-presidential regime. In France, voters elect the President, who is the head of state, chairs the cabinet, and appoints the Prime Minister. The Prime Minister, although selected by the President, must be acceptable to the *Assemblée Nationale* (the lower chamber of Parliament). Power is divided or shared over various policy areas. In practical terms, the President must seek to appoint a Prime Minister who is acceptable to a majority in the national assembly. Otherwise, the *Assemblée Nationale* will vote no confidence in the Prime Minister, who will then have to resign. If the President's party (or coalition) holds a majority of seats in the National Assembly, the President will likely choose a Prime Minister from his own party. When the President does not have majority support in the *Assemblée Nationale*, he or she will likely have to appoint a Prime Minister from a party in the majority bloc. This gives rise to the practice of *cohabitation* (a form of divided government)—in which a president from one political party holds office with a prime minister from an opposing party.

Different definitions of semi-presidentialism make it challenging to identify which countries fit into which regime type. Table 11.1 reports two commonly used typologies of regime type. First, from the World Bank's Database of Political Institutions (DPI), the variable "system" provides a classification of presidential versus parliamentarism. This source defines a regime as parliamentary if "the legislature elects the chief executive" and where this assembly can "easily remove him." According to this source, 32 of the 68 countries in our study are parliamentary while 33 are presidential. Pakistan, South Africa, and Switzerland are neither parliamentary or presidential but regimes that DPI refers to as "Assembly-elected President." Second, Robert Elgie provides a classification scheme that pays closer attention to semi-presidentialism as a unique regime type. His list of system types is reported in column three of Table 11.1. According to his classification, 21 countries in our study are parliamentary, 18 are semi-presidential, and 29 are presidential.

Clearly, different scholars occasionally classify the same country differently. South Korea thus exemplifies the challenge of classifying democratic regimes as presidential or parliamentary. DPI identifies South Korea as a parliamentary system; whereas Elgie classifies South Korea as presidential, explaining his choice as follows:

> South Korea has both a president and a P[rime] M[inister], but this is not a sufficient condition for semi-presidentialism. For there to be semi-presidentialism, the PM and cabinet must be collectively responsible to the legislature. In South Korea, there is only individual responsibility i.e. the legislature may vote for the dismissal of the PM individually. However, even then, in the case of South Korea

Table 11.1 Regime and investiture types

Country	Regime Type	System Type	Parliamentary Investiture
Argentina	Presidential	Presidential	
Australia	Parliamentary	Parliamentary	No Investiture
Austria	Semi-Presidential	Parliamentary	No Investiture
Belgium	Parliamentary	Parliamentary	Reactive Investiture
Benin	Presidential	Presidential	
Bolivia	Presidential	Presidential	
Brazil	Presidential	Presidential	
Bulgaria	Semi-Presidential	Parliamentary	Proactive Investiture
Burundi	Presidential	Presidential	
Canada	Parliamentary	Parliamentary	Reactive Investiture
Chile	Presidential	Presidential	
Colombia	Presidential	Presidential	
Costa Rica	Presidential	Presidential	
Croatia	Semi-Presidential	Parliamentary	Reactive Investiture
Czech Republic	Semi-Presidential	Parliamentary	Reactive Investiture
Denmark	Parliamentary	Parliamentary	No Investiture
Dominican Republic	Presidential	Presidential	
Ecuador	Presidential	Presidential	
El Salvador	Presidential	Presidential	
Finland	Semi-Presidential	Parliamentary	Proactive Investiture
France	Semi-Presidential	Parliamentary	No Investiture
Germany	Presidential	Parliamentary	Proactive Investiture
Ghana	Presidential	Presidential	
Greece	Parliamentary	Parliamentary	Reactive Investiture
Guatemala	Presidential	Presidential	
Honduras	Presidential	Presidential	
Hungary	Parliamentary	Parliamentary	Proactive Investiture
India	Parliamentary	Parliamentary	No Investiture
Indonesia	Presidential	Presidential	
Ireland	Semi-Presidential	Parliamentary	Proactive Investiture
Israel	Parliamentary	Parliamentary	Reactive Investiture
Italy	Parliamentary	Parliamentary	Reactive Investiture
Japan	Parliamentary	Parliamentary	No Investiture
Kenya	Presidential	Presidential	
Liberia	Presidential	Presidential	
Malawi	Presidential	Presidential	
Mexico	Presidential	Presidential	
Nepal	Parliamentary	Parliamentary	Reactive Investiture
Netherlands	Parliamentary	Parliamentary	No Investiture
New Zealand	Parliamentary	Parliamentary	No Investiture

Country	Regime Type	System Type	Parliamentary Investiture
Nicaragua	Presidential	Presidential	
Niger	Semi-Presidential	Presidential	No Investiture
Nigeria	Presidential	Presidential	
Norway	Parliamentary	Parliamentary	No Investiture
Pakistan	Parliamentary	Assembly Elected Presidential	No Investiture
Papua New Guinea	Parliamentary	Parliamentary	Proactive Investiture
Paraguay	Presidential	Presidential	
Peru	Semi-Presidential	Presidential	Reactive Investiture
Philippines	Presidential	Presidential	
Poland	Semi-Presidential	Presidential	Reactive Investiture
Portugal	Semi-Presidential	Parliamentary	No Investiture
Romania	Semi-Presidential	Parliamentary	Proactive Investiture
Senegal	Semi-Presidential	Presidential	No Investiture
Serbia	Semi-Presidential	Parliamentary	Reactive Investiture
Sierra Leone	Presidential	Presidential	
Slovak Republic	Semi-Presidential	Parliamentary	Reactive Investiture
South Africa	Parliamentary	Assembly Elected Presidential	No Investiture
South Korea	Presidential	Parliamentary	No Investiture
Spain	Parliamentary	Parliamentary	Proactive Investiture
Sweden	Parliamentary	Parliamentary	Proactive Investiture
Switzerland	Parliamentary	Assembly Elected Presidential	No Investiture
Taiwan	Semi-Presidential	Presidential	No Investiture
Tunisia	Semi-Presidential	Presidential	Proactive Investiture
Turkey	Presidential	Parliamentary	Reactive Investiture
Ukraine	Semi-Presidential	Presidential	Proactive Investiture
United Kingdom	Parliamentary	Parliamentary	Reactive Investiture
United States	Presidential	Presidential	No Investiture
Zambia	Presidential	Presidential	

the vote is only a recommendation. The president has complete constitutional freedom to decide whether or not to accept the recommendation. So, constitutionally the legislature cannot dismiss the PM and cabinet collectively or even the PM individually. This is why I now class South Korea as presidential, though I am the first to admit that I was confused about this situation for a while in some of my early writings.

Source: http://www.semipresidentialism.com/?p=195

Table 11.2 explores further the politics of regime choice. In this regression analysis the dependent variable equal one if the political system is presidential,

Table 11.2 Presidential system

	(1)	(2)	(3)	(4)	(5)	(6)
Majoritarian	0.06				−0.03	
	(0.15)				(0.13)	
Mixed	−0.17				−0.08	
	(0.15)				(0.13)	
Mean District Magnitude	−0.001				−0.001	
	(0.001)				(0.001)	
Sovereignty		−0.002			0.001	
		(0.002)			(0.002)	
log(GDP per Capita)		−0.10**				−0.06
		(0.04)				(0.04)
GINI		0.03***				0.01
		(0.01)				(0.01)
log(Population)		0.004			0.02	
		(0.04)			(0.04)	
Ethnic Fractionalization		−0.001			0.08	
		(0.24)			(0.23)	
Africa and Middle East			0.67***		0.62***	0.41**
			(0.12)		(0.18)	(0.18)
Asia and Oceania			0.27**		0.27	0.19
			(0.13)		(0.17)	(0.14)
Americas			0.88***		0.86***	0.66***
			(0.12)		(0.14)	(0.17)
Eastern Europe			0.00		0.05	
			(0.14)		(0.19)	
British Colony				0.36**		−0.10
				(0.16)		(0.14)
Other Colony				0.45***		−0.03
				(0.13)		(0.12)
Constant	0.47***	3.06	−0.00	0.11	−1.49	0.26
	(0.09)	(3.73)	(0.08)	(0.11)	(4.18)	(0.50)
N	68	68	68	68	68	68
R^2	0.07	0.48	0.56	0.16	0.57	0.60
Adjusted R^2	0.03	0.44	0.53	0.13	0.50	0.55

Notes: The dependent variable equals 1 if a presidential system and 0 if semi-presidential or parliamentary.
$^*p < .1$; $^{**}p < .05$; $^{***}p < .01$.

and zero otherwise. The results in Table 11.2 suggest that wealthier countries are less likely to have presidential systems. By contrast, countries with more inequality (higher GINI), former colonies, and countries from the African/Middle Eastern, Asian/Oceanic, and American region are more likely to have presidential systems. In the final model (6), only the regional dummies for Africa and the

Americas remain significant. Thus, even though most colonial powers had parliamentary regimes, their former colonies have predominantly adopted presidential constitutions.

11.3 Government Formation under Parliamentarism

In this section, we take a closer look at the formal role of legislative assemblies in government formation—the process by which a cabinet take office. As discussed above, criteria such as that the government "emerges from" parliament can be rather vague. We therefore need more unambiguous and operational criteria. One way to identify the precise role of the legislature in government formation is to look for the presence or absence of an investiture vote in this process. As defined by Rasch et al. (2015: 4) "Investiture consists of a vote in parliament to demonstrate that an already formed or about to be formed government has legislative support."

Not all parliamentary systems have an investiture vote. Negative parliamentarism describes a situation in which a political system is parliamentary but the legislature does not vote on a new government (Bergman 1993). Instead, the legislature's role focuses on termination—the legislature can remove a government but is not formally involved in selecting it. The Netherlands represents a case of negative parliamentarism. A new Dutch government is not subject to an investiture vote in the *Tweede Kamer*. Instead, until proven otherwise it is assumed that the government has the support of the assembly. Legislative assemblies in negative parliamentary systems nevertheless play an important informal role in the government formation process: the partisan composition of legislative assembly matters for which governments are viable, meaning that the assembly is composed of a sufficient number of members that are inclined by party affiliation or otherwise to at least tolerate the government—whereas a non-viable government could be removed by the majority through a no confidence vote.

In our study, 21 legislatures have an investiture vote (see Box 11.1 for reflections on the challenge of identifying the presence or absence of an investiture vote). The last column of Table 11.1 identifies the investiture type, if any, for the parliamentary countries in our study. What factors correlate with the likelihood of a legislative assembly having an investiture vote? To help answer this, Table 11.3 reports the result of a regression analysis where investiture is the dependent variable. The results in Table 11.3 suggest that wealthier countries, countries that gained sovereignty later, and Eastern European countries are more likely to require an investiture vote. This is also true in Model 1 for countries that have a higher mean district magnitude. In comparison, countries from Africa/Middle East, Asia/Oceania, and the Americas appear to be less likely to require an investiture vote than Western Europe (the omitted region).

Table 11.3 Parliamentary investiture

	(1)	(2)	(3)	(4)	(5)	(6)
Majoritarian	−0.14				0.01	
	(0.15)				(0.15)	
Mixed	−0.04				0.01	
	(0.14)				(0.14)	
Mean District Magnitude	0.002*				0.0002	0.0003
	(0.001)				(0.001)	(0.001)
Sovereignty		0.004**			0.001	0.001
		(0.002)			(0.002)	(0.002)
log(GDP per Capita)		0.10*				0.08*
		(0.05)				(0.05)
GINI		−0.01				
		(0.01)				
log(Population)		−0.03			0.02	
		(0.04)			(0.04)	
Ethnic Fractionalization		−0.02			−0.21	
		(0.27)			(0.25)	
Africa and Middle East			−0.30**		−0.26	−0.08
			(0.14)		(0.20)	(0.21)
Asia and Oceania			−0.41***		−0.44**	−0.30*
			(0.15)		(0.20)	(0.17)
Americas			−0.38***		−0.33**	−0.24
			(0.13)		(0.15)	(0.15)
Eastern Europe			0.50***		0.47**	0.54***
			(0.16)		(0.22)	(0.20)
British Colony				−0.17		
				(0.17)		
Other Colony				0.01		
				(0.14)		
Constant	0.34***	−7.41*	0.50***	0.37***	−1.51	−2.80
	(0.08)	(4.31)	(0.09)	(0.11)	(4.70)	(4.19)
N	68	68	68	68	68	68
R^2	0.08	0.24	0.40	0.02	0.41	0.44
Adjusted R^2	0.03	0.18	0.37	−0.01	0.31	0.37

Notes: The dependent variable measures whether legislative investiture of the government is required, with 1 = Yes and 0 = No.
*$p < 0.1$; **$p < 0.05$; ***$p < 0.01$.

From the perspective offered by Rasch et al. (2015), investiture can be concerned with an already formed or an about-to-be-formed government. In an ex ante investiture vote, the legislative assembly votes to select a prospective Prime Minister. Thirteen countries in our study have such an ex ante investiture vote. In Ireland, parliament's lower chamber (the *Dáil*) votes to select the prime minister

Box 11.1 Is the King's Speech an Investiture Vote?

By most accounts, the British Prime Minister is appointed by the Monarch, with little formal role for the House of Commons in the government formation process. By convention, the Monarch (currently King Charles III) will be advised to appoint a Prime Minister who is likely to enjoy the confidence of the House of Commons. The choice of Prime Minister is obvious when one party wins a majority of seats in the House of Commons, as is typically the case at British general elections.

The 2017 British General Election produced an unexpected outcome: the incumbent Conservative Party government enjoyed a parliamentary majority going into the election but lost that majority in the general election. Nevertheless, it remained the largest party in the House of Commons. On the day following the general election, the Prime Minister visited the Queen and received the Queen's consent to remain as Prime Minister. Speaking after the audience with the Queen, Prime Minister May stated that "I have just been to see Her Majesty the Queen, and I will now form a government."[*]

The Prime Minister then set about ensuring she could build the support of a parliamentary majority. This is essential, as a government is quickly tested on whether it has a parliamentary majority in the form of a vote on the King's (or Queen's) Speech. The King's Speech is a speech delivered in parliament by the monarch but written by the government, setting out the government's proposed legislative agenda. The King's Speech is considered a test of the government's ability to command the confidence of the House of Commons. The constitutional convention is that the government resigns if a majority of the House of Commons rejects the King's Speech, as happened for example in 1924.

In 2017, the Conservative Party reached agreement with the Democratic Unionist Party from Northern Ireland, guaranteeing the government's success in the Queen's Speech vote. MPs voted 323 to 309 to approve the Speech, securing the Conservative Party's right to continue in office. Rasch et al. (2015) consider the King's speech to be a form of ex post investiture: the legislature—in this case the House of Commons—votes to confirm a government already in office. For these scholars, the prospect of a test informs bargaining over government formation: a minority party knows it must secure majority support in order to pass the hurdle that is the vote on the King's Speech. Other scholars are less certain about whether the King's Speech really constitutes an investiture vote (for a full discussion, see Kelso 2015).

[*] http://www.independent.co.uk/news/uk/politics/theresa-may-election-results-response-speech-hung-parliament-read-in-full-a7781696.html

(the *Taoiseach*) who is then formally appointed by the President. To be elected Taoiseach, a candidate must receive more "yes" than "no" votes in the legislative division. If the first nominated candidate fails to receive more votes for than against, the *Dáil* then votes on the second nominated candidate, if there is any. Ex ante investiture allows the legislature to be proactive, in that it is actively involved in choosing the government.

Rather than being proactive, the investiture vote may instead take place after the head of state has appointed a new government. That government is formally empowered to act—it has control of the state—but it is required to face a parliamentary vote: if it succeeds in that vote, it continues in office; if it fails, it *is required* to resign and the process of forming a new government starts anew, or parliament is dissolved. Rasch et al. (2015) call this type of investiture vote an ex post investiture. In an ex post investiture, the legislature votes on an already appointed government; in this sense, the legislature ratifies a decision already made. Ten legislative assemblies in our study have an ex post, reactive, form of investiture. Under the Italian constitution, the President of the Republic selects the Prime Minister. On the proposal of the Prime Minister the President then appoints other members of the cabinet, which is then sworn into office by the President. The Government then has ten days from the date of swearing in to obtain the confidence of both the *Camera dei deputati* and the *Senato della Repubblica*. Italy is thus a clear case of ex post confirmation of the government by the national legislature. Formally at least, investiture places the legislative assembly at the heart of government formation. Yet the degree to which a legislative assembly is actively engaged in government formation may depend on the partisan composition of the legislative assembly, as we will discuss next.

11.4 Patterns of Government Formation under Parliamentarism

Few legislative elections endow a single political party with a majority of seats in the legislative assembly (or more specifically the chamber to which the government is responsible). Among the 39 parliamentary and semi-presidential regimes included in this study, only seven are governed by a single party majority government—a cabinet comprised of one political party which has a legislative majority. The United Kingdom, in 2022, was an example of a country with a single-party majority government. The Conservative Party controlled a majority of seats in the House of Commons (though not in the House of Lords).

But what happens when no single party wins a majority of seats in a general election, as was the case even in the United Kingdom following the 2010 and 2017 elections? Typically, the result is a bargaining process aimed at producing a government that has sufficient support to survive a confidence vote in parliament.

The players in this bargaining process are typically the leaders of the parliamentary parties, and it is generally assumed that their most important goals are to secure for their respective parties a place in the governing coalition and as much policy influence and as large a share of government portfolios as possible. None of these assumptions are universally valid. While parties have much to gain by acting in a unitary fashion in coalition bargaining, open splits within parties do happen. Thus, German Christian Democrat Rainer Barzel failed to win the Chancellorship in 1972 because two members of his own party group (both of whom were later found to have been bribed by the East German government) failed to support his motion of no confidence against Social Democrat incumbent Willy Brandt. In Norway, a non-socialist parliamentary majority failed in its 1986 attempt to unseat Prime Minister Gro Harlem Brundtland because of an internal split in the Center Party (Strøm 1994).

And while coalition bargaining is typically a game between political parties, Irish history records several instances in which independent members of the Dáil have been critical actors in such negotiations and in some cases even gained cabinet portfolios (see also Chapter 7). Finally, many minority governments have formed when one or several political parties have declined participation in coalitions they could have joined, which illustrates that parties do not always value office or portfolios above all else.

The rules that govern coalition bargaining are typically informal and often fluid. Nonetheless, it is useful to distinguish between *formateur*-based processes, in which a *formateur* is given (typically by the Head of State) the task of leading the bargaining process, and "free-style" bargaining, in which each party is free to negotiate with whatever partners it may choose (see Laver and Schofield 1990). A *formateur* is typically expected to be the prime minister in whatever coalition he or she forms. *Formateur*-based bargaining is most common in semi-presidential regimes, but also occurs in some regimes with a weaker president (such as Italy) and even in some monarchies (such as Belgium). In contrast, free-style bargaining is most common in regimes with figure-head monarchs, such as New Zealand and Scandinavia. Sometimes bargaining is made redundant, or heavily constrained, by coalition commitments that some of the political parties have made prior to the election (Golder 2006; Müller and Strøm 2008).

The coalition bargaining process typically takes less than two weeks (De Winter and Dumont 2008), but may in extreme cases last much longer, as in the case of Belgium, which in 2010–11 went 549 days without a regular government. When a general election returns a legislature in which no political party has a majority, a number of possible outcomes arise:

1. A majority coalition government. A coalition government, sometimes referred to as a multiparty government or cabinet, is comprised of members from two or more political parties. A majority coalition government is a

coalition government which controls a majority of seats in (the relevant chamber of) the legislative assembly. Our study includes 23 countries with a majority coalition government (table 11.3 identifies the type of government for each parliamentary system in our study). For example, as of January 2022, the Netherlands had a four-party coalition holding 77 of the 150 seats in the Tweede Kamer—giving them a (albeit bare) majority.

2. A single-party minority government. A minority government is a government that controls only a minority of seats in the legislature. We have five cases of single-party minority government—a minority government that is composed of one political party—in our study. As we will discuss below, minority governments used to be considered something of an anomaly in studies of parliamentarism (Strøm 1990). After all, governments need the support of the chamber to remain in office and possibly even to take office. In many cases, minority governments emerge because some parties are willing to offer some form of legislative support but without joining the governing minority party in office. At the time of writing Denmark has a single-party minority government—the Social Democrats hold only 50 of 179 seats. A minority party with strong bargaining power, such as historically many Social Democratic parties in Scandinavia, can form a government with no pre-arranged support and then negotiate parliamentary majorities on an ad hoc basis.

3. A coalition minority government. This is a government composed of two or more parties which jointly still do not have a majority of seats in the relevant legislative assembly. We have four cases of coalition minority government in our study. Following the 2022 parliamentary election, Sweden had a coalition minority government comprising the Moderate Party, the Liberals, and the Christian Democrats, which together held only 103 out of 349 seats in the Riksdag. In 2020, Norway went from having a coalition majority government to a coalition minority government when one party (the Progress Party) withdrew from government but the remaining coalition parties remained in office. After the 2021 parliamentary election, this administration was replaced by another minority coalition government.

4. No agreement, perhaps ultimately necessitating a fresh election. As in the Belgian case of 2010–11, which is mentioned above, a successful coalition bargain cannot always be reached in reasonable time. In some such cases, and in some cases in which only a weak government could form, a new election is called well before the end of the regular term of parliament. Yet, there are often strong formal and informal norms against disregarding the (initial) voice of the people in this fashion, and very early elections tend to be most common where the incumbent prime minister has the constitutional authority to call such election himself. Thus, in 1974 British Prime

Minister Harold Wilson called new elections only a few months after a general election had given his party a precarious parliamentary plurality, but no majority. In contrast, Sweden in 2014 and Germany in 2017 faced difficult parliamentary constellations in which many observers suggested early elections, but in both cases the result was "coalitions of the least unwilling" rather than early elections.

Three central puzzles surround government formation in parliamentary systems: (1) In the absence of a single party majority, what explains which parties coalesce and what sort of coalition they form? (2) How do parties that coalesce share cabinet seats amongst themselves?, and (3) Why do we observe so many minority governments in parliamentary regimes? We discuss each in turn.

What Explains Which Parties Coalesce?

Mathematically, many multiparty assemblies permit a wide range of possible coalitions, even if the coalition needs to control a majority of the assembly seats. Which parties coalesce, and why, has been the subject of significant theoretical and empirical research (Laver and Schofield 1990; Martin and Stevenson 2001; Müller and Strøm 2008). Early theories of coalition formation assumed that parties were interested in maximizing their share of cabinet seats and office spoils. Thus, von Neumann and Morgenstern (1944) and Riker (1962) predicted a **Minimal Winning Coalition**—a coalition supported by a legislative majority but without any parties whose votes were not necessary for that "winning" size.[4]

Later research on coalition bargaining shifted focus to assume that political parties contemplating coalition were motivated by policy. Hence, parties with similar policy preferences should be most likely to form coalitions (De Swaan 1973). Specifically, parties should form *connected* coalitions with those parties adjacent to them in policy space, which in these theories is generally assumed to be unidimensional (Axelrod 1970). Parties far apart on the policy spectrum should be unlikely to coalesce, especially to the exclusion of any parties located between them. Surplus majority coalitions—containing more parties than needed to hold an assembly majority—are thus possible when they ensure that parties in a coalition government are connected in policy space.

In a later policy-oriented approach to coalition formation, Laver and Shepsle's (1996) "Portfolio Allocation Model" assumes that parties are interested in policy, but that policy space is multidimensional and defined by the jurisdictions of

---

[4] Riker extended this approach by predicting that cabinets should be of **Minimum Size**—the minimal winning coalition with the smallest seat share in the legislature, and Leiserson (1966) formulated a related "bargaining proposition," which predicted the formation of a majority coalition with the smallest possible number of parties.

the country's ministerial departments. The assumption underlying the portfolio allocation model is that cabinet ministers have substantial autonomy within their respective policy domains. Coalition bargaining thus becomes a contest over a set of mutually exclusive portfolios, each of which grants its holder significant agenda control over its policy jurisdiction. In this process, parties with policy preferences close to the median on each dimension will be favored.

Sharing Cabinet Seats

Because the cabinet is at the apex of political power in most parliamentary democracies, the partisan distribution of cabinet seats (what scholars term *portfolio allocation*) is a topic of particular real-world significance. The allocation of cabinet seats constitutes one of the most important bargains between parties in a legislature (Baron and Ferejohn 1989). But no formateur or prime minister can dictate portfolio allocation within the coalition, and existing scholarship gives us sharply divergent expectations about this outcome.

Gamson's Law—the suggestion that each party receives "a share of the payoff proportional to the amount of resources which they contribute to a coalition" (Gamson 1961, 376)—dominates empirical research on portfolio allocations in coalition governments. The empirical constancy of Gamson's Law contrasts sharply with predictions from game-theoretic legislative bargaining models. Baron and Ferejohn (1989) model the allocation of portfolios between parties in coalition government as a simple divide-the-dollar game, with instant office payoffs as the prize to be distributed. These authors conclude with the clear prediction that the *formateur's* proposer advantage allows her or his party to retain a disproportionately large share of portfolios. The divergence between the predictions from bargaining theory and the empirical regularity of Gamson's Law leads Warwick and Druckman (2006) to speak of a "portfolio allocation paradox," and Cutler et al. (2016: 31) to note the "notorious contradiction" between one of the most influential models in political science and real-world portfolio allocation.

Minority Governments

As noted above, a minority government is a government that controls only a minority of seats in the legislature. Minority governments arguably represent something of a puzzle or an anomaly in parliamentary systems. Strøm (1990) suggests that the presence of an investiture vote reduces the probability of minority government formation. A formal investiture vote may constrain legislative support parties since they would have to publicly express their support for the government as a whole. As Strøm et al. (1994: 311) note, "some parties may find it acceptable tacitly to lend their weight to a government that they could not openly support in an investiture vote." Strøm (1990) also suggests that where a strong legislative committee system makes it possible for opposition parties to influence public policy, parties may prefer not to join a cabinet with some "uncomfortable" partners and instead remain in opposition (we explore the topic of committees in Chapter 8). Remaining in opposition under such circumstances allows a party to exercise some policy influence without incurring the electoral costs of governing (Narud and Valen 2008).

Bergman (1993) finds that in systems with negative parliamentarism (where the government must only be "tolerated by" the parliament) 48 percent of cabinets are minority governments, as compared to 25 percent in systems with positive parliamentarism (where an incoming government needs to be explicitly supported by the parliament). In their multivariate analysis of 220 coalition bargaining situations in 14 countries, Martin and Stevenson (2001: 37) similarly find that minority governments are less likely to form in the presence of an investiture vote. In contrast, in their study of 842 governments in 32 countries Rasch et al. (2015: 347) find no effect of the mere presence of an investiture vote on the likelihood of minority governments. Minority governments, they find, are equally frequent in systems with some kind of investiture procedure and systems without one. Yet, regimes in which investiture requires an absolute majority see fewer minority governments than regimes with more permissive decision rules.

From our perspective, investiture votes associate with a voters' and members' legislative assembly. Because investiture votes provide a hurdle to government formation, citizens in such systems are relatively more protected from the emergence of a government which does not enjoy majority support. And the higher the hurdle, in terms of the investiture decision rule, the more a government needs to have broad support in order to be formed or confirmed. Similarly, the influence of the assembly's membership is maximized when members get to vote on who should be the executive. And again, the higher the hurdle in terms of investiture decision rule, the more influential the membership, all else equal.

11.5 Government Termination under Parliamentarism

A no confidence vote serves to determine whether the legislative assembly has confidence in the prime minister and his or her government. A confidence vote is a similar measure on which the assembly is asked to express its confidence in the government. If a government in a parliamentary system loses a no confidence vote it must resign. A government must also resign if it fails to win a confidence motion. Typically, the opposition will table a no confidence motion in an attempt to bring the incumbent government down. In contrast, the government itself tables a confidence motion—to demonstrate that it has the confidence of the chamber with regard to a specific policy area. As we will see later, confidence procedures allow policy motions to be attached to the government's survival. The legislative assembly, and in particular dissident members of the governing parties, is then faced with a challenge: reject the motion, and thus see the government removed from office, or accept the motion and allow the government to continue in office and its motion to be adopted.

A constructive no confidence procedure is a particular type of confidence procedure, which requires the legislature to simultaneously elect a new prime minister in order to remove the current office-holder. We know of seven countries that have adopted a constructive no confidence procedure in their constitutions: Belgium, Germany, Hungary, Poland, Slovenia, Spain, and Israel. For example, under the Spanish Constitution, an alternative Prime Minister needs to be proposed simultaneously as part of any valid no-confidence motion. If the constructive no-confidence proposal is successful, the government resigns and the King formally appoints the new Prime Minister and government (Constitution of Spain, Art. 99).

Strøm et al. (1994: 310) describe the constructive no confidence procedure as a "significant qualification of the basic norm of parliamentary democracy." Having to specify an alternative government makes it more challenging to remove the existing one. Thus, the constructive procedure creates a barrier to removing the government, favoring leaders over members. In doing so, it promotes stability—for example by rendering a coalition viable even if it loses its parliamentary majority due to the departure of one or more coalition parties. The constructive vote of no confidence originated in Germany where the 1949 Constitution enshrined this procedure as a way to help avoid the instability of the Weimar Republic (1919–1933)—seen by some as a cause of World War II.

11.6 Other Appointment Powers

Thus far, this chapter has focused on the role of the national assembly in appointing the head of government and his or her cabinet. These are certainly important, even pivotal, political positions in any representative democracy. Yet, legislative assemblies may be involved in the appointment of other public office-holders who also play crucial roles in shaping and implementing public policy. We refer to such powers as a legislative assembly's appointment powers. We don't consider here every possible appointment in which a national legislature may be involved. Instead we focus on two key institutions: the senior judiciary and the leadership of a country's central bank. Virtually all countries have a judiciary and a central bank. Subsequently we consider cases in which the legislature is involved in selecting the head of state.

The judicial branch of the government is often hierarchical, with a superior court or sometimes a separate constitutional court at the apex of the judicial system. The Philadelphia Constitutional Convention of 1787 debated various options for how the judiciary should be appointed. As Epstein et al. (2001: 7) note, who should appoint federal judges "was a—perhaps the—major source of contention pertaining to the federal judiciary, with the delegates contemplating several different plans." Some wanted the legislature to select the judiciary, others wanted the executive to have this authority. The compromise to involve both branches was twice rejected before it was ultimately accepted. As a result, the US President nominates judicial appointees and the Senate may confirm or reject these nominations.

The United States judicial tradition has become increasingly influential worldwide, but how widespread has this method of selecting senior judges become? Must the most senior member of the judiciary (the chief justice) be confirmed by one or more chambers before taking office? The answer is that this procedure is about as common as its absence. For 30 of our 68 countries, the legislature plays no formal role in selecting the chief justice. In 25 countries, only the lower chamber (including relevant unicameral cases) takes part in selecting the chief justice. In nine cases, only the upper chamber is involved in this selection process. And in four cases, both chambers are involved in selecting the chief justice. In Germany, for example, the Bundestag and the Bundesrat take turns in selecting the President of the federal constitutional court, the *Bundesverfassungsgericht*. The decision rule requires a two-thirds vote in favor.

Does regime type affect the role of the legislature in selecting the chief justice? The answer is clearly yes. In the vast majority (18 out of 21) of parliamentary systems, the legislature plays no role in selecting the country's most senior judge (Table 11.4). In contrast, in 10 out of 18 semi-presidential systems, the legislature does have such a role. And in the vast majority of presidential systems (25 out of 29), the legislature must confirm the chief justice. The four presidential systems where this does not happen are Colombia, The Dominican Republic, Ecuador, and the Philippines.

A central bank typically serves as both the government's bank, a regulator of the banking sector, and a central actor in shaping and implementing monetary policy. Examples of central banks include the United States' Federal Reserve, the United Kingdom's Bank of England, and Japan's Bank of Japan. The chief executive officer is the senior official within the bank, often referred to as the Central Bank Governor. Cukierman et al. (1992) suggest that who selects the Central Bank governor may have consequence for the independence of the Central Bank and its capacity to effect monetary policy. At one end of their scale, the selection of the governor is determined by the board itself. At the other end of their scale, a political office-holder (for example, the head of government) appoints the governor. Appointments involving the national assembly represent an intermediate

Table 11.4 Government types in parliamentary and semi presidential regimes

Single Party Majority Government	Coalition Majority Government	Single Party Minority Government	Coalition Minority Government
Canada	Taiwan	Denmark	Israel
South Africa	Australia	New Zealand	Norway
United Kingdom	Belgium	Spain	Sweden
Poland	Greece	Peru	Bulgaria
Senegal	Hungary	Portugal	
Slovak Republic	India		
	Italy		
	Japan		
	Nepal		
	Netherlands		
	Pakistan		
	Papua New Guinea		
	Switzerland		
	Austria		
	Croatia		
	Czech Republic		
	Finland		
	France		
	Ireland		
	Niger		
	Romania		
	Serbia		
	Tunisia		
	Ukraine		

case: having the legislature involved represents some element of central bank independence from the executive, but not as much as when the Bank itself appoints its chief officer.

Table 11.5 reports whether or not the most senior central banker (the Governor) needs to be confirmed by one or more chambers of the national legislature before taking office. In 40 countries, the legislature plays no formal role in confirming the central bank governor. In 16 cases the lower (or unicameral) chamber exclusively is involved in the formal appointment. In eight cases, only the upper chamber participates in selecting the Bank's governor. In the United States, for example, the President nominates the Chair of the Federal Reserve but this nomination must be approved by the United States Senate. In two countries, Japan and Switzerland, both chambers are involved in the appointment process. For example, in Japan, both the *Diet* and the House of Councillors must consent to the Cabinet's nominee for Governor (and Deputy Governor).[5]

---

[5] We are missing data for two countries, Benin and Senegal.

Does regime type affect the role assigned to the legislature in selecting Central Bank heads? Again, the answer is yes, but less strikingly than in the case of chief justices. In just three of our 21 parliamentary systems the assembly participates in appointing the central bank governor. In contrast, 11 of the 17 semi-presidential systems involve the legislature in confirming the central bank head. Somewhat surprisingly, the same is true of only a minority of presidential systems (12 out of 28). Thus, while in parliamentary systems the assembly tends not to be involved in selecting the central bank head, it is not the case that presidential systems exhibit the opposite pattern. Rather, semi-presidential and presidential regimes are roughly evenly divided between those that give their assemblies such powers and those that do not.

One other very important appointment role has to do with the selection of the head of state. Twelve countries in our study are monarchies, meaning that the head of state is a hereditary position. Obviously, in such hereditary constitutional monarchies the national assembly can play no elective role. But even under republican constitutions, the national legislature rarely participates in the selection of the head of state. The vast majority of countries in our study (46 of 68) employ a popular election to select the head of state. Amongst countries in our study, only five national legislatures play a central formal role in selecting the head of state. As noted in table 11.5, these are Greece, Hungary, Israel, South Africa, and Switzerland.[6]

Under article 32 of the Greek Constitution, the President of the Republic is elected by the Hellenic Parliament. On the first vote to elect a president, a successful candidate needs to receive the support of a two-thirds majority of the total number of Members of Parliament. The constitution goes on to specify that: "Should the said majority not be attained, the ballot shall be repeated after five days. Should the second ballot fail to produce the required majority, the ballot shall once more be repeated after five days; the person receiving a three-fifths majority of the total number of Members of Parliament shall be elected President of the Republic. Should the third ballot fail to produce the said qualified majority, Parliament shall be dissolved within ten days of the ballot, and elections for a new Parliament shall be called." Selecting the President is thus not only a process in which the Greek Parliament takes part, but indeed a critical function of that assembly.

Five counties (Germany, India, Italy, Nepal, and Pakistan) employ a form of indirect process to elect the head of state. For example, the President of Germany is elected by a Federal Convention. The Federal Convention comprises the members of the lower chamber of the federal parliament (*Bundestag*) and an equal number of members elected by the state parliaments. The number of representatives which

---

[6] Of the remaining cases, in 12 countries a monarch serves as head of state, in five cases the President is indirectly elected and in 46 cases the head of state is popularly elected.

Table 11.5 Other appointment and dismissal powers

Country	Head of State	Chief Justice	Central Bank Governor	Impeachment
Argentina	Popular Election	Yes, Upper Chamber	Yes Upper Chamber	By Legislature + Other Actor(s)
Australia	Monarchy	No Role	No Role	No Impeachment
Austria	Popular Election	No Role	No Role	By Legislature + Other Actor(s)
Belgium	Monarchy	No Role	No Role	No Impeachment
Benin	Popular Election	Yes, (Lower) Chamber		By Lower/Unicameral Chamber
Bolivia	Popular Election	Yes, (Lower) Chamber	Yes (Lower) Chamber	By Legislature + Other Actor(s)
Brazil	Popular Election	Yes, Upper Chamber	Yes Upper Chamber	By Lower and Upper Chamber
Bulgaria	Popular Election	No Role	Yes (Lower) Chamber	By Legislature + Other Actor(s)
Burundi	Popular Election	Yes, Upper Chamber	No Role	By Lower and Upper Chamber
Canada	Monarchy	No Role	No Role	No Impeachment
Chile	Popular Election	Yes, Upper Chamber	Yes Upper Chamber	By Lower and Upper Chamber
Colombia	Popular Election	No Role	No Role	By Legislature + Other Actor(s)
Costa Rica	Popular Election	Yes, (Lower) Chamber	Yes (Lower) Chamber	By Legislature + Other Actor(s)
Croatia	Popular Election	Yes, (Lower) Chamber	Yes (Lower) Chamber	By Legislature + Other Actor(s)
Czech Republic	Popular Election	Yes, (Lower) Chamber	No Role	By Legislature + Other Actor(s)
Denmark	Monarchy	No Role	No Role	No Impeachment
Dominican Republic	Popular Election	No Role	No Role	By Lower and Upper Chamber
Ecuador	Popular Election	No Role	No Role	By Lower/Unicameral Chamber
El Salvador	Popular Election	Yes, (Lower) Chamber	No Role	By Legislature + Other Actor(s)
Finland	Popular Election	No Role	Yes (Lower) Chamber	No Impeachment
France	Popular Election	No Role	No Role	By Lower and Upper Chamber
Germany	Other Indirect	Yes, Lower and Upper Chamber	No Role	By Legislature + Other Actor(s)
Ghana	Popular Election	Yes, (Lower) Chamber	No Role	By Legislature + Other Actor(s)

Greece	Legislature	No Role	No Role	By Legislature + Other Actor(s)
Guatemala	Popular Election	Yes, (Lower) Chamber	No Role	By Legislature + Other Actor(s)
Honduras	Popular Election	Yes, (Lower) Chamber	No Role	By Lower/Unicameral Chamber
Hungary	Legislature	Yes, (Lower) Chamber	No Role	By Legislature + Other Actor(s)
India	Other Indirect	No Role	No Role	By Lower and Upper Chamber
Indonesia	Popular Election	Yes, (Lower) Chamber	Yes (Lower) Chamber	By Legislature + Other Actor(s)
Ireland	Popular Election	No Role	No Role	By Lower and Upper Chamber
Israel	Legislature	No Role	No Role	By Lower/Unicameral Chamber
Italy	Other Indirect	No Role	No Role	By Legislature + Other Actor(s)
Japan	Monarchy	No Role	Yes, Lower and Upper Chamber	No Impeachment
Kenya	Popular Election	Yes, (Lower) Chamber	Yes (Lower) Chamber	By Lower and Upper Chamber
Liberia	Popular Election	Yes, Upper Chamber	No Role	By Legislature + Other Actor(s)
Malawi	Popular Election	Yes, (Lower) Chamber	No Role	By Lower/Unicameral Chamber
Mexico	Popular Election	Yes, Upper Chamber	Yes Upper Chamber	By Lower and Upper Chamber
Nepal	Other Indirect	No Role	No Role	By Lower/Unicameral Chamber
Netherlands	Monarchy	No Role	No Role	No Impeachment
New Zealand	Monarchy	No Role	No Role	No Impeachment
Nicaragua	Popular Election	Yes, (Lower) Chamber	No Role	By Legislature + Other Actor(s)
Niger	Popular Election	No Role	No Role	By Legislature + Other Actor(s)
Nigeria	Popular Election	Yes, Upper Chamber	Yes Upper Chamber	By Legislature + Other Actor(s)
Norway	Monarchy	No Role	No Role	No Impeachment
Pakistan	Other Indirect	No Role	No Role	By Lower and Upper Chamber
Papua New Guinea	Monarchy	No Role	No Role	No Impeachment

Continued

Table 11.5 *Continued*

Country	Head of State	Chief Justice	Central Bank Governor	Impeachment
Paraguay	Popular Election	Yes, Upper Chamber	Yes Upper Chamber	By Lower and Upper Chamber
Peru	Popular Election	Yes, (Lower) Chamber	Yes (Lower) Chamber	By Lower/Unicameral Chamber
Philippines	Popular Election	No Role	No Role	By Legislature + Other Actor(s)
Poland	Popular Election	No Role	Yes (Lower) Chamber	By Legislature + Other Actor(s)
Portugal	Popular Election	Yes, (Lower) Chamber	No Role	By Legislature + Other Actor(s)
Romania	Popular Election	Yes, Lower and Upper Chamber	Yes Upper Chamber	By Legislature + Other Actor(s)
Senegal	Popular Election	No Role		By Legislature + Other Actor(s)
Serbia	Popular Election	Yes, (Lower) Chamber	Yes (Lower) Chamber	By Legislature + Other Actor(s)
Sierra Leone	Popular Election	Yes, (Lower) Chamber	Yes (Lower) Chamber	By Legislature + Other Actor(s)
Slovak Republic	Popular Election	Yes, (Lower) Chamber	Yes (Lower) Chamber	By Legislature + Other Actor(s)
South Africa	Legislature	No Role	No Role	By Lower/Unicameral Chamber
South Korea	Popular Election	Yes, (Lower) Chamber	No Role	By Legislature + Other Actor(s)
Spain	Monarchy	Yes, Lower and Upper Chamber	No Role	No Impeachment
Sweden	Monarchy	No Role	Yes (Lower) Chamber	No Impeachment
Switzerland	Legislature	Yes, Lower and Upper Chamber	Yes, Lower and Upper Chamber	No Impeachment
Taiwan	Popular Election	Yes, (Lower) Chamber	Yes (Lower) Chamber	By Legislature + Other Actor(s)
Tunisia	Popular Election	Yes, (Lower) Chamber	Yes (Lower) Chamber	By Legislature + Other Actor(s)
Turkey	Popular Election	Yes, (Lower) Chamber	No Role	By Lower/Unicameral Chamber
Ukraine	Popular Election	Yes, (Lower) Chamber	Yes (Lower) Chamber	By Legislature + Other Actor(s)
United Kingdom	Monarchy	No Role	No Role	No Impeachment
United States	Popular Election	Yes, Upper Chamber	Yes Upper Chamber	By Lower and Upper Chamber
Zambia	Popular Election	Yes, (Lower) Chamber	No Role	By Legislature + Other Actor(s)

the individual Länder may send to the Federal Convention is calculated based on the population of each Land.

Table 11.5 presents the results of a regression analysis where popular election of the head of state is the dependent variable. The results in Table 11.5 show that wealthier countries are less likely to popularly elect the head of state. Conversely, countries from Africa/Middle East, Americas, and Eastern Europe, as well as non-British colonies and those that gained sovereignty later, are more likely to popularly elect the head of state, although the strength of this evidence is mixed depending on the model.

11.7 Impeachment

Impeachment is one legal avenue by which presidents in some presidential or semi-presidential systems can be removed from office prior to the completion of their term of office.[7] Impeachment describes "a particular trial of the President by which Congress (sometimes with the necessary agreement of the judiciary) is allowed to remove the President from office" (Pérez-Liñán 2007: 6). Impeachment is thus a quasi-judicial process, typically requiring the legislative body to find that the office-holder is guilty of some form of "high crimes and misdemeanours," such as treason or bribery.

Impeachment procedures under presidentialism can thus be contrasted with no-confidence procedures under parliamentarism. Recall that no-confidence procedures permit the legislature to remove the head of government for whatever reason the legislature chooses; the incumbent need not be accused of committing a crime or any sort of wrongdoing. In contrast, impeachment requires that the office-holder be found guilty by the legislature (and, depending on procedures, the court) of having committed a (typically grave) crime. Impeachment is thus not designed to remove presidents in the same way as no-confidence procedures are designed to allow the legislature to remove a sitting government. The cumbersome nature of impeachment processes may be a deliberate design to make it difficult to remove an elected official, therefore facilitating stability. As Linz (1990: 65) notes "impeachment is a very uncertain and time-consuming process, especially compared with the simple parliamentary vote of no confidence." Yet, it is worth emphasizing that legislatures in presidential systems may have the capacity to remove the president. In fact, as we will see below, the threshold of criminality practically required to remove a president has in many political systems been falling, as new crimes such

---

[7] Impeachment can be contrasted with other constitutional mechanisms to remove a President, such as declaring the President unfit or incapable of holding office, or extra-institutional removal mechanisms such as a presidential coup d'état—where the president is removed from office by force.

as "misperformance in office" have become accepted grounds for impeachment in several Latin American democracies (Pérez-Liñán 2007).

Of the 68 countries in our study, only 14 do not have a mechanism to impeach the head of state (see table 11.5). In most of these cases, the head of state is a hereditary monarch. There are two exceptions. The Finnish President and the Swiss Federal President are not subject to impeachment (of course the Swiss Federal President's term of office is only one year). In nine cases, the lower or unicameral chamber has authority to impeach the head of state. In 12 cases, both chambers have the right to do so. In 33 cases, roughly half the countries in our study, impeachment (also) involves an external actor such as the judiciary.

Thus, impeachment is not a procedure found strictly in presidential systems. The Norwegian Constitution of 1814, for example, included (and still includes) an impeachment process, and in 1884 a Parliament dominated by the Liberal Party successfully impeached a politically conservative cabinet appointed by the king and thereby forced the cabinet to accept their responsibility to the national assembly. Yet, even after the no confidence procedure had been accepted by all parties, the impeachment procedure continued to be used in a total of eight cases, the most recent one being charges against the Prime Minister and six other cabinet members in 1926 (they were acquitted in a split decision).[8]

By conventional accounts, impeachment procedures are rare and unlikely to succeed. Their complicated nature makes successful impeachments difficult to achieve. During his presidency, Bill Clinton was impeached by the US House of Representatives on perjury and obstruction of justice charges but was acquitted by the Senate, as fewer than two-thirds of the senators found him guilty. Similarly, President Donald Trump was twice impeached by the Democrat majority in the House of Representatives, but in both cases acquitted by the Senate. In a broader cross-national study, Kim (2014) cites just one example of a president who was ousted via a completed impeachment process between 1974 and 2003— that case being Madagascar's Albert Zafy, who was removed from office in 1996 by the National Assembly. Yet, as Pérez-Liñán (2007: 3) notes, a wave of attempted impeachments from the 1990s in Latin America means that "Presidential impeachment has emerged as the most powerful instrument to displace 'undesirable' presidents without destroying the constitutional order" (see Box 11.2). While impeachments may not succeed, they can weaken presidents, sometimes to the point where they are forced to resign.

---

[8] Even though the impeachment process had not been used for 80 years, the Norwegian *Storting* (Parliament) decided not to repeal this provision during its thoroughgoing constitutional review process in 2007. Rather, the impeachment process was revised to make it better adapted to the contemporary situation, and interestingly the role of the Supreme Court (vis-à-vis the *Storting*) in the Court of Impeachment was strengthened.

Box 11.2 The Impeachment of the President of Brazil

Brazil provides a recent example of presidential impeachment. Under the Brazilian Constitution, the president can only be removed for "crimes of responsibility." Dilma Rousseff was re-elected President in 2014 but in 2016 faced impeachment. This process began in March 2016, when citizens filed a number of impeachment petitions. The following month, the Speaker of the lower chamber accepted these petitions and established a committee to investigate the complaints against the president. Later in April, the Impeachment committee, by a 38–27 vote, recommended a congressional impeachment procedure, and shortly thereafter the lower chamber of the Brazilian Congress voted for impeachment by the necessary 2/3 majority. The case then went to the Senate, which suspended President Rousseff and gave Vice President Michel Temer presidential powers in an acting capacity. In August, by a vote of 61 to 20, The Senate removed Rousseff from office and the acting President became President.

As two commentators noted:

the case has all the markings of an impeachment born out of a political decision to sack a highly unpopular president that had lost parliamentary majorities ... formal devices were used to recreate the consequences that low public approval and/or the loss of a congressional majority would have in a parliamentary regime. In the end, this amounts to a de facto "parliamentarization" of a presidential system. What's wrong with that? According to the Brazilian Constitution, neither low public approval nor the loss of a congressional majority constitute impeachable offenses. Unlike the vote of no-confidence or a censure motion—which are features of parliamentary systems—impeachment is a legal procedure, not a political one.

Source: https://www.brookings.edu/blog/up-front/2016/11/01/parliamentarism-in-disguise/

It is exceedingly clear that Dilma was not a "good" president, and she had the single-digit approval ratings to prove it. Though the opposition was poised for a smooth victory in the next elections, waiting until 2018 seemed an unappealing prospect when a vote of no confidence could quickly free Brazil from an unpopular administration. The problem is that Brazil does not have a parliamentary system, meaning removal of a head of state must be done on the basis of criminal misconduct.

Source: http://thehill.com/blogs/congress-blog/foreign-policy/294012-brazils-flawed-impeachment-of-dilma-rousseff

11.8 Conclusion

In this chapter, we have examined the role of the national assembly in selecting and terminating the head of government and his or her cabinet. Even an early observer such as Bagehot 150 years ago recognized the "elective function" as the most important role of the House of Commons in British politics. In parliamentary systems, these powers of selection and deselection are enforced through votes of investiture and votes of confidence or no confidence. In presidential systems, the head of government is much more independent of the legislature, and impeachment is the main mechanism by which the assembly can affect and potentially remove the chief executive. But impeachment processes are rare and unlikely to succeed, even though they have recently become more common and effective in several Latin American countries.

In parliamentary countries, the legislative majority controls the executive branch in a much more direct and immediate manner. Yet, parliamentary democracy does not automatically mean that the executive branch is drawn from a majority bloc in the legislature, as minority governments remain remarkably common. Nor does parliamentarism necessarily result in quick and efficient bargaining over government formation.

Although the scholarly literature on parliamentary selection processes has overwhelmingly focused on their impact on prime ministerial and cabinet appointments, many national assemblies have other appointment powers as well. In about half of our countries, the legislature participates in the appointment of the highest judges in the country (specifically in our study, the chief justice of the supreme court). Interestingly, in this context, presidential constitutions tend to give the legislature a more important role than do parliamentary ones. The number of democracies in which the legislature plays a role in selecting the central bank governor is lower, but again this is somewhat less common in parliamentary than in presidential or semi-presidential regimes.

Finally, we have seen that few national assemblies play any significant role in selecting the head of state in their respective countries. In some countries, this is very understandable given that the head of state is a hereditary constitutional monarch. In a larger set of countries, this is a consequence of having a presidential constitution. But under some parliamentary, semi-presidential, and other constitutions (including South Africa, Greece, and Switzerland), the national assembly actually does perform an elective function in this respect as well.

References

Axelrod, Robert. 1970. *Conflict of Interest*. Chicago: Markham.
Bagehot, Walter. 1867. *The English Constitution*. London: Chapman & Hall.
Baron, David P., and John A. Ferejohn. 1989. "Bargaining in Legislatures." *American Political Science Review* 83(4): 1181–1206.

Bergman, Torbjörn. 1993. "Formation Rules and Minority Governments." *European Journal of Political Research* 23(1): 55–66.

Cheibub, José Antonio. 2007. *Presidentialism, Parliamentarism, and Democracy.* New York: Cambridge University Press.

Cox, Gary W. 2014. "Reluctant Democrats and Their Legislatures." In Shane Martin, Thomas Saalfeld and Kaare W Strøm (eds.), *The Oxford Handbook of Legislative Studies.* Oxford: Oxford University Press, 696–716.

Cox, Gary W. 2017. *Marketing Sovereign Promises.* Cambridge: Cambridge University Press.

Cukierman, Alex, Steven B. Web, and Bilin Neyapti. 1992. "Measuring the Independence of Central Banks and Its Effect on Policy Outcomes." *The World Bank Economic Review* 6(3): 353–398.

Cutler, Josh, Scott De Marchi, Max Gallop, Florian M. Hollenbach, Michael Laver, and Matthias Orlowski. 2016. "Cabinet Formation and Portfolio Distribution in European Multiparty Systems." *British Journal of Political Science* 46(1): 31–43.

De Swaan, Abram. 1973. *Coalition Theories and Cabinet Formation.* San Francisco: Jossey-Bass.

De Winter, Lieven, and Patrick Dumont. 2008. "Uncertainty and Complexity in Cabinet Formation." In Kaare Strøm, Wolfgang C. Müller, and Torbjörn Bergman (eds.), *Cabinets and Coalition Bargaining. The Democratic Life Cycle in Western Europe.* Oxford: Oxford University Press, 123–158.

Duverger, Maurice. 1980. "A New Political System Model: Semi-presidential Government." *European Journal of Political Research* 8(2): 165–187.

Elgie, Robert. 1998. "The Classification of Democratic Regime Types: Conceptual Ambiguity and Contestable Assumptions." *European Journal of Political Research* 33(2): 219–238.

Elgie, Robert (ed.). 1999. *Semi-presidentialism in Europe.* Oxford: Oxford University Press.

Epstein, Lee, Jack Knight, and Olga Shvetsova. 2001. "Comparing Judicial Selection Systems." *William & Mary Bill of Rights Law Journal* 10(1): 7–36.

Gamson, William A. 1961. "A Theory Of Coalition Formation." *American Sociological Review* 26(3): 373-382.

Golder, Sona Nadenichek. 2006. *The Logic of Pre-electoral Coalition Formation.* Columbus: Ohio State University Press.

Kelso, Alexandra. 2015. "Parliament and Government Formation in the United Kingdom: A Hidden Vote of Investiture." In Rasch, Bjørn Erik Shane Martin, and José Antonio Cheibub (eds.), *Parliaments and Government Formation.* Oxford: Oxford University Press, 29–48.

Kim, Young Hun. 2014. "Impeachment and Presidential Politics in New Democracies." *Democratization* 2(3): 519–553.

Laver, Michael. 2003. "Government Termination." *Annual Review of Political Science* 6(1): 23–40.

Laver, Michael. 2006. "Legislatures and Parliaments in Comparative Context." In Barry R. Weingast and Donald Wittman (eds.), *The Oxford Handbook of Political Economy.* Oxford: Oxford University Press, 121–140.

Laver, Michael and Norman Schofield. 1990. *Multiparty Government: The Politics of Coalition in Europe.* Oxford: Oxford University Press.

Laver, Michael and Kenneth A. Shepsle. 1996. *Making and Breaking Governments: Cabinets and Legislatures in Parliamentary Democracies.* Cambridge: Cambridge University Press.

Leiserson, Michael. 1966. *Coalitions in Politics: A Theoretical and Empirical Study*. New Haven: Yale University, Doctoral Dissertation.

Lijphart, Arend. 1984. *Democracies: Patterns of Majoritarian and Consensus Government in Twenty-One Countries*. First ed. New Haven: Yale University Press.

Linz, Juan J. 1990. "The Perils of Presidentialism." *Journal of Democracy* 1(1): 51–69.

Martin, Lanny W., and Randolph T. Stevenson. 2001. "Government Formation in Parliamentary Democracies." *American Journal of Political Science* 45(1): 33–50.

Müller, Wolfgang C., Torbjörn Bergman, and Kaare Strøm. 2003. "Parliamentary Democracy: Promise and Problems." In Kaare Strøm, Müller, Wolfgang C., and Torbjörn Bergman (eds.), *Delegation and Accountability in Parliamentary Democracies*. Oxford: Oxford University Press, 3–32.

Müller, Wolfgang C. and Kaare Strøm. 2008. "Coalition Agreements and Cabinet Governance." In Kaare Strøm, Wolfgang C. Müller, and Torbjörn Bergman (eds.), *Cabinets and Coalition Bargaining. The Democratic Life Cycle in Western Europe*. Oxford: Oxford University Press, 159–199.

Narud, Hanne Marthe, and Henry Valen. 2008. "Coalition Membership and Electoral Performance." In Kaare Strøm, Wolfgang C. Müller, and Torbjörn Bergman (eds.), *Cabinets and Coalition Bargaining. The Democratic Life Cycle in Western Europe*. Oxford: Oxford University Press, 369–402.

Pérez-Liñán, Aníbal. 2007. *Presidential Impeachment and the New Political Instability in Latin America*. Cambridge: Cambridge University Press.

Rasch, Rasch, Bjørn Erik., Shane Martin, and José Antonio Cheibub. 2015. "Investiture Rules Unpacked." In Rasch, Rasch, Bjørn Erik., Shane Martin, and José Antonio Cheibub (eds.), *Parliaments and Government Formation: Unpacking Investiture Rules*. Oxford: Oxford University Press, 331–356.

Riker, William H. 1962. *The Theory of Political Coalitions*. New Haven: Yale University Press.

Shugart, Matthew S and John M. Carey. 1992. *Presidents and Assemblies: Constitutional Design and Electoral Dynamics*. Cambridge: Cambridge University Press.

Strøm, Kaare. 1990. "A Behavioral Theory of Competitive Political Parties." *American Journal of Political Science* 34(2): 565–598.

Strøm, Kaare. 1994. "The Presthus Debacle: Intraparty Politics and Bargaining Failure in Norway." *American Political Science Review* 88(1): 112–127.

Strøm, Kaare. 2000. "Delegation and Accountability in Parliamentary Democracies." *European Journal of Political Research* 37(3): 261–290.

Strøm, Kaare., Ian Budge, and Michael J. Laver. 1994. "Constraints on Cabinet Formation in Parliamentary Democracies." *American Journal of Political Science* 38: 303–335.

von Neumann, John, and Oskar Morgenstern. 1944. *The Theory of Games and Economic Behavior*. Princeton: Princeton University Press.

Warwick, Paul V., and James N. Druckman. 2006. "The Portfolio Allocation Paradox: An Investigation into the Nature of a Very Strong But Puzzling Relationship." *European Journal of Political Research* 45(4): 635–665.

12
Executive Oversight

As we have seen in earlier chapters, the roles of a legislative assembly are mani-fold, including helping select the executive (in parliamentary systems) and other office holders, budgeting, and lawmaking. This chapter focuses on a fourth role: oversight of the executive. As Kreppel (2014: 86) notes, legislative oversight of the executive branch is a broad concept, "entailing the monitoring of executive agen-cies tasked with the implementation of policy decisions, and regular engagement with the political executive to insure it is meeting its commitments to the public and adequately addressing the various policy needs of the country."

There are several reasons why the legislature seeks to oversee the executive. All legislative assemblies arguably need to monitor the executive in order to perform their lawmaking role. Moreover, while legislatures may play a central role in mak-ing law, they delegate the implementation of the laws (and sometimes the details of the law) to the executive. And as we have noted throughout this volume, with delegation comes the need for oversight, as a form of ex-post control of the agent by the principal. As McCubbins (2014: 570) noted, "elected representatives have the right to control the bureaucracy, because democracy is built on a *chain of del-egation*: politicians are agents of the people, tasked with deciding law; bureaucrats are the agents of elected representatives, tasked with executing that law." Without oversight, bureaucrats may not faithfully implement the intentions of the legisla-tive assembly, a phenomenon known as bureaucratic drift. Bureaucrats may be tempted either to implement according to their own preferences, or not to bother to implement anything at all. Thus, and particularly in presidential systems, the focus of the legislature's oversight of the executive is often the bureaucracy. It is often assumed that legislative assemblies in presidential systems are less concerned with the performance of the elected part of the executive (sometimes referred to as the core executive), presumably because the elected executive is not *politically* accountable to the assembly under presidentialism. Of course, the possibility of initiating an impeachment process against an elected executive means that, even in a presidential system, the legislative assembly still wants some sense and record of what the political executive is doing.

In parliamentary systems, the executive acts as a direct agent of the legislative assembly. The executive in a parliamentary system is sometimes viewed as a com-mittee of the assembly, emerging from the assembly and politically responsible to the assembly. Because the political executive is an agent of the assembly, the assem-bly has the right and responsibility to monitor the activities of both the political

Legislative Assemblies. Shane Martin and Kaare W. Strøm, Oxford University Press.
© Shane Martin and Kaare W. Strøm (2023). DOI: 10.1093/oso/9780198890829.003.0012

executive and the wider bureaucracy. Otherwise, the executive may not act in line with the interests and preferences of the legislative assembly. As noted in the previous chapter, an executive in a parliamentary system can be held to account for its actions and, if necessary, ultimately dismissed for poor performance (or for no reason at all) at the will of the legislature.

The capacity to oversee the executive shapes the fundamental nature of the legislative assembly. A voters' assembly should have a high capacity to monitor the executive. This follows from the emphasis on transparency that characterizes such assemblies, and this demand for transparency should pertain to the executive as well as to the legislative branch. Whether voters approve or disapprove of the current political performance they observe, they will want to know who is responsible, so that they can apportion credit or blame among different branches of government, political parties, and candidates. Thus, voters need information on the performance of the incumbent executive to decide whom to support at election time. Oversight activities by legislative assemblies are one important means by which voters can obtain this information.

A leaders' assembly, in contrast, may be less inclined to develop and employ tools of executive oversight. This is because party leaders are often the same people who populate (or hope to populate) the executive, which reduces their motivation to allow the legislative assembly the tools to question and potentially sanction or embarrass the executive. Certainly, "opposition" parties may have an incentive to use the legislature to oversee and hold to account parties in the executive. This incentive may be curtailed, however, where alternation in executive office is common—the opposition leadership knows it too will govern and may prefer to keep oversight of the incumbent executive weak—safe in the knowledge that it will soon hold that office and would prefer the prying eyes of the legislature not to be on it. Similarly, in presidential systems, the degree of executive oversight in a leaders' assembly likely depends on whether the polity is unified or divided in partisan terms. When the same party controls the executive and the legislative majority, a leaders' assembly has less incentive to engage in oversight, compared to periods of divided government. To the extent that leaders in a leaders' assembly develop strong oversight mechanisms, they will seek to maintain tight control over the dissemination of the information they gain. Thus, the transparency of these oversight procedures will tend to be much lower than in voters' assemblies.

A members' assembly should ensure that executive oversight is sufficiently strong such that individual legislators can monitor the executive in pursuit of their own goals, be it re-election or some other objective such as may follow from progressive ambition. For example, in a members' assembly, any policy made by the legislature will need implementing and affected legislators will want to ensure the policy solutions which they won in legislative bargaining are being implemented by the executive, so that the members may credibly claim credit for these policies among the voters. This requires effective oversight and, since members want to control the information they share with their voters for credit-claiming purposes, a level of transparency greater than that of a leaders' assembly, though lower than that of voters' assembly,.

Legislative assemblies face a difficult task in attempting to hold the executive to account. As Wheare (1963: 148) notes: "If a general survey is made of the position and working of legislatures in the present century, it is apparent that, with a few important and striking exceptions, legislatures have declined in certain important respects and particularly in powers in relation to the executive government." The typical executive tends to be better resourced, speak with a more unified voice, have informational advantages and operate in a less than fully transparent fashion.

To overcome such structural and informational disadvantages, legislatures are empowered with, or give to themselves, a number of oversight tools. These mechanisms provide a means for the legislative assembly to attempt oversee the executive—either the political executive, the bureaucracy or both. McCubbins and Schwartz's (1984) consider two different forms of oversight, which they metaphorically label "police patrols" and "fire alarms." In the words of McCubbins (2014: 573) police patrols are "centralized, active, direct investigations into the behavior of agencies" whereas fire alarms are "systems of rules, procedures, and informal practices that allow others to alert Congress to abuses of bureaucratic discretion." In the sections that follow, we explore different "police patrol" mechanisms available to legislative assemblies. Specifically, we explore the existence in our various assemblies of (1) questions and interpellations, (2) investigations and hearings, (3) a legislative audit office, (4) powers to make war, (5) powers to make treaties, and (6), arguably the ultimate form of oversight, powers to dismiss the executive (typically meaning the cabinet) or individual members of the executive.

12.1 Parliamentary Questions and Interpellations

Parliamentary questions (PQs) are procedures which permit legislators to formally request members of the executive to provide information about their policies and actions. In an era in which many legislatures are finding it increasingly difficult to counter the informational and strategic advantage of the executive, PQs are one of the few tools which give legislators access to information on the actions and operations of the executive (Martin and Rozenberg 2015) as well as represent interests and perhaps even lobby the executive (Bailer 2011; Huwyler and Martin 2022) Although the rules governing PQs vary widely, they come in two fundamental forms: oral or written.

Oral questions are verbally asked and verbally answered on the floor of the legislative assembly. The time dedicated to oral questions—question time—can be contrasted with other plenary activities, such as lawmaking deliberations, motions, statements, or general debates. Legislative assemblies may provide for a dedicated question time on the floor of the chamber during which members of the executive (typically cabinet members) are expected to make themselves available to reply to questions posed by legislators. Probably the best-known example of oral PQs is Prime Minister's Question's in the British House of Commons (see box 12.1). Prime Minister's Questions can provide for political theatre between the executive and opposition (or even between the executive and co-partisan legislators), and in the United Kingdom tends to be the subject of significant media attention. Because Oral PQs demand an on-the-stop answer, the respondent needs to have a full informational command of their area of responsibility.

Box 12.1 UK Prime Minister's Questions

When the British House of Commons is in session, the Prime Minister comes to the chamber every Wednesday afternoon to answer questions from Members of Parliament (MPs). This (now) 30 minutes session is the most analyzed part of the regular weekly cycle of parliamentary life, and the best attended by MPs. Prime Minister's Questions is, in short, the highlight of the parliamentary week.

The Leader of the Opposition (that is to say, the leader of the largest opposition party in the House of Commons) is permitted to ask six questions—with the Prime Minister responding after each individual question. The leader of the Opposition is privileged in having the right to ask questions. Other party leaders may have similar rights to ask, albeit fewer, questions, depending on the size of their parliamentary group. Limited time remains for backbench MPs.

PMQs tend to be extremely theatrical. The Prime Minister generally receives supportive questions from party or coalition colleagues—providing an opportunity for the Prime Minister to showcase in his or her answer the competency of, and good policies emerging from, government. More challenging questions come from the leader of the opposition, the leader of each of the other major parties not in government, and opposition backbenchers who aim to challenge the Prime Minister on her/his record or the record of the government. Indeed British Prime Ministers, and Leaders of the Opposition are assessed closely on their performance during question time. Prime Minister's questions is covered live on national TV, on radio, and features prominently in news broadcasts. The print media also report and analyze carefully Prime Minister's questions the next day. How key political actors perform during question time is of enormous significance in terms of how they are perceived by voters—in terms of competency, communication skills and the ever-necessary mix of information, empathy, and humor. Margaret Thatcher was considered an excellent performer; she was often able to turn negative questions to her advantage and even embarrass the questioner. Many MPs react verbally to the performance of the Prime Minister or the questioner. Often the Speaker will intervene to ask MPs to become quiet if the chamber is too noisy and boisterous with MPs shouting approval or disapproval and waving their order papers. We return later to the advantages and disadvantages of such theatrical question times.

Given the significance of PMQs to the political standing of the party leaders, it is not surprising that the Prime Minister prepares carefully for the encounter. Note that, with questions from the opposition benches, the Prime Minister is not aware in advance of the question. Thus, the Prime Minister must answer questions within seconds of the question being asked. To prepare for this, the Prime Minister will generally spend much of the morning in advance of question time studying answers to potential questions with policy and communications advisers. The Prime Minister, as head of government, is responsible for all government policy. Consequently, preparing for PMQs is a daunting task. It would typically be unacceptable and politically damaging for a Prime Minister to say "I'm sorry I do not know the answer to that question." The questioner is advantaged by the ability to ask what questions they want without notification of topic, and opposition MPs, including the leader of the opposition party, will try to inflict maximum political damage on the Prime Minister during PMQs. Despite the disadvantage of not knowing the topic of questions, one significant political advantage enjoyed by the Prime Minister during PMQs is that she or he has the last word on any question.

Oral PQs are a common feature of legislative assemblies. In 61 of our 68 cases, legislators can ask questions of the executive on the assembly floor. The seven legislative assemblies lacking a formal question time are Ecuador, El Salvador, Nepal, Nigeria, Paraguay, Philippines, and the United States of America (see Table 12.1). While Oral PQs are most associated with parliamentary systems, they are in fact a feature of legislative assembles in both parliamentary and presidential systems. 23 presidential systems have a procedure for oral PQs, whereas only six presidential countries do not. All semi-presidential systems in our study feature oral PQs. Only one parliamentary system in our study (Nepal) lacks an Oral PQs procedure.

However, regular Oral PQs involve the head of government in only a small majority (36) of our countries. In the remaining 32 cases, the head of government does not appear regularly before the legislative assembly to answer questions. Two other parliamentary systems—Israel and South Africa—join Nepal in not having a question time for the head of government. The only presidential system with a regular question time for the President is Turkey. We conclude from this that while it is not uncommon for presidential systems to have an oral question time procedure for members of the executive, this rarely requires a presidential head of government to appear and answer questions.

Table 12.1 Oversight powers

Country	Oral Questions	Head of Government Questions	Written Questions	Interpellations	Investigations	Audit Office	War Powers	Treaty Powers
Argentina	Yes	No	Yes	Yes	Yes	Yes	Yes	Yes
Australia	Yes	Yes	Yes	Yes	Yes	Yes	No	No
Austria	Yes	Yes (in practice)	Yes	Yes	Yes	Yes	Yes	Yes
Belgium	Yes	Yes (in practice)	Yes	Yes	Yes	Yes	No	Yes
Benin	Yes	No	Yes	Yes	Yes	Yes	No	Yes
Bolivia	Yes	No	Yes	Yes	Yes	No	Yes	Yes
Brazil	Yes	No	Yes	Yes	Yes	Yes	Yes	Yes
Bulgaria	Yes	Yes (in practice)	Yes	Yes	Yes	Yes	Yes	Yes
Burundi	Yes	No	Yes	No	No	Yes	No	Yes
Canada	Yes	Yes	Yes	Yes	Yes	Yes	Yes	Yes
Chile	Yes	No	Yes	Yes	Yes	No	Yes	Yes
Colombia	Yes	No	Yes	Yes	Yes	No	Yes	Yes
Costa Rica	Yes	No	Yes	Yes	Yes	Yes	Yes	Yes
Croatia	Yes	Yes	Yes	Yes	Yes	Yes	Yes	Yes
Czech Republic	Yes	Yes	Yes	Yes	Yes	Yes	Yes	Yes
Denmark	Yes	Yes	Yes	Yes	Yes	Yes	Yes	Yes
Dominican Republic	Yes	No	Yes	Yes	No	Yes	No	Yes
Ecuador	No	No	No	Yes	Yes	Yes	No	Yes
El Salvador	No	No	No	Yes	Yes	Yes	Yes	Yes
Finland	Yes	Yes	Yes	Yes	Yes	Yes	Yes	Yes
France	Yes	Yes	Yes	Yes	Yes	No	Yes	Yes

Country						
Germany	Yes	Yes	Yes	Yes	Yes	Yes
Ghana	Yes	Yes	Yes	Yes	No	Yes
Greece	Yes	Yes	Yes	Yes	Yes	Yes
Guatemala	Yes	Yes	Yes	Yes	No	Yes
Honduras	Yes	No	Yes	Yes	No	Yes
Hungary	Yes	No	Yes	Yes	Yes	Yes
India	No	No	Yes	Yes	Yes	No
Indonesia	Yes	Yes	Yes	Yes	No	Yes
Ireland	Yes	Yes	Yes	Yes	Yes	Yes
Israel	Yes	Yes	Yes	Yes	No	Yes
Italy	Yes	Yes	Yes	Yes	Yes	Yes
Japan	Yes	Yes	Yes	Yes	Yes	Yes
Kenya	No	No	No	Yes	No	No
Liberia	Yes	Yes	No	Yes	No	Yes
Malawi	Yes	No	Yes	Yes	No	Yes
Mexico	Yes	Yes	Yes	Yes	No	Yes
Nepal	Yes	No	No	Yes	No	Yes
Netherlands	Yes	Yes	Yes	Yes	Yes	Yes
New Zealand	No	No	Yes	Yes	Yes	No
Nicaragua	Yes	Yes	Yes	Yes	No	Yes
Niger	Yes	Yes	Yes	Yes	Yes	Yes
Nigeria	Yes	Yes	Yes	Yes	No	Yes
Norway	Yes	Yes	Yes	Yes	Yes	Yes
Pakistan	No	No	Yes	Yes	No	No
Papua New Guinea	Yes	Yes	Yes	Yes	Yes	Yes

Continued

Table 12.1 *Continued*

Country	Oral Questions	Head of Government Questions	Written Questions	Interpellations	Investigations	Audit Office	War Powers	Treaty Powers
Paraguay	No	No	No	Yes	Yes	Yes	Yes	Yes
Peru	Yes	No	Yes	Yes	Yes	Yes	Yes	Yes
Philippines	No	No	Yes	Yes	Yes	Yes	Yes	Yes
Poland	Yes	Yes	Yes	Yes	Yes	Yes	Yes	Yes
Portugal	Yes	Yes	Yes	Yes	Yes	Yes	Yes	Yes
Romania	Yes	Yes	Yes	Yes	Yes	Yes	Yes	Yes
Senegal	Yes	Yes	Yes	Yes	Yes	Yes	Yes	Yes
Serbia	Yes	Yes	Yes	Yes	Yes	Yes	No	Yes
Sierra Leone	Yes	No	Yes	No	No	Yes	Yes	Yes
Slovak Republic	Yes	Yes	Yes	Yes	Yes	Yes	Yes	Yes
South Africa	Yes	No	Yes	Yes	Yes	Yes	No	Yes
South Korea	Yes	No	Yes	Yes	Yes	Yes	Yes	Yes
Spain	Yes	Yes	Yes	Yes	Yes	Yes	Yes	Yes
Sweden	Yes	Yes	Yes	Yes	Yes	Yes	Yes	Yes
Switzerland	Yes	Yes	Yes	Yes	Yes	Yes	Yes	Yes
Taiwan	Yes	No	Yes	Yes	Yes	Yes	Yes	Yes
Tunisia	Yes	Yes	Yes	No	No	No	No	No
Turkey	Yes	Yes	Yes	Yes	Yes	Yes	Yes	Yes
Ukraine	Yes	Yes	Yes	Yes	No	Yes	Yes	Yes
United Kingdom	Yes	Yes	Yes	Yes	Yes	Yes	No	Yes
United States	No	No	No	Yes	Yes	No	Yes	Yes
Zambia	Yes	No	Yes	No	No	Yes	No	No

Since plenary time, as we have noted, is often very limited, Written PQs provide an alternative means for legislators to question the executive. With Written Questions, legislators (or in some legislative assemblies, a legislator's member of staff) submit the question in writing and the answer is provided to the member in writing. Both questions and the answers may also be recorded in the published parliamentary proceedings. In many legislatures, Written Questions are now asked more frequently than Oral Questions. Written PQs entail a far lengthier process than their oral counterpart and may require the relevant executive bureaucracy to undertake research to provide an answer. Again, the vast majority of countries in our study—61 out of 68—have a system of written PQs. The same seven countries in our study that lack an oral PQ procedure are the ones that also lack a written PQ provision (see Table 12.1).

Typically, the executive is obligated to answer a written question, commonly in a timely fashion (for example, within one week in the British case), and in a truthful manner. Because written PQs allow time for the answer to be researched, ministers have less opportunity to say that the information requested is not available. For example, the official United Kingdom civil service guidance on drafting answers to parliamentary questions reminds civil servants to:

> Never forget Ministers' obligations to Parliament which are set out in the Ministerial Code: "It is of paramount importance that Ministers give accurate and truthful information to Parliament, correcting any inadvertent error at the earliest opportunity. Ministers who knowingly mislead Parliament will be expected to offer their resignation to the Prime Minister. Ministers should be as open as possible with Parliament and the public, refusing to provide information only when disclosure would not be in the public interest."[1]

PQs allow the legislative assembly to question the executive on proposed government legislation but also on the implementation of legislation and policy. Ministers and bureaucrats are often highly sensitive to the content of PQs. As such, PQs serve as a form of two-way device of communication and signaling. While the answer will provide information to the questioner, the ministry may also learn by taking note of patterns of questions and using this as a measure of the concerns and preferences of backbenchers. In some legislative assemblies, PQs may be less about holding the executive to account and more about communicating constituents' concerns to the executive (Martin 2011). PQs can provide a voice by which the concerns and interests of constituents can be voiced by their representative. In summary, PQs may serve one or two key functions—oversight and representation.

---

[1] https://www.gov.uk/government/uploads/system/uploads/attachment_data/file/61195/drafting-pq-responses.pdf.

According to Pelizzo and Stapenhurst (2013: 35), interpellations are similar to written parliamentary questions, but more extensive in terms of length and depth of probing. Wiberg (1995: 195) notes that interpellations are "politically heavier" than parliamentary questions. In some countries, they can be a prelude to motions of no confidence. Yet, interpellation procedures are actually even more common than parliamentary questions across the democracies in our sample. As Table 12.1 shows, only five countries in our study (Tunisia, Burundi, Liberia, Sierra Leone and Zambia) lack interpellation procedures.

12.2 Investigation and Inquiries

A parliamentary investigation or inquiry is a vehicle for the legislative assembly to undertake a (relatively) detailed examination of some past event or current issue. It is the level of focus and greater-than-normal resources that differentiate investigations and inquiries from other forms of oversight such as PQs. Investigations can last anywhere from weeks to years. Investigations usually involve a number of stages including that of planning (terms of reference) and formal creation, research by legislative staff, calls for written and/or oral evidence, taking of evidence, committee deliberations, and eventually report formulation and release. Subsequently, the assembly plenary may discuss the report and relevant parties, including the relevant part or parts of the executive, may be given an opportunity to respond. Typically, an existing or specially formed committee undertakes the investigation and then reports back to the plenary. Legislative investigations may be reactive, exploring past events, focused on maladministration or a breakdown in the relationship between an agency of the state and other actors. Some investigations and hearings may have a more forward-looking role, focused on how policy, policy implementation, or public administration could be improved. In Australia, for example, parliamentary inquiries are an important tool of policy evaluation (Rodrigues 2008).

As Table 12.1 shows, in 58 of our 68 cases, the legislative assembly can conduct independent investigations of the chief executive and/or other parts of the executive. Of the 10 assemblies that cannot conduct investigations of the executive, two are parliamentary regimes (Nepal and Pakistan), two are semi-presidential (Tunisia and the Ukraine) and six are presidential (Burundi, Dominican Republic, Kenya, Liberia, Sierra Leone, and Zambia).

The ability to conduct Parliamentary Inquiries matters. In a comparative study investigating what makes national parliaments more or less powerful, Chernykh et al. (2017) suggest that the authority to investigate the executive is one of the most valuable powers a legislative assembly can have.

Yet, inquiries by legislative assemblies are not without their critics. In 2002, Ireland's Supreme Court ruled that Parliament could not hold investigations and inquiries that would result in the making or finding of fact against an individual that would be detrimental to that individual's good name.[2] A citizen's right to natural justice thus overrides the legislature's right to investigate. More specifically, as Mr. Justice Murphy wrote, while it, "is of course agreed that elected representatives should take every opportunity to inform and advise themselves on all matters relevant to their wide-ranging duties as law makers in addition to informing themselves as to the needs, interests and concerns of their constituents." Yet the justice rejected the power or duty of a committee of the *Oireachtas* to make a "finding of fact" against a citizen.[3]

Parliament responded by terminating the two inquiries that were underway. Subsequently, the government and Parliament provided for a referendum to change the Constitution. In October 2011 voters were asked in a referendum to enhance the powers of the Parliament to hold parliamentary inquiries (O'Leary 2014). The result of the referendum was a rejection of the proposed amendment, with 53.34 percent against, 46.44 percent in favor and a turnout of 56 percent. The political elite had failed to persuade Irish voters that parliamentary inquiries were a good thing when individual privacy rights might be at stake.

Table 12.2 presents the results of a regression analysis where the dependent variable is our attempt to capture the capacity of the legislature to question and investigate the executive. The variable *Assembly Powers to Question the Executive* ranges from 0 to 10 according to whether legislature can question ministers through a system of parliamentary questions, has powers of summons over executive branch officials for hearings, and/or can conduct independent investigations of the executive. Scores are calculated as follows: For a legislature with none of these powers, the value equals zero. For any one of these powers, the score is 3.33, for two powers 6.67, and for all three powers 10.

The results in Table 12.2 suggest that presidential, majoritarian, African/Middle Eastern countries, and those with higher district magnitude, are less likely to have means by which the legislative assembly can question the executive (i.e., oral or written questions, interpellation, or investigation powers). By comparison, wealthier countries are more likely to have these means, as are possibly more populous countries (Model 5).

12.3 Financial Audits

As we noted in Chapter 10, passing a government budget is an important legislative function. Yet, the budget process involves more than planning for and approving or rejecting a government's income and expenditure plans. According to Wehner

---

[2] The case of *Ardagh v. Maguire* involved an Oireachtas inquiry into the death of a person at the hands of the police.
[3] *Ardagh v. Maguire* [2002], April 11, 2002, IR 447.

Table 12.2 Powers to question the executive

	Powers to Question the Executive					
	(1)	(2)	(3)	(4)	(5)	(6)
Presidential	-1.34***				-1.00	-0.69
	(0.49)				(0.70)	(0.51)
Majoritarian	-1.55**				-1.36*	-1.29**
	(0.59)				(0.70)	(0.59)
Mixed	0.05				0.30	
	(0.59)				(0.68)	
Mean District	-0.01**				-0.01**	-0.01*
Magnitude	(0.004)				(0.004)	(0.003)
Sovereignty		0.01			0.01	
		(0.01)			(0.01)	
log(GDP per		0.82***				0.38*
Capita)		(0.22)				(0.20)
GINI		0.06				
		(0.03)				
log(Population)		0.12			0.36*	0.26
		(0.18)			(0.21)	(0.18)
Ethnic Fraction-		-0.80			-0.11	
alization		(1.16)			(1.19)	
Africa and			-2.67***		-2.06*	-0.72
Middle East			(0.69)		(1.04)	(0.66)
Asia and			-0.91		-1.05	
Oceania			(0.75)		(0.94)	
Americas			-0.98		-0.17	
			(0.67)		(0.93)	
Eastern Europe			-0.37		-0.18	
			(0.80)		(1.01)	
British Colony				-1.08		
				(0.72)		
Other Colony				-0.18		
				(0.60)		
Constant	10.05***	-19.43	10.00***	9.30***	-17.86	2.00
	(0.40)	(18.31)	(0.48)	(0.48)	(21.98)	(3.64)
N	68	68	68	68	68	68
R^2	0.22	0.30	0.21	0.04	0.35	0.36
Adjusted R^2	0.18	0.24	0.16	0.01	0.22	0.30

Notes: The dependent variables measures the capacity of the legislative assembly to question the legislature. The variable ranges from 0 to 10, according to whether the legislative assembly can question ministers (PQs), has powers of summons over executive branch officials for hearings, and can conduct independent investigations of the executive (Investigate) [0 = 0 of 3; 3.33 = 1 of these 3; 6.67 = 2 of these 3; 10 = 3 of 3].
*p < 0.1; **p < 0.05; ***p < 0.01.

(2010), an ex post review of actual government expenditure and revenue constitutes a last but nevertheless important aspect of the legislative budget cycle. In addition to any power over the government's purse, legislative assemblies may have important oversight powers to review the actual income that enters, and the expenditure that leaves, the public purse.

To gauge the ex post budgetary influence of our legislative assemblies, we examine whether there is a mandatory procedure whereby the legislature reviews an audit of government expenditure. An audit is an official inspection of an organization's financial accounts and procedures. Audits ensure that the organization has proper financial accounting procedures to trace its income, expenditures, assets, and liabilities. Here, our interest is in the formal role, if any, played by the legislative assembly in reviewing the (past) financial activities of its government.

The right to audit the government's finances is potentially a very powerful oversight tool, extending far beyond accounting matters. Most public policy requires expenditure of some sort, and for this reason a review of the executive's expenditure provides legislators powerful insights into the performance and functioning of the executive. Where it exists, the obligation to account for monies raised and spent provides a very strong tool for legislative accountability. In developing countries, enhancing the role of national legislatures in the audit of government expenditure is seen by many as a powerful way to reduce corruption. In developed countries, legislative assemblies may be eager to uncover corrupt practices but may also wish to use the audit procedures to uncover cases of poor public administration (maladministration) and inefficiencies in government spending. In 62 of our 68 cases, the legislative assembly annually reviews an audit of government expenditure (see Table 12.1). The six cases where the legislature has no formal right to do so are Tunisia, France, United States of America, Bolivia, Chile, and Colombia.

In some countries, the role of the legislative assembly in reviewing audits is performed by a specialized committee, often referred to as public accounts committees. The UK Parliament established a Public Accounts Committee in 1861, originally charged with auditing government expenditure. The Comptroller and Auditor General in the UK is an officer of the House of Commons, whose reports inform the work of the public accounts committee. Today, the committee's remit has expanded, to take account of efficiency and effectiveness in public expenditure—"This Committee scrutinises the value for money—the economy, efficiency and effectiveness—of public spending and generally holds the government and its civil servants to account for the delivery of public services."[4] Performance auditing, aiming to review the effectiveness of public programs, is thus a core aspect of the work of some public accounts committees.

As Wehner (2014: 518) notes, this form of ex-post financial scrutiny is most developed in legislative assemblies that developed within the Westminster

[4] http://www.parliament.uk/business/committees/committees-a-z/commons-select/public-accounts-committee/role/.

tradition. Pelizzo et al. (2006: 774) suggest that the impact of public accounts committees depends on the "behavior of committee members, on the availability of independent sources of information, and on the media's interest in scrutinizing government accounts." In other words, when information is relatively plentiful and the media engaged, ex post financial scrutiny can enhance the influence of ordinary assembly members over budgetary matters.

12.4 War Powers

Our next two tools of legislative oversight revolve around the assembly's ability to control and oversee the executive's foreign policy. In particular, we consider two aspects of foreign policy which members of a legislative assembly may wish to oversee: the making of international treaties and the declaration of war. It is sometimes suggested that whereas legislative assemblies may be active in making and overseeing domestic policy, foreign policy is best left to the executive (for a recent review, see Raunio 2014). Yet, in an ever-more connected and globalized world, foreign policy is arguably encroaching more and more into the everyday lives of citizens. As such, the argument that foreign policy should be left exclusively to the executive, with little assembly oversight, may be increasingly impractical. And for member states of such supranational organizations as the European Union, the distinction between foreign and domestic politics is becoming more and more difficult to draw.

An important government function in any polity is to protect its territory and citizenry from foreign threats. Such threats may cause countries to go to war with one another. A legislative assembly may be more or less involved in such decisions to go to war. As was commonly the case before World War I, declaring and operating the war may be the constitutional prerogative of the executive, with no role for the legislature. Alternatively, the legislative assembly may be a veto player in determining whether or not to declare, and thus go to, war.

To understand the role of legislative assemblies in overseeing the executives war policies, the variable *War Powers* in Table 12.1 measures whether the approval of the legislative assembly is necessary for the declaration of war.[5] In 49 of our 68 cases, the executive cannot declare war on another country without the approval of the legislative assembly. In 19 cases, the executive is free to declare war without seeking legislative approval. Of these 19 countries where the legislative assembly is without the right to veto the declaration of war, nine legislative assemblies operate in a parliamentary system, two operate in a semi-presidential one, and eight under presidentialism. Of the 49 cases where the legislative assembly can veto the declaration of war, 13 are parliamentary, 16 are semi-presidential, and

---

[5] Conflict scholars may object that many wars are undeclared. One implication might be that it is important also to look at assemblies' powers to sanction such behavior retrospectively.

20 are presidential. It thus appears that parliamentary regimes tend to have the weakest war powers and semi-presidential systems the strongest. These patterns may be due to the fact the semi-presidential regimes tend to have more recent constitutions than parliamentary ones.

However, the exact role of a legislative assembly in declaring war is not always easy to categorize. On the one hand, take for example of New Zealand, which formally allows the government to declare war without parliamentary approval (and is coded thus in our dataset). However, in its description of the subject the New Zealand Parliament notes that:

> While there is no legal requirement in New Zealand for the government to obtain Parliament's consent to deployments of troops abroad, it has generally been the practice over the last 25 years for significant initial commitments of troops to overseas operations to be debated in Parliament. These debates have sometimes been initiated by the government and sometimes by the opposition, and have taken place both before and after the announcements of decisions on deployments.[6]

In the United Kingdom, the executive declares war, and Parliament has no formal role in the process. However, as in New Zealand British prime ministers may feel it necessary to seek the approval of Parliament before engaging in military intervention. In August 2013, Prime Minister Cameron's government thus introduced a motion in the House of Commons seeking support for planned military action in Syria by British forces. Following an at times heated debate the chamber voted 285-272 against the motion, and the Government lost. Cameron's government had indicated that it would accept the result of the vote, although it was not constitutionally required to do so.[7] Thus, in the cases of New Zealand and the United Kingdom, our codings may lead us to underestimate the political influence of legislative assemblies on government decisions to go to war.

In contrast, the formal war powers of the US Congress may exaggerate its influence (see Box 12.2). What role a legislative assembly plays in declaring war arguably reflects a trade-off between efficiency and democratic legitimacy. Wars are strategic operations, requiring quick action and reaction, and given their modes and speeds of deliberation, legislative assemblies may not be best suited to managing a country's war policy. Balanced against this constraint is the belief that going to war against another country and place a one's armed forces in harm's way is one of the most fundamental and consequential decisions a country can make, and one that therefore should be approved by the directly elected representatives of the people. Still, most recent US presidents have carefully guarded their right to

---

[6] https://www.parliament.nz/en/pb/research-papers/document/00PLLawRP2014051/troop-deployments-abroad#footnote_2_ref.
[7] http://www.bbc.co.uk/news/uk-politics-23892783.

go to war without Congressional approval, with some exceptions. For example, in late August 2013, President Obama announced his desire to intervene militarily in Syria, but agreed to seek Congressional support for this move: "Yet, while I believe I have the authority to carry out this military action without specific congressional authorization, I know that the country will be stronger if we take this course, and our actions will be even more effective."[8]

Box 12.2   US Congressional War Powers

Article I, Section 8 of the US Constitution explicitly and unambiguously grants Congress the right to declare war: "The Congress shall have Power ... To declare War, grant Letters of Marque and Reprisal, and make Rules conquering Captures on Land and Water." Yet, US presidents have frequently gone to war without prior approval by Congress. Examples include the Korean War, the Vietnam War, as well as the invasions of Afghanistan in 2001 and Iraq in 2002. The source of this unilateral executive action lies in Article II, Section 2 of the US Constitution, which designates the President as Commander-in-Chief of the armed forces. The implication is that the President has the right to position and command troops, even without the formal declaration of war. In an effort to rein back influence over foreign military operations after the Vietnam War, Congress passed the War Powers Resolution in 1973. Among other things, the War Powers Resolution requires the President to remove all troops after 60 days if Congress has not granted an extension.

12.5   Treaties

While war between countries may be the ultimate and most dramatic form of inter-state conflict, countries also cooperate with each other and form agreements on a whole host of topics and issues. These agreements tend to be referred to as (inter-national) treaties. As with war powers, legislative assemblies may be more or less involved in the treaty-making process, with consequences for the discretion with which the executive can make such agreements and with what level of oversight by the legislature.

In the vast majority of countries in our study, the national legislature's consent is necessary to ratify treaties with foreign countries. Only in seven countries can the executive enter into treaties without the approval of their national assembly: Australia, India, Kenya, New Zealand, Pakistan, Tunisia, and Zambia.

---

[8] https://www.nytimes.com/2013/09/01/world/middleeast/text-of-president-obamas-remarks-on-syria.html?ref=middleeast&_r=0.

Table 12.3 Assembly treaty power

	Assembly Treaty Power					
	(1)	(2)	(3)	(4)	(5)	(6)
Presidential	0.09				0.18*	0.07
	(0.07)				(0.10)	(0.07)
Majoritarian	−0.31***				−0.19*	−0.04
	(0.09)				(0.10)	(0.11)
Mixed	−0.02				0.11	
	(0.09)				(0.10)	
Mean District	0.0002				0.0004	
Magnitude	(0.001)				(0.001)	
Sovereignty		−0.002			0.0002	
		(0.001)			(0.002)	
log(GDP per		0.01				
Capita)		(0.04)				
GINI		−0.0002				
		(0.01)				
log(Population)		−0.05			0.0004	
		(0.03)			(0.03)	
Ethnic		0.03			0.08	
Fractionalization		(0.19)			(0.17)	
Africa and			−0.20*		−0.30*	−0.10
Middle East			(0.10)		(0.15)	(0.09)
Asia and Oceania			−0.36***		−0.44***	−0.24**
			(0.11)		(0.14)	(0.09)
Americas			−0.00		−0.18	
			(0.10)		(0.14)	
Eastern Europe			0.00		−0.10	
			(0.12)		(0.15)	
British Colony				−0.40***		−0.27**
				(0.09)		(0.12)
Other Colony				−0.03		
				(0.08)		
Constant	0.93***	4.68	1.00***	1.00***	0.68	1.00***
	(0.06)	(3.07)	(0.07)	(0.06)	(3.23)	(0.05)
N	68	68	68	68	68	68
R^2	0.19	0.07	0.21	0.27	0.34	0.36
Adjusted R^2	0.13	−0.005	0.16	0.25	0.21	0.31

Notes: The dependent variable measures whether the legislature's approval is necessary to ratify treaties with foreign countries, with 1 = Yes and 0 = No.
*p < .1; **p < .05; ***p < .01

Table 12.3 presents the results of a regression analysis where a legislative assembly's treaty power is the dependent variable. The dependent variable takes the value one if the legislature's approval necessary to ratify treaties with foreign countries, and zero otherwise. The results in Table 12.3 suggest that countries with majoritarian systems, former British colonies, and countries from Africa/Middle East and Asia/Oceania are less likely to require legislative approval of treaties. By comparison, presidential countries may be more likely to require legislative approval, although this relationship is only significant in Model 5.

In an important contribution, Martin (2000, 198) spells out the advantages of formally involving the legislature in the process of making international treaties:

> As long as legislatures have the capacity to impede implementation of interna-
> tional agreements, closing them out of the initial stages of international cooper-
> ation and attempting to prevent their preferences from influencing the course of
> negotiations has the potential to cause severe commitment dilemmas. Insulated
> executives are not, in the final analysis, strong executives, because they find it dif-
> ficult to implement international agreements. In contrast, bringing legislators into
> the cooperation process in a formalized, regular manner allows states to bargain
> more effectively and to assure others that agreements signed at the international
> table will in fact be put in place at the domestic level.

The US Founding Fathers certainly felt that Congress should be a powerful player in negotiating international treaties. Article II, section 2 of the US Constitution states that the "President shall have Power, by and with the Advice and Consent of the Senate, to make Treaties, provided two-thirds of the Senators present concur." In other words, the US cannot ratify a treaty unless two-thirds of the US Senate agree (note that the House of Representatives is given no role in ratifying treaties). This provision drastically curtails the power of the US President to make inter-national treaties. However, US presidents have responded to this high barrier by entering into international agreements that are not technically classified as treaties. Rather, these are classified as executive agreements, as noted by the US Senate:

> there are other types of international agreements concluded by the executive
> branch and not submitted to the Senate. These are classified in the United States
> as executive agreements, not as treaties, a distinction that has only domestic sig-
> nificance. International law regards each mode of international agreement as
> binding, whatever its designation under domestic law.[9]

In September 2016, the United States accepted the Paris Climate Change Agree-ment of 2015 by executive order (and in June 2017 the United States gave notice of its intention to withdraw, per the terms of the agreement, a decision subsequently reversed in 2022). While the Paris Climate Change Agreement may have looked like an international treaty, it was classified by the US Government as an executive

---

[9] https://www.senate.gov/artandhistory/history/common/briefing/Treaties.htm.

agreement—thus avoiding triggering of the treaty-consent procedure under Article II, section 2 of the US Constitution. Executive agreements do not require the consent of the Senate, but then again, they can also be unilaterally rescinded by a new president (or the original one, for that matter).

To complicate matters further, the US also engages in international trade policy through Congressional-Executive agreements. Thus, international agreements such as the North American Free Trade Agreement (NAFTA), World Trade Organization agreements, and bilateral free trade agreements (FTAs) have been approved by majority vote of each house rather than by a two-thirds vote of the Senate.[10]

12.6 Responsibility

It would be incorrect to conclude any chapter on executive oversight without making reference to the concept of political responsibility inherent in parliamentary and semi-presidential regimes. As we noted in Chapter 11, if a government in a parliamentary democracy loses a no confidence vote, it must resign. A government must also resign if it fails to win a confidence motion. This is also the case in a semi-presidential regime, but not in a presidential one. This is a critical power. The ultimate form of oversight is the ability to dismiss the head of government and his or her cabinet, thus removing the government from office. As we have noted, it is important to distinguish between this form of parliamentary responsibility and impeachment procedures. In parliamentary systems, the legislative assembly can remove the government from office for whatever reason it wishes, or for no reason at all. In presidential regimes, the President can only be removed, if at all, by means of impeachment. Thus, although the majority of assembly members may have no confidence in the president, they have no constitutional power to remove him. Of course, as we saw in Chapter 11, removing a government through a vote of no confidence may be an unwieldy "nuclear" option, and in most parliamentary regimes it happens much less often than one might naively believe. Even though the "big stick" of the no-confidence procedure may be of little day-to-day benefit to parliamentarians seeking to keep tabs on the actions of the executive, executives in parliamentary and semi-presidential systems work and operate in the shadow of parliamentary confidence and no confidence procedures.

12.7 Conclusion

Oversight of the executive is a key function of most legislative assemblies. In parliamentary systems, the political executive acts as a direct agent of the legislative

---

[10] https://fas.org/sgp/crs/misc/97-896.pdf.

assembly. Because the political executive is an agent of the assembly, the assembly needs to monitor the activities of both the political executive and the wider bureaucracy. Otherwise, the political executive or bureaucracy may not act in line with the interests and preferences of the legislative assembly. In presidential systems, the political executive is not appointed by, or politically responsible to, the legislature. Oversight of the government in presidential systems is therefore relatively more focused on the non-political executive (the bureaucracy). Bureaucrats are the agents of elected representatives and legislative oversight is necessary as without oversight, bureaucrats may not faithfully implement the preferences of the legislative assembly, a phenomenon known as bureaucratic drift.

By conventional accounts, legislative assemblies face a difficult task in attempting to hold the executive to account. The typical executive tends to be better resourced, speak with a more unified voice, have an informational advantage and operate in a less than fully transparent fashion. However, this chapter explored a number of oversight tools and monitoring mechanisms available to, or potentially available, to legislators. These tools are (1) questions and interpellations, (2) investigations and hearings, (3) a legislative audit office, (4) powers to make war, (5) powers to make treaties, and (6), arguably the ultimate form of oversight, powers to dismiss the executive (typically meaning the cabinet) or individual members of the executive. These tools, individually and in combination, can be an important resource for members to hold the executive to account.

A voters' assembly and a members' assembly should have a high capacity to monitor the executive. Voters need information on the performance of the incumbent executive to decide whom to support at election time. Likewise, members need information to hold the executive (political and/or bureaucracy) to account and to further their own political careers and the interests of their constituents. A members' assembly should ensure that executive oversight is sufficiently strong such that individual legislators can monitor the executive in pursuit of their own goals, be it re-election or some other objective. A leaders' assembly, in contrast, may be less inclined to develop and employ tools of executive oversight. This is because party leaders are often the same people who populate (or hope to populate) the executive, which reduces their motivation to allow the legislative assembly the tools to question and potentially sanction the executive.

References

Ardagh v. Maguire, 2002. I.R. 21: 2002.

Bailer, Stefanie. 2011. "People's Voice or Information Pool? The Role of, and Reasons for, Parliamentary Questions in the Swiss Parliament." *The Journal of Legislative Studies* 17(3): 302–314.

Chernykh, Svitlana, David Doyle, and Timothy J. Power. 2017. "Measuring Legislative Power: An Expert Reweighting of the Fish-Kroenig Parliamentary Powers Index." *Legislative Studies Quarterly* 42(2): 295–320.

Huwyler, Oliver, and Shane Martin. 2022. "Interest Group Tactics and Legislative Behaviour: How the Mode of Communication Matters." *Journal of European Public Policy* 29(8): 1268–1287.

Kreppel, Amie. 2014. "Typologies and Classifications." In Shane Martin, Thomas Saalfeld, and Kaare W Strøm (eds.), *The Oxford Handbook of Legislative Studies*. Oxford: Oxford University Press, 82–100.

Martin, Lisa L. 2000. *Democratic Commitments: Legislatures and International Cooperation*. Princeton: Princeton University Press.

Martin, Shane. 2011. "Parliamentary Questions, the Behaviour of Legislators, and the Function of Legislatures: An Introduction." *The Journal of Legislative Studies* 17(3): 259–270.

Martin, Shane and Olivier Rozenberg. eds. 2015. *The Roles and Function of Parliamentary Questions*. Abington: Routledge.

McCubbins, Mathew D. 2014. "Common Agency? Legislatures and Bureaucracies." In Shane Martin, Thomas Saalfeld, and Kaare Strom (eds.), *The Oxford Handbook of Legislative Studies*. Oxford: Oxford University Press, 567–588.

McCubbins, Mathew D., and Thomas Schwartz. 1984. "Congressional Oversight Overlooked: Police Patrols versus Fire Alarms." *American Journal of Political Science* 28(1): 165–179.

O'Leary, Eimear Noelle, 2014. "Oireachtas Inquiries Referendum." *Irish Political Studies* 29(2): 318–329.

Pelizzo, Riccardo, and Frederick Stapenhurst. 2013. *Parliamentary Oversight Tools: A Comparative Analysis*. Abington: Routledge.

Pelizzo, Riccardo, Rick Stapenhurst, Vinod Sahgal, and William Woodley. 2006. "What Makes Public Accounts Committees Work? A Comparative Analysis." *Politics & Policy* 34(4): 774–793.

Raunio, Tapio. 2014. "Legislatures and Foreign Policy." In Shane Martin, Thomas Saalfeld, and Kaare W Strøm (eds.), *The Oxford Handbook of Legislative Studies*. Oxford: Oxford University Press, 543–566.

Rodrigues, Mark. 2008. "Parliamentary Inquiries as a Form of Policy Evaluation." *Australasian Parliamentary Review* 23(1): 25–38.

Wehner, Joachim. 2010. *Legislatures and the Budget Process: The Myth of Fiscal Control*. Basingstoke: Palgrave Macmillan.

Wehner, Joachim. 2014. "Legislatures and Public Finance." In Shane Martin, Thomas Saalfeld, and Kaare W Strøm (eds.), *The Oxford Handbook of Legislative Studies*. Oxford: Oxford University Press, 514–525.

Wheare, Kenneth C. 1963. *Legislatures*. New York: Oxford University Press.

Wiberg, Matti. 1995. "Parliamentary Questioning: Control by Communication?" In Herbert Döring (ed.), *Parliaments and Majority Rule in Western Europe*. Frankfurt: Campus, 179–222.

13

Legislative Assembly Types

How can legislative assemblies be compared and contrasted? Our answer, presented in Chapter 1, was to suggest that legislative assemblies could be meaningfully explored by thinking about the relationships between three critical sets of actors: the members who serve in the assemblies, the leaders who seek to control and shape what members do, and the voters who elect them all. All assemblies face challenges of capacity and accountability, but differ in the ways that they confront these challenges. And these institutional responses and designs generate different benefits for members, leaders, and voters. Accordingly, we have developed conceptions of a members' assembly, a leaders' assembly, and a voters' assembly, each representing a bundle of institutional characteristics that particularly reflect the interests of one of these classes of actors.

Our empirical journey through the legislative assemblies of contemporary democracies in the preceding chapters reveals significant institutional variation. Legislative assemblies differ in how they are designed as well as in their functions. For the 68 countries included in our book, we have explored how members are selected and for how long, the degree to which the chambers reflect the electorate, and their cameral designs. We have surveyed their leaderships and resources and the characteristics of legislative parties and committees. And we have examined the roles of legislative assemblies in lawmaking, budgeting, government formation and termination, appointments, and executive oversight. These various analyses have demonstrated at times extraordinary differences and at other times striking similarities between our 68 legislative assemblies. Throughout, we have suggested how such variations and similarities relate to the three types of legislative assemblies set out in Chapter 1.

Our aim in this chapter is to measure more comprehensively the extent to which real-world legislative assemblies in the world's major democracies correspond to the three ideal types we laid out at the outset. In other words, we want to understand to what degree each assembly resembles our ideal types of a members' assembly, a leaders' assembly, or a voters' assembly, and the degree to which these different ideal types overlap in the real world.

These ideal types were derived deductively (based on our assessment of the interests and preferences of members, voters, and leaders) rather than inductively (for example, through a data exercise seeking to identify underlying patterns and correlates between various aspects of legislative designs). Our conceptual categories are thus a product of theoretical deduction, and they are ideal types in

Legislative Assemblies. Shane Martin and Kaare W. Strøm, Oxford University Press.
© Shane Martin and Kaare W. Strøm (2023). DOI: 10.1093/oso/9780198890829.003.0013

the sense that they represent bundles of characteristics that we are unlikely to encounter in their pure form in the real world of legislative politics. Nevertheless, as with all ideal types, we intend them to help us identify common empirical correlates and patterns in legislative institutions. Our objective in this chapter is to capture the essential empirical features that we expect each ideal type to exhibit and to use these to assess the fit between our theory and typologies on the one hand and real-world assemblies on the other.

To do this, we construct an index for each of our ideal types of legislative assemblies. This chapter begins by exploring the rationales and rules we set for constructing these indices. We then introduce the component parts of each index as well as the placement of each of our 68 assemblies on that scale.

13.1 Operationalizing Ideal Types

Typologies can be wonderful things. As Collier et al. (2012: 17) note, typologies are particularly useful for "forming and refining concepts, drawing out underlying dimensions, creating categories for classification and measurement, and sorting cases." Political science is crowded with typologies, in an effort to help us understand, among other things, regime types (for example, democracy versus autocracy), fundamental constitutional choices (for example, presidentialism versus semi-presidentialism versus parliamentarism), party systems (for example, multiparty versus two-party), and party types (for example, catch-all versus cadre). But we also saw in Chapter 2 that, with some notable and important exceptions, typologies are less common in legislative studies.[1]

If typologies are to be useful, they need to be at least descriptively meaningful, which is to say that they must help us compare various real-world manifestations of the phenomenon they are designed to describe. Classification schemes can be particularly useful when they help us recognize and understand ideal types, which describe clusters of characteristics that tend to go together in consequential ways. In our case, these ideal types are the members', leaders', and voters' assemblies, respectively. Through these ideal types, and by building on preceding chapters, we aim to give empirical content and coherence to our survey of legislative assemblies. Here we explain the next step, which is to construct indices for each of our ideal types.

At its simplest, an index aggregates component parts. A useful index helps us measure some multi-faceted latent concept or variable for which there is no adequate single indicator. A latent variable captures regularities in the real world but is not directly measurable. So for example, our three ideal types of legislative

---

[1] The exceptions discussed in Chapter 2 include Bagehot (1867), Polsby (1975), Mezey (1979), and Kreppel (2014).

assemblies are not directly measurable. We can't, for example, point to one identifiable quantity which allows us to determine whether a legislative assembly is a members' assembly. This is at least in part because each ideal type comprises several different features that are commonly found together and that have interactive effects. Instead, an index allows us, a priori, to specify a set of observable measures that each capture some component of what, when aggregated, serves as a measure of our ideal type. These indices, we hope, will explore the most critical features of legislative assemblies from the perspective of our ideal types and the relationships among them.

As the previous chapters have shown, we have a large number of indicators of legislative assembly characteristics. Any number of these indicators could tap into an underlying latent dimension. In developing our indices, we are guided by the following principles:

1. We want our indices to be as parsimonious, that is to say simple to understand, as possible. For this reason, we construct for each ideal type a simple additive index comprised of 10 component parts. An additive index works on the assumption that each indicator is as important as any other indicator and that they all relate to the latent concept in an identical and additive manner. Of course, each of these assumptions could be challenged, but absent evidence to support any alternative construction, we find this to be the simplest and most transparent point of departure. Here we follow the strategies of other legislative studies scholars such as Fish and Kroenig (2009) in their Parliamentary Powers Index and Goplerud and Schleiter (2016) in their Index of Assembly Dissolution Powers.

2. Our indices and their component parts are theoretically motivated. We have a priori specified the relationship between the component parts of our indices and their related latent concepts. In practical terms, this means that we reviewed each variable in our dataset and identified those that in our view best matched each of the three ideal types theoretically. So, for example, we asked ourselves questions such as: Do the rules by which a legislative assembly is elected matter for whether it is a members' assembly? If so, which assembly election variable is most clearly related to that concept? That variable or variables then become part of our index. And of course, while our indices are theoretically motivated this is ultimately an empirical endeavor and no component of an ideal type can be included if it cannot be measured.

3. We want our data and analysis to be accessible for replication and extension. We set out below how we construct our indices, including exactly how we measure the component parts. Our aim is to share sufficient information that the reader can both have confidence in our indices and the ability to replicate these indices from the data collection stage onwards. Hence, it should be possible to replicate our data collection effort, coding cases, index

constructions decisions, and measurements. Equally, it should be easy for anyone to extend our indices, either to cover a different historical time point, or to update our measurement, or to extend our framework to other assemblies beyond the national legislatures of the 68 democracies that we examine in this volume.

As noted above, each of our three indices has been created using 10 components. Where necessary, a component is first rescaled to range from zero to 10. These are then added together to form the respective index. Hypothetically then, each index could range from zero to 100, with higher scores indicating that the legislative assembly comes relatively closer to the ideal type.[2] Details of the 10 components that make up each index are provided below. These descriptions include the variable(s) from our dataset used to construct each component as well as information about sources, range, any outliers, and the scaling technique used. In creating our 10-point scale components, we adopted a strategy of limiting the influence of any outliers. Thus, in constructing our indices, outliers are first removed, the variable is then rescaled from zero to 10, and then finally the outliers are added back in and set to either the minimum (zero) or maximum (10) value of the scale, respectively.

13.2 A Members' Assembly Index

We begin with the construction of an index for a members' assembly. A members' assembly is configured to suit the interests of assembly members. More specifically, a members' assembly is one in which members benefit from opportunities to promote their interests (including career ambitions) through decentralized decision making and relative autonomy from assembly leaders as well as from voters. These forms of decentralization and specialization can also enhance assembly capacity. The members' assembly differs from the voters' assembly in having weaker mechanisms of electoral accountability and therefore more secure legislative incumbents. The members' assembly differs from the leaders' assembly in having less centralized authority, less cohesive parties, and weaker forms of hierarchy.

In members' assemblies, power is widely dispersed among ordinary legislators, who are effectively the principals of the party leaders and in parliamentary systems also of the cabinet members. The members' assembly responds to capacity challenges by facilitating differentiation and specialization among its members. By empowering individual members, this legislative model enables even backbench legislators to respond to voter demands, especially as these demands have to do

---

[2] A component may appear in more than one index and may be scaled differently to reflect whether greater values of the variable are predicted to benefit or disadvantage voters, members, or leaders, respectively.

with case work or issues of local interest. As with each of our ideal types of legislative assemblies, our members' assembly index is formed of 10 parts. We discuss these components of the index below.

The Electoral System: The first variable in our index of a members' assembly is the electoral system. As noted in earlier chapters, an electoral system is the mechanism by which votes are translated into assembly seats. Electoral systems matter for members because they determine whose approval legislators need in order to be re-elected. Some electoral systems are candidate-centered, creating opportunities for politicians to cultivate a personal vote. In contrast, in party-centered systems, the fate of a legislator may rest more with the electoral success of his or her party.

Ideally, members may not wish to be an agent of either the voters (as in a voters' assembly), or the party (as in a leaders' assembly), yet we know of no electoral system that permits them such full independence. And indeed full independence from the voters is hardly consistent with democracy. Electoral systems that allow members to bypass the party and appeal directly to voters, however, grant these members the greatest control over their re-election prospects compatible with popular sovereignty. In this context, then, the interests of voters and members largely coincide. Both prefer electoral rules under which members can differentiate themselves and voters can effectively choose among them. In constructing our members' assembly index, more personal vote-oriented electoral systems hence associate with a members' assembly.

As we discussed in Chapter 3, members can be privileged or constrained by the rules governing assembly elections. Under some electoral systems voters can only choose between political parties and have no ability to express any preference for individual candidates. This is the case, for example, in Portugal. In contrast, other electoral systems allow voters to favor individual candidates, and sometimes even to support candidates from several different political parties. In Ireland, for example, voters can typically rank-order candidates from multiple political parties. Different electoral systems thus provide different incentives for legislators to cultivate a personal vote—the part of a candidate's vote that is based on his or her individual characteristics or record (Cain et al. 1987). Personal vote electoral systems align with our notion of a members' assembly. In contrast, legislators in non-personal vote electoral systems (such as closed-list Proportional Representation) tend to focus their re-election efforts on promoting the party label and staying in the good graces of party leaders, who typically control their ballot access. Electoral systems matter, then, in part because they determine to whom a legislator seeking re-election needs to be responsive.[3]

---

[3] And as we will see later in this chapter, the personal versus party centeredness of the electoral system also has consequences for the degree to which a legislative assembly is a voters' or leaders' assembly.

One empirical measure of how electoral systems shape incentives to cultivate a personal (as distinct from a party) vote is provided by Johnson and Wallack (2012). These authors empirically quantify the dimensions of the personal vote identified by Carey and Shugart (1995) by examining party control over ballot access, the extent to which votes are shared with co-partisans, whether votes are primarily cast for parties or candidates, and district magnitude. Their measure provides an ordinal ranking from one to 13 with higher numbers representing a greater incentive to cultivate a personal vote. Because we want each component part of our index to range from a minimum of zero to a maximum of 10, we rescale Johnson and Wallack's (2012) ordinal ranking so that it runs from zero to 10. The higher the value on this scale, the greater the personal-vote orientation of the electoral system, and, by our logic, the more the legislative assembly resembles a members' assembly.

Job Security: The second component of our members' assembly index captures the job security of assembly members during their tenure of office. We assume that incumbent legislators prefer short-term job certainty over uncertainty. This preference for job security, we suspect, holds among workers in any profession but may be particularly strong in politics. Elected members will be mindful of the precariousness of their political lives. In any functional democracy, voters can deselect incumbents, and all elected members are thus vulnerable to losing their seat through an election.[4]

But some institutional designs make incumbent legislators particularly vulnerable: the threat of being recalled and the lack of a fixed term. Recall, as discussed in Chapter 3, is a relatively rare mechanism to unseat a member between general elections. Loss of office through dissolution and early elections is thus for most members a greater threat. Some legislatures (for example, the Norwegian Storting) remove this latter threat through constitutionally fixed terms—inflexible inter-electoral periods, while other assemblies (as in most parliamentary systems) can be dissolved early and elections called. The United Kingdom House of Commons is a good example of a member-unfriendly assembly with respect to members' short-term security of tenure. British MPs can now be relatively easily recalled (see Chapter 3) and parliamentary elections can happen at any time. In all, 28 of our legislative assemblies (mostly in presidential regimes) have fixed terms, whereas 40 chambers do not.

Empirically, this component of our members' assembly index takes one of four values: The maximum value (10) represents fixed terms and no recall mechanism. Fixed terms with a recall procedure is considered the next best scenario for members (scoring 6.66), followed by flexible terms and no recall (scoring 3.33). Finally,

---

[4] In chambers with staggered elections, though, not all members will be at risk in every general election.

a legislative assembly with flexible terms and a recall provision scores zero, since such assemblies are least compatible with members' short-term job security.

Term Length: The third component of our members' assembly index is the length of the electoral term. Members, we believe, value longer inter-electoral periods as this increases career (and employability) security and arguably their opportunities to devote themselves to policy specialization and the freedom of longer time horizons. Even the most seasoned electoral campaigner presumably fears the judgment of the voters when elections are due. Uncertainty about the future is greater, all else equal, the shorter the (maximum or average) inter-electoral period.

Maximum term length in our sample varies substantially, from the two-year term of the US House of Representatives to the six-year term of the Liberian House of Representatives. As we saw in Chapter 3, the most common term is four years, and the mean for cases included in this volume is 4.28 years. Here, as in the case of dissolution (early elections) and recall procedures, the interests of members and voters conflict. Whereas voters tend to prefer keeping their representatives accountable through short terms, members just as clearly prefer longer terms.

In our members' assembly index, we rescale the maximum constitutional inter-election period such that two- or three-year terms score zero, four-year terms five, and a five-year or six-year term score 10. Our rationale for categorizing term lengths this way is a variant of our procedure concerning outliers. Since the US House of Representatives is the only assembly with a two-year term and the Liberian House of Representatives represents the only six-year term, we do not want to give undue weight to these two cases in our scaling. Again, higher scores indicate a closer fit with our ideal type of a members' assembly. Thus, higher values on this scale (reflecting a longer maximum inter-electoral period) correlate with a members' assembly.

Staff Resources: Tapping the resources available to legislators to help them perform their representative and other functions, the fourth component of our members' assembly index is the number of staff members per legislator. A members' assembly will be well-staffed and have a high ratio of staff to legislators. All else equal, members will presumably prefer having more, rather than fewer, staff members to assist them. Staff provide members with resources to undertake their roles, and potentially aid their prospects of re-election or promotion to other offices. Research services allow members perform their policy roles more effectively and efficiently. And constituency case work is often handled not by the legislators themselves but by their staffers. The latter may be particularly important under personal-vote electoral systems where members may need to dedicate significant time to their constituencies. Indeed, staff resources may be one of the most significant perquisites of office available to members in personal-vote electoral environments.

For this aspect of a members' assembly, we measure staffing as the number of full-time equivalent (or FTE) positions per legislator. Note that we count only staff members whose payroll is processed by the legislative assembly. As we noted in Chapter 6, the legislative chambers in this study have an average of five staff members per legislator. But we observe significant variation in this ratio: The US House of Representatives provides almost 30 FTE staff members per legislator. In contrast, in Sierra Leone's national assembly there is one staff member for just under every two members. Because we are missing staffing data for Nepal, Niger, Nigeria, Papua New Guinea, Senegal, and South Africa, the values for these cases have been imputed. To incorporate average staffing per member into our members' assembly index, we rescale the data to vary between zero and 10. Nigeria (14.8 staff per member), Peru (16.7), Paraguay (16.8), South Africa (17.5), Argentina (20.1), and the United States (29.7) are identified as outliers, and set to 10 in our scale. Higher values in the scale associate with a members' assembly.

Salary: The fifth component of our members' index captures members' salary—the minimum annual salary a legislator is guaranteed. Salaries are self-evidently important in that they help define the attractiveness of any job. A low salary may mean that politicians won't be motivated to seek public office for personal gain (leaving aside the financial benefits that flow from being a current or former legislator) but a low salary may at the same time dissuade the "best and brightest" from a career in politics. Why be subjected to a low salary and all the challenges of public office when one could have an easier life as a banker or academic? Ultimately, salaries define at least in part the monetary returns to being a member of the legislative assembly. Members' assemblies, we believe, will therefore have comparatively high salaries.

It is challenging to compare salaries across countries and this challenge may apply particularly to legislative salaries for at least two reasons. In some countries, legislative salaries are tax-free, whereas in others, legislators pay taxes like all other citizens. Also, members may receive additional financial benefits not accounted for in the salary data, such as pension schemes and expense accounts. We also have to mindful of cost-of-living differences and purchasing power parities across very different societies.

The average salary for a lower-chamber legislator across our study is USD $63,732 (USD equivalents). The lowest salary is in Senegal (USD $2330 per annum), followed by India ($2893). Members of the US House of Representatives have the highest salaries, at $174,000.[5] To include salary in our members assembly index, we take the basic salary in USD equivalents, control for national income, and rescale this from zero to 10. The range after scaling runs from zero (for Senegal) to 10 for the (United States). High values, we believe, associate with a members' assembly.

---

[5] Note that we impute salary data for four countries (Liberia, Malawi, Nicaragua, and Niger), because of missing data.

Percent of Non-Party Legislators: The sixth component of our members assembly' index is the percentage of assembly members who are not affiliated with any political party. Such non-party legislators are sometimes referred to as independents. Parties do many things, but most importantly they provide a hierarchical assembly structure, so that legislators can overcome problems of collective action and preference intransitivities among themselves (Aldrich 2011). For these, and perhaps other and less altruistic purposes, parties shape and control legislators' behavior. Failure to follow the instructions of the party leadership may result in expulsion from the parliamentary party caucus, or even from regular party membership. Such discipline may end a politician's career or at the very least adversely affect career advancement. Thus, party organization and discipline help assemblies make decisions, but at the cost of imposing penalties and restrictions on individual members.

Party leaders will, however, have less power to discipline their members if these members can have a legislative career outside their party. The ability to serve and be re-elected without a party label thus strengthens (ordinary) members relative to party leaders. And we assume that members prefer to enjoy at least some autonomy from the party leadership. Even members who have no desire to shed their party label may benefit in bargaining power from the fact that this avenue is in principle open. We therefore expect a members' assembly to have at least some non-party legislators.

As we note in Chapter 7, 38 of the 68 legislatures in our study have at least one non-party member. Malawi, with 52 non-party legislators (27 percent of the total membership), has the highest relative incidence. To measure the presence of non-party legislators across assemblies, we calculate the percentage of non-party legislators in the lower chamber. We then rescale these scores from zero to 10. France, Bulgaria, Chile, Ireland, Romania, Ukraine, Liberia, Papua New Guinea, and Malawi are, due to the high number of non-party legislators, identified as outliers and thus set to 10.

Committee Service: The seventh component of our members' assembly index focuses on the legislative committee system. Committees are vehicles of differentiation and specialization within legislative assemblies. All else equal, a system of permanent and specialized committees enhances assembly capacity to the benefit of members and voters alike. But the benefits these two categories of actors derive are not exactly the same. Committees benefit voters mainly by facilitating better-informed legislative decisions and by promoting efficient policy making through divisions of labor. Members may similarly benefit from these effects, but are more likely to attracted by their ability to specialize in policy areas of special interest to themselves and their constituents and perhaps to have disproportional influence in such matters. Members may also value enhancing the legislative assembly's capacity vis-à-vis the executive through specialization and gains from trade.

Here we focus on assignments to permanent (standing) committees with substantive policy responsibilities, and in particular on the ability of members to secure membership on some committee of their choice, and preferably several. Multiple committee assignments give members the greatest flexibility over how many, and which, committees they serve on. Specifically we ask two questions: Do all members serve in at least one committee? And if so, are members commonly limited to a single committee assignment? A members' assembly will have a committee assignment process that guarantees each member a committee assignment and does not limit the number of committees on which a member can serve. On our members' assembly index, each legislative assembly is scored either zero (when there is no guarantee of a committee assignment), five (where each member obtains at least one committee assignment but rarely more), or 10 (where each member is guaranteed a committee assignment and it is common for members to serve on multiple committees).

Agenda Control: The eight component of our members' assembly index focuses on the capacity of ordinary members to affect the legislative agenda. Rasch (2014: 455) defines agenda-setting institutions as the rules that "regulate which issues and proposals are to be considered, and how the issues are finally decided." Agenda setting helps determine which of the multitude of possible proposals will be considered and what form and sequence this deliberation will take. Ordinary assembly members can have more or less agenda power. In some legislatures, the executive is granted substantial agenda prerogatives. This may curtail the capacity of ordinary members to influence the business of the legislative assembly (Cox 1987; Koss 2018). In other legislative assemblies, no such rights may exist.

Agenda control matters to ordinary members for several reasons. Whatever ultimate policy effects the legislative agenda rules have obviously affect members as well as their constituents. But in addition the agenda procedure may affect the opportunities that members have to claim credit or avoid blame for particular decisions (Mayhew 1974). We believe that members will prefer more, rather than less, agenda power, and that this is an area in which their preferences conflict with those of the assembly leaders. A pure members' assembly, then, will give members rather than the executive control of the legislative agenda.

In constructing an agenda control indicator for our index, we focus on two issues: whether the government (the executive branch) has formal proposal rights, and whether it can exercise agenda control by ending debate on any proposal and moving it to a vote. For our members' assembly index, we thus classify assembly agenda power as follows: A legislative assembly where the executive has neither agenda control nor formal proposal rights scores 10; where the executive has either agenda control or proposal rights but not both, we assign a score of five; and a legislative assembly scores zero where the executive has both agenda control and proposal rights. Higher scores represent a members' assembly. Our observations range from zero (for 16 legislatures) to 10 (for three assemblies: those of Kenya, Liberia, and the United States).

Budgetary Power: The ninth factor in our members' assembly index is the assembly's budget power. Raising government revenue and deciding how to expend them for public purposes are among the most critical functions of national legislatures. For Montesquieu (1989 [1748]: 164) the power of the purse defined the very notions of liberty versus tyranny: "If the executive power enacts on the raising of public funds without the consent of the legislature, there will no longer be liberty, because the executive power will become the legislator on the most important point of legislation." In Federalist No. 58, James Madison (2009 [1788]: 298) noted that "power over the purse may, in fact, be regarded as the most complete and effectual weapon with which any constitution can arm the immediate representatives of the people, for obtaining a redress of every grievance, and for carrying into effect every just and salutary measure." And Cox (2014: 710) argues that "any measure of legislative power should be mostly about the legislature's power over the purse. If that power fails, the others will likely be illusory."

A members' assembly will have comparatively strong budgetary powers. Because passing an annual government budget implies so many important decisions, members value having influence over, and engagement with, the budgetary process. Members (or at least the more influential ones) may use the budgetary process to seek rents or win personal votes, albeit possibly to the detriment of fiscal discipline. Members will have less interest in serving in an assembly that provides little opportunity to either oversee or otherwise influence the government's budget.

Budgetary capacity differs substantially from one national assembly to another, as we discovered in Chapter 10, with the United States Congress and several European assemblies coming in at the high end of budgetary capacity and less economically developed nations generally scoring much lower. To capture legislative assemblies' power of the purse, we employ Wehner's (2006) index of budgetary powers, which includes (1) the degree to which the legislative assembly can amend the proposed budget, (2) what happens if no budget is agreed (the budgetary reversion), (3) executive discretion in budget implementation, (4) the amount of time available to the legislative assembly for budget deliberations, (5) the role and significance of legislative committees in the budgetary process, and (6) the budgetary information available to the legislative assembly.

Following Wehner (2006), we use these data to create an index of the cross-national variation in the legislative assembly's power of the purse. The observed range of that index before scaling is 16.7 (Senegal) to 89 (United States). We rescale the Wehner index to run from zero to 10, with Senegal scoring zero and the United States 10. High scores indicate greater budgetary powers for the legislative assembly, which we take as an indication of a members' assembly.

Membership Requirement for Cabinet Members: The final component of our members' assembly index explores their opportunities to hold or gain executive office. Specifically, our indicator is whether or not members of the cabinet must typically be selected from amongst the assembly membership. In some political systems, such as the United Kingdom, membership of the legislative assembly is a virtual prerequisite for ministerial office. In other cases, being a legislator may be necessary for some cabinet ministers, but not all. And in other cases, such as Norway, being a legislator is incompatible with holding a cabinet position. In the latter cases, a legislator would need to (temporarily) vacate their assembly seat in order to take up a ministerial appointment. In some presidential regimes, including the United States, the prohibition against holding simultaneous office in the legislative and the executive branch is even stricter.

In a members' assembly, legislators will have exclusive or at least privileged access to cabinet positions. Cabinets are at the apex of political power, particularly in parliamentary regimes. Any cabinet position is typically an office prized by assembly members. In contrast to a regime in which any citizen can become a cabinet minister, restricting cabinet membership to current assembly members dramatically increases the probability that assembly members will become ministers. To the benefit of elected legislators, it thus reduces the supply of what Laver and Shepsle (1994: 302) call "ministrables"—individuals eligible to become cabinet ministers.

To account for the degree to which legislators have privileged access to cabinet membership, we create a scale with the following values: a score of 10 indicates that membership of the legislative assembly is necessary in order to be a cabinet minister. A score of five indicates that assembly membership is required for some, but not all, cabinet ministers. A score of zero indicates that membership of the legislative assembly is either not necessary for, or is incompatible with, a cabinet appointment.

The Members' Assembly

We can now aggregate our scores on these 10 indicators into a members' assembly index. This members' assembly index is presented in Figure 13.1 and ranges from 23.9 for the Tunisian Majlis Nuwwāb ash-Sha'b (Assembly of the Representatives of the People) to 63.7 for the US House of Representatives. Colombia represents the median case.

The Tunisian case—perhaps reflected even in the name of the chamber itself—provides a good example of many of the characteristic we would not expect to see in a members' assembly. Its closed-list, party-centered, electoral system provides little opportunity for legislators to cultivate a personal vote. Terms are not fixed. Staffing per legislator at 1.5FTE is relatively low. Salaries are the 13th lowest

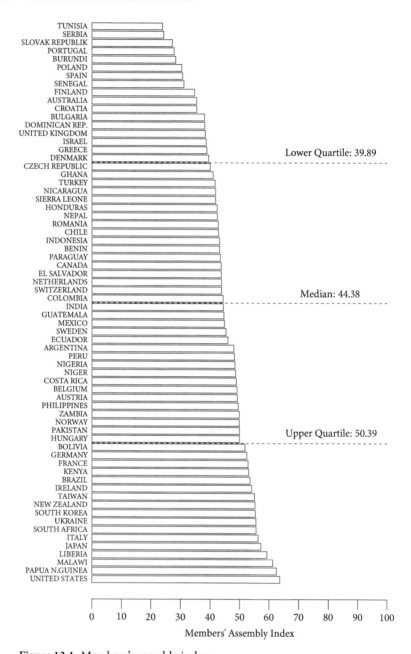

Figure 13.1 Members' assembly index

amongst our cases. There are no non-party legislators in the assembly. Committee assignment rules, by our definition, do not prioritize members' interests. The executive controls the legislative agenda and the assembly is relatively powerless in budgetary matters. And finally, there is no requirement that members of the Tunisian cabinet be drawn from the Assembly. From the members' perspective, the most positive aspect of the Tunisian assembly is that its electoral term is (up to) five years, comparatively long by comparison with most of our 68 assemblies.

At the other end of our members assembly index sits the United States House of Representatives. The single-member district plurality electoral system provides incumbents' with opportunities to cultivate a personal vote, and the primary system of candidate selection gives party leaders little control over ballot access. Members of the House cannot ordinarily be recalled and enjoy the certainty of a fixed term. US House members also enjoy a generous staff—the most generous in our study. Salary is also comparatively generous. Committee assignment rules somewhat privilege members. The executive has few prerogative rights over the legislative agenda. The US Congress' budgetary powers are the strongest in our global comparison. For members, the most important negative is that at two years the term of a member of the US House of Representatives is very short. One disadvantage to being a member of the US House of Representatives is thus that you effectively always live in the shadow of the next election. Also contrary to our notion of a members' assembly is the fact there are few independents in the US House. Finally, appointment to the federal cabinet is in no way restricted to members of the Congress and is in fact incompatible with simultaneous membership of the legislative branch.

Of course, scholars of the US Congress have long realized that the institution serves its incumbent membership well. Re-election rates tend to be very high (see the next chapter), and this is in part due to how Congress organizes itself and the perquisites of membership it bestows on its members. As David Mayhew puts it in his seminal work:

> [T]he organization of Congress meets remarkably well the electoral needs of its members. To put it another way, if a group of planners sat down and tried to design a pair of American national assemblies with the goal of serving members' electoral needs year in and year out, they would be hard pressed to improve on what exists
>
> (Mayhew 1974: 81–82)

Mayhew thus suggests that many institutional features of the US House of Representation serve the purposes of incumbent members by enhancing their prospects of re-election and reducing turnover in office. A wide range of legislative features, such as committee systems, opportunities for legislative initiatives and questions, mechanisms of executive oversight, access to discretionary "pork-barrel" grants, leadership functions, and remuneration schemes promote these incumbent interests. We will return to this theme in the next chapter, when we explore whether such assembly features provide greater electoral security for its members.

Outside the United States, members' assemblies are most commonly found in a motley collection of countries with constitutions drafted in relatively recent decades, such as Papua New Guinea, Malawi, Liberia, South Africa, and South Korea. Though some classically parliamentary systems, such as the United Kingdom, Denmark, and Australia, rate low on this index, some parliamentary regimes with relatively young constitutions, such as Italy and Japan, are among the high scorers. However, Eastern European democracies, such as Serbia, Slovakia, and Poland, generally score low.

In summary, the members' assembly is a form to which collegial assemblies may be easily drawn. Incumbent politicians will naturally favor institutions that reduce their electoral risk, and members' assemblies can do so by generating distributive and particularistic ("pork-barrel") outputs and favors. Powerful committees may build considerable expertise and prestige in their respective jurisdictions and thus aid their members at election time. But members' assemblies are less capable of aggregating interests across policy areas.

13.3 A Leaders' Assembly Index

Leaders' assemblies, in our conception, are as if designed for the purposes of legislative leaders—those individuals capable of dominating the agenda of the assembly and in control of, or competing for control of, executive offices and the policy process. In contemporary legislatures, this means the leaders of the major political parties. The most powerful leaders in modern assemblies are almost without exception the leading members of the strongest political parties within these legislatures. These individuals possess such power largely because of the benefits (and punishments) they can dispense to their respective parties' elected representatives. Party leaders are in the business of winning elections and typically do not survive long unless they do. And the best way to win elections is generally to build (minimal winning) coalitions by offering promises of tangible benefits to sufficiently broad coalitions of voters, tacitly at the expense of others. Thus, assembly leaders will be driven to make compromises and trade-offs between policy formulation and implementation, seeking or holding on to leadership positions and offices, and winning votes at the next election (Strøm 1990; Müller and Strøm 1999).

In a leaders' assembly, party leaders influence their members through centralized decision making, hierarchy, and control of legislators' careers and information flows. Hierarchy is the dominant element of internal legislative organization and the main mechanism by which a leaders' assembly confronts the challenges of capacity and accountability. In its ideal form, hierarchy means that assembly resources can be exploited for a single and coherent purpose and that voters are faced with simple and transparent choices. Note, however, that in a leaders' assembly hierarchy is based on party leadership position rather than seniority. Being able to rein in their assembly co-partisans is thus critically important. Parties provide candidates with labels that voters can employ in making their electoral decisions. Parties also shape their members' legislative behavior and can disrupt their role as agents of the voters who elected them, assuming voters get to choose their representatives in the first place (rather than simply vote for a party). We now discuss the 10 components that will make up our index of a leaders' assembly.

The Electoral System: The first component of our leaders' assembly index is the electoral system. Simply stated, though they generate different incentives for different actors, elections rule everything that happens in legislative assemblies. Since party leaders must seek to win elections, we focus here on their role of in structuring electoral competition. As we have already discussed, some electoral systems provide incentives for incumbent legislators to cultivate a personal vote and for voters to reward such efforts. Other electoral systems are more party- and leader-centered. This may mean that on election day voters only get to choose between political parties, with the parties themse0lves determining the order in which their candidates will be chosen.

Party-centered electoral systems are most conducive to leaders' assemblies. Closed-list electoral systems typically empower leaders because party leaders play a significant role in determining an incumbent's probability of electoral success. A candidate at the top of the list will have a good chance of being elected even with minimal effort and in a "bad year." In contrast, a candidate in a lowly list position often has no chance, regardless of her personal appeal and how hard she campaigns. Thus, in a closed-list system, a member is as much, if not more, an agent of the party leaders as an agent of the citizens in his or her district. All else equal, if leaders control ballot placement, an assembly selected by means of a closed-list electoral system is therefore likely to be leader-centered.

In computing this component of our leaders' index we again rely on Carey and Shugart's (1995) personal vote framework and rescale Johnson and Wallack's (2012) ordinal ranking accordingly. For our leaders' index, we invert the values because higher scores on a leaders' assembly should align with low incentives to cultivate a personal vote.

Term Limits: The next constitutional (or statutory) provision that correlates with a leaders' assembly is term limits. A term limit restricts the right of an officeholder to seek re-election. For example, in Bolivia and Costa Rica, elected representatives can serve no more than two consecutive terms. In the Philippines, members are limited to three such terms. And in Mexico, legislators can serve at most four consecutive terms.

We would not expect to find term limits in a leaders' assembly, since they reduce the ability of leaders to rein in members by controlling ballot access. Under term limits, party leaders sooner or later lose such influence and are left with fewer effective "carrots" and "sticks" to control their members' behavior. Term-limited incumbents need not worry about whether or not the party leaders will support their re-election campaigns. Such members may therefore be less inclined to sacrifice cherished policies or constituency interests to satisfy their party leadership. Granted, for some incumbent politicians term limits may, particularly under federalism or presidentialism, motivate them to look to party leaders for post-legislative career opportunities. But this effect will hardly outweigh the leaders' loss of ballot control. Overall then, term limits will reduce the capacity of party leaders to control their respective members. To incorporate term limits into our leaders' assembly index, we create a scale such that legislative assemblies with any form of term limit score zero and assemblies without term limits score 10.

Dissolution Power: Leaders also derive power from any ability to dissolve the legislative assembly and call early elections. As noted in Chapter 3, most legislative assemblies do not have fixed terms, even though all our democracies have a maximum constitutional inter-electoral period (CIEP). These maximum legislative terms may thus allow for "early elections," though the rules concerning who has the right to call elections under what circumstances vary greatly. Historically, this power has in parliamentary systems tended to rest with the prime minister or cabinet (or before democratization, with the monarch). In Ireland, for example, the prime minister has the power to dissolve parliament. This was also the case in the United Kingdom until 2011 and again since 2022. However, in many recent constitutions the power to dissolve the legislature may instead be vested in its members rather than in its leaders.[6] In yet other countries, the power to call elections is instead vested in a head of state, such as a president.

A leaders' assembly will place dissolution powers in the hands of the party leadership, meaning the prime minister or the cabinet. For one thing, the ability of the prime minister or cabinet to dissolve the assembly and call early elections presents opportunities to time elections strategically to maximize their electoral returns (see Smith 2004). Moreover, dissolution power gives party leaders a tool by which they can control their members. As discussed above, legislators value certainty and job security; dissolution threatens both. A threat by party leaders to dissolve the legislative assembly may help induce loyalty from backbenchers and have them toe the party line—lest they have to face a general election.

To incorporate dissolution powers into our leaders' assembly index, we build on Goplerud and Schleiter (2016) who develop an index of dissolution powers for each of four actors: the prime minister, the cabinet, the legislature, and the president. As an indicator of leadership control, we take the highest score for either the prime minister or the cabinet in the Goplerud and Schleiter index. The scores range from zero for 46 countries to 10 for Australia, Canada, Denmark, Ireland,

---

[6] The (inappropriately titled) UK Fixed Term Parliament Act 2011 did exactly this—removing the power to dissolve parliament from the Prime Minister and instead requiring a two-thirds vote of MPs to dissolve the House of Commons.

New Zealand, and Pakistan. As this score already ranges from zero to 10, no rescaling is required. A higher score indicates that either the prime minister or cabinet have relatively greater control over parliamentary dissolution, features that we associate with a leaders' assembly.

Percent of Non-Party Legislators: The fourth component of our leaders assembly' is the percentage of assembly members who are not affiliated with any parliamentary party. The presence of viable non-party legislators runs counter to our concept of a leaders' assembly. Indeed, and as noted above, the presence of non-party legislators indicates that a legislative career is possible even outside any legislative party. The ability to be elected or at least serve without a party label also strengthens members relative to party leaders, as the threat of a "withdrawal of the whip" (termination of party support) is less credible. In Ireland, for example, party leaders are often reluctant to discipline legislators who break party ranks, because many such members who have been expelled continue to have a successful parliament career as non-party parliamentarians, often increasing their electoral support at subsequent elections.

As in our members' assembly index, we scale the percentage of non-party legislators in a given legislative assembly. However, in our leaders' assembly index, low values indicate that the assembly has a comparatively high proportion of non-party legislators, whereas high values reflect a low share of such "independents." Thus the range after scaling goes from zero for Bulgaria, Chile, France, Ireland, Liberia, Malawi, Netherlands, Papua New Guinea, Romania, Ukraine (countries with relatively "healthy" numbers of non-party legislators) to 10 for 30 countries with no such members.

Majority Control of Committees: In a leaders' assembly, party leaders also dominate the deliberative and policy-making process. The fifth component of our leaders' assembly hence focuses on assembly committees and specifically whether the legislative majority takes control of all committee chairs. Every committee system with which we are familiar makes provision for the selection of a committee chair—a person who presides over the business of the committee. Just as the presiding chair of the plenary session has significant influence and authority (see Chapter 6), so too will committee chairs be able to influence the work of their respective committees. Our specific interest here is whether the majority party or coalition in a presidential system or the government in a parliamentary system controls all the committee chair positions, or whether these must be shared with other parties.

Majority control of all committee chairs associates with our concept of a leaders' assembly. In contrast, a system in which committee chairs are selected based on general or committee seniority reduces the power and influence of party leaders. Similarly, a proportional distribution of committee chairs across parties reduces the influence of majority party leaders and generally limits it to committees within their own bailiwick (those held by their own party members).

To include majority control of committee chairs in our leaders' assembly index, we code each legislative assembly as to whether the majority controls all the committee chairs or whether opposition parties control at least one. To scale this, we score a legislative assembly as zero if at least some committee chairs are assigned to legislators from opposition or the assembly minority parties. If the majority controls all chairs, we assign a score of 10. And of course, higher scores correlate with our ideal type of a leaders' assembly.

Executive Agenda Control: While important parts of assembly deliberation take place in committees, final decisions are almost always made in the plenary according to rules defining the legislative agenda. The sixth component of our leaders' assembly index therefore taps control of the legislative agenda. In a leaders' assembly, agenda powers will be centralized in the hands of party leaders. Agenda setting and agenda control powers confer on the holders prerogatives that can be used to control public policy making and shape policy outcomes. The executive/majority leadership can use agenda powers to dominate the lawmaking process, often at the cost of ordinary legislators and backbenchers. Huber (1996) sheds light on agenda-setting and agenda-controlling instruments designed to aid the executive's legislative hegemony by focusing on the package vote (vote bloqué) arising from Article 44.3 of the Constitution of the French Fifth Republic. The package vote procedure allows the government to demand a vote in either legislative chamber on all or part of a bill, retaining only the amendments that the government has proposed or accepted. It is generally acknowledged that the framers of France's 5th Republic thus aimed to strengthen the executive by means of restrictive legislative procedures favoring the cabinet.

In our index we specifically want to capture whether the executive (or majority leadership in presidential systems) can formally propose legislation and whether this same leadership has the authority to end debate and move any proposed legislation or other bill to a vote. In many parliamentary systems, the executive enjoys a near-monopoly on drafting power (Rasch 2014). In 20 of our cases, the executive has some such capacity to curtail the legislative process to its advantage.

To account for agenda control in our leaders' assembly index, we create a scale with the following values: We score a legislative assembly as 10 where the government has formal proposal rights and can end debate and move the process to a vote (agenda control). Where the executive has only one of these powers, the assembly scores five. Where the executive has neither agenda proposal rights nor the power to curtail the legislative process, the case scores zero. The scale ranges from zero (for Kenya, Liberia, and the United States) to 10 (for 16 countries).

Budgetary Powers: The power of the purse may be the most critical authority vested in legislative assemblies, and therefore the seventh factor in our leaders' assembly index is the assembly's budget power. As noted, budgetary capacity varies substantially from one national assembly to another. Leaders' assemblies will tend to score low on budget powers. We argued above that members will want to be significant players in the budgetary process, offsetting the executives' typical dominance over this process. Leaders, we suggest, want the exact opposite: to retain strict control over the budgetary process. Instead of granting broad budgetary powers to the assembly, leaders want to keep this control for themselves (meaning the executive branch or the party leadership). This control may allow leaders to make coherent and timely budgetary decisions, without the need for transparency and consultation. Moreover, leaders' can in different ways seek to overcome the collective action problems of budgeting for a large number of discrete constituencies and interests. Of course, leaders can also use their broad budgetary powers to effect large-scale redistributions or to generate generous rents for themselves and their supporters.

Again, we use data to create an index of the cross-national variation in the legislature's power of the purse, following Wehner's (2006) Index of Legislative Budget Institutions. Unlike in our members' assembly index, however, in the leaders' index we invert the scores on the Wehner Index so that higher scores indicate stronger executive powers.

External Veto: Assembly leaders will want to protect their legislation and budgetary decisions from "interference" not only by ordinary members or voters, but also by political chief executives (such as presidents) or courts. Next we therefore consider whether a player external to the legislative assembly itself can veto assembly decisions. Tsebelis (1995: 293) defines a veto player as "an individual or collective actor whose agreement is required for a policy decision." An external veto player with regard to lawmaking is an individual or collective actor outside the legislative assembly who can veto bills approved by the legislative assembly and thus prevent them from becoming law. Such external veto players are often heads of state or non-majoritarian institutions, such as constitutional courts or in some cases supra-national institutions.

Under a leaders' assembly, external veto players should be largely absent, since the ability to make decisions and shape public policy should rest with the legislative leadership. Having to share decision making powers with heads of state might reduce the legislative capacity and agenda powers of the leadership, particularly under divided government. This in turn may make it difficult for legislative leaders to sustain a disciplined parliamentary party group or party caucus.

To capture the presence or absence of external players who can veto proposed legislation, we provide the following scores: A legislative assembly operating with no external veto players scores a perfect 10. As noted in Chapter 9, in 18 of our 68 countries, no external agent can veto a bill passed by the legislative assembly and thus prevent it from becoming law. Where only the head of state can veto proposed legislation (regardless of whether and how this veto might be overturned), the score is five. Finally, where either a court or a head of state or other institutions (at least two institutions in total) can veto legislation—meaning that the assembly leadership is dependent on a number of actors accepting, or at least not vetoing, any public policy decision, the legislative assembly is assigned a score of zero. On this component indicator, our cases range from zero (for Croatia, Hungary, Ireland, South Africa, Switzerland, and Tunisia) to 10 for 18 countries. The remaining 44 cases score five.

Appointment Powers: Many legislative assemblies also have or share substantial appointment powers, which may be of great value to party leaders (see Chapter 11). Our ninth indicator therefore taps the degree to which the assembly has such appointment powers. We focus on the role of the legislative assembly and its leaders in three appointment processes in particular: the political chief executive (the head of government), the Governor of the country's central bank, and the Chief Justice of the highest court. In a leaders' assembly, it is permissible and easy for legislative leaders to take control of executive office. Other appointment powers will be vested primarily in the chief executive. In this way, the influence of legislative leaders is maximized. Leaders will not want to worry about controlling ordinary members to win an investiture vote, or a vote to confirm their choice of central banker or senior justice.

Roughly, and with important qualifications, parliamentary systems grant their assemblies decisive powers to seat and unseat cabinets, but leave other appointment powers largely in the hands of the cabinet. In presidential systems, this pattern is reversed: the legislature may select and appoint such officials as judges and bank governors, but has little or no say in the appointment or dismissal of members of the national cabinet. In our study, 21 legislatures have an investiture vote to select or confirm the head of government or the cabinet. In 40 of our 68 cases, the legislature plays no formal role in confirming the central bank governor.

To build this component into our leaders' index we ask if legislative investiture of the government is required, whether the most senior central banker must be confirmed by one or more chambers before taking office, and whether similarly the most senior member of the judiciary must be confirmed by one or more chambers before taking office. An assembly with no involvement scores 10 on this component of our index, reflecting the fact that the appointment power in such cases effectively rests with political leaders. A legislative assembly scores 6.67 if only one of the three above mentioned offices requires a vote in the assembly. A legislature scores 3.33 if two of the three above mentioned offices require a legislative vote of approval. And an assembly scores zero (indicating the lowest fit with a leaders' assembly) if legislative investiture, legislative confirmation of senior central banker, and legislative confirmation of senior judge are all required. The resulting scale ranges from zero (for Croatia, Peru, Romania, Serbia, the Slovak Republic, Tunisia, and Ukraine) to 10 (for 17 countries).

Selection of Presiding Officer: Finally, party leaders will treasure their control over the leading office exercising agenda and other powers within the assembly. The 10th and final component of our leaders' assembly index explores how the presiding legislative officer (in some assemblies referred to as chamber President or Speaker) is selected and more specifically the degree to which party leaders can influence this selection. Here, we focus on whether or not the vote to select the presiding officer is secret.

We expect that in a leaders' assembly voting to select the presiding officer will be open, rather than secret. Secret voting to select the presiding officer reduces the influence of party leaders in this process. In a secret vote, members can ignore, often safely, any directions provided by party leaders. Instead, legislators can vote sincerely for their candidate of choice. This may have important consequences for the openness of legislative work. At one end of the spectrum, the office of presiding officer can be a tool for party leaders. By removing or reducing partisan influences in the selection process, secret voting may result in a more neutral, non-partisan, presiding officer (see Chapter 6). Neutral presiding officers tend to see themselves as agents of all members, rather than of the majority party leadership. And as we noted in Chapter 6, several legislative assemblies, including those of the United Kingdom and Ireland, have introduced reforms to move from open voting to secret voting to select their presiding officers. The object has been to strengthen the presiding officer by reducing the role of party leaders in selecting the officeholder to the advantage of ordinary members. Such a trend conforms to a preference for less of a leaders' assembly.

To account in our leaders' assembly index for how the presiding officer is selected, we score all cases in which the vote to select the presiding officer is secret as zero and all cases where the vote to select the presiding officer is public as 10. A high score thus implies conformity with a leaders' assembly. Empirically, we find that almost two-thirds of our assemblies do not fit the model of a leaders' assembly on this count. In 44 of our cases, voting to elect the presiding officer is conducted in secret. In 24 cases, voting is open.

The Leaders' Assembly Index

Our index of a leaders' assembly is depicted in Figure 13.2. With the lowest score in our index of a leaders' assembly, The Hungarian Országgyűlés (National Assembly), displays, or at least did in 2015 display, many characteristics contrary to our concept of a leaders' assembly.[7] Hungary's electoral system provides opportunities for legislators to be independent of their party leaders. Dissolution power is not vested in the leadership. Not every Hungarian MPs belongs to a political party. The governing party does not control all committee chairs. Executive control of the agenda is only partial. Legislative budgetary power is high. There is external veto

---

[7] Note that Hungary in recent years has undergone significant institutional changes, which some observers characterize as democratic backsliding, with power increasingly concentrated in the hands of Prime Minister Viktor Orbán.

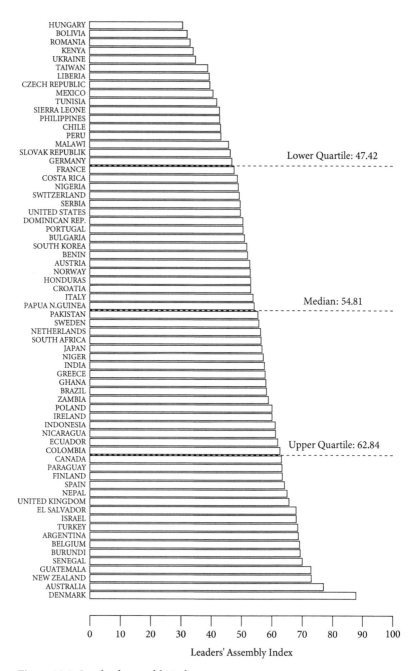

Figure 13.2 Leaders' assembly index

power. And finally, the Speaker is elected by a secret vote. On the other hand, the Hungarian National Assembly does retain some of the characteristics of a leaders' assembly, including the absence of term limits.

At the other end of our leaders' assembly scale lies the Danish Folketing. In terms of incentives to cultivate a personal vote, Denmark's electoral system is relatively leader-centered.[8] There are no term limits. Dissolution power rests with the government. Danish legislators invariably have to be members of a political party. The governing parties control committee chairs. On the other hand, executive agenda control and budgetary power are both modest. There is no external veto. Appointment powers rest with the executive rather than the legislative assembly. The vote to select the Speaker is not secret. And, as we noted in Chapter 7, among the countries for which we have data, party voting unity within the Danish Folketing is not just high, but one of the highest in the democratic world.

In sum, a leaders' assembly is an assembly in which party leaders rule their parties and government through centralized decision making, hierarchy, and control of member careers and information flows. Though Denmark scores higher on this scale than any other democracy in our sample, several Westminster-type parliamentary systems also score high, including Australia, New Zealand, and the United Kingdom itself. However, continental European parliamentary systems, such as France, Germany, and Italy, score only middling to low on this dimension. Not surprisingly, many of the assemblies that score high as members' assemblies have comparatively low scores as leaders' assemblies. Yet, Japan and New Zealand score relatively high on both.

13.4 A Voters' Assembly Index

Recall that a voters' assembly is a body in which citizens can exercise a direct and immediate influence over the legislative assembly. Voters, we believe, value having control over who represents them and having procedures by which their preferences can be represented. Voters also prefer institutions that promote decisional efficiency, openness, and transparency in the legislative process. Their general concern is to ensure good governance and avoid bad policies and practices such as corruption and maladministration. A voters' assembly typically features institutions designed to promote information revelation and transparency. Also, rules and institutions are designed to keep legislators on a "short leash," so as to be at all times mindful of their electoral accountability and their need to satisfy

---

[8] Denmark operates an open-list electoral system, meaning that voters can cast a preference among candidates. There are two kinds of seats in Danish parliamentary elections, with most legislators elected via multimember constituency seats. After constituency seats are awarded, compensatory seats are distributed based on the proportion of the national vote each party receives in order to achieve proportionality.

the demands of their voters. Also, in divisions of authority between their direct (elected legislators) and indirect (non-elected members of the executive branch) agents, voters will favor the former. We next discuss each of the 10 components of our voters' assembly index in turn.

The Electoral System: Central to a voters' assembly is the degree of control voters have over who represents them. The first component of the voters' assembly index hence seeks to measure the direct influence of voters in selecting their representatives. As we discussed in Chapter 3 and above, voters can be privileged or constrained by the rules governing who gets to serve as assembly members. As above, we focus on the degree to which the electoral system allows voters to choose between candidates as well as political parties.

Personal vote electoral systems align with a voters' assembly, as electoral accountability is its very cornerstone. The ability to choose who represents them, and to hold these representatives to account at the next election, places voters at the heart of legislative politics. Personal vote electoral systems promote accountability by allowing voters to choose between individual candidates. In contrast, legislators in non-personal vote electoral systems (such as closed-list Proportional Representation) have few incentives to cultivate relations with individual voters. Thus, these accountability conditions affect the degree to which a legislative assembly matches our concept of a voters' assembly.[9]

Again, we use as our indicator of how electoral systems shape incentives to cultivate a personal (as distinct from a party) vote the measure provided by Johnson and Wallack (2012), rescaled so that it runs from zero to 10. The higher the value on this scale, the greater the personal-vote orientation of the electoral system, and, by our logic, the more the legislature resembles a voters' assembly. In contrast, lower scores indicate a party-centered electoral system that provides little incentive for incumbents to be accountable to their voters.

Recall Provisions: The second component of our voters' assembly index focuses on the ability of voters to remove their representatives between elections. Voters can typically hold legislators to account only at the end of the electoral term, which may be fixed in length. In many other relationships of delegation, however, representatives (agents) are also subject to ongoing scrutiny, and their "contracts" can be terminated at short notice before the end of their term. As discussed in Chapter 3 and above, recall elections are one way in which legislators can be forced to leave office before their term expires. Through recall, citizens can petition to trigger a vote on whether an incumbent representative is permitted to continue in office. In this way, recall provisions mirror immediate accountability mechanisms from other social contexts and increase voter control over their representative.

---

[9] Again, the personal versus party centeredness of the electoral system also has consequences for the degree to which a legislative assembly is a members' assembly versus a leaders' assembly.

This ability to recall aligns with a voters' assembly. The mere presence of a credible recall process will likely affect the behavior of incumbent legislators: they know that they are prone to removal even before the next election, which increases their incentive to faithfully represent their voters. In computing our index of a voters' assembly, we score assemblies with a recall process 10. In contrast, if voters do not have such a mechanism to recall their representatives, a score of zero indicates that the assembly conforms less well with our notion of a voters' assembly.

Term Length: The third component of our voters' assembly index is term length—the maximum period of time a legislative assembly is constitutionally permitted to serve before an election is required. As James Madison, discussing the design of the US House of Representatives, wrote in The Federalist, No. 52: "As it is essential to liberty that the government in general, should have a common interest with the people; so it is particularly essential that the branch of it under consideration, should have an immediate dependence on, and an intimate sympathy with the people." This immediate dependence on, and intimate sympathy with, the people was to be achieved by regular elections at short intervals, with two years as a compromise between those who wanted a one-year term and those who wanted a longer, three-year term.[10]

All else equal, a voters' assembly has relatively short terms. Shorter periods between elections provide voters with the greatest and most immediate control over their representatives. Hence, short terms arguably heighten the responsiveness of incumbents seeking re-election to the needs and policy preferences of voters, precisely because these incumbents know that the next election is never far away.

As noted above, maximum term length in our sample varies from the two-year term of the US House of Representatives to the six-year term of the Liberian House of Representatives. Because relatively shorter term-lengths associate with a voters' assembly, we take the maximum inter-electoral period for each legislative assembly and rescale it so that two- or three-year terms score 10 on our scale, four-year terms score five, and five- or six-year terms score zero.

Electoral Proportionality: The fourth component of our voters' assembly index reflects the degree to which the partisan makeup of the legislative assembly is congruent with the party preferences of the electorate. Partisanship is the most important way in which politicians signal their policy preferences, and a legislature's partisan distribution is therefore the most obvious way to analyze that chamber's policy congruence. Some elections produce proportional outcomes in which each political party's share of assembly seats is approximately proportional to their share of the popular vote. In contrast, other elections generate markedly disproportional outcomes. Take the UK House of Commons as an example. At the 2019 general election, The Conservative Party won just under 44 percent of the

---

[10] https://history.house.gov/Institution/Origins-Development/Biennial-Elections/.

vote but secured 56 percent of the seats. In contrast, the Liberal Democrats won almost 12 percent of the vote, but just 2 percent of the seats. In some previous elections, the winning party has benefited from an even greater disproportionality. Thus, in 2005, the Labour Party needed only 35 percent of the vote to win 55 percent of the seats in the House of Commons.

A voters' assembly will have a membership that broadly reflects the partisanship of the electorate. In a voters' assembly, the partisan distribution of the members should thus correspond, at least approximately, to the partisan preferences of the voters. A commonly espoused normative principle in democratic theory is that a legislature's composition should reflect the preferences of the voters who select it. In other words, as a "representative body," the chamber should be a microcosm of the political preferences of the general population. Although from a broader philosophical perspective such matching might not be desirable if many voters are bigoted, envious, or spiteful, policy congruence is generally considered to be desirable in a democracy and, from our perspective, in a voters' assembly in particular. Such congruence means that the legislative assembly should represent the partisan preferences (and thus the policy preferences) of the voters. And to the extent that political parties structure the chain of political delegation from voters to policy makers, high disproportionality is a problem, especially if over time the same parties are consistently overrepresented or underrepresented.[11]

Since however worthwhile, it may be impossible to measure the partisan preferences of the entire population, including non-voters, partisan congruence can best be measured by comparing the partisan preferences of the citizens who turned out to vote and the party composition of the chamber. The Gallagher Index of Disproportionality (Gallagher 1991) measures how well the seat shares parties receive in the legislative assembly correspond to their vote shares. A low score on the Index of Disproportionality means a high degree of proportionality—indicating that the partisan composition of the chamber is congruent with the voters' partisan preferences. To create a measure of proportionality we take the Gallagher index, invert it (as it is an index of disproportionality), and rescale it zero to 10. In our scale, lower values thus represent disproportionality whereas higher scores reflect more proportional electoral outcomes, in keeping with a voters' assembly.

Gender Representation: The fifth component of our voters' assembly index also focuses on the composition of the legislature and its relation to the population it represents. But here we focus on demographic gender representation and specifically the proportion of the legislative chamber that are women. Despite the

---

[11] Note that the latter has not been the case over the past few decades in our example: elections to the British House of Commons. The party with the largest vote share, whether Conservatives or Labour, has generally benefitted from overrepresentation, whereas the Liberal Democrats have invariably been underrepresented. Yet, "third" parties with a regional base, such as the Scottish National Party, have often been overrepresented rather than underrepresented.

near-parity of women to men in the general population, most democratic legislatures comprise significantly fewer women than men. As we reported in Chapter 4,
on average approximately three out of every four democratic legislators are male.
Yet, there is significant cross-national variation. Since independence, the National
Parliament of Papua New Guinea has never had more than three women members out of a total membership of 111. In contrast, Bolivia's Cámara de Diputados
has the highest percentage of women legislators in our study: 53.1 percent. In fact,
Bolivia is the only chamber in our study with a majority female membership.

A voters' assembly will have a membership in which both males and females are
significantly represented. Since gender is a politically relevant voter characteristic
and the legislative assembly is a "representative body," the chamber should ideally be a microcosm of the general population with respect to gender.[12] Arguably,
this descriptive representation should lead to better substantive representation—
having more women legislators should translate into better representation for and
of women's interests (Phillips 1995).

To account in our index for the percentage of women legislators, we take this
proportion for each legislative assembly, measured as the absolute difference in
percentage terms between the actual proportion of females and 50 percent. This
absolute point distance from 50 percent is then rescaled to a zero to 10 scale and
inverted, so that chambers closer to 50 percent female membership get higher
scores. The extremes before scaling represented by Papua New Guinea (2.7 percent women legislators) and Bolivia (53.1 percent female) thus map on this index
component to a score of zero for Papua New Guinea and 10 for Bolivia. Higher
scores indicate a more gender-balanced legislative assembly, signposting to us that
the chamber more closely associates with a voters' assembly.

Cameral Type: The next component of our voters' assembly explores the legislative assembly's cameral structure. As we discussed in Chapter 5, cameral structure
denotes the number of legislative chambers and, where there is more than one, the
similarities and differences between the chambers. Specifically, we are interested
in whether the legislative assembly has one or two chambers. Secondly, in bicameral cases, how democratic is the process of selecting the members of the second
(upper) chamber?

Citizens, we presume, value elective bicameralism. A popularly elected second
chamber may provide an extra check on the executive (thus adding to transparency in government) and on the lower chamber (thus allowing for more

---

[12] There is today broad agreement that gender is a politically relevant characteristic on which we
value inclusive representation. One might add to this category such variables as ethnicity, faith, age,
income, sexual orientation, disability, and educational attainment, although for some of these there may
be more controversy and for many of them comparable data are difficult to collect. On the other hand,
few would argue that features such as body height or hair color are in themselves politically relevant
variables, though they may in some societies be proxies for other politically relevant characteristics of
voters.

reflective lawmaking). Second chambers thus serve as a constraining influence on the policy-making power of the majority in the first (lower) chamber. In a voters' assembly, citizens benefit from the direct and immediate influence over the selection of members and the ability to remove and replace these representatives in future elections. Elective second chambers, perhaps elected at different intervals and under different electoral rules, can enhance this influence.

But voters' interests may not be served by a second chamber that is unelected or only partially elected. Popular control will not be enhanced in such a second chamber. For any potential utility, an unelected second chamber is contrary to our notion of a voters' assembly—an open legislative assembly where members are highly responsive and accountable to citizens. The UK House of Lords presents a good example of how an unelected form of bicameralism may be contrary to the interests of ordinary citizens. Members of the House of Lords are appointed by the Government or elected by a small group of hereditary Lords. They serve for life, unless they voluntarily retire. They can't ordinarily be removed, the voters never selected them, and the same voters have no opportunity to replace them.

The contemporary world of democracies is pretty evenly divided between unicameral and bicameral assemblies. Of the 68 legislative assemblies in our study, 33 have two chambers while 35 have just one. In about two-thirds (21 of 33) of the bicameral cases, both chambers are popularly elected. In contrast, 12 upper chambers in our study are appointed or somehow indirectly, rather than popularly, elected.

To capture the fit between bicameralism and voters' interests, we create the following scale: Legislative assemblies with an unelected or only partially elected second chamber score zero—indicative of a legislative cameral structure that is least compatible with our concept of a voters' assembly. Unicameral legislatures score five. Countries with a popularly elected second chamber score 10, reflecting our belief that voters value the benefits of second chambers, but only where the second chamber is democratically elected. On this scale, the United Kingdom (with an unelected second chamber), for example, then scores zero, Norway (with a unicameral system) scores five, while the United States (with a popularly elected second chamber) scores 10.

Internal Organization and Committees: Next we turn to the capacity of the legislative assembly to perform the roles and functions expected of it, constitutionally and by citizens. As noted in Chapter 1, the challenge of capacity has to do with the assembly's ability to enact effective policies and to select policy instruments that serve these goals efficiently. Here, we first examine a legislative assembly's committee system. Mattson and Strøm (1995: 249) define a legislative committee as "a subgroup of legislators, normally entrusted with specific organizational tasks." Standing (meaning permanent in membership within a legislative term) committees are critical legislative subunits that permit assembly members to divide their labor and specialize in functional tasks and policy areas.

One of the most basic features of committee systems concerns their sheer numbers. The greater the number of committees, the more assembly members can specialize. Through specialization and gains from trade, committees generally benefit ordinary citizens by enhancing the legislative assembly's deliberative capacity. A larger number of committees broadly corresponds to greater capacity. Yet, the number of assembly committees may matter in less straightforward ways. Too few committees mean that their main advantages—permitting members to specialize and facilitating efficiency by allowing the assembly to consider simultaneously a range of topics and bills—are unlikely to materialize. A large number of committees thus helps the assembly deal with many specialized tasks simultaneously and may give each member multiple avenues of influence. At the same time, though, too many committees may cause legislators to be overburdened with committee work. Thus, there is likely some tradeoff between maximizing the assembly's effectiveness and productivity and burdening members with unreasonable workloads.

Yet, few real-world assemblies are likely to have enough committees to experience negative returns. For the assembly's overall effectiveness, more committees is therefore generally better. Since we believe voters will favor empowering their direct agents over their indirect ones, a voters' assembly should have a relatively high number of standing committees.

To include a measure of committee strength in our voters' assembly index, we take the raw number of substantive "permanent" committees in each legislative assembly and rescale it zero to 10. We count a total of 1418 such substantive committees across our 68 democratic assemblies.[13] This means that the mean (average) number of legislative committees is 20.8. However, there is significant variation in the number of committee between legislative assemblies—Benin's Assemblée Nationale has just five committees while the Nigerian House of Representatives has 84. Three assemblies are outliers on the positive end (Mexico with 52 committees, the Philippines with 58, and Nigeria with 84), and in rescaling we set each of these to 10. After rescaling, the values range from zero (for Benin), to 10 (for Argentina, Mexico, Nigeria, and the Philippines). Recall that higher voters' assembly scores associate with a greater number of substantive standing assembly committees.

---

[13] Substantive committees are those that have responsibilities related to deliberations in specific policy areas (e.g., foreign affairs committees) or to the process of deliberation (e.g., rules committees). We exclude committees that have purely housekeeping functions or that represent specific non-political interests or identities among members (e.g., language communities or chess players).

Agenda Access: Next we consider the ability of citizens to formally inform, or even bypass, the legislative assembly in endeavors to generate new public policy. In a representative democracy, the task of lawmaking, including the process of initiation, is commonly delegated to legislators. However, ordinary citizens can be involved in making new laws in at least two important ways: One way is by having the formal capacity to present policy proposals to the legislative assembly, which may then be required to consider the proposal. In Austria, for example, an initiative (Volksbegehren) requires the signature of 100,000 voters, and the initiative "may take the form of a bill, i.e. contain the concrete wording of a text to be adopted, but it is also sufficient if the movers' concern is described in detail."[14] A second way for citizens to gain agenda power is via an initiative process whereby laws can be made without the involvement of the legislative assembly. For example, citizen-proposed referendums in Switzerland are common, and have included topics such as gambling, nuclear power, the environment, United Nations membership, executive pay, and immigration.

The ability of citizens to formally set the legislative agenda or bypass entirely the legislative assembly tallies with our concept of a voters' assembly: a body in which citizens benefit from direct and immediate influence over members and policies. Of course, the general interests of citizens may not always be well met by the ability of a faction of citizens to set or bypass the legislative agenda. Yet, for better or worse citizens' initiatives certainly empower citizens and provide one avenue whereby the agenda control of the legislature and executive can be diminished. For this reason, such procedures increase voter influence and reduce the powers of members and leaders. Even the prospect that laws may be introduced or passed via initiatives may be enough to induce the legislative assembly to deal preemptively with policy issues which politicians would not otherwise wish to consider. Switzerland's direct democracy system, for example, often forces onto the agenda topics which Swiss politicians might otherwise wish to avoid (Serdült 2018).

To capture the ability of citizens' to engage directly in public policy initiation, we create a scale from zero to 10, with the following possible values: Countries that have neither a citizen initiative process nor give formal legislative proposal rights to citizens score zero. Countries that have both citizen proposal rights and a citizen initiative score 10, and countries with either public proposal rights or a citizen initiative, but not both, score five. Higher scores indicate a higher capacity for citizens to be directly and formally involved in the making of public policy, corresponding to our concept of a voters' assembly.

Budgetary Powers: The ninth factor in our voters' assembly index is the legislative assembly's budget power. The budgetary process is, due to its complexity, one in which legislative assemblies are at a decided disadvantage relative to the executive branch. Economically, this is not always a disadvantage for voters. Assemblies may be driven in their budgetary decisions by wishful thinking and fiscal illusions

---

[14] https://www.parlament.gv.at/ENGL/PERK/GES/WEG/INITIATIVE/index.shtml.

or time inconsistency problems, such that their budgetary decisions for example favor current generations over future ones. If having a weak role for legislative assemblies in the budgetary process reduces over-spending or inefficiencies, then, as a whole and over the long run, citizens will benefit. Overall though, we believe voters will want their representatives in the assembly to be significant players in the budgetary process, adding transparency and accountability to the executives' typical dominance over this process. This reflects our general belief that, all else equal, voters prefer political authority to be vested in their direct, rather than indirect, agents. Hence, legislative assembly power over the budgetary process, we believe, aligns with our notion of a voters' assembly.

Again, for budgetary powers we use Wehner's (2006) Index of Legislative Budget Institutions. We rescale it to range to zero to 10, with Senegal (with the weakest powers) scoring zero and the United States (with the strongest powers) 10. High scores indicate greater assembly budgetary powers, which we take as a correlate of a voters' assembly.

Powers of Executive Oversight: The 10th and final component of our voters' assembly index captures the capacity of the legislative assembly to scrutinize and oversee the executive. As we noted in Chapter 12, legislative assemblies face a difficult task in attempting to hold the executive to account. Compared with the assembly, the typical executive tends to be better resourced, speak with a more unified voice, have informational advantages, and operate in a less transparent fashion. To overcome such structural and informational disadvantages, legislatures are empowered with, or grant themselves, a number of oversight tools.

Effective oversight mechanisms help legislators overcome some of the informational and resource disadvantages they face relative to the executive branch. And the capacity to oversee the executive echoes the fundamental nature of the legislative assembly. In a comparative study investigating what makes national legislatures more or less powerful, Chernykh et al. (2017) thus suggest that the power to investigate the government is one of the most valuable powers a legislative assembly can have.

As we assume that voters prefer to empower their direct rather than their indirect agents, these same devices will generally also serve the interests of voters. A voters' assembly should therefore have a high capacity to monitor the executive. Parliamentary scrutiny and accountability matter to voters because through effective legislative oversight they can hope to induce better public policy and better governance. Moreover, the information that effective oversight generates about the performance of the incumbent executive helps voters decide whom to support at election time.

Specifically, some of the most important oversight devices have to do with whether legislators can question ministers, whether the legislative assembly has power of summons over executive branch officials, and whether the legislative assembly can conduct investigations of such officials. Parliamentary questions (PQs) permit legislators to request members of the executive formally to provide information about their policies and procedures. Oral PQs are a common feature of legislative assemblies. In 61 of our 68 cases, legislators can ask questions of the executive on the assembly floor. According to Pelizzo and Stapenhurst (2013: 35), interpellations, which exist in 63 of our assemblies, are similar to written parliamentary questions, but more extensive, and analogous to a short debate on the activities of a particular member or part of the executive. A parliamentary investigation or inquiry is a vehicle for the legislative assembly to undertake a (relatively) detailed examination of some past event or current issue. In 58 of our 68 cases, the legislative assembly can conduct independent investigations of the chief executive and/or other parts of the executive.

To capture oversight capacity in our index, we construct a scale from zero to 10 capturing the presence or absence of the powers of legislative questions, interpellations, and investigations. A legislative assembly lacking all these oversight mechanisms scores zero. An assembly with one of the three scores 3.33; one with two of the three scores 6.66, and a chamber endowed with all three powers of parliamentary questions, interpellations, and investigations scores 10. Because each of these oversight powers enhances voters' ability to influence and oversee policy, higher scores associate with a voters' assembly. After scaling, legislative assemblies in 53 countries score 10, while no legislative assembly scores zero. Six countries score 3.33, while nine countries score 6.67.

The Voters' Assembly

Our index of a voters' assembly for the 68 countries included in this study is presented in Figure 13.3, which reflects some interesting variation. The average index score across all countries is 44.88, suggesting that, on average, legislative assemblies would require significant reform to come close to our ideal type of a voters' assembly. There is at the same time substantial variation in how real-world legislative assemblies line up empirically. The voters' assembly index ranges from 21.1 to 75.0. Among our 68 major democracies, Burundi's national assembly least resembles our concept of a voters' assembly whereas that of the Philippines most closely approximates this type. Spain represents the median case.

Burundi's Inama Nshingamateka (National Assembly) is elected by a closed-list electoral system giving voters limited control over exactly who represents them, no recall, a relatively long maximum inter-electoral period (five years), relatively few parliamentary committees (eight), little formal capacity for citizens to initiate public policy change, weak budgetary oversight (ninth weakest of 68), only one questioning tool, and sits alongside an indirectly elected second chamber. Burundi does, however, score better on proportionality (23rd most proportional of our 68 cases) and gender representation (15th most balanced).

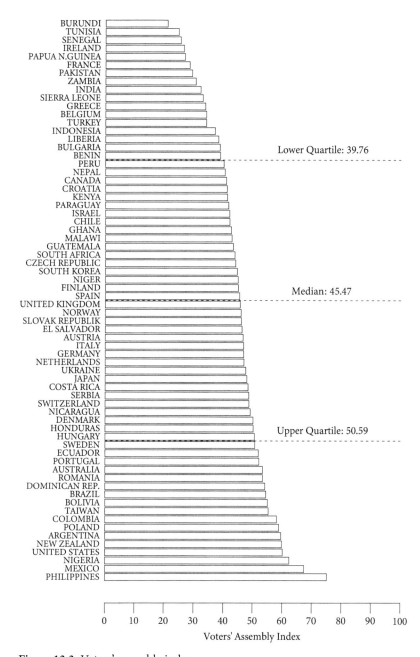

Figure 13.3 Voters' assembly index

As the closest approximation of a voters' assembly, the Philippines House of Representatives scores high across a number of component parts of our index. The House is elected via a mixed-member type electoral system, involving single member constituencies and a list element, which ensures rewards for cultivating personal votes as well as a degree of overall proportionality (although the assembly ranks only 32nd in vote-seat proportionality). The maximum inter-electoral period is relatively short, at three years. Having a directly elected Senate, the Philippines also scores high for cameral type, as well as for the number of House committees (58), for citizens' ability to formally influence public policy, and for legislative oversight capacity. In contrast, the Philippines has no recall procedures and scores only middlingly on legislative budgetary powers (38th out of 68) and gender representation (again 38th).

Overall, the countries at the high end of this scale tend to have relatively recent constitutions, many of them influenced by that of the United States (which itself scores 4th). Many are presidential or semi-presidential regimes. And as the highest-scoring Western European country, Portugal ranks only 15th, whereas four assemblies in this region rank among the bottom 12. New Zealand and Australia are high-scoring Commonwealth countries, whereas other such nations are scattered across the ranks.

13.5 Assembly Types in Comparison

Let us now examine the scores of real-world assemblies on these respective indices. Are the characteristics that make up the three assembly types mutually exclusive? In a strict sense, no. It is no surprise that the three ideal types, as we have constructed and measured them, are not perfectly orthogonal, or mutually exclusive. All three types are, after all, democratic assemblies and share a number of properties by virtue of this commonality. It is also true that operationally, we have employed several of the same variables to construct these different indices. Thus, for example, incentives generated by the electoral system to cultivate a personal vote load positively on the members' assembly index as well as on the voters' assembly measure, but negatively on the leaders' assembly index.

Thus, it is possible for particular legislative assemblies to score high (or low) on more than one of these indices at the same time. An assembly that scores high on our members' assembly index, for example, could also score high on the voters' assembly score, as indeed the US House of Representatives does. As noted above, this well-known assembly scores higher than any other democratic assembly on the members' assembly index. At the same time, it scores fourth on the voters' assembly measure, behind only the Philippines, Mexico, and Nigeria, all of which were strongly influenced by the US model.[15] Yet, it is certainly not the case that

---

[15] All three national assemblies are bicameral, with a smaller Senate and a larger lower chamber, which in the cases of Nigeria and the Philippines is called the House of Representatives (in Mexico the Chamber of Deputies). The framers of Nigeria's Fourth Republic, founded in 1999, clearly modeled their national assembly on that of the United States, which had also been the model for the Second Republic (1979–83) (see Campbell 2013; LeVan 2019).

all polities that score high on the members' index also rank among the high scorers on the voters' assembly index. Indeed, the three assemblies that follow the US Congress on the members' assembly measure, Papua New Guinea, Malawi, and Liberia, all score below the mean on the voters' assembly index.

Over our entire sample of 68 legislative assemblies, the intercorrelations between our three assembly indices are relatively low. As the example above suggests, the two most compatible models are a voters' assembly and a members' assembly, as the correlation between these two indices is 0.13. This is a modest association indeed, as it indicates that although assemblies that score high on one of these indices are slightly more likely to score high on the second as well, at the same time the score on one of the measures explains less than 2 percent of the variance in the other.

The two other intercorrelations are both negative, indicating for one thing that members' and leaders' assemblies do not tend to go together. This is hardly a great surprise, and this correlation is also clearly the strongest and most statistically significant of the three. The result suggests that it is difficult to devise a legislative structure that rewards leaders and ordinary members at the same time. These are the two dominant classes of actors within legislative assemblies, who will inevitably have conflicting interests over many aspects of legislative organization and procedure. The third and final intercorrelation, between a voters' assembly and a leaders' assembly, is negative but only marginally stronger than the one between a voters' assembly and a members' assembly (though reversed in direction). The slightly ominous implication, given the long-term trend toward stronger assembly leaderships, is that this may be more likely to detract from, rather than support, voter sovereignty.

13.6 Assembly Types and Regime Types

Next we might be interested in whatever associations might exist between assembly types and broader regime types. Is there any systematic relationship between regime types and assembly models? Since parliamentary constitutions rely more heavily on executive control of the legislative agenda, we might expect to see a positive relationship between parliamentarism and leaders' assemblies. Indeed, one of components of the leaders' assembly index is whether the executive has the constitutional power to dissolve the assembly, which is commonly present in parliamentary systems but not in presidential ones.

The leaders' assembly index thus seems more straightforwardly associated with specific constitutional traditions and particularly with parliamentarism and perhaps with Westminter parliamentarism in particular.[16] Thus, Australia (second)

---

[16] Although see Russell and Serban (2021) for a criticism of the very notion of a "Westminster model" of parliamentarism, at least when explored comparatively.

and New Zealand (third) are both in the top quartile, along with the United Kingdom and Canada. Most European countries score relatively high on this dimension, especially those that have traditional parliamentary, rather than semi-presidential, constitutions. The European exceptions are some of the Eastern European regimes, such as Hungary and Romania. The United States scores relatively low on this index, along with several (though not all) other presidential systems in the Americas.

Assemblies in parliamentary democracies do tend to score somewhat higher (mean of 59.9) on the leaders' assembly index than legislatures in presidential countries (53.9). Interestingly, though, semi-presidential systems score lower than either of the other regime types (at 49.6). At the same time, presidential assemblies score a bit higher as voters' assemblies, whereas on the members' assembly index, the two regime types have virtually identical means. There is, then, a tendency for pure parliamentary assemblies to resemble leaders' assemblies more than presidential assemblies do, whereas the latter are more likely to approach our voters' assembly type.

On the members' assembly index, many European countries similarly rank among the low scorers. Thus, among the 17 countries in the bottom quartile, 11 are European, whereas the same continent accounts for only five of the countries in the top quartile. This may reflect a tendency for parliamentary systems not to conform to the members' model, but closer inspection suggests that this lesson needs to be qualified. Interestingly, parliamentary countries with a similar political heritage are sometimes far apart on the members' assembly dimension, for example with New Zealand and Ireland in the top quartile and Australia and the United Kingdom near the bottom.[17] Apart from the United States and Brazil, most assemblies in the Americas have remarkably middling scores. African countries, in contrast, seem to cluster near the extremes, with Tunisia and Burundi among the low scorers, and Malawi and Liberia near the top.

Similarly, electoral systems features tend to associate with our indices in fairly straightforward ways. Compared with multi-member district systems, single-member district elections are positively associated with members' assembly scores and negatively with the two others. Most of these differences are fairly small, however, so that our indices of the various assembly types are not simply alternative ways to describe these common ways to classify electoral systems.

Federalism has a less obvious correlation with assembly type, though we expect that the checks and balance with which it is commonly associated will militate against leaders' assemblies. In our sample, federal systems in fact score above unitary ones on all three dimensions, but not by particularly large or significant

---

[17] This is not wholly surprising given that both countries have deliberately deviated in many respects from the UK constitutional model—Ireland following independence in the 1920s (MacCarthaigh 2005), and New Zealand for more pragmatic reasons in the 1990s (Mulgan and Aimer 2004).

margins. Cameral structure has a more intuitive correlation with assembly type, since bicameralism, particular the incongruent type in which the two chambers are elected in dissimilar ways, is likely to constrain the powers of party leaders. Bicameral assemblies (often associated with federalism) do in fact score higher than unicameral ones on the voters' and members' assembly indices, but slightly lower on the leaders' assembly measure, as one might expect. Bicameralism presumably dilutes legislative leadership power and may in fact be designed to do just that.

13.7 Conclusion

At the beginning of this volume, we suggested that it is possible to meaningfully classify legislative assemblies based on the interests of key institutional actors, specifically voters, ordinary members of the assembly, and its leaders. We thus proposed three pure assembly types, based on the extent to which the assembly's rules and procedures favor one or another of these actors: A members' assembly, a leaders' assembly, and a voters' assembly. This chapter has set out to explore systematically how closely real-world legislative designs correspond to our ideal-type assemblies. We have done this by developing an index for each of our ideal types and providing empirical content to these indices. We have also discussed our interpretation of these ideal types in order to better make sense of real-world legislative assemblies.

Some findings provide comfort that our ideal types and indices have face validity: from our general knowledge of legislative politics we would have expected the US House of Representatives to emerge as an example of a members' assembly. Denmark and some Westminster-style parliamentary systems also plausibly emerge as strong cases of a leaders' assembly. And although the specific legislatures that stand out on our index of voters' assemblies are probably less predictable, the fact that they are products of relatively recent constitutions is no great surprise. One question that might follow from our survey is whether such institutional features that benefit members, leaders, or voters have any consequences for elections and representation in democratic assemblies. The next chapter addresses that issue.

References

Aldrich, John H. 2011. *Why Parties? A Second Look. Chicago*: The University of Chicago Press.

Bagehot, Walter. 1867. *The English Constitution*. London: Chapman & Hall.

Cain, Bruce, John Ferejohn, and Morris Fiorina. 1987. *The Personal Vote: Constituency Service and Electoral Independence*. Boston: Harvard University Press.

Campbell, John. 2013. *Nigeria: Dancing on the Brink*. Lanham: Rowman & Littlefield Publishers, 2013.

Carey, John M., and Matthew Soberg Shugart. 1995. "Incentives to Cultivate a Personal Vote: A Rank Ordering of Electoral Formulas." *Electoral Studies* 14(4): 417–439.

Chernykh, Svitlana, David Doyle, and Timothy J. Power. 2017. "Measuring Legislative Power: An Expert Reweighting of the Fish-Kroenig Parliamentary Powers Index." *Legislative Studies Quarterly* 42(2): 295–320.

Collier, David, Jody LaPorte, and Jason Seawright. 2012. "Putting Typologies to Work: Concept Formation, Measurement, and Analytic Rigor." *Political Research Quarterly* 65(1): 217–232.

Cox, Gary W. 1987. *The Efficient Secret: The Cabinet and the Development of Political Parties in Victorian England*. New York: Cambridge University Press.

Cox, Gary W. 2014. "Reluctant Democrats and Their Legislatures." In Shane Martin, Thomas Saalfeld, and Kaare W Strøm (eds.), *The Oxford Handbook of Legislative Studies*. Oxford: Oxford University Press, 696–716.

Fish, M. Steven, and Matthew Kroenig. 2009. *The Handbook of National Legislatures: A Global Survey*. Cambridge: Cambridge University Press.

Gallagher, Michael. 1991. "Proportionality, Disproportionality and Electoral System." *Electoral Studies* 10(1): 3–51.

Goplerud, Max, and Petra Schleiter. 2016. "An Index of Assembly Dissolution Powers." *Comparative Political Studies* 49(4): 427–456.

Huber, John D. 1996. *Rationalizing Parliament: Legislative Institutions and Party Politics in France*. Cambridge: Cambridge University Press.

Johnson, Joel W., and Jessica S. Wallack. 2012. *Electoral Systems and the Personal Vote*. Dataverse Network Project.

Koss, Michael. 2018. *Parliaments in Time: The Evolution of Legislative Democracy in Western Europe 1866–2015*. Oxford: Oxford University Press.

Kreppel, Amie. 2014. "Typologies and Classifications." In Shane Martin, Thomas Saalfeld, and Kaare W. Strøm (eds.), *The Oxford Handbook of Legislative Studies*. Oxford: Oxford University Press, 82–102.

Laver, Michael, and Kenneth A. Shepsle. 1994. "Cabinet Government in Theoretical Perspective: Cabinet Ministers and Parliamentary Government." In Michael Laver and Kenneth A. Shepsle (eds.), *Cabinet Ministers and Parliamentary Government*. Cambridge: Cambridge University Press, 285–310.

LeVan, A. Carl. 2019. *Contemporary Nigerian politics: Competition in a Time of Transition and Terror*. New York: Cambridge University Press.

MacCarthaigh, Muiris. 2005. *Accountability in Irish Parliamentary Politics*. Dublin: Institute of Public Administration.

Madison, James. 2009 [1788]. *The Federalist Papers*. No. 52. New Haven: Yale University Press.

Mattson, Ingvar, and Kaare Strøm. 1995. "Parliamentary Committees." In Herbert Döring (ed.), *Parliaments and Majority Rule in Western Europe*. Frankfurt: Campus Verlag, 249–307.

Mayhew, David R. 1974. *Congress: The Electoral Connection*. New Haven: Yale University Press.

Mezey, Michael. 1979. *Comparative Legislatures*. Durham: Duke University Press.

Montesquieu, Charles de S. 1989[1748]. *Spirit of the Laws*. Cambridge: Cambridge University Press.

Mulgan, Richard G., and Peter Aimer. 2004. *Politics in New Zealand*. Auckland: Auckland University Press.

Müller, Wolfgang C., and Kaare Strøm, eds. 1999. *Policy, Office or Votes? How Political Parties in Western Europe Make Hard Decisions*. Cambridge: Cambridge University Press.

Pelizzo, Riccardo, and Frederick Stapenhurst. 2013. *Parliamentary Oversight Tools: A Comparative Analysis*. Abington: Routledge.

Phillips, Anne. 1995. *The Politics of Presence*. London: Clarendon Press.

Polsby, Nelson., 1975. "Legislatures." In Fred I. Greenstein and Nelson Polsby (eds.), *Handbook of Political Science (Vol. V)*. Reading: Addison-Wesley Press, 557–622.

Rasch, Bjørn Erik. 2014. "Institutional Foundations of Legislative Agenda Setting." In Shane Martin, Thomas Saalfeld, and Kaare W Strøm (eds.), *The Oxford Handbook of Legislative Studies*. Oxford: Oxford University Press, 455–480.

Russell, Meg, and Ruxandra Serban. 2021. "The Muddle of the 'Westminster Model': A Concept Stretched beyond Repair." *Government and Opposition* 56(4): 744–764.

Serdült, Uwe. 2018. "Switzerland." In Matt Qvortrup (ed.), *Referendums around the World*. London: Palgrave Macmillan, 47–112.

Smith, Alastair. 2004. *Election Timing*. Cambridge: Cambridge University Press.

Strøm, Kaare. 1990. "A Behavioral Theory of Competitive Political Parties." *American Journal of Political Science* 34(2): 565–598.

Tsebelis, George. 1995. "Decision Making in Political Systems: Veto Players in Presidentialism, Parliamentarism, Multicameralism and Multipartyism." *British Journal of Political Science* 25(3): 289–325.

Wehner, Joachim. 2006. "Assessing the Power of the Purse: An Index of Legislative Budget Institutions." *Political Studies* 54(4): 767–785.

14

Incumbency and Re-election

In the introductory chapter of this book, we cited James Madison's concerns, in his attempt to design a legislative assembly based on popular sovereignty, about what we have called capacity and accountability: the assembly's powers and resources to make significant political decisions and the degree to which it is beholden to the citizens it is meant to represent. A successful national assembly, Madison believed, must meet both of these challenges. The empirical chapters that have followed have identified three sets of critical actors in contemporary legislative assemblies and sketched out three ideal types of democratic assemblies through which such concerns could be met, namely the members' assembly, the leaders' assembly, and the voters' assembly. None of these models represents a perfect marriage between capacity and accountability, and in different ways each privileges one over the other. And none of the national assemblies of the 68 contemporary democracies we have examined in the previous chapters perfectly match any of our ideal-typical models. Indeed, as we have seen in Chapter 13, the national assemblies of our 68 assemblies all represent different mixes between these pure assembly types.

This characterization of our three assembly models, and the placement of existing legislatures, could serve as a basis for analyzing a variety of questions about the effects that legislative design might have on policy outputs, political success, and regime performance. We do hope that our work will indeed help motivate such research, though for the most part such analysis is beyond the scope of this book. Many such questions would unquestionably need to be raised in a context in which one would have to consider a variety of contextual, historical, and environmental factors and the ways in which they interact with legislative institutions.

Yet in this chapter we shall examine the effects of legislative institutions on an outcome that is both proximate to the operations of these assemblies and critical to their accountability to their citizens: the rate at which elected representatives are re-elected to their offices in subsequent elections. It is easy to see that this is an issue that matters to members as well as to leaders and voters. And, as we shall show, there is a range of assembly features that we expect to have a predictable impact on such incumbent re-election rates. But first, let us simply establish that the variance in re-election rates is large, and that there is every reason to think that it may be consequential.

On February 24, 2014, at the age of 88, Representative John D. Dingell, Jr. (D–MI) announced his retirement from Michigan's 12th congressional district. Dingell was first elected in 1954 when he succeeded his father, John Dingell, Sr.,

Legislative Assemblies. Shane Martin and Kaare W. Strøm, Oxford University Press.
© Shane Martin and Kaare W. Strøm (2023). DOI: 10.1093/oso/9780198890829.003.0014

who had held the seat since 1933. John Dingell, Jr. went on to serve for 30 terms under 11 different presidents and become the longest-serving member of the US Congress in history. He was succeeded in office by his wife Debbie Dingell, who at the time of writing still holds this seat. Thus, for more than 90 years, this district (and its predecessors) has consistently been represented by a member of the Dingell family.

Incumbency can be a powerful factor in legislative politics, but its impact is far from universal. Although the Dingells' case is extreme, many members of the US Congress enjoy long legislative careers, as do many members of the British House of Commons. On the other hand, under very similar electoral laws, in India's *Lok Sabha* incumbents have routinely been defeated by the droves. Thus, in the 2014 general election, no fewer than 12 incumbent cabinet members lost their assembly seats.

Such cross-national contrasts certainly seem noteworthy, yet studies of incumbent re-election rates have focused mainly on the United States. Such research on legislative incumbency in the United States demonstrates not only that incumbency rates are high, but also that important consequences follow. Thus, scholars analyzing Congressional incumbency (e.g., Cox and Katz 1996; Jacobson 2015) have been motivated in part by Fiorina's (1977: 77) observation that "policy change in the Congress results more from the replacement of incumbents than from changes in their behavior." Only recently have political scientists begun to explore incumbency rates in other countries (see, for example, Uppal, 2009; Ariga 2015; Moral, Ozen, Tokdemir 2015; Redmond and Regan 2015; Klašnja and Titiunik 2017; Fiva and Smith 2018). Yet, with two exceptions (Matland and Studlar 2004 and Gouglas, Maddens and Brans 2017), broadly cross-national research is still rare and it is difficult to piece together this existing knowledge. Different studies measure the rate of incumbency differently and cannot reliably be aggregated for comparability. Moreover, the dearth of cross-national research, especially beyond OECD countries, complicates efforts to understand the impact of political institutions, which mainly vary cross-nationally.

How, then, can we explore the cross-national variation in incumbent re-election rates and account for the substantial differences that seem to exist? In this chapter we address these questions by examining variation in legislative re-election rates across our 68 assemblies, on the basis of the assumption that some factors that contribute to differences in the electoral success of incumbents have to do with institutional features of the assemblies in which they serve.

14.1 Incumbency, Capacity, and Accountability

Does the variation in incumbent re-election rates matter? We believe that it does, since incumbency rates may affect assembly capacity as well as accountability.

Presumably, legislative capacity as discussed throughout this volume presupposes some minimum of political experience, as well as skills and knowledge gained in and outside the assembly. Hence, there is good reason to believe that the political careers and experiences of legislators matter. A legislative assembly can only be as effective as the members who comprise it.

High re-election rates and concomitant high levels of experience in key offices (such as committee chairs) may allow legislatures to develop stable and efficient procedures, policy expertise, and strong institutional memories (Krehbiel 1991: 141–143). If in contrast turnover is high, the result may be inexperienced leadership, a lack of expertise, and low professionalism—liabilities that under term limits have affected some American state legislatures (Kousser 2005). Low incumbency rates may thus adversely impact parliamentary deliberation and by extension the quality of governance. High legislative turnover may for similar reasons blunt effective oversight functions and accountability. Finally, low incumbency rates may be concerning to the extent that they reflect a lack of trust or agreement between ordinary citizens and politicians or deter quality candidates from political careers.

On the other hand, high-incumbency assemblies may have their own liabilities (see Krupnikov and Shipan 2020). High re-election rates may reflect an institutional bias favoring incumbents and hurting legislative effectiveness. If sitting members are heavily advantaged electorally, even ineffective incumbents that expend little effort may be returned, thus hurting legislative capacity. Moreover, high re-election rates could depress accountability by building institutional barriers against challengers in general and especially against underrepresented demographic groups, such as women (Phillips 1995; Matland and Studlar 2004; Schwindt-Bayer 2005), working-class individuals, or members of minority ethnic, religious, or language communities. High re-election rates might also contribute to gerontocracy, favor rent-seekers, foster political cronyism, and seed voter apathy or alienation.

Thus, as the incumbency rate increases, the legislative assembly may possibly become a more effective principal of the executive branch, though a less faithful agent of the voters. Assembly capacity may be gained at the expense of accountability. In short, who serves in the legislature, how securely, and for how long are issues of profound normative, theoretical, and real-world significance.

14.2 Comparing Incumbency Rates

Let us therefore examine the variation in incumbency rates among our 68 democratic assemblies. For each country, we have generated legislative incumbency re-election data for each general election from 2000 or since the country became democratic, whichever is most recent, through 2018. We first construct a list of members of parliament (MPs) at the beginning of each "new" parliament (defined as the members taking office immediately following a general election).[1] We calculate the re-election rate of incumbents (or simply: "the incumbency rate") following a general election for each lower or unicameral legislative chamber i, as follows:

$$\text{Incumbency Rate}_{it} = \frac{\sum (\text{MPs}_t \text{ who were also MPs}_{t-1})}{\sum \text{MPs}_t} \times 100$$

where time t is the beginning of the parliamentary session following a general election, and time t–1 is the beginning of the parliamentary session following the previous general election.[2]

The legislative incumbency rate for any given general election, then, is the percentage of representatives elected in that election who were also elected in the previous general election. We calculate such re-election rates for all general elections held in each of our 68 assemblies between 2000 and 2018. We calculate these rates by scraping various electoral records to create legislative membership lists following each general election, which in total adds up to more than 95,000 observations.

The challenge of generating legislative membership lists varies dramatically by country. In some cases, we have relied on existing country datasets or cross-national data collections, such as the Constituency Level Elections Archive (CLEA),[3] which includes an impressive number of constituency-level election results for 74 countries.[4] For many countries, however, membership lists for each legislative term are not accessible in a suitable format. For many smaller and less economically developed democracies especially, information on parliamentary websites tends to be incomplete or non-existent. We therefore used web-scraping techniques to tap a wide variety of electoral sources, such as the records of national electoral commissions. We also accessed websites that preserve historical versions of parliamentary websites in digital archives, such as the Internet Archive project.[5] In still other cases, we started from records of every member who served in a given parliamentary session and then scraped the web for information on those who

---

[1] The Argentine Chamber of Deputies has staggered elections in which half of the members are elected in any one election. For this case, we adjust our calculation to focus only on the portion of the membership that is elected at that time.

[2] The lower bounds are thus 2000 for t and each country's most recent election held before 2000 for t–1.

[3] CLEA. Release 13: June 17, 2019. http://www.electiondataarchive.org.

[4] CLEA does not always include candidate names for all members and all elections, however. The format of candidate names is also not necessarily standardized across elections, making it more difficult to generate inter-election comparisons of incumbency rates. For such cases, we consulted additional sources of information.

[5] Internet Archive Wayback Machine, http://archive.org/web.

entered mid-term (via appointment or by-election) to derive through backward induction a membership list as of the beginning of the term.[6]

As Table 14.1 shows, our dataset covers many countries and elections that have not been included in such previous analyses as those of Matland and Studlar (2004) and Gouglas, Maddens, and Brans (2017). We have thus added more than 40 democracies, including countries in Eastern Europe, Latin America, Asia, and Africa. Our target sample across our 68 democracies consists of 301 elections held between 2000 and 2018.[7] Through extensive data collection efforts, we have been able to collect incumbency rates for 288 of these elections (96%). This corresponds to over 95,000 observations (where an observation is a member-term dyad) and more than 55,000 unique legislators.

Figure 14.1 provides a box plot showing the incumbency rates for each of our 68 democratic assemblies. Note the large cross-national variation, from a 0 percent median incumbency rate in Mexico and Costa Rica to more than 80 percent in the United States. This figure also displays substantial variation between these extremes, with a global mean and median incumbency rate of just over 44 percent. Apart from countries with term limits, our observations are quite evenly distributed between the teens and the low 70s. Only the United States and the United Kingdom have a median incumbency rate above the latter figure.

The four assemblies with the highest incumbency rates are those of the United States and three prosperous Commonwealth countries (the UK, New Zealand, and Australia). Canada similarly scores toward the top end of re-election rates, though with greater internal variance among elections. The three assemblies with the lowest incumbency rates are all Latin American, but they are also legislatures with various term limits. Apart from such rather obvious cases, the assemblies with the lowest re-election rates are dominated by African nations. Inter-election variance within countries is in many cases surprisingly limited, especially at the low end of re-election rates. Yet some countries stand out with much greater differences from one election to the next. Southern European countries, such as Spain, France, Portugal, and Greece, are among these, along with Japan and Latin American countries such as Argentina and El Salvador.

---

[6] Such data collection efforts are always fraught with challenges. For example, different reported names may actually represent the same person, as when individuals have multiple names, alternately choose to list or not list their middle names, go by nicknames, or change their names due to marriage or other circumstances. On the other hand, two seemingly identical names may occasionally represent two different individuals. Consider, as mentioned above, *John D. Dingell, Jr.* v. *John D. Dingell, Sr.* in the Congressional district representing Detroit's western suburbs. Thus, the same name may not always represent the same person (see Smith and Martin 2017).

[7] We calculate incumbency rates only for elections where the preceding election was also held under democratic rule. This decision rules excludes 34 elections across our sample (2000–2018).

Table 14.1 Country elections included in our analysis

Country	Election Years	Data Sources
Argentina	2001[1], 2003[1], 2005, 2007, 2009, 2011, 2013, 2015, 2017	W
Australia	2001, 2004, 2007, 2010, 2013, 2016	W
Austria	2002, 2006, 2008, 2013, 2017	W
Belgium	2003, 2007, 2010, 2014	W
Benin	2003, 2007, 2011, 2015	W
Bolivia	2002, 2005, 2009, 2014	W; Legislatina (2019)
Brazil	2002, 2006, 2010, 2014, 2018	W; Legislatina (2019)
Bulgaria	2001[1], 2005, 2009, 2013, 2014, 2017	W
Burundi	2005[2], 2010, 2015	W
Canada	2000, 2004, 2006, 2008, 2011, 2015	W; CLEA (2019)
Chile	2001, 2005, 2009, 2013, 2017	W
Colombia	2002, 2006, 2010, 2014, 2018	W; Legislatina (2019)
Costa Rica	2002, 2006, 2010, 2014, 2018	W
Croatia	2000[2], 2003, 2007, 2011, 2015, 2016	W
Czech Republic	2002, 2006, 2010, 2013, 2017	W
Denmark	2001, 2005, 2007, 2011, 2015	W
Dominican Republic	2002, 2006, 2010, 2016	W; Legislatina (2019)
Ecuador	2002[2], 2006[2], 2007[3], 2009[3], 2013, 2017	W; Legislatina (2019)
El Salvador	2000[1], 2003, 2006, 2009, 2012, 2015, 2018	W; Legislatina (2019)
Finland	2003, 2007, 2011, 2015	W
France	2002, 2007, 2012, 2017	W
Germany	2002, 2005, 2009, 2013, 2017	W
Ghana	2000[2], 2004, 2008, 2012, 2016	W
Greece	2000, 2004, 2007, 2009, 2012, 2012, 2015, 2015	W
Guatemala	2003, 2007, 2011, 2015	W; Legislatina (2019)
Honduras	2001, 2005, 2009[2], 2013[2], 2017	W; Legislatina (2019)
Hungary	2002, 2006, 2010, 2014, 2018	W
India	2004, 2009, 2014	W; CLEA (2019)
Indonesia	2004[1], 2009[1], 2014	W; CLEA (2019)
Ireland	2002, 2007, 2011, 2016	W; Elections Ireland (2019)
Israel	2003, 2006, 2009, 2013, 2015	W
Italy	2001, 2006, 2008, 2013, 2018	W
Japan	2000, 2003, 2005, 2009, 2012, 2014, 2017	Reed and Smith (2018)
Kenya	2002$∧2$, 2007[1], 2013, 2017	W
Liberia	2005$∧2$, 2011, 2017[1]	W; CLEA (2019)

Continued

Table 14.1 *Continued*

Country	Election Years	Data Sources
Malawi	2004[1], 2009[1], 2014	W
Mexico	2000, 2003, 2006, 2009, 2012, 2015, 2018	W
Nepal	2008[2], 2013[1], 2017	W
Netherlands	2002, 2003, 2006, 2010, 2012, 2017	W
New Zealand	2002, 2005, 2008, 2011, 2014, 2017	W; Nemoto (2014)
Nicaragua	2001, 2006, 2011, 2016	W; Legislatina (2019)
Niger	2004[2], 2009[2], 2011[2], 2016	W
Nigeria	2003[2], 2007[2], 2011[2], 2015	W; CLEA (2019)
Norway	2001, 2005, 2009, 2013, 2017	W
Pakistan	2002[2], 2008[2], 2013, 2018	W
Papua New Guinea	2002, 2007, 2012, 2017	W
Paraguay	2003, 2008, 2013, 2018	W; Legislatina (2019)
Peru	2000[2], 2001[2], 2006, 2011, 2016	W
Philippines	2001, 2004, 2007, 2010, 2013, 2016	W
Poland	2001, 2005, 2007, 2011, 2015	W
Portugal	2002, 2005, 2009, 2011, 2015	W
Romania	2000, 2004, 2008, 2012, 2016	W
Senegal	2001[2], 2007[1], 2012, 2017	W
Serbia	2000[2], 2003[2], 2007[2], 2008, 2012, 2014, 2016	W
Sierra Leone	2002[2], 2007, 2012, 2018	W; SLOEDP (2019)
Slovak Republik	2002, 2006, 2010, 2012, 2016	W
South Africa	2004[1], 2009, 2014	W
South Korea	2000, 2004, 2008, 2012, 2016	Nemoto (2016)
Spain	2000, 2004, 2008, 2011, 2015, 2016	W
Sweden	2002, 2006, 2010, 2014, 2018	W
Switzerland	2003, 2007, 2011, 2015	W
Taiwan	2001, 2004, 2008, 2012, 2016	W
Tunisia	2004[2], 2009[2], 2011[2], 2014	W
Turkey	2002, 2007, 2011, 2015[2], 2015[2], 2018[2]	W
Ukraine	2002, 2006, 2007, 2012, 2014	W
United Kingdom	2001, 2005, 2010, 2015, 2017	W
United States	2000, 2002, 2004, 2006, 2008, 2010, 2012, 2014, 2016, 2018	Voteview (2019)
Zambia	2001[2], 2006[2], 2011[2], 2016	W

Notes: 1 = We are missing the necessary data to compute the incumbency rate for this election; 2 = Either this election or the preceding election was not held under democratic rule (according to Polity) and is thus excluded from our analysis; 3 = Ecuador's national legislature changed from the National Congress to the Constituent Assembly and then the National Assembly. We choose to include these elections in Figure 14.1. For data sources, W = Collected by downloading files or scraping data from the official websites of country legislatures (current or archived via the Internet Archive Wayback Machine).

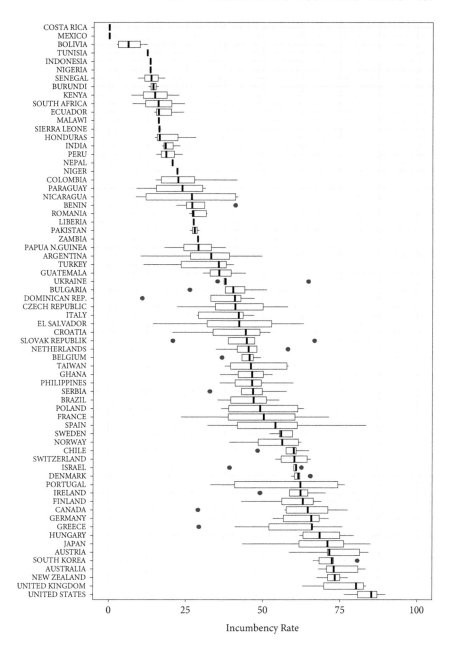

Figure 14.1 Incumbency rates in 68 democracies (2000–2018)

14.3 Understanding Incumbency Rates

How, then, do we explain these large differences among, and in some cases also within, our sample of democracies? One possibility that readily suggests itself is that incumbent re-election rates might be significantly correlated with assembly types. Specifically, we might expect members' assemblies to be conducive to high re-election rates, such as we have observed for the US House of Representatives. As discussed in Chapter 13, the US Congress scores at the very top of our members' assembly index, despite having some distinctly member-unfriendly features (such as two-year terms). In the simplest terms, we would expect incumbent re-election rates to be higher in such members' assemblies than in voters' assemblies, where incumbents may be less well protected against the occasional ire of the electorate. As for leaders' assemblies, we might instead expect substantial variance among members, in such a way that would correlate with the power and standing of each member within her respective political party. Thus, incumbents in leadership positions or favored by their respective leaders should be more electorally successful than those without such advantages.

But such simple expectations ignore the ways in which incumbents may adapt to the electoral threats (or lack of such) facing them. Vulnerable members in voters' assemblies, for example, knowing the electoral risks facing them, may respond by campaigning more intensively and heeding public opinion in their districts more closely. Whereas electorally favored incumbents in members' assemblies may instead direct more of their energies into efforts that enhance their policy specialization or perhaps their preparation for higher office, rather than meeting the demands of their current constituents. In either case, the results may defy our simple expectations.

We should also be mindful of the possibility that not all the institutional features that characterize our respective assembly types may affect the incumbent re-election rate in the same way. In our voters' assembly index we have, for example, included the ease of agenda access for civil society groups and other non-members. While we believe that this institutional feature properly characterizes a voters' assembly, we see little reason to expect it to correlate strongly with the rate of incumbent re-election. And while we also believe that we have correctly associated the members' assembly with long electoral terms, we have no strong expectation that long terms will correlate positively with incumbency rates. Indeed, as we will discuss below, there are good reasons to expect the opposite. Hence, in building our expectations concerning re-election rates, we shall have to consider more closely the choices that lead incumbent legislators to be re-elected (or not) and the specific institutional and situational features that most significantly impinge on these decisions.

Let us begin with the incumbents. Elected politicians generally wish to be re-elected, and hence we expect members' assemblies to be conducive to such ambitions. And yet political ambitions may be more complicated. In a seminal contribution, Schlesinger (1966) differentiated between discrete, static, and progressive ambition. Discrete ambition refers to candidates that seek office for a single term only and have no ambition of being re-elected. Static ambition is what most directly motivates re-election: the desire to hold the same office for several terms. Finally, progressive ambition characterizes candidates who view a given office as a stepping-stone to a higher, more powerful or lucrative, position. Legislators harboring discrete or progressive ambition may well value re-election less or differently than those with static ambition. Understanding legislative re-election rates may therefore require us to account for the impact of discrete or progressive, as well as static, political ambition.

Moreover, incumbent success or failure also depends on the voters that re-elect these incumbents (or not). In their assessment of incumbents, these voters may be influenced by the policies and economic performance they observe but also by their trust in the political system. Thus, in exploring the causes of variation in incumbency rates, we need to consider factors that affect the supply of incumbents seeking re-election, as well as conditions that shape voter demand for these incumbents. Also, some endowments (such as legislative perquisites) that generally favor incumbents may do so only when voters have a reasonable level of confidence in their political system and their incumbents.

What specific features of legislative assemblies, then, do we expect to correlate with high re-election rates? Scholars of the US Congress have long noted that the institution serves the electoral purposes of its incumbents well, in part due to the perquisites it bestows on its members. As David Mayhew puts it in his classic work:

> [T]he organization of Congress meets remarkably well the electoral needs of its members. To put it another way, if a group of planners sat down and tried to design a pair of American national assemblies with the goal of serving members' electoral needs year in and year out, they would be hard pressed to improve on what exists.
>
> (Mayhew, 1974: 81–82)

Mayhew thus suggests that many institutional features of the US House of Representation serve the purposes of incumbent members by enhancing their prospects of re-election. Many of these favorable conditions pertain to the internal organization of the US Congress, in which members are well endowed with electorally valuable resources. Mayhew (1974: 81–82) suggests that these institutional features enhance incumbency rates and limit turnover. These properties include powerful committees with access to discretionary "pork-barrel" grants (Mayhew 1974: 85–91), opportunities for legislative advertising, position taking, and credit claiming (Mayhew 1974: 49–73), personalized control over campaign finance (Mayhew 1974: 41), and generous staffing and remuneration schemes (Mayhew 1974: 84; see also Rohde 1979). Mayhew's argument also implies that alternative forms of legislative organization—where power and resources are shifted from individual legislators to party leaders—may hamper individual members' re-election pursuits (Mayhew 1974: 19–24). We find this argument important and largely persuasive and will in this chapter build on it and examine the extent to which it can be generalized to other assemblies.

Yet, we believe that the Mayhewian perspective may be incomplete for our purposes because it leads us to focus on the conditions that help incumbents satisfy their static ambitions of re-election, which of course are always pressing for members of the US House of Representatives, with its exceptionally short electoral terms. But cross-nationally many legislators may also harbor progressive ambition of one sort or another. Moreover, Mayhew emphasizes the "supply side" of politics, whereas the "demand side" also matters. In other words, any exploration of legislative turnover must also account for voters' preferences. Unless voters trust that their legislators will act in ways that benefit the public, and not just themselves, legislative perquisites may not help incumbents. Hence, cross-nationally, the impact of legislative resources may be constrained by trust-reducing conditions, such as political corruption. When applied globally, and especially to lower-trust societies, Mayhew's supply-side picture of legislative politics thus needs to be supplemented.

14.4 Modeling Re-election Decisions

To incorporate all these considerations, we model the interaction between incumbent legislators and voters and derive a set of testable propositions concerning the cross-national variation in incumbency rates. Re-election rates are driven in part by the supply of legislators willing and able to seek re-election, and in part by voter demand for their continued service. More specifically, the supply of incumbents seeking re-election will be shaped by (1) the legislative resources and perquisites incumbents can employ in their re-election bids, (2) political institutions that affect the re-election motivations of incumbents, and (3) statutory and other constraints on re-election opportunities. The demands of voters will be shaped by (1) their experiences with the national economy, as well as by (2) their confidence in government and politicians, as reflected in perceived levels of political corruption. We develop more specific hypotheses below.

We begin identifying the factors that may account for cross-national and inter-electoral variation in incumbency rates by sketching the process by which legislative incumbents may (or may not) be re-elected (see Figure 14.2). Whether incumbents win re-election is a function of their choices, as well as the choices of their voters. We therefore model this process as an interaction between the incumbent and the decisive voter in the incumbent's constituency.[8] Incumbents

---

[8] For simplicity, we assume the existence of a decisive voter similar to the median voter in a Downsian model. For similar reasons of simplicity, we use male pronouns for the incumbent and female pronouns for the voter.

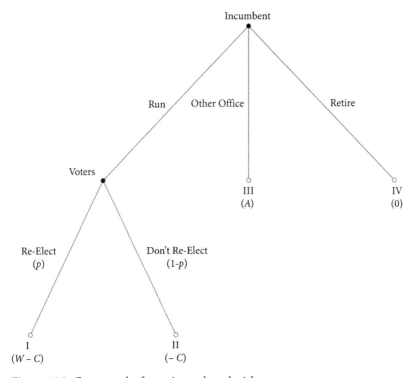

Figure 14.2 Career paths for an incumbent legislator

initially choose among three options: running for re-election, running for (or accepting) some alternative political office, or retiring. The first option, running for re-election, assumes that the incumbent can at least get on the ballot for the next election. Thus, this path excludes candidates that may wish to be re-elected but are denied the opportunity by law, by their respective parties, or by their primary voters. When such barriers are not present, the re-election motive is likely to be prominent in most democratic assemblies, particularly perhaps where alternative career opportunities are not plentiful. If this motive provided a full explanation, however, we should observe high incumbent re-election rates across democratically elected assemblies. And yet significant exceptions, such as India, pose a puzzle: If members of national legislative assemblies generally strive to be re-elected, why do they so often fail?

One potential answer is that some incumbents during their term in the assembly decide to accept or pursue some alternative political office. The alternative office option may encompass a wide range of political positions, including executive office (such as a presidency or governorship or the office of mayor of a major city), membership in a different assembly (such as a Senate seat or in the United Kingdom a life peerage), or appointment to a directorship, a judgeship, or a public sector management council. The third option, retirement, means anything other than service in a political office, such as retirement more literally, a career outside of politics, emigration, or death.

If the incumbent runs for re-election, the next stage of the game is that election, which we model simply as an up-or-down choice by the decisive voter. If she re-elects the incumbent, the game ends with outcome I in Figure 14.2. If she instead opts not to re-elect, the outcome is II. If the incumbent does not run but instead pursues some alternative political office, the outcome is III. And finally, if the incumbent retires, the outcome is IV.

We assume that each outcome generates a particular payoff (reward) for the incumbent. The payoff for winning re-election is W, by which we mean the net value of holding office for the next legislative term, over and above the utility of political retirement or loss of office.[9] We thus discount the value of office by its non-political opportunity costs (such as pensions, non-political pursuits, or the value of leisure). Thus, W may for some incumbents be negative. By running for re-election, the incumbent also incurs a fixed and positive cost, C. If the incumbent wins, he thus captures a payoff of W – C, whereas losing nets him a payoff of –C, which is always negative. The payoff for retirement is zero (0), as for simplicity we assume that retirement is costless and generates no political rewards. We similarly set the value of running and losing as equivalent to retirement, except for the cost of running (–C).

The payoff from alternative office is A, which represents the value of the best other political office the incumbent could attain at that time. There may be a cost associated with the pursuit of alternative office, which could be practically zero for a life peerage for a senior UK politician, or very high for a presidential candidate in the United States. Similarly, there may be a probability distribution over the likelihood of winning any such alternative office. For simplicity, however, we "bake" such considerations into payoff A, which accordingly means the expected net value of the best available outside political office, accounting for the costs of pursuing it, the probability of succeeding, and the non-political opportunity costs.

We assume that before deciding whether to run, the incumbent estimates a subjective probability of winning equal to p and a probability of losing equal to 1–p. We thus expect the incumbent to run for re-election if pW – C > A and pW – C > 0.[10] He will seek alternative office if A > pW – C and A > 0. Finally, he will retire if pW–C < 0 and A < 0 (and also if he is prevented from running by term limits, other constraints, or death). We assume that for the incumbent outcome II is the least desirable, and that no incumbent will seek re-election if he knows that he is certain to lose. Moreover, if his subjective estimate of p (the likelihood of winning) is very

---

[9] Figure 14.2 could be extended by modelling opportunities outside of political office that might generate political rewards, such as lobbying. We instead include these concerns within the W term, which captures the net value of holding office compared to other opportunities.

[10] For simplicity, we assume that the incumbent is not indifferent between any payoffs.

low, the incumbent will run only if W is much larger than the greater of A and 0.[11] In sum, we expect incumbency rates to be increasing in W (the value of re-election) and p (the incumbent's subjective probability of winning) and decreasing in A (the value of the best alternative office) and C (the cost of running for re-election).

We use this framework empirically to analyze the aggregate incumbency rates across our 68 democracies. Each observation is thus an aggregate re-election rate for a particular general election in a given country. To shed light on these re-election rates, we will consider constitutional, statutory, societal, and economic factors that may affect the various payoffs in our model. Thus, we believe that re-election rates depend on what legislators want, what resources the assembly endows them with, what the relevant laws and regulations permit, and, not least, how a typical voter assesses her incumbent representative and his performance in office.

The Re-election Motive

We begin with legislator motivations, and specifically with W, the net value to the incumbent of being re-elected. We expect incumbency rates to correlate with the incidence of static, rather than discrete or progressive, ambition. If many legislators have only discrete ambition, it means that their W (or perhaps their p) is low, and we should observe a high incidence of outcome IV (retirement). Assemblies that include many such members should therefore have low incumbency rates. Similarly, regimes in which alternative offices are plentiful and comparatively attractive (high A relative to W) and where many members have progressive ambition should, all else equal, feature a comparatively high incidence of outcome III. Hence, such assemblies should also exhibit lower re-election rates than those characterized by static ambition.

The paradigmatic legislative chamber dominated by static ambition is the United States House of Representatives. Mayhew (1974: 5) famously depicts its members as "single-minded seekers of reelection." Mayhew's description suggests an assembly in which each member's expected payoff from running for re-election, $pW - C$, exceeds the payoff from retirement (0) or from any alternative political office (A). Of course, Mayhew presumably did not intend his thesis to be taken quite so literally. Most likely, some incumbents face a probability of winning re-election (p) that is sufficiently low to deter them from running. And for some the cost of running (C) can become prohibitive, due to campaign costs, health conditions, family circumstances, or age. For example, when John Dingell, Jr. finally

---

[11] In real life, an incumbent may run even if his probability of winning is very low, for example to please his party and obtain its endorsement for a winnable office later. Such "hopeless" runs may also occur in protest against an opponent the incumbent views as particularly undesirable. Yet, we believe such decisions are sufficiently rare to ignore them for simplicity.

retired, it was presumably not because he despaired of his re-election prospects or aimed for higher office. Thus, even under the most favorable institutional conditions, some incumbents will not seek re-election. But in general we expect that the greater the value of their legislative office and the better the odds of winning, the more likely incumbents will be to seek re-election.

Legislative Resources

What institutional conditions, then, make for a favorable environment for incumbents seeking re-election? Some assemblies allow members to use their perquisites of office to maximize electoral success. Variation in incumbency rates may therefore reflect the legislative resources available to incumbents. Krehbiel (1991: 2) defines legislative organization as "the allocation of resources and assignment of parliamentary rights to individual legislators or groups of legislators." Legislative organization thus defines a set of institutional powers and privileges and a set of legislators to whom those various endowments are assigned (see Chapter 6). Such organizational resources may influence the re-election prospects of assembly members, most likely by helping them meet the cost of running (C) or enhancing their likelihood of winning (p).

Some legislative perquisites that help incumbents win re-election are those that give ordinary members discretionary resources, some autonomy from party leaders, and opportunities to build a personal vote. As noted above, Mayhew identified a number of such legislative resources, and we will build on his argument and generalize it to the assemblies in our study. Specifically, then, we expect incumbency rates to correlate positively with the size of legislative staffs (which can be useful in building a personal vote), with incumbents' access to legislative committees (which can generate benefits for constituents and affected interests), and with their legislative remuneration schemes. In sum, all else equal,

> H1: Incumbency rates will be positively associated with the electorally valuable legislative resources and perquisites available to incumbent legislators.

Regimes and Institutions

Some conditions that affect US House incumbency rates are not internal characteristics of the Congress itself, however, but institutional features that affect the value of retirement or alternative offices (A). While the payoffs from retirement will be highly person-specific (e.g., age and alternative sources of income) and therefore beyond the scope of our analysis, we can identify regime characteristics that correlate with attractive alternative offices and hence promote progressive ambition. Progressive ambition should depress incumbency rates. And we expect more members to act on progressive ambition when A is large, reflecting a generous "supply" of alternative legislative or executive offices. In contrast, factors that render alternative office less attractive or attainable should boost re-election rates.

In some democracies, progressive ambition would hardly ever steer incumbents away from a re-election bid. Consider, for example, New Zealand, which is unicameral, parliamentary, and monarchical. There are precious few alternative political offices for which an ambitious MP would want to give up his seat. Instead, for backbenchers progressive ambition focuses on cabinet positions, the route to which goes through parliament and the ruling party or coalition.

The lure of alternative offices thus depends on regime properties, such as federalism, presidentialism, and bicameralism, which compared with the alternatives (unitarism, parliamentarism, and unicameralism, respectively) all tend to expand the set of attractive alternative offices and thus increase the A term. We thus expect outside options to suppress incumbency rates under bicameralism, as some members of the lower chamber may aspire to join the upper house.[12] We similarly expect presidential or federal systems to have lower incumbency rates, since such regimes tend to feature a larger number of directly elected executive or state government offices that may divert some legislative incumbents from seeking re-election (see, for example, Micozzi 2014). However, outside such bicameral, presidential, and/or federal regimes, progressive ambition, and hence any A term, will rarely be relevant.[13]

We summarize our expectations so far as follows, where each proposition (and also those derived in the following sections) assumes all else equal:

H2: Incumbency rates will be negatively associated with bicameralism.
H3: Incumbency rates will be negatively associated with presidentialism.
H4: Incumbency rates will be negatively associated with federalism.

Yet, none of these regime properties guarantees that any significant number of legislators will pursue alternative office. Note that the United States has all three regime properties favoring progressive ambition. Yet, the likelihood that a Democrat House member from Houston or a Republican representing California's "Inland Empire" will give up their seats in pursuit of statewide or federal office may (due to high cost and low probability of success) be exceedingly small. Hence, we expect the effects of these regime characteristics to be relatively modest.

---

[12] Despite the common designation of second chambers as "upper," their value to political candidates varies. In the United States most federal legislators might, all else equal, prefer to be members of the Senate. In contrast, in the United Kingdom life peerages appeal mainly to senior politicians with no further cabinet aspirations (Chapter 5 discusses cameral structures).

[13] Occasionally, incumbent legislators may pursue alternative office even in countries that have none of these institutional characteristics. For example, some members may hanker after a central bank governorship or some other executive appointment. Or, in member countries, some legislators may seek European Union offices. Although such cases are likely to be rare, they lead us to expect regime effects to be modest.

Electoral Constraints

A further explanation of the variance in incumbency rates may be constraints, including statutory or constitutional rules concerning candidate selection, on the ability of legislators to seek re-election. The most obvious such constraint, of course, is term limits. Their strictest form, employed in Costa Rica and in Mexico until 2014, is a "no re-election rule" limiting occupants of legislative (and executive) office to a single term. Bolivia and the Philippines have more permissive rules, limiting incumbents to two and three terms, respectively. Most of our constitutions, however, impose no formal term limits on national legislators.

Term limits obviously have major and direct effects on re-election rates. Under a strict no re-election rule, virtually all incumbents will be barred from re-election.[14] Under more permissive term limits, re-election rates can be positive, but still systematically depressed. Figure 14.1 above shows that these expectations are indeed borne out by our data. But since our term-limited assemblies are few and idiosyncratic, and the effects obvious, we will not put these expectations to more formal tests.

More indirectly, re-election prospects will depend on election rules, especially those concerning ballot access and opportunities to cultivate a personal vote. Incumbents seeking re-election will be favored when they, rather than their respective parties, control ballot access. They will also benefit from electoral systems that permit candidate voting, as opposed to, for example, closed-list systems of proportional representation.

> H5: Incumbency rates will be positively associated with electoral systems that provide incentives to cultivate a personal vote.

We also expect the legislative term length (or its maximum constitutional length) to affect re-election rates. Under longer terms, more incumbents will die, resign, or run for higher office between elections. And non-political opportunity costs may depress the value of re-election, W, especially for incumbents who qualify for a comfortable pension (see Schlesinger 1966; Brace 1984). When terms are longer, voters may also be more inclined to vote out incumbents because stronger challengers present themselves.

> H6: Incumbency rates will be negatively associated with the maximum constitutional length of the legislative term.

---

[14] Even under a no re-election rule, legislators elected in one general election may occasionally be able to contest the next general election, for example if they resign their seats during the legislative term and then run as challengers in the next general election. However, we expect such cases to be very rare.

Voters, Prosperity, and Political Corruption

Our hypotheses so far have focused on "supply" conditions that make it more or less feasible and attractive for incumbents to seek re-election. But while favorable institutional conditions may be necessary for high re-election rates, they are not sufficient. Whether legislative incumbents succeed at election time ultimately depends on the voters, and the p term in the incumbents' calculus refers to their anticipation of this constraint. We believe that in her judgements of political incumbents, the decisive voter will be guided by two considerations in particular: (1) her assessment of the policy performance of the incumbent government and (2) her trust in the political system. In our analysis, we will capture these two concerns, respectively, through (1) GDP growth and GDP per capita and (2) the level of political corruption.

Our first expectation is based straightforwardly on the extensive scholarship on the economic vote, which argues that voters hold governments accountable for past economic performance (e.g., Duch and Stevenson 2008). We hypothesize that incumbent re-election rates will be boosted by both long-term and short-term economic prosperity:

H7: Incumbency rates will be positively associated with the level of GDP per capita.

H8: Incumbency rates will be positively associated with the rate of GDP growth.

The second concern that we believe will influence the voter's judgments on incumbents is her trust in government, for which our proxy is the level of perceived political corruption. Corruption is commonly defined as "the abuse of public office for private gains," which includes fraud, bribery, and misuse of public funds by elected officials (De Vries and Solaz 2017: 392). Unfortunately, corruption appears commonplace across the world, with real consequences for the quality of governance, economic development, prosperity, and the strength of society (Rothstein and Varraich 2017). Incumbents seeking re-election may not be advantaged when voters have reasons to be skeptical about their public-spiritedness. Voters may have ample reason to harbor such doubts in polities plagued by high levels of political corruption.

Existing studies suggest that when political corruption is rampant, incumbents are disadvantaged (Klašnja 2015; Klašnja and Titiunik 2017). For example, examining the effect of spending audits on mayoral elections in Brazil, Ferraz and Finan (2008: 705) conclude that "voters not only care about corruption, but once empowered with the information, update their prior beliefs and punish corrupt politicians at the polls." Survey experimental evidence suggests a strong link between priming participants with information on corruption and reduced candidate support (e.g., Winters and Weitz-Shapiro 2013; Mares and Visconti 2019;

Agerberg 2020).[15] Klašnja (2015: 928) argues that "the returns from corruption increase over the course of an incumbent's tenure (e.g., because of learning on the job), which forces voters to minimize corruption increase by replacing incumbents frequently, even if challengers are also perceived as corrupt." For these reasons the willingness of voters to reward incumbents may be conditional on a low or moderate level of political corruption. Hence,

> H9: Incumbency rates will be negatively associated with the severity of political corruption.

Conditional Effect of Corruption

Finally, we expect legislative endowments such as those identified by Mayhew to benefit incumbents only in those polities where political corruption is relatively low. Voters may opt to reap the rewards of having an experienced incumbent (for example, where seniority enhances legislators' ability to deliver preferred policies or pork to their respective constituencies), but only where the fruits of incumbency benefit voters and not just the politicians, such as through rent seeking and other forms of corruption. Specifically, therefore, we anticipate that

> H10: The positive association between legislative resources and incumbency rates stipulated in H1 will obtain only under relatively low levels of political corruption.

14.5 Analysis

To test these propositions, we estimate linear regression models in which the dependent variable is the incumbency rate for each observed assembly election. We operationalize this variable as the percentage of legislators elected in a given general election who were also elected in the previous general election. After presenting our initial results, we then employ instrumental variable (IV) regression to address endogeneity concerns and show the robustness of our findings.

For our independent variables, we employ the data reported in earlier chapters on electoral system, cameral structure, and rules, as well as on the resources available to members via legislative staffs, committee assignments, and salaries. Using this data and following Mayhew's argument, we create a Legislative Resources

---

[15] De Vries and Solaz (2017) and Incerti (2020) provide useful summaries of the extensive literature. Yet, the overall effect of political corruption on incumbency rates may be complex, as a significant number of field experiments find that the electoral impact of anti-corruption interventions is "small in magnitude in actual elections" (Incerti 2020: 761).

index that gives equal weight to four factors: (1) the size of the legislative staff (per member), (2) the number of permanent legislative committees, (3) whether a member commonly serves on more than one such committee, and (4) the guaranteed minimum salary per member (divided by GNI per capita). Each indicator varies substantially within our sample; for ease of comparison, we rescale each component from 0 to 1, add them together, and multiply the result by 25, so as to generate a 0–100 scale.[16] The resulting index ranges from assemblies with relatively smaller staffs, lower salaries, and fewer committees (such as the Swiss National Council) to those with much larger staffs, higher salaries, and extensive committee systems (such as the US House of Representatives).[17]

For our other variables, we rely on widely used measures in comparative research. To capture regime characteristics that facilitate progressive ambition, we include binary variables for Bicameral, Presidential, and Federal constitutions.[18] For constraints on re-election opportunities, we use the Incentive to Cultivate a Personal Vote (ICPV) index (Carey and Shugart 1995; Johnson and Wallack 2012). Recall that this index ranges from 1 to 12, with higher scores indicating electoral systems that compared to programmatic party competition provide greater incentives for the personal vote. We also include our Term Length variable to measure the maximum constitutional inter-election period, which in our sample ranges from two to six years.

Finally, for our voter demand variables we use log(GDP per Capita), GDP Growth, and the Corruption Perceptions Index (CPI), all lagged one year, to capture the overall prosperity and level of corruption, respectively, in the year preceding the election. CPI, published by Transparency International (TI), assigns each country an annual corruption score ranging from 0 (extremely corrupt) to 100 (extremely clean). To make our Corruption index easier to interpret, we reverse the TI scale, so that higher values indicate more corruption. Table 14.3 explains the operationalization and source of each of our independent variables and Table 14.4 provides summary statistics on these variables.

Table 14.2 shows the results of our regression analyses. We test each group of variables on their own (Models 1–5) and then jointly in Models 6 and 7. To prevent countries with term limits from biasing our analysis, we exclude Mexico, Bolivia, Costa Rica, Ecuador, and the Philippines, which gives us a total of 262 elections

---

[16] To avoid having outliers distort our scaling approach, we first remove any outliers before scaling and then set them to either the minimum (0) or maximum (1) value. All our results, however, are substantively similar if we do not treat outliers separately from other observations.

[17] We are missing data on staff for six countries (Nepal, Niger, Nigeria, Papua New Guinea, Senegal, and South Africa) and salary for four countries (Liberia, Malawi, Nicaragua, and Niger). We impute these missing values using each country's GDP per capita, time since independence, region, size of parliament, and level of urbanization. We find similar results if we instead exclude these countries from the analyses that follow.

[18] The variable Presidential is equal to 1 if a country has a presidential system, and 0 if it is parliamentary or semi-presidential. We use the coding provided by Robert Elgie (see Chapter 11).

Table 14.2 Legislative resources, corruption, and incumbency

				DV: Incumbency Rate			
	(1)	(2)	(3)	(4)	(5)	(6)	(7)
Legislative Resources	-0.099				0.584***	0.036	0.465***
	(0.153)				(0.193)	(0.079)	(0.157)
Institutions							
Bicameral		-0.426				-3.638	-5.116
		(4.622)				(3.086)	(3.102)
Presidential		-12.059**				-0.979	1.143
		(5.873)				(3.441)	(3.441)
Federal		11.859				0.169	2.592
		(8.158)				(4.256)	(3.868)
Constraints							
ICPV			1.256**			1.008***	0.697**
			(0.521)			(0.367)	(0.346)
Term Length			-13.653***			-7.431***	-5.195**
			(2.628)			(2.405)	(2.250)
Prosperity and Corruption							
log(GDP per Capita)				5.154***		5.555***	6.255***
				(1.849)		(1.732)	(1.549)
GDP Growth				0.619***		0.647**	0.742***
				(0.307)		(0.253)	(0.248)
Corruption				-0.359***	-0.183	-0.267**	0.091
				(0.120)	(0.120)	(0.114)	(0.38)
Conditional Effect							
Legislative Resources x Corruption					-0.011***		-0.009***
					(0.003)		(0.003)
Constant	51.893***	49.221***	97.359***	10.690	52.685***	32.008	0.697
	(5.464)	(3.157)	(11.258)	(21.441)	(5.957)	(23.325)	(24.086)
Observations	262	262	262	262	262	262	262
R²	0.008	0.116	0.272	0.501	0.513	0.594	0.623

Note: ICPV: Incentive to Cultivate a Personal Vote.
*p<0.1; **p<0.05; ***p<0.001

Table 14.3 Operationalization of independent variables

Variable	Description	Data Sources
Legislative Resources Index	Gives equal weight to the four components below, rescaled to be a 0–100 scale	Authors
Number of Committees	Number of substantive, permanent committees	Authors
Staff per Legislator	Number of full-time, permanent staff divided by the number of MPs	Authors
Multiple Committees	Equal to 1 if a member can commonly serve on more than one committee and 0 otherwise	Authors
Log(Salary/GNI per Capita)	Guaranteed minimum salary of an MP divided by the gross national income per capita	Authors
Corruption	Scores countries by their perceived levels of corruption from 0 (extremely clean) to 100 (extremely corrupt)	Transparency International (2000-2018, reverse scale of Corruption Perceptions Index)
Control Variables		
Bicameral	Equal to 1 if a country has a bicameral legislature and 0 if it has a unicameral legislature	IPU (2019)
Presidential	Equal to 1 if a country has a presidential system and 0 if a country has a parliamentary or semi-presidential system	Elgie (2019)
Federal	Equal to 1 if a country has a federal system and 0 if it has a unitary system	IPU (2019)
ICPV	Incentive to Cultivate a Personal Vote index, which ranges from 1 to 12	Carey and Shugart (1995), Johnson and Wallack (2012), Authors
Term Length	Constitutional inter-election period	IPU (2019)
Log(GDP per Capita)	GDP per capita (current US$), lagged 1 year	IMF (2019)
GDP Growth	Annual percentage change in real GDP growth, lagged 1 year	IMF (2019)

Note: Data sources listed as "Authors" involve original data collection by scraping the official websites of country legislatures, direct contact with national legislative staff, and direct contact with country experts.

Table 14.4 Summary statistics

Variable	Mean	SD	Min	Max	N
Incumbency Rate	47.81	(21.012)	7.10	89.7	262
Legislative Resources Index	41.25	(19.180)	3.91	90.33	262
Number of Committees	19.60	(10.218)	5	84	262
Staff per Legislator	5.69	(6.431)	0.40	29.70	262
Multiple Committees	0.61	(0.488)	0	1	262
Log(Salary/GNI per Capita)	1.33	(0.891)	−0.15	4.48	262
Corruption	44.65	(22.804)	3	84	262
Control Variables					
Bicameral	0.52	(0.501)	0	1	262
Presidential	0.32	(0.468)	0	1	262
Federal	0.23	(0.419)	0	1	262
ICPV	5.31	(3.995)	1	12	262
Term Length	4.12	(0.693)	2	6	262
Log(GDP per Capita)	9.31	(1.407)	5.36	11.53	262
GDP Growth	2.90	(3.278)	−9.10	25.00	262

Note: ICPV: Incentive to Cultivate a Personal Vote.

in 63 democracies. All models are estimated with robust standard errors clustered at the country level. We choose not to include fixed effects in our main analyses, given that many of our independent variables do not vary over time within countries, but we find similar results if fixed effects are included where possible or if we take the median values of variables and analyze the data at the country level.

We first find that our Legislative Resources index does not reach conventional levels of significance. Thus, there is no clear evidence that resources such as larger staffs, more extensive committee systems, and higher salaries universally facilitate higher incumbency rates (when we rerun the analyses for each of the four components of the Legislative Resources index, we find similar null effects).

We next consider institutional (regime) effects on incumbency rates. As expected, we find only modest support for our expectations regarding institutions that might promote progressive ambition (raise the value of A) and thus reduce re-election rates. Specifically, there is some evidence that presidential democracies have lower incumbency rates, compared with parliamentary or semi-presidential ones. Model 2 suggests that presidential democracies have an incumbency rate that on average is 12.06 percentage points lower, although this effect largely disappears in Model 6. Thus, the greater supply and attractiveness of alternative offices in presidential systems may modestly lower re-election rates, presumably through their effect on progressive ambition. However, since presidential democracies are also generally less prosperous than parliamentary ones, the effects of regime type and prosperity may be hard to disentangle. We find no evidence of similar effects for bicameralism or federalism.

Concerning electoral constraints, we find that Incentive to Cultivate a Personal Vote (ICPV) has a positive and significant effect on incumbency. Countries with electoral systems that empower individual legislators to make their own reelection decisions and encourage the personal vote have substantially higher incumbency rates than countries where parties control ballot access and citizens have no opportunity to cast a personal vote.

Our results for the effect of Term Length on incumbency are strong, robust, and consistent with our expectations. The shorter the constitutional inter-election period, the higher the incumbency rate. With longer terms, legislators may be more likely to leave their post, either voluntarily (resignation) or involuntarily (e.g., death, scandal), between elections. Moreover, under longer terms incumbents may face stronger challengers motivated by a larger W (value of office).

Table 14.2 also provides strong indications that voter demand matters. As predicted, incumbents are significantly more likely to hold onto their seats under greater economic prosperity (log(GDP per Capita)) and growth (GDP Growth) and less corruption (Corruption). The effects of GDP Growth and Corruption hold even with the inclusion of country and year fixed effects. This suggests that incumbency rates are also sensitive to within-country changes over time: when countries increase their economic growth or limit corruption, their incumbency rate rises.

Finally, we find that the electoral effect of legislative resources indeed depends on corruption levels. The Legislative Resources x Corruption interaction term is negative and significant in Models 5 and 7. Consistently with our hypothesis, legislative resources have a stronger, more positive effect on the incumbency rates of legislators under relatively low levels of political corruption compared to more corrupt countries.[19]

To better understand the relationship between legislative resources and incumbency across different levels of corruption, Figure 14.3 provides a marginal effects plot. The plot includes the linear interaction model (black line) and 95 percent confidence interval (gray shaded area) for Model 7 in Table 14.2 together with a histogram along the x-axis to show the relative distribution of Corruption values in our dataset.

For countries with relatively low corruption, the effects of legislative resources are not only statistically significant, but also substantively strong. For a country with an exceptionally clean government such as Denmark, Finland, or New Zealand (median Corruption: 6), we estimate that a one standard deviation increase in Legislative Resources (19.2 points on our index scale) would increase

---

[19] All four components of Legislative Resources are also negative and significant when interacted with Corruption in our fully specified model.

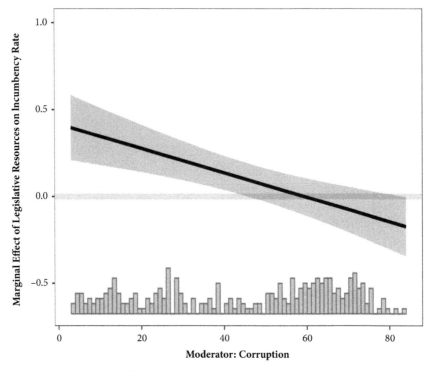

Figure 14.3 Marginal effect of legislative resources on incumbency rate by corruption level

Note: Marginal effects plot generated using the interflex R package (Hainmueller et al. 2019).

the incumbency rate by as much as 7.9 percentage points. For countries that are more corrupt, such as Nigeria and the Ukraine (median Corruption: 74), the estimated marginal effect is actually negative and suggests that a similar increase in Legislative Resources would instead decrease the incumbency rate by about 3.7 percentage points.

In sum, we find more support for the hypothesized main effects of electoral constraints, economic conditions, and corruption, and less for regime effects. Across our full sample of democratic elections, our results suggest some consistent behaviors among legislators and voters. The ambitions of incumbent legislators to seek re-election appear to be constrained by factors such as the electoral system (ICPV) and term length. Likewise, we find strong evidence that voters across these 63 democracies reward incumbents for economic prosperity and punish them for corruption. In contrast, there is scant evidence that institutions which foster progressive ambition significantly affect re-election rates.

Similarly, the legislative resources identified by Mayhew (1974) for the US Congress—large staffs, extensive committee systems, and higher salaries—do not appear to facilitate members' re-election across our full sample of democracies.

Instead, our results suggest that the effect of legislative resources on incumbency is conditional on the level of political corruption. In less corrupt countries, there is strong evidence that legislative endowments help sustain incumbents much in the way that Mayhew suggests. In highly corrupt countries, however, the effect of legislative resources is less visible and may actually disadvantage incumbents that seek re-election.

14.6 Addressing Endogeneity

While the results support our hypothesis that legislative resources conditionally affect incumbency rates, testing the direction of causality presents some inferential challenges. It is possible that higher incumbency rates could influence the availability of legislative resources, or that some other, unobserved factor could drive both legislative resources and incumbency rates. Both reciprocal causation and confounding thus pose challenges for our analysis.

To address these endogeneity concerns, we instrument for Legislative Resources using the word counts of those sections within national constitutions that describe the lower or unicameral legislative chamber. We expect that longer legislative sections are more likely to contain provisions concerning institutional powers and resources that can benefit incumbent legislators. However, this relationship may not necessarily be linear. As suggested by studies of bureaucracies (e.g., Huber and Shipan 2002), at a certain point, more verbose constitutions may constrain the discretion of legislators rather than empower them. We thus follow Rooney (2019) in modeling the instrument's relationship with the endogenous variable and looking for potential non-linearities.

We construct our instrument by drawing on the English-language constitutions provided by the Comparative Constitutions Project, which covers all our 68 countries.[20] We count the number of words in each country's constitution that discuss the structure or powers of the lower (or unicameral) legislative chamber, and take the natural logarithm of this number, given the skew of the word-count data. As an initial validation of this measure, we find that constitutions with longer legislative sections are significantly more likely to elaborate the oversight authority of standing committees and give the legislature, rather than other actors, authority to determine its own members' compensation. In Table 14.5, we thus use legislative word-count to instrument for Legislative Resources.[21]

An instrumental variable (IV) approach can enable causal identification so long as our instrument (legislative word-count) is sufficiently correlated with the endogenous variable (legislative resources) and only influences the dependent

[20] Three countries in our sample (Israel, New Zealand, and the United Kingdom) do not have written constitutions. Nevertheless, the Comparative Constitutions Project identifies for each country the

Table 14.5 Legislative resources, corruption, and incumbency (IV analysis)

	DV: Incumbency Rate			
	(1)	(2)	(3)	(4)
Legislative Resources	−0.096	1.058*	0.460**	1.020***
	(0.164)	(0.579)	(0.220)	(0.384)
Corruption	−0.608***	−0.313***	−0.058	0.335**
	(0.050)	(0.108)	(0.174)	(0.163)
Legislative Resources			−0.013***	−0.015***
x Corruption			(0.004)	(0.003)
Constant	78.940***	13.157	56.369***	−26.309
	(5.716)	(29.870)	(7.973)	(17.848)
Observations	262	262	262	262
Control Variables	No	Yes	No	Yes

Notes: Table presents second-stage results. The IV for Legislative Resources is the natural logarithm of the number of words in each country's constitution that discuss the lower (or unicameral) legislative chamber. Controls include the institutional, electoral constraints, and economic variables from Table 14.1.
$^{*}p < 0.1$, $^{**}p<0.05$, $^{***}p<0.01$.

variable (incumbency rates) through its effect on that same endogenous variable. Our word-count measure satisfies both criteria. First, the F-statistic (21.4) from the first stage of our two-stage least squares regressions exceeds the commonly accepted threshold of 10, suggesting that weak identification is not a problem. Second, while national constitutions can affect legislative behavior in various ways, there is no obvious alternative pathway through which the number of words describing a country's legislature could affect incumbency rates that does not involve the structure or powers of the legislature. Moreover, most of the constitutions in our sample were written well prior to our period of analysis, and few have had their legislative sections revised, making reverse causality unlikely. In sum, our word-count measure is plausibly exogenous, making it a good instrument for Legislative Resources.

Ultimately, our IV analysis (Table 14.5) generates results similar to our earlier models: the presence of greater legislative resources can lead to higher incumbency rates, but only in countries with lower levels of corruption. This causal evidence

document or set of documents that serve a similar function. We use the word counts from these documents in our IV analyses. All our results hold if we instead exclude these three countries. Comparative Constitutions Project, https://www.constituteproject.org/, accessed January 2021.
[21] Corruption is also possibly an endogenous variable, but efforts to find a suitable instrument for it are heavily debated. In particular, two commonly used instruments—ethno-linguistic fractionalization and political stability—are unlikely to satisfy the exclusion restriction of only affecting incumbency rates through their influence on development or corruption. With that being said, we find similar results using either of these two instruments.

consistent with our initial analyses gives us further confidence in our theory regarding the link between legislative resources, corruption, and incumbency.

14.7 Conclusion

In a Schumpeterian view of democracy, it is electoral competition that keeps members on their toes and responsive to their constituents. It is this force that limits rent-seeking and abuses of power and that brings about political innovation. In a world of perfect electoral competition, we would expect tightly contested elections and frequent alternations in office. But precisely these features of electoral competition entail some consequences that may not be entirely benign. Legislative effectiveness requires expertise and experience, which may well go missing in a world of highly competitive elections. A world in which political office-holders come and go, frequently and unpredictably, is not the paradise of your typical citizen. At the other extreme, however, a firmly entrenched politician may be just as autocratic and unresponsive to voters as a firmly entrenched civil servant. A well-functioning legislative assembly cannot sacrifice either capacity or accountability. And whatever the optimal balance between electoral competitiveness and legislative experience, the ability of incumbents to win re-election is an issue of consequence.

In many national legislatures, incumbency is the single most powerful predictor of electoral success. Yet, as this chapter has shown, incumbent re-election rates vary substantially across the world's 68 largest democracies. To understand this variation in re-election rates, we must understand the context in which legislators decide whether or not to pursue re-election and the institutional and societal conditions that can affect such decisions. When incumbents make decisions about re-election bids, they generally have two main alternatives: other (often meaning higher) political office or retirement from politics. And incumbents make such decisions in anticipation of the judgments of the voters that ultimately decide their fate.

In his seminal work, Mayhew (1974) suggests that the high levels of incumbency in the US House of Representatives are due to features of legislative organization that facilitate re-election. We have tested the cross-national generalizability of this argument by constructing an index of legislative resources similar to the features Mayhew identified. While few legislatures endow their members with as generous resources as does the US House, even in those that do (such as Nigeria and the Philippines), incumbents do not fare anywhere near as well as those in the United States. As we have argued and our data has shown, this is because voters may evaluate incumbents more critically if political corruption is rife. Thus, the advantage that incumbents can gain from legislative resources is dependent on a relatively low level of political corruption.

The incumbents' alternatives also matter. While decisions about political retirement are affected by a host of personal and social circumstances that are often idiosyncratic, we have sought to identify institutional conditions under which progressive ambition may drive an incumbent to eschew re-election. Our analysis shows that incumbent re-election rates are somewhat lower in presidential democracies than elsewhere. Overall, however, opportunities for progressive ambition have only modest effects on legislative turnover. Specific electoral rules do matter in more robust ways. Incumbency rates are systematically lower in democracies where there are fewer opportunities for candidates to cultivate a personal vote and where legislative terms are longer.

The interaction between legislative resources and corruption is one of the strongest and most interesting results of our analysis. It suggests that political "engineering" has its limits. Legislative incumbents can indeed be vested with powers and perquisites that contribute to their political longevity, but only as long as most citizens have reason to believe that such resources will be used for the public good rather than in corrupt, ineffective, or self-serving ways. While this lesson may be sobering for political incumbents, it is one for which ordinary citizens have at least a qualified reason to cheer.

References

Agerberg, Mattias. 2020. "The Lesser Evil? Corruption Voting and the Importance of Clean Alternatives." *Comparative Political Studies* 53 2: 253–287.

Ariga, Kenichi. 2015. "Incumbency Disadvantage under Electoral Rules with Intra-party Competition: Evidence from Japan." *The Journal of Politics* 77(3): 874–887.

Brace, Paul. 1984. "Progressive Ambition in the House: A Probabilistic Approach." *American Journal of Political Science* 46(2): 556–571.

Carey, John M., and Matthew Soberg Shugart. 1995. "Incentives to Cultivate a Personal Vote: A Rank Ordering of Electoral Formulas." *Electoral Studies* 14(4): 417–439.

Cox, Gary W., and Jonathan N. Katz. 1996. "Why Did the Incumbency Advantage in US House Elections Grow?" *American Journal of Political Science* 40(2): 478–497.

De Vries, Catherine E., and Hector Solaz. 2017. "The Electoral Consequences of Corruption." *Annual Review of Political Science* 20: 391–408.

Duch, Raymond M., and Randolph T. Stevenson. 2008. *The Economic Vote: How Political and Economic Institutions Condition Electoral Results.* Cambridge: Cambridge University Press.

Ferraz, Claudio, and Frederico Finan. 2008. "Exposing Corrupt Politicians: The Effects of Brazil's Publicly Released Audits on Electoral Outcomes." *The Quarterly Journal of Economics* 123(2): 703–745.

Fiorina, Maurice P. 1977. "The Case of the Vanishing Marginals: The Bureaucracy Did It." *American Political Science Review* 71(1): 177–181.

Fiva, Jon H., and Daniel M. Smith. 2018. "Political Dynasties and the Incumbency Advantage in Party-Centered Environments." *American Political Science Review* 112(3): 706–712.

Gouglas, Athanassios, Bart Maddens, and Marleen Brans. 2017. "Determinants of Legislative Turnover in Western Europe, 1945–2014." *European Journal of Political Research* 57(3): 637–661.

Huber, John D., and Charles R. Shipan. 2002. *Deliberate Discretion?: The Institutional Foundations of Bureaucratic Autonomy*. Cambridge: Cambridge University Press.

Incerti, Trevor. 2020. "Corruption Information and Vote Share: A Meta-Analysis and Lessons for Experimental Design." *American Political Science Review* 114(3): 761–774.

Jacobson, Gary C. 2015. "It's Nothing Personal: The Decline of the Incumbency Advantage in US House Elections." *The Journal of Politics* 77(3): 861–873.

Johnson, Joel W., and Jessica S. Wallack 2012. *Electoral Systems and the Personal Vote*. URL: https://dataverse.harvard.edu/dataset.xhtml?persistentId=hdl:1902.1/17901.

Klašnja, Marko. 2015. "Corruption and the Incumbency Disadvantage: Theory and Evidence." *The Journal of Politics* 77(4): 928–942.

Klašnja, Marko, and Rocío Titiunik. 2017. "The Incumbency Curse: Weak Parties, Term Limits, and Unfulfilled Accountability." *American Political Science Review* 111(1): 129–148.

Kousser, Thad. 2005. *Term Limits and the Dismantling of State Legislative Professionalism*. New York: Cambridge University Press.

Krehbiel, Keith. 1991. *Information and Legislative Organization*. Ann Arbor: University of Michigan Press.

Krupnikov, Yanna, and Charles R. Shipan. 2020. "Voter Uncertainty, Political Institutions, and Legislative Turnover." *Political Science Research and Methods* 8(1): 14–29.

Mares, Isabela, and Giancarlo Visconti. 2019. "Voting for the Lesser Evil: Evidence from a Conjoint Experiment in Romania." *Political Science Research and Methods* 6: 8(2): 315–328.

Matland, Richard E., and Donley T. Studlar. 2004. "Determinants of Legislative Turnover: A Cross-National Analysis." *British Journal of Political Science* 34(1): 87–108.

Mayhew, David. R. 1974. *Congress: The Electoral Connection*. New Haven: Yale University Press.

Micozzi, Juan Pablo. 2014. "From House to Home: Linking Multi-Level Ambition and Legislative Performance in Argentina." *Journal of Legislative Studies* 20(3): 265–284.

Moral, Mert, H. Ege Ozen, and Efe Tokdemir. 2015. "Bringing the Incumbency Advantage into Question for Proportional Representation." *Electoral Studies* 40: 56–65.

Phillips, Anne. 1995. *The Politics of Presence*. Oxford: Clarendon Press.

Redmond, Paul, and John Regan. 2015. "Incumbency Advantage in a Proportional Electoral System: A Regression Discontinuity Analysis of Irish Elections." *European Journal of Political Economy* 38: 244–256.

Rohde, David W. 1979. "Risk-Bearing and Progressive Ambition: The Case of Members of the United States House of Representatives." *American Journal of Political Science* 23(1): 1–26.

Rooney, Bryan. 2019. "Emergency Powers in Democracies and International Conflict." *Journal of Conflict Resolution* 63(1): 644–671.

Rothstein, Bo, and Aiysha Varraich. 2017. *Making Sense of Corruption*. Cambridge: Cambridge University Press.

Schlesinger, Joseph A. 1966. *Ambition and Politics: Political Careers in the United States.* Chicago, IL: Rand McNally.

Schwindt-Bayer, Leslie A. 2005. "The Incumbency Disadvantage and Women's Election to Legislative Office." *Electoral Studies* 28: 227–244.

Smith, Daniel M., and Shane Martin. 2017. "Political Dynasties and the Selection of Cabinet Ministers." *Legislative Studies Quarterly* 42(1): 131–165.

Uppal, Yogesh. 2009. "The Disadvantaged Incumbents: Estimating Incumbency Effects in Indian State Legislatures." *Public Choice* 138(1): 9–27.

Winters, Matthew S., and Rebecca Weitz-Shapiro. 2013. "Lacking Information or Condoning Corruption: When Do Voters Support Corrupt Politicians?" *Comparative Politics* 45(4): 418–436.

15

Democratic Assemblies and Contemporary Challenges

As the various chapters of this book have demonstrated, the legislative assemblies of contemporary democracies vary widely and in many ways. In our first chapter, we quoted James Madison's argument that in a well-functioning republic, legislative assemblies need the skills necessary to make good policy as well as fidelity to the people. The likelihood that a legislative assembly will faithfully serve their democratic principles thus depends on two conditions: (1) the capacity of the assembly to act effectively in public policy making, and (2) the strength and credibility of the electoral mechanisms by which the voters can hold their representatives to account. These are the conditions of capacity and popular accountability, respectively. Yet, capacity and accountability can be established in a number of different ways through a variety of structures and processes, and more or less successfully. Legislative assemblies differ in the ways in which they are designed as well as in their functions. Also, they differ in the trade-offs they make between capacity, accountability, and other values.

For the 68 democratic assemblies analyzed here, we have explored how members are selected and for what length of terms, the degree to which the composition of the chambers reflect the electorate, and their cameral designs. We have surveyed their leaderships and resources and the characteristics of legislative parties and committees. And we have examined the roles of legislative assemblies in lawmaking, budgeting, government formation and termination, and executive oversight.

Yet, the complexity and diversity of the world of democratic legislative assemblies can be appreciated through a relatively simple conceptual lens. We have thus argued that legislative assemblies can be understood by focusing on the interests of the voters that select the assemblies, the members who serve in them, and the leaders who seek to control and shape what members do. All assemblies face challenges of capacity and accountability, and yet there are numerous ways in which they can confront these challenges. These various institutional responses and designs generate different benefits for members, leaders, and voters. Accordingly, we have developed ideal-typical conceptions of a members' assembly, a leaders' assembly, and a voters' assembly, each representing a bundle of institutional characteristics that particularly reflect the interests of one of these classes of actors.

Legislative Assemblies. Shane Martin and Kaare W. Strøm, Oxford University Press.
© Shane Martin and Kaare W. Strøm (2023). DOI: 10.1093/oso/9780198890829.003.0015

Typically, leaders' assemblies prioritize capacity and build it through central-ized and cohesive political parties, whereas members' assemblies rely on more decentralized capacity through permanent committees as well as parties, and vot-ers' assemblies on civil society organizations and public transparency as well as on internal assembly resources. The capacity-enhancing role of assembly com-mittees in turn depends their access to expertise and private information about specific policy areas and the administrative and regulatory institutions that control them.

Accountability is in all democratic assemblies attained mainly through free, fair, and competitive elections and guarantees of such civil rights as freedom of speech, assembly, and association, but again there are differences between assembly types. Leaders' assemblies vest accountability mainly in political parties and in regular, though not necessarily frequent, elections. Members' assemblies rely more exten-sively on the accountability and responsiveness of individual legislators to their respective constituencies, whereas voters' assemblies are characterized by frequent elections, the availability of recall mechanisms, information transparency, and by various forms of direct citizen access to the legislative arena.

What determines the relative power of members, leaders, and voters in existing legislative politics? The rules and routines that characterize different legislative assemblies certainly matter. Some rules, typically those concerning cameral struc-ture, eligibility, and voting rights, are constitutional and thus often well entrenched and of long standing. Others are statutory and contained in ordinary legislation. Much of the fine print of legislative organization and procedure, however, is typi-cally found in the standing orders which are easily amendable by the assembly itself (Sieberer et al. 2016). Yet other rules exist simply by convention. Thus, Norway has the second oldest written constitution in the democratic world, dating back to 1814. But many of the contemporary rules that govern the legislative process in Norway bear little resemblance to the formal provisions of the Constitution. Thus, the effective rules governing legislative assemblies may diverge from the formal ones and are rarely static, but evolve over time.

In a previous chapter (Chapter 13) we sought to map and measure more thor-oughly the extent to which real-world legislative assemblies in the world's major democracies approximate the three ideal types we laid out in our first chapter. Our aim was to understand the degree to which each of our real-world legisla-tures is a members' assembly, a leaders' assembly, or a voters' assembly, and how these different types of assemblies overlap in the real world. For these purposes, we constructed an index for each of our three types of assemblies and scored each of our 68 national legislatures accordingly. We found substantial cross-national variation but observed also that few existing national assemblies closely approx-imate any one of our ideal types. More commonly, existing national assemblies represent mixes and compromises between these legislative ideal types. We also found only modest empirical correlations between our three indices, so that it is entirely possible for particular legislatures to score high on two assembly indices simultaneously. This is most notable for a members' assembly and a voters' assembly, as indicated for example by the high score of the US House of Representatives on both indices, whereas a match between a members' assembly and a leaders' assembly is less in evidence. The latter result is partly a consequence of our index constructions, but more fundamentally a reflection of the fact that the most important institutional conflicts of interest in legislative design run between party leaders and ordinary members.

In this concluding chapter we will discuss the circumstances that might lead legislative assemblies to resemble one or the other of these categories. We will also discuss the place of legislative assemblies in autocratic societies and the paths that might lead democratic assemblies to transition into non-democratic ones. We conclude by exploring the prospects for democratic legislative assemblies in the contemporary world.

15.1 The Forces that Shape Legislative Assemblies

What are the forces that shape legislative assemblies, and to what extent do such assemblies change over time? It would be comforting to think that legislative assemblies are typically constitutionally designed to be voters' assemblies, and that any deviation from such forms must be unintended. Though such assumptions may seem naïve, there may be a kernel of truth even in optimistic beliefs. The institutional features of legislative assemblies are among the first issues confronting constitution makers in such situations as the fall of a dictator, the resolution of a civil or interstate war, or the successful conclusion of a struggle for national independence. In such constitutional moments, those who design assembly institutions may genuinely desire most of all to make them represent popular opinion, at least in a form reflected through elite concerns and considerations. Surely, the American founders desired to make their House of Representatives more of a voters' assembly than any national assembly that existed at that time (while at the same time they intended the Senate to be much more of a members' assembly). Such concerns may be especially prominent in cases where the framers are not themselves candidates for political leadership, or closely allied with those who are. Thus, we expect voters' assemblies to be most likely where the framers themselves have the lowest prospects of inhabiting these bodies, or where the constitutional negotiations take place under something approaching a Rawlsian veil of ignorance (Rawls 1971), in which those who design the constitution have no reliable information about the roles that they are likely to play within it.[1]

---

[1] One way to involve voters more in issues of institutional design has been to create citizens' assemblies as part of constitutional amendment initiatives. Citizens' assemblies are mini-publics, usually

When these conditions do not hold, however, the desire to make assemblies responsive to voters may be tempered not only by efficiency or competence concerns (assembly capacity, in our language), but also by calculations of personal advantage among potential candidates for elective office (see Bucur et al. 2018; Elster et al. 2018). Under such circumstances, the preferences that are constitutionally embodied will vary with the offices and powers of those who write them, as well as with the circumstances in which they were drafted. Thus, the Constitution of the French Fifth Republic prescribes an assembly much more committed to the interests of its leaders, and less to those of its members, than its Fourth Republic predecessor. No doubt a major reason was that the 1958 Constitution which introduced the Fifth Republic was drafted under the supervision of the incumbent prime minister and prospective president, Charles de Gaulle (see Huber 1996; Jackson 2018). Generally, we would expect that the more the rules are designed by incumbent or prospective rulers, the more they will favor such leaders. Moreover, France in 1958 was in a crisis mode, in which the costs of a prolonged colonial war and the prospect of domestic civil conflict lent strength to demands for stronger leadership, providing the opportunity for a move to a leaders' assembly.

Regardless of the initial concerns of the constitutional framers, the powers, functions, and procedures of legislative assemblies will typically evolve, often in ways unanticipated by the original framers, or even directly contrary to their desires. The best guide to such changes will typically be the interests of those who come to populate these assemblies, and especially their members and leaders. Thus, legislative bodies with common origins may over time come to take on more of the typical features of a leaders' assembly, as in Victorian Britain (Cox 1987), or those of a members' assembly, as in the United States Congress for much of the twentieth century. The divergence between these two trajectories may be explained by the existence of the confidence vote in the British constitution, by the greater regional divisions of American politics, by the federal institutions that reflected these divisions, or by the more pressing need for political efficiency in a monarchy frequently engaged in or threatened by armed conflict. At any rate, both assemblies evolved, and it is indeed likely that institutional drift generally is likely to weaken, rather than strengthen, the typical features of a voters' assembly. Hence, all else equal, the voters' assembly type may be most common in relatively young regimes, whereas more "mature" assemblies will tend to drift toward either

comprising randomly selected citizens charged with deliberating and making recommendations on political reforms or policy issues (Ratner 2004). For example, the 2006 Dutch Civic Forum included 140 randomly selected citizens who were tasked with exploring electoral system reform. The Irish Citizens' Assembly 2016–18 involved 99 randomly selected citizens, whose mandate included discussing fixed-term parliaments and the electoral system.

a members' model, or, more likely perhaps, a leaders' type (where leaders within the assembly can cartelize power away from both voters and members).

Indeed, on our voters' assembly index, most high scorers are countries with relatively recent constitutions, such as the Philippines and Nigeria. Regionally, most of these regimes are located in Asia or the Americas. Interestingly, the top 12 voters' assemblies include only one European country, Poland. Indeed, the top three European countries are Poland, Romania, and Portugal, underscoring the tendency for recent constitutions to account for comparatively high scores on this index. Conversely, many of the more mature European democracies boast only low (France) to middling (the United Kingdom) scores as voters' assemblies.

15.2 Challenges to Legislative Assemblies

In democratic societies, legislative assembly gain their authority through electoral delegation from the citizens they serve. In the first chapter of this book, we noted that competitive elections are critical to democracy and that sustaining effective democratic delegation through competitive elections is a tall order. Delegation, though often mutually beneficial, is always risky. Moreover, delegation through democratic elections differs from delegation in other walks of life, such as economic exchanges, in ways that often make political delegation riskier. One such difference is that in politics delegation is not a purely voluntary and temporary granting of authority. When I go to my attorney with my legal concerns or to my car mechanic with my auto problems (and preferably not the other way around), I can revoke my grant of authority at any time (though I may owe my agent a fee). In politics, delegation is commonly neither voluntary nor temporary. I do not have the option of not being represented (or taxed) by anybody, and though I can (with the help of other voters) kick the present rascals out, I cannot avoid having somebody (perhaps the devil I don't know) represent me.

A second important difference is that in many other situations in which we delegate authority, we can choose among numerous potential agents. And even if there are few good attorneys or car mechanics in my town, I can take my business elsewhere. This is typically not so in politics, where the "supply side" of agents is typically highly restricted and often cartel-like or even monopolistic. If I live in the United States and like neither Democrats nor Republicans, my options are not promising. If I live in North Korea and do not like Communists (or specifically the Kim family), my predicament is considerably worse.

Finally, and most ominously, political delegation means giving my agent coercive powers, which he could use against me. In most situations of non-political delegation, this is not true, and the risks are accordingly lower. And while the financial risks in economic delegation may be large, there is, unlike politics, typically no prospect of physical harm or even loss of life.[2] Thus, the fact that politics ultimately rests on powers of coercion makes political delegation a much riskier undertaking than most other ways in which we conditionally grant authority in social or economic life.

Political delegation is thus risky and effective accountability essential. If accountability in legislative assemblies is compromised, the result is often that the likelihood of alternation in control of the legislature (and possibly also the executive branch) is reduced. The ultimate threat is that any prospect of a lawful and institutionalized transfer of power is eliminated. Thus, any discussion of the potential downfalls of legislative assemblies as vehicles of popular representation will need to consider the risk of backsliding into a particular type of non-democratic assembly, which we call a dictator's assembly.

Our description of democratic party leaders and the leaders' assembly assumes that they can and will freely compete for control of the assembly with a realistic expectation of turnover. This obviously contrasts with an assembly dominated by a singular leader in which there is no prospect of alternation in this office and perhaps no plausible scenario in which such a change could happen because "the rules of the game" are so thoroughly rigged. This latter situation is what we would expect in autocratic, hegemonic, or semi-democratic societies such as Mexico until the 1990s or the Russian Federation at the time of writing. In such assemblies, policies will be dictated by the preferences of this leader, whose policies will typically provide generous rents to the leader himself or herself, as well as to the leader's assembly supporters, entourage, family, and winning coalition (Bueno de Mesquita et al. 2005), and with little prospect of popular accountability. This type of assembly fails Madison's requirements on at least one dimension, and indeed commonly on both. Specifically, a dictator's assembly is not accountable to ordinary citizens, because it is instead responsive to, and indeed dominated by, some autocrat or autocratic institution. For much the same reason, its subservience to an autocratic ruler, the dictator's assembly typically also lacks capacity.

15.3 The Dictator's Assembly

The dictators' assembly has received minimal attention in our book, since it is an assembly type associated with autocracy, rather than democracy. The actor whose interests it serves, the autocratic ruler, is one that by definition we should not find in a democracy. And our concern in this volume, of course, is with democracies and their national assemblies. Yet, the dictators' assembly is sadly relevant in

---

[2] Except in medical situations or if I for example ask for assistance from a member of a syndicate of organized crime.

the real world, even in regimes ostensibly committed to democratic ideals. This is because of the risk that a democratic assembly may transition to a dictators' assembly as elected representatives and their leaders pursue their own interests and the political "good life" and weaken their bonds of accountability.

Dictators' assemblies may take many forms. Some, such as the Supreme Soviet of the USSR during much of Stalin's rule, may be nothing more than transparently sham assemblies, with no real authority and no accountability to anybody but the supreme leader. Yet, the variety and importance of dictators' assemblies have increased, as the autocratic world has come to consist of fewer totalitarian regimes, such as Stalin's USSR, and more hegemonic and hybrid regimes, as in many parts of the developing world today (Gandhi 2008; Schuler and Malesky 2014).

Recent scholarship has shown that legislative assemblies can be highly institutionalized even in autocratic regimes, and that they may perform a range of identifiable political functions. At a minimum, establishing and sustaining a legislative assembly may bolster the legitimacy of autocrats domestically and internationally. This may be particularly important for relatively weak and needy autocrats in regions such as the Middle East or Central America who seek the support of leaders in the United States or the European Union (Rustow 1985; Malesky and Schuler 2009; Levitsky and Way 2010). Such concerns may have been particularly prominent after the end of the Cold War in the early 1990s, when many Western governments were keen to shift their attention from global security concerns to promotion of democracy and human rights and to support regimes that promised them.

Another function of dictators' assemblies may be to provide information to rulers about their support and about political preferences among regular citizens. Dictators' assemblies may also function as venues for the distribution of patronage (Lust-Okar 2005) or as vehicles with which to co-opt at least the more moderate or pliable parts of the opposition (Gandhi 2008). Finally, even dictators' assemblies, though hardly popularly accountable or highly effective, may play some role in decision making and power sharing (Svolik 2012).

Transitions to a dictator's assembly can happen in any number of ways, but at least two of them are worth discussing in particular. One is dramatic, such as a coup d'état by a group of military commanders or insurgents, as in Nigeria in 1983, and may be more or less pre-meditated or the result of unforeseen circumstances. The other is much more covert but also much more likely to be part of a deliberate power-grabbing design of the executive or some powerful actor within that branch of government (Levitsky and Ziblatt 2009). Although the incumbent chief executive is certainly not the only actor that could instigate such a regime threat, he or she certainly deserves special attention in this discussion.

The first avenue toward creeping autocratization is through the establishment of executive emergency powers, often confirmed or at least tolerated by the national assembly. The recent COVID-19 pandemic has witnessed a series of grants of authority to political executives that would hardly have been imaginable a year or two previously (Bolleyer and Salát 2021). In some cases, these emergency powers were clearly in violation of constitutional principles. In a substantial number of cases, they greatly encroached on established civil rights and liberties, such as freedom of association and privacy rights. In many cases, these measures were adopted with little legislative input and without the regular measures of accountability.

To what extent these emergency powers will pave the way for an erosion of civil liberties as well as legislative power remains to be seen. But there are certainly historical cases in which emergency powers have been used to undermine the constitutional powers of the legislative assembly and to usher in a flagrantly autocratic regime, in which the legislature would play at best a subordinate role as a dictator's assembly.

The prime historical example of such a transition is the emasculation of the German Reichstag (Parliament) after Adolf Hitler's ascent to the chancellorship in 1933. The Weimar Republic's Constitution, adopted shortly after the end of World War I, included Article 48, which granted the president broad emergency powers to circumvent the Reichstag and even impose emergency taxes. Article 48 had been intended for situations of social unrest and economic crisis, which Germany certainly experienced in the 1920s. But in the early 1930s, President Hindenburg invoked these emergency powers to sustain minority governments that would otherwise have found it difficult to survive in the badly polarized national assembly. When Hitler gained the chancellorship on February 1, 1933, he quickly persuaded Hindenburg to dissolve the Reichstag and call new elections, while the emergency powers were also used to suppress press freedom, repeal basic rights, and subjugate those German states, led by Bavaria, that resisted National Socialism. Hitler then moved quickly to dismantle German federalism, abolish the Reichstag through the Enabling Act of March 1933, and in July 1933 to dissolve all parties other than the NSDAP (see Bracher 1973).

Although the German transition was remarkably swift and brutal, similar developments have taken place in other previously democratic countries. The Italian Fascists traveled the same route to the subjugation of all parliamentary opposition, but at a slower pace and while maintaining the façade of the Italian monarchy and tolerating a substantial presence of the Catholic church in Italian social life. In Japan, the Meiji Constitution of 1889 established a bicameral national assembly, with a popularly elected lower chamber and a hereditary upper chamber, much along the lines of the British Parliament. Power was shared between the two chambers and the Emperor, though cabinet ministers were responsible to the latter alone. From 1890 until about 1930, parliamentary democracy seemed to take root, with a consolidating party system, an increasingly inclusive franchise, and an assertive role for the national assembly. Over the course of the 1930s, however, a new emperor (Hirohito) took on a more assertive role, embraced a militaristic agenda, and increasingly selected military officers for his cabinet, thereby sidelining the national assembly. The last elections prior to the fall of the Empire were held in 1937 (Congleton 2011: 485–521).

In more recent times, Venezuela's President Hugo Chávez, in power almost continuously from 1999 to 2013, in various ways gradually undermined the powers of his country's national assembly and transformed it into a dictator's assembly. One of his strategies was to establish an alternative body that could undermine the authority of the national assembly. In a 1999 constitutional reform, Chávez established a constituent assembly, in which his supporters won an overwhelming majority. This constituent assembly subsequently drafted a constitution that made censorship easier and expanded the president's powers. The constituent assembly voted to give itself the power to abolish government institutions and to dismiss officials perceived as corrupt or as operating only in their own interests. The national assembly's authority declined with the growing claims of the constituent assembly and as Chávez himself grew more powerful, eventually extending his presidential term of office and abolishing the term limits that the Constitution had imposed on the president. He packed the courts with his own supporters and arrested or harassed opposition politicians who dared speak out against his government or its policies.

The trajectory of Venezuela's slide into a dictator's assembly under Hugo Chávez is in many ways similar to the path taken by his contemporary Vladimir Putin in the Russian Federation. Putin came to power late in 1999, inheriting the institutions of a complex but largely presidentialist constitution created under Boris Yeltsin and approved by Russian voters in 1993. The Russian Federation borrowed many institutional features from the United States and others from the French Fifth Republic, though with a stronger presidency and a less independent judicial branch than either of those countries. The latter differences would facilitate the erosion of legislative capacity and accountability under Putin's long dominance of Russian politics in the early twenty-first century.

Like Chávez, Putin weakened the constitutional constraints on his presidency by circumventing its term limits and lengthening his presidential term of office. He stifled resistance by extending his control of the mass media and through brutal intimidation and harassment of any political opposition. The bicameral national assembly was weakened and federalism enfeebled through changes in the electoral laws and the powers of the subject territories within the Russian Federation (the Russian "states"). In a peculiarly Russian manner, several of the main opposition parties also obliged by adopting particularly nasty programs or running seriously anachronistic candidates. Like Chávez, Putin also consolidated his own standing among the general population by providing better and more reliable social benefits for people of ordinary means and by attacking members of the upper classes and the business elites (the "oligarchs") (see Fish 2005; Ostrovsky 2017). And, while as Remington (2019) has noted, parliamentary elections were central to Russia's democratization in the 1990s, subsequent reductions in the Duma's capacity and popular accountability ensured that it did not threaten Putin's consolidation of power and the emergence of a semi-authoritarian regime.

Thus, a transition to a dictator's assembly can occur in a number of ways but seems a particular risk in polities with a strong, ambitious, and sometimes charismatic chief executive. The mechanisms by which the transitions takes place can be manifold, but include such ostensibly democratic mechanisms as referendums and constituent assemblies. Emergency powers are certainly useful, and harassment or intimidation of the opposition and any critical media seems a constant. Control of the armed forces or paramilitary organizations is also commonly associated with such transitions.

One disturbingly common feature of executive transgressions on democratic regimes is when incumbent presidents repeal or subvert one of the most common limitations on their power: term limits. Formal or informal term limits for democratic executives have been common since George Washington in 1796 established the precedent of limiting himself to two terms in presidential office. Although this convention was not ratified as the 22nd Amendment to the United States Constitution until 1951, Franklin D. Roosevelt (in 1940 and 1944) was the only president to violate it during the intervening 155 years. Term limits were incorporated into a number of presidentialist constitutions globally during the nineteenth and twentieth centuries, but have in many parts of the world been contravened with alarming frequency (Baturo 2014). Autocratization can also be aided through an erosion of the checks that judicial institutions place on chief executives, for example through court-packing schemes as imposed by Hugo Chávez in Venezuela, or by several presidents since Juan Perón in Argentina, or as threatened by US President Franklin D. Roosevelt in 1937 but stymied by a Congress in which his own party held large majorities. As Acemoglu and Robinson (2012: 329) observe, "Congressmen and senators understood that if the president could undermine the independence of the judiciary, then this would undermine the balance of power in the system that protected them from the president and ensured the continuity of pluralistic political institutions."

One of the ways in which executive powergrabs and democratic backsliding in general can be contained is through various forms of powersharing. Graham et al. (2017) examine the effects of different forms of powersharing in sustaining democracy across 180 countries between 1975 and 2010. In all, these states experienced 37 transitions to autocracy over this period. Graham et al. examine the annual incidence of 19 indicators of powersharing across this global sample and find that they cluster into three distinct forms: inclusive, dispersive, and constraining powersharing. Examples of such institutions include reserved political offices for ethnic groups (inclusive), federalism (dispersive), and judicial review and judicial independence more generally (constraining).

Controlling for a host of socio-economic conditions, Graham et al. (2017) find that only constraining powersharing has a strong and statistically significant sustaining effect on democracy. Inclusive powersharing helps democracy survive only in societies that have recently experienced severe social conflict (such as civil war), whereas dispersive powersharing has no discernible positive effect on democracy. Thus, attempts to protect democratic assemblies from autocratization should focus not only on the assembly itself, but also on constraining powersharing features such as independent and empowered courts, civilian control of the armed forces, and protections of basic civil rights such as the freedoms of speech, faith, and assembly. Key among the protections against autocratization are the independence of judicial institutions and in the most general sense the rule of law.

But while transitions to a dictator's assembly can be dramatic, violent, and tragic, they may ultimately be less common than less overt developments that nevertheless undermine the capacity and accountability of the national assembly and render it incapable of playing a leading role in democratic policy making. One important legislative function that has proven susceptible to manipulation and subversion is the power of the purse—a power which, as we saw in Chapter 10, is at least shared between the executive and the legislative assembly in most countries. As Cox (2014, 2016) shows, the English Bill of Rights of 1689 paved the way for parliamentary supremacy by establishing Parliament's power to deny, amend, or approve new taxes, public debt, and the state's annual expenditures. These powers were enforced by threats of a vote of no confidence, which succeeded impeachment procedures as the favored mechanism of parliamentary control of the executive. This power of the purse that the Glorious Revolution vested in Parliament became the cornerstone of parliamentary democracy as it evolved through the eighteenth and nineteenth centuries and established itself as an influential model for democratizing countries, especially in the Commonwealth and in Europe.

Yet, as Cox notes, transplanting English parliamentarism has not always been easy, and the devil has commonly been in the details. The formal authority to control executive taxing and spending decisions may easily become illusory unless the critical enforcement mechanisms are in place. And ambitious and spendthrift executives can be counted upon to try to circumvent the legislature's power of the purse for their own benefit. One advantage executives commonly enjoy is an agenda-setting right: Under most existing constitutions the executive has the right to make the first budget proposal. Procedures that constrain legislators from proposing budgets or amendments that significantly differ from the executive's proposal will then of course favor the executive. The same may be the case for budgetary reversion rules that favor the executive, for example by stipulating that in case of a budget deadlock, or if the legislature fails to adopt an alternative budget within an allotted time period, the resulting budget will be the executive's proposal or perhaps last year's budget.

Cox refers to such provisions as executive-favoring reversions (EFRs) and show that they are both common and consequential. The percentage of the world's countries having EFRs thus rose from 33 in 1875 to 68 in 2005. And such budgetary provisions may drastically affect the likelihood that initially democratic regimes will survive. Thus, in his study of 130 electoral democracies after 1875, Cox finds that parliamentary regimes with legislature-favoring reversions remained democratic for an estimated 58.6 percent of their "lives," whereas similar parliamentary regimes with executive-favoring reversions were democratic for only 16.6 percent of their duration.

15.4 Prospects

Legislative assemblies have a long history, dating back to the first meeting of Iceland's Alþingi in 930 AD. No democracy that we know of is without a legislature. Yet, the decline of legislative assemblies has been discussed and lamented for decades. Ostrogorski (1902) warned that legislatures were being fundamentally weakened by the rise of party organizations. Bryce (1921) famously wrote of the decline of legislatures. And Hollis (1949) titled his study of the British Parliament *Can Parliament Survive?*

The answer to the latter question is surely yes, but each of these works, and more recent examples, point to the challenges faced by legislative assemblies, even if the decline-of-parliament thesis has been overstated (Flinders and Kelso 2011). In the closing section of this volume, it seems appropriate to reflect on the current challenges and prospects facing legislative assemblies around the world. In so doing, we remain mindful of the observations from the preceding empirical chapters on variation in how legislatures function and Madison's reflections on the need for legislative assemblies to have the capacity to act effectively in public policy making as well as be accountable to the electorate. We begin by reflecting on one long-discussed if nonetheless contemporary challenge to the capacity of legislative assemblies: the threat of executive dominance.

Executive dominance can be thought of as an imbalance in the relative power of the executive versus the legislature (Lijphart 1999: 129), where this imbalance favors the executive. Indeed, the rise in relative influence of the executive is one of the primary reasons some scholars speak of the decline of legislative assemblies. According to this logic, legislatures have all but lost their significance in the legislative process, becoming mere "rubber-stamps" for the executive's policies, and with little meaningful oversight. As Huber (1996: 280) notes, "scholars have devoted thousands of pages to parliamentary forms of government, and a good share of these pages have stressed the subordination of members of parliaments to leaders in governments." A shift to corporatist-style extra-legislative decision making in the 1960s and 1970s arguably exacerbated the decline of legislatures, leading some to talk of "post-parliamentary democracy" (Richardson and Jordan 1979).

Certainly, as we have seen in this volume, legislative assemblies tend to be over-shadowed in size and resources by the executive. And as we discussed above, the Covid-19 pandemic illustrated the limitations in the capacity of legislative assemblies to respond fully to the emerging public health crisis, and play a meaningful role in setting the legal framework and monitoring the performance of national governments' responses to the pandemic. In many ways, legislative assemblies appeared side-lined during the pandemic, with executives often declaring emergency powers and relying heavily on executive decrees. The Covid-19 pandemic seemed to leave many legislative assemblies struggling to function, with operational questions around matters such as how to meet and how to vote often taking priority over the substantive business of the legislative assembly.

Yet, much of the tone of the "decline of parliament" literature may stem from a misunderstanding of exactly what legislative assemblies do and how they do it (as distinct from how well they do what they should be doing). Moreover, the balance of power between the legislature and executive is an ever-turning tide, influenced by among other things how both camps are resourced and organized, the political and other skills of the leadership, and electoral outcomes. On the latter, for example, executive-legislative relation tends to look very different in a parliamentary system under minority as opposed to majority government (Strøm 1990; Field 2016) or in a presidential system under divided government (Cox and Kernell 1991). Under these circumstances, legislative assemblies may experience a resurgence and even an activation of powers that had previously been dormant or controversial, such as audits and formal investigations.

And organizationally, legislative assemblies do change. The US Congress is a good example. As Sundquist (1981) noted in his aptly titled volume, *The Decline and Resurgence of Congress*, the US Congress from 1973 onwards began to take back many of the roles and powers that it had lost in earlier decades to an increasingly dominant presidency. And as Congress, particularly during periods of divided government, has continued to make the life of US Presidents difficult, the struggle for power and influence between President and Congress goes on.

Even in the United Kingdom, recently scholarship has questioned the near-conventional wisdom that the House of Commons is ineffectual (Russell and Gover 2017). Reflecting on the resurgence of the House of Commons, especially in the form of a more engaged membership, a more inquisitive chamber, and a strengthened committee system, Norton (2017) notes that in terms of its influence and control over the executive it is "the best of times" (at least since the 1800s) for the UK Parliament. In response to executive dominance, other legislatures as well have attempted organizational reform to strengthen their capacity. Such legislative capacity building programs—a broad term to describe institutional reforms and additional resource allocation aimed at allowing legislative assemblies to more effectively perform their constitutional function—are now common in both well-established democracies and countries in transition to democracy. When it comes to executive–legislative relations, legislative assemblies are fighting back, or at least attempting to do so.

Yet Norton (2017) also notes that in terms of popular perceptions these are the "worst of times" for parliament, which brings us to the second challenge facing many, if not all, legislative assemblies: legitimacy and popular support. Historically at least, strong mechanisms of accountability such as democratic, free, and fair elections ensured that legislative assemblies derived broad popular legitimacy from the electoral process. And as we know, even many autocratic rulers go to great lengths to create the impression of free and fair elections, for example by inviting international organizations to monitor legislative elections, to achieve this approbation. Yet in some countries, including the United States, the legitimacy of some election procedures as well as the fairness of election outcomes have been challenged by leading politicians of both major parties. But the broader challenge to the legitimacy of legislative assemblies arguably comes not in the form of citizens' unhappiness with elections but with their unhappiness with the legislative assembly itself. With some notable exceptions, confidence in, and respect, for national legislatures appears to be in decline (Holmberg, Lindberg, and Svensson 2017). While specific election procedures can in most cases be reformed, countering a loss of diffuse support for a key democratic institutions is a more daunting prospect.

In the United Kingdom, for example, and as discussed in Chapter 6, a major scandal erupted in 2009 when a national newspaper began reporting details of the expenses of members of the House of Commons. The impact was to reduce significantly citizens' trust in their parliamentarians. And as Russell (2021, 454) notes, during heated hearings on the Brexit issue, "[c]ontroversy over proper use of parliamentary procedure hence became increasingly heated, and politicised" with voters divided as to the proper role and function of the House of Commons. Norton (2019: 1007), himself a practicing legislator, argues that "[d]eference to Parliament has been undermined by popular cynicism, a less interested and less informed media, and the emergence of social media, all of which have contributed to a more distracted population, one wanting instant gratification, and with a short attention span."

Whether or not this portrait is accurate, legislative assemblies have no doubt been slow to adapt to the new information age, where soundbites carry more weight than in-depth parliamentary discourse. The procedures of many legislative assemblies appear, to many people, ritualistic and arcane and unable to appeal to a broad range of voters, certainly including Generation Z and Generation Alpha.[3] Growing popular indifference to legislative assemblies and their members is

---

[3] Contrary to this perspective, we do note a movement in a number of countries to reduce the voting age for parliamentary elections and an attempt by some legislative assemblies to appeal to younger voters.

arguably far greater a threat to democratic assemblies than executive dominance ever was.

Popular skepticism toward legislative assemblies and their members has broader consequences, in particular in terms of how it impacts who wants to become and remain a legislator. Observing the abuse thrust upon some legislators, particularly over social media, one may be forgiven for asking why anyone would want such attention. This brings us to our third challenge facing legislative assemblies: the membership challenge.

Quite simply, the lack of trust or respect experienced by elected politicians may dissuade well-qualified candidates from political careers and thus exacerbate problems of adverse selection in politics. And a legislative assembly can only be as effective as the members who comprise it. Assemblies vary in their members' experience levels, skills, and ambitions. And as we note in Chapter 14, assembly capacity requires members to have some minimum of political experience, as well as skills and knowledge gained in and outside the assembly. Hence, there is good reason to believe that the quality of legislators (in terms of personal characteristics such as intelligence, inter-personal skills, formal education, and lived experience) has consequences for the capacity of a legislative assembly to perform its roles. In short, one challenge facing legislative assemblies is the ability to recruit and retain quality legislators.

Finally, the most radical challenge is whether legislative assemblies can be made redundant altogether. As extreme a proposition as this may sound, it is one that we need to contemplate at a time of rapidly evolving technology and declining support for legislative assemblies. It is indisputably true that legislative assemblies are the cornerstone of representative democracy and in many political systems the only directly elected entity at the national level. But do technological advances mean that we don't need representative democracy? As we saw earlier in the volume, Switzerland has only a part-time legislature, and many of the important policy questions are decided not by parliament but through referendums. Referendums, particularly where they can be initiated by citizens, certainly empower voters and provide one example whereby a core function of most legislative assemblies can be usurped. Given that in many countries most people have access to a mobile communications device, could politics not operate via some form a decision app— where, for example, each day, voters are asked questions and vote to approve or reject? And in such a world, would we need legislative assemblies? Or could they at a minimum be relegated to broad agenda-setting functions, upon which citizens could then give their judgments? In a less radical fashion, the emergence of citizens' assemblies or mini-publics provides alternative avenues to making public policy which can bypass or sidestep legislative assemblies. And leaving decisions to voters may have its advantages, including the time horizons problem associated with much political decision making. Would some countries' environmental policies, for example, be more consistent and sustainable if made by voters who care about the medium to long term, compared with legislators or other elected officials who must worry about the shorter-term consequences of their decisions, such as re-election?

But despite these contemporary challenges and more, we very much doubt that legislative assemblies will disappear anytime soon, at least in advanced democracies. Institutions, particularly ones prescribed by national constitutions, tend to be sticky—evolving (albeit at times very slowly) in the face of challenges rather than disappearing or altering fundamentally. And any attempt to eliminate institutions as well-entrenched in the constitutional order as legislative assemblies would surely come with unanticipated consequences, some of which might not at all be appreciated. As we have seen in this volume, legislative assemblies do perform central functions in modern democracies and would not be easily replaced. Certainly though, legitimacy and broad-based approval can surely only be achieved by real world legislative assemblies moving closer in design and operation to our notion of a voters' assembly—an assembly based on transparency, access, accountability, and effective oversight of the executive, and hopefully making sound public policy in the interest of the common good.

Legislative assemblies thus differ in many ways and may come to change and differ even more in years to come. This volume has suggested that much of this variation can be understood in view of the ways in which these assemblies reflect the interests of the members and leaders that populate these institutions and the voters that elect them. In addition, there is always a risk that a purportedly democratic assembly can degenerate into a dictator's assembly.

We see a number of avenues for future research. First, it may be fruitful to extend our empirical research in two ways: by expanding the number of countries beyond the 68 largest democracies but also by extending the study from a temporal snapshot to an inter-temporal study, exploring how the key characteristics and roles of legislative assemblies have evolved over time. Second, future research ought to investigate more fully the consequences of different types of legislative assemblies for the adoption of more responsive public policy and more generous and effective provisions of public goods. Would legislatures more akin to members' assemblies, for example, more effectively incentivize members to develop specialized skills and cater closely to the preferences of their constituents? And could institutions with a stronger tilt toward leaders' assemblies more successfully produce coherent and responsible policy packages?

We have no specific or confident answers to these questions, but we do believe that understanding different legislative templates and the actors and concerns that drive them is critical to any such endeavors. Legislative assemblies remain and we expect will continue to be a cornerstone of representative democracy. Like all public bodies, however, they face challenges and uncertain prospects, and must continually adapt to meet the changing preferences and needs of the groups they host and serve: citizens, members, and leaders. Finding ways to elicit the best and most constructive efforts from each of these classes of actors will remain the fundamental challenge of legislative politics.

References

Acemoglu, Daron, and James A. Robinson. 2012. *Why Nations Fail: The Origins of Power, Prosperity, and Poverty*. New York: Random House.

Baturo, Alexander. 2014. *Democracy, Dictatorship, and Term Limits*. Ann Arbor: University of Michigan Press.

Bolleyer, Nicole, and Orsolya Salát. 2021. "Parliaments in Times of Crisis: COVID-19, Populism and Executive Dominance." *West European Politics* 44(5-6): 1103–1128.

Bracher, Karl Dietrich. 1973. *The German Dictatorship: The Origins, Structure, and Consequences of National Socialism*. London: Penguin.

Bryce, James. 1921. *Modern Democracies*, Vol. 2, London: Macmillan.

Bucur, Cristina, José Antonio Cheibub, Shane Martin, and Bjørn Erik Rasch. 2018. "Constitution Making and Legislative Involvement in Government Formation." In Jon Elster, Roberto Gargarella, Vatsal Naresh, and Bjørn Erik Rasch (eds.), *Constituent Assemblies*. Cambridge: Cambridge University Press, 186–206.

Bueno de Mesquita, Bruce, Alastair Smith, James D. Morrow, and Randolph M. Siverson. 2005. *The Logic of Political Survival*. Cambridge: MIT Press.

Congleton, Roger D. 2011. *Perfecting Parliament*. Cambridge: Cambridge University Press.

Cox, Gary W. 1987. *The Efficient Secret*. Cambridge: Cambridge University Press.

Cox, Gary W. 2014. "Reluctant Democrats and Their Legislatures." In Shane Martin, Thomas Saalfeld, and Kaare W Strøm (eds.), *The Oxford Handbook of Legislative Studies*. Oxford: Oxford University Press, 696–716.

Cox, Gary W. 2016. *Marketing Sovereign Promises*. Cambridge: Cambridge University Press.

Cox, Gary W., and Samuel Kernell. eds. 1991. *The Politics of Divided Government*. Boulder: Westview Press.

Elster, Jon, Roberto Gargarella, Vatsal Naresh, and Bjørn Erik Rasch, eds. 2018. *Constituent Assemblies*. Cambridge: Cambridge University Press.

Field, Bonnie N. 2016. *Why Minority Governments Work: Multilevel Territorial Politics in Spain*. New York: Palgrave Macmillan.

Fish, M. Stephen. 2005. *Democracy Derailed in Russia: The Failure of Open Politics*. Cambridge: Cambridge University Press.

Flinders, Matthew, and Alexandra Kelso. 2011. "Mind the Gap: Political Analysis, Public Expectations and the Parliamentary Decline Thesis." *The British Journal of Politics and International Relations* 13 (2): 249–268.

Gandhi, Jennifer. 2008. *Political Institutions under Dictatorship*. New York: Cambridge University Press.

Graham, Benjamin A.T., Michael K. Miller, and Kaare W. Strøm. 2017. "Safeguarding Democracy: Powersharing and Democratic Survival. *American Political Science Review* 111(4): 686–704.

Hollis, Christopher. 1949. *Can Parliament Survive?* London: Hollis & Carter.

Holmberg, Soren, Staffan Lindberg, and Richard Svensson. 2017. "Trust in Parliament." *Journal of Public Affairs* 17(1–2): Article e1647.

Huber, John D. 1996. "The Vote of Confidence in Parliamentary Democracies." *American Political Science Review* 90(2): 269–282.

Jackson, Julian. 2018. *De Gaulle*. Cambridge, MA: Belknap Press.

Levitsky, Steven, and Lucan Way. 2010. *Competitive Authoritarianism: Hybrid Regimes after the Cold War*. New York: Cambridge University Press.

Levitsky, Steven, and Daniel Ziblatt. 2009. *How Democracies Die*. New York: Crown.

Lijphart, Arend. 1999. *Patterns of Democracy*. New Haven: Yale University Press.

Lust-Okar, Ellen. 2005. *Structuring Conflict in the Arab World: Incumbents, Opponents, and Institutions*. New York: Cambridge University Press.

Malesky, Edward, and Paul Schuler. 2009. "The Single-Party Dictator's Dilemma: Information in Elections without Opposition." *Legislative Studies Quarterly* 36: 491–530.

Norton, Philip. 2017. "Speaking for Parliament." *Parliamentary Affairs* 70(2): 191–206.

Norton, Philip. 2019. "Is the House of Commons Too Powerful? The 2019 Bingham Lecture in Constitutional Studies, University of Oxford." *Parliamentary Affairs* 72(4): 996–1013.

Ostrogorski, Moisej J. 1902 [2010]. *Democracy and the Organization of Political Parties*—vol. 1, New York: Kessinger Publishing.

Ostrovsky, Arkady. 2017. *The Invention of Russia*. New York: Penguin.

Ratner, Robert S. 2004. "British Columbia's Citizens' Assembly: The Learning Phase." *Canadian Parliamentary Review* 27(2): 20–26.

Rawls, John. 1971. *A Theory of Justice*. New York: Belknap Press.

Remington, Thomas. 2019. *Parliaments in Transition: The New Legislative Politics in the Former USSR and Eastern Europe*. New York: Routledge.

Richardson, Jeremy J., and A. Grant Jordan 1979. *Governing under Pressure: The Policy Process in a Post-parliamentary Democracy*. Oxford: Robertson.

Russell, Meg. 2021. "Brexit and Parliament: The Anatomy of a Perfect Storm." *Parliamentary Affairs* 74(2): 443–463.

Russell, Meg, and Daniel Gover. 2017. *Legislation at Westminster: Parliamentary Actors and Influence in the Making of British Law*. Oxford: Oxford University Press.

Rustow, Dankwart A. 1985. "Elections and Legitimacy in the Middle East." *The Annals of the American Academy of Political and Social Science* 482(1): 122–146.

Schuler, Paul, and Edward J. Maleski. 2014. "Authoritarian Legislatures." in: Shane Martin, Thomas Saalfeld, and Kaare W. Strøm (eds.), *The Oxford Handbook of Legislative Studies*. Oxford: Oxford University Press, 676–695.

Sieberer, Ulrich, Peter Meißner, Julia F. Keh, and Wolfgang C. Müller. 2016. "Mapping and Explaining Parliamentary Rule Changes in Europe: A Research Program." *Legislative Studies Quarterly* 41(1): 61–88.

Strøm, Kaare. 1990. *Minority Government and Majority Rule*. Cambridge: Cambridge University Press.

Sundquist, James L. 1981. *The Decline and Resurgence of Congress*. Washington: Brookings Institution Press.

Svolik, Milan W. 2012. *The Politics of Authoritarian Rule*. New York: Cambridge University Press.

Index

For the benefit of digital users, indexed terms that span two pages (e.g., 52–53) may, on occasion, appear on only one of those pages.

Introductory Note

References such as '178–9' indicate (not necessarily continuous) discussion of a topic across a range of pages. Wherever possible in the case of topics with many references, these have either been divided into sub-topics or only the most significant discussions of the topic are listed. Because the entire work is about 'legislative assemblies', the use of this term (and certain others which occur constantly throughout the book) as an entry point has been restricted. Information will be found under the corresponding detailed topics.

absence, unexcused 82
abstentions 171–172
acclamation 225–226
accountability 2–4, 17, 27, 34–35, 352–354, 383
  electoral 22–23, 26, 33, 58, 335–336
  legislative 17–18, 23–24, 134, 247, 303
  mechanisms 20–22, 34–35, 336
  popular 1, 34, 58, 131–132, 383, 388, 391–392
ad hoc committees 192–193, 211
affluence 24, 42, 49, 51, 237
Africa 76, 78, 93, 109, 117, 130, 138, 154, 162, 165, 168, 205, 231, 234, 242, 248, 257, 268, 270, 302, 307; *see also individual countries*
age 5, 7, 12, 62–63, 100–101, 120, 365–367
  minimum
    to stand for election 59, 62–63, 101, 120
    voting 62, 87–88, 101
  profiles 95, 100
  requirements 41–42, 62–63, 120
agency, loss 21–22, 86–87, 186–187
agenda
  control 15, 23, 31, 227, 321–322, 330, 342
  legislative 16–17, 223, 226–227, 321, 324–325, 330, 342
  powers 8, 17, 29–30, 35, 321, 330–331
  setting 227, 330, 393
agents 18–22, 86–87, 148, 291–292, 327, 387–388
agricultural committees 188–189
alternative offices 26–27, 363–367, 374–375
alternative vote 65, 73, 83, 92, 125, 148
Althingi 5, 11
ambitions 28, 30, 40, 42, 44–45, 360–361, 365, 376

discrete 26, 360–361, 365
static 26, 360–362, 365–366
amendment powers 241–242, 245–246
amendments 123, 127, 208–209, 216, 219, 222, 226–227, 241–245
  constitutional 23, 114–115, 141–143
Americas 77–78, 93, 109, 117, 130, 137–138, 153–154, 165, 168, 205, 231, 234, 248, 257, 268–270, 302, 307; *see also individual countries*
André, Audrey 68–69, 72
appointment 24, 122, 123, 125, 186–187, 261, 278, 282
  powers 47–48, 132, 261–262, 278, 332, 335
Argentina 60–62, 65, 90, 104, 108, 122, 128, 142, 151, 162, 194, 219, 223, 228, 242, 245, 246–247, 249, 250, 253–254, 266, 282, 296, 318–319, 323–325, 333–335, 341, 345–346, 356, 357, 392
armed forces 305–306, 392, 393
Asia 76, 78, 93, 109, 117, 130, 138, 154, 165, 168, 205, 231, 234, 248, 257, 268, 270, 302, 307; *see also* individual countries
assembly types 26–27, 32–33, 35, 36, 40–41, 312; *see also individual types*
  in comparison 346
  and House of Commons 317, 328, 337–338
  and Houses of Representatives 318–319, 325, 337, 346–347
  operationalizing ideal types 313
  and regime types 347
audit committees 242, 250–252
audits 242, 395
  financial 301

Australia 13, 60, 65, 73, 77, 82, 90, 104, 127, 151, 154–155, 162, 173, 194, 211, 219, 228, 242, 245–246, 280, 282, 296, 300, 306, 323–326, 328–329, 333–335, 345–348, 356–357
Austria 60, 65, 90, 104, 141–143, 151, 153, 162, 173, 194, 219, 222, 223, 228, 242, 245, 280, 296, 323–325, 333–335, 342, 345–346, 357
authority 15–16, 20–22, 127, 144, 248, 251, 387
  budgetary 47
  elective and appointment 47
  formal 14–16, 134, 393
  oversight 48
autocracies 2–3, 13–14, 23, 32, 88–89, 313, 388–389, 392
autonomy 2, 28, 59, 64–65, 275–276, 320, 366
  partisan 40–41

backbenchers 135–136, 170–171, 177–178, 184–185, 299, 315–316, 328, 330
background variables 49–50, 56, 95
backsliding, democratic 3–4, 333–335, 392
Bagehot, Walter 7–9, 40–41, 178, 260, 288, 313
balance 108, 140–141, 160, 258, 348–349, 392, 395
ballot access 46, 73–74, 83, 316–317, 325, 327–328, 368
ballots 68–69, 73–75, 82–83, 108, 176, 281, 363
  secret 148–149
banks, central 260, 278, 279–280, 332
bargaining
  coalition 272–273, 275–276
  processes 272–273
Barnes, Tiffany D. 97, 105–106
Baron, David P. 242, 276
Belgium 52–53, 60, 65, 90, 102–104, 127, 151, 162, 173, 194, 219, 228, 232, 242, 251–252, 273, 278, 280, 282, 296, 323–325, 333–335, 345–346, 357
Benin 52–53, 60, 65, 74–75, 90, 104, 151, 162, 194, 204, 219, 228, 242, 251–254, 280, 296, 323–325, 333–335, 341, 345–346, 357
Bergman, Torbjörn 9, 262, 269, 277
"best and brightest" 98–99, 150, 156–157, 319
bicameral assemblies/legislatures 113–117, 119–120
bicameral rivalry 191
bicameral systems 26–27, 62–63, 102–103, 116–117, 119, 120, 152–153, 191
bicameralism 44–45, 113–117, 120, 121, 126, 131–132, 138, 367, 372, 373–374
  incongruent 44, 126

bills 126–127, 210–211, 215, 216, 222, 224, 232–233, 235
  government 208–209, 215
  legislative 46–47, 215, 222, 225
  money 127–128
Blais, André 13, 62, 164
block votes 122
Boix, Carles 51–52
Boix-Miller-Rosato (BMR) coding 54
Bolivia 26, 60, 63, 65, 90, 103, 104, 148, 151, 162, 194, 207–208, 219, 228, 242, 249, 253–254, 296, 303, 323–325, 327, 333–335, 338–339, 345–346, 357, 368, 371–374
bottlenecks
  collective 28–29
  legislative 120
  plenary 116, 136, 155–156, 178–179, 186–187, 226–227
Brazil 16–17, 52–53, 60, 65, 71, 90, 104, 151, 162, 164, 194, 219, 228, 235, 242, 249, 253–254, 282, 286, 296, 323–325, 333–335, 345–346, 348, 357, 369–370
British colonies 52–53, 75, 78, 93, 108–110, 117, 138, 154, 165, 168, 205, 231, 248, 270, 302
Bryce, James 2, 394
budget committees, specialized 251–252
budget institutions, legislative 254, 257, 331, 343
budgetary authority 47
budgetary capacity 253–254, 256–258, 322
budgetary committees 194, 211
budgetary decisions 47, 239–241, 256, 330–331, 342–343
budgetary information 241, 252–253, 322
budgetary powers 47, 241, 242, 245–246, 254, 322, 330–331, 342–343
  legislative 333–335, 345
  measuring 241
  variation 253
  Wehner Index 257
budgetary process 47, 53, 209, 211, 212, 239, 322, 330–331, 342–343
  amendment powers 241
  executive flexibility during implementation 247
  measuring budgetary powers 241
  reversionary budgets 242, 246, 248
  time for scrutiny 250
  variation in budgetary powers 253
budgetary scrutiny 253
budgets 151, 154–155, 241–245, 246–249, 251–252
  draft 245, 250–251
  implementation 241, 249–250, 322

institutions 256
    reversionary 242, 246, 248
Bueno de Mesquita, Bruce 7, 388
Bulgaria 60, 65, 90, 104, 151, 162, 219, 222–223,
    228, 242, 296, 320, 323–325, 329,
    333–335, 345–346, 357
Bundesrat 116–117, 122–123, 279
Bundestag 73, 82, 116–117, 175–176, 279,
    281–285
bureaucracy 145, 291–293, 309–310, 377
bureaucrats 215, 291, 299, 309–310
Burundi 51, 60, 65, 90, 104, 106, 151, 162, 194,
    219, 228, 242, 282, 296, 300, 344–346,
    357
by-elections 79–80, 355–356

cabinet 177–179, 260, 261–266, 276–277,
    328–329
    members 9, 18–19, 204, 286, 293–294,
        315–316, 323
    ministers 31, 206, 275–276, 323, 390–391
    positions 26–27, 206, 323, 367
    seats 177–178, 275, 276
    sharing seats 276
California 42, 74, 81–82, 119, 223–224, 367
cameral congruence 126
cameral powers 126
cameral structures 35, 44, 55, 113, 135, 191, 339,
    348–349
    broader representation 119
    design 113, 115
    federal versus unitary countries 116
    future of second chambers 129
    higher quality representation 120
    House of Commons 113–114, 116, 120,
        123–125, 127
    House of Lords 113–114, 120–127
    membership selection 121
    and population 116
    powers 126
    regional and historical effects 121
    senates 113, 119, 120, 125, 127–128, 131
campaigns 67–69, 327, 361–362
Canada 52, 60, 65, 76–79, 90, 97, 104, 162,
    166–167, 173, 194, 219, 222, 242,
    245–246, 250–251, 280, 296, 323–325,
    328–329, 333–335, 345–348, 356–357
candidate selection 30, 32–33, 48–49, 73–75, 83,
    176, 325
    procedures 28, 73–74, 180
    processes 74
candidate-centered electoral systems 45, 64–65,
    68–69, 167, 177–178

candidates 25–26, 35, 67–75, 106, 148, 168, 177,
    363
    party 176
capacity 27–28, 34–35, 352, 383; see also
        Introductory Note
    budgetary 253–254, 256–258, 322
    committee 210–211, 242, 250–252
    institutional 1, 62, 132, 256, 257
    legislative 3–4, 14–16, 27, 134–135, 155–156,
        194, 353–354
careers 28, 30, 97–99, 150, 156–157, 318, 319
    political 101, 108–110, 173–174, 310,
        353–354, 397
Carey, John 14, 28, 68, 74–75, 177, 179, 371, 373
Carroll, Royce 144
cartel party theory 189–190, 192, 210–211
case selection 36, 41
case work 17, 28–29, 68–69, 315–316
Catholic orders 12
Catholics 12
caucuses, party 160, 170, 225, 331
censure motions 286
central bank governors 47–48, 261–262,
    279–282, 288, 332
central bankers 280, 332
central banks 260, 278, 279–280, 332
chain of delegation 18–19, 22, 29–30, 160,
    260–261, 291
    democratic 29–30, 86–87, 180, 223
chairs 144, 148, 170, 194, 208, 265, 280, 330
    committee, see committee chairs
    majority 194
    opposition 194
challengers 354, 368, 369–370, 375
chambers 44–45, 113, 114–115, 138, 187–188,
    191, 194, 205, 224–225, 282, 338–340; see
        also Introductory Note
    chamber size 134–135, 137
    lower 44–45, 90, 104, 106, 114, 119, 125–127,
        132, 162, 168, 204–205
    number of 115
    second, see second chambers
    size 135
    unicameral 108–110, 153, 286
Chávez, Hugo 391–392
chief justices 279, 281, 282, 288, 332
Chile 60, 65, 90, 104, 151, 162, 194, 206, 219,
    226–228, 233, 242, 245, 253–254, 264,
    296, 303, 320, 323–325, 329, 333–335,
    345–346, 357
choice of electoral system 64–65
CIEP (constitutional inter-electoral period),
        see constitutional inter-electoral period
        (CIEP)

citizen initiatives 223–224, 342
citizen interests 14, 121, 136, 186, 216, 340
citizenship 13, 41–42, 59–61, 82, 223–224
　rights 12
civil rights 101–102, 384, 389–390, 393
civil servants 8–9, 19–20, 299, 303, 379
civil wars 25, 106, 148, 393
class 95–98, 110
classification schemes 41, 265, 313
CLEA (Constituency Level Elections
　　Archive) 355–357
closed list systems 65, 67–68, 71, 72–73, 102,
　　106–108, 176–177
coalition bargaining 272–273, 275–276
coalition formation, reasons for 275
coalition governments 208, 273, 275–276
coalition minority government 273
coalition parties 208, 273, 278
coalitions 30–31, 208, 210–211, 273–276, 278
cohesion 172, 175–176, 180–181
cohesive parties 16–17, 172–173, 315, 384
collegial assemblies 29, 326
Colombia 60, 65, 90, 102–104, 151, 162, 194,
　　210, 219, 223–224, 233, 242, 250, 279,
　　296, 303, 323–325, 333–335, 345–346,
　　357
colonial powers 53, 268
colonies 53, 78, 93, 109, 117, 130, 138, 147, 165,
　　205, 231, 270, 302
　British 52–53, 75, 78, 93, 108–110, 117, 138,
　　　154, 165, 168, 205, 231, 248, 270, 302
committee chairs 12, 17, 98–99, 159, 160, 194,
　　208, 329–330
　legislative 17, 29
committee stage in legislative process 208–209,
　　211, 216
committees 184; see also Introductory Note
　ad hoc 192–193, 211
　agricultural 188–189
　assembly 193, 329, 341, 384
　audit 242, 250–252
　bicameral rivalry perspective 191
　budgetary 194, 211
　capacity 210–211, 242, 250–252
　cartel party perspective 189
　comparison of systems 192
　congressional 189–190
　deliberations 206, 300
　distributive perspective 188
　informational perspective and efficiency 186
　legislative 46, 192, 193–194, 204, 208–211,
　　250
　members 187–188, 194, 206, 212, 303–304
　membership 206

　number 193
　permanent 190, 192, 193–194, 210–211, 341,
　　373
　portfolio 242, 251, 252
　portfolios 209, 212
　powerful 29, 326, 361–362
　powers 208
　preferred 189–190
　public accounts 251–252, 303–304
　reasons for 186
　rules 190, 341
　sectoral 251
　service on 187, 320
　specialized 29, 46, 184–185, 187–188, 303,
　　320
　systems 184–187, 189–190, 192, 210–211
　　legislative 185, 210, 320
　work 187, 193, 341
Commons, see House of Commons
competition 19–20, 25, 64–65, 68–69, 72, 180,
　　191, 258
　electoral 2, 23, 34–35, 327, 379
competitive elections 23, 379, 384, 387
competitiveness, electoral 25–26, 379
conditions 22–23, 25–26, 49, 212, 214–215,
　　361–362
Confederation Congress 1–2
confidence 262–264, 270–272, 277–278, 286,
　　288, 309
　motions 277–278, 309
　procedures 179, 262–263, 277–278, 286, 309
　votes 179, 263, 269, 272–273, 277–278, 309,
　　386–387
Congleton, Roger D. 1–2, 7, 390–391
congresses 3–4, 245, 260–261
　federal 1
congruence
　cameral 126
　descriptive 93, 110
　jurisdictional 209–210
　and membership 86
　partisan 89–92, 338
consecutive terms 60, 63, 96, 99, 168, 327
consent 8, 22, 240, 247–249, 280, 308–309, 322
Conservatives 79–80, 96, 97, 173–174, 270, 272,
　　337–338
constituencies 30–31, 68–69, 79–80, 179–180,
　　188, 318
Constituency Level Elections Archive, see CLEA
constituency service 20, 68–69, 186
constituent assemblies 357, 391
constituents 68–69, 79–80, 187, 188–189,
　　225–226, 299

constitutional amendment 23, 114–115, 141–143
constitutional conventions 68–69, 270, 279
constitutional courts 260, 279, 331
constitutional functions 2–3, 17–18, 192, 395–396
constitutional inter-electoral period (CIEP) 77, 318, 328, 371, 373, 375
constitutional monarchies 232, 281
constitutional powers 129, 309, 347, 390
constitutions 106, 114–115, 128, 139–141, 232–233, 278, 377–378, 385–386
  Brazil 286
  Burundi 106
  Norway 35, 114–115, 286, 384
  parliamentary 214–215, 263, 264, 347
  presidential 9, 179–180, 288
  South Africa 139–140
  United States 147, 214–215, 305–306, 308–309
constructive votes of no confidence 262, 278
contracts 21–22, 79, 336
control variables 373–374, 378
conventions 35, 123, 270, 384, 392
coordination 11, 18, 20
co-partisans 31, 47–48, 68–69, 74–75, 161, 167, 171, 172–173
corrupt countries 375–377
corruption 369–376, 378–379
  conditional effect 370
  Corruption Perceptions Index (CPI) 371, 373
  levels 371, 375
  political 194, 362, 369–370, 379
Costa Rica 26, 60, 63, 65, 90, 104, 135, 151, 162, 194, 211, 219, 242, 246, 264, 282, 296, 323–325, 327, 333–335, 345–346, 356, 357, 368, 371–374
councils 3–4, 7
  federal 116–117
courts 219, 223, 228, 232–233, 235–236, 331
  constitutional 260, 279, 331
Cox, Gary 31, 159, 160–161, 177, 189–190, 239–240, 393–394
CPI (Corruption Perceptions Index) 371, 373
credibility 7, 34, 177, 263, 337, 383
Croatia 52–53, 60, 65, 90, 102–104, 114–115, 151, 162, 194, 219, 222–223, 228, 232–233, 242, 280, 282, 296, 323–325, 331–335, 345–346, 357
cross-national variations 41–42, 48–49, 206, 239–241, 322, 331
cultures 62, 75, 101, 108–110, 123

Czech Republic 52–53, 60, 65, 71, 90, 104, 219, 228, 250–252, 280, 282, 296, 323–325, 333–335, 345–346, 357

Dahl, Robert A. 18, 25, 59, 94
Dáil 148–149, 270, 273
data collection 53–54, 373
Database of Political Institutions (DPI) 54, 265
death 6, 79, 300–301, 363–365, 375
decision rules 76–77, 142, 147–148, 225, 279, 356
declarations of war 304–305
delegates 8, 18–20, 86–87, 98–99, 116–117, 123, 139
delegation 17–23, 116–117, 260–261, 387–388
  effective 20, 22–23
  political 18–19, 21, 91–92, 170, 338, 387–388
deliberations 2, 33, 120, 215–216, 224, 227, 341
  budgetary 250, 322
  committee 206, 300
  legislative 91–92, 226, 293–294
democracies 1–2, 24–25, 40, 41–42, 51–52, 54, 173, 355–356, 359, 374, 388–389, 393
  contemporary 3, 18–19, 36, 42, 48–49, 51, 214–215
  liberal 1–2
  parliamentary 19–20, 59, 180–181, 276, 278, 288, 390–391, 393
  participatory 139–140
  presidential 7–8, 19–20, 264, 374–375, 380
  representative 3–4, 94, 116, 125, 278, 342, 397–398
  stable 95, 264
democratic assemblies 10–11, 34, 194, 346–347, 349, 352, 363, 383
  and challenges to legislative assemblies 387
  and dictator's assemblies 32, 388, 398
  and forces shaping legislative assemblies 385
  prospects 394
democratic backsliding 3–4, 333–335, 392
democratic chain of delegation 29–30, 86–87, 180, 223
democratic countries 41–42, 77, 78–79, 191, 239, 390–391
democratic legislatures 21, 40–41, 47–48, 58, 103, 214–215, 239–240
democratic legitimacy 123, 129, 305–306
democratic societies 9–11, 18, 50, 236, 387
democratic stability 2–3
Democrats 79–80, 96, 97–98, 162, 273, 337–338, 387
demographics 23–26, 43–44, 86, 110

Denmark 7, 23, 60, 65, 71, 90, 104, 108–110, 121, 151, 162, 172–173, 194, 210, 219, 228, 242, 249, 253–254, 273, 280, 282, 296, 323–326, 328–329, 333–335, 345–346, 349, 357, 375–376
Depauw, Sam 172–173, 177, 179
dependence on the people 32–33, 337
dependent variables 50, 76, 77–78, 205, 231, 233–234, 248, 257, 267–270, 302, 307–308
deputies 68–69, 86, 106, 120, 148, 162, 216, 346–347
deputy members 206
descriptive congruence 93, 110
descriptive representation 92–93, 100–102, 339
dictators 7, 385, 388–389
dictator's assemblies 32, 388, 398
Diermeier, Daniel 114, 191
diets 3–4, 58, 168, 280
differentiation 17, 46, 121–122, 184–185, 262, 315–316, 320
Dingell family 63, 352–353, 355–356, 365–366
disability 79, 95, 339
discipline 172, 175–176, 180–181, 320
    fiscal 47, 240–241, 258, 322
    party 172, 175, 176–178
discrete ambition 26, 360–361, 365
discretion 24–25, 35, 73–74, 83, 177, 181, 232
dismissal powers 47–48, 261–262, 282
disproportionality 54, 89–93, 337–338
    indices of 89–91, 338
dissolution 35, 76–77, 264–265, 317, 318, 328
    early 30, 76–77, 83
    powers 328–329, 333–335
distribution, partisan 88–91, 276, 337–338
distributive perspective 188–190
districts 17, 19–20, 28–29, 61–62, 65, 68–69, 87–88, 122, 188
    electoral 68–69, 72, 73, 87–88, 126
    magnitude 65, 68–69, 90, 92–93, 109, 165, 168, 231, 234, 248, 257, 268–270, 302, 307
divided government 265, 292, 331, 395
dominance, executive 394–397
Dominican Republic 60, 65, 90, 104, 119, 126, 154–155, 207–208, 228, 233, 279, 296, 300, 323–325, 333–335, 345–346, 357
DPI (Database of Political Institutions) 54, 265
draft budgets 245, 250–251
Duverger, Maurice 164, 264–265

early dissolution 30, 76–77, 83
early elections 76–77, 273, 317–318, 328

Eastern Europe 76–77, 93, 117, 130, 138, 154, 165, 168, 205, 231, 248, 257, 268, 302, 307
Ecuador 60, 62–63, 65, 79, 90, 104, 151, 162, 194, 219, 222–223, 235, 241–245, 250, 266, 279, 295, 296, 323–325, 333–335, 345–346, 357, 371–374
education 95–98, 105–106, 110, 123, 192
effective delegation 20, 22–23
effective oversight 206, 292–293, 343, 398
effectiveness 193, 206, 216, 222–223, 303, 341
EFRs (executive-favoring reversions) 394
El Salvador 60, 65, 77, 90, 104, 151, 194, 219, 228, 242, 295–296, 323–325, 333–335, 345–346, 356–357
elected assemblies 1–2, 24, 363
elected members/legislators 25, 74, 100–101, 116–117, 123, 177, 180, 317
elected presidents 16–17, 235, 264–265, 281
elected representatives 9, 18, 20, 22, 159–160, 291, 326–327
elected second chambers 20, 339–340, 344
election laws 23
election time 23, 25–26, 29, 48, 61–62, 68–69, 83, 160
elections 12–13, 25–26, 106–108, 122, 162, 166–168, 337–338, 355–357
    competitive 23, 379, 384, 387
    democratic 25, 376, 387
    early 76–77, 273, 317–318, 328
    fair 22, 41–42, 396
    general 79–80, 270, 272–273, 317, 354–355, 370
    legislative 41–42, 58, 89–91, 144, 192, 272, 396
    new 179, 273, 390
    parliamentary 273, 317, 335, 391–392, 396–397
    popular 18–19, 83–84, 123, 281–282, 285
    primary 32–33, 72, 176
    procedures 396
    process 148–149, 156
    recall 79–82, 336
    rules 126, 368
    single-member district 348
    staggered 125, 317, 354–355
    of women 106
elective and appointment authority 47
elective function 9, 47–48, 260
    defining regime types 262
    government formation under parliamentarism 269, 272
    government termination under parliamentarism 277

House of Commons 260, 263–264, 270, 272, 288
House of Lords 272
Houses of Representatives 286
impeachment, *see* impeachment
other appointment powers 278
reasons for coalition formation 275
senates 263–264, 279, 280, 286
sharing cabinet seats 276
and voters, members and leaders 260
elective powers 47–48, 261–262
electoral accountability 22–23, 26, 33, 58, 335–336
electoral colleges 168, 260, 263–264
electoral competition 2, 23, 34–35, 327, 379
electoral competitiveness 25–26, 379
electoral constraints 368, 375, 376, 378
electoral districts 68–69, 72, 73, 87–88, 126
electoral incentives 16–17, 31, 177–178
electoral laws 25, 82, 88–89, 353, 391–392
electoral proportionality 90, 93, 337–338
electoral rules 64–65, 82–84, 108, 316, 339–340, 380
electoral success 316, 327, 353, 366, 379
electoral systems 35, 54, 64, 72, 73–76, 92, 122, 125–126, 164, 316–317, 327, 336, 345
    candidate-centered 45, 64–65, 68–69, 167, 177–178
    closed-list 67–68, 75, 176, 327, 344
    mixed 73, 164
    open-list, *see* open-list systems
    party-centered 64–65, 67, 68, 327, 336
electoral terms 30, 35, 78–79, 83, 318, 324, 336
electorates 43–44, 87–91, 98–99, 102–103, 168, 223–224, 337–338
Elgie, Robert 264–265, 371, 373
eligibility 35, 59, 62, 79–80, 101, 120, 384
elites
    business 391–392
    political 68–69, 114–115, 129, 301
emergency powers 389–390, 392, 395
endogenous variables 377–379
endowments 14–15, 361, 366
environment 42, 188, 342, 366
ethnic fractionalization 52, 76, 77–78, 93, 109, 117, 130, 138, 154, 165, 168, 205, 227, 231, 234, 248, 257, 268, 270, 302
ethnic groups 106, 392
ethnic minorities 12, 93–94, 102, 106
ethnicity 12, 95, 339
European Parliament 4, 42, 160, 207–208, 225–226
European Union 26–27, 123, 214, 304, 367, 389
executive agenda control 226, 231, 330, 335

executive appointments 26–27, 179, 260, 367
executive branch 1–2, 8, 35, 256, 258, 288, 342–343
executive dominance 394–397
executive flexibility 242, 247, 249–250
executive office 1–2, 9, 47–48, 83, 167, 261–262, 292, 323
executive oversight 28–29, 48, 152–153, 156–157, 186–187, 192, 208–209, 291
    authority 48
    capacity 48, 254, 344–345
    effective 206, 292–293, 343, 398
    financial audits 301
    House of Commons 293–294, 303, 305
    investigation and inquiries 300
    parliamentary questions and interpellations 293
    powers 296, 302, 344
    procedures 27, 292
    and responsibility 309
    senates 308–309
    tools 293, 310, 343
    treaties 306
    war powers 304
executive powers 8, 40–41, 178, 240, 322, 331
executive-favoring reversions (EFRs) 394
executives 214–215, 218, 219, 235–236, 239–240, 393
expectations 32, 41, 120, 191, 205, 367, 368, 374–375
expenditure 239–240, 245, 248–249, 258, 302–303
    budgeted 249
    government 247, 251–252, 258, 302–303
    public 239, 252, 254, 303
expenses 26–27, 30–31, 34, 79–80, 150, 179, 194
    systems 79–80, 150
experience
    legislative 95, 99, 379
    political 29, 353–354, 397
expertise 17, 29, 206–209, 379, 384
experts 55, 207, 215
    national 53, 55
expulsion 79, 82, 320
external transparency 35
external vetoes 228, 233, 331, 333–335
    players 232, 234, 331

fair elections 22, 41–42, 396
faith 24, 110, 339, 393; *see also* religion
federal countries 116, 204–205, 247
federal legislators 81–82, 367
federal parliaments 60, 116–117, 252, 281–285

federal systems/regimes 26–28, 116, 119, 247, 348–349, 367, 373
federalism 16–17, 26–27, 116–117, 119, 348–349, 367, 391–392
Federalist 1, 8, 15, 23–24, 32–33, 240, 322, 337
Federalists 29, 32, 46
females, *see* women
Ferejohn, John A. 242, 276
Ferguson, Sir Alex 79
Fifth Republic 204, 227, 330, 386, 391
filibusters 15, 144–145
final passage
    of legislation 138–139, 141–143, 155–156, 235–236
    rule 142
financial audits 301
financial benefits 62–63, 150, 156–157, 319
financial bills 127–128
financial legislation 127, 218, 236
financial legislative powers 129–130
Finland 3–4, 13, 44, 50–51, 60, 65, 71, 74, 90, 102–104, 108–110, 151, 162, 172, 173, 194, 210, 219, 228, 242, 253–254, 280, 282, 296, 323–325, 333–335, 345–346, 357, 375–376
first chambers 113, 119, 120, 126, 191
first choice candidates 68–69
first preference votes 73
fiscal discipline 47, 240–241, 258, 322
fiscal powers 245–249
fixed terms 28, 65, 76–77, 263, 317–318, 325, 328
flexibility, executive 242, 247, 249–250
football managers 79
foreign policies 304
formal authority 14–16, 134, 393
formal powers 123, 126, 129
formal proposal rights 216, 218, 219, 223, 321–322, 330
formal roles 138–139, 210–211, 269, 270, 279, 280
formal rules 138–139, 194
formateurs 273, 276
four-chamber assemblies 44
fractionalization
    ethnic 52, 76, 77–78, 93, 109, 117, 130, 138, 154, 165, 168, 205, 227, 231, 234, 248, 257, 268, 270, 302
    ethno-linguistic 378–379
France 60, 65, 72, 90, 104, 131–132, 151, 154–155, 162, 173, 194, 204, 210, 219, 228, 239, 242, 245, 249–252, 265, 280, 296, 303, 320, 323–325, 329, 330, 333–335, 345–346, 356, 357, 386, 387

Fifth Republic 139–140, 227, 330, 386, 391
functions
    constitutional 2–3, 17–18, 192, 395–396
    elective 9, 47–48, 260
    institutional 7

Gallagher Index 54, 92, 338
Gamson's Law 276
gatekeeping powers 189, 210–211
GDP 76, 93, 109, 117, 130, 138, 154, 165, 205, 231, 248, 257, 270, 302, 307, 369, 371–373, 375
    growth 369, 371, 372–373, 375
    per capita 51, 78, 168, 234, 268, 369, 373–374
gender 12, 44, 93–95, 103, 106–108, 110, 339
    quotas 104, 106, 108
    representation 110, 338–339, 344, 345
general elections 79–80, 270, 272–273, 317, 354–355, 370
Germany 52–53, 60, 65, 68–69, 74, 82, 90, 92, 104, 116–117, 122–123, 151, 162, 173, 194, 210, 219, 222, 228, 232, 242, 249, 250–254, 273, 278–279, 281–285, 296, 323–325, 333–335, 345–346, 357, 390
    Bundesrat 116–117, 122–123, 279
    Bundestag 73, 82, 116–117, 175–176, 279, 281–285
    Länder 116–117, 122–123
Ghana 6, 50–51, 60, 65, 82, 90, 104, 151, 162, 194, 219, 228, 242, 253–254, 282, 296, 323–325, 333–335, 345–346, 357
Gilligan, Thomas W. 187
GINI coefficients 51–52, 76, 78, 93, 109, 117, 130, 137, 138, 153, 154, 165, 168, 205, 227, 231, 234, 248, 257, 268, 270, 302
Glorious Revolution 5, 8, 263, 393
Google Scholar 55
Google Translate 55
governance 116, 139, 194, 335–336, 354, 369
governing parties 31, 179, 208, 215, 277–278, 333–335
government bills 208–209, 215
government budgets, *see* budgets
government departments 210, 251
government expenditure 247, 251–252, 258, 302–303
government formation 116–117, 145, 268–272, 275, 277, 288
    under parliamentarism 269, 272
government termination under parliamentarism 277

Greece 60, 65, 90, 104, 151, 162, 194, 210,
        219, 228, 242, 251–252, 280, 281–282,
        288, 296, 323–325, 333–335, 345–346,
        356–357
Guatemala 60, 65, 90, 104, 151, 162, 194, 219,
        228, 242, 282, 296, 323–325, 333–335,
        345–346, 357

heads of government 170, 260, 263–265, 288,
        295–296, 332
heads of state 228, 232–233, 264–265, 281, 282,
        285, 286, 331–332
hearings 215, 293, 300–302, 310
hereditary peers 24, 122
hierarchy 16–17, 29–30, 46, 159, 184–185,
        326–327
Honduras 60, 65, 90, 104, 151, 162, 194, 219,
        228, 242, 282, 296, 323–325, 333–335,
        345–346, 357
House of Commons 4–5, 9, 10–11, 19–20, 33,
        135, 396
    assembly type 317, 328, 337–338
    contemporary challenges 395–396
    electing 58, 72, 76–77, 79–80
    elective function 260, 263–264, 270, 272, 288
    executive oversight 293–294, 303, 305
    and incumbency 353
    membership and congruence 97, 103,
        108–110
    organization and leadership 136, 144–146,
        148, 150
    parties 170–171, 178–179
    structures 113–114, 116, 120, 123–125, 127
House of Lords 4–5, 10–11, 19–20, 24
    assembly type 340
    elections in Canada 62–63
    elective function 272
    organization and leadership 144
    structures 113–114, 120–127
housekeeping committees 192–193
Houses of Representatives 98, 100–101
    assembly type 318–319, 325, 337, 346–347
    committees 190, 194
    contemporary challenges 384–385
    electing 61–63, 72, 73, 77, 83
    elective function 286
    executive oversight 308
    and incumbency 359–362, 365–366, 370–371,
        379
    lawmaking 222, 224
    Liberia 48–49, 77, 318, 337
    Nigeria 194, 341
    organization and leadership 141–142,
        145–146, 150, 153

parties 167, 170
structures 114, 119, 120, 125, 127
United States 26, 28, 32, 48–49, 63, 72,
        77, 83, 96–97, 99, 100, 119, 141–142,
        145–146, 150, 153, 161–163, 170, 222,
        286, 318–319, 323, 325, 337, 346–347,
        349, 361–362, 365–366, 370–371, 379,
        384–385
Huber, John 178–179, 204, 227, 330, 377, 386,
        394
Hungary 60, 65, 90, 104, 151, 162, 194, 206, 219,
        223–224, 228, 232–233, 242, 246–247,
        250, 254, 278, 280–281, 296, 323–325,
        331–335, 345–348, 357
Hutus 106

Iceland 5, 12, 97, 101, 173, 176
ICPV (incentives to cultivate a personal
        vote) 65, 75, 76, 168, 371–375
ideal agents 86
ideal types 36, 40, 41, 312–315, 349, 352,
        384–385
    operationalizing 313
impeachment 79, 282, 285, 288, 309
    President of Brazil 286
    procedures 285–286, 309
    processes 263–264, 285–286, 288, 291
incentives 62–64, 68–69, 74–76, 292, 316–317,
        336, 372–374
    to cultivate a personal vote, see ICPV
    electoral 16–17, 31, 177–178
incomes 51–52, 150, 249, 302, 303, 339, 366–367
    inequality 51–52, 75, 137
incongruence 126
incongruent bicameralism 44, 126
incumbency 100, 352
    analysis 370
    capacity and accountability 353
    conditional effect of corruption 370
    electoral constraints 368, 375, 376, 378
    and House of Commons 353
    and Houses of Representatives 359–362,
        365–366, 370–371, 379
    rates 353–357, 359, 366–367, 372, 374–378
        comparing 354
        and legislative resources 370, 375, 377
        understanding 359
    regimes and institutions 366
    and senates 367
    voters, prosperity, and political
        corruption 369
incumbent governments 277–278, 369
incumbent re-election rates, see re-election, rates

independence 52–53, 64–65, 71–72, 147, 148, 316, 392–393
independent variables 49–50, 256, 370–371, 373, 374
independents 166–167, 320, 325, 329
India 13, 42, 52, 60, 65, 82, 90, 99, 101–104, 150, 151, 154–155, 162, 194, 207–208, 210, 219, 228, 233, 242, 249, 251, 253–254, 280, 281–285, 296, 306, 319, 323–325, 333–335, 345–346, 353, 357, 363
indices
  disproportionality 89–91, 338
  leaders' assemblies 326, 333, 334
  legislative budget institutions 254, 331, 343
  legislative resources 373–374, 379
  members' assemblies 315, 324
  parliamentary powers 54, 314
  voters' assemblies 335, 345
Indonesia 52–53, 60, 65, 90, 104, 151, 162, 194, 219, 228, 242, 253–254, 296, 323–325, 333–335, 345–346, 357
information
  budgetary 241, 252–253, 322
  flows 16, 30, 326–327, 335
informational disadvantages 32, 100, 293, 343
initiatives 188, 214–215, 219, 223–224, 342
  citizen 223–224, 342
  legislative 28–29, 325
inquiries, parliamentary 300–301
institutional capacity 1, 62, 132, 256, 257
institutional constraints 35
institutional designs 48–49, 52, 317, 385
institutional features 27–28, 34–36, 55, 56, 360, 361–362
institutional functions 7
institutions 13–14, 42, 214–215, 228, 331–332, 335–336, 366, 372, 398
  budget 256
  government 187–188, 391
  legislative 2–4, 312–313, 352
    budget 254, 257, 331, 343
  and regimes 366
inter-electoral period 43, 58–59, 77, 78, 318, 344–345
interest groups 21–22, 166, 171, 215
interests
  citizens 14, 121, 136, 186, 216, 340
  special 208, 320
  voters 33, 44, 132, 184–185, 193, 343
  women 94, 105, 339
international agreements 308–309
international treaties 304, 308–309
interpellations 292–293, 300, 301, 310, 343–344
investigations 44, 48, 293, 296, 300–301, 310
investiture 266, 269, 270–272, 277, 288, 332

Ireland 5, 23, 48–51, 53
  assembly membership and congruence 90, 104
  assembly type 316, 320, 323–325, 328–329, 331–335
  budgetary process 242, 249–251, 254, 257
  cameral structures 114–115, 136
  committees 194, 208, 211
  elections 60, 65, 68–69, 71–72, 74–75
  elective function 264–265, 270, 280, 282
  executive oversight 296
  incumbency and re-election 357
  lawmaking 219, 226–228, 232–233
  organization and leadership 148–149, 151, 153
  parties 162, 167, 172–173, 177–178, 180
Irish Citizens' Assembly 385
Israel 60, 65, 90, 104, 151, 162, 173, 194, 219, 222–223, 228, 232, 242, 249, 278, 281, 295, 296, 323–325, 333–335, 345–346, 357, 377
Italy 60, 65, 90, 92, 104, 114–115, 120, 130–132, 148, 151, 162, 173, 194, 210, 216, 219, 223, 224, 228, 233, 242, 246, 251–254, 272, 273, 280, 281–285, 296, 323–326, 333–335, 345–346, 357
IV analysis 378–379

Japan 6, 58, 60, 65, 90, 104, 142, 151, 154–155, 162, 168, 194, 219, 222–223, 228, 242, 250, 279–280, 282, 296, 323–326, 333–335, 345–346, 356, 357, 390–391
Jesuits 12
Jews 12, 102
Johnson, Joel W. 54, 74–76, 317, 373
judicial review 223, 236, 392
judiciary 127, 140, 223, 225, 260, 278–279, 285, 286; see also courts
jurisdictional congruence 209–210

Kenya 60, 65, 82, 90, 104, 106, 114–115, 128, 142, 148, 151, 162, 194, 219, 222–223, 228, 242, 249–250, 253–254, 296, 300, 306, 321–325, 330, 333–335, 345–346, 357
kings 4–5, 7, 8, 122, 145–146, 191, 232; see also monarchs
King's Speech 270
Klašnja, Marko 353, 369–370
knowledge 2, 15, 33, 123, 126–127, 181, 187, 292
Korea
  North 25, 387
  South 60, 90, 104, 142, 151, 194, 219, 228, 242, 253–254, 266, 282, 296, 323–325, 333–335, 345–346

Krehbiel, Keith 17, 187, 354, 366

labels 29–30, 68, 145–146, 160, 252, 293, 326–327
Labour Party 79–80, 96, 97–98, 123, 160, 168, 337–338
Labrador 87–88
Länder 116–117, 122–123
Latin America 6, 121, 286, 356;
    see also individual countries
Laver, Michael 260–263, 273, 275–276, 323
lawmaking 7–8, 46–47, 152–153, 155, 156–157, 184–185, 214, 231
    authority 46, 214
    executive agenda control 226, 231, 330, 335
    external vetoes, see external vetoes
    legislative productivity 216, 228, 232–233, 235, 237
    procedures 8
    process 130, 215, 218, 222, 223–227, 235–237
    proposal rights 218, 321–322
    stages of deliberation and voting mechanisms 224
lawyers 11, 96
LDP (Liberal Democratic Party) 168
leaders 11; see also Introductory Note; party leaders
    assembly 11, 27, 28, 30–31, 35, 134, 315, 321
    legislative 12, 47–48, 215, 261–262, 331, 332
    political 7, 9, 26, 82–83, 191–192, 332
    powerful 46, 159, 326
    religious 5
leaders' assemblies 29, 35, 74, 76, 98–99, 193, 240–241, 245–246
    index 326, 333, 334
leadership 11, 76, 147, 149, 330–331, 333–335, 383, 386
    functions 11, 325
    legislative 11–12, 140, 145–146, 178, 331
    party 64, 68, 71–72, 176, 177, 320, 327–328
    positions 24, 31, 144, 155, 326, 359–360
Legislatinas 357
legislation 116–117, 126–128, 210–211, 215–216, 222–223, 232–233, 235, 331–332; see also bills
    financial 127, 218, 236
    government 210–211, 216, 299
    non-financial 127–128, 218
    volume of 178–179, 216, 235
legislative accountability 17–18, 23–24, 134, 247, 303
legislative agenda 16–17, 223, 226–227, 321, 324–325, 330, 342
legislative approval 242, 246, 247–249, 307–308

legislative assemblies 4; see also Introductory Note
    accountability, see accountability
    capacity 14
    challenges to 387
    comparison 40
    elections 58
    forces shaping 385
    institutional functions 7
    members, leaders, and voters 9
    reasons for 4
    types, see assembly types
legislative audit office 293, 310
legislative bills 46–47, 215, 222, 225
legislative budget institutions 254, 257, 331, 343
legislative budgetary power 333–335, 345
legislative capacity 3–4, 14–16, 27, 134–135, 155–156, 194, 353–354
legislative chambers, see chambers
legislative committees 46, 192, 193–194, 204, 208–211, 250
    systems 185, 210, 320
legislative divisions 171–172, 180–181, 225–226, 270
legislative elections 41–42, 58, 59, 62–63, 89–91, 144, 192, 272
legislative experience 95, 99, 379
legislative institutions 2–4, 312–313, 352
legislative investiture, see investiture
legislative leaders 12, 47–48, 215, 261–262, 331, 332
legislative leadership 11–12, 140, 145–146, 178, 331
legislative majorities 262–264, 272, 275, 292, 329
legislative office 43–44, 59, 62–63, 82, 106, 160, 365–366
legislative organization 45, 56, 134, 139–141, 184, 191–192, 366
    centralized 45
    internal 16, 45, 134, 144, 326–327
legislative parties 159–162, 164–165, 167–169, 173–174
    cohesive 16, 172–173
    number 161
    organizational structure 167
    and political parties 160
legislative politics 13, 35, 40, 55, 58, 167, 349, 353
legislative power(s) 52, 114, 115, 125, 126–128, 178–179, 390
    financial 129–130
    levels 47, 241

legislative process 126–128, 208–211, 224–225, 227, 231, 330
  committee stage 208–209, 211, 216
legislative productivity 228, 232–233, 235, 237
legislative proposals 178, 193, 214–215, 222
legislative resources 366, 372, 375–379
  and incumbency rates 370, 375, 377
  and re-election 366
Legislative Resources Index 373–374, 379
legislative rules 14, 100, 134, 140, 141, 143
legislative salaries 150, 319
legislative seats 22, 59, 64, 87–92, 106
legislative state of nature 45, 134, 135, 155–156
legislative terms 59, 74–77, 184–185, 207–208, 368
  length 75
legislative turnover, see turnover
legislative votes 170–171, 176, 262–263, 332
legislators 62–64, 76, 151, 153, 154, 162, 168, 173–178, 194, 206–208, 219, 225–226, 318–319, 373; see also Introductory Note
  backbench 170–171, 315–316
  control over behavior 160, 320
  elected 160, 177, 180, 323, 335–336
  federal 81–82, 367
  former 150, 156–157, 319
  independent 166–167
  lower-chamber 114, 125, 150, 319
  national 58, 60, 62–63, 116, 159, 368
  non-party 166, 168, 320, 324, 329
  women 93–94, 103, 104–106, 108–110, 338–339
legitimacy 123, 389, 396, 398
  democratic 123, 129, 305–306
liberal democracy 1–2
Liberal Democrats 79–80, 96, 97–98, 168, 337–338
Liberia 48–49, 60, 65, 74–75, 77, 90, 104, 142, 150, 151–153, 162, 167, 194, 204, 219, 222, 228, 242, 250, 253–254, 282, 296, 300, 318–326, 329, 330, 333–335, 337, 345–348, 357, 370–371
liberty 8, 240, 322, 337, 389–390
life peers 122–123
Lijphart, Arend 30, 44, 115, 123, 126, 129, 262, 394
Linz, Juan J. 263–264, 285–286
list proportional representation 122
lobbyists 191, 218
Lords, see House of Lords
lower chambers 44–45, 90, 104, 106, 114, 119, 125–127, 132, 162, 168, 204–205

McCubbins, Mathew 12, 16, 31, 159, 161, 177, 189–190, 293
Madison, James 1–4, 14, 15, 17–18, 27, 32–34
Magna Carta 4–5, 8
majoritarian systems 92–93, 108–110, 164–165, 168, 231, 234, 248, 257, 268, 270, 302, 307–308
majorities
  legislative 262–264, 272, 275, 292, 329
  parliamentary 8, 270, 272–273, 278
  plenary 142
  of seats 99, 214–215, 263, 265, 270, 272–273
  of votes 72–73, 168
majority chairs 194
majority control 30, 329–330
majority parties 30, 99, 145–146, 167, 208, 263, 329
majority support 31, 265, 270, 277
Malawi 60, 65, 90, 104, 142, 150, 151–153, 162, 166–167, 194, 219, 228, 233, 242, 249, 253–254, 282, 296, 319, 320, 323–326, 329, 333–335, 345–348, 357, 370–371
Māori 103
Massachusetts 10, 12
Mattson, Ingvar 184, 206, 340–341
Mayhew, David 26, 28, 83, 325, 361–362, 365–366, 376–377
mean district magnitude 93, 165, 168, 231, 234, 248, 268, 270
members 10; see also Introductory Note
  assembly 12–13, 15–16, 22, 179–180, 323
  cabinet 9, 18–19, 204, 286, 293–294, 315–316, 323
  committee 187–188, 194, 206, 212, 303–304
  deputy 206
  elected 25, 74, 100–101, 116–117, 123, 177, 180, 317
  elections of 101–102
  incumbent 28, 36, 61–62, 71–72, 184–185, 240–241, 325, 361–362
  independent 166–167, 181, 273
  legislative 33, 82–83
  party 73–74, 168, 329
  women 103, 109, 119, 338–339
members' assemblies 28, 35, 76, 323
  index 315, 324
Members of Parliament, see MPs
membership 11, 43, 60, 62–63, 90, 95, 99, 121–122, 194, 323
  age profiles 100
  committees 206
  composition 43–44, 99, 110
  and congruence 86
  descriptive representation and congruence 93

and education 98
female 103, 338–339
and gender 101
ideal agents 86
and legislative experience 99
and partisan affiliations 88
party 168
restrictions 59–60
rules 55, 59
selection 43, 59, 121–123
   rules 43
size 10–11, 52, 153
and socio-economic background 95
total 24, 106, 320, 338–339
Mexico 60, 63, 65, 90, 104, 142, 151–153, 162,
   194, 219, 242, 296, 341, 346–347, 356,
   357
Middle Ages 4, 7
Middle East 76, 78, 93, 109, 117, 130, 154, 165,
   168, 231, 234, 248, 257, 268, 270, 302,
   307; see also individual countries
minimum ages
   to stand for election 59, 62–63, 101, 120
   voting 62, 87–88, 101
mini-publics 385, 397–398
ministers 68–69, 116–117, 170, 206, 209,
   248–249, 299
   cabinet 31, 206, 275–276, 323, 390–391
ministries 210
minorities 51–52, 102–103, 141–143, 216,
   280–281, 354
   ethnic/racial 12, 93–94, 102, 106
   religious 43–44, 93–95, 101, 102, 192–193
minority governments 167, 273–276, 280, 288
   coalition 273
   single-party 273
minority parties 139, 167, 270, 273
mixed electoral systems 73, 164
mixed member systems 65, 73, 92
Mixed-Member Proportional (MMP)
   systems 68–69
monarchies 5, 273, 281, 386–387; see also kings;
   monarchs
   constitutional 232, 281
monarchs 7–8, 11, 232, 270, 281, 328; see also
   kings
money bills 127–128
motions
   censure 286
   confidence 277–278, 309
motivations 18, 20, 144–145, 188–189, 194, 292,
   310
MPs (Members of Parliament) 79–80, 96,
   97–98, 135–136, 150, 281, 293–294, 373

Müller, Wolfgang C. 30–31, 114, 148, 159, 262,
   273, 275, 326
multi-member districts 67, 71, 335, 348
Myerson, Roger B. 114, 191

national assemblies 76, 96, 106, 139, 140, 194,
   261, 286, 288, 352, 357, 390–391
national experts 53, 55
national legislative office 62–63, 160
national legislators 58, 60, 62–63, 116, 159, 368
Nebraskan State Assembly 166–167
negative parliamentarism 269, 277
Nepal 60, 65, 74–75, 90, 102–104, 114–115, 119,
   142, 151, 152–153, 162, 194, 206, 219,
   228, 233, 242, 251, 280, 281–285, 295,
   296, 300, 318–319, 323–325, 333–335,
   345–346, 357, 370–371
Netherlands 60, 65, 90, 104, 142, 151, 162, 194,
   219, 228, 242, 251, 269, 273, 280, 296,
   323–325, 329, 333–335, 345–346, 357
neutrality 145–146, 148–149, 156
New Zealand 13, 16–17, 60, 65, 74, 77, 90,
   102–104, 142, 151, 173, 180, 194,
   219, 228, 266, 273, 280, 296, 305–306,
   323–325, 328–329, 333–335, 345–348,
   356, 357, 367, 375–377
Nicaragua 60, 65, 90, 104, 142, 150, 151,
   154–155, 162, 194, 219, 228, 233, 242,
   249, 250, 296, 319, 323–325, 333–335,
   345–346, 357, 370–371
Niger 52–53, 60, 65, 90, 102–104, 106, 142,
   150, 151–153, 162, 194, 206, 208, 210,
   219, 223, 233, 242, 249, 280, 282, 296,
   318–319, 323–325, 333–335, 345–346,
   357, 370–371
Nigeria 53, 60, 62–63, 65, 79, 90, 104, 121,
   142, 151, 152–155, 162, 194, 219, 242,
   253–254, 282, 295–296, 318–319,
   323–325, 333–335, 341, 345–347, 357,
   370–371, 376, 379, 387, 389
no re-election rule 63, 368
no-confidence procedures 285–286, 309
nominations 122, 168, 279–280
non-financial legislation 127–128, 218
non-partisans 147, 166
non-party legislators 166, 168, 320, 324, 329
non-personal vote systems 316, 336
Nordic countries 5–6, 9, 97, 101; see also
   individual countries
North Korea 25, 387
Norton, Philip 8, 115, 125, 214, 216, 395–396

Norway 12–13, 35, 59–60, 65, 76–77, 90, 102, 104, 108–110, 114–115, 142, 151, 162, 173, 194, 219, 228, 242, 254, 272–273, 282, 286, 296, 323–325, 333–335, 340, 345–346, 357, 384

observers 63, 135–136, 273, 333–335
Oceania 93, 109, 138, 269, 302, 307–308; *see also individual countries*
officeholders 46–47, 159, 225, 279–280, 285–286, 327, 333, 379
open legislative assemblies, *see* voters' assemblies
open-list systems 65, 71–72, 177, 335
opposition 44–45, 147, 194, 276–278, 293–294, 389, 392
  chairs 194
  parties 88–89, 276–277, 292, 293–294, 391–392
oral questions 293–296, 299, 343–344
ordinary citizens 9–10, 18–19, 83, 214–215, 341–342
ordinary legislation 35, 384
ordinary members 40–41, 82–83, 135, 156, 181, 321
organizational choices 48
outliers 52, 128, 235, 315, 318–320, 370–371
oversight, *see* executive oversight

Pakistan 60, 65, 82, 90, 102–104, 106, 142, 151, 162, 194, 210, 219, 228, 235, 242, 253, 265, 280, 281–285, 296, 300, 306, 323–325, 328–329, 333–335, 345–346, 357
Papua New Guinea 3–4, 50–52, 60, 65, 73, 103–104, 142, 151–153, 167, 219, 228, 242, 250, 266, 280, 282, 296, 318–320, 323–326, 329, 333–335, 338–339, 345–347, 357, 370–371
Paraguay 60, 65, 90, 104, 142, 151, 162, 194, 219, 228, 233, 242, 295–296, 318–319, 323–325, 333–335, 345–346, 357
parliamentarism 262–265, 268, 269–270, 272, 277, 347–348
  government formation under 269, 272
  government termination under 277
  negative 269, 277
parliamentary assemblies 19–20, 348
Parliamentary Budget Office (PBO) 254
parliamentary constitutions 214–215, 263, 264, 347
parliamentary control 263, 393
parliamentary countries 269, 288, 348
parliamentary democracies 19–20, 59, 180–181, 276, 278, 288, 390–391, 393

parliamentary elections 273, 317, 335, 391–392, 396–397
parliamentary government 262–263
parliamentary inquiries 300–301
parliamentary majorities 8, 270, 272–273, 278
parliamentary parties 11–12, 272–273, 329
Parliamentary Party Group (PPG) 160, 331
Parliamentary Powers Index 54, 314
parliamentary procedures 141, 396
parliamentary questions, *see* questions
parliamentary systems 19–20, 253–254, 260–263, 268, 273–275, 286, 291–292, 295
parliamentary votes 263, 272
parliaments, *see Introductory Note*
participatory democracy 139–140
parties 46; *see also Introductory Note*
  coalition 208, 273, 278
  cohesive 16–17, 172–173, 315, 384
  governing 31, 179, 208, 215, 277–278, 333–335
  House of Commons 170–171, 178–179
  influence on roll-call behavior 171
  leadership 64, 68, 71–72, 176, 177, 320, 327–328
  legislative, *see* legislative parties
  in the legislature 159
  minority 139, 167, 270, 273
  opposition 88–89, 276–277, 292, 293–294, 391–392
  parliamentary 11–12, 272–273, 329
  political and legislative distinguished, *see* political parties
  ruling 26–27, 122, 367
partisan affiliation 88, 90
partisan autonomy 40–41
partisan composition 44–45, 90, 91–92, 114–115, 269, 272
partisan Congress 29, 148
partisan congruence 89–92, 338
partisan distribution 88–91, 276, 337–338
partisan preferences 88–91, 338
partisanship 44, 72, 86, 88–89, 95–96, 148–149, 162, 337–338
party affiliation 68, 145–146, 171, 173–174, 269
party candidates 176
party caucuses 160, 170, 225, 331
party cohesion 16–17, 30, 172, 175
party discipline 172, 175, 176–178
party groups 89, 164–165, 207–208, 222–223, 226–227, 272–273
party labels 68–69, 72, 82–83, 166, 316, 320, 329
party leaders 29–32, 168, 170–171, 176, 177–178, 190, 194, 327–328, 332–333

ability 175, 177–178
  control 67, 71–72, 83, 176, 190
  influence 71–72, 106, 326–327, 329, 333
  national 176, 207–208
  power 46, 176, 181, 348–349
  role 31, 148–149, 333
party lists 67–68, 75, 106–108, 176
party members 73–74, 168, 329
  votes 168, 171
party membership 168
party politics 2, 166, 181
party quotas 104
party unity 68–69, 172, 173, 175, 176–177,
      179–181
party-centered electoral systems 64–65, 67, 68,
      327, 336
payoffs 25–26, 276, 364–367
PBO (Parliamentary Budget Office) 254
peers
  hereditary 24, 122
  life 122–123
performance sensitivity 25–26
permanent committees 190, 192, 193–194,
      210–211, 341, 373
  legislative 17, 370–371
  substantive 192–193, 210
personal characteristics 68, 72, 397
personal votes 54, 68–69, 74–76, 177, 316–317,
      336, 345, 371, 372–375
Peru 60, 65, 90, 104, 114–115, 129, 130, 142,
      151, 162, 194, 219, 228, 242, 246,
      253–254, 280, 296, 318–319, 323–325,
      332, 333–335, 345–346, 357
Peters, Ronald M. 147–148
petitions 79–80, 286, 336
Philippines 26, 60, 63, 65, 77, 90, 104, 120,
      122, 142, 151, 162, 194, 219, 222–224,
      226–228, 242, 279, 295, 296, 323–325,
      327, 333–335, 341, 344–347, 357, 368,
      371–374, 379, 387
Phillips, Anne 94, 105, 339, 354
plenary bottlenecks 116, 136, 155–156,
      178–179, 186–187, 226–227
plenary majorities 142
plenary supermajorities 142
plenary time 45, 116, 134–135, 155–156,
      186–187, 226–227, 299
PLS (pre-legislative scrutiny) 216
plurality 65, 72, 73, 125, 142, 148, 252
  single member district 72, 125, 167, 325
PMQs (prime minister's questions) 33, 293–294
Poland 50–53, 60, 65, 90, 104, 122, 142, 151,
      162, 194, 219, 228, 242, 278, 282, 296,
      323–326, 333–335, 345–346, 357, 387

police 21, 155, 300–301
policy congruence 88–89, 110, 187, 337–338
policy influence 189–191, 272–273, 276–277
policy jurisdictions 16, 184–185, 210, 275–276
policy making 8, 64, 101, 123, 129, 188–189,
      194, 393–394
policy preferences 64, 88–90, 172–174, 275–276,
      337–338
  voters 77, 88–89, 337
policy specialization 17, 77, 318, 360
political agendas 23, 218
political ambitions 26, 360–361
political candidates 87, 176, 367
political corruption 194, 362, 369–370, 379; *see
      also* corruption
political delegation 18–19, 21, 91–92, 170, 338,
      387–388
political elites 68–69, 114–115, 129, 301
political institutions 51–53, 258, 353, 362, 392
political leaders 7, 9, 26, 82–83, 191–192, 332
political office 14, 95, 97–98, 100–102, 363–364
  alternative 26–27, 363–367
political parties, *see also* parties
  and legislative parties distinguished 160
political power 5, 105–106, 264–265, 276, 323
political scientists 55, 74–75, 86, 138–139, 143,
      180–181, 263, 353
political systems 9–10, 123, 127, 232–233, 263,
      267–269, 361
politics
  legislative 13, 35, 40, 55, 58, 167, 349, 353
  party 2, 166, 181
Polsby, Nelson W. 2, 40–41, 313
popular accountability 1, 34, 58, 131–132, 383,
      388, 391–392
popular election 18–19, 83–84, 123, 281–282,
      285
popular vote 58, 337–338
population 116
  size 50–52, 116, 119, 137
populous countries 10–11, 75, 92, 153, 167, 301
pork-barrel
  grants 28–29, 325, 361–362
  outputs and favors 29, 326
  projects 188
portfolio allocations 276
portfolio committees 242, 251, 252
portfolios 170, 194, 242, 248, 251, 273, 276
Portugal 60, 65, 90, 104, 142, 151, 162, 194, 210,
      219, 228, 242, 282, 296, 316, 323–325,
      333–335, 345–346, 356, 357, 387
positions, cabinet 26–27, 206, 323, 367
powers, *see also Introductory Note*
  agenda 8, 17, 29–30, 35, 321, 330–331

powers, *see also Introductory Note* (*Continued*)
  amendment 241–242, 245–246
  appointment 47–48, 132, 261–262, 278, 332,
    335
  assembly 14, 41, 250, 301
  broad 5, 186–187
  budget 245–246, 330–331
  budgetary 47, 242, 248, 252–254, 257, 322,
    342–343
  cameral 126
  colonial 53, 268
  committees 208
  constitutional 129, 309, 347, 390
  to delay 123, 128, 129–130
  dismissal 47–48, 261–262, 282
  dissolution 328–329, 333–335
  elective 47–48, 261–262
  emergency 389–390, 392, 395
  executive 8, 40–41, 178, 240, 322, 331
  financial legislative 129–130
  fiscal 245–249
  formal 123, 126, 129
  gatekeeping 189, 210–211
  institutional 366, 377
  legislative 52, 114, 115, 125, 126–128,
    178–179, 390
  oversight 296, 302, 344
  policy-making 40–41, 339–340
  political 5, 105–106, 264–265, 276, 323
  of the purse 8, 239–241, 322, 330–331, 393
  of second chambers 127–128
  veto 15, 23, 126–128, 130, 131, 232–233
  war 304
powersharing 52, 106, 392–393
PQs, *see* questions
PR, *see* proportional representation
predictors 49–50, 137, 254
preferences 21–22, 86–87, 90, 120, 161,
    173–175, 207–208, 226, 309–310
  partisan 88–91, 338
pre-legislative scrutiny, *see* PLS
presidential constitutions 9, 179–180, 288
presidential countries 129, 233, 295, 307–308,
    348
presidential democracies 7–8, 19–20, 264,
    374–375, 380
  stable 264
presidential government 262–263
presidential impeachment 286
presidential systems/regimes 20, 260–261,
    263–264, 268, 279–281, 291, 295, 373
presidentialism 26–27, 58, 178–179, 253–254,
    262, 263–264, 367

presidents 130–131, 232–233, 263–266,
    270–272, 285–286, 392
  elected 16–17, 235, 264–265, 281
presiding officers 135, 142, 144, 147–149, 156,
    206, 332–333
  neutral 145–146, 333
  non-partisan/partisan 147
  office 135, 144, 156, 333
primary elections 32–33, 72, 176
  system 72–74
prime ministers 122–123, 168, 263–265,
    270–272, 293–294, 328–329
  former 114
Prime Minister's Questions 33, 293–294
principals 18–20, 21–22, 29–30, 86–87, 160
procedural rights 45, 134, 178–179
productivity 184–185, 193, 228, 233, 235, 341
  legislative 216, 228, 232–233, 235, 237
professional politicians 17–18, 22, 32, 97
progressive ambition 26–27, 179–180, 360–361,
    366–367, 374–375, 380
promotion 44–45, 114, 131–132, 136, 176–177,
    318, 389
proportional representation 30, 67, 92, 102–103,
    106, 122, 125–126, 164
  closed-list 67, 316, 336
  list 122
proportionality 89–91, 92, 335, 338, 344, 345
  electoral 90, 93, 337–338
proposal rights 218, 321–322
  formal 216, 218, 219, 223, 321–322, 330
prosperity 369, 371, 374–375
Protestant Reformation 5
Przeworski, Adam 3–4, 13, 25–26, 51
public accounts committees 251–252, 303–304
public expenditure 239, 252, 254, 303
public office 150, 156–157, 319, 369
public policy 192, 194, 208–210, 214, 239, 330,
    331, 345
public scrutiny 35
purse, power of the 8, 239–241, 322, 330–331,
    393
Putin, Vladimir 391–392

question time 293–295
questioners 293–294, 299
questions 135, 293–296, 299, 301–302, 310, 352
  oral 293–296, 299, 343–344
  prime minister's 33, 293–294
  written 299
quotas 68–69, 108, 206
  gender 104, 106, 108
  party 104

race 93–95, 101
Rasch, Bjørn Erik 9, 216, 225–227, 269, 270–272, 321, 330
recall 30, 35, 67, 79–83, 317–318, 335–337
   elections 79–82, 336
   mechanisms 23, 317–318, 384
   procedures 23, 28, 35, 317–318, 345
   process 79–80, 337
   provisions 33, 79, 81–82, 336
re-election 26–27, 61–63, 73, 75, 78–79, 99, 176–177, 352; see also incumbency
   bids 362, 367, 379
   and legislative resources 366
   likelihood of 82–83, 189
   modelling decisions 362
   motives 26–27, 363, 365
   no re-election rule 63, 368
   opportunities 362, 371
   rates 353–354, 356, 359–361, 363, 368–369, 374–375
   value of 364–365, 368
referendums 68–69, 123, 131, 214, 219, 223–224, 301, 397–398
reforms 33, 52, 81–84, 122, 130–131, 144, 254
regime types 235–236, 253–254, 256, 260–261, 264–266
   and assembly types 347
   definition 262
regimes and institutions 366
regression analysis 75, 77, 164, 167, 227, 233, 267–269
religion 95, 110; see also faith
religious leaders 5
religious minorities 43–44, 93–95, 101, 102, 192–193
rents, generous 330–331, 388
representation
   broader 119
   descriptive, see descriptive representation
   higher quality 120
   substantive 94, 103, 105
representative bodies 10–11, 14, 87–88, 258, 338–339
representative democracy 3–4, 94, 116, 125, 278, 342, 397–398
representatives 18–20, 63, 78–79, 82–83, 96, 99–100, 142, 162, 168, 194, 318, 325, 336–337
   elected 9, 18, 20, 22, 159–160, 291, 326–327
Republicans 162, 173–174, 367, 387
re-selection 176
reserve funds 242, 249
reserved seats 102–104, 106–110
residency 61–62

requirements 59–62
resources 15–16, 45, 134–135, 149, 151, 164–165, 318, 361–362
   legislative 366, 372, 375–379
responsibility and executive oversight 309
responsiveness 28–29, 32, 34, 67, 160, 337, 384
retirement 352–353, 363–367, 379
reversionary budgets 242, 246, 248
review, judicial 223, 236, 392
rights
   civil 101–102, 384, 389–390, 393
   procedural 45, 134, 178–179
   proposal, see proposal rights
   voting 12–13, 18, 35, 41–42, 58, 102–103, 126
Riksdag 14, 145, 206, 254, 273
risk 20–21, 25, 75, 179, 317, 387–389, 392
roll-call behavior 170–174, 176, 178–179, 225–226
   party influence on 171
roll-call votes 171, 175, 190, 226
Romania 60, 65, 90, 102–104, 122, 142, 151, 162, 167, 194, 207–208, 219, 228, 235, 242, 249, 253–254, 280, 282, 296, 320, 323–325, 329, 332–335, 345–348, 357, 387
rule of law 5–9, 393
rules 138
   committee assignment 324–325
   committees 190, 341
   electoral 64–65, 82–84, 108, 316, 339–340, 380
   formal 138–139, 194
   legislative 14, 100, 134, 140, 141, 143
ruling parties 26–27, 122, 367
Russell, Meg 113, 115, 116, 123, 216, 347–348, 395–396
Russian Federation 2–3, 388, 391–392

salaries 149–151, 155, 319, 323–325, 370–371
   legislative 150, 319
   low 150, 156–157, 319
sample 51–52, 249, 250, 356, 370–371, 376–378
Samuels, David J. 16–17, 30, 51–52, 87–88, 179
scandals 2, 79, 150, 194, 375, 396
Scandinavia 5, 121, 273; see also individual countries
Schlesinger, Joseph A. 44–45, 114, 159, 161, 360–361, 368
Scottish National Party (SNP) 97, 338
scrutiny 79, 215, 216, 235–236, 250, 336
   budgetary 253
   public 35
   time for 250

seats
  cabinet 177–178, 275, 276
  legislative 22, 59, 64, 87–92, 106
  majority 99, 214–215, 263, 265, 270, 272–273
second chambers 113–119, 122, 125–126, 128, 129–132
  appointed 132
  elected 20, 339–340, 344
  future 129
  powers 127–128
  relatively powerless 44–45
  unelected 44–45, 113–114, 123, 340
secondary sources 54–55
secret ballots 148–149
secret votes 149, 333, 334
secret voting 148–149, 156, 225–226, 333
sectoral committees 251
security 76, 153, 207, 318
selection 21, 35, 36, 130–131, 147–149, 168, 281; see also candidate selection
  jury 23–24
  presiding officers 142, 147–148, 332–333
  processes 148–149, 279, 333
selectorate 73–74, 168
semi-democracies 2–3, 23
semi-presidential systems/regimes 264–265, 272, 273, 279, 281, 285, 304–305, 309
semi-presidentialism 179, 235–236, 253–254, 264–266, 313
senates 1, 3–4, 24, 385
  assembly type 346–347
  elective function 263–264, 279, 280, 286
  executive oversight 308–309
  and incumbency 367
  lawmaking 224
  parties 167
  structures 113, 119, 120, 125, 127–128, 131
Senato della Repubblica 130–131, 272
senators 24, 102, 114, 120, 122–123, 125, 130–131, 194
Senegal 52–53, 60, 65, 74–75, 90, 91–92, 104, 142, 150, 151–153, 162, 164, 194, 219, 228, 233, 242, 253–254, 280, 282, 296, 318–319, 322, 323–325, 333–335, 343, 345–346, 357, 370–371
senior members 29, 122–123, 135–136, 279, 332
seniority 17, 29, 30, 63, 99–100, 326–327, 370
Serbia 50–51, 60, 65, 74–75, 90, 104, 142, 151, 162, 194, 219, 242, 253–254, 280, 282, 296, 323–326, 332, 333–335, 345–346, 357
shared grievances 2–3
Shepsle, Kenneth A. 188–189, 208, 275–276, 323
short terms 15, 77, 318, 337
Shugart, Matthew S. 28, 30, 68, 74–75, 177, 179, 371, 373

Sieberer, Ulrich 35, 74, 114, 140–141, 143, 175–176, 179, 384
Sierra Leone 60, 65, 74–75, 142, 148, 151, 152–155, 161–163, 194, 219, 228, 235, 282, 296, 300, 318–319, 323–325, 333–335, 345–346, 357
simplicity 21, 32, 362–365
Single Member District Plurality, see SMDP
Single Transferable Vote, see STV
single-member districts 72, 83, 348
single-party minority governments 273
skills 9, 18, 21, 23–24, 87, 94, 395, 397
Slovak Republic 52–53, 60, 65, 90, 104, 142, 151, 162, 194, 219, 228, 242, 266, 280, 282, 296, 323–325, 332, 333–335, 345–346, 357
SMDP (Single Member District Plurality) 72–73, 122, 125, 167, 325
Smith, Alastair 7, 24, 25–26, 100, 328, 353, 355–357
SNP (Scottish National Party) 97, 338
social choice theorists 2
social democratic parties 97, 273
socio-economic background 95
South Africa 50–52, 60, 65, 91–92, 104, 113, 139, 140, 142, 151–153, 194, 219, 228, 232–233, 241–245, 249–252, 254, 257, 265, 281–282, 288, 295–296, 318–319, 323–326, 331–335, 345–346, 357, 370–371
South Korea 52–53, 60, 65, 90, 104, 142, 151, 194, 219, 222, 228, 235, 242, 246–247, 252, 253–254, 265, 266, 282, 296, 323–326, 333–335, 345–346, 357
sovereignty 18–19, 76, 78, 93, 108–110, 116–117, 130, 138, 154, 165, 168, 205, 231, 234, 248, 257, 268–270, 302
Spain 60, 65, 90, 104, 122, 142, 151, 162, 194, 219, 223–224, 242, 246–247, 249, 251–252, 266, 278, 280, 296, 323–325, 333–335, 344, 345–346, 356–357
speakers 11–12, 144–148, 334, 335
speakerships 11, 17, 145–148, 156
specialist committees 251
specialization 17, 28–29, 184–187, 315–316, 320
  policy 17, 77, 318, 360
stability
  democratic 2–3
  political 378–379
staffing 15, 149–150, 152–153, 155, 156–157, 323–325
  levels 49, 52, 152–153
staggered elections 125, 317, 354–355
standing orders 35, 138, 141–142, 144–145, 173–174, 384

state governments 116–117, 122–123
state legislators 2
state legislatures 42, 155, 214–215
    United States 15, 63, 155
Storting 20, 102, 114–115, 286
structures 14, 36, 41–42, 210, 377–378, 383
    cameral, *see* cameral structures
Stuart monarchs 4–5
STV (Single Transferable Vote) 32–33, 68–69,
    71–75, 83, 92, 122
subnational legislatures 42, 63
substantive representation 94, 103, 105
supermajorities 142, 148, 228
    plenary 142
supporters 214, 240–241, 258, 330–331, 391
Sweden 6, 10, 44, 60, 65, 90, 97, 104, 108–110,
    142, 151, 160, 162, 173, 194, 206, 210,
    219, 228, 242, 247, 249, 253–254, 257,
    273, 296, 323–325, 333–335, 345–346,
    357
    Riksdag 14, 145, 206, 254, 273
Switzerland 51, 59, 60, 65, 71, 76–77, 90,
    97–98, 104, 122, 126, 142, 151, 162, 194,
    210, 219, 223–224, 228, 242, 247, 251,
    263, 265, 280, 281, 288, 296, 323–325,
    331–335, 342, 345–346, 357, 397–398

Taagepera, Rein 92, 116, 136–137, 164
Taiwan 60, 65, 90, 102–104, 142, 151, 162, 194,
    207–208, 219, 223–224, 228, 232, 242,
    245, 249–250, 252, 264, 266, 280, 296,
    323–325, 333–335, 345–346, 357
Tanzania 6
taxes 4–5, 14, 150, 319
tenure 23, 28–29, 63, 194, 207, 317
terms 58–59, 65, 75, 77, 79, 168, 318, 337,
    359–360
    consecutive 60, 63, 96, 99, 168, 327
    electoral 30, 35, 78–79, 83, 318, 324, 336
    fixed 28, 65, 76–77, 263, 317–318, 325, 328
    flexible 317–318
    legislative, *see* legislative terms
    length 59, 78, 318, 337, 372, 375, 376
    limits 60, 63–64, 99, 327–328, 334, 356, 368,
        392
    longer 77, 318, 368, 375
    short 15, 77, 318, 337
    six-year 77, 83, 318, 337
trade-offs 30–31, 83, 86–87, 245–246, 326, 383
transformative legislatures 40–41
transitions 32, 388–390, 392, 393, 395–396
transparency 32–34, 139, 140, 148, 292–293,
    335–336
    external 35
    in government 113, 339–340
Transparency International 371, 373

treaties 293, 296, 306, 310
    international 304, 308–309
Tsebelis, George 113, 115, 116, 131–132, 232,
    331
Tunisia 50–51, 60, 65, 74–75, 90, 104, 142, 151,
    162, 194, 206, 219, 222, 228, 232–233,
    242, 249, 253–254, 280, 282, 296, 300,
    303, 306, 323–325, 331–335, 345–346,
    348, 357
Turkey 60, 65, 74–75, 90, 104, 142, 148, 151, 162,
    194, 206–208, 219, 242, 245, 252, 282,
    295–296, 323–325, 333–335, 345–346,
    357
turnover 3–4, 17, 28, 32, 99, 325, 354, 362
Tutsis 106
two-party legislatures 89, 161–163
two-party systems 164, 173–174
two-round systems 72, 122
typologies 40–42, 48–49, 192, 265, 312–313

Ukraine 51–53, 60, 65, 90, 104, 142, 148, 151,
    162, 167, 194, 206, 219, 223–224, 228,
    242, 249, 280, 296, 300, 320, 323–325,
    329, 332–335, 345–346, 357, 376
unelected second chambers 44–45, 113–114,
    123, 340
unexcused absence 82
unicameral chambers 108–110, 153, 286
unicameral legislatures 117, 130, 373
unicameralism 26–27, 113, 115, 129, 130–131,
    367
United Kingdom 10–11, 16–17, 32
    assembly membership and
        congruence 87–88, 90, 97–98,
        104
    assembly type 323–326, 328, 333–335, 340
    budgetary process 239–240, 245, 246, 250,
        251
    cameral structures 114–116, 120, 121–123,
        126–127, 131–132
    committees 208, 211
    contemporary challenges 387, 395–396
    elections 58, 60, 62, 65, 72, 76–77, 79–80
    elective function 263, 272–273, 282
    executive oversight 293–294, 296, 303, 305
    House of Commons, *see* House of Commons
    House of Lords 10, 19–20, 24, 120–121,
        123–127, 340
    incumbency and re-election 356–357,
        363–364, 377
    lawmaking 214, 216, 219, 226–228, 232
    organization and leadership 141–142, 147,
        149–151, 154–155
    parties 179–180
United States 2, 6, 12, 26, 35, 42

United States (*Continued*)
  assembly membership and congruence 90, 98, 99–102, 104
  assembly type 318–319, 322–323, 345–348
  budgetary process 245, 247, 249–254, 256–258
  cameral structures 116, 119, 121–122, 126, 142
  committees 194
  Congress 28–29, 152–153, 189–190, 263–264, 325, 361–362, 395
  Constitution 147, 214–215, 305–306, 308–309
  contemporary challenges 387, 389, 391, 396
  elections 59–63, 65, 73–74, 81–82
  elective function 263–264, 279, 280
  executive oversight 295–296, 303, 308–309
  House of Representatives 99–100, 142, 145–146, 153, 318, 325, 361–362, 379
  incumbency and re-election 353, 356, 357, 364, 367, 379
  lawmaking 219–224, 228, 233
  organization and leadership 114, 145–146, 151, 154–155
  parties 176
  President 233, 263–264, 279, 305–306, 308, 395
  Senate 1, 29, 114, 119, 120, 125, 144, 280, 308
  state legislatures 15, 63, 155
unity, party 68–69, 172, 173, 175, 176–177, 179–181
upper chambers 44–45, 116–117, 120, 121, 131, 279, 282

variables 49, 51–52, 194, 242, 249–250, 302, 313–315, 371–374
  background 49–50, 56, 95
  control 373–374, 378
  dependent 50, 76, 77–78, 205, 231, 233–234, 248, 257, 267–270, 302, 307–308
  endogenous 377–379
  independent 49–50, 256, 370–371, 373, 374
vetoes 126–130, 210–211, 232–233, 304–305, 331–332
  executive 236
  external, *see* external vetoes
  partial 233
  players 189, 232–233, 235, 304, 331
  power 15, 23, 126–128, 130, 131, 232–233
voters 12; *see also* Introductory Note
  ability to hold to account 64, 75, 225–226, 336
  decisive 362–364, 369
  eligible 13, 87–88
  interests 33, 44, 132, 184–185, 193, 343
  policy preferences 77, 88–89, 337

voters' assemblies 32, 35, 44–45, 76, 98–99, 113–114, 240–241, 340
  index 335, 345
votes 65, 68–69, 72–73, 148, 168, 171–172, 175–176, 225–226, 242, 248, 266, 270–272, 332–333
  candidate 68, 74, 316
  confidence 179, 263, 269, 272–273, 277–278, 309, 386–387
  first preference 73
  formal 168, 225
  investiture 269–272, 276–277, 288, 332
  legislative 170–171, 176, 262–263, 332
  majority 72–73, 168
  non-personal 316, 336
  parliamentary 263, 272
  party members 168, 171
  personal 54, 68–69, 74–76, 177, 316–317, 336, 345, 371, 372–375
  roll-call 171, 175, 190, 226
  secret 149, 333, 334
  single transferable 32–33, 83, 122
voting 68–69, 148–149, 156, 168, 172–173, 225–226, 333
  behavior 68–69, 171, 172, 180–181, 226
  cross-partisan 32–33, 68
  mechanisms 224
  procedures 225–226
  rights 12–13, 18, 35, 41–42, 58, 102–103, 126
  secret 148–149, 156, 225–226, 333
  unity 171–173, 175
  unity scores 171

Wallack, Jessica S. 54, 74–75, 317, 327, 373
war powers 304
wealth 48–49, 51, 63, 95–96
wealthier countries 77, 268, 269, 285, 301
Wehner, Joachim 241, 250–254, 258, 322
Weingast, Barry R. 188–189, 208
Wilson, Harold 273
Wilson, Woodrow 212
women 13, 93–94, 103, 104–110, 119, 338–339
  candidates 106–108
  elections of 106
  interests 94, 105, 339
  legislators 93–94, 103, 104–106, 108–110, 338–339
  members 103, 109, 119, 338–339
  reserved seats for 104, 106, 108, 110
World Bank, Database of Political Institutions (DPI) 54, 265

Zambia 60, 65, 76–77, 82, 90, 104, 142, 151, 154–155, 162, 194, 206, 219, 228, 242, 245, 253–254, 296, 300, 306, 323–325, 333–335, 345–346, 357